POST
A CHRONOLOGY OF INTRIGUING
EVENTS IN THE MAILS AND PHILATELY
DATES

About the author

Stamps have been a major part of Ken Wood's life for half a century. A collector since the early 1930s, he soon became aware that stamps complemented his interest in history by recalling the past and reflecting the present.

Wood was editor of *Stamp Collector* from 1968 to 1980 and has been writing about the hobby for some 25 years. He is the author of the encyclopedia *This is Philately,* the philatelic atlas *Where in the World,* and the handbook for new collectors, *Basic Philately.*

A Fellow of the Royal Philatelic Society, London, Wood is a holder of the Phoenix Award given by the Arizona State Philatelic Hall of Fame for service to philately. In 1974, he was named Distinguished Philatelist of the Year by the Northwest Federation of Stamp Clubs. In 1979, the American Topical Association elected him to its Roll of Distinguished Topical Philatelists, and in 1984, he was named to the Writers Hall of Fame of the Writers Unit #30 of the American Philatelic Society.

Born at Hastings, England, a few miles from the site of the 1066 battle, a proximity he holds responsible for his fondness for history, Wood served in the British Army during World War II, spending several years in Egypt, Cyrenaica, and other Mediterranean countries. After the war he traveled extensively and lived in Guyana, Trinidad, and Canada, before settling with his wife, Hilda in the United States.

POST

A CHRONOLOGY OF INTRIGUING
EVENTS IN THE MAILS AND PHILATELY

DATES

by

Kenneth A. Wood

Published by
Van Dahl Publications
Box 10,
Albany, OR 97321

For Hilda: My favorite date.

First edition, September 1985
Copyright © 1985 Van Dahl Publications

Library of Congress Cataloging in Publication Data

Wood, Kenneth A., 1926-
  Post Dates
  Bibliography: p.
  Includes index.
  1. Postal service — History — Chronology.
  2. Postage stamps — Collectors and collecting — History — Chronology.
I. Title.
HE6041.W66   1985   383′.49   85-3253
ISBN 0-934466-08-4

Printed in the United States of America.

Foreword

Time is but the stream I go a-fishing in.
— Thoreau

This volume is unlike most books about stamps, postal history, or other aspects of philately. It is a chronological account, from the very beginning, of written communications.

The coming of the adhesive postage stamp is woven into our story as one of the strands of postal history. That 1840 event generated a pastime that has grown from a basic acquisitive urge into something of a science — for those who wish to make it so — without losing any of its great appeal.

Opening with the tireless runner of ancient empires and progressing to the technological wonder of satellite communications, the story unfolds to become a mirror of mankind's development.

The day when marks were incised into clay and baked before being sent by messenger on a journey across an ancient landscape is a far cry from the satellite beeping its message through space, but it is those contrasts that are encompassed within this story.

Inevitably, some of the events recorded here have their foundation in political and sociological areas, but it is this weaving of history into the fabric of our hobby that emphasizes how much of the story of the post is the story of our relationships with each other as individuals and nations.

Dates have always played an important role in our hobby. Ever since the first adhesive postage stamp franked a letter on May 2, 1840, collectors have wanted to know the "whens" as well as the "whats."

"May 2, 1840? But I thought the Penny Black was issued on May 6," you ask. For the answer to that, look inside and see for yourself what a fascinating world is the one that links events to dates.

A familiarity with the dates that tie philately to the story of our society can be valuable as well as interesting. Such knowledge can pay handsome dividends when we spot a date on a postal item, the significance of which only we recognize. There are many desirable items identifiable only by the date they bear.

In postal history particularly, dates assume a great importance and the day on which a stamp was issued, a postal marking introduced, or a service inaugurated, can be critical in assessing a postal item.

So, let us wander through the years as we explore the story of the post.

Kenneth A. Wood, FRPS,L.

Appreciation

Many philatelists and writers, past and present, played a part in compiling this book and a list of sources and suggested reading is included at the end of the text.

To list everyone who helped would be impossible, but there are some friends who must be thanked. They include: Henry W. Beecher, Clyde Carriker, Peter Collins, Dr. Arthur A. Delaney, Belmont Faries, Philip Halward, Ernest A. Kehr, James Kingman, Ernest J. Roscoe, Rodney Slanga, and Mike Street.

For his patience and expertise in preparing the illustrations, special thanks must go to Warren Burgess, chief photographer of the *Albany Democrat-Herald*.

In the production department, Manager Mary Meacham and printing technicians Christy Conley, Mona Conley, Rachel Derksen, and Teresa James applied much dedication to setting type, proofing, and preparing pages.

I am grateful to Michael Green and Kyle Jansson for editorial assistance, to James Magruder II for his faith, and to Arlene Van Dahl for her encouragement.

That there are omissions in this book is inevitable, but because of the constrictions of space I have, by necessity, been arbitrary and responsibility for inclusions and exclusions is mine alone.

Contents

Suggestions for use

The arrangement of this book has been made as straightforward as possible. If you want to know what happened at a specific time, then all you need do is to follow the dates at the head of each page until you come to the one you want.

If you wish to find out when something happened, turn to the appropriate listing in the index. There you will find the dates you seek. Because of its chronological arrangement, page numbers are not necessary and the index is arranged to take you directly to the item.

Events for which only the year is known can be found at the beginning of that year. Where month and year are known, the event is located at the beginning of the appropriate month. Items for which day, month, and year have been established are listed in their proper sequence.

The index is alphabetized as though each listing were one word.

Monarchs are listed under first name, as "George V," "Elizabeth II."

For dates of first 19th century stamps, there are index entries under both country name and "First stamps."

International inaugural air mail, or proving flights, are listed under the originating country as well as under "Air mail." In some cases they may also be indexed under the airline name.

For ease of location, all United States-related entries are grouped under "US" headings.

Extensive cross-referencing has been provided and the use of the "q.v." *(quod vide:* which see) reference indicates that the item preceding it has its own index listing.

4000 BC - 1599
In the beginning

4000 BC

Although some sources indicate that a form of courier or messenger service existed in China, postal historian Wang Shih-ying states that China's postal history probably starts in the Chou Dynasty of 1122-221 BC. Records prior to this time are not reliable, according to Wang Shih-ying.

Reports exist that there was a form of message delivery service in the Indus Valley during this period. Parts of the area were located in what is now India and Pakistan.

3000 BC

At about this time, merchant settlers from Assyria, who had settled in an area of central Asia Minor known as Cappadocia, developed a form of letter writing. They used clay tablets which were baked after being inscribed and were then inserted in clay envelopes.

The earliest recorded clay-tablet letter dates from 2095 BC and was found in Sumer, according to Kandaouroff. The ancient Egyptians also used clay tablets and operated a courier service. They are known to have communicated in this fashion with Assyria and Babylon.

2000 BC

Near this time, an Egyptian is said to have warned his son that if he wanted to be a government letter carrier, he would do well to make his will immediately! Letter carriers, he claimed, were in constant danger from wild animals and the unfriendly population of areas through which they had to pass, according to Codding.

1550 BC

From about this time to approximately 1250 BC, Egypt had an efficient courier service linking outposts, local princes and outlying areas with the central government. Horses, introduced about 1700 BC by the Hyksos invaders had an impressive effect in speeding communications in an empire that soon extended its territory into what is now Turkey and Iraq.

1122 BC

During the Chou Dynasty (1122-221 BC) in China, a postal service existed, according to Wang Shih-ying. Prior to this time, oral messages sent via a messenger and beacon fires were among the chief methods of communications used.

But in the Chou Dynasty, a postal service came into being, based on a network of post houses. Service was by horse carts and messengers on foot and on horseback. The emphasis at first was on the horse-drawn carts, but they were gradually eliminated and the other two methods became the ones commonly used for written messages.

559 BC

At this time, Cyrus of Persia developed a "secret" method of carrying messages, Bowyer reports. A courier's head would be shaved and the message written on his scalp. He would then be locked up until his hair grew to conceal the message, when he would be sent on his way! At the destination, his head was again shaved and the message "delivered."

551 BC

Confucius (551-479 BC) is reported to have said "The flowing progress of virtue is more rapid than the transmission of imperial orders

Confucius: Man of many sayings.

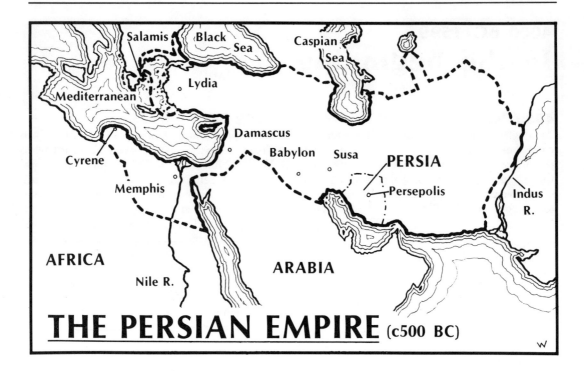

THE PERSIAN EMPIRE (c500 BC)

by postal stages and couriers." This may well be the first recorded criticism of a postal service!

500 BC

The Persian Empire featured a well-organized system of couriers, or post riders. Darius I (522-486 BC) improved an earlier network of routes along which were posting stations at intervals of one day's journey. Royal messengers used these routes, traveling in relays. Of these messengers, the historian Herodotus wrote: "They are stayed by neither snow or rain, nor darkness from accomplishing their appointed course with all speed."

The routes traversed Asia Minor from Persia, extended south into Egypt and east to India. Xerxes used the system to send back to Persia news of the Battle of Salamis (480 BC) and his invasion of Greece, a journey that took the couriers just over a week.

221 BC

During the Chin Dynasty (221-207 BC), China became unified and a centralized system of government was established. This required improved communications and a massive highway construction program began. Post houses were set up three to four miles apart, with major stations every ten miles.

Stables and cart stations provided for the transmission of correspondence and the transportation of officials, according to Wang Shih-ying (see 1122 BC).

206 BC

During the Han Dynasty in China (206 BC-AD 220), the post stations system operated in a similar fashion to that of the Chin Dynasty (221-207 BC). Carts drawn by horses were favored and there were several categories depending on the number and quality of horses used. Many new post stations were established during this period. An account from the eastern Han Dynasty period mentions the Roman Empire, called Tachin by the Chinese. It is described as having a similar network of post stations, which are noted as being painted white.

105 BC

Paper began to be used in China following its development by Ts'ai Lun, a Chinese court official. Prior to this, the Chinese used woven cloth. Other ancient peoples had written on a variety of materials including papyrus, parchment, bark and clay tablets.

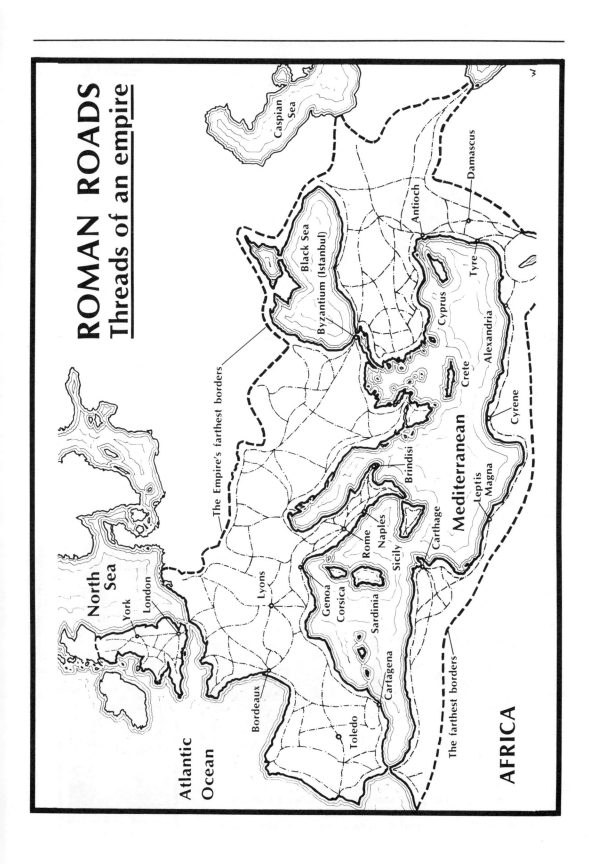

ROMAN ROADS
Threads of an empire

Caspian Sea

Black Sea

Byzantium (Istanbul)

Antioch

Damascus

Tyre

Cyprus

Crete

Alexandria

Cyrene

The Empire's farthest borders

Brindisi

Leptis Magna

Carthage

Mediterranean

Rome

Naples

Sicily

Genoa

Corsica

Sardinia

Cartagena

Toledo

Bordeaux

Lyons

York

London

North Sea

Atlantic Ocean

The farthest borders

AFRICA

The art of papermaking did not spread beyond the borders of China for about 500 years. By the 10th century AD, paper was being made in Egypt, but it did not reach Europe (via Morocco) until the mid-12th century.

A vehicle of the *cursus publicus*.

AD 100

The Romans utilized an extensive network of relays to carry messages within their empire via the magnificent highway system they built across Europe, North Africa, and Asia Minor. At intervals of 25 miles were lodging places known as *mansiones* and between these about every 10 miles were relay stations called *mutationes.*

Postal vehicles were drawn by two horses and had two wheels. Specifications for these vehicles were laid down by law. The prefect of the Praetorian Guard, responsible only to the emperor, was in charge of the Roman system, or *cursus publicus,* as it was known.

AD 220

Contemporary reports of the Wei Dynasty (AD 220-265) speak of Ansi (Chinese for Persia) as being prosperous, with carts plying its highways and a postal station network similar to China's, according to Wang Shih-ying. He claims that both the Romans and the Persians had based their post system on that of China.

During this dynasty, the cart system was abolished because of its expense, and letters were carried either by messengers on foot or horseback.

AD 645

A system of horse couriers and relay stations was established between important centers in Japan.

1100

During the 12th century, the so-called Butchers' Post (Metzger Post) was created by the Guild of Butchers in Germany. Because butchers had occasion to travel and thus had a horse and cart, they began to carry letters. Eventually this developed into a postal administration that lasted into the 1500s. Mail carriers carried a curved horn to announce their arrival and to them belongs the credit for introducing what became the post horn, that ubiquitous instrument so widely used as a symbol of the post. The Butchers' Post was eventually taken over by the postal service of the Holy Roman Empire.

The horn used by the Butchers' Post eventually became the post horn, an instrument used to warn of the coming of the post and today used as a symbol by many postal services. These stamps from Belgium, Germany and Austria depict it in both roles.

1150

By the middle of the 12th century, a municipal post had been established by the Hanseatic League in the German town of Bremen. From this port, routes extended to other League ports.

1160

By this year, there was a mail system in the Spanish city of Barcelona. A lay brotherhood, the members of which were known in Catalan as "troters," supplied mail service to area towns and villages, wore a uniform, and had to keep postal accounts. Van Dam notes that this may have been the first organized European postal system since the days of the Roman *curcus publicus* (q.v.).

1200

For about 500 years, the universities of Europe operated messenger services for the use of students who, because of travel difficulties, would often remain at the universities for the duration of their studies. The messengers of the University of Paris carried messages for private individuals as well as students, on a system covering most of Europe, according to Kandaouroff.

1263

King Jaime I of Aragon (1208-1276) issued a postal decree that set up a system of hostels for use by couriers during their travels. These were called Hostels de Correus, and it is from this that the Spanish term *correos* is derived, according to Van Dam.

1290

The courier service known as the Corrieri Bergamaschie was established in the Republic of Venice, by Amadeo Tasso. By the 1400s, Tasso's post was expanding and extending into the Holy Roman Empire. The Tasso and Della Torre families were united by marriage, to later become the famous House of Thurn and Taxis (q.v.).

1322

The earliest mention of a municipal postal service can be traced back to this year. The city of Strasbourg in modern-day France operated a

A medieval messenger typical of the period is seen on this Austrian stamp.

postal service, whose messengers had to take an oath of good behavior and were not permitted to gamble. The service carried letters of civic officials and could be used by the public. By the early 1500s, the Strasbourg service sent messengers to all parts of Europe. Other cities operated similar services and they eventually became the basis of state postal systems.

1402

In China, the Ming Emperor Yung Lo opened the Imperial Courier Service to those who wished to send private letters.

1444

July 20: Postal authorities in Barcelona, Spain, issued specific instructions regarding the handling of mail. Among these rules: bundles of letters were not to be untied, letters should only be delivered to the addresses at their residences, and a special delivery service should be made available at additional cost.

1450

Roger, Count of della Torre and Tassis and Valassina, went to Germany from Italy and was knighted by Frederick III. He germanized the title to Von Thurn and Taxis and laid the foundation of the family posts by establishing a post in the Tyrol.

1459

The House of Thurn and Taxis organized a post in Europe, between Frankfurt and Leipzig.

1464

June 19: King Louis XI of France decreed the formation of a body of couriers for royal use. Relay stations were set up at 12-mile intervals

A royal messenger of France; ancestor of today's French mailman.

and the couriers were to gallop from one to the other. Robinson states that private individuals could use the facilities by permission and the payment of a fixed sum for the use of horses kept at the stations. The decree stated that postmasters were forbidden to hire out horses to unauthorized persons on pain of death, according to Kandaouroff. This French postal system is said to be the oldest state postal service still existing.

1477

Although most postal historians give the year that French King Louis XI established a Royal Post as 1464, Codding states that research in France indicates that it was formed in 1477.

1481

King Edward IV of England set up a "post" for relaying dispatches during a war with Scotland. It was not a permanent system and was not available to the public. Robson Lowe notes that a relay of riders stationed every 20 miles would pass on messages and that using this method, letters could travel up to 100 miles a day. While mostly temporary, this system seems to have been permanent on the route from London to Dover.

1489

Johann von Taxis was named the first Imperial Postmaster of the Holy Roman Empire, with headquarters at Augsburg in what is now the Federal Republic of Germany and established a government post in Austria.

1505

Jan. 18: In return for 12,000 livres a year, Franz von Taxis signed a convention with Spain to set up and operate a postal system between the Low Countries (now Belgium and the

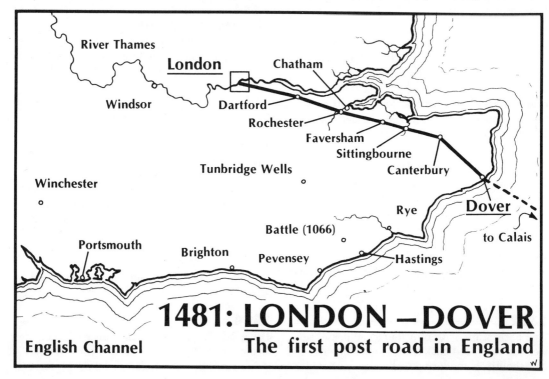

1481: LONDON — DOVER
The first post road in England

Netherlands), the Court of Maximilian in Germany, and the courts of the kings of France and Spain. It also served the French cities of Paris and Lyons and the Spanish cities of Toledo and Granada. Von Taxis made Brussels his headquarters and, when he received permission to carry private mail, the international postal service was born. The House of Thurn and Taxis served the empires and nations of Europe up to 1867, when the last remaining routes were sold to Prussia.

1510

Brian Tuke was appointed Master of the Posts by King Henry VIII of England. Tuke's function was to organize the carrying of the royal correspondence and state documents.

1512

Franz von Taxis received a title of hereditary nobility from the Emperor Maximilian.

1516

Franz von Taxis established a post between Brussels and Vienna. This was extended to Rome, Verona, and Naples and linked up with his brother Roger's post between Austria and points in what is now Italy.

1520

Johann Baptista, a nephew of Franz von Taxis was made General Postmaster by Karl V of the Holy Roman Empire over "all those lands under the Habsburg-Spanish rule."

1525

The appointment was confirmed of Luis Homem as Grand Master of the Posts by King Emmanuel I of Portugal. Homem was instructed to maintain couriers for the king's service and for the public and to fix rates depending on distance and time taken.

1533

In England, Master of the Posts Brian Tuke was criticized for the inefficiency of the mails. He responded that the Treasury was at fault for not allowing funds to keep horses in readiness at posts and that when needed, horses often had to be taken from ploughs and farm carts, "wherein there can be no extreme diligence."

1548

Leonard I von Taxis became head of the Thurn and Taxis postal system and under his control posts were established from the Belgian city of Ghent to Liege, Treves, and Spire, as well as Augsburg and Innsbruck.

1557

In this year, Richard Harrison was recorded as a freeman "of the mystery and art of printing." From that beginning can be traced the firm of Harrison and Sons (High Wycombe) Ltd., one of the best-known of the world's stamp printers and a producer of stamps for the British Post Office since 1934.

These three stamps depict members of the House of Thurn and Taxis. They are from the left, Franz von Taxis (June 19, 1464); Johann Baptista, a nephew of Franz (1520); and Leonard I von Taxis (1548). The stamps are part of a Belgian set issued May 14, 1952 marking the 13th Universal Postal Union Congress, held at Brussels.

1561

Jan. 10: A postmaster general was appointed in Piedmont, in the Duchy of Savoy, to form a postal service.

1562

Nicholas Fitzsymon of Dublin was appointed the first official postmaster of that Irish city. His duties were to receive and dispatch the Queen's letters plus, when convenient, those of the public. He was still in office 20 years later, according to Reynolds.

1564

The Irish mails were expensive and a letter from Carlingford to Carrickfergus is reported as costing the equivalent of about $6.

1571

In England, a government proclamation ordered that no one was to carry letters to and from overseas except those named by the "Master of the Posts" or the "Masters of the Postes General." It ordered that all baggage of unauthorized people be searched to ensure that it contained no letters.

1573

Thomas Randolf was commissioned to set up a series of posts on the London-Holyhead road, so that the mails between London and Ireland could be carried from stage to stage by postboys on official post horses.

1590

William Brewster, one of the founders of the Plymouth Colony, was named Master of the Post at Scrooby, England. He received 20 pence a day and held the post until he left England in 1607.

1598

Fixed posts were set up in England from London to Ireland via Holyhead and another via Milford Haven. An order referring to official letters being entered in a book, with all others passing as by-letters, indicates that this post was open to private letters.

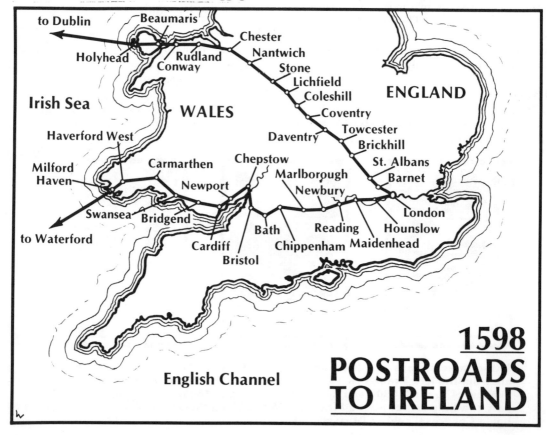

1598 POSTROADS TO IRELAND

1600-1774
Postal services develop

1608

Feb. 1: What is believed to be the first item of postal stationery was released. The letter sheets sold in Venice, featured the city's coat of arms as an indicium. Their use was mandatory for written communications to and from government officials. They continued in use until 1797 and it is believed that they were delivered free of further charge, according to the late Dr. Rodney L. Mott.

1615

Lamoral von Taxis, head of the postal service of the House of Thurn and Taxis, was appointed hereditary postmaster general of Germany by the Emperor Matthias. The appointment granted that the title be hereditary through the male line. He was also raised to the rank of a Baron of the Empire.

1619

Ships rounding the Cape of Good Hope called there and left letters under inscribed stones to be picked up by ships bound in the other direction. The British, Portuguese, and Dutch used this system, according to Robson Lowe.

1620

The birth of the Swedish postal service can be traced back to this year when Gustaf II Adolf established a mail route between Stockholm and Hamburg.

1624

Dec. 24: The Danish Post Office was formed when King Christian IV established a postal service for his people. It was managed by representatives of the four trade companies. These were the Icelandic Company, the East India Company, the Cloth Company, and the Silk Company.

1627

Cardinal Richelieu of France is reported to have established a regular public postal service between Paris, Dijon, Toulouse, Lyons, and Bordeaux. No special wrappers or postal markings were used, according to Ward.

1633

What is regarded as the world's first packet boat service ran between Dover, England and Calais, France.

April: In England, Thomas Witherings, Postmaster-General for Foreign Parts, wrote in a letter to Secretary of State Sir John Coke that the House of Thurn and Taxis had established stages from Antwerp to Calais and requested that similar stages be set up from London to Dover. This was done and the post to Dover ran day and night.

It was intended that it reach Dover while daylight remained for crossing the English Channel. Mail arriving from the Continent was to be displayed in order that it could be claimed. This indicates that the post was used by the public.

1634

The colony of Curacao was founded by the Dutch. The Geoctroyeerde West-Indische Compagnie, formed in 1621, was given a monopoly in trading between the Netherlands,

A Danish messenger of 1624 and a postrider of about 1780 are seen on this stamp, one of a 1974 set marking the 350th anniversary of the Danish Post Office (Dec. 24, 1624).

King Gustaf II Adolf, father of the Swedish Post Office in 1620.

the West Indies and Suriname. Thus, it was responsible for carrying the mails between Curacao and the homeland.

1635
July 31: Thomas Witherings, English Postmaster-General for Foreign Parts, was charged with the establishment of a new domestic "Letter-Office." This new postal service was to be similar to that of the House of Thurn and Taxis. Rates were set at fourpence for 80-140 miles, sixpence over that, and eightpence to Scotland. Unfortunately, the onset of the English Civil War and the coming to power of Oliver Cromwell made these reforms impossible.

1636
Sweden's General Post Office came into being. Although a major power at that time, Sweden had only one million inhabitants and Stockholm's population was about 12,000.

1637
July: A royal order of King Charles I of England limited the postal service to letters on the King's business and to those connected with the government.

1639
Nov. 5: The first record of any official action concerning postal matters in the American colonies was the appointment by the General Court of Massachusetts of Richard Fairbanks, whose house in Boston was designated as the place to which all foreign letters were to be brought, whether incoming or outgoing. He was paid 1d for each letter he sent on its way as it was directed.

The appointment contained the reservation that "no man shall bee compelled to bring his letters thither except hee please." No provision was made at this time concerning domestic letters.

1650
About this time, private courier systems were established in Japan to carry letters and money for the general public.

1652
An early reference to the franking system in England occurred in this year when a Council of State decreed that letters of members of parliament and certain public officials should go free. Abuse of this system led to postal reform in the 19th century.

1653
In Ireland, post roads were established from Dublin to Belfast, Coleraine, Derry, Sligo, Galway, and Cork and the post was "carried to the remotest parts of Ireland twice weekly," according to a contemporary report.

July 16: King Frederick III gave control of the Danish Post Office to Paul Klingenberg of Hamburg, who introduced improvements, especially on the Copenhagen-Hamburg route. His administration lasted for 30 years.

Aug. 8: Jean-Jacques Renouard de Villayer (some authorities give his name as Francois de Velayer) established a postal service in Paris under a royal mandate from King Louis XIV. Letters were attached to a wrapper called a *Billet de Port Paye* (Receipt for Postage Paid), which were sold for five centimes.

The mailer wrote the day, month, and year of mailing on the *billet* before depositing it attached to the letter in one of the letter boxes that De Villayer had set up around Paris. The letter was then picked up and delivered without further charge, after removing and destroying the *billet*. It could be argued that these were the first postage stamps, since they served a similar purpose and were attached to the letter. However, the service was not a success, as those opposed to it deposited garbage in the letter boxes and rendered them unusable. None of the *billets* are known to have survived.

1657
In England, Oliver Cromwell's Post Office Act emphasized the importance of a centralized, government-controlled post office as a means, not only of promoting trade, but also of discovering what later autocratic regimes have called "subversive elements."

The prevention of the exchange of ideas unfavorable to the Commonwealth by monitoring citizen's correspondence rather than any desire for an efficient postal service, seems to have been Cromwell's aim; an aim often duplicated in more modern times. The Act established the monopoly of the British Post Office in the carriage of mail, a monopoly it has retained ever since.

1659

In one of history's strange coincidences, John Hill, an attorney of York, England, published a pamphlet, *A Penny Post*. He was a believer in private enterprise and had set up stages on the London-York road. Robinson notes that Rowland Hill, a later advocate of the penny post, was not related. It is claimed that he knew nothing of the earlier Hill's pamphlet until his own reforms were in effect. In any event, the 1659 ideas of John Hill were ignored.

1660

Authorities in the Dutch colony of New Amsterdam (now New York) set up a box in the office of the Secretary of the Province for the deposit of all letters addressed out of the colony. Regulations governed ships captains carrying letters and fines were levied for violations.

With the Restoration and coming to the throne of King Charles II as ruler of England, Parliament enacted what came to be known as the Post Office Charter. It established a General Post Office under a postmaster general appointed by the king on payment to him of a fee.

June: Colonel Henry Bishop was named postmaster general of England by King Charles II. He paid £21,500 a year to "farm" the Post Office (see Aug. 12, 1661). Bishop was bought out of his post in 1663 by Daniel O'Neale.

1661

The first slogan postmark was used in London. It was applied to letters to addresses along the road into Kent and comprised a nine-line inscription in a large circle reading "THE POST/ FOR ALL KENT/ GOES EVERY/ NIGHT FROM/ THE ROVND HO/ VSE IN LOVE/ LANE & COMES/ EVERY MOR/ (NING)."

The Virginia Assembly passed an act whereby domestic mail was to be carried from plantation to plantation under penalty of supplying one hogshead (350 pounds) of tobacco each time this was not done.

Aug. 12: British PMG Colonel Henry Bishop introduced the "Bishop Mark." It was in the form of a circle divided horizontally, with the day of the month in the upper half and the month in the lower half.

Bishop described it as "A stamp is invented that is putt upon every letter shewing the day of the moneth that every letter comes to the post office, so that no letter carryer may dare to detayne a letter from post to post, which before was usual."

The marking was used until 1787 and a variation without the dividing line was used in the American colonies.

1666

A regular letter post was established in Russia between Moscow and Courland. Mail was carried by postriders, according to Prigara.

1668

June 13: A mail service was established between Harwich, England, and Helvoetsluis, in the Netherlands. Mail left London on Tuesdays and Fridays, and Helvoetsluis on Wednesdays and Saturdays. English packet boats were used.

Strangely, the service was not interrupted

Seen from the left are the earliest known slogan postmarks (1661), a 1960 British stamp commemorating the 300th anniversary of the establishment of the General Post Office (1660), and a typical "Bishop Mark" (Aug. 12, 1661).

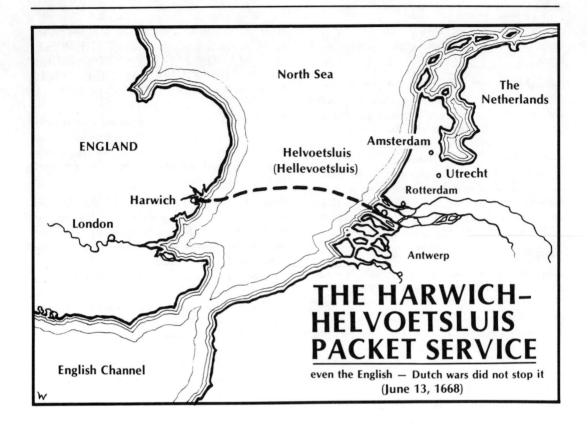

North Sea

ENGLAND

The Netherlands

Amsterdam

Helvoetsluis
(Hellevoetsluis)

Utrecht

Rotterdam

Harwich

London

Antwerp

THE HARWICH-HELVOETSLUIS PACKET SERVICE

even the English — Dutch wars did not stop it
(June 13, 1668)

English Channel

during the Third Dutch War of 1672. There seems to have been a tacit agreement that neither side would stop the service if each permitted the other's letters to pass unhindered.

1670

Aug. 13: The earliest known Irish "Bishop Mark" bears this date.

1671

Oct. 31: Gabriel Martin was belatedly appointed postmaster of Jamaica. King Charles II had instructed the lieutenant governor of the island to establish a post office as early as 1663. Even so, little was done. When Thomas Neale was given the job of setting up a postal system in the American colonies in 1692, colonies in the Caribbean were included. Jamaica was one of these.

1673

The earliest recorded example of a forwarding agent's marking is that of Ezekiel Wright of London in this year, according to Rowe.

When a missionary named Friar Domingo Navarette visited the South Atlantic island of Ascension, he reported that a "bottle post office" had been established there. Passing ships would drop off letters placed in bottles to be picked up by ships travelling in the opposite direction. It was still being used in 1769, when Louis de Bougainville, commander of the ship *Boudeuse,* called at the island.

Today, Ascension plays a major role in space communications. It has a satellite and space shuttle tracking facility and the British Broadcasting Corporation beams its international service to the Western Hemisphere via a relay station on the island.

Jan. 1: Governor Lovelace of New York established a monthly mail service from New York City to Boston. Letters could be sent by depositing them at the office of the Colonial Secretary and paying the stipulated fee. However, the first messenger did not leave New York until Jan. 22. The service was not a

History of Mail Transport

ASCENSION
17th century bottle post
8p 1980

THE BOTTLE POST
The Ascension "bottle post" became an established practice in the 17th century. The procedure was recorded in 1673 by a visiting missionary, Friar Domingo Navarrete, and was still in use when Louis de Bougainville, captain of *La Boudeuse*, called in 1769.

ASCENSION
19th century chance calling ship
12p 1980

CHANCE CALLING SHIPS
Until 1857 communication with Ascension was through chance calling ships such as the 19th century English 36-gun frigate shown. The scene is at Clarence Bay (then called Sandy Bay) with Fort Cockburn in the background.

ASCENSION
Regular mail service from 1863
15p 1980

REGULAR MAIL SERVICE
A regular mail service started in 1857 when the Union Steam Ship Co Ltd contracted to collect UK destined mail. In 1900 the Company amalgamated with the Castle Mail Packets Co Ltd to form the Union-Castle Mail Steamship Co Ltd, whose ship *Garth Castle* is shown beyond the old Canteen store where the mail bell until recently hung.

ASCENSION
Mail services 1980
50p 1980

MAIL SERVICES TODAY
Surface mail is now carried by the *RMS St Helena*, shown here against the coastline of Ascension. Airmail is carried in this scene by a Lockheed C141 aircraft of the Military Airlift Command of the USAF, completing the picture of the current Ascension mail services.

ASCENSION ISLAND

The 8p stamp in this souvenir sheet issued by Ascension in 1980 describes the Ascension Bottle Post (1673).

success because of interference by Indians and the Dutch. It ceased when the Dutch recaptured New York on Aug. 9, 1673.

1675

First mention of the envelope was made when a French book on etiquette advocated their use as "a mark of respect to one's superiors." They did not come into general use for mail until 1840, when British postal reform introduced low-cost mail and charged by weight rather than the number of pieces of paper a letter contained.

1676

Eugene Alexander von Taxis assumed management of the Thurn and Taxis posts.

1678

During its war with the Netherlands, France took over the Thurn and Taxis posts operating in that country. They were restored within a year.

1680

April 1: William Dockwra began a postal service in London, England, called the Penny Post. It offered a cheap postal service where none at all was provided by the General Post Office.

A contemporary announcement reads: "A Penny Well Bestowed, or a Brief Account of the New Design contrived for the great Increase of Trade, and the Ease of Correspondence, to the great Advantage of the Inhabitants of all sorts, by Conveying of Letters or Pacquets under a Pound Weight, to and from all parts within the cities of London and Westminster; and the Out Parishes within the weekly Bills of Mortality, for One Penny."

The final phrase referred to the parishes in and around London from which returns of deaths were made. One of the important aspects of Dockwra's operation was the postal markings he used. The service was prepaid and the triangular marking he used is regarded as the very first postage stamp, since it indicates

Examples of Dockwra's postal markings. The heart-shaped ones are morning and afternoon time markings and the triangular one indicates that the postage on the item was paid. Thus it can be regarded as the world's first postage stamp. Dockwra's original markings can be distinguished from the later ones used by the government after it had taken over, by the position of the bottom word in the triangle; in Dockwra's it is always the right way up, while the government's are invariably inverted (April 1, 1680).

the payment of the letter. He also used time markings.

1682

Nov. 23: Dockwra's Penny Post in London had been suppressed and on this date was reopened as part of the government postal service operated by the Duke of York. Dockwra had made the mistake of devising a profitable operation! Similar but identifiable postal markings were used by the post under royal management.

1683

William Penn set up a post office and established a weekly post from Philadelphia to New Castle, Penn., and Maryland. Henry Waldy operated the post, which had its office at the sign of the "Death of the Fox" in Strawberry Alley, Philadelphia, according to Konwiser. Rich quotes rates as being from 3d to 9d per single letter.

1684

Governor Dongan of New York proposed a chain of post houses from Nova Scotia to the Carolinas. He received permission for them from the Duke of York, who had been granted the revenues of the British Post Office, and whom the governor thought should also have a portion of the colonial postal revenue. The governor was instructed to set up the system and ensure that the duke received "not less than one tenth." However, the ambitious plan was never implemented.

1685

Nov. 23: Edward Randolph was appointed postmaster by James II of Great Britain and Ireland for his Dominion of New England. The appointment terminated upon the fall of James II and the collapse of the scheme.

Dec. 8: The Danish Post Office came under the control of the 11-year-old son of King Christian V with actual operation being by administrators appointed to act on his behalf.

1689

Russia concluded a postal agreement with China concerning the transportation of mail between the two countries.

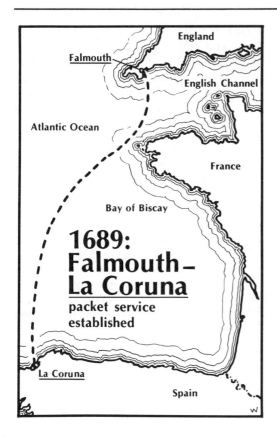

1689: Falmouth– La Coruna packet service established

October: A packet service was established between Falmouth, England, and La Coruna, Spain. The war between France and England prompted the service. The mail for Spain had previously gone by way of France. Ironically, the Spanish Armada had sailed less than 100 years before from La Coruna to battle the English. Two ships were used on the packet service's 450-mile voyage and a third was soon added in order to maintain a fortnightly service.

1690

May: William Dockwra was granted an annuity by the English Crown of £500 a year for seven years "in consideration of his good service in inventing and settling the business of the Penny Post Office."

July: A regular post was begun between Boston, Providence, Bristol, and Newport, Rhode Island, according to Blake and Davis.

1692

Feb. 17: Thomas Neale, Master of the British Mint, was given permission by the British Crown to set up posts in the American colonies.

April 4: Andrew Hamilton, Governor of New Jersey, was appointed the deputy of Thomas Neale to establish and maintain a postal system in the North American colonies. Neale never visited North America.

After six years, Hamilton reported a regular service between Portsmouth, N.H. and Philadelphia, but from 1693 to 1697, he only collected about £400 a year in postage.

Nov. 11: Following his appointment to establish a postal service in the American colonies, Andrew Hamilton sought the help of the colonial governments. New York responded first and passed an act on this date to set up a General Letter Office in New York City. New York set a fine of £100 for people competing with this official post.

Only four other colonies — Pennsylvania, New Hampshire, Massachusetts, and Connecticut — set up postal systems under the Neale patent. (See May 15, 1693; June 5, 1693; June 9, 1693; and May 10, 1694.) The other colonies chose not to establish postal systems.

1693

May 1: On this date an intercolonial post was set up in North America between Portsmouth, N.H. and Philadelphia, under the patent granted to Thomas Neale. The system staggered along without any great success, largely because of letters carried outside the system. The British Crown bought the system in 1707 following Neale's death. Andrew Hamilton's son, John, was made Crown postmaster general.

May 15: Pennsylvania passed legislation establishing a postal system under the patent granted to Thomas Neale, with Andrew Hamilton as his North American deputy.

June 5: New Hampshire passed a postal act granting Thomas Neale a monopoly in that colony, but set a £5 fine for each failure of the mail.

June 9: The colony of Massachusetts passed an act establishing a postal system under the patent granted by the British Crown to Thomas Neale. Rates were set and penalties provided for delaying the mail. The act required letters to be postmarked showing day, month, and year in which they were received. Rich states that this is the first provision relating to postmarks in North America.

However, the Privy Council in London disallowed the act on the grounds that it seemed to be "prejudicial to the office of Postmaster General." The council favored instead an act designed by Neale.

1694

May 10: Connecticut passed legislation granting a postal monopoly to Thomas Neale's post, under his North American deputy, Andrew Hamilton.

1700

Eugene Alexander von Taxis was appointed Postmaster General of the Posts of the Empire and the Low Countries. His title in German was *Kaiserlicher Erbgeneraloberpostmeister.* This title was passed down as a princely fief.

1701

Jan. 1: Cypher stamps were introduced in Great Britain. They were intended to be stuck on the back of a legal document covering the metal staple with which a duty stamp was affixed. These stamps prevented the removal and re-use of the duty stamp. The *London Gazette* noted their introduction on this date.

The name is derived from the fact that they are imprinted with the royal cypher of the reigning monarch. William III and Queen Anne cypher stamps are the earliest known examples of printed stamps, according to Barefoot. Cypher stamps were used until 1921, during the reign of King George V.

These may well have inspired Rowland Hill, since they were of the same size as the *Penny Black* and used a system of numerals, later, letters to indicate their position in the sheet. They also bore plate numbers, according to L.N. and M. Williams.

1702

Oct. 21: The ship *Bridgeman* sailed from Falmouth, England for the West Indies. This

The face of an 1873 Will showing the duty stamp affixed to the document with a metal staple and tied with a circular date stamp is seen at the left and the cypher stamp on the back of the same document covering the staple is shown at the right (Jan. 1, 1701).

was the first of the mail packets in a regular service operated by Edward Dummer who had contracted to provide a monthly service using five 150-ton vessels. *Bridgeman* was captured by privateers on her second voyage and the service was never successful. There were more losses of ships, but Dummer managed to continue operating until 1711, when he lost his remaining ships to his creditors.

1705

A regular courier service began between the cities of Quebec and Montreal in what is now the Canadian province of Quebec, but which was then known as New France. The couriers traveled by boat, as there were no roads, and carried government dispatches and private mail. A fee was charged for carrying private mail.

England and Portugal signed a treaty regulating the exchange of mail between the two countries.

July: Following the Oct. 21, 1702 establishment of Dummer's packet service to Jamaica, Thomas Wood was appointed deputy postmaster of the island under the authority of the General Post Office in London.

1706

King Philip V of Spain bought the Thurn and Taxis postal system operating in his country and set up the Royal Establishment of the Mail, Post Houses, and Roads. This gave the Spanish government control over the mails.

1707

The British Post Office bought the postal service in the American colonies from its operators. It appointed Andrew Hamilton's son John as Deputy Postmaster General in America at a salary of £200 a year.

1709

New Jersey established a postal system under the supervision of John Hamilton.

1711

June 1: The British Post Office Act of 1711 united the Post Offices of England, Ireland, and Scotland, and regulated postal service in the West Indies, New York, and other British colonies in North America. It banned postal officials from engaging in political activities.

Overseas postal rates were set at 1/6 for a single letter to La Coruna, Lisbon, and the West Indies. To the Netherlands and France a single letter cost 10d, while the rate to Italy was 1/-.

In the American colonies, the rate was fixed at 4d for a single letter less than 60 miles and 6d from 60 to 100 miles. Over 100 miles, the rate would be fixed from New York to an important place plus 4d or 6d from there on.

The act legalized the 1d charge of the London Penny Post, which had been established by William Dockwra in 1680, and taken over by the Crown. The boundaries were set as being a 10-mile distance from the London Post Office. Parcels up to one pound in weight were to be carried at the same rate as for a letter.

July 20: The West Indian packet service closed. It had been started by Edward Dummer on Oct. 21, 1702 (q.v.). Despite great efforts and much dedication, Dummer's losses of ships and delays by the British Government in reimbursing him for his expenses, contributed to his failure.

Dummer had begun with four ships and subsequently built 19, of which two were wrecked and 10 captured by enemy ships.

Sept. 25: Following a period of private administration, the Danish Post Office returned to state control and has remained so ever since.

1712

In Great Britain, the newspaper tax stamp was introduced. This stamp did dual duty. It paid the tax on newsprint and its impression on the paper on which news was subsequently printed indicated that the item was to be carried through the mails free of further charge, according to Batchelor and Picton-Phillips.

However, authorities differ and some claim that it was strictly a revenue stamp. At first the stamp bore a denomination of ½d, but later denominations ranged up to 4d. Similar stamps were used in the American colonies (see Nov. 1, 1765).

April 1713 - 1737

The impression of a British newspaper tax stamp (1712).

1713

April: Edward Dummer died, bankrupt and brokenhearted at the failure in 1711 of his packet service from Falmouth to the West Indies. There was no organized mail service to Jamaica and the other islands until a new packet service was established in 1755.

1715

The total amount of free franked mail in Great Britain during 1715, if charged at the current rates, amounted to some £25,000. The abuse of free franking led to the British postal reforms in the 19th century. See 1764.

1716

A postal administration and post office was established in St. Petersburg, then the capital of Russia. Post offices were subsequently set up in Moscow, Riga, Vyborg, Revel, and other major centers in the Russian Empire.

Dec. 7: A Spanish postal decree required that all government mail be stamped with a postal marking featuring the national coat of arms. This was to be used by the king, his court, and ministers in Madrid and Barcelona. It was the first known official postal marking in Spain. Several types were in use until 1854.

1720

Ralph Allen was awarded the farm (contract) for all "by" or "cross post" letters carried in England. He retained the contract until his death almost 50 years later.

A "by letter" was one that traveled between towns on a post road but which did not go into London. A "cross post letter" was one carried across country from one of the post roads that radiated from London to a town on a different post road.

Allan, later mayor of Bath, is an important figure in the history of the post in England and did much to raise the standard of service.

1721

John Hamilton was replaced as Deputy Postmaster General of America by John Lloyd of Charleston, S.C. Robinson reports that the service proved so unprofitable that it owed Hamilton some £350 in back salary.

1730

Alexander Spotswood was appointed Postmaster General of America. A former governor of Virginia, he had taken an active part in the attempts to settle the hinterland. His salary was to be £300 a year, plus 10 percent of Post Office profits. His most important contribution to postal affairs was the 1737 appointment of Benjamin Franklin as deputy postmaster of Philadelphia.

1734

A post road was opened between Quebec and Montreal in the French North American colony of New France. Post houses were established every nine miles and couriers were permitted to carry private mail, although their main duty was to carry government dispatches.

1737

Benjamin Franklin appointed deputy postmaster at Philadelphia by Alexander Spotswood, Postmaster General of America.

Benjamin Franklin, a postal pioneer (1737).

1742

John Palmer was born at Bath, England, the son of a brewer and theater proprietor. He received a good education from his wealthy father at a local school in the fashionable town of his birth and then at Marlborough, one of Britain's better public schools. He was to become noted for the introduction on Aug. 2, 1784 of the mailcoach.

The earliest known example of a forwarding agent's marking in North America is that of Wm. Coffin Jr. of Boston in this year, according to Rowe.

Feb. 8: The posts in Saarbrucken, now part of the Federal Republic of Germany, were taken over by Thurn and Taxis. They were relinquished in 1797, but were regained from Dec. 2, 1815 to July 1, 1816, after which they were operated by Prussia.

1745

December: The packet service from Falmouth, England, to the West Indies was re-established. It was discontinued in 1749.

1750

Thomas Harrison established the firm that is now Harrison & Sons (High Wycombe) Ltd. It produced the first stamps of Great Britain to be printed using the photogravure process.

The earliest known pictorial postmark used in Great Britain is the so-called *Perth Lamb,* which features a lamb and a flag in a shield with the name of the Scottish town of Perth below.

The Perth Lamb, Britain's first pictorial postmark.

1753

Aug. 10: Benjamin Franklin and William Hunter appointed by the British Post Office to

On June 1, 1976, the US and Canada issued a pair of "twin" stamps honoring Benjamin Franklin for his pioneer work in establishing postal services in North America.

the joint position of "Deputy Postmaster and Manager of all His Majesty's Provinces and Dominions on the Continent of North America." The salary was £600 a year between them, "to be paid out of the money arising from the postage of letters." By 1761 a profit of £494 had been remitted to London; the first ever, according to the British Treasury book. For the period 1761-64, the profit was £2,070.

1754

April 27: The Halifax, Nova Scotia, *Gazette* reported that a post office had been established and that the public could, on payment of one penny, have overseas letters delivered to the captain of the first vessel bound for the place to which the letter was addressed. This so-called Outward Post Office was the first post office in the area that is now Canada, according to Robson Lowe.

1755

April 28: The British established a post office at Halifax, Nova Scotia, according to Holmes. Robson Lowe notes the date as April 27, 1754 (q.v.).

May 1: The first embossed revenue stamps used in the American colonies were introduced in Massachusetts on this date. They had been authorized by an act of Jan. 8, 1755 and were used until April 30, 1757. Denominations were ½d, 2d, 3d, and 4d. There were two dies of the ½d stamp and each denomination featured a different design.

Nov. 15: The British Post Office established a packet service between Falmouth, England, and New York. The first ship in this service sailed on this date. There were supposed to be two sailings monthly and the service continued through the Revolutionary period, according to Robson Lowe. However, Scheele gives Sept. 18 as the date the service began, and notes that it was both slow and irregular.

1756

February: The first ship in the new transatlantic packet service arrived in New York from England.

1757

Jan. 1: The colony of New York placed in use embossed revenue stamps under an act of Dec. 1, 1756. They were used until Dec. 31, 1760 and bore denominations of ½d, 1d, 2d, 3d, and 4d. Designs were the same except for the figure of denomination.

1758

A Bishop Mark, similar to that used in Britain, was used in the American colonies from this year to 1800. Unlike that used in Britain, it had no line between day and month, according to Robson Lowe. They are known struck in five sizes and eight different colors. Month abbreviations used were: IA (January), FE (February), MR (March), AP (April), MA (May), IV (June), IY (July), AU (August), SE (September), OC (October), NO (November), and DE (December). (See Aug. 12, 1661).

An American Bishop Mark; the lack of a line between day and month identifies it.

1761

William Hunter died and was replaced by John Foxcroft. Hunter had been appointed jointly with Franklin as deputy postmaster of North America on Aug. 10, 1753 (q.v.).

1763

A monthly post service was established between Montreal and New York.

August: Postmasters General of the American colonies Benjamin Franklin and William Foxcroft arranged with Hugh Finlay in Quebec to operate a regular postal service between Quebec and Montreal, following the defeat of the French by the British and the signing of a peace treaty in 1763.

The single rate between the two cities was set at eight pence. Finlay received a 20 percent commission from the revenue. Post offices were established at Montreal, Three Rivers (Trois Rivieres), and Quebec City. On this post road were post houses at nine-mile intervals, each under a "post master."

1764

By this year the amount of free-franked mail carried in Great Britain, if charged at the current rate, amounted to £170,000. This abuse led Parliament to pass an act in 1764 "for preventing frauds and abuses in relation to the sending and receiving of letters and packets free from the duty of postage." Those found guilty could be transported to a penal colony for seven years. See 1715.

The earliest postal markings used in Canada were straight-line markings of Quebec and Montreal. They were introduced by Hugh Finlay (see August 1763).

Jan. 16: In a letter bearing this date, Benjamin Franklin wrote, "I will not only mention that we hope in the spring to expedite the communication between Boston and New York and we have already that between New York and Philadelphia by making the mails travel by night as well as by day, which has heretofore not been done in America."

Dec. 19: Benjamin Barons was appointed Deputy Postmaster General for the Southern

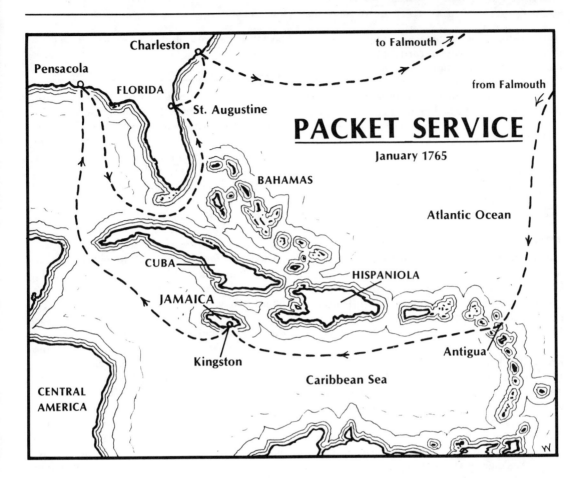

PACKET SERVICE
January 1765

Charleston · to Falmouth · Pensacola · FLORIDA · from Falmouth · St. Augustine · BAHAMAS · Atlantic Ocean · CUBA · HISPANIOLA · JAMAICA · Kingston · Antigua · CENTRAL AMERICA · Caribbean Sea

District of the American colonies. His instructions noted the areas under his authority as North and South Carolina, Georgia, East and West Florida, and the Bahamas. The Northern District was then under Franklin and Foxcroft.

1765

A Penny Post was established in Dublin, after the pattern of the one in London begun by Dockwra. It does not appear to have been a success. As late as 1809 the staff comprised only three clerks and 14 letter carriers, 10 of whom operated in the outlying districts. In 1831, the Penny Post operation was merged with the General Post Office.

January: A packet service was begun from Falmouth, England, to the West Indies, calling at the Leeward Islands, Jamaica, Pensacola, and St. Augustine, Fla., Charleston, S.C., and then back to Falmouth, according to Robinson. Robson Lowe gives the date as February 1764.

This route proved too long and was later divided with the West Indies being served by one and the Florida ports having their own service connecting at Jamaica. Later, St. Augustine and Charleston had their own service direct from Falmouth. (See Sept. 7, 1768).

Oct. 10: A British Act of Parliament, effective on this date, set postal rates in the American colonies at four pence from one port to any other port in America, 4d from any post office in America to any place by land transport up to 60 miles, from 60-100 miles the rate was 6d. The sum of 2d was to be added for each additional 100 miles.

Nov. 1: The British Parliament passed an act on March 22, 1765, which became effective on this date, imposing various taxes on the American colonies, including those in Canada and the West Indies. The taxes were paid by means of embossed revenue stamps. There were stamps for almanacs, pamphlets and newspapers, and playing cards, plus a general purpose range in numerous denominations. They were embossed without color, generally on a document, or on a separate piece of paper which was then attached to the document with a metal staple (see also cypher stamps under Jan. 1, 1701). The stamps were used until May 1, 1766.

Although some sources refer to these items as "Teaparty Stamps," they were never used to collect that tax, which was not enacted until 1767.

1768

Sept. 7: The packet service from the West Indies to Pensacola, St. Augustine, and Charleston, formerly part of the service from England established in January 1765 (Robson Lowe notes the starting date as February 1764), was made a separate monthly service.

Dec. 15: A notice bearing this date advertised an express service between Quebec and Montreal by S. Sills. This was the first express business to be established in North America, according to Robson Lowe. A small parcel service was operated every two weeks, taking about four days for the journey under normal conditions. A sleigh was used during the winter months.

1772

April 1: A so-called *Kleine Post* (Little Post) was established in Vienna, Austria, to deliver and pick up mail within the city. Men walked the streets sounding a wooden clapper to alert people to send and receive mail. This came to be known as the Clapper Post, according to Hornung. Mueller gives the date of establishment as March 1, 1772.

November: Hugh Finlay was appointed Surveyor (Inspector) of the Post Offices and Post Roads on the Continent of North America. Robson Lowe notes that he began his survey on Sept. 13, 1773 and ended it in June 1774. Finlay had been made Postmaster of Canada by Franklin in August 1763 (q.v.). The position of surveyor was the forerunner of today's postal inspectors and the Postal Inspection Service.

1774

What must have been the world's first "stamp" collection was formed in this year by John Bourke, Receiver-General of Stamp Duties in Ireland. He compiled a collection of duty stamps by mounting them in a book and writing them up much as one would today, according to L.N. and M. Williams. Bourke titled it *A Collection of the impressions to be made on every Skin, or piece of Vellum or Parchment, or every sheet of Paper, in manner and form as hereinafter expressed.* Although Bourke was obviously referring to handstamped markings, rather than today's adhesive label, there can be no doubt that his collection cast the shadow of a future hobby.

Jan. 31: Benjamin Franklin was dismissed from the post of Deputy Postmaster for the Northern District of the American Continent (see Dec. 19, 1764). The reasons were not entirely political and it seems that his absences in England where, as agent for Massachusetts he was working for the repeal of the Stamp Act, caused postal affairs to be neglected. This neglect of his duties provided the British government with a valid reason to get rid of him and to punish him for his activities concerning the Stamp Act.

Jan. 31: Hugh Finlay was appointed Deputy Postmaster for the Northern District of America, which extended from Quebec to Virginia. He replaced Benjamin Franklin.

July 2: William Goddard, a Baltimore printer and former postmaster, who had been working on a plan to establish a postal system in the colonies independent of the British, announced in his *Maryland Journal* that the system needed only the support of Maryland and Virginia to render it possible. The developing revolution by the colonies made necessary such a system and in the following year steps were taken to establish an American Post Office. Goddard's postal system adopted the 1765 postal rates set for the colonies by the British Parliament.

From postboy to mailcoach

1775

March: The General Post Office in London advised its postmasters in the seething American colonies that the best it could expect from them was that they should act with discretion to the best of their ability and judgment. In other words, they were pretty much on their own as far as the ability of the British to protect them from the rebels was concerned.

A postrider of Colonial America.

May 29: The Continental Congress appointed a committee under the chairmanship of Benjamin Franklin to organize a postal system. Some colonies had already acted along the lines previously suggested by William Goddard (see July 2, 1774).

July 26: Benjamin Franklin was appointed Postmaster General of the new Continental Post Office. His son-in-law, Richard Bache, became his comptroller and William Goddard was made Surveyor to the Post Office. Franklin's salary was $1,000 a year, which he gave for the relief of wounded soldiers.

The Continental Post Office established rates 20 percent lower than those set by the Act of Parliament of 1765.

Sept. 30: The postal rates set by the Continental Post Office on July 26 were suspended. The 1765 British single sheet rates were adopted, but were expressed in terms of pennyweight (dwt) and grains (gr) of silver (24

grains equaled one pennyweight). For 60 miles or less, the rate was 1dwt 8gr. For 60-100 miles, the rate was 2dwt. Each additional 100 miles or fraction thereof cost 16gr.

Nov. 13: The Continental Army moved into Canada and occupied Montreal until June 1776. An American post office was established there under postmaster George Measam.

Dec. 25: The Secretary of the British Post Office at New York announced that, because of the "interruptions to the couriers" in the American colonies, the inland postal service would end on that date. This brought to a close the operations of the General Post Office in the American colonies.

1776

Jan. 9: Free franking was granted to private soldiers in the Continental Army providing that the letters were franked by an officer in charge.

July 9: Jacob Perkins, founder of the British printing firm of Perkins, Bacon & Petch, later known as Perkins, Bacon & Co., is reported to have been born on this date at Newburyport, Mass. He moved to Britain in 1819.

Aug. 30: The Continental Congress adopted a resolution that called for post riders to be stationed every 25 or 30 miles. The riders were to travel their stage three times every week, setting out immediately upon receipt of the mail and traveling with it day and night until it was delivered to the next rider.

Nov. 7: When Benjamin Franklin went to France as agent for the colonies, Richard Bache became Postmaster General of the Continental Post Office.

1777

Oct. 17: The Continental Congress increased the postal rates of Sept. 30, 1775 (q.v.) by 50 percent.

1778

July 9: The Confederation Post Office, forerunner of the United States Post Office, came into being. Robson Lowe notes that this organization had no authority over internal services within the various colonies and the Confederation itself was a loose union of the colonies. It was not until the federal system came into being in 1789 that there was a United States Post Office.

1779

Feb. 15: Don Teodoro de Croix, Governor of the Interior Provinces of New Spain, issued a decree establishing a mail route between settlements in what is now Texas and the towns in Chihuahua and Arispe. Crossing the Rio Grande, it passed through San Antonio de Bexar (today's San Antonio) and reached as far east as Nacogdoches. Service was monthly.

April 16: The Continental Congress doubled the postal rates of Oct. 17, 1777 (q.v.).

Dec. 28: The Continental Congress increased the July 26, 1775 (q.v.) rates twenty-fold.

1780

By this year, the staff of the Confederation Post Office serving the ex-colonies in America comprised a postmaster general, a secretary/comptroller, three surveyors, one inspector of dead letters, and 26 post riders.

May 5: The Continental Congress established new postal rates at 40 times the July 26, 1775 rates.

Dec. 12: The Continental Congress established that postal rates payable in specie should be 50 percent of the rates of Sept. 30, 1775.

1781

Feb. 24: The Continental Congress increased the postal rates to double those of Sept. 30, 1775.

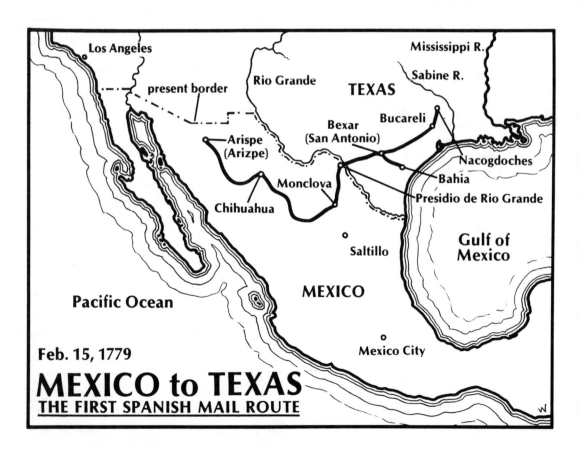

Feb. 15, 1779

MEXICO to TEXAS
THE FIRST SPANISH MAIL ROUTE

1782

Jan. 28: Ebenezer Hazard replaced Richard Bache as Postmaster General of the Continental Post Office. He continued in the office until replaced Sept. 27, 1789 by Samuel Osgood.

Oct. 18: The Continental Congress restored the postal rates of Sept. 30, 1775 effective on this date.

Oct. 18: The Continental Congress passed an act reorganizing and codifying the Post Office. It provided, according to Rich, that "...a continued communication of posts throughout these United States shall be established and maintained under the direction of the Postmaster General of the United States, to extend to and from the State of New Hampshire and the State of Georgia inclusive, and to and from such other parts of these United States, as from time to time he shall judge necessary, or Congress shall direct." The postmaster general received $1,500 a year and his assistant $1,000.

Oct. 18: The franking privilege was granted to members of the Continental Congress, Secretary of the Congress, Commander-in-Chief of the Armies, and the departments of Finance, War, and Foreign Affairs.

1783

The first post office opened at St. John, in what is now the Canadian province of New Brunswick.

June 10: Russia and Turkey signed an agreement providing for the transmission of mail between the two countries and a Russian Postal Agency was established at Constantinople. Packet boats carried mail on a Black Sea route.

Sept. 3: The Treaty of Paris was signed, ending the American Revolution and resulting in the establishment of the United States. On this date, all British operations officially ceased in what had been the American colonies.

Nov. 14: Russia was divided into postal zones and postal communications were established between important cities as a result of an Imperial Order.

1784

Jan. 11: The Deputy Postmaster for the Northern District of America, by then restricted generally to what is now Canada, sent a French Canadian named Durand off on a trial mail trip to the Maritime colonies in an attempt to set up an all-British route following the American Revolution. Mail had previously gone from Upper and Lower Canada (Quebec and Ontario) to New Brunswick and Nova Scotia by way of New York and Boston. It took Durand six weeks to reach Halifax and 102 days for the return journey. Regular service was not inaugurated until 1787 (q.v.).

Jan. 31: J. Stockdale, printer and publisher of the *Bermuda Gazette*, announced a postal service in Bermuda between Hamilton and other communities on the islands. The cost was 4d for a single letter (5d after 1800) and 8d for a letter or packet up to two ounces. According to Stockdale's announcement "...the approach of the letter carrier will be announced by the blowing of a horn." The service was operated by Stockdale until his death in 1803 and subsequently by his son-in-law, Charles Beach, until the Post Office Act of November 1818.

March 3: John Foxcroft was appointed British agent at New York for the packet boat service which was resumed between Great Britain and the former colonies, now the United States of America.

May 14: Under an act of Parliament of this year, the Irish Post Office became independent of the General Post Office in London, an independence it was to enjoy for almost 50 years. The system grew and the profits soared from £15,000 in 1786 to £108,000 in 1831. By 1809, there were 325 post towns in Ireland with daily posts to 223 of them, according to Reynolds.

July 7: Hugh Finlay was named Deputy Postmaster General of Canada.

Aug. 2: In accordance with a proposal by John Palmer that mailcoaches be used to transport mail and to reduce travel time in Britain, the first such coach left the *Swan Tavern*, Bristol at 4 p.m. It called at the Three Tuns at

Bath and arrived at the *Swan With Two Necks* tavern in London at 8 a.m. the following morning. The Bristol-London route proved so successful that other routes were soon established and a new era of mail transportation had begun that was only to be supplanted by the coming of the railway half a century later.

1785

March 28: Following the successful trial of mailcoaches on the Bristol-London route in England by John Palmer, the second of what soon became a network of mailcoach routes was established when a route between London and Norwich began operating on this date.

It was not long before the idea of the mailcoach spread across the world. All major countries had a network of routes and adopted designs most suited to conditions and needs. The culmination was the famous Concord coach that came to symbolize the opening of the American West (q.v.).

April 25: An advertisement in the *New York Packet* noted that the first stage line in New York was to be established in June, 1785, along the east side of the Hudson River between New York City and Albany. The twice-weekly schedule was later made three times a week. Konwiser states that mail was carried.

Dec. 31: US Postmaster General Ebenezer Hazard contracted with stagecoach operators to carry mail on segments of a route between Portsmouth, N.H. and Savannah, Ga. The trips were to be three times a week from May 1 to Nov. 1 and twice weekly from Nov. 1 to May 1. The total cost to the Post Office was $19,000 annually, according to Konwiser. In subsequent years, cross posts were established connecting with this main route.

1786

October: John Palmer was appointed Surveyor and Comptroller General of the Mails in Britain. His salary was £1,500 a year plus 2.5 percent of any increase in net revenue above £240,000 a year. He was directly responsible to the British Treasury and not answerable to the postmaster general.

1787

An "all-British" mail route was established between the cities of Quebec, Upper Canada and Halifax, Nova Scotia, following the American Revolution.

John Palmer (1742-1818) after a painting by Gainsborough.

John Palmer's first mailcoach. The 200th anniversary of the Aug. 2, 1784 Bristol-to-London run was marked in 1984 by a number of stamp issues. These are part of the British set and one of an issue from Lesotho.

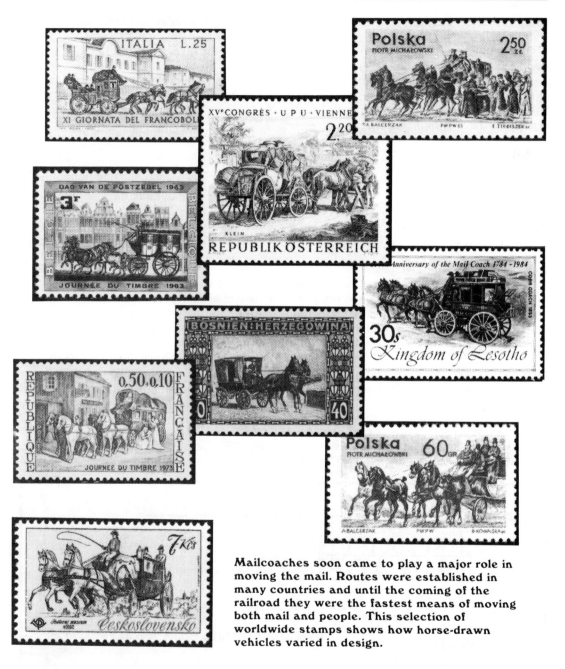

Mailcoaches soon came to play a major role in moving the mail. Routes were established in many countries and until the coming of the railroad they were the fastest means of moving both mail and people. This selection of worldwide stamps shows how horse-drawn vehicles varied in design.

Feb. 28: This is the earliest known date of use of hand-impressed postage stamps in England. This example took the form of two side-by-side circles, one containing "POST/ PAID" and the other, the date "28. FE" in upper and lower halves respectively. Later impressions combined both into one marking. They came in a variety of shapes.

Dec. 7: Delaware was the first of the original 13 states to ratify the Constitution.

Dec. 12: Pennsylvania was the second of the original 13 states to ratify the Constitution.

Dec. 18: New Jersey was the third of the original 13 states to ratify the Constitution.

1788

Jan. 2: Georgia entered the Union as the fourth of the original 13 states to ratify the Constitution.

Jan. 9: Connecticut was the fifth of the original 13 states to ratify the Constitution.

Feb. 4: A straight-line postmark of St. Petersburg bearing this date is the earliest-known Russian postal marking, according to Prigara. The markings are believed to have been introduced about 1782, during the postal reforms of Catherine the Great.

Feb. 6: Massachusetts was the sixth of the original 13 states to ratify the Constitution.

April 5: The US Congress reduced postal rates about 25 percent. The new rates were expressed in pennyweight and grains of silver to standardize them among the various states.

The rates were set at: up to 60 miles inland, 1 dwt; from 60-100 miles, 1 dwt. 8 gr; from 100-200 miles, 2 dwt; from 200-300 miles, 2 dwt. 16gr; from 300-400 miles, 3 dwt; and from 400-500 miles, 3 dwt. 8 gr. Incoming ship letters had 16 gr. added to the inland rate.

April 28: Maryland entered the Union as the seventh of the original 13 states to ratify the Constitution.

May 23: South Carolina was the eighth of the original 13 states to ratify the Constitution.

June 21: New Hampshire entered the Union as the ninth of the original 13 states to ratify the Constitution.

June 26: Virginia was the 10th of the original 13 states to ratify the Constitution.

July 3: This was the inaugural date of mail service westward from Philadelphia to Pittsburgh. Post riders went weekly to Chamberstown and every two weeks from there to Pittsburgh. The route was via Lancaster, Yorktown, Chamberstown, and Bedford.

July 26: New York was the 11th of the original 13 states to ratify the Constitution.

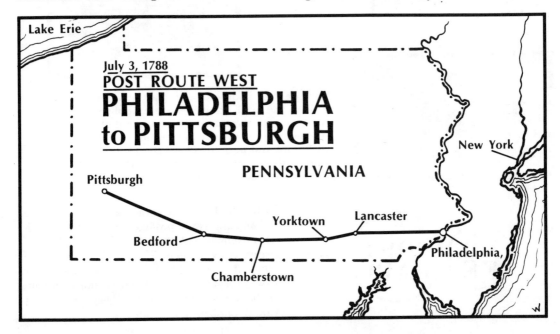

July 3, 1788
POST ROUTE WEST
PHILADELPHIA to PITTSBURGH
PENNSYLVANIA

Aug. 29: Congress authorized the postmaster general to establish a weekly post between the Delaware towns of Wilmington and Dover, according to Konwiser.

1789

Sept. 22: On this date the US Congress passed a Postal Act, thus ending the colonial period of the new country's postal history. The act did not cover North Carolina and Rhode Island, which did not become states until Nov. 21, 1789, and May 29, 1790 respectively.

Sept. 26: Samuel Osgood was appointed first Postmaster General of the newly formed United States by President George Washington. A total of 75 post offices operated in the United States at this time, according to Robson Lowe. They were served by 2,000 miles of post road. Konwiser records that Osgood's headquarters in the New York Post Office had a staff of one assistant and one clerk.

Nov. 21: North Carolina was the 12th of the original 13 states to ratify the Constitution.

1790

Jan. 22: In his first report as postmaster general, Samuel Osgood said rates of postage were too high in some places and too low in others; that receipts totaled about $25,000 a year; that if the average letter rate was set at 5c, a quantity of 500,000 letters would be sent (shades of Rowland Hill!); that cross roads must be established; and that there were about 20 different contracts for carrying mail.

May 29: Rhode Island was the 13th of the original 13 states to ratify the Constitution.

1791

March 4: Vermont entered the Union as the 14th state.

Aug. 12: Timothy Pickering appointed US postmaster general, succeeding Samuel Osgood.

Dec. 28: The first post office was established at the Cape of Good Hope by the early Dutch settlers. A postmaster was appointed and postal rates set.

1792

Feb. 20: The US Congress authorized the Post Office as a permanent organization. Up to this time, it had not been certain whether it should be a department of federal government, be operated by the individual states, or be farmed to private operators.

June 1: On this date, US postal rates were established at 6c for up to 30 miles, 30-60 miles at 8c, 60-100 miles at 10c, 100-150 at 12½c, 150-200 miles at 15c, 200-250 miles at 17c, 250-350 miles at 20c, 350-450 miles at 22c, and over 450 miles at 25c. Newspapers cost 1c for up to 100 miles and 1½c each for over 100 miles. Rates were also set on ship letters, according to Wierenga. These depended on distance traveled from port of arrival plus a 4c charge, which went to the ship's master.

June 1: Kentucky entered the Union as the 15th state.

June 1: A postal convention between the United States and Canada became effective. Under it, letters from Canada could be prepaid right to their US addresses, instead of only "to the lines" (US-Canadian border) as was the case before. Canada received 20 percent of US postage collected in the course of acting as an agent for the US. However, the US Post Office refused to collect Canadian postage on letters going the other way and letters to Canadian addresses could only be prepaid to the lines or sent unpaid. Canada ceased to collect US postage on Nov. 16, 1847, following the release of US postage stamps. (See April 6, 1851.)

1793

Jan. 9: Jean-Pierre Blanchard is reported to have carried a letter from President George Washington on his balloon flight from Philadelphia, but it seems likely that the letter was more in the nature of a safe-conduct pass than an item of mail. In those days, a balloonist was often in more danger from the pitchforks of frightened farmers than from the elements!

March 24: Thomas de la Rue was born at Le Bourg in the parish of La Foret, on the island of Guernsey. He was to found the printing house that bears his name.

May and June: Two small, unmanned balloons carrying packages of letters were released from the besieged fortress of Conde and nearby Valenciennes, according to Cohn. Both balloons were intercepted by the besieging Austrians and thus the mail did not reach its destination, Cohn notes.

Oct. 1: Delaware placed embossed revenue stamps in use in denominations of 5c, 20c, and 50c. Stamps in denominations of 3c, 33c, and $1 were called for but are not known, according to Scott. The stamps were effective until Feb. 7, 1794.

1794

Feb. 13: The first packet boat, the 80-ton *Royal Charlotte* sailed from Weymouth on the south coast of England to the English Channel islands. Aboard was a GPO surveyor, Christopher Saverland, who named Ann Watson postmaster of Guernsey and Charles William le Geyt postmaster of Jersey.

Feb. 15: The first post office was opened on the English Channel island of Jersey.

March 22: The first post office was opened on the English Channel island of Guernsey.

May 8: The US Congress established a General Post Office to have supervision over postal affairs with a postmaster general in charge. Samuel Osgood had been the first postmaster general. Timothy Pickering was serving as postmaster general on this date.

June 1: The drop letter rate in the United States was set at 1c, or 2c if delivered locally. A drop letter is one that is either picked up or delivered from the same post office at which it was mailed.

1795

Feb. 25: Joseph Habersham appointed US postmaster general, succeeding Timothy Pickering.

Dec. 3: Rowland Hill was born at Kidderminster, a manufacturing town about 20 miles southwest of Birmingham, England. At an early age he became a teacher at his father's school — reports tell of him teaching mathematics at the age of 12!

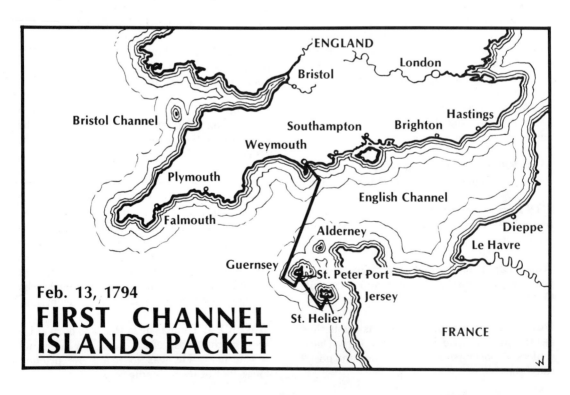

Feb. 13, 1794
FIRST CHANNEL ISLANDS PACKET

1796

June 1: Tennessee entered the Union as the 16th state.

1797

July 6: The US Congress approved on this date "An Act Laying Duties on Stamped Vellum, Parchment, and Paper." It was to take effect on Jan. 1, 1798. However, the difficulty of obtaining and distributing the various stamp dies delayed it until July 1, 1798 (q.v.).

1798

During the occupation of the Cape of Good Hope by the British from 1795-1803, a post office opened for overseas letters.

Jan. 20: A Portuguese royal decree created the Correios Maritimos to supervise the carriage of mail to Brazil, South America and Angola, Africa and to arrange the dispatch of two mail boats every two months from Portugal to Assu, Pernambuco, and Bahia. The decree provided that mail be carried in closed bags bearing the name of the vessel in which it was to sail. Onward transmission to Angola was to remain in private hands. It also decreed that postal administrators be appointed at Madeira, the Azores, and the Angolan cities of Luanda and Benguella.

May 7: An act of Congress of April 7, 1798 became effective, making Mississippi a territory.

July 1: The first US embossed revenue stamps became legal. Congress had approved legislation July 6, 1797 to allow them. They were in use until Feb. 28, 1801. These stamps were issued separately for the states of Connecticut, Delaware, Georgia, Kentucky, Maryland, Massachusetts, New Hampshire, New Jersey, New York, North Carolina, Pennsylvania, Rhode Island, South Carolina, Tennessee, Vermont, and Virginia. Denominations known are 4c, 10c, 20c, 25c, 30c, 50c, 75c, and $1. Higher values for some states are known. Sets of dies were sent to the various state officials who would apply them to documents upon payment of the appropriate tax.

Sept. 3: The Swiss Republic decreed that postal service was a monopoly of the state and assumed control of the cantonal services. However, by 1803, the cantons had regained control of their own postal services. It was not until 1849 that state control was finally assumed.

1799

March 2: Congress set US postal rates at 8c for up to 40 miles, 40-90 miles at 10c, 90-150 miles at 12½c, 150-300 miles at 17c, 300-500 miles at 20c, and over 500 miles at 25c. A drop letter rate of 1c went into effect. Wierenga also notes that the act reduced the 4c payment to ship's masters on ship letters to 2c, with changes to the rate structure on ship letters from the port of arrival.

Sept. 10: A Ship Letter Office was opened in London in an attempt by the General Post Office to prevent the handing of incoming letters to coffee houses and the avoidance of postage charges. No vessel was allowed to break bulk until letters it carried were handed over to the GPO, which charged 4d in addition to the regular domestic rate, 2d of which went to the ship's captain. Many outbound letters continued to be handed directly to ships' masters, thus avoiding the high rates then in effect.

1800

When the US Post Office moved its headquarters from Philadelphia to Washington, D.C., all of its furniture, postal records, and supplies required only two wagons.

July 4: Indiana became a Territory "from or after July 4" according to the act under which it was established. The Supreme Court interpreted this to mean July 5.

1801

London's Penny Post became a Twopenny Post when the lowest rate went from one penny to twopence.

The first post office opened on Cape Breton Island at Sydney. The area is now part of the Canadian province of Nova Scotia.

The Peace of Luneville, following the upheaval of the French Revolution, fixed the boundary of France and Germany on the Rhine River and caused the House of Thurn and Taxis to lose control of its postal service west of the river.

March 1: The US Congress enacted legislation effective on this date that created the second federal issue of embossed revenue stamps. There was a single issue for all states in denominations of 4c, 10c, 20c, 25c, 30c, 50c, 75c, $1, $4 and $10.

The stamp was in two parts, a circular eagle and shield design with denomination and a tombstone-shaped stamp with stars in a circular wreath and the denomination. Scott notes that the tombstone-shaped design was usually impressed below the circular design. The series was valid until June 30, 1802. These stamps were only applied to government-sold paper and the stamping was done in Washington, D.C.

March 6: US Postmaster General Joseph Habersham changed the title of "surveyor" to "special agent" when he appointed Phineas Bradley to investigate delay in mail handling on a route to Kentucky. See June 11, 1880.

Nov. 28: Gideon Granger was appointed US postmaster general, succeeding Joseph Habersham.

1803

The first US post office was opened in Detroit.

March 1: Ohio entered the Union as the 17th state.

June: The Dutch reoccupied the Cape of Good Hope from 1803 to 1805 and set up a post office. Routes were established between Cape Town and Simonstown and from Cape Town to Stellenbosch. The system was retained by the British when they returned in 1805.

July 10: The Sydney *Gazette* reported that the charge was 2d for letters carried by boatmen between Sydney and Parramatta in New South Wales. Robson Lowe notes this as the first mention of postal services in Australia.

1804

July 29: Laurenz Koschier (sometimes spelled Koshir or Kosir) was born at Unter-Luscha in the Austro-Hungarian Empire. He attended school at Laibach (now the Yugoslavian town of Ljubljana). It is claimed that he submitted the idea for adhesive postage stamps to Austro-Hungarian postal authorities on Dec. 31, 1835 (q.v.).

Oct. 1: This was the effective date of an act of Congress creating the District of Louisiana. The area was administered from the Territory of Indiana and took in the land obtained in the Louisiana Purchase of 1803 north of 33 degrees N. The portion to the south became the Territory of Orleans.

1805

April 18: In a letter bearing this date, Francis Freeling, secretary to the General Post Office, London, approved the appointment of Simon Solomon to be postmaster at St. John's, Newfoundland, and the opening of a post office in that town.

July 1: On this date, the Territory of Michigan came into being.

Laurenz Koschier has been honored on stamps of Austria and Yugoslavia.

A packet boat of the early 1800s.

July 4: This was the effective date of an Act of Congress making the District of Louisiana the Territory of Louisiana.

1806

Dec. 2: The British postmaster general was authorized to operate a packet service between Falmouth and Gibraltar and Malta, where the post offices were branches of the General Post Office in London.

1807

The mailcoach running between Montreal, Canada and Boston took four and a half days under normal conditions to make the 312-mile journey.

Aug. 27: Curacao was occupied by the British, who established a post office at Willemstad to serve the islands of Curacao, Aruba, and Bonaire. Postal markings were introduced and were the first used in the islands.

1808

June 2: Johann Peter Colding launched an unmanned balloon carrying letters from Nyborg addressed to Copenhagen on the Danish island of Zealand, then blockaded by the British fleet.

One of Colding's balloons sailing over the British fleet (June 2, 1808).

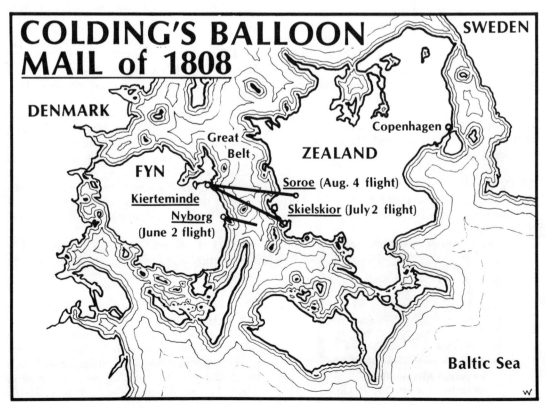

COLDING'S BALLOON MAIL of 1808

SWEDEN

DENMARK

Great Belt

FYN

ZEALAND

Copenhagen

Kierteminde

Nyborg
(June 2 flight)

Soroe (Aug. 4 flight)

Skielskior (July 2 flight)

Baltic Sea

This was the first of several mail-carrying balloon flights and had the official blessing of the Danish king. It is not recorded whether the mail was delivered, but a British vessel is reported to have found a balloon floating in the waters of the Great Belt between the islands of Fyn and Zealand. Two subsequent flights on July 2 and Aug. 4 were successful.

July 2: Johann Peter Colding's second mail-carrying balloon made a successful flight from Kierteminde to the Danish island of Zealand and was delivered to the postmaster of Skielskior (Skaelskor) for delivery to Copenhagen.

Aug. 2: The earliest known use of a postal marking in Curacao is recorded for this date. It was introduced during the 1807-1816 period when Britain administered the Caribbean island, now part of the Netherlands Antilles.

Aug. 4: Johann Peter Colding's third balloon flight carrying mail from Kierteminde to the Danish island of Zealand for transmission to Copenhagen was successful. The balloon was found on Sept. 21 and the contents delivered.

1809

March 1: Illinois became a Territory "from or after March 1," according to the law under which it was established. The Supreme Court interpreted this to mean March 2.

Oct. 31: The first post office was established at Belize, later capital of British Honduras, now the independent country of Belize.

1812

Jan. 23: A river steamer first carried mail on the Mississippi River from New Orleans to Natchez, Miss.

A typical Mississippi steamboat (Feb. 27, 1813).

April 30: The District of Orleans, which had been that part of the Louisiana Purchase to the south of 33 degrees N., became the state of Louisiana and the 18th state of the Union.

Dec. 7: The Territory of Missouri was established on this date.

1813

May 1: The state of Virginia used embossed revenue stamps from this date to Feb. 27, 1816. There were two separate designs used in a variety of denominations. Both are circular and depict a twig and arrow with the state name above and denomination below.

May 10: Montgomery Blair was born in Franklin County, Kentucky. He was later to become US postmaster general and one of the chief advocates of international cooperation in the handling of mail and the development of a simple accounting system between various countries.

Feb. 27: Congress authorized contracts for the carriage of mail by steamboat, according to Konwiser.

1814

Jan. 1: The US Congress passed legislation on Aug. 2, 1813, effective on this date, authorizing the third federal issue of embossed revenue stamps. The design is circular and comprises the eagle, shield, and denomination. Denominations are 5c, 10c, 25c, 50c, 75c, $1, $1.50, $2, $2.50, $3.50, $4, and $5. All stamps were embossed in Washington on paper sold by the government. The taxes were imposed to pay the expenses of the War of 1812. This issue was used until Dec. 31, 1817.

April 11: Return J. Meigs appointed US postmaster general, succeeding Gideon Granger.

Dec. 23: Congress approved a law, effective Feb. 1, 1815, that increased all US postal rates by 50 percent in an attempt to raise revenue to help pay for the War of 1812. The rates charged on ship letters were also affected, although the 2c payment to ship's masters remained in effect. The act was repealed on Feb. 1, 1816.

1815

Feb. 1: This was the effective date of the act of Congress on Dec. 23, 1814 that increased postal rates by 50 percent to help pay for the War of 1812.

March: A national post was set up in the Netherlands and the Thurn and Taxis postal services were further reduced. Following the Napoleonic Wars, Thurn and Taxis began to lose much of its vast system of posts throughout Europe, as national postal systems became established.

April 24: Anthony Trollope was born in Bloomsbury, London, England. His family was a literary one and he was educated at Winchester and Harrow. In reduced circumstances because of his father's long illness, in 1834 Trollope obtained a position at £90 a year in the Post Office and rose to the position of surveyor (inspector).

1816

John Loudon MacAdam (1756-1836) built 11 miles of road in England between Bristol and Old Down. He used a process he had devised, which involved installing proper drainage by raising the road surface above the surrounding land and surfacing it with clean, graded stones. This resulted in enormous improvements in road condition, led to greater speeds, and played a part in speeding the carriage of mail. It was the work of men such as MacAdam that made possible the network of mailcoaches that rose to its peak just as the railway appeared.

Feb. 1: Congress approved the repeal of the War of 1812 postal rates, which represented a 50 percent increase of previous rates in an attempt to raise funds to pay for the war. The repeal became effective on March 31, 1816. See Dec. 23, 1814.

March 31: This was the effective date of the Act of Congress on Feb. 1, 1816 that restored the War of 1812 postal rates to their prewar level. They had been raised by 50 percent to raise money to pay for the war.

May 1: US postal rates were set at 6c for up to 30 miles. Zone rates were 30-80 miles at

10c, 80-150 miles at 12½c, 150-400 miles at 18½c, and more than 400 miles at 25c.

Dec. 11: Indiana entered the Union as the 19th state.

1817

June 5: A letter written by the master of the Spanish ship *Bilboena*, driven ashore at Rottingdean, near Brighton, on England's south coast, provides the earliest known cover with a manuscript inscription identifying it with a wreck, according to Hopkins.

However, in the January 1985 issue of *Scott Stamp Monthly*, L. N. Williams reports the existence of a 1799 letter bearing a marking identifying it as being from the wreck of the British warship HMS *Lutine*, which went down during a storm off the Dutch coast on the night of Oct. 9, 1799. The marking is reported to read "Sav'd from/ the Wreck of/ the Lutine/ Frigate" in a circle.

Aug. 15: On this date, Alabama became a territory.

Nov. 18: A decree by the Austrian government required all post offices and letter-collecting agencies to procure postmarks and use them beginning Jan. 1, 1818. A little more than 1,000 post offices throughout Austria and its provinces obtained and used the postmarks, which were supposed to be applied to the address side of letters.

Dec. 10: Mississippi entered the Union as the 20th state.

1818

Jan. 6: The first building in Ireland designed specifically as a post office was opened on Sackville Street in Dublin.

May 1: The state of Maryland issued embossed revenue stamps on this date under an act of Feb. 11, 1818. Only the 30c denomination is known, according to Scott. The issue was effective until March 7, 1819. The act was ruled unconstitutional by the Supreme Court.

Nov. 17: The Kingdom of Sardinia began the sale of stamped paper. It bore an indicium depicting a horseman at full gallop blowing a

Reproduced on a modern Italian stamp, the Cavallini's octagonal frame indicated that it was a 50c denomination, good for over 35 miles (Nov. 17, 1818).

posthorn. This was enclosed in either a circle, an oval, or an octagon. These were for letters going up to 15 miles, 16-35 miles, or over 35 miles, and their cost was 15, 25, and 50 centesimi respectively.

There were two issues; the first printed in blue and the second in colorless embossing. Known as *Cavallini* (little horseman), there is some confusion as to their status. Dehn notes that they represent an attempt to collect a fee on letters that were sent outside the mail. However, Kanadouroff claims that they were a "tax designed to exercise government control on correspondence and cannot be regarded as postage stamps in the true sense, though of course, such sheets were often exempt from further payments of postage." All of which does little except to indicate that varied opinions are held!

Dec. 3: Illinois entered the Union as the 21st state.

1819

Jacob Perkins, an American, went to England. He founded the firm of Perkins, Bacon & Petch that was to produce the *Penny Black* and *Twopenny Blue*, the world's first adhesive postage stamps. As Perkins, Bacon & Co. the firm lasted until 1936, when it was liquidated.

May 24: Birth of Alexandria Victoria, later Queen Victoria of England, to Edward, Duke of Kent, fourth son of King George III and Victoria Mary Louisa, daughter of the Duke of Saxe-Coburg.

March 2: Arkansas was made a territory by Congress on this date. It became effective

"from or after July 4." The Supreme Court interpreted this to mean July 5.

Dec. 14: Alabama entered the Union as the 22nd state.

1820

Carlo Meratti, an Italian living in Egypt, established a local post in Alexandria. For a fee, he visited incoming ships and delivered letters to the addressees. He soon opened an office where people could bring letters for dispatch by ship, according to Kehr.

March 15: Maine entered the Union as the 23rd state.

1821

Aug. 10: Missouri entered the Union as the 24th state.

1822

March 30: Florida became a territory on this date.

1823

In the United States, waterways and canals were declared to be post roads, thus giving the Post Office a monopoly on their use to carry mail.

July 1: John McLean appointed US postmaster general succeeding Return J. Meigs.

Aug. 23: The Guernsey Post Office set up a department to handle mail to and from the island of Alderney and points on the French coast. It was known as the Foreign Post Office and existed until the 1840s, when a post office was opened on Alderney.

1825

During this year, the title US Post Office Department came into use. Previously, it had borne the name General Post Office following the style of the British General Post Office.

Dead Letter Office established by the US Post Office Department.

May 1: The rate for way letters in the United States (those letters picked up by a mail carrier on his route for deposit at the next post office) was set at 1c in addition to normal postage. The charge had been 2c since June 1, 1794.

The steam packet *Curacao*
(April 26, 1827).

1826

May 18: Stephen F. Austin, in a letter to the chief postmaster of Texas under Mexican administration, recommended the appointment of Samuel May Williams as postmaster of San Felipe de Austin, the center of the American colony in Texas, according to ter Braake. Williams was appointed shortly afterwards. San Felipe was one of only four post offices of the Mexican administration in all of Texas. The others were at San Antonio, Bahia and Nacogdoches.

1827

Prince Maximilian Karl von Taxis assumed control of the Thurn and Taxis posts as his hereditary right. By this time the organization served only 19 small states and the free cities of Hamburg, Bremen, and Lubeck.

January: A prepaid city post was established in Berlin. The city was divided into 36 districts with a total of 60 collection points. There was a staff of 40 mail carriers. Letters could also be sent collect.

Jan. 7: Sir Sandford Fleming born at Kirkaldy, Scotland. He became famous for his work on the transcontinental railroad across Canada, for devising time zones, and as designer of Canada's first adhesive postage stamp, the 3d *Beaver* (q.v.).

April 26: The steam packet *Curacao* sailed from the Netherlands for Curacao, in the West Indies. She was the first steamship to make the westbound transatlantic crossing. She took 44 days for the voyage and made a portion of the crossing under sail. She subsequently made several mail-carrying voyages.

Oct. 12: Thomas Leavitt, inventor of the first practical machine for mechanical cancelation, was born at Hingham, Mass.

1828

A postal service was established in Greece.

This set of four stamps was issued by Greece on May 15, 1978 to mark the 150th anniversary of the Greek Post Office. From the top left the stamps show a postrider and a cancelation of the period, the packet ship *Maximilianos* and the first Greek stamp, a mail train and one of the 1896 Greek Olympic stamps, and modern mailmen on motorcycles and a 1972 stamp picturing a young stamp collector.

Oct. 4: A post office act of this date in Van Diemen's Land (Tasmania) called for the establishment of a post office in Hobart, the appointment of a postmaster, fixed rates, and arranged for the conveyance of letters.

1829

Feb. 7: When Don Jose Ignacio Esteva was appointed postmaster general during the Mexican administration of Texas, he took strong measures to try and control the abuse of the franking privilege.

Texas postmasters were threatened with fines of 20 times the lost postage, suspension of pay for three months and dismissal for subsequent offenses. The problem obviously was not confined to the major nations of that time. It played a large part in bringing about Rowland Hill's postal reform in Great Britain.

April 6: William T. Barry appointed US postmaster general, succeeding John McLean.

September: A new General Post Office building was opened at St. Martin's le Grand, London.

Dec. 4: The harbor master at Fremantle in the British colony of Western Australia was appointed postmaster.

The General Post Office Building at St. Martin's le Grand, London opened in September 1829.

1830 - 1859
Postal reform & postage stamps

1830

France opened a postal agency in Alexandria, Egypt, for the convenience of French citizens in the city. There was no Egyptian postal service available to the public. In succeeding years post offices were opened by Great Britain (1831), Austria (1838), Russia (1857), Greece (1859) and Italy (1863), according to Kehr.

In the Mexican Post Office of the 1830s, social responsibilities were highly developed. Financial support was provided for widows and orphans of postal workers and there was a contributory pension plan, according to ter Braake.

Feb. 13: An early wreck cover bearing an imprinted cachet identifying it as a wreck cover is from the ship *Lady Holland*, wrecked on Dassan Island off the South African coast on this date. The cachet reads "From the wreck/ of the/ Lady Holland."

Hopkins believes it to have been applied at Madras, India, where salvaged mail was taken. The cover is addressed to Calcutta from Bath, England, and was postmarked "Madras G.P.O. Ship Letter" and dated April 24, 1830. (See June 5, 1817.)

March 17: Captain W. Waldegrove of HMS *Seringapatam* wrote the earliest known letter from Pitcairn Island. It was addressed to the Colonial Office in London. The earliest known letter from a resident was written in September 1844 (q.v.) to the resident chaplain of the British community in Valparaiso, Chile, thanking the community for gifts received.

Sept. 15: The first carriage of mail by railway occurred on the Liverpool and Manchester Railway in England.

Oct. 27: The Russian government authorized the postmaster general to establish a City Post in St. Petersburg, the Russian capital. The city was divided into 17 districts with two mailmen for each. Offices were opened in stores and other suitable places and mailboxes were set up.

1831

Jan. 7: Heinrich von Stephen was born at Stolp, Pomerania. He was to become head of the postal service of the North German Confederation. Like Montgomery Blair (q.v.) he worked for the creation of an international organization that would solve the great problems of international mail rates and the accounting procedures necessary for countries to be compensated for handling each other's mail.

Jan. 15: The *Best Friend of Charleston* locomotive on the South Carolina Railroad carried the first mail by railroad in the United States. The locomotive soon came to a sad end, when someone tied down the safety valve in order to get more power!

April 6: The Irish Post Office returned to the control of the General Post Office, London. This resulted in a general reform to bring the operation up to standard. Pay scales were reviewed and the practice of one individual holding down more than one position was eliminated.

1832

March 1: The security printing firm of Rawdon, Wright, Hatch & Co. was formed. In 1847, it changed its name to Rawdon, Wright, Hatch & Edson.

Nov. 30: Stage contractors on the Philadelphia-Lancaster, Penn., route were granted an allowance of $400 a year for carrying the mail on the railroad as far as Westchester, a distance of 30 miles, effective Dec. 5, 1832.

1833

Jan. 17: The Russian City Post began home delivery of mail in St. Petersburg.

May 7: Abraham Lincoln was appointed postmaster of New Salem, Ill. He held the position for about three years. His income is

Abraham Lincoln

Royal William (Aug. 18, 1833).

reported to have been around $1 a week in commission on receipts!

August: Robert Wallace, a member of the British Parliament for Greenock, whose criticism of the British Post Office did much to prompt reform, stated during a speech that "the Post Office ought to be conducted on more liberal principles." This was the first shot in a campaign by Wallace to improve the operation of the Post Office.

Aug. 18: On this date the steamship *Royal William* left Pictou, Nova Scotia, for London, taking 25 days on the voyage. She is reported to have carried unofficial mail, but none has been recorded, according to Staff.

1834
June 30: Indian Territory established. It was previously called Indian Country. With Oklahoma Territory, it became the state of Oklahoma Nov. 16, 1907.

1835
Edward Maxwell of Louisville, Ky., is recorded as making envelopes in the United States. This appears to be the first mention of envelope making in this country.

By this year, according to Robson Lowe, there were 30 post office employees in Van Diemen's Land (Tasmania) and a twice-weekly post carried mail over 434 miles of post road in the colony.

During a speech on the need for British Post Office reform, Robert Wallace told Parliament that letters should be charged by weight, and that the extra charge for letters having envelopes or more than one piece of paper, should be discontinued.

Jan. 8: A mail route across Egypt to link with sea transportation in the Mediterranean and Red seas was advertised by Thomas Waghorn. The fee was 5/- for a letter, in addition to the normal postage for the sea portions of the journey.

The service operated for about 10 years and was a great improvement over the long sea voyage around the Cape of Good Hope. In 1858, a railway linked Suez and Alexandria and from 1869, the new Suez Canal enabled ships to pass between the Mediterranean and Red seas. Covers bearing the inscription "Care of Mr. Waghorn" are greatly prized.

A train similar to this carried...

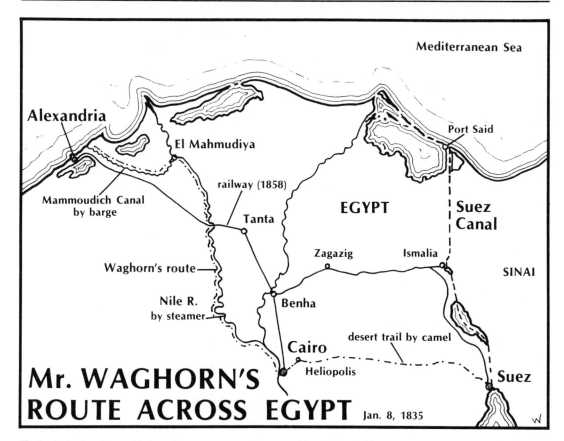

Mr. WAGHORN'S ROUTE ACROSS EGYPT Jan. 8, 1835

Feb. 14: Josef von Hohen Blum, an Austrian, received the first patent for a pneumatic tube system. These tube systems were widely used for mail in Europe and North America during the 19th and early 20th centuries.

May 1: Amos Kendall appointed US postmaster general, succeeding William T. Barry.

Oct. 30: When the postal service of the new Republic of Texas was being planned, a committee headed by Stephen F. Austin recommended a plan very likely unique as a means of funding a postal service — public subscription! ter Braake quotes the following recommendation: "...that a general subscription be opened and put in circulation under the superintendance of said director (PMG), to raise funds to defray the expenses of carrying weekly mails." Support was enthusiastic but even when added to postal revenues was never sufficient. ter

...the first mail by rail in 1830.

Braake says it received $410 within the first 11 months.

Dec. 1: US Postmaster General Amos Kendall wrote on this date that a contract to carry mail had been arranged with operators of steamboats on the Ohio and Mississippi rivers. The cost of a three-times-a-week service during the period of navigation between Pittsburgh and Cincinnati was stated to be $1,800 a year. Kendall also noted that arrangements had been made for a service between Louisville and St. Louis and Louisville and New Orleans at a cost of $30,000 a year.

Dec. 7: A post office department in what soon became the Republic of Texas was created by a law signed on this date by the lieutenant governor following a meeting of the leaders of Texas in San Felipe. The department largely resembled the United States Post Office. Governor Henry Smith approved the plan on Dec. 13. John Rice Jones was named postmaster general.

Dec. 31: Laurenz Koschier presented to the Austro-Hungarian postal authorities ideas for postal reform that included a suggestion for using "letter tax stamps," an idea that was not adopted. In 1954, *L'Union Postale*, the journal of the Universal Postal Union, published documents that Koschier had placed before the 1874 UPU Congress as a claim that he had conceived the idea of postage stamps and submitted it to the Austrian government. It had been rejected as "impractical."

1836

The Eastern Pony Express inaugurated service between cities in the eastern United States. See July 1839.

When the Australian colony of South Australia was founded, it appointed a postmaster at Adelaide. He received and distributed the mail from his house.

Jan. 1: The US postmaster general was authorized to contract for transporting mail by railroad between Philadelphia and Mauch Chunk, Pa., according to Konwiser.

June 15: Arkansas entered the Union as the 25th state.

July 2: Congress increased the way letter rate from 1c to 2c.

July 4: The territory of Wisconsin came into being.

1837

The first official mail service to and from Andorra operated between Seo de Urgel, Spain, and St. Julia de Loria in Andorra. Andorran couriers picked up the mail at St. Julia de Loria and distributed it within Andorra, according to Jacques.

January: Rowland Hill, a schoolmaster, published a pamphlet entitled *Post Office Reform: Its Importance and Practicability.* Initially, he had no connection with or knowledge of the workings of the British Post Office. "I have never been inside the walls of a post office," he claimed.

After much study of the problems he concluded that the most important requirements were a

THE *Original* BATH Mail Coach *of 1784* · AN *Attack on the* EXETER Mail *in 1816* · THE NORWICH Mail

Highlights of the...

Sir Rowland Hill.

uncle, King William IV, as Queen Victoria of the United Kingdom of Great Britain and Ireland and, from 1876, Empress of India.

September: A steamer service run by Wilcox and Anderson as the Peninsular Company (later the famous Peninsula and Oriental Steam Navigation Company or P&O Line) won a contract to carry mail between Falmouth, England, (later from Southampton) and Gibraltar with calls at Vigo, Oporto, Lisbon, and Cadiz. Service was later extended to Alexandria. With the completion of the Suez Canal direct service to India became possible.

Nov. 23: The British House of Commons formed a committee to study the problems of the Post Office as a result of the public clamor following the publication of Rowland Hill's pamphlet on postal reform. The result was the reform of 1840, of which the introduction of the adhesive postage stamp was a part.

uniform charge regardless of destination, a postal charge levied on weight rather than number of pieces and prepayment of letters. He also proposed the use of postal stationery and the adhesive postage stamp as a means of prepaying postal charges.

Hill's proposed reforms were a clear and impressive illustration that the spectator often sees more of the game than does a player. Certainly, he knew what was needed and was even more radical in his thinking than was Wallace (see 1835).

Jan. 26: Michigan entered the Union as the 26th state.

April 13: The first post office opened at Melbourne, Australia, in what became the colony of Victoria in 1851. Prior to achieving colony status, the area was known as the Port Phillip District and was under the administration of New South Wales.

June 20: Alexandria Victoria succeeded her

1838

At the height of the British mailcoach era, one of the many coach proprietors was William Chaplin. In 1838, he operated 70 coaches and used 1,800 horses on his various routes.

Large numbers of horses were needed to maintain the high speeds and a stage was generally only about 10 miles. On the London-to-Scotland route 400 horses were required, according to Robinson.

Changing horses bore all the hallmarks of an Indy 500 pit stop as the four horses were unhitched and a fresh team brought out. This could be done in less than one minute.

Jan. 4: In England, Nathaniel Worsdell was granted a patent for a device for picking up and

...mailcoach era.

The steamship *Sirius*.

depositing mailbags from a moving train. However, the British Post Office offered only £500 for the use of the device. Worsdell refused and the BPO "re-devised" the equipment itself. Presumably Worsdell received nothing. See Oct. 27, 1838.

Jan. 24: The first railway post office that worked mail enroute went into use on the British Grand Junction Railway and operated between Birmingham and Liverpool. It was a converted horse-box and proved so successful that the Post Office decided to make Travelling Post Offices (TPO) a permanent feature of British railways. Their use soon spread to the railways of the world.

Feb. 22: Samuel Allan Taylor was born in the Scottish fishing village of Irvine, a few miles north of Ayr. In 1850 he moved to the United States and then to Montreal, where he began publication of the first North American philatelic periodical.

Eventually, he returned to the United States to become one of the world's great creators of bogus stamps, including one that reproduced his own portrait! He was several times charged with counterfeiting, although the charges were either dropped or the sentence deferred. He died in 1913 and is buried at Everett, Mass.

April 4: Russian letters were carried on the first railroad opened in that country. The track ran for several miles from St. Petersburg.

April 4: The British steamship *Sirius* sailed from Cork for New York. She took 17 days for the crossing and made the return voyage in a similar time. *Sirius* was the first steamship to carry official mail on a transatlantic voyage.

April 5: A letter from James Chalmers of Dundee, Scotland, published in the *Post Circular* advocated the introduction of a stamped slip with a device resembling that of a newspaper stamp and "rubbed over the back with a strong solution of gum." However, this appeared over a year after Rowland Hill had published his adhesive stamp proposal.

There is no conclusive evidence that Chalmers had developed his idea prior to Hill, despite the controversy that arose between their sons after the death of both men. Neither did Chalmers mention an adhesive postage stamp in his entry in the British Treasury's competition for postage payment ideas prior to Hill's 1840 reforms, according to Robinson.

May 18: Scheele quotes a newspaper article of this date describing the working of way mail by a typical route agent on a US train. The agent was responsible for sorting mail for post offices along the line, emptying the mailbox affixed to the train, and either distributing its contents for post offices on the route or handing it, together with the through mail, to the postmaster at the end of the run. The route agent system had operated in the US since 1837.

July 4: Iowa became a territory on this date.

July 7: The US Congress declared all railroads to be post roads. Konwiser quotes the act as providing "that each and every railroad within the limits of the United States which now is or may hereafter be completed, shall be a post route, and the Postmaster General shall cause the mail to be carried thereon."

There was then a total of 1,913 miles of line

on the country. The act limited the cost of railroad transportation of mail to "not more than 25 percent over what similar transportation would cost in post coaches."

Sept. 20: The earliest known railroad postmark in the United States was a circular marking reading "BALTIMORE RAIL-ROAD SEP 20."

Oct. 27: A device designed by the British Post Office to exchange mailbags with a moving train was used on the London and Birmingham Railway. The device was complicated and there were operational problems. A simplified version was designed and was ready for testing by 1848. See Jan. 4, 1852.

Nov. 1: The postmaster general at Sydney, New South Wales, issued what can clearly be regarded as an item of postal stationery. It was in the form of a lettersheet with a colorless embossing of the colony's seal as an indicium. The sheets cost two pence each, which included delivery within the city, then a town of some 20,000. The indicium was canceled by stamping the hour of delivery across it, according to Mott. The items were reprinted several times before the die was destroyed in 1898, according to Hornadge.

1839

A post office opened at Crater (Aden). About 1858 it moved to a new building at Steamer Point. The original office was re-named Aden Cantonment, later Aden Camp sub-office.

February: William Harnden began his express operation between Boston and New York.

May 4: An agreement between the British Admiralty and Samuel Cunard provided for the carriage of mail between Liverpool, England, Halifax, Canada, and Boston. The agreement required vessels to be steam powered and of 300 horsepower. The contract was for seven years at £55,000 per year.

June: Henry Corbould received a commission from the printers, Perkins, Bacon & Petch, to produce a drawing for the engraving of the die for the first adhesive postage stamp, Britain's

Penny Black. The artwork was based on William Wyon's medal featuring a profile of the young Queen Victoria. The medal had been struck to commemorate the Queen's first visit to the City of London on Nov. 9, 1837.

July: Railroads now provided sufficiently fast schedules so that the extra expense of the special service that has come to be called the Eastern Pony Express was no longer justified and it was discontinued. It was begun in 1836 to provide fast service between cities of the east and the southern cities of St. Louis, New Orleans, Mobile, and Charleston, S.C.

Riders on horseback rode around the clock to carry news of commodity price fluctuations, news, government dispatches and private letters. Letters were charged at three times the normal postal rates. It took a little over six days to make the run between New York and New Orleans, with available railroads and steamboats used on portions of the route.

July: Thomas Spring-Rice, British chancellor of the exchequer, proposed a resolution in the House of Commons to "...reduce the postage charged on letters to one uniform rate of one penny ... Parliamentary privilege of franking to be abolished and official franking strictly regulated; this House pledging itself at the same time to make good any deficiency of the revenue which may be occasioned by such alteration of the rates of the existing duties." The resolution passed by a two-to-one majority.

Aug. 17: Royal assent to the British Postal Reform Bill made it law. The law provided for the introduction of a uniform one-penny postal rate throughout the country on Jan. 10, 1840. It was intended that the adhesive 1d and 2d postage stamps and the Mulready envelope and letter sheet also should be released on that date. However, they were not ready and became valid for use on May 6, with the 2d stamp becoming available on May 8.

Aug. 23: The British Treasury opened a competition to determine the design and type of a means of prepaying postal charges. Some form of label was contemplated, as Hill had outlined in his pamphlet (see January 1837). The result was more than 2,600 entries. Although none

Charles Whiting's entry in the British Treasury Competition.

of the suggestions were used, four were considered to deserve a reward. They were a joint entry by James Bogardus and Francis Coffin and individual submissions by Benjamin Cheverton, Henry Cole and Charles Whiting. Each received £100.

Dec. 5: As a prelude to the introduction of uniform penny postage in Great Britain, the postal cost of a letter was reduced to 4d per half ounce, regardless of the number of sheets or the distance the letter was to be carried. This new rate was widely perceived as an attempt to avoid having to introduce the 1d rate and even Rowland Hill was criticized for the half-hearted act. It was this clamor that led Hill and the Treasury to introduce the 1d rate in January 1840, although the stamps would not be ready in time.

1840

A postmaster was appointed on Norfolk Island and handstamps provided for the postmarking of mail. Stamps of Tasmania were used from 1853 but Robson Lowe notes that no used examples canceled with the island's number "102" obliterator are known. Subsequently, stamps of New South Wales were used, then, when they were issued, stamps of the Commonwealth of Australia.

Edward Stanley Gibbons was born during this year at 15 Treville St., Plymouth, England. He founded the stamp dealing and publishing firm that still bears his name. He is reported to have owned a collection by 1854 and in 1856 began dealing in stamps in an area of his father's

pharmacy in Plymouth.

His business was first known as E.S. Gibbons, then E. Stanley Gibbons, followed by Stanley, Gibbons and Company. The comma was presumably intended to lend importance to the endeavor. Gibbons' catalog, first published in 1865, has become one of the world's best known and widely used.

January: The first official post office in New Zealand was established at Kororarika.

Jan. 10: The one penny postal rate was introduced throughout Great Britain as part of Rowland Hill's postal reform. Adhesive postage stamps were to have been released at this time, but were not ready. The one penny stamp, the *Penny Black*, was placed on sale May 1, with postal validity from May 6. The *Twopenny Blue* stamp was available from May 8.

March 20: The Royal Mail Steam Packet Company, which had been formed Sept. 26, 1839, received a contract to carry mail between England and the Americas. The contract required bimonthly sailings and payment for the service amounted to £240,000 a year. The main route started at Falmouth, England, and went via several of the Caribbean islands to Jamaica. A number of feeder lines served areas ranging from Demerara (Guyana) to Mexican ports; Panama; New York; and Halifax, Canada.

March 26: Rowland Hill authorized preparation of *Penny Black* and *Twopenny Blue* adhesive postage stamps with the letters "VR" in upper corners, for use as Official stamps, according to L.N. Williams. A plate was prepared for the *Penny Black* "VR" stamp and a

The "VR" Penny Black.

TO ALL POSTMASTERS
AND
SUB-POSTMASTERS.

GENERAL POST OFFICE,
25th April, 1840.

IT has been decided that Postage Stamps are to be brought into use forthwith, and as it will be necessary that every such Stamp should be cancelled at the Post Office or Sub-Post Office where the Letter bearing the same may be posted, I herewith forward, for your use, an *Obliterating Stamp,* with which you will efface the Postage Stamp upon every Letter despatched from your Office. *Red Composition* must be used for this purpose, and I annex directions for making it, with an Impression of the Stamp.

As the Stamps will come into operation by the **6th of May,** I must desire you will not fail to provide yourself with the necessary supply of Red Composition by that time.

Directions for Preparing the Red Stamping Composition.

1 lb. Printer's Red Ink.
1 Pint Linseed Oil.
Half-pint of the Droppings of Sweet Oil.
To be well mixed.

By Command,

W. L. MABERLY,
SECRETARY.

This British Post Office notice stressed the importance of stamp cancelation (April 25, 1840).

number of sheets printed. Specimens were circulated to postmasters but the stamp was never issued, although some, presumably "escaped," since specimens are known used. The *Twopenny Blue* "VR" stamp was never produced.

April 15: The firm of Perkins, Bacon & Petch began printing the *Penny Black*, the world's first adhesive postage stamp. Intaglio printing from a design engraved on steel was used, a process that remains basically unchanged to this day. This technique generally produces the highest quality stamp combined with the greatest degree of human artistry.

April 25: The British Post Office published a circular giving instructions for canceling the upcoming adhesive postage stamps and giving the formula for the red canceling ink that was to be used. There was great concern about the possible cleaning of the canceling ink from used stamps and their re-use. Considerable experimentation was done to devise a canceling ink that would be as difficult as possible to remove. If a stamp on á letter was determined to be a previously used one, the Post Office had a stamp bearing the letters "O.S." (old stamp) that would be applied and the letter charged as unpaid.

May 1: The *Penny Black*, the world's first adhesive postage stamp went on sale, although it did not become valid to prepay postage until May 6. Use prior to that date is known (see May 2).

Rowland Hill noted in his diary, "May 1 — Rose at 8 am — stamps issued to the public for the first time."

May 2: The oldest known cover bearing an adhesive postage stamp was mailed at Bath, England. Although placed on sale May 1, the *Penny Black* did not become officially valid to prepay postage until May 6. Some postmasters misinterpreted their instructions and other pre-May 6 usages are known, but this is the earliest.

May 6: The world's first adhesive postage stamp became valid to prepay postage. This was the *Penny Black* of Great Britain. It went into use together with the Mulready envelope and letter sheet. These latter items proved un-

The *Penny Black*:
It set the standard.

A typical "Maltese Cross" cancel and a postage due from Malta depicting the real Maltese Cross.

popular and were soon withdrawn amidst great ridicule.

May 6: The first canceling device intended to obliterate an adhesive postage stamp to prevent its re-use is the incorrectly named Maltese Cross killer. Issued to British post offices when the *Penny Black* stamp was officially placed in use, the cancelation is actually based on the Tudor Rose and bears little resemblance to the true Maltese Cross.

At first struck in red, it was soon changed to black. Because the *Penny Black* did not show up a black cancelation to advantage, the color of the stamp was changed to a red-brown on Feb. 10, 1841 (q.v.). This came to be known as the *Penny Red*.

May 8: The *Twopenny Blue*, the world's second adhesive postage stamp, was released by the British Post Office.

May 16: *Unicorn*, the first in a long line of mail-carrying Cunard steamships sailed from Liverpool, England and arrived at Boston,

W. MULREADY. R A.   *POSTAGE ONE PENNY.*   JOHN THOMPSON

The Mulready letter sheet and envelope design generated so much public ridicule that it was promptly taken off sale and many were destroyed. It was a triumph for the British sense of honor over Victorian pomposity.

Mass. on June 2. She had been purchased by the British and North American Royal Mail Steam Packet Company, which became the Cunard Line, to carry mail between Pictou, Nova Scotia and Quebec.

Although this was her delivery voyage, she carried mail across the Atlantic to Boston before entering her Canadian service and thus became the first of the Cunard steamships to carry transatlantic mail.

Unicorn was of 650 tons and had a length of 162 feet.

May 26: John M. Niles appointed US postmaster general, succeeding Amos Kendall.

June: Daniel Webster introduced a resolution in the US Congress calling for "connecting the use of stamps or stamped covers with a large reduction of the present rates of postage." This reflected a public desire for change and simplification, as well as a reduction in cost of postal service in the United States. However, there were no immediate radical changes.

July 4: The Cunard steamer *Britannia* sailed from Liverpool, England on her maiden transatlantic mail and passenger voyage. Although often cited as the first Cunard steamer to make the crossing, she had been preceded by *Unicorn* (see May 16, 1840). *Britannia* traveled to Boston in 14 days, eight hours, including a stop at Halifax, Nova Scotia.

July 14: A mail service was inaugurated from St. John's, Newfoundland, to Halifax, Nova Scotia, to connect with the Cunard packet from Liverpool. The ships *Sandwich* and *Charles Buchan* provided the service every two weeks between 1840 and 1844.

December: Postmaster General Thomas Allen Stayner, who ran the Post Office in Upper and Lower Canada as a deputy of the General Post Office, London, introduced a registration system for mail.

1841

German economist J. von Herrfeldt published the first of several articles advocating specific

The *Penny Black* set a high standard of design and production, and only a very few modern stamps have managed to approach its artistry. Interestingly, all of these beautiful and colorful stamps were produced by the very same printing process that was used for the *Penny Black*. (May 6, 1840).

international mail reforms and the establishment of an international organization with which to achieve them.

He suggested the elimination of transit charges by countries for passing international mail through their territories, on the basis that they would be balanced by similar services provided by other countries. The Universal Postal Union, more than 20 years later, adopted this accounting method.

Jan. 6: A registered mail service went into effect in Great Britain. It initially cost 1/-, but was reduced to 6d in March, 1848.

Jan. 17: This is the earliest known date of use of the British *Penny Red* stamp. The color had been changed from black to permit more effective cancelation. Gibbons notes the official issue date as Feb. 10, 1841.

Feb. 10: The color of the British *Penny Black* postage stamp was changed to red. (See Jan. 17, 1841.)

March 8: Francis Granger succeeded John M. Niles as US postmaster general.

May: Canadian steamboat service began on the St. Lawrence River between Montreal and Quebec City, with calls at Three Rivers, Port St. Francis, and Sorel. There were also steamboat services between Montreal and Toronto; Hamilton, Bytown (Ottawa), and Grenville.

June 10: A sea-link for mail was established between Sydney, Australia, and Melbourne. It was operated by the steamer *Sea Horse*.

Aug. 10: The first post office building was opened at Melbourne, Australia, and home delivery instituted.

Oct. 11: The General Post Office, London, administered the postal service in New Zealand from this date to 1848.

Oct. 13: Charles A. Wickliffe appointed US postmaster general, succeeding Francis Granger.

1842

Carlo Meratti opened a branch of his Alexandria, Egypt, local post in Cairo. His growing organization was named Posta Europea. During the 1850s, following Meratti's death and the succession of the service's new leader, fellow Italian Giacomo Muzzi, Posta Europea expanded across the country to the extent that the Egyptian government suspended its own inefficient system and allowed Posta Europa to handle its postal affairs.

Jan. 1: RMSP *Thames*, the first of the Royal Mail Steam Packets, sailed from Falmouth on the new mail service between England and the Caribbean, with feeder service to other parts of Central and North America. RMSP vessels maintained the service until World War I, according to Foster.

Feb. 1: In New York City, the City Despatch Post issued a 3c stamp for letters carried by the service. This is the first adhesive postage stamp to be issued outside Great Britain. It is the world's third issue, following the *Penny Black* (May 6, 1840) and the *Twopenny Blue* (May 8, 1840).

RMSP *Thames*.

Engraved and printed by Rawdon, Wright & Hatch, it features a portrait of George Washington. Since it was a private issue used for local post, it is not included in lists of first government-issued adhesive postage stamps. The US government did not issue its first general adhesive postage stamp until July 1, 1847.

Aug. 1: The Port Phillip District, in what was to become the Australian colony of Victoria, was made a separate postal entity and the postmaster of Melbourne was placed in charge of its three post offices.

Aug. 16: Because the City Despatch Post, operating in New York City, had become such a success and was handling 450 letters a day to the US Post Office's 250, the US postmaster of New York decided to compete with the private service by buying it out. This was done and the service began operating under US Post Office control as the United States City Despatch Post on this date. The stamps continued in use with the addition of the words "United States" to the inscription.

Aug. 29: The Treaty of Nanking opened certain Chinese ports to outside trade. These came to be called "treaty ports."

British postal agencies operated at the following places (with opening and closing dates): Amoy (April 16, 1844-Nov. 30, 1922), Canton (April 16, 1844-Nov. 30, 1922), Foochow (April 16, 1844-Nov. 30, 1922), Ningpo (April 16, 1844-Nov. 30, 1922), Shanghai (April 16, 1844-Nov. 30, 1922), Swatow (1881-Nov. 30, 1922), Hankow (1872-Nov. 30, 1922), Kiungchow (1873-Nov. 30, 1922), Tientsin (1882-Nov. 30, 1922), and Chefoo (a British post office 1903-Nov. 30, 1922).

There were periods when these offices were closed.

Treaty ports in Japan were: Kanagawa — later Yokohama (1859-Dec. 31, 1879); Nagasaki (1860-Sept. 30, 1879); Hiogo — later Kobe (1869-November 1879); and Hakodate (Hakodadi) (1870s).

November: The first post office was opened at Hong Kong.

Nov. 29: Brazilian Minister of State C.J. d'Aranjo issued a decree directing the release

of adhesive postage stamps, making Brazil the second country to have national, government-issued adhesive postage stamps. It issued its first stamps on Aug. 1, 1843.

December: Jean Jacques Barr became chief engraver of the Paris Mint. He engraved the dies of French stamps prior to 1863. His son, Desire Albert, succeeded him in the post.

1843

A postal convention between Great Britain and France provided for the exchange of mail between various British and French ports and the English Channel islands. Moveable boxes *(boites mobiles)* were used at ports and taken aboard ships at sailing time.

The contents were deposited at the post office in the port of arrival, where they received a special postal marking. This ranged over the years, from a simple "MB" in a box to boxed markings including port, country and date, as well as the "MB." Ship's masters received 1d per letter carried. A postal agreement, signed Sept. 24, 1856, refined the service, which operated until the outbreak of World War II on Sept. 3, 1939.

Feb. 23: A Russian decree of this date ordered two naval frigates to carry mail on the Black Sea between Odessa and Constantinople. There were sailings every 10 days.

March: Stamps issued by the Swiss canton of Zurich. Apart from a frame, the entire design was filled by the figure of denomination. Two denominations were issued; four rappen and six rappen.

Aug. 1: Brazil issued its first adhesive stamps. The three stamps had denominations of 30 reis, 60r, and 90r. The design consisted of a large figure of denomination within a decorated

Brazil's famous
Bull's Eyes.

The numeral obliterators of
Great Britain.

oval. Their "eye-like" effect is responsible for their nickname of *Bull's Eyes.*

The country was second to release postage stamps for national use.

Oct. 1: The Swiss canton of Geneva issued its first postage stamps. The single 10-centime stamp was designed in the form of two 5c stamps side-by-side.

Oct. 10: Henry and Calvert Toulmin of London received a contract to carry mail on a monthly service between England and Sydney, New South Wales. This was the first regular mail service between England and the Australian colonies, but it proved unsatisfactory and lasted only until 1848. They used sailing ships. The first, named *Mary Sharpe,* took 131 days for the voyage.

Dec. 1: Postmaster General Stayner of Canada ordered that the rating of letters was to be by weight instead of the number of sheets as had been the case up to then.

1844
April 2: The first steam packet from Halifax, Nova Scotia, arrived at St. John's, Newfoundland. It went into regular service on the run and replaced the previous sailing vessels (see July 14, 1840). Sailing vessels served the route during the winter months until 1849, when Cunard began a steamship service.

May: The first numeral obliterators, also called "killers," were used in Great Britain. Post offices used different styles: England (oval), Scotland (rectangular), and Ireland (diamond).

When numerals up to three figures were exhausted, a letter-numeral combination was used. These obliterators were gradually retired in the second half of the 19th century, but some remained in post office use until the 1950s.

June 11: The first contract mail packet from Great Britain to Australia, the ship *Mary Sharp,* arrived at Sydney.

Aug. 14: First known use of a precanceled stamp. The precancelation comprised intersecting black ruled pen lines on Hales' local stamp, according to personal correspondence from James Kingman. Established at New York, Hale & Co. operated in New England, New York, Philadelphia and Baltimore, according to Scott.

September: The earliest known letter from a resident of Pitcairn Island was written to the resident chaplain of the British community of Valparaiso, Chile, thanking the community for gifts received.

1845
A mailbox is reported to have been in use in the Swiss town of Basel. It is illustrated on one denomination of Switzerland's 1979 Europa issue.

United States postmasters provisional stamps issued at Baltimore, Md. and New Haven, Conn.

The Basel mailbox (1845).

An early French RPO (March 1, 1845).

Sir Sandford Fleming seen on a 1977 stamp of Canada (June 5, 1845).

Jan. 1: A city post was established in Moscow, Russia. It was similar to the post already operating in St. Petersburg. By 1874, there were city posts in 47 Russian cities delivering local and out-of-town mail.

Jan. 14: William Harnden, founder of the US express company, Harnden and Company, died at the age of 31.

March 1: The first French railroad post office inaugurated service on the Paris-Rouen line, according to Rock. However, France issued a stamp on June 10, 1944 to mark the centenary of France's traveling post offices. Rock says that the first traveling post office was an open flat car on which mail could not be worked. This work was not done until a closed car was introduced on Aug. 1, 1845.

March 3: Florida entered the Union as the 27th state.

March 3: The US Congress legislated postal charges based on weight. This law took effect July 1, 1845 (q.v.).

The same act specified steamship rates. These should not be confused with ship letter rates, where payment of a fee was made to the master of a US ship not having a contract to carry bagged mail, according to Wierenga.

The steamship rates specified included 24c for items not over one half ounce to ports in Britain, France, or others not less than 3,000 miles distant, plus US domestic postage from point of mailing to port of departure. Up to one ounce cost 48c and 15c for each additional half ounce or fraction. To West Indian and Gulf of Mexico ports the charges were set at 10c for ½

oz., 20c for 1 oz., and 5c each additional ½ oz., although these did not go into effect until 1849.

March 7: Cave Johnson succeeded Charles A. Wickliffe as US postmaster general.

May 10: The state of Maryland placed a range of embossed revenue stamps in use. They had been authorized by the state government on March 10, 1845 and were used until March 10, 1856.

June 5: The young Sandford Fleming, who designed Canada's first stamp, landed at Quebec. He had traveled with his elder brother David aboard the steamer *Brilliant* from Glasgow, Scotland.

July 1: The Swiss canton of Basel issued its first stamps. These were also the first multicolored postage stamps, being produced in black, crimson, and blue.

July 1: Beginning on this date, letters in the United States were charged by weight. Congress authorized the procedure on March 3, 1845. The rates, based on a letter weighing one half ounce, were 5c (under 300 miles), 10c (over 300 miles), 2c for a drop letter, circulars 2c per sheet, and a carrier fee was set at 2c. Additional charges were one rate per additional half ounce.

Although it had made postal rates uniform, Congress did not authorize the introduction of adhesive postage stamps for national use and individual postmasters created their own stamps. These are known as Postmasters' Provisionals and the first was used during July in New York City.

July 15: Earliest known use of New York postmaster provisional stamp.

November: The first of the postmasters' provisionals at St. Louis, Mo. were issued. These were the *St. Louis Bears,* a name referring to the design which features the city's coat of arms showing two bears.

Nov. 2: John Walter Scott was born in London, England. He moved to the United States in 1863. After an initial try at stamp dealing in New York, he traveled in the West. By the mid-1860s, he had returned to the stamp business in New York. Beginning in 1867, he published pricelists that developed into the catalog that has become the major one used in the United States. He also conducted the first stamp auctions in this country (May 28, 1870) and in London (March 18, 1872). He died in 1916.

Dec. 1: Russia issued a five-kopeck stamped envelope for use in the city posts of St. Petersburg and Moscow.

Dec. 17: The end of the British mailcoach era was in sight when the London-to-Louth mailcoach was returned to London on a railroad flatbed car from Peterborough after making its run to the Lincolnshire town from the capital. As the railways spread cross Britain, they replaced the coaches and the sound of the coachman's horn was replaced by the toot of the steam whistle.

Dec. 29: Texas became the 28th state of the Union.

The final humiliation. A mailcoach returns to London by train as depicted in a contemporary print (Dec. 17, 1845).

1846

Between 1846 and 1850, *Natal Witness*, a newspaper at Pietermaritzburg, Natal, in South Africa, operated a runner service to Durban for the carriage of letters and newspapers. The trip took two days.

US postmasters' provisional stamps issued at Alexandria, Va.; Annapolis, Md.; Boscawen, N.H. (date in doubt); Brattleboro, Vt.; Lockport, N.Y.; and Millbury, Mass.

April 3: The days of the British long-distance mailcoaches ended when the last of the London-based coach routes left on a run to Norwich via Newmarket.

April 24: Francois Fournier, one of the best-known of the philatelic forgers, was born in Switzerland. In May 1904, he bought the "facsimile" business of Louis-Henri Mercier. He advertised his creations as being better than the originals!

May 29: The postal service of the former Republic of Texas became part of the US Post Office Department. A mail route was established between New Orleans and Galveston, Texas, with service every five days.

Aug. 16: The Danube Steam Navigation Company received exclusive rights to trade on the Danube until 1880. In return it agreed to carry government mails free.

Aug. 24: A US postmaster provisional stamp was issued at Providence, R.I.

Nov. 25: "Nov. 25" is the month and day postmarked on a cover bearing the only known copy of the Alexandria, Va. postmasters' provisional printed on blue paper. The year is believed to be 1846. The letter it contained is a proposal of marriage addressed to a Miss Jannett Brown. The letter and cover were found by her daughter in 1907 among family correspondence. The cover is the first single philatelic item to sell for $1 million (see May 8, 1981).

Nov. 28: The United States City Despatch Post in New York City was sold by the US Post Office to Abraham B. Mead, who began to operate it on Nov. 30. It subsequently changed hands again, and little is recorded after 1851.

December: Rowland Hill appointed Secretary to the Postmaster General.

Dec. 28: Iowa entered the Union as the 29th state.

1847

The first post office opened at Victoria on Vancouver Island (then Vancouver's Island), Canada. It was located in the office of the Hudson's Bay Company accountant. Until 1857, the company transmitted mail to and from the United States without charge, according to Robson Lowe.

These three stamps were issued by Austria on March 13, 1979 to mark the 150th anniversary of the Danube Steamship Company. Vessels operated by the company at various times are depicted (Aug. 16, 1846).

March 3: Congress authorized the postmaster general to release national postage stamps (see July 1, 1847).

The same act authorized two mail routes; one from Independence, Mo. to Santa Fe, N.M. which went into effect July 1, 1850, and one from Independence to Astoria, in what is now Oregon, at the mouth of the Columbia River.

According to Hafen, the same law authorized the postmaster general to contract for a route to Astoria via the isthmus of Panama, with mail going by ship from Charleston, S.C. to Chagres, Panama, and up the Pacific coast by sea to Astoria (see following entry).

March 3: An act of Congress of this date provided for contract steamship routes to Havana, Cuba; Chagres, Panama; and Astoria, Oregon. The Chagres service originated at Charleston, S.C., calling at St. Augustine and Key West, Fla., and if necessary, at Havana. From Panama on the Pacific side of the isthmus, the route went north to Astoria, calling at Monterey and San Francisco. The rates were 20c to or from Chagres, 12½c to or from Havana, to or from Panama 30c, and to or from Astoria or any US Pacific coast territory was 40c.

March 20: In a letter of this date, the New York printing firm of Rawdon, Wright, Hatch & Edson wrote to the US Post Office Department quoting a price of 25c per thousand to produce 5c and 10c stamps. The company stated that "the stamps are to be executed in the best style of line engraving, and the dies and plates to belong to, and to be held for the ex-

clusive use of the Post Office Department."

In a letter of March 31, the firm offered to print the figures of denomination on the stamps in a different color from the rest of the design, and also reduced the single-color price to 20c per thousand and 25c for the bicolored stamps. The post office accepted the 20c, single-color price.

April 24: The famous *Lady McLeod* stamp used to frank mail carried by the ship of the same name between Port of Spain, Trinidad, and the southern Trinidad port of San Fernando was issued.

Named for the wife of Trinidad Governor Sir Henry McLeod, the ship was an iron-hulled paddle steamer built by Robert Napier of Goven, Scotland. The ship was taken off the Port of Spain — San Fernando service in 1851 and was broken up in 1854, according to Coffey.

May 9: The House of Thurn and Taxis announced the use of stamped envelopes by its post in the German city of Stuttgart. The use of such envelopes was extended to other areas later that month.

June 1: The steamship *Washington* became the first US steamship to carry mail from this country in transatlantic service when she began her maiden voyage on this date. She sailed to Bremerhaven with a call at Southampton, England.

June 26: On this date the firm of Rawdon, Wright, Hatch & Edson, printers of the first US stamps, wrote to the US postmaster

This 1972 stamp from Trinidad and Tobago reproduces the *Lady McLeod* stamp and indicates on a map the two towns it served (April 24, 1847).

The first government postage stamps issued for national use by the United States (July 1, 1847).

general to tell him that the postage stamps he had ordered, were ready. These are the 5c and 10c stamps issued July 1, 1847.

July 1: The US government issued its first adhesive postage stamps for national use. None are known canceled on the issue date. The stamps have denominations of 5c (Benjamin Franklin) and 10c (George Washington).

Sept. 1: The postmaster at Wheeling, Va. began canceling 5c and 10c 1847 stamps with a red device that covered four stamps. Some consider this a form of precancelation, while others, including Ashbrook, do not.

Sept. 21: Mauritius issued the famous 1d and 2d *Post Office* stamps. These are the first stamps of the British crown colony in the Indian Ocean and had been engraved and printed locally. A jeweler, Joseph Barnard, engraved them. Much has been made of the supposed mistake in inscribing the stamps "POST OFFICE" but it seems likely that Barnard merely followed the inscription used in the island's postmarks for many years.

Nov. 16: The Canadian Post Office ceased to collect postage due on letters from the United States on behalf of the US Post Office. Canada had collected the postage since 1792 and received a 20 percent commission.

1848

Postmasters W.B. Perot of Hamilton and James H. Thies of St. Georges issued local stamps in Bermuda. Perot devised his stamps to prevent the loss of income that occurred when people deposited letters and cash after office hours. He had found that the amount of cash often was less than that required by the number of letters deposited and had no way of determining the offenders.

The stamps were created by using a date stamp, deleting the day and month, substituting a manuscript "One Penny" and signing them. A second type using a crowned circle "paid" handstamp is known.

May 29: Wisconsin became the 30th state of the United States.

This 1948 stamp marks the Perot stamp centenary and shows a Perot stamp.

The Perot house in Hamilton, Bermuda is restored to its original state and Perot's post office functions for tourists and collectors who make the pilgrimage to this philatelic shrine. The building is also pictured on one of Bermuda's beautiful 1962-65 definitive stamps. Photo courtesy of Dr. Arthur A. Delaney.

Oct. 1, 1848
CHARLESTON to ASTORIA
The route via Panama

Aug. 1: The oldest named mail train is the *Irish Mail* from London to Holyhead, which made its first run on this date.

Aug. 14: The US Congress set the basic rate between the Atlantic coast and points on the Pacific in California at 40c. The rate within California was made 12½c.

Aug. 14: The Oregon Territory was established by the US Congress on this date.

Oct. 1: A monthly mail service by sea from the east coast of the United States to its west coast began. It started from Charleston, S.C. to Chagres, Panama, across the isthmus of Panama, and then up the Pacific coast by ship to San Francisco and Astoria, Ore. The steamship *California* left New York Oct. 6, 1848 to serve on the Pacific coast link.

Nov. 1: US Postmaster General Cave Johnson appointed William Van Voorhies special agent. Van Voorhies proceeded to California to establish postal operations as a result of the gold strike and the establishment of a steamer service carrying mail from Panama to points on the California coast.

Dec. 1: The steamship *Falcon* sailed from New York for Chagres. She belonged to the United States Mail Steamship Company, which had received a contract to carry mail on that section of the route between New York and the Pacific coast via the isthmus of Panama.

Dec. 1: Russia issued stamped envelopes valid for use throughout the Russian Empire. Denominations were 10-kopeck, 20k, and 30k.

1849

Jan. 1: France issued its first stamps. These are the 20 centime black and the 1 franc vermilion in the Ceres design.

Jan. 17: The steamer *California*, which had left New York on Oct. 6, 1848, arrived at Panama after a long voyage around Cape

Horn. She picked up mail and miners bound for the California goldfields.

Feb. 28: *California* arrived at San Francisco from Panama. While in port the entire crew, except for the captain and one boy, deserted for the goldfields! However, another crew must have been found, because the ship is reported to have sailed for Panama on April 12, carrying the first eastbound mail of the federal government's contract.

March 3: Congress set the US rate for letters weighing from a half ounce to one ounce at double the then-current single rate and at two additional rates for each succeeding ounce or fraction thereof.

March 3: On this date, Congress created the territory of Minnesota.

March 5: Brigham Young created the unofficial state of Deseret, which ceased to exist upon the formation of Utah Territory on Sept. 9, 1850.

March 8: Jacob Collamer appointed US postmaster general, succeeding Cave Johnson.

May 14: A postal convention between the United States, Great Britain, and the British North American colonies, allowed mail between the United States and the British colonies to be sent at the domestic rates. Mail could be fully prepaid or unpaid. Prepayment did not become compulsory until 1875.

May 25: The legislative assembly of the colony of Canada passed a resolution to adopt adhesive postage stamps, but the first stamp was not issued until April 23, 1851 (q.v.).

July 1: Belgium issued its first stamps. They picture King Leopold I and are in denominations of 10c and 20c.

July 13: Jacob Perkins, founder of the firm of Perkins, Bacon, and Petch (later Perkins, Bacon & Co.), died in Scotland. The firm printed the *Penny Black* and *Twopenny Blue*, the first adhesive postage stamps, using a process known as "Perkins Mill and Die process." Today, the process is known as intaglio printing.

Oct. 1: The United States established a post office in the town of Santa Fe, in what is now New Mexico. It appointed William S. Knight as postmaster.

November: John T. Little was appointed postmaster at Coloma, Calif., the first post office to be opened in the gold country, according to Wiltsee.

Nov. 1: Stamps were first issued by the kingdom of Bavaria. The first design had a denomination of one kreuzer and featured a large denomination figure at the center. It was printed by typography and not perforated.

1850

Austria became the first country to begin using true duplex cancelers, where the date stamp and obliterating device was combined in a single marking.

The Austro-German Postal Union was formed. This organization originated as a treaty between Austria and Prussia, by which both countries agreed to simplify and speed the transit of the other's mail through its territory, to set modest transit charges, and establish uniform rates. Eventually, 15 other German postal administrations and the Thurn and Taxis postal system became members of the union. Although it lasted only about 12 years, the union proved that states could cooperate to render international mail service simple, cheap, and fast.

Jan. 1: Spain issued its first stamps. They depict the profile of Queen Isabella II, facing to the left on the six-cuarto denomination and to the right on the 12c, five real, 6r and 10r values. Production was by lithography.

Jan. 1: The British colony of New South Wales issued its first stamps. These are known as the *Sydney Views* because they show a view of the settlement of Port Jackson, later named Sydney. The view is claimed to derive from the colony's seal. Denominations were 1d, 2d, and 3d. Only the 2d stamp was ready on the issue date, the others coming out a few days later.

Jan. 3: The first stamps for the Australian colony of Victoria were issued on this date. They came in denominations of 1d and 3d and depict a full-face portrait of Queen Victoria. Issued imperforate, they were produced by lithography.

Jan. 20: Liberia signed a postal convention with Great Britain.

Jan. 23: On this date, Spain placed special cancelations in use. They were designed to cancel a stamp while leaving the portrait of Queen Isabella unmarred. The queen's vanity matched that of her uncle, King "Bomba" Ferdinand of the Kingdom of the Two Sicilies, who also had a frame-like cancel for stamps bearing his features.

The queen is reported by Van Dam to have had a blacksmith make a specimen of the desired device. It consisted of four joined half circles, from the outside of which four arrows projected in the form of a cross. The open area in the center was supposed to contain the royal features.

April 5: The federal administration of Switzerland issued stamps. The design features the country's coat of arms and M. Durheim of Berne lithographed them.

June 1: Austria issued its first postage stamps. They feature the national coat of arms and were also used in Hungary. This latter portion of the Austro-Hungarian Empire did not get its own stamps until 1871.

June 1: Lombardy-Venetia (Austrian Italy) issued its first stamps. They are in the same design as the first issue of Austria, except for the denominations, which are in centesimi and lira instead of the Austrian kreuzer.

June 29: The kingdom of Saxony issued its first stamp. It was a three-pfennig stamp featuring a large figure of denomination.

July 1: A mule-drawn mail wagon set out from Independence, Mo. for Santa Fe, in what was to become New Mexico. This is the first mail vehicle to traverse the Great Plains under a mail contract. The firm of Waldo, Hall and Co. had received a four-year contract from the US Post Office Department to transport mail on the 800-mile Santa Fe Trail, using the Cimarron Cutoff. It arrived in Santa Fe on July 28. The firm held the mail contract until 1862.

July 1: The US Post Office Department granted a mail-carrying contract to Col. Samuel Woodson for the route between Independence, Mo., and Salt Lake City. He used pack mules to carry to the mail.

July 1: The colony of British Guiana issued its first stamps beginning on this date. They were released in denominations of 2c, 4c, 8c, and 12c, and are known as *Cotton Reels* from their likeness to a label on the end of a reel of sewing cotton. They are primitive in design and production, but are major rarities. All were printed in black on rose, orange, green, and blue paper respectively. There are variations of paper color. They were printed at the office of the *Royal Gazette* in Georgetown.

July 23: Nathan K. Hall appointed US postmaster general, succeeding Jacob Collamer.

Sept. 9: On this date, the Territory of Utah came into being.

Sept. 9: California became the 31st state in the United States.

Sept. 27: The US Post Office Department extended service to the territories of Utah and New Mexico. The rates were the same as for the Pacific coast (see Aug. 14, 1848).

Nov. 15: The first stamps were issued by the kingdom of Prussia. They feature the profile of King Frederick William IV. Intaglio printed, they were engraved by Schilling and Eichens of Berlin.

Nov. 15: The German state of Schleswig-Holstein issued its first stamps. They depict the state's coat of arms. The one schilling and two schilling stamps were printed in two colors plus embossing.

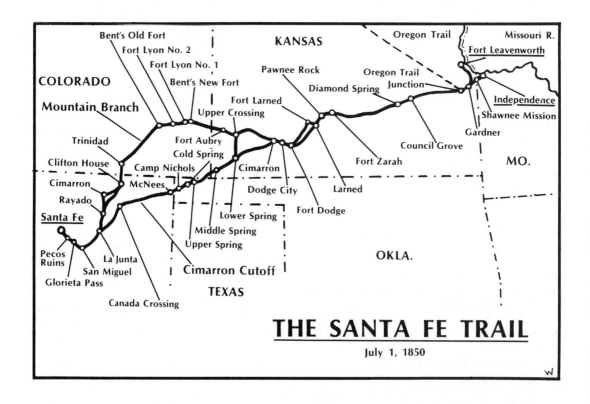

THE SANTA FE TRAIL

July 1, 1850

Dec. 1: The German state of Hanover issued its first stamp. It depicts the state's coat of arms. In square format, the one groschen stamp was typographed from a design by A. Jurgens. The engraver was J.F. Fickenscher and it was printed by Culemann of Hanover.

Dec. 13: The US Congress established the Territory of New Mexico on this date.

Dec. 14: The Russian Post Office began to supply stocks of its 10-kopeck, 20k, and 30k stamped envelopes for use in the Russian-controlled kingdom of Poland.

1851

The earliest known telegraph stamp was issued in Great Britain by the Electric Telegraph Co. It took the form of a 1/- indicium on the message form, according to Joseph and Stephen Rich. The firm issued adhesive stamps in 1854.

The International and Colonial Postage Association was formed in London. It proposed reforming international mail handling by achieving a simple and uniform international mail service at a low rate. The association received support from most major countries, but on the death of its main worker, Manuel de Ysasi, the organization disbanded. Despite its lack of concrete success, the association planted the idea of international postal reform, notes Codding.

Jan. 1: Austria issued the first stamps to prepay postage on newspapers and periodicals. The three stamps were undenominated and their face value was indicated by color. A fourth stamp was issued in 1856. The designs feature a rather crude representation of Mercury, messenger of the gods.

Jan. 1: The postal administration of the kingdom of Poland was subordinated to that of the Russian Empire. When Russia introduced adhesive postage stamps in 1858, they went into use in Poland also.

Jan. 1: The kingdom of Sardinia issued its first postage stamps. They depict King Victor Emmanuel II. Sardinia formed the basis of the unified Kingdom of Italy.

March 3: An act of Congress setting new postal rates on this date became effective on June 30, 1851 (q.v.). The act also declared streets and roads in many US cities to be post roads.

March 22: The kingdom of Wurttemberg bought the postal rights in the kingdom from Prince Maximilian Karl von Taxis for 1.3 million florins.

March 22: The first advertisement seeking to buy and exchange stamps, was inserted in the London *Family Herald,* according to Hornung. There had been previous ads seeking used stamps, but they were for purposes other than what we think of today as philatelic.

April 1: Denmark issued its first postage stamps. The issue comprised two stamps in denominations of two and four rigsbank dalers.

From the left are the first stamp of Hanover (Dec. 1, 1850), Austria's first newspaper stamp (Jan. 1, 1851), the first stamp of Wurttemberg (March 22, 1851), and Denmark's first issue (April 1, 1851).

The first Canadian stamp to feature the Chalon portrait of the young Queen Victoria (June 14, 1851) was followed by similar stamps from other parts of the British Empire and a selection is shown here.

April 1: The Italian state of Tuscany issued its first stamps. The design used for the nine-stamp issue depicts the Lion emblem of the state. The first printing was on blue paper.

April 6: The Post Office in Upper and Lower Canada was transferred to the government of the new province of Canada from the General Post Office, London. James Morris was appointed postmaster general. The May 14, 1849 (q.v) agreement between Canada, and the United States was continued.

April 7: An example of the New Carlisle, Quebec, Canada, postmaster's provisional envelope bears this date. It has a denomination of three pence and is signed by the postmaster, R.W. Kelly. It is addressed to Toronto. Although thought by many authorities to be unique, Robson Lowe notes a second copy was sold in 1928.

April 16: Russia introduced mail cars operated by postal employees on its St. Petersburg-Moscow Railway.

April 23: The province of Canada issued its first postage stamp. It is the well-known 3d Beaver and was designed by Sir Sandford Fleming (1827-1915). He was also responsible for the introduction of time zones in Canada, an idea later adopted worldwide, and chief engineer of the Canadian Pacific Railway.

April 23: From this date to June 30, 1851 letters from Canada to the United States could be franked with stamps of each country for the respective portions of the journey. Canadian stamps were issued April 23. Beginning July 1, 1851 letters could be prepaid entirely with Canadian stamps.

May 1: The grand duchy of Baden issued its first postage stamps. Their design comprises a large figure of denomination. Engraved by C. Naumann of Frankfurt, the four-denomination set was typographed by Hasper of Karlsruhe.

May 1: The first mail route between California and Salt Lake City, Utah, was established when George Chorpenning left Sacramento on this date and reached Salt Lake City on June 5. Chorpenning and Absalom Woodward had received a contract from the US Post Office Department for a monthly service for $14,000 a year. Woodward was killed by Indians in Utah later that year, but the service continued operating for several years under conditions of great difficulty, especially during the winters.

June 14: Canada issued the first stamp reproducing the beautiful Chalon portrait of Queen Victoria. It is the famous 12d black. Other members of the British Empire later used the portrait on a number of stamps.

July 1: US letter rates were set up to 3,000 miles, at 3c (not prepaid 5c) and over 3,000 miles, at 6c (not prepaid 10c). Drop letters were 1c. This was the effective date of a March 3, 1851 act of Congress. The same act established a fund to cover postal deficits, along with a provision that no postal route would be discontinued because of loss of revenue. Under the same act, steamship rates were reduced to 10c for under 2,500 miles and 20c for over that distance.

July 1: Legislation became effective under which the US Post Office delivered letters in a number of US cities for an additional charge of 1c. Two official carriers' stamps were issued. Several cities also issued semi-official carriers' stamps. Carrier fees were discontinued June 30, 1863, but a drop letter rate of 1c continued.

July 1: The Newfoundland Legislature assumed control of the postal service in the colony. It had previously been run by the General Post Office, London.

July 6: The British colony of New Brunswick assumed responsibility for its own postal affairs.

July 30: Wiltsee records that there were only 60 post offices in the whole of California on this date and, despite the more than 100 gold mining camps in the gold country, only 25 were located in that region.

Aug. 5: This is the postmark date on the famous *Miss Rose Cover* of British Guiana. The cover, franked with a vertical pair of the British Guiana 2c "Cottonreels" of 1851, was donated by a church member in 1896 to a fund to pay off the mortgage on Christ Church in Georgetown. Church officials sold it for $1,005 and it has since resided in a number of the world's great collections, including Dauveen, Hind, Theodore Champion, and Lichtenstein. The cover's name comes from the fact that it is addressed to a Miss Rose, Blankenburg, a sugar estate on the coast of British Guiana.

Aug. 14: The first stamps for the British colony of Trinidad were issued on this date, according to Gibbons. The design features the seated figure of Britannia from a drawing by Edward Henry Corbould for the printer, Perkins, Bacon & Co. The stamps have no figure of denomination and came in various colors, although all were supposed to represent a face value of 1d.

Sept. 1: The British colony of Nova Scotia issued its first stamps. Denominations were 3d, 6d, and 1/-, with a 1d stamp being added May 12, 1853.

Sept. 5: This is the issue date reported by Gibbons for the first stamps of the British North America colony of New Brunswick, although Poole quotes a postmaster general's report that states the stamps were in circulation from Sept. 6. Denominations were 3d, 6d, and 1/-.

Oct. 1: The first stamps were issued by the kingdom of Hawaii. They were the famous *Missionaries.* Their name came from the fact that they were mostly used by missionaries in the islands to frank correspondence. Denominations were 2c, 5c, and 13c.

Oct. 15: The kingdom of Wurttemberg issued its first postage stamps. The design features a large figure of denomination.

November: British Post Office surveyor and novelist Anthony Trollope proposed in a report that "...letter boxes should be erected, letter carriers and sorters should not be overworked, that they should be adequately paid and have some hours to themselves, especially on Sundays." See Nov. 23, 1852.

1852

The French colony of Reunion, an island in the Indian Ocean, off Madagascar, received its first stamps. The designs are primitive and locally produced.

The duchy of Brunswick issued its first stamps. The design features a running horse engraved by K. Petersen and printed by J.H. Meyer of Brunswick.

Jean-Baptiste Moens began to deal in stamps at his bookstore in Brussels, Belgium, becoming the first recorded stamp dealer. He went on to become one of the leading philatelic dealers and publishers.

Although mailboxes did not go into general use until the middle of the 19th century, the Bottle Post of Ascension could claim to use mailboxes in the form of bottles, as the first stamp shows (see 1673). Other mailboxes around the world are depicted, included the familiar one used today in this country. (November 1851).

The first recorded exhibition of postage stamps as collectible items is said to have been made by Philip Vandermaelenm. He exhibited a picture frame of stamps at his museum in Brussels, Belgium, according to L.N. Williams in the January 1981 issue of *Scott's Monthly Stamp Journal*.

Jan. 1: The grand duchy of Luxembourg joined the Austro-German Postal Union. Membership required the use of adhesive postage stamps. The government followed the example of Belgium, which had set up its own government printing works, and arrangements were made for stamps to be produced. The results appeared on Sept. 15, 1852 (q.v.).

Jan. 1: The House of Thurn and Taxis issued stamps for use throughout its postal system. At this time, two different currencies were in use in the area it served, which made it necessary to have two stamp issues, one for each currency. The Northern District used silbergroschen, 30 of which equaled one thaler and the Southern District used kreuzer, 60 of which were equal to one gulden.

Jan. 1: The first stamps were issued for the Roman States. The designs varied, but all feature the crossed keys emblem. The states originally comprised most of the central Italian peninsula, but by 1870 they had ceased to exist as separate political entities. The stamps of Italy then were in use.

Jan. 1: The Netherlands issued its first postage stamps. They depict King William III. Engraved by J.W. Kaiser of Brussels, intaglio printing was by the Netherlands Mint at Utrecht.

Jan. 1: The Panama Railroad contracted to carry mail across the isthmus of Panama for the US Post Office Department. The railroad was completed in late January 1855.

Jan. 4: Nathaniel Worsdell's patent for a device for exchanging mailbags with a moving train expired on this date. Because the British Post Office was unable to reach an agreement with Worsdell, it had devised its own equipment. After a period of use, it was found unsuitable. A simplified device was designed, but, the BPO was concerned that it was too much like Worsdell's and did not place it in general use until Worsdell's patent expired.

Jan. 5: The grand duchy of Oldenburg issued its first stamps. The designs feature figures of denomination, which are expressed in fractions of a thaler. Gerhard Stalling used lithography at his printing plant in Oldenburg to produce the stamps.

Jan. 29: The British Africa Steam Navigation Company was granted a contract to carry mail to and from the British colony of Lagos, now the capital city of Nigeria.

March 3: New South Wales made compulsory the use of stamps to prepay postage, except on mail to Great Britain.

March 18: Henry Wells and William G. Fargo met with a group of interested associates at the Astor House in New York. They agreed to form a banking and express business to serve the gold rush country of California. This was the birth of the famous Wells, Fargo & Co.

The first stamps issued by the House of Thurn and Taxis. The stamp for the Northern District is at the left (Jan. 1, 1852).

The first stamp of the Netherlands (Jan. 1, 1852).

The first stamp of Oldenburg (Jan. 5, 1852).

April 15: The British colony of Barbados issued its first stamps. Barbados was the second British West Indian colony to issue stamps. It shared the stamp design with Trinidad, which had been the first. The only difference is the colony name.

May 20: The firm of Wells, Fargo & Co. announced in a New York *Times* advertisement that it had organized and that Samuel P. Carter and R.W. Washburn had been appointed agents in California.

June 1: The Italian state of Modena issued its first postage stamps. They feature the Modena coat of arms and were printed by the State Stamp Office from electrotypes made by the firm of Rocca, Rinaldi, and Algeri, Modena.

June 1: The Italian state of Parma released its first postage stamps. They feature a crown and fleur-de-lis. Typographic printing was by D. Bentelli.

June 20: The Spanish government looked upon stamp collecting with an extremely jaundiced eye. A decree of this date stated "...stamps are forbidden for resale; in fact they are considered contraband, and people apprehended selling same will be fined no less than three times and no more than six times the value of the stamp sold."

If registered mail in Spain was opened and found to contain used postage stamps, the sender would be subject to "diligent and scrupulous investigation for evading the law."

Fortunately for philately, Spaniards generally ignored the law. It was officially repealed in 1901, according to Van Dam.

July: The Royal Mail Ship *Australian* brought the first direct European mail to Albany, Western Australia. In the years immediately after, mail took an average time of about 83 days to travel between the colony and Britain; a marked improvement over the time taken previously.

July 1: The *Scinde Dawk* stamps were issued in Sind Province, India, under the authority of British Commissioner Sir Bartle Frere. The stamps were supplied to the postmaster at Karachi, from whom officials throughout the district received them. The stamps were withdrawn in October 1854.

July 2: A story in the San Francisco *Daily Herald* announced the opening of Wells, Fargo & Co. offices at 114 Montgomery St. The company also established agencies initially at jumping off points for the gold country — Sacramento, Marysville, Stockton, and Auburn.

September: When the Duke of Wellington died, mail service to New Zealand was so slow that not until January 1853 did the inhabitants of the city of Wellington — named for the duke — receive the news from Britain.

Sept. 14: Samuel D. Hubbard succeeded Nathan K. Hall as US postmaster general.

The first stamp of Barbados (April 15, 1852).

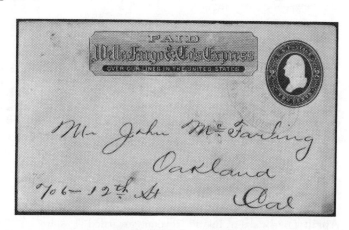

A Wells, Fargo cover.

Sept. 15: The grand duchy of Luxembourg issued its first stamps. They depict Grand Duke William III and were intaglio printed by M. Barth-Wahl of Luxembourg.

Oct. 1: The United States set the printed matter postal rate at 1c for up to three ounces, and 1c for each additional ounce anywhere in the United States. The Post Offices charged double for unpaid printed matter. Previously, printed matter had been charged on a distance basis.

Nov. 23: Anthony Trollope, British Post Office surveyor and novelist, had pillar boxes (letter boxes) installed in St. Helier, Jersey. These are generally considered to be the first British letter boxes. In announcing the new service, the postmaster of St. Helier stated that on this date "Roadside Letter Boxes" would be opened at "David Place, nearly opposite the Rectory; New Street, in front of Mr. Fry's, Painter & Glazier; Cheapside, top of the Parade; and St. Clements Road, corner of Pleasance," according to J. Maurice Hicks.

1853

Feb. 1: The Italian state of Modena issued its first newspaper tax stamps.

March 1: Austria issued the first newspaper tax stamp. The labels did not pay postage and represented a tax collected by the post office on newspapers.

March 2: On this date the Washington Territory came into being. It entered the Union as the state of Washington on Nov. 11, 1889.

March 8: James Campbell was appointed US postmaster general succeeding Samuel D. Hubbard.

April: The Board of Inland Revenue awarded a four-year contract to the firm of Thomas de la Rue to produce British fiscal (revenue) stamps, using the firm's relief printing process. This was the firm's first stamp-printing contract and led to a long involvement with stamp production for many British colonies and foreign countries, including the Confederate States of America.

April 14: A mail route between New Orleans and Vera Cruz, Mexico, was inaugurated, being served by the steamships *Texas* and *Orizba*. However, by September 1856 both vessels had been transferred to the Nicaragua route, according to Wierenga. The route ended with the outbreak of the American Civil War.

June: Duplex cancelers featuring a datestamp and obliterator combined in one instrument were first used in Great Britain. Some collectors define these as "double stamps" since they are separate markings, although applied at the same time. They define a duplex marking as one that combines both functions in a single marking, as in a squared-circle marking.

July: Portugal issued its first postage stamps. They depict Queen Maria II and were designed and engraved by F. Borja Freire. The royal profile was embossed.

July 1: Chile's first stamps, issued on this date, picture Christopher Columbus. They were released in denominations of five and ten centavos.

July 1: The United States issued its first stamped envelopes. They were printed by George F. Nesbitt & Co. of New York.

August: The first post office cars in Canada went into operation on the St. Lawrence and Atlantic (Grand Trunk) Railroad between Montreal and Sherbrooke. By 1857, they operated on railroads throughout the areas that later became Canada.

Sept. 1: This is the issue date of the first triangular stamps of the British colony of Cape of Good Hope. These famous and popular stamps were also the first for the colony. Denominations were 1d and 4d and they were intended for domestic use. The 1d stamp paid the newspaper rate, while the 4d paid the letter rate of 4d per half ounce.

Oct. 20: The use of adhesive postage stamps was made compulsory on all letters from the Australian colony of New South Wales to neighboring colonies.

Nov. 1: Van Diemen's Land (later Tasmania) released its first postage stamps. The issue comprised two stamps in denominations of 1d and 4d. The designs were very primitive profiles of Queen Victoria.

1854

Rowland Hill was named Secretary of the Post Office in Britain, replacing Col. W.L. Maberly, whose job he had long sought.

Jan. 28: British stamps began to be perforated as an aid to separation. The perforating device's inventor, Henry Archer, had first approached the government in 1847 with the suggestion that such a separation device be adopted. Critics have claimed Rowland Hill's lukewarm attitude toward perforating stamps may have been due to the fact that it was not his idea. Hill said of perforating that "it would be useful and acceptable to the public to a certain extent." Hardly the words of a devotee of postal efficiency!

Feb. 1: The Philippine Islands, under Spanish rule, issued its first stamps. They were printed in Manila from plates made locally.

April 22: A contract to carry mail between Santa Fe and San Antonio was awarded to David Wasson. The compensation was $16,750 a year. The contract required a monthly service using two-horse coaches with a time of 25 days for the trip. In 1858, the service began weekly runs using six-mule coaches.

May 30: Kansas became a territory.

May 30: The territory of Nebraska was established.

July 1: The Waldo and Hall partnership was dissolved prior to the granting to Hall of another four-year contract to carry mail on the Santa Fe Trail from Independence, Mo., to Santa Fe, in what is now New Mexico. John M. Hockaday joined Hall in a new partnership.

July 1: Spain issued what are claimed to be the world's first Official stamps (stamps for use on government correspondence) on this date. They were unusual in that they were denominated, not in currency, but by the amount of weight they would frank, i.e. in *onzas* (ounces) and *libras* (pounds).

Aug. 1: The first stamp for the British colony of Western Australia was issued on this date.

The first stamp of Van Diemen's Land (Tasmania) was a very primitive profile of Queen Victoria, as can be seen on this reproduction on a stamp of Norfolk Island (Nov. 1, 1853).

This stamp of the Cape of Good Hope is the world's first triangular stamp (Sept. 1, 1853).

This 1d stamp in the famous *Black Swan* design was intaglio printed by Perkins, Bacon & Co. of London. Stamps in denominations of 4d and 1/- were lithographed locally soon after.

The famous "invert" occurred in the 4d stamp. Often called the "inverted swan," it is the stamp's frame that is inverted. This happened when the printers prepared the lithographic printing base. They laid one frame down inverted, all the swan vignettes being correct. This improper frame placement has been proven with the discovery of an invert with part of the adjacent stamp showing a correctly placed frame. The error was discovered during production and corrected. Only a few examples are known.

Oct. 1: The Italian state of Tuscany issued a newspaper tax stamp. The stamp represented payment of a tax on newspapers coming from a foreign country.

Oct. 1: British India issued its first stamp for use throughout the colony on this date, although Gibbons notes that copies dated up to two weeks earlier are known. The stamp had a denomination of ½ anna and was soon followed by 1a, 2a, and 4a stamps.

Oct. 11: Rowland Hill announced the planned installation of pillar boxes (letter boxes) on the streets of London, England. They were to be installed one half mile apart on main streets.

Oct. 14: The East India Company accepted De La Rue's bid to print four-anna and 8a stamps for use in the area of India it administered. The stamps were issued in October 1855. This led, within a few years, to De La Rue producing all stamps and postal stationery for the company.

Oct. 15: This is the issue date of an Indian four-anna stamp on which the inverted head error occurs. Because the stamp was printed in two colors it required two passes through the press. It is believed that at least six sheets were printed with the blue Queen's head inverted.

Oct. 19: The postmaster general of the British colony of Nova Scotia authorized the bisecting of the current 3d stamp, each half to be used as a 1½d stamp in conjunction with the 6d stamp to pay the 7½d letter rate to Great Britain. No 7½d stamp was available.

Dec. 1: Victoria, the British colony in Australia, is believed to have been the first postal entity to issue special stamps for use on registered mail. It is a 1/- stamp featuring a profile of Queen Victoria.

1855

The first stamp collector in the United States is believed to have been William H. Faber of Charleston, S.C. He is quoted by Harlow as stating in the *Metropolitan Philatelist* of New York in 1918, that he began collecting when he was a boy.

The Free City of Bremen, in what is now West Germany, issued its first postage stamp. It was a three-grote denomination picturing the city's coat of arms.

The New York City and Suburban Printing Telegraph Co. was organized. It issued the first telegraph stamps in the United States. The issue date of the stamps is not known but is probably about 1859. The first issue is certainly prior to the pre-1861 takeover by the American Telegraph Co.

The first recorded special-event cancel was used during this year at an international exposition in Paris.

January: Norway issued its first postage stamp. It is a four-skilling denomination depicting the Norwegian coat of arms. The die was engraved by M. Zarbell and typographic printing was by Wulfsberg of Christania (Oslo).

Above is a Black Swan stamp of Western Australia (Aug. 1, 1854) and on the right is the first issue of the free city of Bremen (1855).

Norway's first stamp (January 1855), the first pillar box set up in London (March 1855), and the beautiful first stamp of New Zealand (July 18, 1855).

Jan. 1: Stamps first issued for the colony of South Australia. This issue was a 2d denomination intaglio printed by Perkins, Bacon & Co. The 1d and 6d stamps followed on Oct. 26, 1855.

Jan. 1: The Australian colony of Victoria issued "Too Late" stamps for use on mail accepted for delivery to a ship after the normal mail had closed. This represents the first use of this class of stamp. Beginning in 1886, several other stamp-issuing entities released such stamps.

Feb. 28: The first post office in Western Canada was established at Winnipeg, in what is now the province of Manitoba.

March: The first pillar box (letter box) was installed in London as a result of Rowland Hill's Oct. 11, 1854 announcement. It is reported to have been located at the corner of Fleet and Farringdon streets. Installation of the boxes soon spread across the country. Both Hill and the novelist Anthony Trollope claimed the credit for its invention. Trollope was for many years a Post Office Surveyor and had a pillar box installed at St. Helier, Jersey, in 1853.

April: Stamps went into use in Cuba, then a colony of Spain. The same stamps were to have been placed on sale in neighboring Puerto Rico at the same time, but apparently were not officially introduced there until July 25, 1856 (q.v.).

April 1: The prepayment of mail by adhesive stamps, stamped envelopes, or cash became compulsory in the US.

April 1: The British North American colony of Prince Edward Island instituted a mail registration system.

April 1: US mail rates were set at 3c per half ounce for under 3,000 miles and 10c per half ounce over 3,000 miles. Drop letters remained at 1c and domestic mail prepayment made compulsory. Wierenga notes that unpaid ship letters were still accepted. They were charged at the regular domestic rates in addition to the 2c paid to ship's masters, except that regular letters addressed to the port of arrival continued to be charged at 6c.

May 18: Jessey Johnson appointed US stamp agent with an office in Philadelphia. It was his function to take delivery in the name of the United States government of newly printed postage stamps from the printer and forward them to Washington. See Feb. 1, 1869.

May 31: The Canadian Post Office introduced the registration of letters, according to Robson Lowe. Boggs says that registration had been started in December 1840 in Upper and Lower Canada.

July 1: A mail registration system went into effect in the United States, which charged a fee of 5c. There was no indemnity.

July 1: Sweden became the second country to issue stamps perforated for easy separation when it released its first stamps on this date. Stamps of Great Britain were the first perforated stamps issued for public use (see Jan. 28, 1854).

July 18: New Zealand issued its first postage stamps. They feature the beautiful Chalon portrait of Queen Victoria.

July 31: The first relief (letterpress) printed stamp of Great Britain was issued. It had been produced by Thomas de la Rue Ltd. from a design by Joubert de la Ferte.

Oct. 8: Great Britain's Board of Inland Revenue inaugurated a "printed to private order" service on this date. This meant that private individuals could have postal indicia imprinted on their own paper, envelopes, and postcards. As postal rates increased, mailers re-submitted paper for the impression of additional indicia to make up the new rate. The British discontinued the service on Oct. 31, 1973.

Oct. 11: From this date until the appearance of Empire of India stamps in 1882, Indian stamps bore the inscription "East India Postage." This referred not to a geographic area, but to the area administered by the East India Company.

Nov. 10: The Danish West Indies, now the US Virgin Islands, issued its first stamps.

1856

Edward Stanley Gibbons founded his stamp business in this year. It is the world's oldest stamp firm still in operation.

During this year, the Crown Colony of British Guiana issued a stamp that has since become the most famous of all philatelic items. It is usually referred to as the *British Guiana 1c.* Only one copy is known to exist and considerable mystery surrounds its discovery in Georgetown by a young boy, L. Vernon Vaughn. From his collection it eventually passed into the possession of Thomas Ridpath, a stamp dealer in Liverpool, England, who sold it to Count Philippe de la Renotiere von Ferrary. American Arthur Hind bought it when the Ferrary collection was sold on April 5, 1922 (q.v.). Hind's widow kept the stamp until 1940, when she sold it to Frederick T. Small, an Australian living in Florida. Small kept it until 1970, when a group headed by Irwin Weinberg of Wilkes-Barre, Penn., bought it at auction for $280,000, then a record price for a single stamp. It most recently changed hands on April 5, 1980 (q.v.).

Jan. 1: The prepayment of domestic letters by means of postage stamps or stamped envelopes

Edward Stanley Gibbons (1856).

The British Guiana 1c and the press on which it is believed to have been printed. It was at the office of the *Royal Gazette*, Georgetown (1856).

St. Helena's first stamp seen on a recent commemorative (Jan. 1, 1856) and the first stamp of Finland (March 1, 1856).

became compulsory in the US. Congress provided for this in an act of March 3, 1855, according to Norona.

Jan. 1: The South Atlantic island of St. Helena issued its first postage stamp. It was a 6d stamp in blue depicting a profile of Queen Victoria.

March 1: Finland issued its first postage stamp. Released under Russian domination, the stamp has a denomination of five kopecks and reproduces the Finnish coat of arms.

May 1: Registered mail began to be exchanged between the Eastern states and California and Oregon.

May 1: The postal administrations of the United States and Great Britain began the exchange of registered mail.

May 30: The steamer *Propontis* sailed from London for St. John's, Newfoundland with mail. Its owners hoped to establish direct regular mail service between Great Britain and Newfoundland, but the ship made only one voyage. Other shipping companies tried to establish the service but none was successful. Eventually, postal officials gave up the idea of a mail contract and in 1889 announced that mail could go by any ship.

July 1: The grand duchy of Mecklenburg-Schwerin released its first postage stamp. It was a one-schilling denomination that could be divided into four ¼s stamps.

July 25: Puerto Rico placed stamps in use, according to a decree dated July 11. The stamps

were the same as those used in Cuba since April 1855. The reason for a delayed official announcement is not known. Preston and Sanborn note that stamps are known used prior to this date. They add that usage did not become common until some time after the official announcement.

Aug. 1: Mexico issued its first postage stamps. They bear the portrait of Miguel Hidalgo y Costilla and are handstamped with district names.

Aug. 21: The Argentine province of Corrientes issued its first postage stamp. The one-real stamp is very similar to the first French stamp design.

Two of the several *Boites Mobiles* markings (Sept. 24, 1856).

Sept. 24: A postal convention signed by Great Britain and France concerned the exchange of mail between the two countries, including the system of moveable boxes *(boites mobiles)*. See 1843.

October: Stamps were issued in Tlacotalpan, a village in the Mexican state of Veracruz.

Oct. 1: Uruguay issued its first postage stamps. These are the so-called "Carrier Issue."

Oct. 1: The US Post Office Department began the exchange of registered mail with Canada.

December: The US steamship rate was 10c for under 2,500 miles and 20c for letters traveling more than 2,500 miles. In December 1856, the distance between Panama and New York was made less than 2,500 miles for rating purposes, although the actual distance was greater, according to Wierenga.

1857

The US Congress authorized the establishment of a mail service between a point on the Mississippi River and San Francisco. The route was to begin at both St. Louis, Mo., and Memphis, Tenn., join at Fort Smith, Ark., and continue to El Paso, Fort Yuma, and San Francisco. On Sept. 15, 1858, the Butterfield Overland Mail began service on the route.

The first post office was established on the English Channel island of Sark. A man named Queripel was the first postmaster and the office was located at La Heche in a small store. Fishermen carried mail to and from Guernsey.

Jan. 1: Newfoundland issued its first stamps on this date. The issue comprised nine denominations; 1d, 2d, 3d, 4d, 5d, 6d, 8d, and 1/-. They were intaglio printed by Perkins, Bacon & Co. of London.

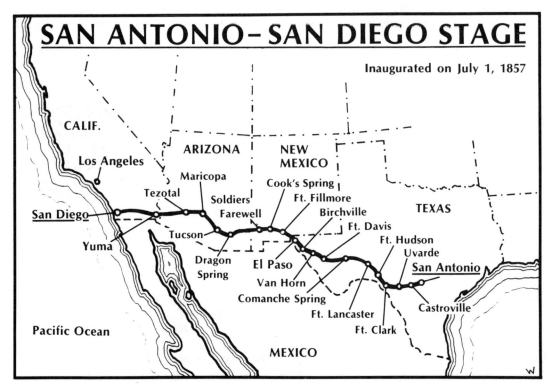

SAN ANTONIO-SAN DIEGO STAGE

Inaugurated on July 1, 1857

CALIF.

ARIZONA

NEW MEXICO

TEXAS

Los Angeles

Maricopa

Tezotal

Soldiers Farewell

Cook's Spring

Ft. Fillmore

Birchville

Ft. Davis

San Diego

Tucson

Ft. Hudson

Uvarde

Yuma

Dragon Spring

El Paso

Van Horn

San Antonio

Comanche Spring

Castroville

Ft. Lancaster

Ft. Clark

Pacific Ocean

MEXICO

Feb. 6: The United States first issued stamps perforated for easy separation, according to Cabeen.

March 7: Aaron V. Brown succeeded James Campbell as US postmaster general.

April 1: The British colony of Ceylon, now Sri Lanka, released its first stamp, a 6d issue. It was intaglio printed by Perkins, Bacon & Co. of London, England.

May 26: The British African colony of Natal issued its first stamps. They were produced in colorless embossing on colored paper by the firm of May and Davis at the Natal Treasury in Pietermaritzburg, according to Poole. Denominations were 3d, 6d, 9d, and 1/-. A 1d denomination was added the following year.

July 1: A private carrier, under a contract with the US Post Office Department, established a mail-carrying stage route between San Antonio, Texas, and San Diego, Calif. The contract called for two trips a month, with 30 days allowed for each trip. Payment for this service amounted to $149,800 a year. See December 1858.

September: Pearson Hill, the son of Sir Rowland Hill, made the first attempt at solving the problem of mechanized cancelation. The new machine, which operated either by steam or a foot treadle, was tested in London beginning in September 1857. After his machine apparently proved unsuccessful, Hill produced in 1858-59 a new machine called the "parallel motion" machine. Experiments made in Edinburgh, Scotland produced the celebrated "Brunswick Star" (q.v.) postmarks of

Pearson Hill's machine.

1863-73. The machine saw wide service in Britain until about 1900.

Sept. 16: John Butterfield and a group of associates received a six-year contract to carry mail from St. Louis, Mo., and Memphis, Tenn., west to San Francisco via Fort Smith, Ark., and El Paso, Texas. The contract required service every two weeks and the remuneration was fixed at $600,000 a year. The journey was to take 25 days.

Dec. 1: Provisional stamps supplied by the Pacific Steam Navigation Company became the first stamps of Peru. Regular issues followed on March 1, 1858.

The concord coach; it carried the mail of the Old West (1858).

1858

British adhesive postage stamps were placed in use in the colony of British Honduras, now the independent country of Belize.

A postmaster provisional handstamp was issued at Tuscumbia, Ala.

J.S. and E.A. Abbott built the first American Concord coach. For a brief moment, the coach represented the peak of mail-carrying technology in the US. It became a symbol of the opening of the American West. The coach was "... tidy and graceful as a lady, as inspiring to a stagefaring man as a ship to a sailor, and has — like the lady and the ship — scarcely a straight line in its body," a contemporary writer said.

Built until about 1865 by the Abbotts and then by Abbott, Downing & Co., the coach's secret was its suspension. It did not use conventional springs, which gave a violent up and down motion. Instead, the coach body was suspended on strips of leather laminated to a thickness of several inches. The coaches were rugged and designed to be as difficult as possible to capsize.

The first mail box is reported to have been placed in use in the United States in Boston. Reports indicate that boxes were also placed in New York during the same year. Konwiser notes that mail boxes existed in Charleston, S.C., as early as 1849 and at Cincinnati in 1854. He also reports that mail boxes were installed on San Francisco Bay ferries by 1857.

January: The first stamps inscribed "Tasmania," formerly Van Diemen's Land, were issued.

Jan. 1: Russia issued its first adhesive postage stamp, an imperforate and ungummed 10-kopeck item. However, since Jan. 1, was a public holiday, the stamp was not available until Jan. 2. Russia had intended to issue 10k, 20k, and 30k stamps perforated and gummed but production delays occurred. Prigara states that all three were finished and available by Jan. 10.

The Scott catalog gives Dec. 10, 1857 as the issue date of the first stamp, but this is the date of the circular announcing the stamps. Russian-occupied Poland also used the stamps.

Jan. 1: The Kingdom of Naples issued its first postage stamps. They were replaced by stamps of the Neapolitan Provinces in February 1861.

March 1: Peru released its first regular issues. They feature a coat of arms design and were lithographed by Emilio Prugue of Lima. Peru's first stamps, issued Dec. 1, 1857 (q.v.), had been supplied by the Pacific Steam Navigation Co.

April 29: Buenos Aires, a province of Argentina, issued its first stamps. The design, which depicts an early steamship, was by Pablo Cataldi. The stamps were typographed by the Banco y Casa de Moneda in Buenos Aires.

May 1: Argentina issued its first national postage stamps under the name of the Argentine Confederation. The design shows a rising sun over two clasped hands symbolizing the confederation. The stamps were lithographed by Carlos Riviere.

May 1: The American Bank Note Company was formed by a merger of Toppan, Carpenter & Company of New York; Rawdon, Wright, Hatch & Edson (printers of the US 1847 5c and 10c stamps); and a number of other firms.

May 11: Minnesota entered the Union as the 32nd state.

May 31: Russia introduced numeral cancelations.

June: British Post Office surveyor and novelist Anthony Trollope, reported to London from

Egypt that he considered the delay in completing a rail link from the Mediterranean Sea to the Red Sea was a result of pressure by the P & O Steamship Company. He said the company feared competition from other companies if fast, easy transit became possible across the land bridge.

Trollope arranged with the Egyptian government to have the transit time for mail not exceed 24 hours. Thus, even before the Suez Canal was opened, India was only one month from England via the Mediterranean.

July: By this date an overland mail service operated from Independence, Mo. through to Placerville, Calif. via Salt Lake City. The scheduled time taken was 38 days.

July: Wells, Fargo & Co. established an express at Victoria, Vancouver Island, and on the mainland of what is now the Canadian province of British Columbia through other companies. The company sold its own envelopes, and when stamps became available they had to be affixed. Until the official stamps were sold, the company took its envelopes to the post office which stamped them upon payment of the postage.

July 1: Jacob Hall began his third four-year mail contract along the Santa Fe Trail. John Hockaday had left and Hall's new partner was Judge James Porter. The new contract required weekly service using six-mule coaches with iron axles and elliptical springs. The coaches departed every Monday at 8 a.m. from each end. The maximum running time was set at 20 days, five days less than the previous contract.

July 15: Moldavia, later part of Romania, issued stamps. Their design features a bull's head and a post horn.

September: Joseph Sloper obtained a British patent for a device that perforated initials or a design on postage stamps as a security measure. These perforated stamps are known as perfins.

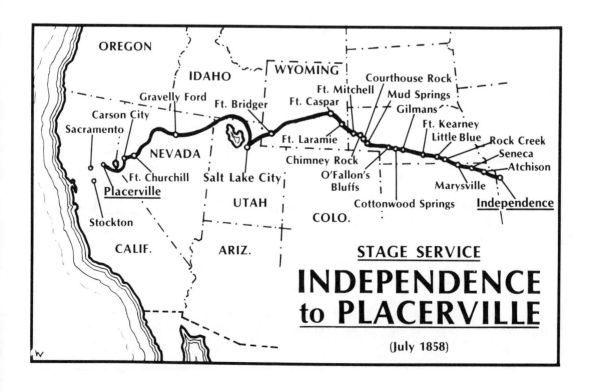

STAGE SERVICE

INDEPENDENCE
to PLACERVILLE

(July 1858)

Sept. 15: The Butterfield Overland Mail began service from both ends of a route between St. Louis, Mo., and Memphis, Tenn., and San Francisco, via Fort Smith, Ark., El Paso, Texas, and Fort Yuma, Ariz. The establishment of a transcontinental mail route had been authorized by Congress in 1857. The first westbound trip took 23 days, 23 hours, while that to the east took 24 days, 18 hours, and 26 minutes.

Oct. 27: The first US mail left New Orleans, La., on a new route to California. This was the so-called Tehuantepec Route. A steamer took mail to Minatitlan at the narrowest point in Mexico, where a river steamer and coach took it to the Pacific coast. The Panama steamer picked it up there and took it north to San Francisco. The mail arrived there on Nov. 14, proving this to be the fastest route to the West Coast. It was highly regarded by passengers. However, an economy-minded postmaster general, Joseph Holt, who had just assumed office, did not renew its one-year contract.

Oct. 28: Cordoba, a province of Argentina, issued its first stamps. The design features the coat of arms of the province. The stamps were lithographed in sheets of 30 stamps by Larsch of Buenos Aires.

Nov. 1: India became a crown colony of Great Britain. It had previously been administered in trust by the East India Company.

Charles Connell

BUTTERFIELD OVERLAND MAIL
(Sept. 15, 1858)

St. Louis
Tipton
Warsaw
Bolivar
Springfield
CALIF.
San Francisco
Visalia
ARIZONA
NEW MEXICO
OKLA.
Ft. Smith
Sherman
Memphis
Yuma
Tezotal
Tucson
Gainesville
Ft. Belknap
Boggy
Colbert's Ferry
Los Angeles
Ft. Chadbourne
Jacksboro
El Paso
Horsehead Crossing
TEXAS
Pacific Ocean

Nov. 1: Charles Connell became postmaster general of the British North American colony of New Brunswick. He later resigned as a result of the famous 5c stamp that bore his portrait and which caused such a fuss. See May 9, 1860.

Nov. 23: Jim Saunders began the first journey of his express line between Fort Laramie, Wyo., and Denver, Colo., following the gold strike at Denver that summer. He made the journey in a small wagon drawn by four ponies, returning to Denver on Jan. 8, 1859. The express had a short life and in the spring of 1859 the Leavenworth and Pike's Peak Express replaced it.

December: The duplicated service between El Paso, Texas, and Fort Yuma, Ariz., by the Butterfield stage from the east to San Francisco, and the San Antonio-San Diego stage, resulted in the latter having its El Paso-Fort Yuma segment removed. The two separated segments were then increased to weekly.

1859

January: The Free City of Hamburg issued its first postage stamps. They were engraved by J. F. R. Ziensenist and printed by T. G. Meissner of Hamburg.

January: France issued the first postage due labels. They are inscribed "Chiffre taxe," with a denomination figure representing the amount of postage due on a piece of mail.

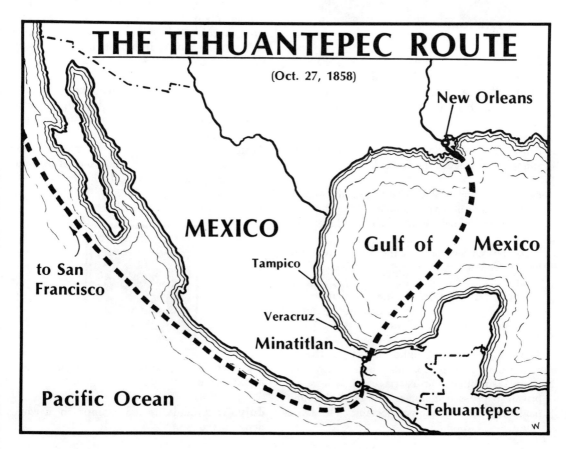

THE TEHUANTEPEC ROUTE
(Oct. 27, 1858)

Jan. 1, 1859 - July 1, 1859

Jan. 1: The free city of Lubeck, now in West Germany, issued its first postage stamps. They were lithographed by H. G. Rathgens of Lubeck.

Jan. 1: Sicily issued its first postage stamps. They depict King Ferdinand II, the infamous "King Bomba", who earned international disgust for his murderous treatment of his subjects.

Jan. 1: Venezuela issued its first postage stamps. They depict the country's coat of arms.

Jan. 1: Parcel post service began in Canada. The weight limit was one pound, later increased to three pounds and in 1914, to 11 pounds.

Feb. 14: Oregon became the 33rd state of the United States.

March 14: President James Buchanan appointed Joseph Holt US postmaster general, succeeding Aaron V. Brown.

May 4: The postal authorities of the British colonies of British Columbia and Vancouver Island permitted the carriage of letters by private express companies, providing the mail paid the required colonial postage. The basic rate was 2½d or 5c.

May 7: The first coach of the Leavenworth and Pike's Peak Express arrived at Denver, Colo., from Leavenworth, Kans. The journey had taken 19 days, a time that was soon reduced to seven days. The distance is given at 687 miles. The company did not have a mail contract. US mail service to the Denver area was not established until August 1860, when a weekly service began.

May 15: Three stamps were issued for the Ionian Islands. Located off the west coast of Greece, the group was a British protectorate from 1814 to 1864. The stamps are in denominations of ½d, 1d, and 2d. The denominations are identified only by the stamp's color, which are orange (½d), blue (1d), and carmine (2d). Intaglio printing was by Perkins, Bacon & Co.

June 10: The Bahamas issued its first stamp. The 1d stamp featuring the Chalon portrait of Queen Victoria, bears the inscription "INTERINSULAR POSTAGE." This indicated that the stamp was intended for domestic use, although it was used on mail out of the colony after May 1, 1860.

June 26: The government of Uruguay issued its first stamps.

July 1: Canada issued stamps in decimal denominations.

August: A provisional government in the Italian state of Parma issued new postage stamps.

August: The Granadine Confederation, the forerunner of the modern state of Colombia issued its first stamps.

Aug. 17: Balloonist John Wise carried mail aboard his balloon *Jupiter* when he ascended from Lafayette, Ind., hoping to fly to the East Coast. He did not find the expected westerly wind and came down at Crawfordsville, Ind., 35 miles away. The mail was forwarded by train. Only one piece of mail is known from this flight.

Aug. 22: Running time of the Independence-Santa Fe mail route along the Santa Fe Trail was reduced from 20 to 15 days. Not long afterward, the operators reported that the mail usually arrrived within 14 days.

Sept. 1: The Italian state of Romagna issued its first postage stamps.

Sept. 21: The crown colony and British protectorate of Sierra Leone released its first postage stamp. It bears a denomination of 6d and was relief printed by De La Rue & Co. of London.

Oct. 15: New stamps were issued by a provisional government in the Italian state of Modena.

Oct. 24: The unofficial territory known as Jefferson was created. It became part of Colorado Territory on Feb. 28, 1861.

December: Prior to the founding of Queensland as a separate British colony in Australia, its postal affairs had been administered by New South Wales. Queensland was then known as the Moreton Bay District.

December: The earliest known letter from the area of the South African Republic (Transvaal) bears this date. It was sent from Potchefstroom, the old Boer capital, to Cape Town.

John Wise ascends from the Indiana town of Lafayette, Ind. hoping to fly to the East Coast and prove his theory that a strong westerly wind existed. Could he have guessed about the jet stream? Unfortunately, he did not find it and came down with the mail he carried only 35 miles away at Crawfordsville. This US stamp was issued on Aug. 17, 1959 to mark the 100th anniversary of the flight.

The age of empires

1860

Liberia issued its first postage stamps. The design shows a figure entitled "Liberia" and a ship. The stamps were lithographed by Dando, Todhunter & Smith of London.

The first stamp dealer in New York City is generally considered to have been William P. Brown, although Harlow quotes him as stating that John Bailey was already established as a dealer when Brown commenced trading about 1860.

William H. Russell, organizer of the Pony Express, advertised for riders as follows: "Wanted: Young, skinny, wiry fellows not over 18. Must be expert riders willing to risk death daily. Orphans preferred." Before being hired, the riders had to swear on a Bible not to "cuss," fight, or abuse their animals and to conduct themselves honestly.

Jan. 1: A provisional government in the Italian state of Tuscany issued stamps on this date. The stamps of Tuscany were replaced by those of Sardinia in 1861.

Jan. 1: Poland, under Russian control, issued a single stamp. The 10-kopeck stamp was printed in Warsaw. It is in a similar design to contemporary Russian stamps except that its inscription is in Polish. Russian stamps were reintroduced in April 1865.

Jan. 1: The French colony of New Caledonia issued its first postage stamp. The design features a primitive portrait of Napoleon III and was printed from a plate of 50 subjects, which were all drawn individually by a French Army soldier stationed on the island. The stamp was in use until Sept. 17, 1862, from which date the general issues of the French colonies were used until 1881.

Jan. 1: The British North American colony of Nova Scotia adopted decimal currency.

February: Stamps of Parma were replaced by those of the kingdom of Sardinia in that Italian state.

February: Stamps of the kingdom of Sardinia replaced those of Romagna in the Italian state.

William Russell's ad for Pony Express riders (1860) and the first stamp issued for use in what is now Poland (Jan. 1, 1860).

February: The Central Overland California and Pike's Peak Express Company absorbed the Leavenworth and Pike's Peak Express. See also May 11, 1860.

March 16: Jarrett reports that this is the earliest date he had seen for Canadian stamped envelopes, which were first used in this year. The envelopes were issued with 5c and 10c indicia. They were made by George F. Nesbitt of New York for the British American Bank Note Co.

April 1: The British Honduras government assumed control of the colony's Post Office from the General Post Office, London.

April 3: The US Post Office Department established a rate of 1c for drop letters delivered by carrier.

April 3: The Pony Express was inaugurated on this date, when riders left San Francisco eastbound and St. Joseph, Mo. westbound. The eastbound rider traveled by boat partway to Sacramento, beginning his ride from there the following day. Relays of riders and ponies carried the mail in each direction.

The westbound mail took 10½ days to reach San Francisco and it is recorded that 75 ponies were required to cover the route from St. Joseph to San Francisco. The distance gradually diminished as the telegraph line and railroad closed the gap from each end, and by

Stamps of the United States honoring the Pony Express in 1940 and 1960.

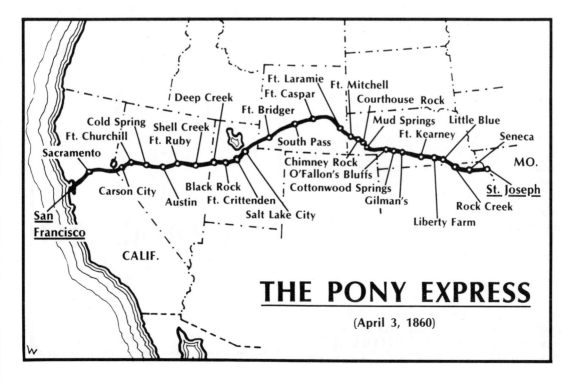

THE PONY EXPRESS

(April 3, 1860)

November 1861 the need for the service, which had meantime been taken over by Wells, Fargo & Co., had ended.

April 21: The San Francisco *Bulletin* reported that a total of 205 letters were dispatched via the Pony Express on that date. Generally, a greater volume of mail went east than was sent west.

May 1: Colonial authorities on the island of Nevis assumed control of postal services. Stamps inscribed for the island were issued during 1861.

May 1: On this date, the crown colony of Hong Kong assumed responsibility for its own postal system. Prior to this, it had been under the control of the General Post Office in London.

May 9: The lieutenant governor of the British colony of New Brunswick accepted the resignation of Postmaster General Charles Connell, as a result of government supression of a 5c stamp bearing Connell's portrait. The stamp was replaced with one picturing Queen Victoria. The Connell stamps were ordered destroyed and this appears to have been done except for about 50 copies, according to Argenti.

May 9: The crown colony of India released its first stamps. Stamps had circulated since 1854 under the administration of the East India Company.

May 11: US Postmaster General Holt annulled the mail contract held by George Chorpenning (see May 1, 1851) for the Salt Lake City, Utah, to Placerville, Calif., route and a new contract was made with the Central Overland California and Pike's Peak Express Company. This firm then had control over the entire central mail route to the Pacific.

July 1: A British post office is reported to have opened in Yokohama, Japan.

July 30: This is the earliest known use of the first stamp issued for joint use in the British colonies of British Columbia and Vancouver Island. It is inscribed "BRITISH COLUMBIA" and "VANCOUVERS ISLAND." The stamp

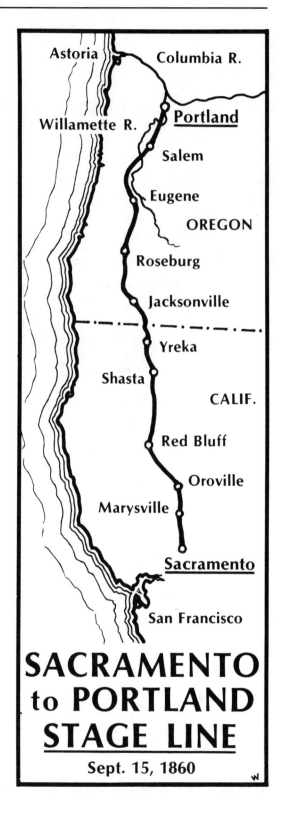

SACRAMENTO to PORTLAND STAGE LINE
Sept. 15, 1860

has a denomination of 2½d and was printed by De La Rue & Co. of London.

Sept. 15: Daily mail service in stages between Sacramento, Calif., and Portland, Ore. began. The service was scheduled to take seven days during the summer and 12 days in the winter.

November: By this month, the Pony Express route had been shortened to the distance between Fort Kearny, Neb., and Fort Churchill, Nev.

Nov. 1: The British colony of Queensland, Australia, issued its first stamps. Featuring the Chalon portrait of Queen Victoria, the stamps are in denominations of 1d, 2d, and 6d. They were intaglio printed by Perkins, Bacon & Co. of London.

Nov. 16: John N. Luff, well-known collector and philatelic writer was born at South Haven, N.Y. He was president of Scott Stamp & Coin Co. from Oct. 1, 1903, until March 1, 1905, when he moved to Stanley Gibbons, Inc. of New York. He wrote *The Postage Stamps of the United States,* first published in 1902.

Nov. 23: The first stamps of the British colony of Jamaica were issued on this date. Denominations are 1d, 2d, 4d, 6d, and 1/-. The stamps were printed by De La Rue & Co. of London.

Dec. 1: The first stamp inscribed for the British colony of Malta was issued. It is a ½d denomination and paid the domestic rate of ½d per half ounce. It was not valid for use outside Malta and is thus classified as a local postage stamp. Stamps of Great Britain were used for overseas mail.

Dec. 18: St. Lucia issued its first stamps. They were intaglio printed by Perkins, Bacon & Co. of London in three denominations designated only by their color. These are lake (1d), deep blue (4d), and green (6d).

Dec. 20: South Carolina voted to secede from the United States, becoming the first state to leave the Union.

Dec. 23: Announcements in Kansas City and Independence, Mo. stated that Hall and Porter had sold their Santa Fe mail service to the Missouri Stage Company, operated by Preston Roberts, Jr. The mail contract was not assigned and Hall remained the sole contractor until 1862.

1861

India became the first country to release government telegraph stamps for the prepayment of telegrams, according to Rich and Rich.

Stamps in four denominations became the first issues for the British colony of Nevis. The denominations are 1d, 4d, 6d, and 1/-. The stamps were intaglio printed by Nissen & Parker of London.

Stamps of the United States of New Granada followed those of the Granadine Confederation. It is now the South American country of Colombia.

Jan. 1: First stamps issued for the British colony of Prince Edward Island, now a province of

First stamps from Malta (Dec. 1, 1860), St. Lucia (Dec. 18, 1860), and Prince Edward Island (Jan. 1, 1861).

Canada. They were released in denominations of 2d, 3d, and 6d. Production was by the London firm of Charles Whiting.

Jan. 9: Mississippi voted to secede from the United States.

Jan. 10: Florida seceded from the United States.

Jan. 11: Alabama seceded from the United States.

Jan. 19: Georgia became the fifth state to secede from the United States.

Jan. 26: Louisiana seceded after 48 years as part of the United States.

Jan. 29: Congress made Kansas the 34th state.

February: Stamps of the Neapolitan Provinces superceded those of the kingdom of Naples. They were in turn replaced by stamps of the kingdom of Italy in 1862.

Feb. 1: Texas voted to secede from the United States. It ratified the decision on Feb. 23.

Feb. 9: The Confederate States of America passed a law to continue in force certain laws of the United States of America. These included postal laws, regulations, and rates.

Feb. 12: Horatio King succeeded Joseph Holt as US postmaster general.

Feb. 21: The Confederate States of America approved a law to establish a post office department.

Feb. 27: The US Congress amended the ship letter charges to eliminate the inequity where a ship letter addressed to a port of arrival was charged 6c, while one going up to 3,000 miles beyond paid only 3c plus the 2c fee for the ship's master. The 6c port of arrival charge was reduced to 5c, according to Wierenga. See April 1, 1855.

Feb. 27: An act of the US Congress authorized the use of wrappers for the mailing of newspapers. The wrapper bears an indicium and is gummed on one end. First issued in October 1861, the wrappers were discontinued in 1934.

Feb. 28: The US Congress made Colorado a territory.

March 2: Dakota became a territory. On Nov. 2, 1889, it became the states of North and South Dakota.

March 2: The US Congress enacted legislation transferring the Butterfield mail route between St. Louis-Memphis and San Francisco, to the Central Route between St. Joseph, Mo., and San Francisco. For this new service, which was to be daily, the Butterfield firm agreed to a million-dollar contract.

Although the looming Civil War would have rendered this move necessary, the need for shorter, more direct communications with the West was the chief reason for the change.

March 2: The territory of Nevada was established on this date.

March 9: President Abraham Lincoln appointed Montgomery Blair US postmaster general, succeeding Horatio King.

April 1: This was the issue date of stamps for mail carried on the Pony Express by Wells,

Fargo & Co., according to Boggs. The denominations are $2 and $4. Nathan states that the earliest known use of the $2 stamp is May 1, 1861. He doubt's that the $4 stamp was ever used.

April 17: Virginia voted to secede, except for the area that became the state of West Virginia. The secession was ratified on May 23.

May 1: The earliest-known use of the $2 stamp issued by Wells, Fargo & Co. for use on the Pony Express. Nathan notes that the stamps were, for an unknown reason, used only on the eastbound Pony Express. For westbound mail, a special stamped envelope with franking on the left side was used.

May 6: Arkansas voted to secede from the United States.

May 8: St. Vincent issued its first stamps in denominations of 1d and 6d. They were intaglio printed by Perkins, Bacon & Co. of London.

May 7: Tennessee voted to secede from the United States. It ratified its decision on June 8.

May 21: North Carolina voted to secede from the United States becoming the final state to join the Confederate States of America.

May 28: The US Post Office Department suspended postal service in the Confederate States of America and invalidated existing US postage stamps, according to US Postmaster General Montgomery Blair in a July 12, 1861 letter to Congress.

May 31: By this date, 923 post offices operated in Texas. The state had 19,664 miles of mail routes, 2,095 of which were operated

by steamboats. Railroads served 180 miles of mail routes, according to Scheele.

June 1: The first stamps of the British colony of Grenada were placed on sale on or about this date, according to Poole. Intaglio printed by Perkins, Bacon & Co. of London, the stamps have denominations of 1d and 6d.

June 1: The Confederate States of America took over the operation of the US Postal Office Department within its boundaries.

June 18: President Lincoln approved formation of the United States Sanitary Commission. Its activities included staging "sanitary fairs" to raise funds to ease the lot of the Union troops during the Civil War. At some of these fairs, semi-official stamps were issued. The first fair opened on Feb. 22, 1864 at Albany, N.Y. (q.v.).

July 1: After this date, the Pony Express operated under contract to the US Post Office as a mail route. Its rate dropped to $1 per half ounce, plus 10c US postage. An additional 10c was charged for the 10c US Post Office stamped envelope from San Francisco, Calif., to Placerville, Calif., for a total of $1 plus 20c.

July 1: The first daily Butterfield stagecoach over the central route left St. Joseph, Mo., and arrived in San Francisco on July 18. (See March 2, 1861).

July 12: US Postmaster General Blair reported to Congress that all US mail service in the seceded states had been discontinued with the exception of the western counties of Virginia (later to become West Virginia) where the population remained loyal to the US government.

August: The United States issued a 3c letter sheet, according to Thorp-Bartels. The letter sheet came in two sizes, notes Dr. Rodney L. Mott of the United Postal Stationery Society. The larger letter sheet was intended primarily for the use of troops, while the smaller one was for "ladies' correspondence." They were withdrawn in April 1864.

Aug. 26: US Postmaster General Blair directed officers and agents of the Post Office Department to end all written communications with the 11 seceded states.

Sept. 27: The government of the Australian colony of Queensland established its own printing operation and beginning with the 1868-74 issue, printed stamps for use in the colony. Between this date and 1868 its stamps were produced by Ham & Co. of Brisbane.

October: It is believed that the United States introduced the use of newspaper wrappers during this month. They had been authorized by Congress on Feb. 27, 1861. The first wrapper had a denomination of 1c. Wrappers were discontinued in 1934.

Oct. 1: Greece issued its first stamps. These are the *Hermes Heads,* the first issue of which was printed in Paris.

Oct. 16: This is the earliest known postmark date on the general issue of the Confederate States of America.

Oct. 24: Completion of the transcontinental telegraph line spelled doom for the Pony Express. The end came in November, 1861. The receipts for the entire Pony Express operation, according to Scheele, amounted to only $91,404 and it had cost its operators an estimated half million dollars.

Nov. 1: The German city of Bergedorf issued its first postage stamps. Originally owned jointly by the free cities of Hamburg and Lubeck, Bergedorf was bought by Hamburg on Aug. 8, 1867.

Dec. 11: A postmaster was appointed for the Seychelles. The islands used stamps of Mauritius until April 5, 1890, when stamps were issued for the Seychelles group. Its location is to the north of Madagascar in the Indian Ocean.

Dec. 21: Alfred Potiquet published the first stamp catalog in Paris. The 10-page listing claimed to include all the world's postage stamps issued to that date.

1862

In this year, the US Congress passed the Revenue Act that authorized many taxes to help pay for the Civil War. Affixed to all sorts of products, including matches and medicines, the stamps are known as "Match and Medicine" revenues.

Their proper name is Private Die Proprietary Stamps, since manufacturers were permitted to have dies engraved and plates made at their own expense in exchange for a discount on the value of the tax stamps. The stamps were usually torn in opening the container on which they were used. The stamp tax was repealed effective July 1, 1883.

Justin Henri Lallier of Paris is said to have published the first stamp album. Some sources note that publication took place in 1863, while others give credit to an A. Oppems of London for producing a stamp album in 1862.

The first recorded philatelic periodical, *The Stamp Collectors' Review and Monthly Advertizer,* published by Edward Moore & Co. in Liverpool, England, sold for one penny a copy and ran for 19 issues before ceasing publication in 1864.

Stamps were first issued by the United States of Colombia, now the Republic of Colombia.

Jan. 1: A US Post Office Department announcement to postmasters stated that after this date US stamps then current would no longer be good for postage, according to Brookman. This act, taken at the beginning of the Civil War, was to prevent stocks of stamps then held in the South from being sent north to raise money for the Confederate cause.

Jan. 11: The first stamps were issued under the name of the Argentine Republic.

March: Stamps were issued for the newly formed kingdom of Italy. The frame was typographed in color, while the profile of King Victor Emmanuel II is in colorless embossing.

March 5: Posta Europe, a private postal system operating in Egypt, received a 10-year postal monopoly in Lower Egypt. Posta Europa is the organization that in 1864 (q.v.) issued the first Interpostal Seals.

April: H & C Treacher of Brighton, England, published the book, *Aid to Stamp Collectors: Being a List of English and Foreign Postage Stamps in Circulation Since 1840.* The author is identified as "A Stamp Collector." Later editions gave the author's name as Frederick Booty.

May: Great Britain's first special event postmark was used at a post office at the international exhibition held in London from May to November 1862.

May: The British collector and dealer, Mount Brown, published his *Catalog of British, Colonial, and Foreign Stamps,* according to Hallgren. It is regarded as the ancestor of today's stamp catalog.

June 25: The joint principalities of Moldavia-Walachia issued their first stamps. The principalities formed the basis of the country of Romania.

July 11: Congress authorized the US Treasury Department to have bank notes or portions of them printed at the department, thus creating the Bureau of Engraving and Printing. The bureau began operating on Aug. 29, 1862 (q.v.).

July 28: The first US railway post office is claimed to have been a mail sorting car of the Hannibal and St. Joseph Railroad introduced on this date. Cabeen reported it to be the idea of W. A. Davis, a postal employee. See Aug. 28, 1864 for another claim to this honor.

Railway sorting cars had been used in Great Britain since 1838 and in France since 1850. In the United States, route agents had operated on trains since the late 1830s. (See May 18, 1838).

August: The crown colony of Antigua issued its first stamp. It is a 6d stamp intaglio printed by Perkins, Bacon & Co. of London.

Aug 4: US Postmaster General Montgomery Blair wrote a letter to Secretary of State William Seward urging international cooperation to organize and simplify international mail traffic and postal rates. The letter was instrumental in convening the Paris Postal Conference of May 11-June 8, 1863.

Aug. 11: Wells, Fargo & Co. inaugurated a Pony Express between San Francisco and Virginia City, Nev. It had no connection with the transcontinental Pony Express, which ceased operation in November 1861. The new service lasted until early 1865 and used 10c brown stamps and 25c stamps in both red and blue. Ponies were used only between Virginia City and Placerville, Calif. The Placerville-Sacramento section used railroads and the Sacramento-San Francisco portion used boats.

Aug. 12: John Gault of New York City obtained a patent for encased postage stamps. He wanted to provide a protective case for postage stamps which were used as currency during a coin shortage caused by the Civil War. During

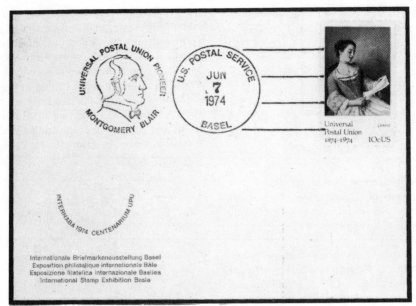

This cover bears a cancel honoring US PMG Montgomery Blair as a UPU pioneer and represents a rare instance of a US post office operating and canceling mail in a foreign country. The event was an international stamp exhibition in Basel, Switzerland in 1974 (Aug. 4, 1862).

the inflation following World War I, a number of European countries also used encased postage stamps as currency.

Aug. 21: To relieve the shortage of small-denomination coins in the United States during the Civil War, postage stamps affixed to Treasury Department paper were used as currency. On July 17, 1862, Congress authorized the production of postage stamps printed directly on Treasury paper and they were first issued on this date. Denominations are 5c, 10c, 25c, and 50c. The 25c and 50c items are imprinted with the necessary number of 5c and 10c stamp impressions. They were used until May 27, 1863.

Aug. 29: The Bureau of Engraving and Printing was established when two men and four women working in an attic of the main US Treasury building in Washington, D.C., began overprinting the Treasury seal and signatures on $1 and $2 notes. The notes had been printed privately. The bureau gradually absorbed the functions of private contractors. On July 1, 1894, the BEP began to produce all US postage stamps. Until the late 1860s, the BEP

was called the First Division National Currency Bureau (see January 1869).

Oct. 1: Effective on this date, revenue stamps were imprinted on checks, drafts, receipts, insurance policies, bonds, and stock certificates in the United States. The designs of many are highly complex and very attractive. Discontinued on July 1, 1882, the United States briefly revived them with a series in 1898 for the Spanish-American War.

Dec. 2: Nicaragua issued its first stamps, which the American Bank Note Company had intaglio printed.

Dec. 8: The British colony of Hong Kong released its first stamps. In denominations of 2c, 8c, 12c, 18c, 24c, 48c, and 96c, they were relief printed by De La Rue & Co. of London. Their use was not made compulsory until Feb. 16, 1864.

1863

The Colombian state of Bolivar issued stamps.

The District of Wenden in Latvia released stamps.

J.B. Moens, one of the world's pioneer stamp dealers and philatelic publishers is pictured on this Oct. 13, 1973 stamp with se-tenant label issued to mark the 50th anniversary of the Belgian Stamp Dealers' Association (1863).

J. B. Moens published the first European philatelic periodical, *Le Timbre Poste*. The periodical lasted for 38 years. The second British philatelic periodical also began publication in this year. This was the *Stamp Collectors Magazine*, published in Bath, England by the Smith brothers. The first British publication had appeared in 1862 (q.v.).

January: Russia began the release of special stamps for use on mail to and from seaports in the Turkish Empire (Levant).

January: Stamps were issued for use in Russian offices in the Turkish empire.

Jan. 1: The Russian Company for Steamshipping and Trade began to carry mail between the Levant ports of Batum, Trebizond, Mytilene, Smyrna, Mersina, Alexandretta, Beirut, Jaffa, Alexandria, Athos, and Salonika. By the end of the century, the company operated 77 steamships.

Jan. 1: Using the central design feature of the tughra (mark or monogram) of the sultan, the Turkish Empire issued its first stamps.

Feb. 3: This is the earliest known use of the famous *Brunswick Star* cancelation. The Edinburgh, Scotland, Post Office used the cancelation during the 1860s and up to 1873, according to Vallancey. There were several variations, but all feature an arrangement of radiating lines in the form of star-burst from the central numerals "131" (See September 1857).

Feb. 11: Italian government sources state this is the date of issue for the first true Italian stamp. Prior to this, the stamps of Sardinia had been used. This new stamp was the first to be inscribed "FRANCOBOLLO ITALIANO;" according to *Italy: Documents and Notes* published in 1974 by the Presidency of the Council of Ministers.

Feb. 24: The US Congress made Arizona a territory.

March 3: Idaho became a territory of the United States.

March 18: The government of Bolivia granted a contract to carry mail to Justiniano Garcia, who prepared postage stamps. The contract was canceled April 29 and the stamps never officially issued.

Four variations of the Brunswick Star cancelation used at Edinburgh, Scotland during the 1860s and 1870s (Feb. 3, 1863).

France and Great Britain were among a number of countries that issued stamps in 1963 to mark the 100th anniversary of the Paris Postal Conference (May 11, 1863).

April: The first stamps of Costa Rica were engraved and intaglio printed by the American Bank Note Co.

May 1: A philatelic periodical reportedly began publication in Leipzig, Germany.

May 11: The Paris Postal Conference opened. It ran until June 8. Representatives of Austria, Belgium, Costa Rica, Denmark, France, Great Britain, the Hanseatic cities of Bremen, Hamburg, and Lubeck, Italy, the Netherlands, Portugal, Prussia, the Sandwich Islands (Hawaii), Spain, Switzerland, and the United States attended. Montgomery Blair, the United States postmaster general, concerned by the difficulties of foreign mail handling and the lack of coordination among nations, was one of those who instigated the conference.

This meeting paved the way for the Postal Conference of 1874 in Berne, Switzerland.

May 27: Minting of silver coins replaced the postage stamp-imprinted Treasury paper in the United States. Postage currency had been in use from Aug. 21, 1862 in the US as a substitute for coinage, during a shortage.

June 1: In the British *Stamp Collectors Magazine* of this date, author Rev. Henry H. Higgins refers to collecting stamps according to the subject of their design. This is believed to be the earliest reference to topical collecting and was reported by Mary Ann Owens and George T. Guzzio, according to George Griffenhagen.

June 4: A US post office opened at Bent's Old Fort, where the route to Denver branched from the main Sante Fe Trail. Lewis Barnum served as its postmaster. His wife was a great-granddaughter of Daniel Boone.

June 15: M. Cottrill and Company received permission to make Kansas City its eastern Santa Fe Trail terminus for the mail contract, instead of Independence, Mo.

June 20: West Virginia became the 35th state of the United States.

The US issued this stamp on Oct. 26, 1963 for the centenary of City Mail Delivery (June 30, 1863).

June 30: The United States designated letter mail as "first-class mail." Authorized by Congress on March 3, 1863, the law also set the domestic letter rate at 3c per half ounce for any distance. Drop letters were 2c. It eliminated all carrier and way charges, resulting in free city delivery in 49 larger US cities.

Ship letters were to be charged double rate, but this also paid the fee for the ship's master. The law stipulated prompt depositing of all ship letters at the post office in the port of arrival, with 2c paid on letters from foreign ports and 1c on those from other US ports.

July: The Shanghai, China, Municipal Council established the Shanghai Local Post Office. Despite its name, the service operated over a large part of China to such distant places as Swatow, Tientsin, Peking, and Chungking, according to Dougan.

July 1: The US registration fee went to 20c. This included a return receipt but provided no indemnity.

July 1: The United States released the 2c stamp known as the *Black Jack*. It depicts Andrew Jackson and looks very modern and effective with its close-cropped portrait of Jackson. None are known used on the first day.

July 27: John Walter Scott sailed from England aboard the ship *Hecla* bound for New York, where he established himself as an outdoor stamp dealer. See Nov. 2, 1845.

Sept. 3: Russian postal authorities issued a 50-kopeck stamp for use by the St. Petersburg and Moscow city posts. They later extended the stamp's use to city posts in other cities.

Oct. 20: The Confederate States of America established an express mail service between its area east of the Mississippi River and those parts on the west side. Letters and packages would be carried, according to the CSA postmaster general.

Westbound mail had to be marked "via Meridan or Brandon" and eastbound mail had to be inscribed "via Shreveport or Alexandria." All mail was to be prepaid at the rate of 40c for a single letter of one half ounce and 40c for each additional half ounce or fraction.

November: Capt. Robert Todd began the La Guaira-St. Thomas mail service when he obtained a contract from the Venezuelan government. Starting in 1868, the service included the Dutch island of Curacao. By that time, however, Jesurun & Sons of Willemstad operated the service. It issued its first stamps in 1864. They depict an early steamship.

Dec. 17: Because of New Zealand's isolation and the delay of mail coming via the service from Britain to Australia, New Zealand contracted for a service across the Pacific via Panama. However, not until June 15, 1866 (q.v.) did a service actually start.

1864

Alexander II of Russia permitted the establishment of the so-called Zemstvo postal systems. Local governments could thus begin operating a postal service within their own areas, most of which were not served by the Imperial Postal Service. The services acted as a link between the rural resident and the Imperial service.

Many areas issued stamps, which were valid only to carry mail within that Zemstvo or to a point served by the Imperial system, when regular Russian stamps had to be used. If a letter was addressed to an area served by another Zemstvo, then stamps of that service had also to be used, making three stamps necessary. The first Zemstvo stamp was issued in September 1865. They were used in some areas until World War I.

During this year Posta Europea, which operated a mail service in Egypt, introduced so-called Interpostal Seals. These large round

On the left is the US stamp known as the *Black Jack* (July 1, 1863), while to the right is an example of the stamps used on the steamship mail service between La Guaira, Venezuela and St. Thomas, with service to Curacao beginning in 1868 (November 1863).

Examples of
the Interpostal
Seals used by
the Posta
Europea (1864).

seal-like adhesive stamps were generally placed on the back of a letter to seal the flap. Although they bore no denomination, Kehr notes that they were valid to frank a piece of mail of any weight.

When the Egyptian government bought Posta Europa, the use of these stamps continued. When Egypt issued postage stamps on Jan. 1, 1866 (q.v.), the seals were subsequently used only by government officials. Their most recent use was in. 1891, according to Kehr.

Prussia issued telegraph stamps.

Rowland Hill resigned his position as Secretary of the Post Office. His full salary was continued as a pension for life.

Feb. 15: The first North American philatelic periodical began publication in Montreal, Canada. S. Allan Taylor published two issues of *The Stamp Collectors' Record* before moving to the United States. The publication lasted until 1876.

Feb. 22: A sanitary fair opened at Albany, N.Y. at which "stamps" were issued. The fair was held to raise funds for the United States Sanitary Commission, which existed to help maintain the health and well being of the Union troops during the Civil War. The fair closed March 30.

Six other fairs that issued these "stamps" took place during 1864 at Boston, Mass.; Brooklyn, N.Y.; New York City; Philadelphia, Pa.; Springfield, Mass.; and Stamford, Conn. Not valid in the US mails, the stamps appear to have been souvenir and money raising items.

March 1: The German federal commissioners of the duchy of Holstein issued stamps.

April 1: The Netherlands Indies issued its first stamps.

May 26: The territory of Montana was established.

May 30: The Ionian Islands ceased to issue its own stamps when Great Britain ceded the islands to Greece.

June 1: The appointment was confirmed of Dr. James H. Starr of Nocogdoches, Texas to be Agent of the Post Office in the Confederate States west of the Mississippi River. He became virtually a postmaster general of the area, because of the poor communications between the two parts of the CSA caused by Union control of the river.

This information is reported by Ashbrook, but Kreiger quotes Shenfield as noting that Starr's appointment did not take place until March 12, 1864, thus indicating some delay in the appointment being confirmed by the Confederate Congress.

June 1: Austrian adhesive postage stamps went into use at that country's post office at Larnaca, Cyprus.

June 15: Stanley Gibbons published his first-known advertisement in *The Stamp Collector's Review*. Among other items, it offered "Old Spain, 1852-53-54, 3d each, 1/3 per hundred" and "New issued, Monte Video, unused and warranted genuine, 1/-each."

June 20: From this date to Nov. 1, 1865, the 2½d stamp of British Columbia and Vancouver Island was sold for 3d and paid postage to that amount.

June 30: Congress set the steamship rate beginning July 1, 1864, at 10c per half ounce regardless of distance carried, according to Wierenga. This rate did not apply to mail to and from countries with which the United States had postal conventions that specified different rates.

July 1: Steamship rates set by the US Congress on June 30, 1864, became effective.

Aug. 28: The United States placed a railroad mail sorting car in service on the Chicago-Clinton, Iowa, run of the Chicago and North Western Railroad. George B. Armstrong, assistant postmaster of Chicago, is credited for this service. Another claim sets July 28, 1862 (q.v.) as the first day of service. In any event, the idea soon spread to other lines and by 1872 railway post offices operated on most of the nation's lines.

Oct. 1: The grand duchy of Mecklenburg-Strelitz issued its first stamps. They were printed and embossed by the Prussian State Printing Office, Berlin.

Oct. 1: US Postmaster General Montgomery Blair resigned. President Lincoln picked up support from his party's radicals in the 1864 election as a result of Blair's resignation.

Oct. 1: President Lincoln appointed William Dennison to succeed Montgomery Blair as postmaster general.

Oct. 26: The British colony of Vancouver Island ceased to use the 2½d stamp inscribed for British Columbia and Vancouvers Island. Until stamps inscribed for Vancouver Island were placed on sale Sept. 19, 1865, franking was by handstamp, according to Poole.

Oct. 31: Nevada became the 36th state of the United States.

November: The Indian feudatory state of Soruth issued stamps.

Nov. 1: US Post Office Department introduced money order service. This had been authorized by Congress on May 17, 1864.

Nov. 3: The first recorded use of the word "philately" occurred in the Nov. 3, 1864 issue of *Collectionneur de Timbre-Poste,* a French periodical. George Herpin used the term.

1865

Having bought the Italian-run Posta Europea, the Egyptian government began to operate it. The former operator, Giacomo Muzzi, became postmaster general. The postal service continued to use Interpostal Seals, the large round postage stamps introduced during 1864 (q.v.).

The South American country of Ecuador issued its first postage stamps. They depict the country's coat of arms and were typographed by M. Rivadeneira of Quito.

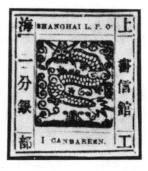

The Shanghai Local Post in that Chinese city issued stamps.

Stamps were first issued by the duchy of Schleswig. They depict a large figure of denomination in an oval frame and were typographed by the Prussian State Printing Works.

Jan. 1: Romania issued its first national postage stamps. They depict Prince Alexandru Ioan Cuza and were lithographed at Bucharest.

Jan. 21: The Santa Fe Stage Company, which had just replaced M. Cottrill & Co., advertised a US mail and express weekly from Kansas City to Santa Fe with connections there for Fort Craig, Mesilla, and El Paso, Texas.

March 17: Nathan records this date as that of the last known letter carried by the San Francisco-Virginia City Pony Express.

April 1: Russia re-introduced its stamps in the Russian-controlled kingdom of Poland. Special stamps had been used since January 1860.

September: The first postage stamp issued by a Zemstvo postal service was by the Vetluga district in Kostroma province. By 1870, about 20 Zemstvo postal services used stamps, according to Lagerloef. By the time the services ended in 1917, a total of 2,427 different stamps had been produced by more than 100 Zemstvos.

September: The United States began the use of newspaper and periodical stamps. The stamps were not affixed to newspapers, but to the memorandum of mailing used with bulk shipments and retained by the post office. They were discontinued July 1, 1898.

Vancouver Island's first stamp (Sept. 19, 1865).

Sept. 7: The French opened a post office in Yokohama, Japan.

Sept. 19: Gibbons catalog gives this as the issue date for the first stamp inscribed "Vancouver Island." Jarrett notes the date as July 1865. A stamp issued in 1860 had been inscribed "British Columbia and Vancouvers Island."

Sept. 25: Bermuda released its first regular postage stamps. Beginning in 1848, the famous postmasters' stamps had been used.

Oct. 19: The Dominican Republic issued its first stamps. They were typographed by Garcia Hermanos of Santo Domingo.

Oct. 30: The steamer *North America* sailed from New York to inaugurate a mail service between that port and Rio de Janeiro, Brazil. The service included stops at St. Thomas, Pernambuco, and Bahia. The New York and Brazil Steamship Company owned the ship and received an annual payment of $240,000, according to Wierenga.

November: A pneumatic tube mail system was inaugurated in Berlin. The first route was between the Royal Main Telegraph Office and the stock exchange, a distance of about 1½ miles. The system was later expanded, but did not open to the public until 1876. By 1913, the system had 73 tube offices.

November: First published during this year, the earliest known edition of the Stanley Gibbons catalog is dated "November 1865." The monthly list cost 2d and was actually a pricelist of the stamps that Gibbons offered for sale.

In his *A Descriptive Price List & Catalogue of British, Colonial & Foreign Postage Stamps*, a mint *Penny Black* cost 1/6, a Canada 12d Black in mint condition cost 10/.-, and an India four annas blue and red was offered at 3d.

Nov. 1: A 3d stamp inscribed for British Columbia was issued. It was typographed by De La Rue & Co. of London.

Nov. 15: Newfoundland introduced decimal currency.

Dec. 29: The first recorded philatelic auction took place in Paris and consisted of the stock of a deceased stamp dealer named Elb. It realized 800 francs, according to L.N. and M. Williams.

1866

Friedrich Jeppe became postmaster of Potchefstroom, the capital of the South African Republic (Transvaal). He reorganized the postal service and established a system of native runners to carry mail to points outside the country. Stamps of Natal, Orange Free State, and the Cape of Good Hope were obtained for use on mail addressed to points outside the country.

Serbia issued its first postage stamps. They depict the country's coat of arms and were printed in Belgrade.

The South American country of Bolivia issued its first postage stamps. They picture a South American condor and were engraved by a Senor Estruch of La Paz. There are many plate varieties.

The British Virgin Islands issued its first postage stamps. They depict the badge of the colony and were lithographed by Nissen and Parker from dies produced by Waterlow & Sons.

Tennessee became the first state in the Confederate States of America to be re-admitted to the United States.

January: British Honduras (now Belize)

issued its first postage stamps. Depicting a left-facing profile of Queen Victoria wearing a crown, the stamps were typographed by De La Rue.

Jan. 1: Egypt issued its first general postage stamps under Turkish suzerainty.

Jan. 1: The Republic of Honduras released its first stamps.

March: Stamps were issued by the Indian feudatory state of Jammu and Kashmir.

April 13: A contract to carry US mail three times a week between the railhead at Lawrence, Kansas, and Santa Fe, in what is now New Mexico was granted to Jared L. Sanderson. The contract later went to Barlow, Sanderson and Co.

April 15: The Danube Steam Navigation Company issued a 17-Kreuzer stamp for use on mail carried on its Danube River services. The company maintained many agencies along the river and ran express services as well as local steamers calling at all points. Established in Vienna in 1829, the ships of the company ran from Linz, Austria, as far as Odessa, on the Black Sea. Postal service ceased about 1879.

May 31: By decree, Guatemala reduced postal rates by 50 percent, mandated the prepayment of postage, and ordered the preparation of adhesive postage stamps. The stamps were issued March 1, 1871.

The first stamp issued by the British Virgin Islands (1866), Egypt's first stamp reproduced on a 1946 commemorative (Jan. 1, 1866), and the first stamp of British Honduras (January 1866).

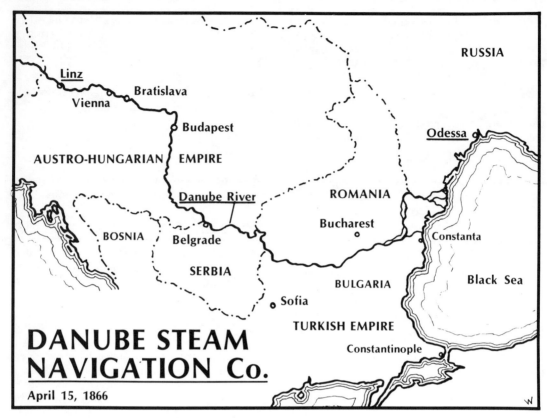

RUSSIA

Linz

Bratislava

Vienna

Budapest

Odessa

AUSTRO-HUNGARIAN EMPIRE

Danube River

ROMANIA

Bucharest

BOSNIA / Belgrade

Constanta

SERBIA

BULGARIA

Black Sea

Sofia

DANUBE STEAM NAVIGATION Co.

TURKISH EMPIRE

Constantinople

April 15, 1866

June 15: The steamship *Kaikoura* began a service from Sydney, Australia, to Panama via New Zealand. The service connected with another ship on the Caribbean side of the Panama isthmus. On the return voyage *Kaikoura* brought mail that had left Britain only 54 days earlier — a vast improvement over the time taken via Australia.

July 1: The first post office opened on the British North Sea island of Heligoland. It was administered by the General Post Office, London. Stamps of Hamburg were used until April 15, 1867, when Heligoland stamps were issued.

July 25: President Andrew Johnson appointed Alexander W. Randall as US postmaster general, succeeding William Dennison.

Aug. 1: India issued its first Official stamps.

They were definitive stamps overprinted "Service."

Oct. 1: The stamps of Prussia replaced those of Hanover in that German state.

November: Wells, Fargo & Company bought the Holladay Overland Mail and Express Company, the Overland Mail Company, and the Pioneer State Company. The new organization was called Wells Fargo and Company and it had almost exclusive control of express and stage routes from the Missouri River to the Pacific Ocean, including many branch lines.

Nov. 19: The colonies of Vancouver Island and British Columbia merged into a territory called British Columbia. It joined Canadian Confederation on July 20, 1871.

1867

The Central American country of El Salvador issued its first postage stamps. They depict an erupting volcano and 11 stars representing the

11 departments comprising the republic. Intaglio printing was by the American Bank Note Company.

Local stamps were issued in the Mexican state of Chiapas.

Handstamped provisionals were issued in the Mexican towns of Cuautla, Cuernavaca, and Guadalajara.

Pneumatic mail service inaugurated in Paris.

March 1: Nebraska entered the United States as the 37th state.

March 3: The South Atlantic island of Ascension placed stamps of Great Britain on sale.

April 4: Stamps were first issued by the Turks Islands.

April 9: An Imperial Russian Decree transferred postal operations in the waters of the Turkish Empire to the Russian Company for Steamshipping and Trade. There had previously been an agreement between Russia and Turkey for the exchange of mail.

April 15: The then-British colony of Heligoland issued its own stamps. All Heligoland stamps were printed by the Imperial Printing Works, Berlin.

June: The Austrian Post Office issued stamps for use at Austrian post offices in the Turkish Empire.

June 1: The first stamps of the dual monarchy of Austria-Hungary were issued. The joint stamps ceased in 1871, when the individual regions issued their own stamps.

June 30: The remaining postal services operated by the House of Thurn and Taxis

were sold to Prussia. At its peak, the posts operated by the House had employed 20,000 people and had offices in most of the major towns of Europe.

July: John Walter Scott published his first catalog. It was a single-page listing.

July 1: The colony of Canada, comprising Ontario and Quebec, combined with the colonies of New Brunswick and Nova Scotia to form the Dominion of Canada. Other former stamp-issuing colonies joined the Dominion on July 20, 1871 (British Columbia and Vancouver Island); July 1, 1873 (Prince Edward Island); and April 1, 1949 (Newfoundland). The provinces of Manitoba, Alberta, and Saskatchewan, which make up the rest of the 10 Canadian provinces were never stamp issuing entities.

July 23: The first US post office in newly purchased Alaska was authorized at Sitka. John H. Kinkead served as its first postmaster.

July 27: A US post office was opened at Yokohama, Japan.

Aug. 8: The city of Lubeck's interest in the city of Bergedorf was purchased by the free city of Hamburg.

Sept. 1: The Straits Settlements issued its first postage stamps. They consisted of overprints on the stamps of India.

Oct. 22: The United States granted Charles F. Steel of Brooklyn, N.Y., a patent for a device to apply an embossed grill to postage stamps. The idea was to break up the paper fibers and allow the cancelation ink to be absorbed to the point that it could not be removed.
  John N. Luff is reported by Cabeen to have believed that grilled stamps were in use by early August 1867. Brookman expresses doubt that Steel had produced any practical device at the time he applied for the patent. The US grilled issues have been widely studied, but little is known about the grilling process, who actually devised it and exactly how it was done. In any

event, it appears not to have been particularly effective and in 1871, the United States discontinued grilling.

1868

A post office under the administration of India opened at Zanzibar in the latter part of this year. It was closed in 1869.

On the island of Cyprus from 1868, when postage stamps were first issued in the Turkish Empire, up to 1878, when the British assumed responsibility for the island's administration, the average annual post office receipts amounted to about $50.

Portugal issued stamps for the Azores. The Azores is an island group in the Atlantic Ocean and is part of Portugal.

Iran, using a design featuring the Persian Lion, issued it first stamps. The original die for each denomination was engraved by A. Barre and the stamps were typographed from copper cliches at Teheran.

The first non-US precanceled stamp is claimed to have been issued in France during this year.

The Colombian state of Antioquia released stamps.

Jan. 1: Overprints on stamps of Portugal served as the first stamps for Portugese Madeira.

Jan. 1: The independent republic of Orange Free State, a Boer state in South Africa, issued its first stamps.

Jan. 1: The North German Confederation issued stamps featuring a large figure of denomination. The stamps were typographed by the Government Printing Works in Berlin.

Jan. 1: A transatlantic letter rate of 12c (6d) went into effect between the United States and Great Britain.

Jan. 1: Italy issued its first postage due labels.

Jan. 1: Stamps of the North German Confederation replaced individual stamps of Bergedorf, Bremen, Brunswick, Hamburg, Holstein, Lubeck, Mecklenburg-Strelitz, Mecklenburg-Schwerin, Oldenburg, Prussia, Saxony, and Schleswig.

March: Anthony Trollope resigned from the British Post Office.

March 13: Joseph Sloper, inventor of a device to perforate initials or a design on postage stamps as a security measure, received written permission to use it from the British Post Office. Permission had previously been denied. Not until a year later (see March 1, 1869) did the authorization appear in the official *Postal Official Circular*. The perforating was to be done privately.

March 24: The Danube Steam Navigation Company informed the Austrian Ministry of Commerce that its 17-kreuzer charge for a letter carried on its ships had been reduced to 10k. The 17k rate had been considered excessive. These charges were in addition to the usual Austrian postage. A new stamp with a denomination of 10k was released prior to November 1867, the date of the earliest known usage.

From the left are the first stamps of the Azores (1868) and the Orange Free State (Jan. 1, 1868), with the 10-kreuzer stamp of the Danube Steam Navigation Company on the right (March 24, 1868).

April 1: The Large Queen design of Canada went on sale. It had been authorized by Post Office Order #2 dated March 1, according to Reiche, although earlier dated copies are known and Gibbons notes the issue date as sometime in March. Denominations were ½c, 1c, 2c, 3c, 6c, 12½c, and 15c. Letter rates effective on the same date were 3c per half ounce within the Dominion (5c unpaid), 6c per half ounce to the US (10c unpaid), 15c per half ounce to the UK via New York (plus a fine of 12c for unpaid or partially paid). Drop letters were 1c and letters to soldiers were 2c.

April 1: The colony of South Australia began the release of Official stamps. They were overprinted with red, blue or black letters representing specific government departments (eg. A — Architect, A.G. (Attorney-General, etc.) A total of 53 different departments received such stamps. The cumbersome system lasted until 1874, when stamps overprinted "O.S." for all departments were introduced.

April 1: The stamps of Nova Scotia, which had joined Canadian Confederation July 1, 1867, were replaced by those of Canada.

June 22: Arkansas became the second Confederate state re-admitted to the United States.

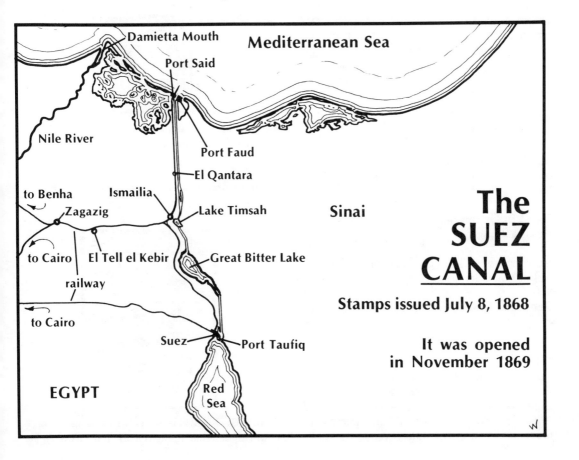

June 25: The US Congress re-admitted Alabama, Florida, Georgia, Louisiana, North Carolina, and South Carolina to the United States.

July: John Walter Scott, New York stamp dealer, produced the first Scott stamp album. Called *Scott's American Album*, it sold for $2.50.

July 8: On or about this date, the Suez Canal Company, then in the process of building the canal from both the Red Sea end and the Mediterranean, placed on sale its own postage stamps. The company operated a postal service for the large numbers of foreign workers who needed mail facilities. The release of the stamps caused Egypt to speed the opening of its postal facilities to serve the area in which the company was operating. See map on previous page.

Egyptian stamps became available on Aug. 16, 1868 and the company's stamps were in use for only a little over one month. The resulting scarcity of used material and the fact that mint stamps were remaindered on the philatelic market has offered fakers a grand opportunity to satisfy an obvious demand. Counterfeit stamps also abound.

July 27: Congress authorized the establishment of a US postal agency at Shanghai. The Shanghai consul general operated the agency until Sept. 25, 1907, when a postal agent was appointed, according to Konwiser. See July 1, 1919.

July 29: On this date, the territory of Wyoming was formed.

September: The Spanish colony of Fernando Po. issued its first stamps.

Dec. 19: France issued its first newspaper stamps.

1869

It is thought that the first example of an overprint being used to indicate the purpose of a stamp occurred in Natal, when the word "Postage" was overprinted on stamps to designate postal rather than revenue usage.

Spain issued what is believed to be the first franchise stamp when it provided writer Diego Castell with stamps for his personal use in mailing copies of his book on postal history. A number of similar stamps have been released by several countries for use by various organizations. Scott and Gibbons note the year of this first stamp as being 1869, but the Spanish catalog *Hevia* gives the year as 1868. Such stamps represent the granting of free postage to individuals or organizations.

The first stamps were issued for St. Thomas and Prince Islands. Gibbons notes the year of issue as 1870.

Transvaal issued its first stamps.

January: It is not known exactly when the title of Bureau of Engraving and Printing came into being. Morris notes that its first known use was in a report by the US Secretary of the Treasury during this month.

January: The Gambia issued the first of the so-called Cameo embossed stamps.

Jan. 1: The US registration fee went to 15c. A return receipt was included but no indemnity provided.

Jan. 26: An article by Dr. Emmanuel Herrmann of Vienna appeared in that city's *Neue*

Freie Presse in which Herrmann advocated the introduction of postal cards. The idea was adopted and the first one placed on sale on Oct. 1, 1869. The cards became an immediate success. According to the *Czechoslovak Specialist* (June 1984), the earliest known use is Sept. 30, 1869.

Feb. 1: The United States stamp agent, who accepted delivery of newly printed US postage stamps, began to deliver them via the New York Post Office's registry division directly to local postmasters who had ordered them, according to Rohrbach and Newman.

Feb. 1: The registration of letters was introduced in Canada. The fee was 2c plus the regular postage.

The three white rulers of Sarawak.

March 1: The first stamps were issued for Sarawak. Because they were only valid locally and to frank mail to Singapore, stamps of the Straits Settlements were made available for international mail. When Sarawak entered the Universal Postal Union in 1897, its stamps became internationally valid.

March 1: Perfins (stamps with initials or a design perforated in them by business firms to prevent their theft and re-sale to the post office by dishonest employees) earned their first official authorization. According to Samuel, the following notice appeared in the British Post Office's *Postal Official Circular* of this date:

"In consequence of representations made to the Post Office by various Firms that there is reason to believe that their postage stamps are purloined by persons in their employ, the Department has recommended that the name or initials of Firms, etc. be either printed on the back of stamps, or perforated through the stamps by a machine devised for the purpose, so that, inasmuch as the sale of such stamps would be thereby rendered difficult, the temptation to steal them might be lessened or altogether removed. Postmasters will take care not to purchase any postage stamps thus marked which may be offered to them for sale." It should be noted that the British Post Office would buy back any postage stamps offered to them. Hence, the concern that employees would steal them to sell to the Post Office.

March 6: John A. J. Creswell appointed US postmaster general to succeed Alexander W. Randall. President Ulysses S. Grant made the appointment.

March 27: One cent, 2c, and 3c denominations of the US 1969 Pictorial issue were released on this date, according to Scott. The 6c, 10c, 12c, 15c, 24c, 30c, and 90c values appeared during the following weeks.

Brookman notes that when the stamps first appeared, the philatelic press praised them, but

The 1c, 2c, and 3c stamps in the US 1869 pictorial issue (March 27, 1869).

they soon became disliked. The reason for this is not known. The issue has since become very popular with collectors.

April: Invented by Francis Wirth in Germany, the first high-speed canceling machine was tested by the British Post Office. It had been introduced in Germany by J. C. Azemar, but was not considered successful.

April 2: The United States issued the 15c denomination in the 1869 Pictorial series. This was the first postage stamp to be intaglio printed in more than one color.

April 10: The Philatelic Society, London, was formed. In 1906, it was granted the title "Royal" and became the Royal Philatelic Society, London.

May 10: The driving of the last spike at Promontory, Utah, was the largest nail in the coffin of the stagecoach as a mail vehicle. The stagecoach staggered on for a few more years serving communities off the main railroad lines. But the mail now went from coast to coast by rail.

The world's first postal card (Oct. 1, 1869).

Sept. 8: The Indian feudatory state of Hyderabad released stamps.

Oct. 1: Austria issued the world's first postal card. It had been suggested by Dr. Emanuel Herrmann. The card proved popular and by the end of the year a total of three million had been sold. Other countries soon adopted the idea.

November: The Suez Canal opened, greatly facilitating the journey from Britain to India and Australia. The British Post Office did not permit mail to travel through the canal until 1873, preferring the quicker transit by rail between Alexandra and Suez.

1870

The ancestor of the modern aerogramme was born during the 1870-71 siege of Paris by the Prussians when mail was flown out of the surrounded city by balloon. The letter form is small and printed on lightweight paper. It bears the inscription "PAR BALLON MONTE" and a box for the stamp. This was what would now be called a formula item of postal stationery, in that adhesive postage stamps had to be affixed. See Sept. 23, 1870.

The first conventional stamp exhibition took place in Dresden, Germany, according to L.N. and M. Williams.

The Colombian departments of Cundinamarca and Tolima issued their first stamps.

The use of the attractive New York foreign mail cancels began in 1870, according to Van Vlissingen and Waud.

Although cancels of a special design had been used prior to 1870, the extremely varied, mostly geometric killer devices associated with the New York foreign mail operation are found only during 1870-1876. They were applied to mail that originated in New York addressed to foreign destinations.

Mail leaving New York for overseas destinations, but which originated at other US post offices did not receive these markings, having been canceled at the place at which they entered the mails.

Just a few of the many attractive New York foreign mail cancels.

The ancestor of today's aerogramme was this letter sheet prepared for mail leaving beseiged Paris during the Franco-Prussian War of 1870-71.

Five years after the end of the Civil War, Virginia was re-admitted to the United States.

Feb. 17: Congress re-admitted Mississippi to the United States.

March 3: Texas gained re-admission to the United States.

March 23: The Russian government declared postal service in Mongolia to be a private enterprise under Russian government supervision.

April: The National Bank Note Company began to produce US stamps and did so until May 1873.

April 1: Stamps inscribed "St. Christopher" were released by St. Kitts.

May 1: The Boer South African Republic (Transvaal) issued stamps, according to Robson Lowe. Scott and Gibbons say the issue date is 1869. Until the South African Republic joined the Universal Postal Union in 1893, its stamps were valid only on domestic mail and stamps of neighboring countries had to be used on international mail.

May 28: John Walter Scott organized in New York the first philatelic auction conducted in the United States. According to a contemporary report, S. Allan Taylor (q.v.) attended the sale. The total realization was about $500.

July 1: Stamps were first issued for the Portuguese colony of Angola.

July 1: The colony of British Columbia signed a postal agreement with the United States. Prior to this, colonial residents usually obtained and affixed US postage stamps to letters intended for that country. The letters remained uncanceled until arrival in the US postal system.

Aug. 1: Paraguay issued its first stamps. They depict a lion holding a cap of liberty and were lithographed by R. Lange of Buenos Aires, Argentina.

A stamp issued by France to mark the centenary of the Paris balloon mail service during the Franco-Prussian War of 1870-71 and a letter flown out of the city, probably by the balloon *Armand Barbes* on Oct. 7, 1870. The flight also carried French Minister of the Interior Gambetta from the beseiged city (Sept. 23, 1870).

From the left is an early issue of Afghanistan (1871), a German stamp honoring Heinrich von Stephen (April 1871), and a French stamp noting the centenary of the Bordeaux Issue (Nov. 13, 1870).

September: The first stamps were issued for areas of France occupied by the Germans during the 1870-71 Franco-Prussian War, including the provinces of Alsace and Lorraine.

The grand duchy of Luxembourg issued its first postal card.

Sept 5: Between this date and Oct. 3, small, unmanned balloons carried some letters out of the besieged French town of Metz during the Franco-Prussian War.

Sept. 23: The balloon *Neptune* flew the first mail out of Paris during the Franco-Prussian War. Some 67 balloons flew from the surrounded city, until the last one left on Jan. 28, 1871.

Although it was the world's first air service for passengers and mail, mail had been carried by balloon prior to the flights from Paris. *Neptune* landed safely at Evreux and its 275 pounds of mail deposited at the post office at Craconville. It took 3 3/4 hours to make the 75-mile flight.

October: The British Post Office issued its first newspaper wrapper.

Oct. 1: Finland, Great Britain, and Switzerland first issued postal cards.

Nov. 1: The Manitoba government established a regular post office at Fort Garry, now Winnipeg. The city was the capital of the province, which had formed on July 15, 1870. The Manitoba government operated the post office and controlled the mails until July 1871, when the Canadian Post Office assumed responsibility.

Nov. 1: The mail service operated in Fiji by the *Fiji Times* newspaper issued stamps. They were primitive, simple designs typeset at the newspaper's office at Levuka. They are inscribed "FIJI TIMES EXPRESS."

Nov. 13: France issued the first stamps of the Bordeaux Issue.

Nov. 15: US Postmaster General John A. Cresswell, in his annual report, recommended the release of postal cards. These were first issued on May 13, 1873 (q.v.).

Nov. 24: The ballooon *Ville d'Orleans* ascended from the Gare du Nord in besieged Paris to begin an epic journey. It landed some 15 hours late in south-central Norway.

1871

Afghanistan issued its first stamps as the kingdom of Kabul. The stamps were of a primitive design depicting a tiger's head and were canceled by having a piece of the stamp torn out.

Jan. 1: Belgium and the Netherlands issued their first postal cards.

March 1: Guatemala issued its first adhesive postage stamps. Printed in France, they feature the shield of Guatemala. Denominations are 1c, 5c, 10c, and 20c.

April: Heinrich von Stephen was appointed postmaster general of the North German Confederation.

April 1: Denmark issued its first postal card.

April 20: Japan established a state-run postal service and released its first postage stamps. They are known as the Dragon Series and consist of four intaglio-printed denominations.

May: Hungary depicted the profile of Franz Josef I on its first stamps.

May 1: Canada issued postal cards. By the end of that year, a total of 1,470,600 had been issued.

July 20: The British colonies of British Columbia and Vancouver Island joined the Dominion of Canada and became a province under the single name of British Columbia. See July 1, 1867; July 1, 1873; and April 1, 1949.

October: The Cape of Good Hope took over mail service in Griqualand West, although the colony was not absorbed by it until 1880.

Oct. 1: Stamps issued for Portuguese India.

Oct 11: In Fiji, a "Public Mail Notice" announced arrangements for the receipt and transmission of mail by the Government Post Office. A service known as the Fiji Times Express had been operated by the Fiji *Times* but the service was soon supressed. (See May 8, 1872.)

Dec. 3: The government of Fiji released its first stamps, according to Robson Lowe. Gibbons notes the issue date as November 1871.

Dec. 25: Norway issued its first stamp with a post horn design. The design, with minor modifications, is still in use and is claimed to be the oldest in continuous use. Norwegian architect Wilhelm von Hanno designed it. He received the equivalent of about 60 kroner for his work.

1872

Handstamped provisionals were issued in the Mexican state of Chihuahua.

A more recent version of Post Office official seal.

The US Post Office Department began using post office seals. Originally intended to seal the flap on registered mail, they are now used to reseal mail that has either been damaged in the mail handling operation or has been opened.

Jan. 1: Norway, Russia, and Sweden issued their first postal cards.

Norway's "post horn" design. An original issue at the left is contrasted with the current issue, while a stamp marking the design's centenary is in the center (Dec. 25, 1871).

Jan. 1: The German Empire featured the German Eagle on its first stamps.

Jan. 1: The stamps of the German Empire replaced the stamps of Baden.

Jan. 4: A set of stamps was issued by Prince Edward Island in decimal currency, replacing the previous sterling currency stamps. The denominations are 1c, 2c, 3c, 4c, 6c, and 12c.

February: The first postal card with reply paid card attached was issued by the German state of Wurttemberg, according to the late Dr. Rodney L. Mott.

Feb. 14: A US Post Office Department announcement to postmasters introduced a new system of handling registered mail. All registered mail was to be enclosed in a special envelope, with a large seal placed over the flap, struck with the cancelation of the office concerned.

The first of the special envelopes did not arrive at the Post Office Department until the end of June, so the system could not have gone into effect until later in 1872. In 1875, the department introduced a new envelope and since this did not require the use of a seal, they were discontinued. Perkal and Kazman say that the seals are believed to have been used for a further period to seal shipments of stamps to post offices from the Postage Stamp Agency.

March 18: John Walter Scott organized the first philatelic auction in Great Britain which was held in London by Sotheby. The sale realized about $1,250.

May 8: The Fiji *Times* newspaper, which had been operating a postal service within the island group, announced that the Fiji govern-

ment had ordered the service discontinued. (See Oct. 11, 1871.)

June 8: Congress authorized US post offices at Panama City and Colon in Panama.

June 8: The US Post Office Department became an executive department of the federal government.

1873

The Dutch colony of Suriname (Dutch Guiana), located on the north coast of South America, issued its first stamps.

Stamps were overprinted for use in the Spanish colony of Puerto Rico. Stamps had been issued in 1855 for both Cuba and Puerto Rico. The 1873 stamps specifically for use in Puerto Rico were overprints on that issue.

Jan. 1: The Icelandic Post Office came into being and the first stamps of the island were issued.

Jan. 1: New Zealand issued a newspaper stamp claimed to be the only country within the British Empire to do so. Subsequent issues followed in 1875 and 1892.

Jan. 31: The US Congress abolished the franking privilege as of July 1, 1873 and instructed the postmaster general to prepare Official stamps. Stamped envelopes were also prepared and issued. Like the stamps, they bear indicia inscribed for the various government departments by which they were to be used. All became obsolete on July 5, 1884.

April 1: Japanese domestic postal rates were revised. A fixed rate was established for the entire country instead of being based on distance as had formerly been done.

May 1: The Continental Bank Note Company received a contract to produce US stamps. The National Bank Note Co. previously had the contract.

May 12: The first use of a US postal card is reported to have been one sent by S. S. Bumstead of Springfield, Mass., to H. M. Burt, editor of the *New England Homestead,* also of Springfield. This was one day prior to their official release, according to Hallgren.

May 13: The first US postal card was officially issued. (See May 12, 1873.)

May 23: Curacao released its first stamps. They feature a portrait of King William III of the Netherlands, of which Curacao was a colony.

July 1: The first US Official stamps and postal stationery issued. They were inscribed for the various government departments that were to use them. Free franking of mail was abolished effective on this date, according to Scheele. He states that during the first full year of the new system, the US Post Office gained $1,769,301 from the sale of the Official stamps and stationery.

In 1877, the post office department introduced the system of penalty envelopes and restored the franking privilege to various elected politicians and other office holders.

Departments for which the stamps were inscribed were Agriculture, Executive, Interior, Justice, Navy, Post Office, State, Treasury, and War.

July 1: Under the authority of Don Carlos, pretender to the Spanish throne, the Spanish provinces of Biscay, Navarre, Guipuzcoa, and Alava introduced stamps during the Second Carlist War of 1872-76.

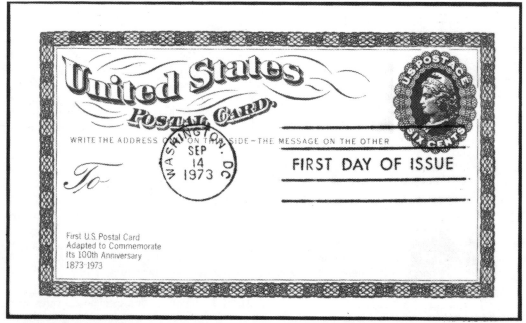

The US Postal Service issued this postal card to mark the centenary of the first one, released May 13, 1873.

July 1: The British colony of Prince Edward Island joined the Dominion of Canada to become a province of that country.

Oct. 6: The earliest known surviving letter complete with cover from Pitcairn Island bears this date. Benjamin Stanley Young, great grandson of *Bounty* mutineer Edward Young, sent the letter. Young had recently returned from serving as a sailor and the letter was to a former shipmate, according to Hornadge.

Dec. 1: Japan issued its first postal card.

1874

One of the strangest mistakes in stamp production occurred in the Russian Zemstvo of Tikhvin, when the person making the handstamp from which the Zemstvo's stamp impression was made, forgot that the handstamp would need to be carved in mirror image in order for the impression to come out right! Thus the impression itself is a mirror image of that intended! The Zemstvo used the stamp in that form.

Stamps issued for the Indian feudatory state of Jind.

The last British horse-drawn mailcoach run ended. It had operated in the north of Scotland, according to Robinson. Watson, however, notes that the last horse-drawn mailcoach ran between Campbeltown and the Mull of Kintyre, Scotland as late as 1914.

Jan. 1: The US registration fee went to 8c. A return receipt was included but no indemnity was provided.

Jan. 1: Spain issued what are claimed to be the first war-tax stamps.

April 15: The Carlists issued stamps for use in the Spanish province of Catalonia.

May: Montenegro issued its first postage stamps. They depict ruler Prince Nicholas I and were typographed by the Austrian Imperial Printing Works, Vienna.

May 4: The island of Dominica in the British West Indies issued its first postage stamps.

They feature a left-facing profile of Queen Victoria and were typographed by De La Rue.

June 10: Stamps were first issued for the British West African colony of Lagos, now part of Nigeria. Featuring a left-facing profile of Queen Victoria, the stamps were typographed by De La Rue.

July 7: Jas. W. Marshall succeeded John A. J. Creswell as US postmaster general.

September: The Carlists released stamps for use in the Spanish province of Valencia.

September: Stamps of the Cape of Good Hope were overprinted for use in Griqualand West.

Sept. 1: President Ulysses S. Grant appointed Marshall Jewell as US postmaster general, succeeding Jas. W. Marshall, who had served less than two months in the post.

Sept. 15: The Postal Conference in Berne, Switzerland, resulted in the formation of the General Postal Union (later the Universal Postal Union) and was a giant step forward in international mail-handling cooperation.

Countries represented at the meeting were Austria-Hungary, Belgium, Denmark, Egypt, France, Germany, Great Britain, Greece, Italy, Luxembourg, the Netherlands, Norway, Portugal, Romania, Russia, Serbia, Spain, Sweden, Switzerland, Turkey, and the United States. The US representative was delayed and did not arrive until Sept. 21.

The conference lasted until Oct. 9. The agreements signed during the conference concerning rates, transit fees, and other postal matters took effect July 1, 1875.

October: The Montreal, Canada, Post Office inaugurated free delivery. The service proved so successful and generated so much mail that a similar service was introduced in Toronto, Quebec City, Ottawa, and Hamilton in 1875, London, Ontario, in 1880, and Winnipeg in 1882, according to Robson Lowe.

1875

Campeche, Mexico, issued local provisional stamps.

Jan. 5: The Japanese foreign postal system inaugurated service at the Yokohama Post Office. The rate for a letter to the US was 15 sen. Since British and French post offices remained in Japan, letters to those countries were sent through those facilities.

March 6: The United States granted a patent to Timothy G. Palmer and Henry F. Clark of New York State, for a canceling machine.

May 12: The Mexican Post Office announced the introduction of the so-called "Porte de Mar" labels, which were to indicate the payment of a fee to a British or French shipping company for carrying the Mexican letter to an overseas port. The announcement stated that denominations would be 10 centavos, 25c, 35c, 60c, 75c, 85c, and 100c.

The labels were not sold to the public but were affixed to the backs of letters to indicate that the fee had been paid. The charge had been in effect since February, but the labels did not become available until about six months later, according to R. R. Billing. There were several issues of the labels and Gibbons notes that they were discontinued on Mexico's entry into the Universal Postal Union on April 1, 1879.

July: The British colony of the Gold Coast issued its first stamps. They depict a left-facing profile of Queen Victoria and were typographed by De La Rue and Co.

July 1: The US registration fee went to 10c. A return receipt was provided but there was no indemnity.

July 1: The treaty signed Oct. 9, 1874 at the founding congress of the General Postal Union

took effect. The organization changed its name to Universal Postal Union at the second congress on May 2, 1878.

July 1: The US postmaster general reduced the basic steamship rate from 10c to 5c to bring the rate into line with the General Postal Union rate on mail to and from foreign countries.

July 1: In accordance with the provisions of the Postal Treaty of Berne dated Oct. 9, 1874, the grand duchy of Luxembourg introduced Official stamps to frank correspondence to points outside the country. They consisted of regular postage stamps overprinted "OFFICIEL."

Sept. 15: The General Postal Union opened its first headquarters in a building at the intersection of Bundesgasse and Gurtengasse in Berne, Switzerland.

Sept. 16: The US Post Office, in cooperation with various railroad companies, instituted the use of special mail trains. The first such train left New York for Chicago. Operated by the New York Central & Hudson River and the Lake Shore & Michigan Southern Railroads, it comprised four postal cars carrying 33 tons of mail, to be worked enroute. The 900-mile run was completed in 26 hours, according to Scheele.

Fast mail trains became common, climaxing in 1889 with a coast-to-coast schedule of 108 hours and 45 minutes. It was a far cry from the 24 days taken by the Butterfield Overland Mail between St. Louis and San Francisco only 31 years earlier.

Oct. 1: The post office at Zanzibar was opened as a foreign post office having special relations with the Indian Post Office. It used stamps of India. In 1890, the Sultan of Zanzibar requested that he be placed under British protection and on Nov. 10, 1895, the post office was transferred from Indian to British East African administration.

Oct. 15: The prepayment of postage in Canada was made compulsory.

Nov. 15: Canada issued its first registration stamps. They were in denominations of 2c, 5c, and 8c to cover the domestic registration rate and that to the US and Great Britain respectively.

This stamped envelope indicium was issued Oct. 15, 1976 to mark the 100th anniv. of the 1876 envelopes. (1876).

1876

The United States issued what can be considered the world's first postal commemorative item in the form of stamped envelopes with an indicium marking the centenary of the United States. It features communications and depicts a pony express rider, telegraph lines, and a train.

The Indian feudatory states of Bhopal and Poonch issued their first stamps.

The Chinese National Postal System began when the special courier service between five major cities of China was opened to the public.

January: Gibralter joined the General Postal Union.

Jan. 6: The first trial of a canceling machine in the United States took place at the Boston, Mass. Post Office during January, 1876. The earliest known example bears this date, according to F. G. Floyd. Hanmer notes that by 1880, about two dozen post offices used these Leavitt machines and that they remained in use until 1892.

Jan. 18: A special meeting of the General Postal Union convened at Berne, Switzerland, to consider the problem of colonies joining the union. The discussion had been prompted when Britain applied for membership on behalf of India. GPU members agreed that British India and French colonies be admitted, but postponed a decision on the Dutch and Spanish colonies.

March 28: Thomas Leavitt and his brother, Martin, were granted a patent for an "Improvement in Rotary Postmarking and Canceling Presses." They received four additional patents for improvements, the last on Dec. 28, 1880.

April 5: A Japanese post office opened at Shanghai, China.

May 17: Japan began the release of the so-called Koban issue of definitive stamps. These were Japan's first typographed stamps.

June: The Indian feudatory state of Sirmoor issued stamps.

July: The Malayan state of Johore released its first stamps.

July: Portugal issued stamps for its colony of Mozambique.

July 1: The Portuguese Madeira Islands released newspaper stamps. They were newspaper stamps of Portugal overprinted for the islands.

July 13: James N. Tyner became US postmaster general, succeeding Marshall Jewell.

July 1: India became a member of the General Postal Union (now UPU). At that time, India included what are now the Republic of India, Pakistan, Bangladesh, and Burma.

Aug. 1: Colorado became the 38th state of the United States.

September: The British West Indian island of Montserrat issued its first stamps. They consisted of stamps of Antigua overprinted

"MONTSERRAT" with a bar obliterating the inscription "ANTIGUA."

Sept. 1: Barlow and Sanderson's Southern Overland Mail had been restricted to the 200-mile run between Trinidad, Colorado and Santa Fe, New Mexico, by this date. The route was traversed in 36 hours running time. The heyday of the Santa Fe Trail was soon to be over as the railroads closed the gap.

1877

Ceylon became a member of the General Postal Union.

Stamps were first issued for the Indian feudatory state of Alwar.

Thomas Rossell y Moles was appointed postmaster in Andorra and sold both Spanish and French stamps. Jacques notes that the postmaster did not have a canceling device and letters were canceled at Seo de Urgel for Spain and Porte for France.

First stamps were issued for the Indian feudatory state of Nowanugger (Nawanagar).

Mauritius and the Seychelles joined the General Postal Union.

Queen Victoria, Queen of the United Kingdom and Ireland became Empress of India.

San Marino issued its first stamps.

Jan. 1: The Portuguese administration of the Cape Verde Islands issued stamps.

March 3: The US Congress approved a law establishing the penalty envelope system. The act stipulated that there would be a fine of $300 for improper use and this was imprinted on the envelope, hence their name of "penalty envelopes." The penalty has remained unchanged, as the modern penalty indicium of the US Postal Service indicates.

March 13: President Rutherford B. Hayes appointed David McK. Key to succeed James N. Tyner as US postmaster general.

March 16: The US Post Office Department arranged for a supply of seals to be delivered to the Dead Letter Office. They were intended to be used to seal letters sent there as undeliverable. Inscribed "OFFICIALLY SEALED," they were the first in a continuing series of similar seals.

They are now used generally to seal mail opened in error or accidently, but only the Dead Letter Office used the first one. The background of its design consisted of many tiny repetitions of the Latin phrase *post obitum* (after death). Subsequent seals omitted this. The same general design was used, although several printing methods were utilized, until the US Postal Service was created in 1971, when the inscription and layout were changed to conform to the new title and logo.

U.S. POSTAL SERVICE
Customer Service
Washington, DC 20265-9997

PENALTY FOR PRIVATE USE TO AVOID
PAYMENT OF POSTAGE $300

OFFICIAL BUSINESS

Address Correction Requested

FIRST CLASS

Editor
Stamp Collector
Post Office Box 10
Albany, OR. 97321-0006

Label 80-B, June 1982

PENALTY FOR PRIVATE
USE TO AVOID PAYMENT
OF POSTAGE. $300

Two variations of the USPS penalty indicia (March 3, 1877).

April: Stamps of the South African Republic were overprinted "V.R. TRANSVAAL" when, at the request of Boers, the British took over administration of the bankrupt South African Republic.

April 1: Bermuda joined the General Postal Union.

April 1: The Straits Settlements became a member of the General Postal Union.

June 1: Japan became a member of the General Postal Union.

The Buffalo balloon stamp.

June 18: When Samuel Archer King ascended from Nashville, Tenn., in his balloon, *Buffalo,* he carried the first balloon mail franked with a special adhesive postage stamp. The stamp was a privately produced blue 5c label inscribed "BALLOON POSTAGE" and depicting the balloon.

Although unofficial, it is the world's first air mail adhesive and occupies a place of honor in air mail history. King's flight landed at a point near Gallatin, Tenn. Two covers are known to have survived and several unused examples of the stamp exist.

July 1: Brazil became a member of the General Postal Union.

Aug. 1: The tiny Republic of San Marino, enclaved within Italy, issued stamps. The Italian Government Printing Works in Turin produced them in denominations of 2c, 10c, 20c, 30c, and 40c. The dies were engraved by Enrico Repettati.

Sept. 1: Iran, then known as Persia, became a member of the General Postal Union.

A Samoan Express stamp
and cover on a modern stamp.

Oct. 1: The Independent Kingdom of Samoa issued its first stamps. These were inscribed "Samoa Express" and were issued by the Samoan Express Post Office, a postal service operated by authority of King Malietoa of Samoa. The post office lasted until 1881.

Oct. 6: The first Canadian stamped envelopes were issued following Confederation in 1867. They were in denominations of 1c and 3c.

1878

The Malay state of Sungei Ujong, later absorbed into Negri Sembilan, issued its first stamps.

Panama, then a department of Colombia, issued stamps.

The Malay state of Perak released its first stamps.

Jan. 1: Great Britain issued the first registered envelope. It was in the form still in use in a number of countries. The envelope is strong and bears an indicium representing the registration fee. It also has imprinted blue lines vertically and horizontally to indicate an item of registered mail.

April 1: Argentina became a member of the General Postal Union.

May 2: The second conference of the General Postal Union convened at Paris, France. At this conference, the name was changed to Universal Postal Union. The name of the basic document of agreement concerning international postal affairs changed to "convention" from "treaty." The Conference also decided to hold future conferences every five years, instead of every three years.

June 19: The Falkland Islands' first adhesive postage stamps were issued. They feature a right-facing profile of Queen Victoria and were intaglio printed by Bradbury Wilkinson.

July 1: Canada became a member of the Universal Postal Union.

July 27: A British post office was opened at Larnaca, Cyprus, following the establishment of a British administration over the island on July 1. The post office used contemporary British stamps and postal rates.

Aug. 26: The first stamps inscribed "Transvaal" were issued. Stamps previously used in the area had been overprints on stamps of the South African Republic.

October: The Chinese experiment of 1876 in opening a government courier service to the public was judged a success. The number of cities it served expanded to 13 from five and it issued its first adhesive postage stamps. The stamps are in three denominations and have a common design featuring the Imperial Dragon. The Chinese Imperial Maritimes Customs operated the service.

Oct. 1: The US introduced registration service for third-class mail. There was no indemnity.

1879

The British colony of Lagos joined the Universal Postal Union.

The Colombian department of Cauca issued stamps.

The Indian feudatory native states of Bhor and Faridkot issued their first postage stamps.

Jan. 1: Newfoundland joined the Universal Postal Union.

Jan. 1: The British colony of the Gold Coast, now the country of Ghana, joined the Universal Postal Union.

Jan. 1: The Gambia joined the Universal Postal Union.

Feb. 4: The American Bank Note Company took over the Continental Bank Note Company and began printing US stamps.

April 1: The following countries joined the Universal Postal Union: British Honduras, El Salvador, Honduras, Liberia, Mexico, and Peru.

April 1: The British issued postal cards bearing a 1d indicium and the inscription "Great Britain." The Irish protested this designation and in October, 1879, cards were issued inscribed "Great Britain and Ireland."

May: The British crown colony of Labuan issued its first stamps.

May 1: The US introduced registration service for fourth-class mail, a class of mail newly created. There was no indemnity.

May 1: Penalty envelopes replaced US Official stamps (Departmental stamps), which were declared obsolete July 5, 1884. Official stamps were not re-introduced until Jan. 12, 1983.

June 1: Bulgaria issues its first stamps. Gibbons notes the date as May 1, 1879.

June 1: The island of Heligoland, then a British colony, became a member of the Universal Postal Union.

June 27: The British firm of De La Rue & Co. received a contract for the relief (letterpress) printing of British 1d stamps which had been intaglio printed by Perkins, Bacon & Co. The 1d stamp was issued Jan. 1, 1880.

July 1: Bulgaria became a member of the Universal Postal Union.

July 1: India issued its first postal cards. One variety had a denomination of ¼ anna and was for domestic use, while the other bore a 1½-anna indicium and was for foreign mail. The cards were inscribed "EAST INDIA POST CARD."

July 1: Austria issued stamps for Bosnia and Herzegovina.

July 1: The United States placed postage due labels into official use. Some denominations had been issued on May 9, 1879.

Aug. 1: The first stamps for the British colony of Tobago were issued. They feature a left-facing profile of Queen Victoria and were typographed by De La Rue.

Aug. 1: The first known use of the so-called New York "pearls," a precancel device found only on postage dues, took place according to James Kingman (personal correspondence). The device comprised the letters "NYC" intertwined within a circle of small dots, or "pearls." It is a representative of some precancel designs used in the United States from about this time into the 1890s.

Aug. 7: Laurenz Koschier died in Vienna, Austria.

Aug. 27: Sir Rowland Hill died. His burial took place in Westminster Abbey.

September: The first squared circle postal marking was used in Great Britain at Leeds. Other countries eventually used this type of postmark. The marking is a true duplex postal marking in that it combined both killer and postmark dater in one marking.

Statue of Sir Rowland Hill outside the General Post Office, London (Aug. 27, 1879).

A British squared circle postmark (September 1879).

Britain's first letterpress-printed postage stamp (Jan. 1, 1880).

Dec. 1: The United States issued its first international postal card. The card bears a 2c Liberty indicium in blue. The earliest known use is reported as Dec. 12, 1879.

1880

The Indian feudatory state of Rajpipla issued stamps.

The post office in the Faroe Islands handled a total of 2,111 letters during this year. By 1900, the amount had increased to 32,612, according to Wowern.

Eastern Rumelia, now part of Bulgaria, issued stamps.

Jan. 1: Great Britain issued its first letterpress-printed stamp. It was produced by De La Rue & Company (see June 27, 1879).

Jan. 1: Venezuela became a member of the Universal Postal Union.

Jan. 24: Barlow and Sanderson's Southern Overland Mail ceased operations and the stage service on the Santa Fe Trail came to an end.

Feb. 11: The first legislation relating to the postal service of the Falkland Islands became effective on this date. It required the master of every vessel calling at Port Stanley or any other port in the islands, to receive mail. For this the master was to receive one penny for each letter and one farthing (¼d) for each newspaper, book, or packet. Incoming mail was to be delivered to the postmaster before customs clearance.

This stamp of Cyprus shows the first stamp and a numeral obliterator of the period.

March 31: The French post office in Yokohama closed. This was the last foreign post office in Japan.

April 1: British stamps overprinted "CYPRUS" became the first stamps issued for the island of Cyprus.

June 11: The US Congress enacted legislation establishing the position of chief post office inspector and changed the designation of special agent to inspector. Then-Postmaster General David McK. Key, had recommended the change as "more appropriate and less liable to confusion with others in public and private employment."

July 1: Ecuador joined the Universal Postal Union.

July 1: Uruguay became a member of the Universal Postal Union.

July 1: The Bureau of Engraving and Printing moved into its first new building located at 14th and B streets in Washington, D.C.

Aug. 25: Horace Maynard was appointed US postmaster general by President Rutherford B. Hayes to succeed David McK. Key.

October: The stamps of Griqualand West became obsolete, when the area became part of the colony of the Cape of Good Hope.

Oct. 1: The Dominican Republic joined the Universal Postal Union.

Oct. 9: A Paris Postal Conference of the Universal Postal Union convened to draft a parcel post convention. Delegates of 23 member countries attended the conference.

December: The Swiss printing firm of Helio Courvoisier SA was formed. It is still owned by the Courvoisier family and prints high-quality stamps for many countries.

1881

At the end of the first Boer War, the Boers again established the South African Republic in the Transvaal and issued stamps. The British finally occupied the area in 1900 and it eventually became part of the Union of South Africa.

Portuguese Guinea issued its first stamps, which consisted of the stamps of Cape Verde overprinted "GUINE."

The Malay state of Selangor released its first stamps.

January: The Peruvian department of Arequipa issued stamps because of a stamp shortage caused by the Chilean occupation of Lima and Calleo during the war between Peru and Chile.

February: Four Peruvian areas issued stamps during a stamp shortage caused by the Chilean occupation of Lima and Calleo in the war between the two countries. The four stamp-issuing areas were Ayacucho, Cuzco, Moquegua, and Puno.

March 8: President James A. Garfield appointed Thomas L. James US postmaster general to succeed Horace Maynard, who had been postmaster general for only six months.

April 1: Chile became a member of the Universal Postal Union.

May 16: Nepal issued its first stamps during 1881. This date represents the earliest known usage, according to Haverbeck.

July 1: Colombia, Haiti, and Paraguay became members of the Postal Union.

July 1: The Republic of Haiti issued its first stamps. They depict the head of Liberty and were designed by M. Laforesterie. The die was engraved in wood and the stamps printed from electrotypes in Paris by M. G. Richards.

July 1: The first specially printed stamps of Cyprus were issued. They were in the standard British Empire key type design, which featured a profile of the monarch, territory name, and denomination. This design was utilized for several areas of the British Empire and was adopted as a means of producing stamps for a number of areas at lower cost than if different designs had to be created.

Aug. 1: Guatemala joined the Universal Postal Union.

1882

The Kingdom of Hawaii became a member of the Universal Postal Union.

The second Boer republic in the Transvaal issued its first stamps.

Belgian postal authorities released the first letter cards.

Jan. 5: Timothy O. Howe succeeded Thomas L. James as US postmaster general.

April 27: Stamps of the Straits Settlements overprinted "B" were issued for use at a British post office in Bangkok, Siam (Thailand). The stamps were withdrawn July 1, 1885, when Siam became a member of the Universal Postal Union. A Straits Settlements' postal card was also overprinted.

May 1: Nicaragua became a member of the Universal Postal Union.

June 9: The French administration for Tahiti issued its first stamps. The stamps were general issues of the French colonies overprinted and surcharged.

Oct. 1: A British Post Office circular announced on Sept. 26, 1882 that British stamps overprinted "I.R./ OFFICIAL" would be used from Oct. 1, 1882 by "certain officers of Inland Revenue stationed outside the Metropolis (London)." The Inland Revenue is similar in function to the US Internal Revenue Service. Gibbons notes the earliest date of use as Sept. 27, 1882. Denominations issued were ½d, 1d, and 6d. Some authorities claim that these and subsequent similar issues for this and other departments of government are Departmentals rather than Officials.

1883

Frederick John Melville was born in England. He became the best known of the English philatelic journalists and founded the Junior Philatelic Society (now the National Philatelic Society). Melville formed the society because he had been refused admission the Philatelic Society, London (now the Royal Philatelic Society, London), on the grounds of age. He served as president of the JPS until his death on Jan. 12, 1940. His last book *Modern Stamp Collecting,* was published May 6, 1940.

The Malay state of Kedah used stamps of Siam (Thailand) until 1909, when it began using stamps of the Straits Settlements and Federated Malay States stamps.

Jan. 1: Costa Rica joined the Universal Postal Union.

April 11: President Chester A. Arthur appointed Walter Q. Gresham US postmaster general to succeed Timothy O. Howe.

June: North Borneo, under the administration of the British North Borneo Company, issued its first stamps.

July 1: British stamps overprinted "GOVt/ PARCELS" were issued for use by all government offices on parcels of more than three pounds in weight. They were withdrawn in 1904 together with other British Official stamps.

July 23: Former US Postmaster General Montgomery Blair died. However, his work lives on in the form of the Universal Postal

Union, which he was instrumental in forming. He is regarded by many as the greatest United States postmaster general. Benjamin Franklin, another great American postmaster general, held office under a British administration and the Continental Congress and did not hold postal office under a United States administration.

Aug. 1: The British Post Office introduced a parcel service. Initially, it cost 3d a pound up to a limit of seven pounds. By 1900, a parcel could be sent for 1d a pound up to 11 pounds.

Aug. 4: The Kingdom of Siam, now Thailand, issued its first stamps. They depict King Chulalongkorn and bear only a small inscription in Thai. Intaglio production was by Waterlow & Sons.

Oct. 1: The domestic letter rate in the United States became 2c per half ounce to any address in the country.

1884

Carle Bushe, A Frenchman, obtained a British patent for a device that would print a "stamp" on an envelope and record the amount of postage by means of a counting device, or meter. No working model of this first recorded idea for a postage meter is known to have been built.

The Colombian department of Santander released stamps.

The Indian convention state of Patiala released stamps.

Jan. 1: On this date, the Australian colony of Victoria made all stamps, whether postage or revenue, valid for both postal and revenue use. Subsequent to this, stamps were issued inscribed "Stamp Duty" to serve all purposes. These newer stamps are properly called Postage and Revenue Stamps, while the stamp duty stamps issued prior to Jan. 1, 1884 and which then became valid for postal use are correctly referred to as Postal Fiscals.

Jan. 25: The German Empire issued stamps surcharged for use at German post offices in the Turkish Empire.

Feb. 1: Stellaland issued its first stamps. On Sept. 30, 1885, the area was incorporated into British Bechuanaland.

Feb. 23: The French colony of Guadeloupe issued its first stamps.

March: Stamps were issued for use by the British Consular Mail in Madagascar.

March 1: Portugal issued its first stamps for use in Macao.

April: Ancachs, Chachapoyas, Chala, Chiclayo, Huacho, Paita, Pasco, Pisco, Piura, and Yca — all areas of Peru — issued stamps. They became necessary because of a stamp shortage caused by the Chilean occupation of Lima and Calleo during the war between those two countries.

April 4: This is the date of the earliest known use of stamps of Stellaland, according to Robson Lowe.

April 17: A. W. Cooke of Boston, Mass., applied for a patent for a stamp booklet. The US patent office granted it on Oct. 14, 1884. Cooke offered the idea to the US Post Office Department, but it showed no interest and the idea was dropped. Booklets were introduced by Luxembourg (see 1895) and Sweden (see 1898). The United States issued its first booklet on April 16, 1900 (q.v.).

July 1: Italy issued what are claimed to be the first parcel post stamps. In conventional format, they reproduce a profile of King Humbert I.

July 5: US "Departmental" Official stamps were declared obsolete on this date.

Oct. 14: Frank Hatton was appointed US postmaster general, succeeding Walter Q. Gresham.

Oct. 14: Jean de Sperati, one of philately's best-known forgers, was born at Pistoia, Italy. Tyler states that Sperati learned his "trade" from his mother and two brothers! He moved to France where his forgeries were so good that in 1943 he was forced to admit in a French court that his stamps were forgeries in order to avoid charges of exporting capital in the form of rare stamps. He produced identical stamps to prove to the court that the stamps he was sending abroad were not really of value! He was then fined 5,000 francs for forgery!

November: The Kingdom of Korea issued its first stamps.

1885

The Indian feudatory states of Gwalior and Jind issued their first stamps.

Monaco issued its first stamps. They depict Prince Charles III.

The Costa Rican province of Guanacaste issued stamps.

January: The French colony of St. Pierre and Miquelon issued its first stamps.

Jan. 1: The postal administration of the British colony of Malta was transferred from the General Post Office in London to the colonial authorities in Malta.

Feb. 4: The third full congress of the Universal Postal Union convened at Lisbon, Portugal. By this date, there were 54 member nations. Special delivery service and reply-paid postal cards were added to the international postal service on a voluntary basis.

March 7: President Grover Cleveland appointed Wm. F. Vilas US postmaster general to succeed Frank Hatton.

May: The Indian convention state of Nabha issued its first stamps.

July 1: Siam (now Thailand) became a member of the Universal Postal Union.

July 1: The United States established a domestic letter rate of 2c per ounce.

July 1: Stamps of the Straits Settlements overprinted "B" were withdrawn from use at a British post office in Bangkok, Siam (Thailand).

Aug. 1: Great Britain surcharged its stamps in Turkish currency for use at British post offices in the Turkish Empire.

Aug. 5: France issued stamps surcharged in Turkish currency for use at its post offices in the Turkish Empire. Later, stamps were specifically released for Cavalla, Dedeagh, Port Lagos, and Vathy.

Sept. 22: South Bulgaria issued stamps that superseded those of Eastern Rumelia.

Sept. 30: British Bechuanaland became a British crown colony. The colony issued stamps in December, 1885.

Oct. 1: The United States introduced special delivery service and the first US special delivery stamp was issued. Initially this service operated only from post offices serving communities with a population of more than 4,000 and known as "free delivery" offices. This involved a total of 555 post offices. The fee was

10c in addition to the letter postage. The service proved popular and was extended on Oct. 1, 1886 (q.v.).

December: British Bechuanaland issued stamps.

Dec. 2: Stellaland withdrew its stamps.

1886

The Protectorate Kingdom of Tonga issued stamps that depict King George I. They were typographed by the Government Printing Office in Wellington, New Zealand.

The Indian convention state of Chamba issued its first stamps.

The French colony of Gabon issued stamps. They took the form of overprints "GAB" and surcharges on the general issue of the French colonies.

The first issue of the Republic of Colombia came in two designs, one showing an eagle and coat of arms and the other depicting Simon Bolivar.

Jan. 1: The Congo Free State, later the Belgian Congo, issued its first stamps.

Jan. 1: The Congo Free State became a member of the Universal Postal Union.

Jan. 1: The New Republic, a Boer state established in Zululand, released its first stamps.

Jan. 1: Gibraltar issued its first stamps and its post office came under administration of the colony. Stamps of Bermuda overprinted with "GIBRALTAR" were used because there was insufficient time to prepare special stamps. Denominations overprinted were ½d, 1d, 2d, 2½d, 4d, 6d, and 1/-. The post office had been a branch of the General Post Office, London.

Jan. 1: The stamps of Gibraltar went on sale at the British post office at Tangier and other Moroccan ports where consular offices acted as postal agencies. This change came about as a result of the Gibraltar Post Office coming under the British Colonial Office. It had previously been part of the General Post Office, London. Stamps of Gibraltar continued to be used until 1898 when they were first overprinted "Morocco Agencies."

February: Portuguese Timor issued its first stamps according to Gibbons. Scott gives the issue date as 1885.

April 1: Bolivia joined the Universal Postal Union.

July: The French colony of Martinique issued stamps. They consisted of overprints "MQE" and surcharges on the General Issues of the French colonies.

July 4: The first transcontinental mail train across Canada arrived at Port Moody, near Vancouver, British Columbia, from Montreal. Although Jarrett gives the year as 1885, Robson Lowe and railroad history sources cite this 1886 date.

Aug. 4: The individual states making up the United States of Colombia became departments in the Republic of Colombia. They did, however, retain the right to issue their stamps and some did so until 1904.

Aug. 18: The United States issued a letter sheet with a 2c green indicium depicting President Ulysses S. Grant. It was withdrawn June 30, 1894.

Aug. 20: Paraguay issued its first Official stamps.

Sept. 13: The American Philatelic Society formed as the American Philatelic Association. It became the American Philatelic Society in 1897, but reverted to its original name a few months later. In September 1908, it again assumed its present name.

Oct. 1: The United States Post Office Department, using authorization granted by Congress on Aug. 4, 1886, extended special delivery service to all US post offices on this date. It prepared a new special delivery stamp with an amended inscription, but did not issue the stamp until Sept. 6, 1888 so that supplies of the obsolete stamps could be used up.

December: French Guiana issued its first stamps. They consisted of the General Issues of the French colonies overprinted and surcharged.

1887

A French courier service carried mail to and from Andorra beginning this year. Two couriers, paid by France, operated between Porte and Andorre la Vielle (the French spelling of the tiny country's capital city. The Spanish spelling is Andorra la Vieja).

The French colony of Senegal issued stamps.

The Indian feudatory state of Jhalawar released its first stamps.

Jan. 1: Faridkot, an Indian convention state, issued its first stamps.

Jan. 10: The first issue of *The American Philatelist,* journal of the American Philatelic Association (now the American Philatelic Society) appeared on this date. It was edited by W. R. Fraser and ran until May, 1887. In October 1887, the association resumed publication of the journal.

Feb. 1: The first German post office opened in German Cameroon. It used stamps of Germany until April 1, 1897, when stamps were overprinted for use in the colony.

June 1: Japan became a member of the Universal Postal Union. It was dropped from the membership rolls in 1948 and restored in 1949.

July 22: Although the United States did not introduce domestic parcel post service until 1913, many foreign countries provided the service a great deal earlier. With the forming of the Universal Postal Union, the United States found itself involved in parcel post operations as far as reciprocating service with other countries was concerned. On this date, the United States signed its first parcel post convention. It was with the British Caribbean colony of Jamaica (see Oct. 1, 1899).

1888

During this year, the British colony of New South Wales released a series of stamps bearing an inscription marking the 100th anniversary of the establishment of the first British settlement. These stamps are considered to be the first government-issued, adhesive commemorative stamps.

Stamps were first issued by the Indian feudatory states of Bamra and Wadhwan.

Jan. 1: British Honduras adopted decimal currency.

Jan. 17: President Grover Cleveland appointed Don M. Dickinson as US postmaster general, succeeding Wm. F. Vilas.

Jan. 21: The French Indo-China provinces of Annam and Tonkin first issued stamps.

March: The earliest known use of machine cancelers made by the International Postal Supply Company of New York, was in Brooklyn, N.Y. the machines came to be widely used except in Boston and a few other centers where machines of the American Postal Machine Company were preferred, according to Hanmer.

March 12: When a severe blizzard had New York City smothered, two Bayonne, N.J., residents created a local post stamp to frank mail carried to the New York Post Office. The mail was also franked with the proper US postage, according to Konwiser. The local stamps bore the coat of arms of New Jersey and were inscribed "Blizzard Mail."

May 1: Zululand issued stamps.

July 1: The French Protectorate of Tunisia became a member of the Universal Postal Union.

July 1: The French Protectorate of Tunisia issued stamps.

Aug. 7: The Mafeking-Bulawayo Runner Post inaugurated service on this date. It ran from Mafeking, British Bechuanaland, north to Bulawayo in what is now Zimbabwe (formerly Southern Rhodesia). It lasted for about one year, when a mail cart service replaced it. Five postal agencies were established. From Mafeking north they were Kanye, Molepolole, Shoshong, Tati, and Bulawayo. The first stamps of the Bechuanaland Protectorate were issued on this date and used on the runner post.

Sept. 4: The southern portion of the eastern half of New Guinea was proclaimed a British protectorate. Great Britain administered it with participation by the colonies of New South Wales, Queensland, and Victoria. The protectorate opened post offices at Port Moresby and Samarai at which stamps of Queensland were sold.

Oct. 16: The Indian feudatory state of Travancore first issued stamps.

1889
The island of Madagascar released its first stamps.

January: Stamps were issued for the Malay state of Pahang.

January: French Indo-China first issued stamps.

Feb. 1: Brazil issued its first newspaper stamps.

March 6: Benjamin Harrison, newly inaugurated as US president, appointed John Wanamaker as postmaster general, succeeding Don M. Dickinson.

March 11: The first stamp exhibition in the United States is reported to have taken place at the Eden Musee in the New York area. The Brooklyn Philatelic Club, the National Philatelic Society, and the Staten Island Philatelic Society provided exhibits.

April: Stamps of Jamaica went into use in the Cayman Islands, which were then a dependency of Jamaica.

May: The French colony of Nossi Be, an island of the northwest coast of Madagascar, issued its first stamps.

May 4: Nicholas F. Seebeck, representing the Hamilton Bank Note Company of New York, signed an agreement with the director general of posts and telegraphs of Nicaragua to supply Nicaragua with free postage stamps in return for the right to receive unsold remainders when new stamps were issued and to make reprints for the philatelic market. A few weeks earlier similar contracts had been signed with El Salvador and Honduras. Two years later Ecuador also signed. Stamps issued under this arrangement are believed to be the 1890-99 issues of Nicaragua and El Salvador, the 1890-95 issues of Honduras, and the 1892-96 issues of Ecuador.

June 5: A Post Office sorting van was used on the railway between Perth and Albany, Western Australia, since the British mails were usually landed at the latter place and then sorted enroute to Perth.

July: Gibraltar issued stamps denominated in

Spanish currency, since Spanish coinage was commonly in circulation and the exchange complicated transactions. The first stamps were surcharges on sterling Gibraltar issues. Specially printed stamps became available in November 1889.

July 1: Norway issued its first postage due labels.

Oct. 18: Swaziland issued its first stamps while under joint protection of Great Britain and South African Republic.

Nov. 2: North and South Dakota became states.

Nov. 8: Montana became the 41st state of the United States.

Nov. 11: The Congress made Washington the 42nd state of the United States.

1890

The Leeward Islands, comprising Antigua, Dominica (to Dec. 31, 1939), Montserrat, Nevis, St. Christopher, St. Kitts-Nevis, and the British Virgin Islands issued its first stamps

They were in the standard British colonial key type design, which was retained right up to July 1, 1956, when Leeward Islands stamps were discontinued. The only non-omnibus commemorative issue to be released by the Leeward Islands was the set marking the 60th anniversary of Queen Victoria's reign, an overprint on the key type stamps.

The French colony of Diego Suarez, located in northern Madagascar, released its first stamps.

Jan. 1: The British Crown Colony of Labuan was placed under the administration of the North Borneo Company and used stamps of North Borneo overprinted "Labuan."

Feb. 2: Peru issued its first Official stamps.

Feb. 5: The Shanghai Local Post appointed H. J. Wood to run its agency at Amoy. Stamps of the Shanghai Local Post were available there beginning on March 1, 1890.

April 5: The first stamps were issued for the Seychelles, while it was a dependency of Mauritius.

Five reigns — one design! One would not collect the stamps comprising the Leeward Islands' general issue for their variety, but a page of these stamps can be surprisingly attractive.

This British commemorative stamped envelope marks 50 years of Penny Postage.

May: British East Africa issued its first stamps. The British East Africa Company administered the colony.

May 2: The territory of Oklahoma was established.

May 19: When the then-Duke of Edinburgh opened the first London Philatelic Exhibition on this date, he referred to Prince George, later King George V, as a stamp collector. It is likely that the prince gained his interest in philately from his uncle, the Duke of Edinburgh, according to John B. Marriott, keeper of the Royal Collection.

The Duke of Edinburgh served as honorary president of the Philatelic Society, London (now the Royal Philatelic Society, London) for 10 years before his death in 1900. The collection he presented to Prince George formed the basis of today's Royal Collection. During the duke's presidency, the future King George V joined the society in March 1893 and was named honorary vice president.

July: Charles J. Phillips bought the stamp and philatelic publishing business established by Stanley Gibbons, for £25,000. It then became a private limited company with Gibbons as chairman of the board and Phillips as managing director.

July 2: The British Post Office issued a 1d stamped envelope commemorating the 50th anniversary of penny postage. It features mail transport and delivery in 1790, 1840, and 1890. The item included a "correspondence card," which featured a portrait of Sir Rowland Hill and the inscription "HE GAVE US PENNY POSTAGE." Thomas De La Rue printed the envelope and card.

July 3: Idaho became the 43rd state of the United States.

July 10: Wyoming joined the United States as the 44th state.

Aug. 10: The German Post Office took over the postal administration of the former British island of Heligoland, following the exchange of the island for German interests in Zanzibar.

Sept: 11: A regular horse post, the Mashonaland Mail Service, began with the completion of a route from Mafeking in British Bechuanaland north to Salisbury (Harare). It used the stamps of British Bechuanaland.

1891

The French Congo issued its first stamps.

Fiji became a member of the Universal Postal Union.

January: A stamp was issued to frank mail from Tierra del Fuego to Argentina and Chile. Julio Popper, a Romanian engineer who had obtained a concession to mine for gold in the portion of the island claimed by Argentina, produced the stamp.

Intended to frank mail to the nearest post office on the mainland, little is known of the stamp's use. Covers exist, but they are extremely rare. The stamps were in use for only a short time as Popper died in Buenos Aires in 1893. The design features a miner's pick and hammer.

Jan. 1: French stamps surcharged in local currency, were issued for use at French post offices in Morocco.

Jan. 2: New Zealand issued the first stamps for Official use by its Life Insurance Department. Until 1947, they depicted a stylized lighthouse, but in that year began an attractive series of stamps picturing specific lighthouses. In 1967, there were several surcharges of decimal currency on sterling denominations and in 1969 the first series in decimal currency was released.

February: North Borneo became a member of the Universal Postal Union. Prior to this, the stamps of North Borneo had only limited local validity and stamps of the Straits Settlements or Labuan were used to frank mail sent beyond its borders.

April: Stamps of Rhodesia were overprinted for use in British Central Africa, which became the Nyasaland Protectorate from July 6, 1907.

May 20: The Fourth Congress of the Universal Postal Union convened at Vienna, Austria. It established cash-on-delivery (COD) service in international mail. It also made the supply of reply-paid postal cards mandatory for all member postal administration.

August: Stamps first issued for the Malay state of Negri Sembilan. The first stamp was a 2c denomination of the Straits Settlements overprinted "Negri/ Sembilan."

Oct. 1: The Australian colonies of New South Wales, Queensland, South Australia, Tasmania, Victoria, and Western Australia joined the Universal Postal Union.

November: The stamps of Great Britain were used without overprint in the Oil Rivers and Niger Coast Protectorate until July 20, 1892 (q.v.).

1892

The French island of Mayotte, located between Madagascar and the African mainland, issued its first stamp.

Horta, a district in the Portuguese Azores, released its first stamp.

The French West African colony of Benin received its first stamp issue. It took the form of the 1881 general issue of French colonial stamps handstamped "BENIN." In 1895, Benin was incorporated into the colony of Dahomey. See also Benin, People's Republic of.

The Italian colony of Eritrea issued its first stamps, which were Italian stamps overprinted "Colonia Eritrea," according to Scott. Gibbons gives 1893 as the year of issue.

Ponta Delgada, a district of the Portuguese Azores, released stamps.

The Mozambique Company issued stamps for the area of the Portuguese African colony of Mozambique that it administered.

The Portuguese administrative area of Angra, located in the Azores, received its first stamp issue. They depict King Carlos of Portugal. The stamps were used until 1906, when stamps of the Azores were issued. In 1931, stamps of Portugal replaced Azores' stamp.

Jan. 2: Stamps inscribed "British South Africa Company" were issued for use in what later became Rhodesia.

February: The Indian feudatory state of Nandgaon issued stamps.

Feb. 1: The town of Obock, located within the French Somali Coast, now the Republic of Djibouti, released its first stamps.

April 1: Funchal, a district of Portuguese Madeira, issued its first stamps.

April 1: The Indian feudatory state of Cochin released stamps.

April 19: This is the date quoted by Gibbons for the first stamps of the Cook Islands. Robson Lowe notes that this was the date the stamps arrived at the islands. He adds that official announcements state the issue date to be May 7, 1892. He also claims that stamps known canceled with the April 19 date presumably represent souvenirs for officials.

June 24: The Commerce and Navigation key type of the French Colonies was issued inscribed for New Caledonia. Previous stamps had been overprints and surcharges on French colonial general issues, except for the first stamp, issued in 1860.

July 2: British New Guinea became a member of the Universal Postal Union.

July 20: Stamps of Great Britain were overprinted "BRITISH/ PROTECTORATE/ OIL RIVERS" for use in what became the Niger Coast Protectorate and is now part of Nigeria.

Oct. 25: The US Post Office Department issued its first reply paid postal card.

November: The French Oceanic Settlements, now French Polynesia, issued its first stamps.

November: The French colony of Ivory Coast issued its first stamps.

November: French Guinea issued its first stamps.

November: Anjouan, an island in what is now the Comoros located between Madagascar and the African mainland, issued its first stamps. The island was then a French colony.

November: French India released its first stamps.

Dec. 5: By this date, the St. Louis, Mo., and Suburban Railroad had established a number of street-car routes on which post-office cars operated. Workers sorted, canceled, and distributed mail in these cars. Eventually, about 14 routes with post-office cars operated in the St. Louis system.

Other cities to have street-car mail service were Brooklyn, N.Y. (Aug. 8, 1894); Boston (May 1, 1895); Philadelphia (June 1, 1895); New York (Sept. 23, 1895); Chicago (Nov. 11, 1895); Cincinnati (Nov. 11, 1895); Washington, DC (1896); Baltimore (1896); San Francisco (1896); Rochester, N.Y. (1896); Pittsburgh (1898); Seattle, Wash. (1905); Cleveland (1908); and Omaha, Neb. (1910). Most of these systems were ended by 1915, although a few survived longer. Baltimore's lasted until Nov. 9, 1929.

1893

The Duke of York, later King George V, joined the Philatelic Society, London, becoming president in 1896. He held that position until ascending the British throne in 1910. He exhibited at the 1906 London International Stamp Exhibition and won two silver medals.

French stamps overprinted "Cavalle" were issued for use at a French post office in what was then a Turkish town on the Aegean Sea. It is now the Greek port of Kavalla.

French stamps were overprinted "Dedeagh" for use at a French post office in the town when it was a Turkish port city. It is located on the Aegean coast and is now part of northern Greece. The French issued stamps inscribed for the town in 1902. The town is now named Alexandroupolis. Alternative spellings of Dedeagh are noted as Dedeagatch, Dedeagatz, or Dedeagach.

French stamps were overprinted "Vathy" for use at a French post office in the town, which is located in the Aegean Sea on the island of Samos. At the time it was part of Turkey, but became Greek in 1912.

The Indian feudatory state of Duttia (Datia) issued stamps.

The stamps of Germany were surcharged for use in German East Africa.

Jan. 1: Egypt issued its first Official stamps, according to the general catalogs.

Jan. 1: The US registration fee went to 8c. There was no indemnity (see July 1, 1898).

Jan. 2: The United States issued the Colum-

bian series commemorating the Columbian Exposition and the 400th anniversary of the discovery of the Western Hemisphere by Columbus. These stamps are the first US adhesive commemorative stamps. Denominations range from 1c to $5. The 8c denomination was not issued until March 3, 1893.

February: This is the earliest date of use known for stamps of New Zealand bearing commercial advertisements printed on their backs. As an experiment, an agency was given a contract to sell space. A number of ads appeared for products that are still well known, including Cadbury's chocolate, Sunlight soap, and Fry's cocoa. The scheme was not a success because of production problems and complaints from mailers who feared bad effects from licking the ink under the gum. Advertisers are reported to have been unhappy about their ads disappearing when the stamp was stuck on a letter, although it is surprising that they did not anticipate that possibility! The experiment lasted only for about a year.

Feb. 3: The US Post Office Department authorized the use of a cancel reading "Street R.P.O. No. 1" on the St. Louis, Mo., street car service. This was the first such service, the second being established Aug. 8, 1894, in Brooklyn, N.Y. See Dec. 5, 1892.

Feb. 13: Tonga issued its first Official stamps.

Feb. 22: British Central Africa Protectorate was proclaimed, although the name British Central Africa had been used since 1891. The former name was Nyassaland District.

March 1: A six-inch, double pneumatic tube line was inaugurated to move mail between Philadelphia's Central Post Office and the Chestnut Street Station. Items took two minutes to make the half-mile trip, a significant savings over the 15 minutes or more by horse and wagon. By 1898, the system had been expanded to connect the city's Broad Street Station and the Reading Terminal.

March 1: The first US international reply postal card was issued. Each card bears a 2c Liberty indicium in blue. The earliest known

use is April 3, 1893, from New York to Berlin, according to the *United States Postal Card Catalog.*

March 7: Wilson S. Bissell succeeded John Wanamaker as US postmaster general.

April 1: France issued stamps for use at its post office at Port Lagos in the Turkish Empire.

April 1: The British colony of the Cape of Good Hope took over the postal service of British Bechuanaland. The area was annexed Nov. 16, 1895, and Cape of Good Hope stamps were used from that time.

May 12: The name Oil Rivers Protectorate was changed to Niger Coast Protectorate. New stamps reflecting the change were released in November, 1893.

May 20: The Hankow, China, Local Post, issued stamps and took over the agency of the Shanghai Local Post. The stamp design shows a coolie carrying two chests of tea suspended from a pole across his shoulders. The stamps were produced in strips of 10 and also in stamp booklets of 100. The post operated until Feb. 2, 1897.

June 1: Belgium introduced stamps with perforated labels attached A bilingual text on the label stated "Do not deliver on a Sunday." These are known as "Dominical Lables" and were used up to 1914. When Sunday delivery was not desired the label was left attached to the stamp. If it was removed, then the letter would be delivered on Sunday if necessary.

Oct. 6: The local post at Chefoo, China, issued stamps on this date. The post is believed to have begun operations earlier in 1893. The post eventually used a range of postal stationery.

Nov. 1: The Chungking, China, Local Post began operations. It is believed to have first issued stamps in December 1893, according to Dougan. The service operated until March 1897.

December: Liberia issued registration labels. With an unstated face value of 10c, the stamps bore the names of five principal ports on the Liberian coast. They were Buchanan, Greenville, Harper, Monrovia, and Robertsport. The labels had a space for the registration number to be inserted.

Dec. 2: Belgium issued its first precanceled stamps.

1894

France began to use French and Indo-China stamps overprinted "Chine" at its post offices in China.

France issued French stamps surcharged for use at its post office in Zanzibar.

Ethiopia (Abyssinia) issued stamps.

The Portuguese colony of Lourenco Marques began issuing stamps this year and continued until the 1920s, when they were replaced by the stamps of Mozambique.

The French colony of Djibouti issued stamps.

The Indian feudatory state of Charkhari issued stamps.

About this time, precancels such as the Fort Wayne "tombstone" and the Lansing "spider" appeared on US stamps, according to correspondence from James Kingman.

Jan. 2: William Barry of Syracuse, N.Y., received a patent for a canceling machine. By 1895, he had a contract to supply 100 of his machines to the US Post Office Department at an annual rental of $150 each.

March 9: Japan issued its first commemorative postage stamps. They marked the 25th wedding anniversary of the Emperor and Empress Meiji.

April: The French colony of St. Marie de Madagascar, an island off the east coast of Madagascar, issued stamps. It used stamps of Madagascar after 1896.

April 12: Using surcharged stamps of the French colonies general issue, the French Sudan issued its first stamps.

May: The first stamps were issued for the Indian feudatory state of Bundi.

June 1: The Kewkiang, China, Local Post, organized earlier in 1894, issued its first stamps.

June 30: The US Post Office Department withdrew the letter sheet it had issued on Aug. 18, 1886 (q.v.).

July 2: The American Bank Note Co., which had been printing US postage stamps, transferred all dies, rolls, working plates and postage stamps to the Bureau of Engraving and Printing. The BEP took over the production of postage stamps and with a few exceptions has continued to produce them to the present day.

July 4: Hawaii proclaimed itself a republic, with Sanford Ballard Dole as its president.

July 6: The Fresno, Calif., to San Francisco bicycle mail service began during a railroad strike. It used a special stamp and a stamped envelope. The service ran until July 18.

July 18: The 6c US stamp picturing President James Garfield, the first stamp in the 1894 issue and the first produced by the Bureau of Engraving and Printing, was issued. With some exceptions, the BEP has printed US stamps ever since.

Aug. 1: The post office of the Wuhu, China, Local Post opened. Stamps are thought to have been placed on sale in November, 1894.

Aug. 5: The Portuguese Congo, also known as Cabinda, issued stamps.

Aug. 6: The Chinkiang Local Post in China issued stamps. Later, it released postage due labels, Official stamps, and postal stationery. The post operated until Feb. 2, 1897, when the Chinese Government Post took it over.

Oct. 31: First flag cancel used. It was applied by an American Postal Machine Co. model "H" at the Boston, Mass., Main Post Office.

November: Zambezia, an area in Mozambique, issued its first stamps.

Dec. 1: The Ichang Local Post in China placed stamps on sale. The post had been formed earlier in 1894.

1895

The duchy of Luxembourg issued the first stamp booklet.

January: The so-called British Inland Mail was organized by the British Consulate of Antananarivo, Madagascar. Adhesive stamps were issued for the runner service, which took letters to the port of Vatomandry for sea transport to Durban, where they were placed in the mailstream. The service ceased in September, 1895.

Jan. 1: The Foochow Local Post opened a post office in that Chinese city. It replaced the agency of the Shanghai Local Post that had operated there. The local post was discontinued on Feb. 2, 1897, when the Chinese Government Post took over.

Feb. 28: The town of Majunga, on the northwest coast of Madagascar, placed its first stamps on sale.

March 20: Uganda issued the famous "typewritten" stamps. They were also the first stamps of the protectorate of Uganda.

This is a reprint of the stamp issued for the Fresno, Calif. to San Francisco bicycle mail. It was printed from a defaced die. Note the corrected spelling "Francisco." (July 6, 1894).

April 4: President Grover Cleveland appointed William S. Wilson as US postmaster general, succeeding Wilson S. Bissell.

June 8: Having established its own local post independent of, but cooperating with, the Shanghai Local Post, Amoy introduced its own stamps. The Chinese Government Post took over the Amoy post on Feb. 2, 1897.

June 14: Canada issued a 2c stamped envelope for drop letter use. A drop letter is one that is picked up at or delivered from the same post office at which it was mailed.

June 20: The Indian feudatory state of Bussahir (Bashahr) released its first stamps.

June 30: The US Post Office Department contract for the rental of Hey & Dolphin canceling machines expired and was not renewed. Instead, the post office department awarded William Barry a contract to supply 100 machines at an annual rental of $100 each (the Hey & Dolphin machines had cost the US $400 a year each). However, Funk and Bond note that all of the 100 machines were never in service. Only 52 were in service by the end of 1896 and they report a maximum of 93 in 1899.

July: A set of 10 stamps inscribed for Brunei was placed on sale. Ranging from ½c to $1, the stamps feature a five-pointed star over a landscape flanked by two palm trees. Strictly local in nature, the stamps resulted from a deal made by J. C. Robertson, manager of a commercial company in Borneo, and Sultan Hashim of Brunei.

The stamps could be used to frank mail to Labuan and Sarawak, but beyond that, stamps of Labuan had to be used, according to Collins. Although local stamps, they are listed by Gibbons, beginning with that catalog's 1983 edition.

July 1: The Portuguese colony of Inhambane, located in Mozambique, had stamps issued in its name. They were later replaced by the stamps of Mozambique.

July 17: The Detroit River mail service, established to provide mail service to crews of ships plying the Great Lakes, began. Konwiser notes that the service was discontinued June 30, 1948.

Aug. 1: The Foochow Local Post in China issued stamps printed by Waterlow & Sons. The nine denominations range from ½c to 40c. The common design shows a Dragon Boat with ships and mountains in the background.

October: The Balkan country of Montenegro issued its first acknowledgement-of-receipt stamps.

Nov. 10: The Indian-administered post office at Zanzibar came under the administration of British East Africa. Indian stamps were overprinted "ZANZIBAR."

1896

The Indian feudatory state of Indore placed its first stamps on sale.

Jan. 1: A daily philatelic magazine, *The Daily Stamp Item*, began publication. It ran for a full year before ceasing. Published by the C. H.

Mekeel Stamp and Publishing Co. of St. Louis, Mo., its masthead stated that it appeared "every day in the week except Sunday" and was "edited by the office cat."

Jan. 4: Utah entered the Union as the 45th state.

March 24: British stamps were converted to Official stamps (Departmentals) for use by the Office of Works by overprinting them "O.W./ OFFICIAL." The stamps were used on official correspondence from London and departments in various major British cities and by Clerks of Works at various British embassies abroad. They were withdrawn in 1904.

July 1: The Federated Malay States was formed. It included Negri Sembilan, Pahang, Perak, and Selangor. The federation issued stamps in 1900.

Sept. 1: British stamps overprinted "ARMY/ OFFICIAL" were issued for use by British Army paymasters on local correspondence. Along with other British Official stamps, they were withdrawn in 1904.

Sept. 20: The Nanking, China, Local Post placed stamps on sale. The founding date of the post is not known.

October: St. Helena joined the Universal Postal Union.

Oct. 1: The US Postal Office Department established a Collection and Distribution Wagon Service in New York City and Washington, D.C. These were intended to augment the Street Car Mail Service and worked mail en route. The service later operated in Buffalo, N.Y., and St. Louis, Mo. There was also a service over a 30-mile route in Maryland from 1899 to 1905. See April 3, 1899.

Oct. 1: The first experimental US Rural Free Delivery (RFD) routes were established in West Virginia. Initially, there were three routes, each about 20 miles in length and based in the towns of Uvilla, Hallstown, and Charlestown. The idea worked and was soon expanded.

Oct. 5: The Collectors Club (of New York) was founded. Its facilities are located at 22 East 35th St., New York City.

1897

Grand Comoro Island issued stamps in the French colonial Commerce and Navigation key type inscribed "Grande Comoro" for the island located off the coast of Madagascar.

German stamps overprinted for use in German South West Africa were placed in use.

Germany overprinted its stamps for use in German New Guinea.

The British Post Office used a steam-powered road vehicle to carry mail between London and Redhill, Surrey.

German stamps overprinted "Marschall-Inseln" became the first stamps of the German Marshall Islands.

Stamps were first issued for the Indian feudatory states of Dhar and Las Bela.

Nyassa, an area located in the northern part of Mozambique, released its first stamps.

By this date, the Russian Empire had more than 9,730 post offices. A staff of 51,590 handled about 220 million letters each year.

The German Empire issued stamps overprinted "China" for use at German Treaty Port post offices.

Jan. 2: The Chinese Government Post issued its first stamps.

Feb. 2: The Chinese Government Post officially took over all postal systems in China.

March 1: The Anglo-Egyptian Condominium administration of the Sudan issued its first stamps. They are Egyptian stamps overprinted "SOUDAN" plus the Arabic equivalent.

March 6: President William McKinley appointed James A. Gary postmaster general. He replaced William S. Wilson.

March 17: An inter-island postal service in the New Hebrides issued stamps inscribed "The Australasian New Hebrides Company Limited." Denominations are 1d and 2d. Robson Lowe notes the stamps were valid to frank mail to Sydney, Australia.

April 1: Germany overprinted its stamps for use in German Cameroon.

April 8: Heinrich von Stephan died. He had been postmaster general of Prussia and a moving force behind the formation of the Universal Postal Union.

May 5: The Fifth Congress of the Universal Postal Union convened in Washington, D.C. Free transit for international mail through a country enroute to another was debated. South American members proposed it, but European nations opposed it because a large amount of mail passed through their systems to other areas. They said it would be an unfair burden on them. The proposal was not adopted.

May 14: The Great Barrier Island Pigeon Post began operating between the island and the New Zealand mainland. The island is located about 50 miles northeast of Auckland. Several stamp issues appeared.

June 19: Canada issued the Diamond Jubilee stamps. They were released to mark the 60th anniversary of the reign of Queen Victoria. Denominations are ½c, 1c, 2c, 3c, 5c, 6c, 8c, 10c, 15c, 20c, 50c, $1, $2, $3, $4, and $5. This is the first Canadian commemorative issue, and the first to be printed by the American Bank Note Co., Ottawa.

June 22 and 28: On these dates, the British colony of New South Wales issued stamps with a postal validity of 1d and 2½d, but bearing denominations of 1/- and 2/6. The difference went to provide funding for a home for consumptives. The stamps are the world's first semi-postal issues.

June 26: Sarawak became a member of the Universal Postal Union.

June 30: By this date, the US Rural Free Delivery (RFD) system had been expanded to cover 29 states with 82 routes. It had been introduced on Oct. 1, 1896 (q.v.).

July 22: The Leeward issued its only non-omnibus commemorative set when it overprinted eight of its regular key type stamps to mark Queen Victoria's Diamond Jubilee.

October: The US post office opened pneumatic tube lines in New York, and extended them across the Brooklyn Bridge into Brooklyn by 1898.

Oct. 19: A balloon carried mail from Leipzig, Germany, to Tarnow. Captain L. Goddard piloted the aircraft.

December: The General Post Office in Boston, Mass., was connected by pneumatic tube with the North Station.

Dec. 31: The British annexed Zululand to their colony of Natal, although its stamps were continued until June 30, 1898.

1898

After the United States occupation of Puerto Rico and the expulsion of Spanish forces, a stamp shortage caused the release of a provisional stamp at Ponce. It took the form of a round handstamp reading "POSTAGE/ CORREOS" with "5 cts." in the center. Forgeries exist.

Stamps of Gibraltar were issued overprinted "Morocco/ Agencies" for use at British post offices in Morocco.

The stamps issued by Portugal in 1898 to mark the 400th anniversary of the discovery by Vasco da Gama of the route to India, represent the first of the omnibus issues. Sets featuring a common design were issued by Portugal and the Portuguese colonies of the Azores, Macao, Madeira, Portuguese Africa, Portuguese India, and Timor.

March 1: The first stamps specially produced for the Sudan were issued. These are in the "Camel Postman" design, which was in use until the late 1940s.

April: Portugal issued stamps for general use in its African colonies.

April: During this month, France leased from China the port of Kouang-Tcheou (Kwangchow) and surrounding area. The port issued stamps in 1906. The area reverted to China in February, 1943.

April 6: Greece issued a set of 12 stamps marking the first international Olympic Games of the modern era, which were held at Athens.

April 21: Turkey issued military stamps for its forces in Thessaly during that country's 1897-98 war with Greece. These are believed to be the first military stamps and are well known because of their unusual octagonal shape.

April 22: Charles Emory Smith succeeded James A. Gary as US postmaster general.

May 24: The United States established postal facilities in the Philippines following the defeat of the Spanish fleet in Manila Bay. The first post office was opened at Cavite on July 30, 1898. This and other subsequent offices were made branches of the San Francisco Post Office until after the signing of a peace treaty with Spain on Dec. 10, 1898.

June 17: The United States issued the Trans-Mississippi series commemorating the Trans-Mississippi Exposition at Omaha, Neb., from June 1 to Nov. 1, 1898. It is this set that contains the famous *Western Cattle in Storm* $1 stamp (q.v.).

June 17: *Western Cattle in Storm* was the title of the $1 stamp design in the Trans-Mississippi Exposition issue. At the time, postal officials said the $1 design represented a herd of cattle in the Western United States during a storm and was based on an engraving by C. O. Murray. However, according to Brookman, the engraving is based on the painting, *The Vanguard,* by J. A. MacWhirter, of a group of cattle in the West Highlands of Scotland, owned by Lord Blythswood!

When this was discovered, the US Post Office Department rendered an apology to the owner via the British Ambassador in Washington. Despite its depiction of Scottish Highland cattle in some rather thick Scottish weather instead of a blizzard on the plains of the American West, it is still a remarkably handsome stamp!

June 28: Canada issued its first special delivery stamp. It remained on sale until 1922, when a new design replaced it.

June 30: The use of Zululand stamps ceased and stamps of the British colony of Natal went into use in the area. Zululand had become part of Natal on Dec. 31, 1897.

July 1: The US Post Office Department introduced an indemnity of up to $10 on registered first-class mail.

July 1: The Canadian post office instituted a special delivery service for first-class mail and issued a special 10c stamp that had to be affixed to the letter in addition to the normal postage. The service had gone into effect on June 28 in Brantford, Ont.; Fredericton, N.B.; Halifax, N.S.; Hamilton, Ont.; Kingston, Ont.; London, Ont.; Montreal, PQ; Ottawa, Ont.; Quebec City, PQ; St. John, N.B.; Toronto, Ont.; Vancouver, B.C.; Victoria, B.C.; and Winnipeg, Man.

July 30: The first US post office at Cavite in the Philippines was opened following the defeat of Spain during the Spanish-American War. It was a branch of the San Francisco Post Office.

August: The US military established provisional mail service in Puerto Rico following the expulsion of Spain from the island during the Spanish-American War. After occupying the island, the United States changed its spelling to Porto Rico but objections of the inhabitants forced an almost immediate return to the original version. However, stamps issued subsequently still bore the "Porto" version.

Aug. 3: The first US post office in Puerto Rico, a military postal station at La Playa de Ponce, opened.

Aug. 12: Hawaii became a territory of the United States.

Aug. 14: A stamp shortage developed at the town of Coamo in Puerto Rico and a provisional 5c stamp was issued. It is a primitive typeset production in settings of 10, with a number of variations caused by different typefaces being used. There are forgeries.

Oct. 1: Gibraltar re-issued stamps in sterling currency after about nine years of stamps in Spanish currency denominations.

Nov. 17: The Great Barrier Island Pigeongram Service issued its first stamps. A pigeon mail service inaugurated May 14, 1897 from Great Barrier Island to Auckland, New Zealand, the service ended Sept. 5, 1908, when a telegraph service began operating.

Nov. 25: The area of Crete under British administration issued stamps. Robson Lowe gives the issue date as Nov. 28.

Dec. 7: Canada issued the 2c *Map Stamp* to mark the Dec. 25, 1898 introduction of Imperial Penny Postage. The design features a map of the world using Mercator's projection, with British possessions shown in red. Various printing irregularies magnify some of the red areas and the distortion of the projection used makes the area of Canada appear to be much larger than it actually is.

The ocean areas are in a blue that varies from lavender to light blue with shades ranging to a deeper blue and a bluish green, according to Robson Lowe. The rest of the stamp is in black. A total of 20 million copies was produced. In addition to being unusual for a 19th century stamp, it also forecast the modern trend towards combination production with the black being an intaglio impression and the other colors being typographed.

Dec. 13: The United States placed stamped envelopes overprinted with "PORTO RICO" below the indicium on sale in Puerto Rico.

Dec. 19: The Cuban town of Puerto Principe (now Camaguey) experienced a stamp shortage during the takeover of the island by the United States. The postmaster ordered the surcharging of Cuban stamps to create needed supplies of 1c, 2c, 3c, 5c, and 10c stamps. Numerous varieties were made and counterfeits are common.

Dec. 25: Imperial Penny Postage went into effect between Great Britain and Canada. Other countries in the British Empire soon enjoyed the same privilege.

Dec. 29: On this date, the Canadian Post Office reduced the domestic letter rate from 3c to 2c, prompting the production of the so-called Port Hood Provisional. The postmaster of Port Hood, Nova Scotia, bisected some 3c stamps into one third surcharged 1c and two thirds sur-

Despite its inscription, the Canadian Map Stamp was not issued to commemorate Christmas, but to mark the introduction of Imperial Penny Postage.

charged 2c in order to meet the new rate until supplies of 2c stamps became available.

Boggs quotes the postmaster as saying that the provisionals were in use for one day (Jan. 5, 1899) and that not more than 200 of the 2c ones were made.

1899

France issued stamps for use at its post office at Port Said, Egypt. They were French stamps overprinted "PORT-SAID ."

Stamps of France were overprinted "ALEXANDRIE" for use at a French post office in the Egyptian city of Alexandria. Beginning in 1902, stamps were issued inscribed "ALEXANDRIE."

Germany overprinted its stamps "Karolinen" for use in the Caroline Islands, then a German colony.

The Colombian department of Boyaca issued stamps.

The Indian feudatory state of Kishangarh placed its first stamps on sale.

The French colony of Dahomey issued stamps.

Negri Sembilan became a member of the Universal Postal Union. It is now part of Malaysia.

Jan. 1: The "Chrysanthemum Series" of postage stamps was issued by Japan. These feature the imperial crest with a stylized chrysanthemum in the center of the design.

Jan. 1: In Cuba, the United States overprinted and surcharged US stamps. Postage due labels and special delivery stamps were also issued. The US military issued stamps inscribed for Cuba later in the year.

Jan. 5: Most postal history authorities agree that this is the only day on which the Port Hood provisional was used. See Dec. 29, 1898.

Jan. 24: Elmer E. Wolf of Springfield, Ohio, obtained a US patent for a postal franking device. Nothing came of it.

March 15: US stamps overprinted "PORTO RICO" were issued for use on the island of Puerto Rico, which had been taken from Spain during the Spanish-American War.

April 3: A two-horse mail collection and delivery wagon inaugurated service over a 30-mile route in Carroll County, Maryland. Mailboxes were set up every half mile along the route and the wagon collected and sorted the mail enroute. The service was considered a success and additional wagons were introduced beginning Dec. 20, 1899 (q.v.). The wagons carried two postal clerks.

May: The area of Crete under Russian administration issued stamps.

May 1: A Philippine Postal Service was established. Following the US occupation of the islands, post offices there had been considered branches of the San Francisco post office and regular US postal paper had been used.

June 30: US stamps overprinted "PHILIPPINES" began to be sold in the island group.

July 7: US stamps overprinted "GUAM" were placed on sale on Guam while it was under US naval administration. The United States introduced stamps without the overprint on March 29, 1901, although the overprinted stamps remained in use for some time.

July 19: The earliest known machine slogan cancel in the United States was made on a Barry machine and advertised the Pan-American Exposition. The Buffalo, N.Y. Post Office used the cancel.

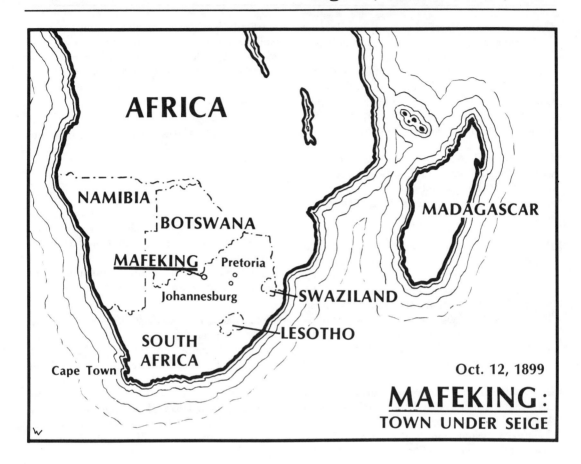

MADAGASCAR

AFRICA

NAMIBIA

BOTSWANA

MAFEKING · Pretoria

Johannesburg

SWAZILAND

LESOTHO

SOUTH AFRICA

Cape Town

Oct. 12, 1899

MAFEKING:
TOWN UNDER SEIGE

Aug. 15: The United States administration on Guam did not cancel mail until this date, according to Murphy, who adds that only five pieces of mail were canceled on Aug. 15. Beginning on July 7, 1899, mail had been canceled aboard USS *Yosemite.*

Aug. 16: The Philippines issued its first postage due labels.

Aug. 18: The Philippines under US administration issued its first stamped envelope. It was a 3c Washington envelope with "PHILIPPINES" overprinted below the indicium.

September: The Spanish Mariana Islands placed its first stamps on sale. They were Spanish Philippine stamps overprinted "MARIANAS/ ESPANOLAS." The overprint was handstamped vertically reading either up or down and was boxed.

Sept 1: A British post office began operating at Wei-Hai-Wei, a small British colony located on the north side of the Shantung Peninsula and leased from China. It was a dependency of Hong Kong. A second post office opened at Port Edward, in the European section of Wei-Hai-Wei, in 1904. Both offices closed Oct. 1, 1930, when the area reverted to China.

Oct. 1: The United States signed a parcel post convention with Germany, its first with a European country. The United States made its first parcel post agreement with Jamaica on July 22, 1887. Such foreign parcel post exchanges eventually resulted in a domestic parcel post service in the United States. Special interests, such as the express companies and small town merchants, who felt their business threatened, opposed it. The parcel post service in the United States formally started on Jan. 1, 1913 (q.v.).

Oct. 12: The town of Mafeking, now located in the Republic of South Africa, was besieged during the Boer War. The siege led to stamps being produced on March 24, 1900, for local use by the British forces bottled up in the town. Colonel Baden-Powell, the defender of Mafeking, later became even more famous as the founder of the Boy Scout movement.

November: The town of Vryburg, Cape Province, during an occupation by Boer forces during the Boer War, issued stamps. British forces also issued stamps for it after liberating it in early 1900.

Dec. 2: On this date, Germany and the United States divided the Samoan Islands. Great Britain had relinquished its claim in return for acquisitions elsewhere. The western group became a German colony and issued stamps in March 1900. These were German stamps overprinted "Samoa." In December 1900, stamps in the Royal Yacht *Hohenzollern* key type were issued.

Dec. 20: Three additional collection and distribution wagons joined the one introduced April 3, 1899, serving rural areas of Carroll County, Maryland. The wagons served feeder routes at designated junctions and special postal markings were used on the wagons. Similar wagons were later introduced in other areas of Maryland, Pennsylvania, Missouri, and Georgia. The service was discontinued prior to 1905, when one-man routes became able to provide more economical service.

Dec. 20: The German Empire issued stamps overprinted and surcharged for use at German post offices in Morocco.

Dec. 20: *The Horseless Age* reported the successful Post Office test of a Winton truck in Cleveland, Ohio. The vehicle was used during a snowstorm on a mail collection run of 22 miles. It completed the run in 2½ hours. A horse and wagon under good weather conditions took more than six hours over the same route.

Dec. 30: The earliest known Doremus machine cancel impression bears this date, according to Langford. At the end of 1899 some 12 US post offices had the machines and this increased rapidly to a peak of 315 machines. Langford says the last known use of the machine was in 1933. Hand-operated and simple, the machine was more suited to smaller post offices than to an office handling a large mail volume.

1900 - 1919
The Edwardian era & war

1900

During this year, the postal service of Puerto Rico was merged with the US Post Office Department. Overprinted US stamps for the island were discontinued and regular US stamps placed in use.

Italian stamps were overprinted "La Cana" for use at an Italian post office in Crete.

The Federated Malay States, comprising Negri Sembilan, Pahang, Perak, and Selangor, issued stamps.

The Turks and Caicos Islands placed its first stamps on sale.

Jan. 1: The Empire of Korea became a member of the Universal Postal Union. During the 1910-1945 Japanese occupation, the country was known as Chosen and became a member under that name in 1922. The UPU dropped it from membership in 1948. The current Republic of Korea (South Korea) joined in 1949.

Jan. 1: The postal system in the Oil River and Niger Coast Protectorate was merged into that of Southern Nigeria.

February: The US administration of the Philippines issued postal cards. They are US items with "PHILIPPINES" overprinted below the indicium.

March: Northern Nigeria issued its first stamps.

March 1: The government of the Mediterranean island of Crete issued stamps, which were used until union with Greece in 1913.

March 1: German Samoa issued its first stamps. They took the form of German stamps overprinted diagonally "SAMOA."

March 19: Following the occupation of the Orange Free State by British forces, its stamps were overprinted "V.R.I." (Victoria Regina Imperatrix). Denominations of ½d, 1d, and 2½d were placed on sale on this date, with other values following.

March 24: The besieged city of Mafeking issued its first stamps during the South African Boer War.

April 1: By this date, all private city posts had ceased operating in the German Empire. The Reichspost had taken control of the posts, including Berlin's popular and efficient Berliner Packetfahrt.

April 9: The two famous Siege of Mafeking stamps depicting Cadet Sgt. Major Goodyear (1d) and Colonel Baden-Powell (3d) were issued. Produced in Mafeking using a photographic process, the stamps were intended for local mail only.

April 16: The United States issued its first stamp booklets, according to Scott, although Cabeen gives the date as April 2. There were three types: a 25c booklet containing two panes of six 2c stamps, a 49c booklet containing four panes of six 2c stamps, and a 97c booklet containing eight panes of six 2c stamps. The

This is a stamp from the first issue of overprints produced in the beseiged town of Mafeking during the Boer War (March 24, 1900).

booklets sold for 1c over the total face value of the stamps and featured the 2c denomination of the 1894 issue bearing a profile of George Washington.

May: Stamps of Germany were overprinted "Marianen" for use in the Mariana Islands, which Germany had acquired from Spain.

May 9: Stamps of German post offices in China were surcharged for use at Kiautschou.

June: Stamps were issued for the South African town of Wolmaransstad while under British occupation during the Boer War.

June 14: Stamps of the United States replaced those of Hawaii in the Islands.

June 18: The second British occupation of Transvaal prompted the issuance of stamps for the area.

June 23: Stamps were issued for the British occupation of the South African town of Rustenburg during the Boer War.

July 2: This date saw an event that was to prove a harbinger of future postal history. The first flight took place of Count Ferdinand von Zeppelin's first rigid dirigible.
  LZ-1, as it was labeled was not an unqualified success. Clumsy and underpowered, it made only three brief test flights over Lake Constance in southern Germany, but it pointed the way to the successful, mail-carrying Graf Zeppelin and a handful of other dirigibles that carried mail during the period between the two world wars.

July 2: An Extraordinary Congress of the Universal Postal Union convened in Berne, Switzerland, to mark the organization's 25th anniversary. The UPU used the effective date of the first congress as the beginning of the organization instead of the Oct. 9, 1874 signing date. This 1900 UPU Congress voted money for the construction of the UPU monument. Switzerland issued a set of three stamps marking the anniversary.

July 16: Stamps of Straits Settlements were authorized for use in the Federated Malay States during a shortage of stamps. Authorization was withdrawn Jan. 1, 1902, according to Robson Lowe, but it is not unusual to find copies bearing a later date.

July 20: The United States established a post office on American Samoa. US stamps have always been used there.

August: By this date, the harbor facilities at Fremantle, Western Australia, were equipped to handle ships from Great Britain and the mails were landed there instead of at Albany, 260 miles to the south.

August: Stamps were issued for the British occupation of the South African town of Schweizer Renecke during the Boer War.

Aug. 1: The postmarking of mail on US Rural Free Delivery routes became mandatory and carriers were provided with handstamps for this purpose. The US ceased issuing the postmarkers in July 1903.

Aug. 10: Stamps of the Cape of Good Hope overprinted "ORANGE/ RIVER/ COLONY" went on sale in the new colony after stamps overprinted "V.R.I." had been exhausted.

Aug. 24: The first franking device (postage meter), which had been invented by Charles A. Kahrs, was placed in use in the lobby of the General Post Office in Christiana (Oslo), Norway. It was withdrawn from use on Dec. 19, 1900.

September: Stamps were issued by the British in the occupation of the South African town of Lydenburg, during the Boer War.

November: The Cayman Islands issued its first stamps.

1901

Jan. 1: The Commonwealth of Australia was formed. It included the colonies of New South Wales, Queensland, South Australia, Tasmania, Victoria, Western Australia, plus the Northern Territory.

Queen Victoria.

Jan. 22: Queen Victoria died. The Prince of Wales succeeded to the throne of Great Britain as King Edward VII.

March: The British colony of Southern Nigeria issued stamps.

March 1: Postal control of the Commonwealth of Australia, formed on Jan. 1, 1901, was assumed by the central government. However, the ex-colonies of New South Wales, Queensland, South Australia, Tasmania, Victoria, and Western Australia continued to use their own stamps. A common stamp issue was not released until Jan. 1, 1913, although postage due labels were issued in July 1902.

Until Commonwealth stamps were issued, stamps bearing the individual states' names were released. These were valid for use in any part of the Commonwealth and Rosenblum suggests that they could well be classed as "regional" issues, as they were issued under Commonwealth authority.

March 20: The Boers issued their first stamps for the South African town of Pietersburg. They were withdrawn on April 9, 1901, when British forces captured the town.

March 29: The United States placed its own stamps on sale on the island of Guam. Prior to this, US stamps had been issued overprinted "GUAM."

March 30: The US Post Office Department took over postal operations on Guam from the US Navy.

April 9: Stamps issued by the Boers for the South African town of Pietersburg were withdrawn upon the the town's capture by British forces.

May 1: The United States released the Pan-American Exposition issue. The stamps depict various forms of transportation in use at that time.

June 11: The island of Aitutaki became a dependency of New Zealand and issued stamps on June 12, 1903 (q.v.). These were replaced by Cook Island stamps on March 15, 1932. Its own stamps were re-introduced on Aug. 9, 1972.

June 11: The island of Penrhyn became a dependency of New Zealand and stamps were issued May 5, 1902. Stamps of the Cook Islands replaced them on March 15, 1932, but Penrhyn re-introduced its own stamps on Oct. 24, 1973.

July 1: British New Guinea issued stamps inscribed with its name.

Sept. 28: The United States administration for the Philippines issued newspaper wrappers. They comprised US items with "PHILIPPINES" overprinted below the indicium.

Oct. 15: The first Philippine Islands special delivery stamp went on sale.

Nov. 19: New Zealand opened a post office on the Pacific island of Niue.

Dec. 9: Arthur Hill Pitney applied for a patent on the postage meter he had invented.

1902

The stamps of the German Empire replaced those of Wurttemberg. However, Wurttemberg's Official stamps continued in use until 1923.

Spanish Guinea issued stamps.

Jan. 1: Great Britain issued its first stamps depicting King Edward VII.

Jan. 4: The New Zealand dependency of Niue issued its first stamps.

Jan. 15: President Theodore Roosevelt appointed Henry C. Payne to succeed Charles Emory Smith as US postmaster general.

Feb. 19: Britain overprinted its stamps with "BOARD/ OF/ EDUCATION" for use by that government department. They were withdrawn, together with other British Official stamps, in 1904.

Feb. 19: British stamps overprinted "R.H./ OFFICIAL" were issued for us on correspondence by the royal household. They were withdrawn in 1904, when the use of Official stamps ceased, according to L. N. Williams

Feb. 25: The Dominican Republic issued its first Official stamps.

March: British forces occupying the South African town of Volksrust during the Boer War, issued stamps for the town.

May 5: Penrhyn Island, in the Cook Islands issued its first stamps, according to Gibbons. Robson Lowe notes the issue date as Jan. 27. They were stamps of New Zealand overprinted and surcharged.

May 27: This is the earliest known use of the so-called "Garbage Card", a 1c US postal card featuring a full-face portrait of President McKinley. The production had proven unsatisfactory and the postmaster general ordered the entire printing destroyed.

However, one box of 500 cards was sold to the New York firm of Booth, Daley & Ivins for use by the firm's garbage barge captains in reporting locations and condition of garbage barges or dumpers. Hence their name. The cards are correctly classified as prepared for use but not issued.

July: French Somali Coast, subsequently the French Territory of Afars and Issas and now the Republic of Djibouti, issued its first stamps.

July: The Commonwealth of Australia issued postage due labels for use in all states except Victoria. They had been made from the plates used for the New South Wales dues with "N.S.W." removed from the bottom of the design.

July 1: The US Post Office Department increased to $25 the indemnity on registered first class mail.

Aug. 9: During a "Coronation" balloon post flight, cards were dropped over Kent, England at Leeds Castle, near Canterbury, and near Dover. Only six cards are known.

Sept. 20: The first "Lifeboat Saturday" balloon post took place when more than 4,000 postcards were dropped from a balloon that had ascended from Manchester, England. Only one card is known to have survived from this flight.

Sept. 30: The Republic of Cuba issued its first stamps.

Oct. 3: French post offices on the island of Crete issued stamps. The post offices were located at Canea, Rethymnon, Candia, San Nicolo, Sitia, and Hierapetra. The stamps were those of France overprinted "CRETE."

Oct. 4: Cuba became a member of the Universal Postal Union.

Oct. 14: Arthur Hill Pitney obtained a US patent for a franking device. In 1902, he also formed the Pitney Postal Machine Co., which became the American Postage Meter Co. in 1910. Pitney and Walter H. Bowes met in 1919 and formed the Pitney-Bowes Postage Meter Co. in April 1920.

Nov. 29: The New Zealand Post Office opened a postal agency on Fanning Island. On Jan. 27, 1916, it was placed under the administration of the Gilbert and Ellice Islands.

This marking meant deliver on Christmas Day.

Dec. 17: The British Post Office began an experiment at Rochdale, Lancashire, by accepting mail to be held for Christmas Day delivery. The period of acceptance was Dec. 17-22 and an oval marking was applied reading "POSTED IN ADVANCE FOR DELIVERY ON CHRISTMAS DAY 1902." This mail had to be handed over the post office counter and could not be deposited in mail boxes. About 19,000 pieces of mail were handled this way in the experiment. In 1903, the scheme was tried at 28 post offices in the United Kingdom. In subsequent years up to 1909 it operated at various post offices. The service had a number of disadvantages, not the least of which was the large amount of mail that had to be delivered on the one day at considerable expense. A number

of varied markings were used, several of which incorporated a prominent black cross to designate the special mail.

Dec. 18: Guatemala issued its first Official stamps.

1903

Mauritius, in the Indian Ocean, issued its first special delivery stamps.

East Africa and Uganda placed its first stamps on sale.

The Spanish colonies of Eloby, Annobon, and Corisco issued stamps.

March: Definitive stamps depicting a profile of King Edward VII were placed on sale in the Orange River Colony, formerly the Orange Free State.

March: An Austrian post office in Crete, surcharged stamps of Austria for use there.

March 3: British stamps overprinted "ADMIRALTY/ OFFICIAL" were issued for use on official Admiralty correspondence. They were withdrawn in 1904 when the use of Official stamps by Great Britain ceased.

April 1: The most familiar of all French stamp designs, *La Semeuse,* better known as *The Sower,* made its debut. It proved a longlived design, being used well into the 1960s, although details of the design have varied over the years. It is the work of artist Louis Oscar Roty, who took it from a miniature in the Louvre, according to Patrick Hamilton. It depicts a female figure carrying a bag of seed, which she is sowing by hand. It had also been

used by Roty for the obverse of a 50-centime French coin he designed.

April 26: Indian postal authorities opened the first of several temporary post offices in Tibet during the first Francis Younghusband expedition into Tibet. An unofficial overprint reading "Tibet" was applied to Indian stamps. After waiting five months to meet with the Dalai Lama, the expedition withdrew. It returned on Dec. 12 of the same year as a punitive expedition.

May 26: The US Post Office Department specified that precancel devices should comprise city name and state between two parallel lines, according to correspondence from James Kingman.

June 1: Italy issued express letter stamps for domestic use. Similar stamps for foreign mail were issued in September 1908.

June 1: British Somaliland joined the Universal Postal Union and issued Indian stamps overprinted "BRITISH/ SOMALILAND". In 1904, special stamps were released inscribed for use there.

June 1: A post office was opened on the island of Aitutaki as a sub-post office of the Cook Islands.

June 12: The island of Aitutaki in the Cook Islands issued stamps. They were stamps of New Zealand overprinted "AITUTAKI."

June 15: Norwegian Karl Uchermann first devised the nearest approach to the postage meter as it now exists. It was used in Christiana (Oslo), Norway, on this date. The last date of use was Jan. 2, 1905. During that period seven machines were used, three by private firms and four by the Norwegian Post Office.

July: The French colony of Senegambia and Niger issued it first stamps.

Sept. 5: The second "Lifeboat Saturday" balloon post took place when a balloon ascended and postcards were dropped over England. Six flown cards are known to exist from this flight.

October: Italian Somaliland issued its first stamps, which were inscribed "BENADIR."

Nov. 10: The Republic of Panama, which had seceded from Colombia with the encouragement of the United States, issued its first stamps, according to Gibbons. Scott gives the date as Nov. 16.

Dec. 12: A British military expedition entered Tibet as a result of the failure of the first Younghusband expedition to meet Tibetan officials. The expedition reached Lhasa on Aug. 3, 1904. A treaty was signed on Sept. 7, 1904. The expedition withdrew from the Tibetan capital on Sept. 23, 1904, reentering India on Oct. 25, 1904. A number of field post offices using Indian stamps, operated during the expedition. As a result of the treaty, British postal agencies were opened in Tibet.

1904

Christmas seals, an idea of Danish postal employee Einar Holboell, were first placed on sale in Denmark, Norway, and Sweden, according to Cabeen. Other countries adopted this method of raising money and today the seals are used in many parts of the world.

In New Zealand, the Automatic Stamping Company Ltd. was formed to produce postage meters. It was later renamed Automatic Franking Machine Co. (NZ) Ltd.

The Indian feudatory state of Jaipur released its first stamps.

January: The first precancel catalog was published, according to James Kingman. Entitled *The Catalog of the Precancelled Postage Stamps of the United States,* it was compiled and edited by F. L. Smith and George F. Duck.

April 28: Congress authorized the use of permit imprints instead of adhesive postage stamps. The law took effect Oct. 1, 1904.

April 30: The United States released the Louisiana Purchase Exposition issue. The stamps depict Robert R. Livingstone (1c), Thomas Jefferson (2c), James Monroe (3c), William McKinley (5c), and a map of the territory purchased (10c).

May: British Official stamps overprinted for use by various departments of government were withdrawn from use on either May 12 or May 14, according to L. N. Williams.

June: The Christchurch, New Zealand, Post Office place in use a coin-operated franking device. It had been invented by Ernest Moss. Postal officials withdrew the machine at the end of a two-week test period in Christchurch and a three-week test at the Wellington Post Office.

June 11: Panama became a member of the Universal Postal Union.

June 24: The US Canal Zone Postal Service went into operation and issued its first stamps.

July 11: New Zealand Post Office trials of a Moss #2 postage meter began at Christchurch Meat Co. The test lasted until Aug. 10.

Sept. 10: The third Moss postage meter was submitted to New Zealand postal authorities.

Oct. 1: The US permit imprint system established by Congress on April 28, 1904, became effective on this date.

Oct. 10: President Theodore Roosevelt appointed Robert J. Wynne as US postmaster general, succeeding Henry C. Payne.

1905

Greenland, the world's largest island, issued stamps for the prepayment of parcels. The island came under Danish influence about 1721 when settlements were established. Prior to Dec. 1, 1938 (q.v.), its mail was carried free between Greenland and Denmark.

This set of five stamps was issued to commemorate the Louisiana Purchase Exposition held April 30-Dec. 1, 1904 at St. Louis, Mo.

A Greenland parcel post stamp (1905).

The Spanish colony of Rio de Oro released stamps.

January: Stamps of the Sudan were overprinted "ARMY/ OFFICIAL" and issued for use by military personnal stationed there.

March 7: President Theodore Roosevelt appointed his third postmaster general, George B. Cortelyou. He succeeded Robert J. Wynne.

June 1: Japanese forces occupying Korea withdrew Korean stamps and placed stamps of Japan in use.

June 1: The Bavarian Post Office introduced a postbus service between Bad Tolz and Long-gries using a 29 horsepower Daimler.

July 12: Several balloons ascended in conjunction with the Beckenham, Kent, England, Flower Show. Postcards were dropped, of which seven are known. They are inscribed "Dispatched from the Clouds by Balloon Post from the Beckenham Flower Show, Wednesday, July 12, 1905".

July 14: German colonial authorities opened a post office on the Pacific island of Nauru. Stamps of the German Marshall Islands were used.

Aug. 15: Following this date, stamps of Great Britain overprinted "LEVANT" were placed in use for packages at British post offices in the Turkish Empire. The offices were located at Beyrout (Beirut), Constantinople (Istanbul), Salonica (Thessalonika), Smyrna (Izmir), and Stamboul (sub-post office of Constantinople). British post offices also operated in Egypt, which was then part of the Turkish Empire.

Aug. 23: The Netherlands Post Office began the sale of Curacao stamps as a service to those who wished to include return postage in a letter. Similarly, stamps of the Netherlands were made available in Curacao.

Oct. 26: Norway repealed union with Sweden and became an independent kingdom.

1906

King Edward VII gave permission to The Philatelic Society, London, to use the prefix "Royal."

The French colony of Mauritania issued its first stamps.

The French colony of Upper Senegal and Niger placed its first stamps on sale.

Jan. 14: Romania issued its first semi-postal stamps.

Feb. 8: A Moss Mark II postage meter was installed at offices of Christchurch Meat Co., Christchurch, New Zealand. A Mark IV (Model C) machine soon superseded it. By October 1906, five machines had been installed in the offices of private firms.

April 5: The US Congress approved a bill allowing the use of Consular Service Fee stamps at US consulates beginning on June 1, 1906.

April 7: The Sixth Congress of the Universal Postal Union took place in Rome, Italy. It created the international reply coupon. Picture postcards were authorized under the same conditions as postal cards. The UPU's actions took effect on Oct. 1, 1907.

June 1: US Consular Service Fee stamps went into use. They were used on all documents for which a fee was prescribed as an indication that the fee had been paid. They were discontinued Sept. 30, 1955.

Sept. 9: The first stamps for the Maldive Islands, consisting of overprints on stamps of Ceylon, went on sale.

Oct. 1: The US Post Office contracted for two Columbia motor trucks to collect mail from street mailboxes in Baltimore. They were so successful that motor vehicles in other cities began to replace horse-drawn carts.

Oct. 6: The condominium administration of New Hebrides by Britain and France began on this date.

Oct. 11: The first internationally valid postage stamps were issued for Brunei. Its first post office, located at Brunei Town, opened.

Oct. 30: The British placed the colony of Labuan under the administration of the Straits Settlements. In 1912, Labuan became a separate entity in the Straits Settlements and remained so until the Japanese invasion in December 1941.

Nov. 8: The stamps of British New Guinea were overprinted "Papua" to reflect the administrative change for the area constituting the southern portion of the eastern half of the island of New Guinea. The Australian colonies of New South Wales, Queensland, and Victoria, plus Great Britain had administered the area. Beginning Sept. 1, 1906 the Australian federal government assumed the role played by the former colonies. The name was changed at this time, from British New Guinea to the Territory of Papua.

Nov. 15: Brazil issued its first Official stamps.

Nov. 26: Luxembourg issued a souvenir sheet containing 10 stamps of its 1906 10c stamp to mark the accession of Grand Duke William IV to the throne of the Grand Duchy. This is the world's first souvenir sheet.

Dec. 1: The Netherlands issued its first semi-postal stamps. The surtax went to tuberculosis research.

1907

The French colony of Middle Congo issued its first stamps. See also Congo Republic.

Great Britain overprinted its stamps "MOROCCO/AGENCIES" for use at British post offices in Morocco.

Jan. 25: Barbados issued its first semi-postal stamp, which had a 1d surtax in aid of the Kingston Relief Fund.

Feb. 9: The Canal Zone Postal Service placed its first postal card on sale. It was a 2c Republic of Panama card overprinted and surcharged "1c."

Feb. 14: The British Solomon Islands Protectorate placed its first stamps on sale.

March 4: George von L. Meyer was appointed US postmaster general by President Theodore Roosevelt, succeeding George B. Cortelyou.

April 25: San Marino issued its first special delivery stamp.

April 26: The United States released the Jamestown Exposition issue. Designs feature Captain John Smith (1c), the founding of Jamestown (2c), and Pocahontas (5c).

July 6: The name British Central Africa Protectorate was changed to Nyasaland Protectorate. Stamps featuring the new name were issued July 22, 1907.

September: The British Solomon Islands Protectorate became a member of the Universal Postal Union.

Oct. 1: Algeria, Australia, New Zealand, and the US Possessions became members of the Universal Postal Union.

Oct. 14: A balloon flight sponsored by the *Daily Graphic* newspaper ascended from England and drifted to Tosse, Sweden. About 15,000 postcards were dropped during the flight. Few survive today.

Nov. 16: Oklahoma became the 46th state of the United States.

Dec. 7: Christmas seals were first placed on sale in the United States. Through the efforts of Emily P. Bissel, the Delaware chapter of the American Red Cross conducted sales. Beginning in 1919, after 10 years of selling them on behalf of the Red Cross, the National Tuberculosis Society produced and sold them, according to Cabeen.

1908
The Spanish post office in the Moroccan town of Tetuan issued stamps.

Jan. 1: Ernest Shackleton left New Zealand in the ship *Nimrod* on an expedition to Antarctica. He took with him a supply of New Zealand 1d stamps overprinted "King Edward VII Land" in green and had been sworn in as a New Zealand postmaster. A total of 23,492 stamps was carried, according to Pirie. After leaving Shackleton's expedition in Antarctica, *Nimrod* returned to New Zealand. It carried mail franked with the stamps, which were canceled by a round handstamp reading "BRIT. ANTARCTIC EXPD." The expedition left Antarctica on March 4, 1909 aboard *Nimrod*, which had returned to pick them up.

Feb. 18: The first official US coil stamps went into use. They were the 1c and 2c in the 1902-03 series and came perf 12 either horizontally or vertically. The 5c value was issued perf 12 horizontally on Feb. 24. Coils containing 500 or 1,000 were made. The 1c and 2c stamps were also available in imperforate coils, according to Cabeen.

May 8: The US Post Office Department authorized the use of perfins in the United States. Perfins are designs, initials, or numerals perforated in postage stamps by private firms and governmental agencies, as a security device to discourage stamp theft and misuse. Some 6,000 different perfins are

recorded in the United States, with about 40,000 different existing worldwide.

June: Stamps of the Netherlands Indies were overprinted "JAVA" for use on that island and on Madura, and "BUITEN/BEZIT." for use on other islands of the colony.

July 1: The first post offices aboard US naval vessels went into operation. A total of 69 ships initially had post offices.

July 1: Count Zeppelin dropped a personal card from the airship LZ-4 over Zurich, thus making it the first dropped Zeppelin mail.

July 22: The first stamps reflecting the change in name of British Central Africa Protectorate to Nyasaland Protectorate were released.

September: Italy issued express letter stamps for foreign mail.

Sept. 5: The Great Barrier Island-Auckland Pigeon Post Service ended when a telegraph service went into operation.

Oct. 1: "Penny Postage" went into effect between Great Britain and the United States. The rate from Great Britain was 1d per ounce, while that from the United States was 2c per ounce. These were reductions from 2½d and 5c respectively.

Oct. 29: Stamps inscribed in English were issued for the British-French condominium administration of the New Hebrides.

Nov. 1: Ethiopia became a member of the Universal Postal Union. It was dropped in 1937 after the Italian invasion and occupation. The UPU restored it as a member in 1945.

Nov. 15: Belgium annexed the Congo Free State as the Belgian Congo. The new colony issued its first stamps on Jan. 1, 1909.

Nov. 21: The British-French condominium administration of the New Hebrides issued stamps inscribed in French.

The "Merry Widow."

Dec. 12: On this date, the United States issued a 10c special delivery stamp featuring Mercury's hat. Since the headgear so closely resembled a woman's hat of the Edwardian period and the musical comedy *The Merry Widow* was a popular hit of the day, the stamp became known as the "Merry Widow."

1909

Stamps of the Straits Settlements and the Federated Malay States went into use in the Malayan state of Kedah, replacing stamps of Siam (Thailand), which had been used from 1883.

Until this year, stamps of Siam (Thailand) were used in the Malayan state of Perlis. The state used stamps of the Federated Malay States until 1912.

Jan. 1: The Belgian Congo issued its first stamps.

March 6: Frank H. Hitchcock succeeded George von L. Meyer as US postmaster general.

March 28: This date is found on a Le Havre, France, arrival stamp applied to a letter originating on Kerguelen Island, located in the Kerguelen Archipelago on the fringe of Antarctica in the southern Indian Ocean. A postal ser-

vice operated from the island from about 1912 to 1925, the earliest and latest dates known on mail. The community was tiny and no regular service to or from the island appears to have existed. Varied transit markings found on mail suggest that mail was taken by visiting ships. Island residents used the stamps of France canceled with a special circular "Iles Kerguelen" handstamp.

June 1: The Alaska-Yukon-Pacific Exposition issue was released by the United States. The 2c stamp features the profile of William H. Seward, who as Secretary of State was instrumental in the purchase of Alaska from Russia in 1867 for $7.2 million. The stamp exists both perforated 12 and imperf.

July: From this date, stamps of the Federated Malay States were used in the Malayan state of Kelantan. Prior to this, stamps of Siam (Thailand) had been used. Stamps inscribed for Kelantan went into use in January 1911.

July: Postage due labels of the same design as those used in the Australian state of Victoria, but inscribed "AUSTRALIA," were issued by the Commonwealth of Australia for use in all states.

Oct. 4: The monument to the Universal Postal Union was dedicated at Berne, Switzerland, the UPU headquarters. The monument had been decided upon at the UPU's 1900 Extraordinary Congress to mark the organization's 25th anniversary. The monument, with its five figures floating around the globe, has appeared on many of the world's stamps.

Nov. 1: The US registration fee went to 10c. For first-class mail, this provided a $50 indemnity.

Nov. 20: To serve the growing whaling community and more effectively administer the area, the Falkland Islands appointed a postmaster for the island of South Georgia, a dependency. The post office opened Dec. 3 and the first mail dispatched on Dec. 23. Mail volume grew and by 1913 the annual mail had reached 139 mailbags.

The Universal Postal Union monument

A selection of the many stamps from around the world that picture the UPU monument in Berne, Switzerland (Oct. 4, 1909).

Dec. 3: The Falkland Islands government opened a post office at Grytviken, South Georgia. No datestamp was provided and mail went to the Falkland Islands for cancelation and onward transmission. The first South Georgia cancelation was used in July 1910.

1910

The US Pitney Postal Machine Co. was reorganized as the American Postage Meter Co. this was the first public use of the term "postage meter."

The Malay state of Trengganu issued stamps.

February: China invaded Tibet and occupied the country. During the Chinese revolution that began in October 1910, the Tibetans drove the Chinese out, but not before the Chinese had established an efficient postal service using their own stamps.

Feb. 6: The first aviation meet on the African continent took place Feb. 6-13 during Aviation Week at Heliopolis, near Cairo, Egypt. A special cancelation was provided by a post office set up for the event, which read "Heliopolis Aerodrome." Some cards were flown as personal favors, but no official air mail was carried.

May 1: Argentina marked the 100th anniversary of the republic with a set of 16 stamps reminscent of the US Columbian series and the Canadian Diamond Jubilees.

May 6: King Edward VII of Great Britain died. He was succeeded by his son, who became King George V. The new king was an experienced philatelist and had served as president of the Royal Philatelic Society, London.

May 31: The Union of South Africa was created from the former colonies of Cape of Good Hope, Natal, Transvaal, and the Orange River Colony. Areas of these that had once been Orange Free State, Griqualand West, New Republic, and Zululand were also included.

June 1: Belgium issued its first semi-postal stamps. Post offices sold the stamps at double their face value with the excess going to an anti-tuberculosis organization.

June 1: South Africa became a member of the Universal Postal Union.

June 19: Between this date and June 28, the DELAG Zeppelin LZ-7 dropped mail during flights over Germany. The mail consisted of scenic postcards imprinted with the Zeppelin Company's handstamp and a handwritten marking indicating drop location.

Aug. 6: A special cancelation was used at an aviation meet held at Lanark, Scotland, from Aug. 6-13. Although it does not designate mail flown at the event, it was the first postal station operated at an aviation meeting in Great Britain.

Aug. 14: The first semi-official air mail stamp was issued in France for an Aug. 14-21 aviation meet held at Nantes. Its use was necessary for an item to be carried by air during the meet, according to Kronstein.

Aug. 17: The first airplane mail was carried in Great Britain when Claude Graham-White took off from Blackpool. Bad weather ended the flight at Southport. The mail was sent on to London and deposited in the mails there. No special postal marking was used.

Sept. 23: Postcards were issued and flown at an aviation meeting during September and October at Milan, Italy, to honor Jorge Chaves. Chaves became the first man to fly across the Alps from Switzerland to Italy. But after taking off from Brig, Switzerland, and successfully crossing the Simplon Pass, he crashed and was killed near his landing place at Domodossola, Italy. His native Peru has issued stamps in his honor.

Nov. 3: Mail had been scheduled to be flown from the German liner *Kaiserin Augusta Victoria* at sea to New York by A.D. McCurdy, but bad weather canceled the attempt. The US postmaster general had approved the flight.

Nov. 4: The Union of South Africa issued its first stamp. This 2½d stamp commemorated the opening of the first Union Parliament by the Duke of Connaught. It met at Cape Town. The

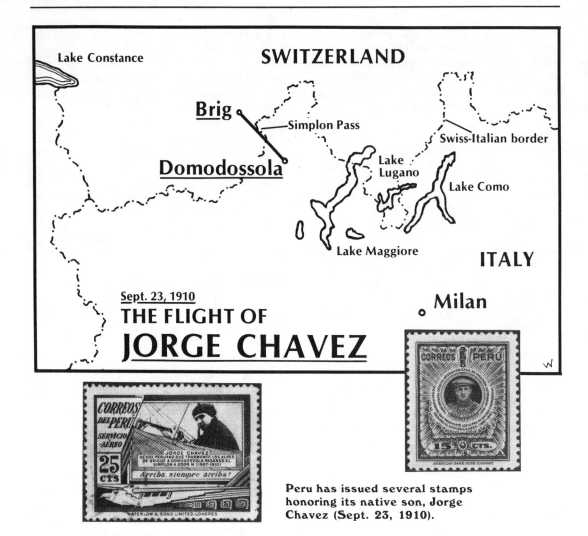

Peru has issued several stamps honoring its native son, Jorge Chavez (Sept. 23, 1910).

Union did not issue its first definitive stamps until Sept. 1, 1913. In the meantime, stamps of the component colonies were valid for use throughout the country.

Nov. 29: Captain Robert Falcon Scott left New Zealand aboard the ship *Terra Nova* on an Antarctic expedition. He carried 23,100 New Zealand 1d stamps overprinted "Victoria Land" and a circular datestamp similar to that provided to Ernest Shackleton (see Jan. 1, 1908). He also had been sworn in as a New Zealand postmaster. During 1912, a quantity of 1,910 ½d stamps similarly overprinted was sent to Scott. The first mail sent by the expedition left on Jan. 19, 1911 and the last on Jan. 18, 1913. There were two additional dispat-

ches in between, according to Pirie. Following the death of Scott and four companions after they had reached the South Pole on Jan. 18, 1912, the expedition was evacuated on Jan. 19, 1913.

Dec. 1: Japan issued its first military stamp.

Dec. 22: The United States issued Official stamps for use on correspondence resulting from the administration's newly established postal savings plan. The stamps were issued in denominations of 1c, 2c, 10c, 50c, and $1. They were withdrawn from use under a law approved Sept. 23, 1914.

1911

January: The Malayan state of Kelantan placed its first stamps on sale.

Jan. 1: First stamps issued for the British Protectorate of the Gilbert and Ellice Islands. They were stamps of Fiji overprinted "GILBERT & ELLICE/ ISLANDS."

Jan. 3: The US Post Office Department issued the first Postal Savings stamps. These were redeemable as a credit to Postal Savings accounts. They were withdrawn March 28, 1966.

Jan. 13: A competition opened in Australia for a design to be used for the first definitive series of stamps for the Commonwealth. Although the contest generated 1,051 entries, none were deemed suitable. Blamire Young, an artist in the Victoria Artists Association, was invited to submit a design. His design, with a few changes, became the kangaroo and map stamp, first issued Jan. 1, 1913.

Jan. 24: Scott states this is the issue date of the 3c so-called Orangeburg Coil, considered the rarest of all US coil stamps. Reports of the quantity bought range from a single roll of 500 stamps by Jacob Kayne, an employee of Bell & Company, the pharmaceutical firm that is believed to have been the sole user, up to a possible total of 223,500 stamps, according to Griffenhagen. The stamp is a flat plate printing in the Washington head design on a single-line watermark paper and is perforated 12 vertically. Its color is deep violet.

Feb. 2: The South American Postal Union was formed at a Latin-American congress in Montevideo. In 1921, it became the Pan-American Postal Union. After it admitted Spain in 1923 and Canada in 1931, the organization assumed the name of the Postal Union of the Americas and Spain.

Feb. 18: The world's first official airplane mail was flown in India during the United Provinces Industrial and Agricultural Exhibition at Allahabad. French pilot M. Pequet carried the mail about five miles to Naini Junction and it received a large magenta cancelation. This depicted a side view of the Humber-Sommer biplane flying over a mountain range and bearing the inscription "FIRST AERIAL POST" around the top and "U.P. EXHIBITION ALLAHABAD" around the bottom. About 6,500 pieces of mail were carried.

March 1: New Hebrides became a member of the Universal Postal Union.

May 1: The Australian colonies that had federated to form the Commonwealth of Australia made their postal rates uniform.

May 7: The Dusseldorf flight of Zeppelin LZ-8 carried mail. An "On Board" handstamp was applied.

June 22: Great Britain issued the first stamps bearing a portrait of King George V. This was the infamous Downey Head, which presented a less-than-flattering royal image and was soon

A strip of five of the Orangeburg coil (Jan. 24, 1911).

Above are two examples of the large magenta cancel used on the Feb. 18, 1911 air mail flights at Allahabad, India. Also shown are the three stamps India issued for the 50th anniversary of the event in 1961. The stamps show the 1911 aircraft and reproduce the cancel (Feb. 18, 1911).

The Downey Head was less than flattering to King George V (June 22, 1911).

replaced by an issue featuring a profile of the king.

July 1: The US Post Office Department introduced an indemnity of up to $25 on registered third and fourth-class mail.

July 16: The first passenger flight of the Zeppelin LZ-10 *Schwaben* took place.

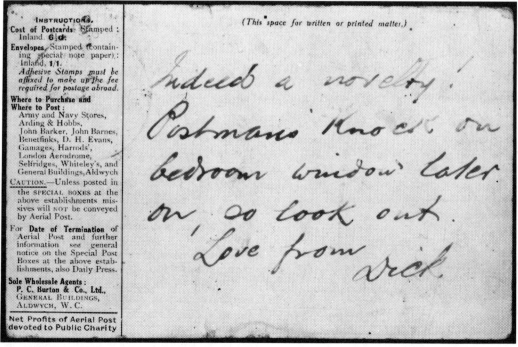

The front and back of a postcard carried on the British "Coronation Aerial Post" from Hendon (London) to Windsor (Sept. 9, 1911).

July 19: The Zeppelin LZ-10 *Schwaben* made a flight over Austria. Covers from this flight are franked with Austrian stamps.

September: The Cherifien Administration of Posts, Telegraphs, and Telephones formed in Morocco under French guidance. The administration began issuing stamps in May 1912.

Sept. 1: Until this date, the colonies of Cape of Good Hope, Natal, Transvaal, and Orange River Colony, which had merged to form the Union of South Africa on May 31, 1910, retained their own postal regulations. Henceforward, a central Postal Department headquartered at Pretoria, the administrative capital of South Africa, regulated postal affairs.

Sept. 2: Robert Svendsen carried Europe's first experimental airplane mail in Denmark. The flight covered about 10 miles from the city of Middlefart, on the island of Fyn, across a body of water to the town of Frederica. It is reported that about 150 postcards printed by a newspaper and showing the aircraft, were carried to Frederica. About 80 flew on the return flight. The pilot signed the cards. This mail was not officially sanctioned and the cards were franked with regular Danish stamps. They were placed in the mail at the destination and bear no special markings.

Sept. 9: The first flight of the first official British airplane mail service, the Coronation Aerial Post between Hendon (London) and Windsor, took place. Special cards and envelopes were used. They bear a cachet showing an aircraft over Windsor Castle. The flights continued until Sept. 26.

Rodger's "Vin Fiz" label (Sept. 17, 1911).

Sept. 17: Calbraith Perry Rodgers left Sheepshead Bay, Long Island, on a transcontinental flight. He flew a Wright aircraft and had 12 major crashes during the 84-day flight. Although the US Post Office Department played no part in the flight, Rodgers did carry mail between some stops. In addition to US postage, the mail bore a 25c label, named the Vin Fiz label for the soft drink company that sponsored the flight. "Vin Fiz" was one of its products.

Sept. 23: The first official US airplane mail was carried by Earle L. Ovington at the International Aviation Tournament at Garden City, N.Y. He carried 640 letters and 1,280 postcards. The flights continued until Sept. 30, although no mail was carried on Sept. 29. Planes carried the mail about three miles to the Mineola Post Office where it was dropped from the aircraft in flight. The mail received a special cancel and a one-line cachet reading "AERIAL SPECIAL DISPATCH."

Sept. 26: The Coronation Aerial Post made its last flight between London and Windsor, England. (See Sept. 9, 1911).

Sept. 30: The final flight was made carrying mail at Garden City, N.Y. (See Sept. 23, 1911).

October: Greece issued stamps for the Aegean island of Icaria.

October: The Solomon Islands joined the Universal Postal Union.

Oct. 2: The first air mail flight took place in Norway when Baron Cederstrom dropped copies of a newspaper in addressed wrappers over the airfield at Trondheim with a request that finders deposit them in the nearest letter box. No further air mail flights are recorded in Norway until 1920.

Oct. 4: Portugal issued its first postal tax stamp.

Oct. 4: The first mail carried by airplane west of the Mississippi River was flown from Kinloch

Field to Fairgrounds Park, St. Louis by Walter Richard Brookins. A special cancel was used. Brookins had been the first American student pilot of the Wright brothers in 1910. When he was 22, in 1910, he had set an altitude record of 6,259 feet over Atlantic City, N.J.

Oct. 8: Hugh Robinson flew mail in his hydroplane (seaplane) over and under all the bridges across the Mississippi River at St. Louis, Mo. A special four-line postal marking reading "HYDRO-AEROPLANE/ MAIL SERVICE/ ST. LOUIS, MO./ OCT 7. 1911" was applied to the items of mail.

Oct. 11: An official test of the Pitney postage meter was held in Washington, D.C.

Oct. 13: On this date and on Oct. 14, an experimental flight carried postcards from Freshfield to Southport, England.

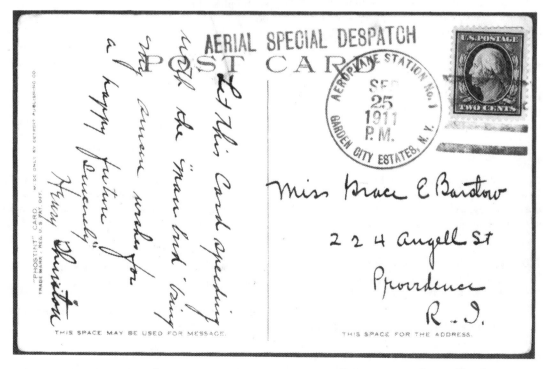

A postcard carried by Earle L. Ovington at the International Aviation Tournament, Garden City, N.Y. The stamp pictures the Bleriot aircraft similar to that used by Ovington. It is a British-built flying replica (Sept. 23, 1911).

Oct. 17: Hugh Robinson left Minneapolis, Minn., flying his hydroplane (seaplane) down the Mississippi River to New Orleans. However, he ran out of money Oct. 21 at Rock Island, Ill. and terminated the attempt. Mail had been delivered and picked up at his various stops. The mail carried bears a manuscript notation.

Oct. 17: The first aerial parcel post was flown in England when parcels containing boots were delivered by air by a Northampton firm to Hendon Aerodrome, near London. Each order included a souvenir certificate stating that the order was delivered by air.

Oct. 21: Famous US pilot Lincoln Beachey made his first air mail flight at Rochester, N.Y., during an aviation meet. He flew about 15,000 pieces of mail two miles during two flights from Crittenden Park to Genessee Valley Park. The mail received a special cancel.

Nov. 3: Clifford Turpin carried mail Nov. 3-5 at an "Aero Military Tournament" at Louisville, Ky. It received a special cancel.

Nov. 6: At an air meet held Nov. 5-6 at Fort Smith, Ark., Lincoln Beachey and Beckwith Havens carried mail by airplane from the airfield and dropped it at the Federal Building. A special cancel was used.

Nov. 16: Members of the Curtiss Flying School, among whom was Lincoln Beachey, flew mail from the postal station to a post office during a Nov. 16-18 air meet at Atlanta, Ga. A special cancel was used.

Nov. 25: Beckwith Havens flew mail on Nov. 25 and Nov. 28 at an aviation meet at Savannah, Ga. The mail received a special cancel.

Dec. 1: The US Post Office Department issued a 10c registration stamp, but since regular postage stamps could also be used to pay the registration fee, the special stamp was not widely used. On May 5, 1913, the department ordered discontinuance when existing stocks were used. The stamp could have been

**The US 10c
registration stamp.**

properly used up to March 31, 1913, when the rate changed, according to Markovits.

Dec. 12: Mail was flown at an aviation meet held Dec. 12-13 at Columbus, Ga. A special cancel was used.

Dec. 27: The first mail flight took place in South Africa. Several flights were made beginning on this date between Kenilworth and Muizenburg. Special cards were sold at 1/- each plus ½d domestic and 1d overseas postage.

Dec. 28: Thornwall Andrews flew mail at an aviation meet at Albany, Ga. It received a special cancelation.

1912

The newly formed Republic of China issued stamps. The first stamps were overprints on issues of the Imperial Chinese Post.

Stamps of Kedah were used beginning this year in the Malayan state of Perlis until replaced by stamps of the World War II Japanese occupation in 1942.

Italy issued stamps for its new colony of Libya. They took the form of Italian stamps overprinted "Libia."

Greece released the first stamps for the Aegean island of Lemnos.

Jan. 2: Walter Brookins piloted a plane carrying mail at an aviation meet at Wilmington, N.C. The mail received a special cancelation. The flight had been scheduled for Jan. 1, but was delayed by bad weather.

Jan. 6: New Mexico became the 47th state in the United States.

Jan. 20: Glenn L. Martin flew the first mail on the opening day of the Dominguez Field Aviation Meet near Los Angeles. He flew the mail to the Compton Post Office, which sent it by train to Los Angeles. The mail was flown twice a day during the nine-day event.

Jan. 24: The General Post Office, London, began to use a franking device. It had been invented by F. Wilkinson and made by Automatic Stamp Sealing Machines Ltd. The post office took the machine out of service on Aug. 31, 1912.

Jan. 29: The Principality of Liechtenstein released its first stamps.

Feb. 14: Arizona entered the United States as the 48th state.

Feb. 17: Farnum T. Fish flew mail at an aviation meet held Feb. 17-25 at Oakland, Calif. Mail was flown on each day of the meet except Feb. 19-21. A special cancelation was used.

Feb. 18: An aircraft built by Hans Grade made a series of mail-carrying flights from the German town of Bork and nearby communities. Various semi-official stamps were used during the period of the flights, which lasted until June 25, 1913.

March 2: Glenn L. Martin and Phil Parmalee flew mail at a March 2-3 aviation meet held at Sacramento, Calif. A special cancelation was used.

March 4: The Zeppelin LZ-11 *Viktoria Louise* made its first passenger flight. It made more than 1,000 additional flights before Oct. 8, 1915, when it was wrecked.

March 12: Air mail was carried at an aviation meet held March 12-16 at Hot Springs, Ark. Only two pieces of the specially canceled mail are known.

March 12: Paul Studensky flew mail 15 miles from an aviation meet at Galveston, Texas, to La Marque and returned to the airfield. The mail received a special cancelation.

March 24: A special marking was applied to mail to be carried at a Houston, Texas aviation meet. However, the mail was not flown.

March 31: The last horse-drawn mailcoach route in Denmark was ended.

April 6: One bag of mail was flown from an aviation meet at San Diego, Calif., to a beach and dropped. A seaplane picked up the mail there and flew it to Point Loma. The bag of mail was then taken to a post office.

April 10: An experimental flight taking only 91 minutes to make a 90-mile flight from New Orleans, La., to Baton Rouge carried mail. The planned return flight was canceled because of damage to the aircraft while landing at Baton Rouge. The mail received a special cancel reading "US AERIAL MAIL SERVICE."

April 14: When the White Star Line's *Titanic* sank on her maiden voyage, five mail sorters on board, two British and three American, were lost. A total of 3,366 bags of letter mail and much parcel mail was also lost.

April 21: Specially canceled mail was flown at an aviation meet in Eureka, Calif.

May: The Cherifien Administration of Posts, Telegraphs, and Telephones, which had been formed in Morocco in September 1911 issued adhesive postage stamps.

May 9: During the week beginning May 9, the United States made test mailings using the Pitney postage meter and the idea of a detachable meter component was conceived.

May 15: Only four postcards are known of about 1,500 carried by an airplane piloted by Lincoln Beachey at an aviation meet held May 15-16 at Marietta, Ohio.

May 18: Mail was prepared but not flown at an Altoona, Pa. aviation meet. Pilot Walter Brookins canceled the flight when crowds could not be cleared from the field.

May 25: An experimental flight flew mail carried from Bath, England, to Hendon, near London. A special cachet was applied and cards were postmarked at Hendon on May 28.

May 30: At Salem Depot, N.H., mail was to have been officially flown during an aviation meet. Bad weather forced pilot Lincoln Beachey to cancel the flight.

May 30: Specially canceled mail was flown at an aviation meet held at the fairgrounds in Milwaukee, Wis.

May 30: An aviation meet at Cliftondale, Mass., included the flying of mail. It bears a special cancel reading "AERO/ POSTAL Sta./ SAUGUS/ Mass." in a circle.

May 30: At a tri-city aviation meet held May 30-June 2 in the Cicero-Elmhurst-Wheaton, Ill. area, pilots flew mail to the the three cities. The mail received an "AERIAL MAIL" marking.

June: During June and August, the *Daily Mail* newspaper sponsored "around Britain flights" at various points on the British coast. Pictorial postcards were flown and a commemorative cachet was applied.

June 1: A flight between Eslof and Akarp carried the first mail flown in Sweden.

June 2: A roundtrip flight between Shibaura (Tokyo) and Yokohama harbor transported the first air mail in Japan.

June 3: Mail bearing the marking "U.S. OFFICIAL/ AERIAL/ MAIL STAMP" was to have been carried at a June 3-9 aviation meet at Lexington, Ky.

June 6: A special cancel depicting an aircraft

This card was carried by the Zeppelin LZ-10 *Schwaben* during the *Gelber Hund* flights to various Rhine and Main river cities (June 10, 1912).

had been applied to mail carried at an aviation meet held June 6-8 at Evansville, Ind.

June 6: Lima, Ohio, was the site of a June 6-8 aviation meet at which specially postmarked mail was carried.

June 7: Six unflown postcards are all that are known to have survived from a June 7-8 aviation meet held at Mansfield, Ohio.

June 10: The Zeppelin LZ-10 *Schwaben* made flights to various cities on the Rhine and Main rivers in conjunction with the airplane *Gelber Hund,* to raise money for charity. Special cards were printed and sold and franked with stamps produced for the flights. The aircraft carried the mail between the cities of Darmstadt, Frankfurt, Mainz, Offenbach, and Worms.

June 27: Portsmouth, Ohio, was the site of a June 27-28 aviation meet at which mail was specially canceled and flown.

June 28: The Zeppelin LZ-10 *Schwaben* crashed during a flight. Mail had been dropped at Coblenz, Germany, before the crash.

June 30: Lincoln Beachey, Glenn L. Martin, Archie Freeman, and Blanche Scott performed at an aviation meet held at Squantum, Mass. Specially canceled mail had been authorized by the US Post Office to be carried to New York, but was not flown.

July: During July and August a waterplane (seaplane) tour was sponsored in Britain by the *Daily Mail* newspaper. Cards flown show pilot Henry Farman and his aircraft. The postmaster general prohibited the carrying of the cards, but permitted those already accepted and postmarked to be placed in the British mailstream.

July: The Malayan state of Kedah issued stamps.

July 4: Mail was flown on the second day of an aviation meet held July 3-4 at Bedford, Ind.

Two types of two-line cachets were applied to mail.

July 4: An aircraft carried specially marked mail at a hydroplane (seaplane) meet held at a South Amboy-Perth Amboy, N.J.

July 12: Specially canceled mail was flown at a July 12-13 aviation meet at Hamilton, Ohio.

July 17: At an aviation meet at Benton Harbor, Mich., an airplane flew specially-canceled mail on July 17-18.

July 19: At an aviation meet July 19-22 at Cincinnati, Ohio, specially cacheted mail was flown.

July 20: Dubuque, Iowa, was the site of a July 20-21 aviation meet at which mail was flown. It received a commemorative cachet.

July 21: Bad weather prevented mail from being flown at a Connersville-Rushville, Ind., aviation meet July 21-29. An oval cachet had been prepared.

July 22: No special marking was applied to mail flown at a July 22-27 aviation meet held at Providence, Ky., although the flights had been officially authorized by the US Post Office.

July 30: Japan issued a series of postage stamps known as the Tazawa Series. Named for their designer, Masakoto Tazawa, an official of Japan's Printing Bureau, the occasion marked the death of the Emperor Meiji and the succession of the Emperor Taisho. The series was in use until 1937.

Aug. 3: The Zeppelin LZ-13 *Hansa* made its first passenger flight. Between this date and July 1914, it made a number of mail-carrying flights. Various handstamps were applied to mail carried.

Aug. 3: An aviation meet at Hohokus, N.J., featured flown mail. It received a special cancelation.

Aug. 3: Planes flew mail between the New Jersey cities of Ocean City and Stone Harbor during an Aug. 3-10 aviation meet.

Aug. 6: An aviation meet at which mail was carried took place Aug. 6-8 at Fort Recovery, Ohio. A special cancel was applied.

Aug. 7: The first motor vehicle used in the Rural Free Delivery (RFD) system ran in Bennington County, Vt., on this date.

Aug. 10: The first air mail was flown in the Pacific Northwest, when a plane carried it seven miles from Portland, Ore. to Vancouver, Wash. A special cancelation was applied. Flights took place on both Aug. 10-11.

Aug. 20: A Rockport, Ind., aviation meet that took place Aug. 20-23 included the flying of mail.

Aug. 23: Mail was carried on Aug. 23-24 during an aviation meet held at Plainfield, N.J. A special cancel was used.

Aug. 24: Alaska became a territory of the United States.

Aug. 25: The first mail was carried by air in Uruguay.

Aug. 28: A special cancel featuring an aircraft was placed on mail flown at an aviation meet Aug. 28-31 at Boonville, Ind.

Sept. 6: Lincoln Beachey flew mail during an aviation meet held Sept. 6-7 at Cedar Falls, Iowa. A special cachet was applied.

Sept. 9: During the Gordon Bennett International Balloon Races and aviation meet, held Sept. 9-15 at Cicero, Ill., mail was flown from the flying field to Chicago.

Sept. 10: A plane carried the first air mail flown in Tennessee. The flight took place during an aviation meet held Sept. 10-12 at Columbia. A special cancel was used.

Sept. 16: An aviation meet took place Sept. 16-22 at Chicago. A number of pilots carried mail each day except Sept. 18. The mail received a special cancel.

Sept. 21: Glen Head, Long Island, N.Y., was the site of demonstration flights made on this and other dates during August, September, and October by Charles Wald of the Wright Company. While the flights showed off the company's standard aircraft fitted with pontoons, the one on this date carried mail to New Rochelle. The mail received a special cachet. Only one cover is known.

Sept. 26: Mail was carried on a flight during an aviation meet Sept. 25-26 at Bluffton, Ind. A special cachet was applied.

Sept. 26: Horace Kearney carried air mail during a Sept. 26-28 aviation meet at McLeansboro, Ill.

Sept. 28: An air mail flight was made between Puyallup, Wash., and Tacoma, Wash. under the name "Crawford's Puget Sound Aerial Mail."

Oct. 4: At the Oct. 4-12 Springfield-Williamsville, Ill. aviation meet, airplanes carried mail on some days. A special cancelation was used.

Oct. 12: Only two covers are known from a mail flight made at Birmingham, Ala., during an aviation meet. The aircraft crashed shortly after takeoff, killing the pilot, Joseph Stevenson.

Oct. 12: Pennsylvania's first air mail flight took place during an aviation meet at Lock Haven, Pa. An oval cachet reading "U.S. Official Aerial Mail Stamp 1912" was applied.

Oct. 12: Between this date and Nov. 7, 1912, the German Zeppelin LZ-11 *Viktoria Louise* made flights between Frankfurt and Wiesbaden to raise money for the National Aviation Fund. Special cards were produced and carried on the flights.

Oct. 31: An aviation meet held Oct. 31-Nov. 2 at Cuthbert, Ga., featured the flying of mail.

November: Canada issued 1c and 2c stamps in the Admiral series in coil form. These were Canada's first official coil stamps.

November: Greece issued stamps for the Aegean islands of Metelin (Mytilene) and Samos.

Nov. 24: Henry Crawford flew 47 postcards at an aviation meet at San Francisco. He landed at the Presidio, near the Golden Gate.

Nov. 27: The US Post Office Department issued Parcel Post postage due labels. They had been approved by Congress on Aug. 24, 1912.

December: The Tibetan government issued its first specially printed stamps. They were placed on sale only at Lhasa, and were not available at other post offices until 1913. They consisted of five denominations in sheetlets of 12 stamps. They are primitive in production and feature the Tibetan Lion. They are imperforate and issued without gum. The stamps were used until 1933 and were valid only within Tibet. Mail going out of the country went mostly by way of India and was franked with Indian stamps. Some printings of this first issue were made using European enamel paint!

Dec. 14: The Republic of China issued its first specially-printed stamps. Preceding issues earlier in 1912 had been overprints on issues of the Imperial Chinese Post. The new stamps feature a portrait of Dr. Sun Yat-sen.

Dec. 16: The first postage stamp depicting an airplane went on sale. This was the 20c denomination in the US Parcel Post series. Although the aircraft shown appears to be a Wright model, the picture varies considerably from any known Wright aircraft.

Dec. 31: The registration service for fourth-class mail was withdrawn upon the introduction of an insurance service.

1913

Belgium issued the world's first air mail

This photograph represents the closest-appearing Wright aircraft to that seen on the 20c US Parcel Post stamp. There are differences in detail, but it is possible that the photograph influenced the stamp designer (Dec. 16, 1912).

stamped envelope, according to Mackay. It is inscribed "POSTE AERIENNE."

Greece issued stamps overprinted with a Greek inscription for use in the town of Cavalla when it was occupied. It had previously been Turkish.

The Indian feudatory state of Orchha released stamps.

The united colony of Trinidad and Tobago placed its stamps on sale.

Stamps are believed to have been issued by an autonomous government in Western Thrace following the withdrawal of Bulgarian forces and prior to the occupation by Greece.

Tete, a district of Portuguese Mozambique, issued stamps.

A district of Portuguese Mozambique, Quelimane, issued stamps. Gibbons gives the issue date as 1914.

Jan. 1: The United States released the Panama-Pacific Exposition issue. It comprised four stamps, although the 10c value comes in two shade varieties. The stamps show Vasco Nunez de Balboa (1c), the Pedro Miguel Locks on the Panama Canal (2c), the "Golden Gate" to San Francisco Bay (5c), and the discovery of San Francisco Bay (10c).

Australia's first postage stamp.

Jan. 1: The first adhesive postage stamp bearing the name of the Commonwealth of Australia, which had been formed on Jan. 1, 1901, was officially issued. The Com-

monwealth had issued postage due labels for all states except Victoria in July 1902 and a postal card had been released in April 1911. The first Commonwealth stamp was a 1d denomination and because Jan. 1 was a holiday, Jan. 2 was the actual first day of use. The stamp was the first in a long series in the map and kangaroo design. Other denominations appeared during 1913.

Jan. 1: A law, approved by the US Congress on Aug. 24, 1912, establishing a domestic parcel post service took effect. The weight limit was 11 pounds, but within a year this was increased to 50 pounds for local parcels and 20 pounds for long-distance service. A system of eight zones governed the rates charged.

Jan. 1: The US Post Office Department began the use of a series of parcel post stamps authorized by Congress on Aug. 24, 1912. It has been claimed that confusion was caused by all stamps being of the same color. However, Gobie states that more problems were likely caused because the stamps came in the unusual format of 45 to the pane and thus created accounting problems for clerks more accustomed to stamps in panes of 50 or 100. The problems certainly indicated that the new system had not been well planned.

By July 1, 1913, the stamps had been declared valid for all postal purposes in an attempt to use up stocks as quickly as possible. Their subsequent use on letters and postcards continues to puzzle new collectors and remains as a mute witness to a good idea poorly executed. In addition to the 12 stamps, five parcel post postage due labels were also issued.

Jan. 13: Harry M. Jones left Boston, Mass., carrying parcel post and first-class mail destined for New York on the first official parcel post flight in the United States. Jones had been sworn in as the first US Aerial Parcel Post Carrier. The flight was a slow one and it was March 4 before Jones crashed at Oakhurst, N.Y., not far from his Governor's Island destination.

Feb. 11: During Aviation Week at Gosforth, near Newcastle, England, parcels of tobacco were flown to nearby towns. A green adhesive label showing a Bleriot aircraft was placed on

On Jan. 1, 1913, the US Post Office Department began to use this set of 12 parcel post stamps. They are all in the same red color and were produced in sheets of 45 stamps. Thus they were confusing to use and accounting was more difficult than the usual 50 or 100-stamp panes. By July 1913, it was decided to use them for general postage in an attempt to use up the stocks. No more were issued.

Above is the label used on shipments of tobacco that were flown from Gosforth Park racecourse during an aviation meet (Feb. 11, 1913), while at top right is a Swiss stamp depicting Oscar Bider (March 30, 1913), and the third stamp is an Italian pneumatic post stamp (April 1913).

the packages and was canceled at Gosforth Park, a racecourse that was the site of the event.

Feb. 13: British stamp dealer Edward Stanley Gibbons died at his home in Baker Street, London.

March 5: President Woodrow Wilson appointed Albert S. Burleson as US postmaster general, succeeding Frank H. Hitchcock.

March 9: Some 5,000 postcards were flown on the first airplane mail flight in Switzerland. The flight was from Basel to Liestal. Some sources note the pilot as being Oscar Bider, the famous Swiss aviator, but the *American Air Mail Catalogue* states only that the pilot was "a military aviator." A special semi-official air mail stamp was placed on the mail carried in addition to regular Swiss stamps, raised money for a fund to advance Swiss aviation.

March 29: A seaplane attempted an air mail flight from Corpus Christi, Texas, to Port Aransas, Texas. However, the aircraft only completed three of its 20-mile flight, when a broken propeller forced it down.

March 30: Pilot Oscar Bider made a mail-carrying flight in Switzerland from Berne to Burgdorf and back. Special semi-official stamps were used in addition to regular Swiss postage stamps. The money thus raised was devoted to the advancement of Swiss aviation. Different stamps were used for each flight. About 13,000 were used from Berne and some 2,760 were applied at Burgdorf.

April: The first stamp specifically intended to frank mail carried by a pneumatic mail service was issued by Italy. Although a number of cities used the pneumatic tube systems, Italy is the only country to issue adhesive postage stamps. Some other countries used special postal stationery items.

April 13: Demonstration air mail flights took place at La Paz, Bolivia, from April 13-15.

April 19: At Sacramento, Calif., an aviation meet held April 19-20 included the flying of mail that had a special cancelation.

May: The first air mail was flown in Belgium in conjunction with an exposition at Ghent.

May: Greece issued stamps for the Aegean island of Chios.

May 4: The Zeppelin LZ-17 *Sachsen* made its first passenger flight. It made mail-carrying flights until August 1914.

May 17: At an aviation meet held May 17-18 at Santa Rosa, Calif. an airplane flew mail.

May 25: The Mexican state of Sonora issued stamps.

May 29: US Post Office Department executive order H7136 discontinued the use of the 10c registration stamps that had been issued Dec. 1, 1911. Markovits quotes the order as stating "...the slight advantage of the distinctive registry stamp was outweighed by the confusion arising from its attempted use for prepayment of postage by persons unfamiliar with its true function." However, existing stocks were allowed to be used up.

June 16: Albania issued its first stamps. They were stamps of Turkey overprinted with a double-headed eagle device.

Britain's Sea Horse design.

June 30: The first stamp in Great Britain's handsome and popular Sea Horse design was issued. The series remained in use until replaced by the King George VI high values. Denominations were 2/6, 5/-, 10/-, and £1.

July: The US Post Office Department issued its only Official postal card. Used for transmitting monthly reports of business transacted at post offices in the Postal Savings System, the card was in use only for a brief period.

July 1: A US cash-on-delivery (COD) system whereby buyers of merchandise by mail paid for it at the time the post office delivered it, was introduced.

July 1: US parcel post stamps became valid for any postal purpose. The parcel post stamps had not proven successful and it was intended that stocks should be used up as quickly as possible.

July 1: The US Post Office Department first authorized payment for precancel devices. Previously, they had been supplied by permit holders or postmasters "at no cost to the department," according to correspondence from James Kingman. At the same time, the Post Office allowed contractors to make precancel devices for local post offices, an offer that resulted in thousands of precancel types from both large electroplates and small rubber handstamp devices.

July 18: Greece issued stamps for the city of Dedeagh (now Alexandroupolis).

August: Stamps of Greece are believed to have been overprinted for use in Thrace prior to its occupation by Greek forces.

Sept. 2: Rutland, Vt., was the site of an aviation meet at which mail was flown. During a flight on this date, the aircraft crashed, killing pilot George Schmitt and seriously injuring a passenger. A four-line cachet was applied to mail.

Sept. 4: At an aviation meet held Sept. 4-6 at McLeansboro, Ill., mail with a special cancel was flown about five miles on each day.

Sept. 9: "MAILED VIA AIRSHIP" is the cachet applied to mail flown Sept. 10-11 by airplane at an aviation meet held Sept. 9-11 at Carmi, Ill.

Sept. 15: Bad weather prevented authorized air mail flights from taking place Sept. 15-20 at the Hicksville, Ohio aviation meet.

Sept. 23: At the Montana State Fair, Katherine Stinson became the first woman to officially carry air mail. She had been sworn in as a carrier by the Helena postmaster the day before. She flew the mail and dropped it at the fairgrounds postal station. During the fair she carried about 1,335 souvenir postcards and letters.

Oct. 4: An experimental air mail flight was attempted from Natrona, Pa. to Pittsburgh. The flight was not made, but the mail was flown around the airfield and received a special cachet.

Oct. 17: Mail flown at an aviation meet held at Woodstock, Va., received a special cachet. Although only about 10 pieces were carried, it represents the first mail flown in the state of Virginia.

Oct. 27: An international philatelic exhibition in New York City began on this date and continued to Nov. 1.

Nov. 20: Hungary issued its first semi-postal stamps. The surtax went to aid flood victims.

Dec. 1: Switzerland issued the first semi-postal stamp in its Pro Juventute series. The inscription means "for the young" and the surtax is devoted to child welfare and other charitable work connected with the young. With the exception of 1914, they have been an annual issue since then.

1914

Jan. 1: The Crown Colony of Nigeria was formed from the former protectorates of Northern and Southern Nigeria. The new postal entity issued stamps, which were in the key type design common to many of the British colonies.

Jan. 4: A French pilot, Marc Pourpe, took off from Heliopolis, near Cairo, Egypt, for Khartoum, Sudan, on the first air mail flight in Egypt. Carrying one letter, he arrived on Jan. 12. Several letters were carried on the return flight, which he completed on Feb. 3. The aircraft was a Morane Saulnier with a Gnome 50 hp engine. Jean Gravelat notes that a total of 37 pieces of mail have been recorded as flown. Some souvenir postcards had been taken up at an aviation meeting at Heliopolis on Feb. 6-13 (see Feb. 6, 1910).

Jan. 18: Tom Gunn flew the first mail in Hawaii while on a demonstration flight over the island of Kauai. Only one cover is known to have survived, according to the *American Air Mail Catalogue*.

Jan. 28: Several Chicago businesses began test mailings using the Pitney postage meter device. The tests lasted until May 28.

Marc Pourpe lands at Khartoum, after a flight from Cairo, Egypt. He was carrying one letter, but several were flown on the return flight (Jan. 4, 1914).

February: Prior to Greek occupation, Epirus issued stamps.

Feb. 17: The first mail-carrying flight along the Suez Canal was made from Suez to Port Said. The pilot, Marc Pourpe, made a flight to the Sudan the previous month (see Jan. 4, 1914).

Feb. 24: An attempted flight by Jaime Gonzalez from Cienfuegos to Havana, Cuba, carried mail, but the aircraft crashed on takeoff and the mail was forwarded by regular means, according to the *American Air Mail Catalogue*.

March 1: What was then the Republic of China became a member of the Universal Postal Union. It is now the People's Republic of China.

March 31: The German state of Bavaria began to issue the world's first photogravure-printed stamps. The Stanley Gibbons catalog notes that these stamps run badly in water. The portrait depicted is that of the Bavarian monarch, Ludwig III.

The photogravure process involves the creation of a printing cylinder using photographic methods where a series of dots of varying depth are chemically etched. Other than the photographic printing cylinder preparation, the printing method is similar to intaglio printing (see Printing, intaglio).

April 1: Souvenir cards bearing an air mail vignette were carried by aircraft participating in the Monaco Aerial Rally.

April 20: Great Britain released its first postage due labels.

May 3: A post office under the authority of the US Post Office Department operated from May 3 to Nov. 3 in Vera Cruz, Mexico, during the period of occupation by US Marines.

May 18: Ernest Moss developed a multi-denominational postage meter which was installed in the Christchurch, New Zealand, Post Office for a trial that lasted until May 27.

May 30: Between May 30 and Sept. 7, experimental air mail flights made by a seaplane flown by Alfred Engle took place over Chautauqua Lake, N.Y. The flights served several communities and the flown mail bears a special cachet.

June 28: During the Bishop, Inyo, Mono, and Alpine Counties Aviation Week in California June 28-July 2, mail was flown. On June 23, pilot Silas Christofferson had set a US altitude record of 15,728 feet while flying over Mount Whitney.

June 30: The United States issued its first stamp printed by a rotary press. This press was

Three designs of Bavaria's 1914 definitive series that was the world's first photogravure-printed issue (March 31, 1914).

A souvenir card carried by one of the competing aircraft (April 1, 1914).

the Stickney press, developed by Benjamin Stickney of the Bureau of Engraving and Printing. The stamp was an imperforated 2c denomination in the Washington Head design.

July 16: The first air mail was flown in Australia between Melbourne and Sydney.

July 22: Spanish stamps overprinted "MARRUECOS," were issued for use in Spanish Morocco. Stamps had been used at Spanish post offices in the area. Those were Spanish stamps bearing the overprint "CORREO ESPANOL/ MARRUECOS."

Aug. 1: The French protectorate of Morocco issued stamps. They were French stamps overprinted "Protectorat Francais."

Aug. 11: France issued its first semi-postal stamp. It features the well-known Sower design and has a denomination of 10c+5c, with the surtax going to the Red Cross.

Sept. 3: When New Zealand forces occupied German Samoa at the beginning of World War I, they overprinted the German colonial stamps with "G.R.I." and surcharged them in sterling denominations.

Sept. 17: Mail was flown during a Sept. 17-18 aviation meet at Clayton, N.M.

Sept. 18: Trinidad issued a Red Cross seal that was permitted to prepay postage of ½d for one day.

Sept. 28: The Anglo-French occupation forces in the ex-German colony of Togo issued stamps. Robson Lowe notes the date as Oct. 1, 1914.

Sept. 29: New Zealand overprinted its stamps for use in Samoa, then under New Zealand military control.

October: Monaco issued its first semi-postal stamp.

Oct. 4: Austria issued its first semi-postal stamps.

Oct. 6: The first mail was flown from the beseiged fortress of Przemysl by the Austrian defenders during World War I.

A German colonial registration label overprinted "G.R.I." and surcharged is reproduced on this 1973 stamp of Papua New Guinea.

Oct. 17: Australian forces occupying the former German New Guinea issued stamps. These consisted of German colonies issues overprinted "G.R.I." and surcharged in sterling currency. Registration labels and German colonial stamps of the Marshall Islands were similarly treated.

Oct. 17: William C. Robinson left Des Moines, Iowa, flying a monoplane he had designed and completed a 370-mile nonstop flight towards Chicago in four hours, 44 minutes. Three days later, he flew on to Chicago. A special cachet was applied to mail.

Nov. 3: Katherine Stinson flew mail at the Nov. 3-8 Troy, Ala., aviation meet.

1915

By this year, a total of 56,571 miles of pneumatic tube lines in the United States moved mail between post offices and railroad stations. Cities with such services were Boston, Brooklyn, New York, Philadelphia, Chicago, and St. Louis. The last pneumatic tube service operated in New York until Dec. 31, 1953.

Ubangi-Shari-Chad, a group of central African French colonies, issued stamps, according to Scott. The stamps are those of Middle Congo overprinted "OUBANGUI-CHARI-TCHAD." Gibbons gives the year of issue as 1916.

January: The British occupiers of Mafia Island, off the coast of former German East Africa, placed stamps on sale.

February: The French colony of Madagascar issued its first semi-postal stamps.

February: The French protectorate of Tunisia issued its first semi-postal stamps.

Feb. 20: Pilot Gustave Strohmer flew from Tacoma, Wash., to Seattle, Wash., carrying actress Jane O'Roark. She had been designated as the mail carrier by the Post Office and was in charge of the small amount of mail carried. The 20-mile flight took 27 minutes. A three-line cachet was applied to the mail.

March 15: Australian stamps overprinted "N.W. Pacific Islands" were placed on sale at Rabaul, following occupation by Australian forces of former German territory in and around New Guinea during World War I. Con-

sidering their overprinted inscription, the stamps can be rather misleading, since the area of their use did not correspond. The stamps had been intended for use in other ex-German areas, but the Japanese had taken them and the stamps were used without being amended. They remained in use until replaced by special stamps in 1925. They had replaced the German colonial issues overprinted "G.R.I." used when the area was first taken.

April 28: Austria issued stamps for use by Austro-Hungarian military authorities in occupied areas during World War I.

May: Stamps of the Gold Coast were overprinted for use in the captured German colony of Togo.

May: The French Caribbean island of Guadeloupe issued its first semi-postal stamps.

May 15: Semi-postal stamps were issued for the French island of Martinique.

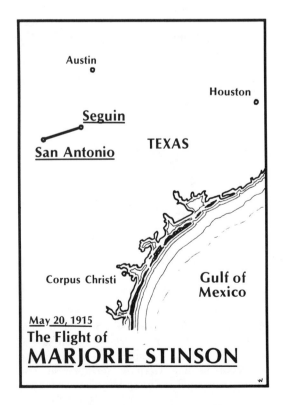

Austin

Houston

Seguin

San Antonio

TEXAS

Corpus Christi

Gulf of Mexico

May 20, 1915
The Flight of
MARJORIE STINSON

May 20: Marjorie Stinson, sister of Katherine Stinson, made an experimental air mail flight between Seguin, Texas, and San Antonio, Texas. A special cancelation was used. Only one cover is known.

June 10: The Netherlands Indies issued its first semi-postal stamps. The surtax went to the Red Cross.

June 30: After this date, all British Queen Victorian stamps were no longer valid for postage, although Robson Lowe reports that the £5 denomination was on sale at a London post office as late as 1921.

July: Shortly after the outbreak of World War I in 1914, a German ship was captured bearing a consignment of stamps for German Cameroon. These were overprinted "C.E.F." (Cameroon Expeditionary Force) and placed on sale in the British-occupied colony during July 1915.

July 1: San Marino became a member of the Universal Postal Union.

July 9: The Germans surrendered German South West Africa to Union of South Africa forces. Until Jan. 1, 1923, the territory used South African stamps. On that date, overprinted stamps were placed in use.

July 22: Sir Sandford Fleming died. The legacy he left Canada included the transcontinental railroad, the system of time zones around the world, and Canada's first adhesive postage stamp, the 3d "Beaver."

Aug. 7: Port Huron, Mich., was the site of the state's first air mail flight which took place at an aviation meet. A special cachet was applied to the small mail.

Aug. 14: A commemorative cachet was applied to mail flown Aug. 14-15 at a Rock Island, Ill., aviation meet.

Aug. 15: During the British occupation of Bushire, a town on the Iranian shore of the Persian Gulf, stamps were issued.

A stamp created for use during the British occupation of Bushire, Persia (Iran).

Sept. 6: Mail was flown during an aviation meet Sept. 6-14 at Detroit, Mich. It received a special cachet.

Sept. 13: At an aviation meet Sept. 13-17 at Milwaukee, Wis., mail was flown to a nearby post office. It received a special cancelation.

Sept. 16: Mexico resumed stamp issues following the revolutionary period.

Sept. 21: Mail was flown during a Sept. 21-24 aviation meet at Chippewa Falls, Wis. A three-line cachet was used.

Oct. 16: Persia (Iran) resumed control of the post office at Bushire following a brief British occupation.

November: Italy issued special delivery stamps for its colony of Libya.

Nov. 4: Katherine Stinson flew mail each day of a Nov. 4-6 aviation meet held at Tucson, Ariz. A special cancelation was used.

Nov. 15: Italy issued its first semi-postal stamps. The surtax went to the Red Cross.

1916

John Walter Scott died in New York. He has been called the father of United States philately.

The Malayan state of Johore became a member of the Universal Postal Union.

The Turks and Caicos Islands placed on sale the first of several War Tax stamps.

The Spanish northwest African colony of Cape Juby issued stamps.

An experimental US bureau precancel (January 1916).

During this year, the US Post Office Department made experiments to find out if the Bureau of Engraving and Printing could produce precanceled stamps at a cost less than the individual post offices could obtain them locally. Of the reporting cities, only Augusta, Maine; New Orleans, La.; and Springfield, Mass., were paying a price higher than the BEP quotation. Consequently, the BEP overprinted existing stamps for those cities. These are the forerunners of the 1923 so-called Bureau precancels (see May 3, 1923). Sources vary as to the date of these tests; some give 1916, while others state 1917. It seems likely that the experiment started in 1916 and the stamps may have been sent to the three cities through 1917.

Jan. 1: A special delivery service was inaugurated between Canada and the Bahamas. The Bahamas overprinted its regular 5d stamp with "SPECIAL/ DELIVERY" and handed a quantity of 600 to the Canadian postal authorities. Canada placed these stamps on sale at Ottawa, Toronto, Westmount, and Winnipeg for use on mail to the Bahamas on which special delivery service was desired. Canada terminated the arrangement after a short period. Robson Lowe gives the inaugural date as May 1, 1916.

Jan. 1: Brunei became a member of the Universal Postal Union.

A stamp used during the French mandate over the island of Rouad (Arwad).

Jan. 12: The first stamps were issued under the French mandate over the island of Rouad (Arwad), located off the coast of Syria. The stamps are those of France overprinted "ILE ROUAD."

Jan. 25: This is the intended issue date of a set of six stamps for the area of Mount Athos on the Chalkidiki Peninsula of Greece. The British considered occupying the holy community on the most easterly of the three-pronged peninsula. There are two unusual aspects of the stamps; they were produced aboard the British aircraft carrier HMS *Ark Royal* and the denominations were expressed in three currencies, British, Greek, and Russian. As the stamps were never issued, they must be regarded as "prepared for use, but not issued."

Jan. 27: Fanning Island was placed under the administration of the Gilbert and Ellice Islands. However, the New Zealand postal agency continued to operate until Feb. 13, 1939!

Feb. 28: Great Britain overprinted "Levant" on its stamps for use at the British Army Field Post Office at Salonica.

March 6: Austria issued stamps for its occupation of Serbia during World War I.

April 24: The Canal Zone Postal Service released its first stamped envelopes. They comprised 1c and 2c envelopes of Panama with the words "CANAL ZONE" added to the vignette die by the American Bank Note Co.

May 7: The first occupation stamps were issued for Long Island, an Aegean island occupied by British forces from May 7-26, 1916. Turkish revenue stamps were overprinted "G.R.I. POSTAGE" and surcharged in British currency, but it is the stamps made on a typewriter that are best known. Only a few hundred of these latter stamps were prepared.

May 26: British forces withdrew from Long Island, located in the Aegean. This brought to an end the provisional stamp issues. See May 7, 1916.

May 29: Portuguese forces occupying Kionga, an area formerly part of German East Africa, issued stamps.

June 23: The German submarine *Deutschland* left Heligoland carrying mail for the United States. It evaded the British blockade and arrived in Chesapeake Bay July 9. Two subsequent voyages were made and special postal markings were used on mail.

July: Local stamps bearing the name of Christmas Island (Pacific Ocean) and depicting the schooner *Ysabel May*, are said to have been issued at this time. However, James Kyle notes that the earliest covers known are dated early in 1918. The island later issued stamps in 1924, 1926, and 1934. According to Kyle, it is doubtful that much of the mail was non-philatelic.

July 3: Boise, Idaho, was the site of a mail flight during an air mail demonstration. An aircraft attempted a flight on July 4, but it crashed on takeoff and could not be repaired in time. Of the mail carried, only one example is known.

July 18: Mail was flown from Smithville, Mo., to Kansas City. Only one item is known from this flight.

August: The Sherifate of Mecca in Hejaz, later part of the Kingdom of Saudi Arabia, issued its first stamps.

Oct. 5: Mail was flown from West Branch, Mich., to a nearby post office. A special cancelation was used.

Oct. 13: An experimental air mail flight had been scheduled at Ithaca, N.Y. for this date, but bad weather delayed it until the next day. The pilot then dropped the mail into a wooded area and it was not found and postmarked until Oct. 16.

Stamp of Nauru (Oct. 23, 1916).

Oct. 23: British stamps overprinted "NAURU" were issued for the island of Nauru, which had been taken from the Germans by Australian forces during World War I.

Nov. 2: A "dawn to dusk" air mail flight from Chicago to New York began. Pilot Victor Carlstrom reached Hammondsport, N.Y., that evening and spent the night there. He flew to Governors Island in New York City the next morning. The flight was sponsored by the *New York Times*, which had special postcards prepared.

Dec. 21: Sweden issued its first semi-postal stamps.

1917

Stamps of Kenya overprinted "G.E.A." were used during the British occupation of the former German East Africa.

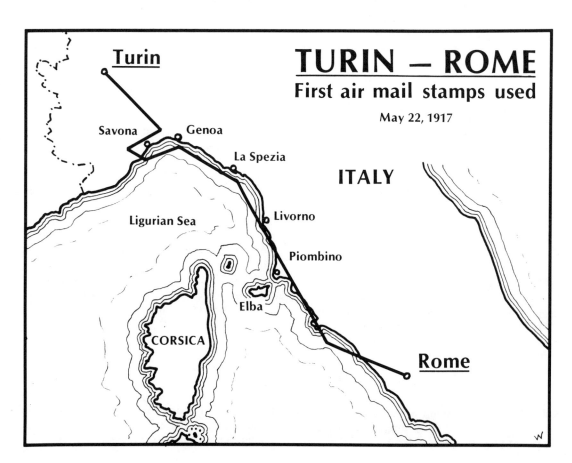

Turin

Savona
Genoa
La Spezia

ITALY

TURIN — ROME

First air mail stamps used

May 22, 1917

Ligurian Sea

Livorno

Piombino

Elba

CORSICA

Rome

"Lathework" began to appear on some bottom sheet margins of Canada's Admiral issue. There are four different designs known and they appear on most values in the series, according to Hans Reiche. The reason for this art work is unknown and there has been considerable speculation as to its purpose. It was not used after 1924.

A stamp for Wei-Hai-Wei.

Jan. 1: Stamps of Hong Kong overprinted "CHINA" were issued for use at British treaty ports in China and at Wei-Hai-Wei. They continued in use until the treaty port post offices closed on Nov. 30, 1922 and Wei-Hai-Wei reverted to China on Oct. 1, 1930.

Feb. 5: The Venizelist provisional government of Greece issued stamps.

March 1: Austria issued stamps for its occupation of the Kingdom of Montenegro.

March 31: The Danish West Indies became the property of the United States at a price of $25 million. For six months, mail could be franked with either DWI or US postage or combinations of the two.

May: The first air mail flight took place in Albania. Military aircraft made flights during May and June from Valona to Brindisi, Italy. Mail flown on the flight bears a special cachet.

May 16: Italy issued the world's first air mail stamps for the experimental air mail flights between Turin and Rome (See May 22, 1917).

May 18: The Bahamas issued its first semi-postal stamp. The government released it to raise money for the Red Cross.

The first air mail stamp.

May 22: Experimental air mail flights began between Turin and Rome, Italy. The world's first air mail stamps were issued by Italy for the flights (see May 16, 1917).

May 30: The earliest known letter from the American Expeditionary Force in France bears this date.

June 28: Mail flown on an experimental air mail flight between Naples and Palermo, Sicily, was franked with the world's second air mail stamp.

July 6: A government-authorized experimental air mail flight between Mexico City and Pachuca, Mexico, is the first of its kind in Mexico.

July 10: Army Post Office #1 opened at St. Nazaire, France, for the American Expeditionary Force.

July 12: Francois Fournier died. His career as a forger caused thousands of forged postage stamps to be spread among the world's collections. Many are still hiding therein and continue to plague the hobby. The Philatelic Union of Geneva purchased the Fournier stock from his successor's widow, in order to remove as many as possible from the philatelic market. After creating a number of reference albums of marked Fournier creations, the group burned the remainder.

July 13: The American Expeditionary Force in France, under General Order #15 established censorship.

July 16: Postmaster General A. S. Burleson authorized a special postal rate of 1c on magazines handed to a postal employee for delivery to members of the armed forces on active service in a theater of war. This order, published in *Postal Bulletin* 11399 of July 17, applied to magazines that had printed on the upper right of the cover "Notice to reader/ when you finish reading this magazine place a 1-cent stamp on this notice, hand same to any postal employee and it will be placed in the hands of our soldiers or sailors at the front./ NO WRAPPING — NO ADDRESS/ A. S.

The world's second air mail stamp (June 28, 1917).

Burleson,/ Postmaster General." A revised order took effect on April 3, 1918 (q.v.).

September: Stamps were issued for the British occupation of Baghdad, in what is now Iraq, during the World War I campaign against the Turkish Empire.

Oct. 3: The US Congress authorized free franking for US troops overseas. The service was implemented on Oct. 20, 1917, under General Orders, #48.

Nov. 1: Austria issued stamps for its occupation of Romania.

Nov. 2: This was the effective date of the US War Revenue Act of Oct. 3, 1917, which, among other increases, raised the first-class letter rate to 3c per ounce from 2c. The additional cent was a war tax.

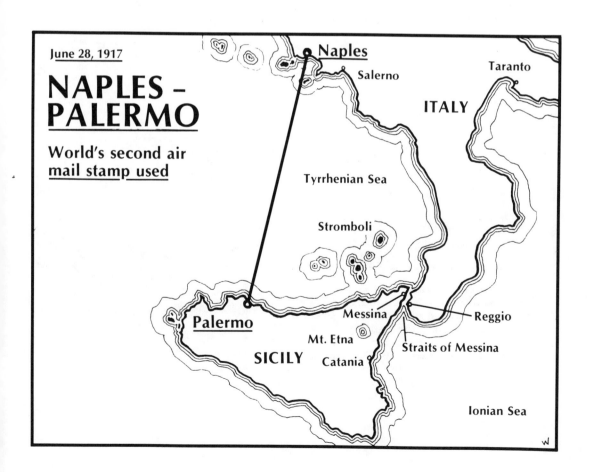

June 28, 1917

NAPLES – PALERMO

World's second air mail stamp used

Naples
Salerno
Taranto
ITALY
Tyrrhenian Sea
Stromboli
Palermo
Messina
Reggio
Mt. Etna
Straits of Messina
SICILY
Catania
Ionian Sea

Nov. 7: The Russian Socialist Federal Soviet Republic was formed in the former Russian Empire.

Dec. 1: The US Treasury Department released War Savings stamps. The last stamp was issued Aug. 5, 1945. They were redeemable in the form of US treasury bonds, war certificates, defense bonds, or war bonds. What is called a Treasury Savings stamp was issued Dec. 21, 1920. This $1 stamp could be exchanged for War Savings stamps or Treasury savings certificates.

Dec. 10: Great Britain placed in service its

first machine cancel slogan postmark. It consisted of a box containing the inscription "BUY NATIONAL/ WAR BONDS/ NOW."

Dec. 15: San Marino issued its first semipostal stamps.

1918

The Western Ukraine, a shortlived state in what had been the Austro-Hungarian province of Galicia, issued stamps. The country soon came under Polish administration.

January: Thailand issued its first semi-postal stamps. The stamps were sold for more than

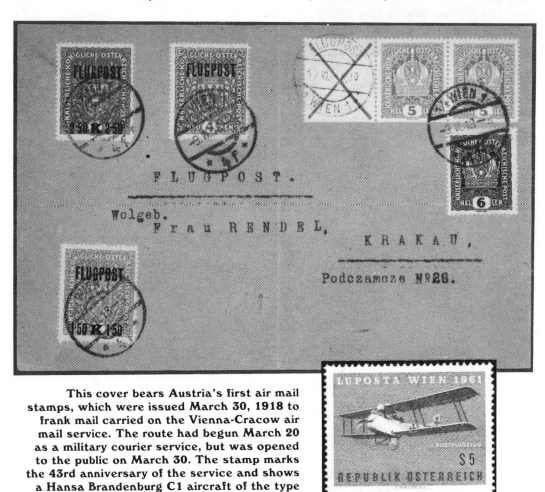

This cover bears Austria's first air mail stamps, which were issued March 30, 1918 to frank mail carried on the Vienna-Cracow air mail service. The route had begun March 20 as a military courier service, but was opened to the public on March 30. The stamp marks the 43rd anniversary of the service and shows a Hansa Brandenburg C1 aircraft of the type used on the route.

their face value, with the excess going to the Red Cross.

Palestine's first stamp.

Feb. 10: Palestine issued its first stamps following its liberation from Turkish rule by British forces during World War I.

Feb. 12: Finland became a member of the Universal Postal Union.

Feb. 21: The Bahamas issued its first War Tax stamp.

March 20: Austria inaugurated a military courier air mail service from Vienna to Lemberg via Cracow.

March 30: Austria issued its first air mail stamps for the inauguration of civilian air mail on the Vienna to Lemberg via Cracow route. The service had begun as a military courier service on March 20.

April 3: Regulations governing the 1c magazine rate to members of the US armed forces on active service announced July 16, 1917 (q.v.) were revised in *Postal Bulletin* 11617 of this date. The notice to be printed on the covers of magazines was changed to read "mail the magazine" instead of "hand same to any postal employee" and "destined to proceed overseas" instead of "at the front." Postal rate authority Henry W. Beecher believes this to be the only instance in US postal history in which it was permissible to mail an article bearing no address of any kind.

May 13: The first US air mail stamp, which was also the world's first purpose-designed air mail stamp went on sale. It was to be used on the Washington, Philadelphia, and New York air mail service inaugurated on May 15. This is the stamp of which the inverted center variety is one of philately's best-known errors. The 24c per ounce air mail rate included special delivery service.

May 14: W. T. Robey purchased a sheet of 100 of the 24c air mail stamp with the aircraft printed in an inverted position. The stamp had been placed on sale the previous day. Robey sold the sheet to Philadelphia dealer Eugene Klein for a reported $15,000. Klein is said to have sold the sheet to Col. Green for $20,000.

The notice printed on a magazine cover giving instructions for mailing to servicemen during World War I. A stamp was applied, indicating that the magazine buyer took the trouble to mail it at the special 1c rate.

New York

Belmont Park

Philadelphia

Trenton

Wilmington

Atlantic Ocean

Baltimore

Washington

May 15, 1918

FIRST REGULAR GOVERNMENT AIR-MAIL SERVICE

This stamp depicts a Curtiss Jenny of the type used on the Washington, Philadelphia, and New York air mail service. It was issued May 15, 1968 to mark the 50th anniversary of the service (May 15, 1918).

May 15: The US Post Office Department established the first air mail service between Washington, Philadelphia, and New York. The world's first purpose-designed air mail stamp had been issued on May 13 (q.v.) for this service. See July 15, 1918 and Dec. 15, 1918.

May 26: The National Republic of Georgia was established. It became part of the Transcaucasian Federation on March 12, 1922, after being a Soviet republic since Feb. 25, 1921. Georgia first issued stamps during 1919.

May 27: The Republic of Azerbaijan was formed, lasting until April 28, 1920. It first issued stamps during 1919.

May 28: The Republic of Armenia was created for the first time. It lasted until Dec. 2, 1920, but existed again from Feb. 18, 1920 to April 2, 1921. The republic began issuing stamps in 1919.

June: The British colony of the Gold Coast issued a War Tax stamp.

June: The British protectorate of the Gilbert and Ellice Islands became a crown colony.

June 24: Capt. B. A. Peck piloted a Curtiss JN-4 Canuck aircraft of the Royal Air Force from Montreal to Toronto on the first recorded air mail flight in Canada. With Corporal W. C. Mather as passenger, Peck's plane took off at 10:30 a.m. with 124 pieces of mail. The aircraft arrived in Toronto at 4:55 p.m.

June 30: The US Post Office department discontinued pneumatic tube service because of what were considered excessive operating costs and the belief that improved motor transporation could handle the mail at less cost. Service was restored on some lines in New York on Oct. 2, 1922 and Boston on Aug. 1, 1926.

July: The Ukraine released its first stamps.

July 1: By this date, the US Post Office owned 1,004 trucks operating in 12 cities. It employed 1,200 mechanics, drivers, and other vehicle personnel, according to Scheele.

July 4: Hungary issued its first air mail stamps on this date.

July 9: Katherine Stinson flew mail from Calgary, Alberta, to Edmonton, Alberta. She carried about 250 letters, which are now considered rare.

July 15: The US air mail postal rate, which had been 24c per ounce since its introduction on May 15, 1918, was reduced to 16c for the first ounce and 6c for each additional ounce. This included the 10c special delivery fee.

July 15: Captain Ben Lipsner of the US Army was appointed superintendent of the Aerial Mail Service for the US Post Office Department. The department took over from the War

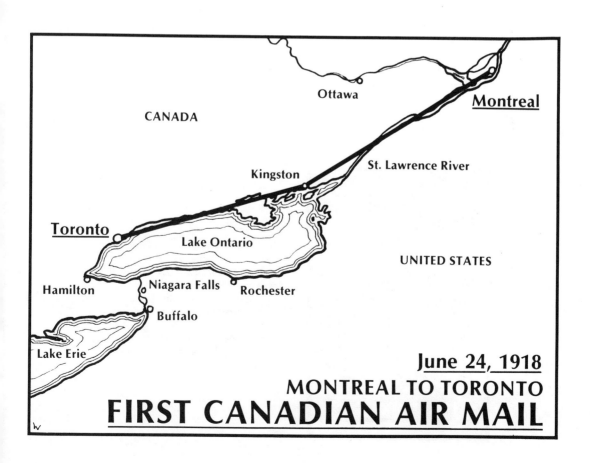

June 24, 1918
MONTREAL TO TORONTO
FIRST CANADIAN AIR MAIL

Department the operation of the fledgling air mail service between Washington, Philadelphia, and New York on Aug. 12, 1918.

Aug. 6: Mafia Island, off the coast of Tanganyika (formerly German East Africa), came under the administration of Tanganyika. The island had been occupied by British forces since Dec. 16, 1914 and it used German East Africa stamps that had been overprinted. When these stocks were exhausted, overprinted Indian stamps were utilized.

Aug. 12: The US Post Office Department took over the operation of the New York, Washington, and Philadelphia air mail service from the War Department, which had been responsible for it since the service had been inaugurated May 15, 1918.

Aug. 17: The first usage of an "Air Mail" sticker (known as an "etiquette") is reported to have been on this date on a French air mail service between Paris and St. Nazaire.

Aug. 24: The first air mail flight in Russia took place when a plane flew diplomatic mail from Kiev to Berlin, Germany.

Aug. 26: A mail-carrying flight from Toronto to Ottawa took place on this date, with a return flight to Toronto made the next day. The letters had a special label issued by the Aero Club of Canada, which shows a German Zeppelin being shot down in flames.

Sept. 1: Iraq, following liberation of the area by British forces from Turkish rule during World War I, placed its first stamps on sale.

Nov. 3: Trentino, Trieste, and Venezia Giulia, — territory of Austria acquired by Italy at the end of World War I — issued stamps.

Nov. 17: Polish stamps were issued at Warsaw.

Nov. 19: The establishment of the Estonian Postal Service was announced. At first, mail was franked in manuscript until stamps were issued on Nov. 22.

Nov. 22: The first government-issued postage stamps of the new nation of Estonia were released.

Dec. 2: The Allied occupiers of Fiume issued stamps.

This Canadian semi-official air mail stamp was used on mail carried between Toronto and Ottawa, Ontario. It depicts a German Zeppelin dirigible being shot down in flames by a British aircraft. The flight was sponsored and the stamp issued by the Aero Club of Canada (Aug. 26, 1918).

Dec. 5: Austrian stamps overprinted "POLSKA POCZTA" were issued at Lublin, Poland.

Dec. 13: A military aircraft made the first direct air mail flight from London to Karachi, India (now Pakistan).

Dec. 15: The US air mail rate, which had been 16c per ounce for the first ounce and 6c for each additional ounce since July 15, 1918, was reduced to 6c per ounce, but did not include special delivery service.

Dec. 18: Czechoslovakia issued its first postage stamps. The design featured a view of Hradcany Castle, Prague.

Front and back of a Latvian stamp printed on the back of a German military map.

Dec. 19: Latvia placed its first stamps on sale. These stamps were printed on the backs of German Military maps in sheets of 228 stamps, arranged in 12 horizontal rows of 19 stamps. The size of the maps dictated this arrangement since a paper shortage made it necessary to fully utilize the available stock.

Dec. 25: Mexico issued its first semi-postal stamp.

Dec. 27: The first stamps issued for independent Lithuania are two stamps with denominations of 10 skatiku and 15sk. These are known as the First Vilnius issue. A quantity of 5,000 of each is reported.

1919

During this year, groups fighting the Bolsheviks in South Russia issued stamps. Among these were the Don Government's Rostov issue and the Kuban Government's Ekaterinodar, Crimean, and Denikin issues.

The National Republic of Georgia issued its first stamps.

Jan. 1: The first air mail flight in Chile was made between Valparaiso and Santiago.

A surcharged stamp used in the Faroes.

Jan. 3: The first stamp of the Faroe Islands was a bisect of the Danish 4 ore stamp to meet a need for 7 ore stamp because of a rate increase. The bisected stamp was used with a 5 ore stamp to make up the rate. The diagonal bisect was made in two variations; northwest to southeast and the more scarce northeast to southwest. Postal officials even cut the 4 ore indicia from newspaper wrappers and bisected them. Later in January, 5 ore stamps were surcharged to 2 ore.

Jan 10: Poland issued its first postage due labels.

Jan. 27: Separate stamp issues were released for use in northern and southern Poland.

Jan. 29: When Poland occupied the portion of Lithuania containing the capital city of Vilnius, the Lithuanian government was re-established at Kaunas where it produced and issued a set of stamps. This is known as the First Kaunas issue.

Jan. 30: Two US Navy aircraft carried mail from Nassau, Bahamas, to Miami, Fla.

February: Italy released general stamp issues for use in areas of Austria occupied during World War I. See also Trentino and Trieste.

February: Turkish revenue stamps were overprinted and surcharged for use by British and Indian forces occupying the town of Mosul in what is now Iraq. The area had been taken from Turkey during World War I.

Feb. 17: The first mail carried by air in Siam (Thailand) was flown from Bangkok to Chandhaburi.

Feb. 17: The first Lithuanian stamps in color were printed in Berlin and issued on this date. Previous stamps had been locally produced provisional issues in black.

March 1: Military air mail service began between England and British Occupation Headquarters at Cologne, Germany.

March 3: The first air mail flight, between Canada and the United States took place from Vancouver, British Columbia, to Seattle, Wash. The flight was made in a Boeing C-3 seaplane by Eddie Hubbard with W. E. Boeing as passenger. The flight took three hours with one fuel stop.

March 4: Stamps were issued in an area known as South Lithuania during a period of Russian occupation. The stamp-issuing area centered on the town of Grodno.

March 4: French occupiers of Cilicia issued stamps.

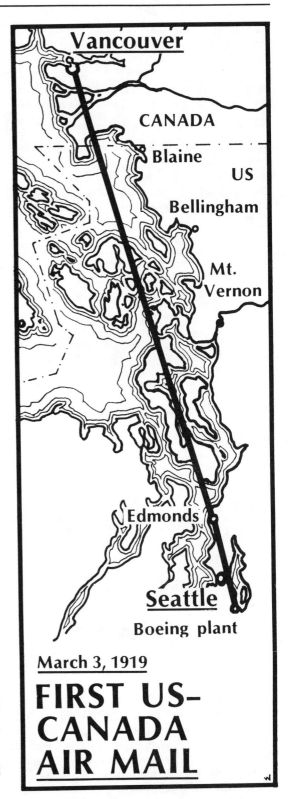

March 3, 1919

FIRST US–CANADA AIR MAIL

April: From this month until March 16, 1932, stamps used in the Cook Islands were inscribed for Rarotonga, the chief island in the group.

April: The French protectorate of Tunisia issued its first air mail stamp.

April 4: The Black Sea port city of Batum had stamps issued for it during the Dec. 1, 1918-July 7, 1920 occupation by British forces.

April 4: Ruth Law carried postcards on a flight in the Philippines in conjunction with the Manila Exposition. The cards are inscribed "AERIAL POST CARD TO COMMEMORATE the First Aerial Mail Service in the Philippines, April 4 and 5, 1919." Cards dated on April 5 were not flown, according to the *American Air Mail Catalogue*.

April 12: Newfoundland became the first British possession to issue an air mail stamp, when a 3c definitive in the Caribou design was overprinted for use on mail carried on the unsuccessful Harry G. Hawker/ Mackenzie Grieve transatlantic flight.

April 15: Portuguese India issued a pair of war tax stamps.

May: Poland issued stamps overprinted "LEVANT" for use on mail handed in at the Polish consulate in Constantinople.

May 1: Poland became a member of the Universal Postal Union.

May 1: Stamps were issued for Dalmatia under Italian occupation.

May 1: The Republic of Germany issued its first semi-postal stamps.

May 3: Guatemala issued its first postal tax stamps.

May 3: Poland issued its first semi-postal stamps. The stamps commemorated the first Polish philatelic exhibition and the surtax went to the Polish White Cross Society.

May 7: Souvenir covers were carried through the Panama Canal from the Caribbean Sea to the Pacific Ocean by the US submarine *C3*. The mail was carried as souvenirs for those who subscribed to a Victory Loan drive. No stamps were used on the covers, which were postmarked at Christobal, with a receiving postmark being applied at Balboa.

May 14: Experimental civilian air mail service began between London and Paris.

May 18: A flight from Victoria, British Columbia, to Seattle, Wash., dropped invitations

A cover carried by submarine through the Panama Canal (May 7, 1919).

to visit Victoria while flying over Seattle. Only three letters are reported to have been carried on the flight, which was sponsored by the Aerial League of Canada.

May 18: Harry Hawker and Major K. MacKenzie Grieve took off on a mail-carrying flight across the North Atlantic from St. John's, Newfoundland. Their Sopwith aircraft was forced down, fortunately near the Danish steamer *Mary*, which picked them up. Newfoundland postal authorities had overprinted the 3c Caribou stamp "FIRST/ TRANS-/ ATLANTIC/ AIR-POST/ April, 1919." According to the *American Air Mail Catalogue*, a total of 200 copies were so overprinted, with 95 being used on mail.

May 18: A transatlantic flight from Newfoundland was attempted by Major F. P. Raynham and Major C. F. W. Morgan in a Martinsyde aircraft. They tried a takeoff on the same day that Harry Hawker and MacKenzie Grieve left, but crashed. The small mail was held for a further attempt on July 17, which was also a failure. Raynham carried the mail to Britain, by ship, but forgot to hand it to postal authorities until Jan. 7, 1920!

May 20: Portuguese Guinea issued a set of three war tax stamps.

May 24: Stamps were issued for use from the US postal agency at Shanghai, China. The stamps went on sale July 1, 1919 in Shanghai. They were withdrawn in December, 1922.

June 9: The 15c stamp in Newfoundland's 1897 definitive series was overprinted "Trans-Atlantic. AIR POST/ 1919/ ONE DOLLAR" to frank mail carried by John Alcock and Arthur Whitten-Brown on their transatlantic flight. (See June 14, 1919.)

June 14: A Soviet republic was established in Hungary following World War I and the col-

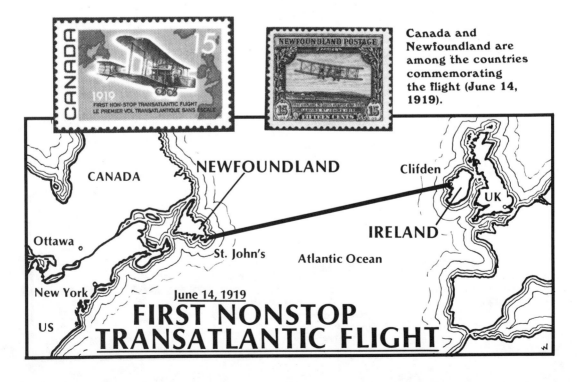

Canada and Newfoundland are among the countries commemorating the flight (June 14, 1919).

CANADA

NEWFOUNDLAND

Clifden

UK

IRELAND

Ottawa

St. John's

Atlantic Ocean

New York

US

June 14, 1919

FIRST NONSTOP TRANSATLANTIC FLIGHT

lapse of the Austro-Hungarian Empire. It issued stamps on this date.

June 14: The first nonstop transatlantic air mail was carried by John Alcock and Arthur Whitten-Brown in their Vickers Vimy aircraft from Newfoundland to Clifden, Ireland.

June 18: The first air mail was carried in Colombia.

June 28: Great Britain received a Treaty of Versailles mandate over Tanganyika (formerly German East Africa). In 1935, Tanganyika's postal service joined with those of Kenya and Uganda. This was known as the East African Customs and Postal Union.

July 1: The domestic letter rate in the United States was reduced to 2c per ounce following the period of 3c postage during World War I.

July 2: The British dirigible R-34, which made the first east-to-west flight and the first round-trip crossing of the Atlantic Ocean, carried some mail on its July 2-6 flight.

July 3: Two US Army seaplanes flew mail from Pearl Harbor to Hilo, Hawaii, according to Crampon. He reports that a mailbag was carried containing letters bearing 2c postage stamps and 10c special delivery stamp. The planes carried mail on the return flight.

July 9: The British dirigible R-34 began its return flight from New York to Pulham, Norfolk, England. It carried mail which had a special marking applied by the British Post Office on arrival in London.

July 11: Censorship of mail from US forces overseas ended.

July 17: Pilot Major F. P. Raynham with Lt. C. H. Biddlescombe as navigator made a second attempt to fly the Atlantic from Newfoundland, but their repaired aircraft again crashed on takeoff (see May 18, 1919). The flight was then abandoned. Raynham carried the mail to England by ship, but forgot to hand it to postal officials for several months. It was eventually backstamped in London on Jan. 7, according to Harmer.

July 18: A US Postmaster General's Order effective this date discontinued specific air mail service and provided that mail would be flown at the regular first-class letter rate of 2c per an ounce on a space-available and airplane-available basis, according to the *American Air Mail Catalogue.*

Aug. 1: The Northwestern Army in Russia under General Yudenitch, who was fighting the Bolshevicks, issued stamps.

Aug. 5: German stamps were overprinted and issued for use in the Poznan area of Poland.

Aug. 7: Capt. Ernest C. Hay flew a mail-carrying plane from Vancouver, British Columbia, to Calgary, Alberta. Flying a Curtiss JN-4 Canuck, Hoy made the first aerial crossing of the Rocky Mountains in the course of the flight. Several stops were made to drop and pick up mail. The aircraft crashed at Golden, B.C., on Aug. 11 during the return flight. Very little of the mail has survived.

Aug. 11: The Portuguese colony of Macao issued a pair of war tax stamps. The same stamps were also valid in Portuguese Timor.

Aug. 14: The first shore-to-ship air mail delivery was made on this date when C. J. Zimmerman, flying a seaplane, delivered mail to the SS *Adriatic* two hours after the ship had left New York.

Aug. 24: The first passenger flight of the Zeppelin LZ-120 *Bodensee* took place. Until Dec. 5, the aircraft made a number of flights, including several between Friedrichshafen and

The first German air mail stamps (Nov. 10, 1919).

Berlin, on which it carried mail. On July 3, 1921, LZ-120 was delivered to Italy as war reparations.

Aug. 25: The first air-mail flight from Toronto, Ontario, to New York City took place. The Aero Club of Canada produced a special label to be placed on mail that was carried.

September: Following an agreement between the governments of France and Great Britain, an air mail service began operating between London and Paris. The cost of a letter on this service was 3/6. In May 1920, the rate was lowered to 2/2½ per ounce. The route was flown from London by Air Transport and Travel Ltd. and a French airline carried mail from Paris.

September: The Northern Army in Russia under General Rodzianko, who was fighting the Bolsheviks, released stamps.

Oct. 3: Japan issued its first air mail stamps.

Oct. 5: The earliest recorded flight to the Channel Islands from England took place when copies of *Lloyds Weekly News* were flown. The flight terminated in the sea near Alderney. The newspapers bore the inscription "By seaplane, Special Edition," according to Gibbons.

Oct. 8: The Zeppelin LZ-120 made a mail-carrying flight to Stockholm, Sweden from its base in Germany.

At the right, inscribed "FIRST Aerial Post," is the label applied to mail carried on the first Britain-Australia flight. Great Britain, Singapore, and Australia are among countries issuing stamps marking the flight (Nov. 12, 1919).

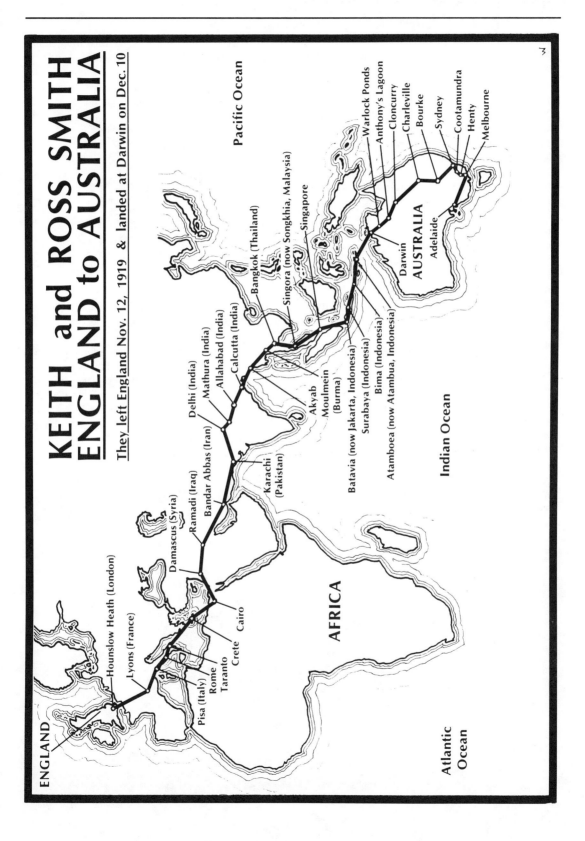

KEITH and ROSS SMITH
ENGLAND to AUSTRALIA

They left England Nov. 12, 1919 & landed at Darwin on Dec. 10

Pacific Ocean

ENGLAND

Hounslow Heath (London)
Lyons (France)
Damascus (Syria)
Ramadi (Iraq)
Bandar Abbas (Iran)
Karachi (Pakistan)
Pisa (Italy)
Rome
Taranto
Crete
Cairo

AFRICA

Atlantic Ocean

Delhi (India)
Mathura (India)
Allahabad (India)
Calcutta (India)
Akyab
Moulmein (Burma)
Bangkok (Thailand)
Singora (now Songkhia, Malaysia)
Singapore
Batavia (now Jakarta, Indonesia)
Surabaya (Indonesia)
Bima (Indonesia)
Atamboea (now Atambua, Indonesia)

Indian Ocean

Warlock Ponds
Anthony's Lagoon
Cloncurry
Charleville
Bourke
Sydney
Cootamundra
Henty
Melbourne
Darwin
AUSTRALIA
Adelaide

3

Oct. 10: Stamps were issued by the Western Army in Russia under Colonel Avalov-Bermondt, which was fighting the Bolshevists in Courland, Latvia.

Nov. 10: The first German air mail stamps went on sale. The two designs feature a post horn with wings and a stylized rendition of a contemporary aircraft.

Nov. 12: A flight from England to Australia began on this date. Ross and Keith Smith flew some mail in their Vickers Vimy aircraft, which arrived at Darwin on Dec. 10. A special label was produced and affixed to the mail on Feb. 25, when the aircraft arrived in Melbourne. The label is one of the major rarities in both air mail and Australian philately. Of a total of 451 copies printed only 364 were used on mail, leaving 87 mint stamps.

Nov. 15: Iceland became a member of the Universal Postal Union.

Nov. 16: A monarchy replaced the shortlived soviet republic in Hungary and issued stamps on this date.

Nov. 19: The first stamps issued for Syria under French occupation following its liberation from Turkey by British forces during World War I went on sale, according to Gibbons. The Scott catalog gives the date of the first stamps as Nov. 21.

Nov. 25: The first inter-island mail flight made in the Philippines was from Manila to Cebu by two Philippine National Guard pilots. The flight returned to Manila on Nov. 28. Only three covers are known to have survived.

December: Bulgarian stamps were over-printed "THRACE INTERALLIEE" following its occupation by Allied forces.

Dec. 12: Czechoslovakia issued its first air mail stamps. These were overprints on stamps of Austria. The overprint reads "FLUGPOST" and "POSTA CESKOSLOVENSKA 1919." The Scott catalog does not list these, although Gibbons does. According to Scott, Czechoslovakia issued its first air mail stamps during 1920.

Dec. 16: The first official air mail was flown in New Zealand. Walsh Bros. and Dexter Ltd. carried the mail between Auckland and Dargaville.

1920 - 1939
The inter-war years

1920

The free city of Danzig issued stamps. They were overprints on stamps of Germany.

Stamps of Upper Senegal and Niger overprinted "HAUTE-VOLTA" went on sale as the first stamps for the French colony of Upper Volta.

The French colony of Wallis and Futuna Islands issued its first stamps. They consisted of stamps of New Caledonia overprinted "ILES WALLIS/ et/ FUTUNA."

Jan. 25: Stamps were issued for use in the plebiscite area of Schleswig.

Jan. 30: The Saar released stamps. They were stamps of Germany overprinted "Sarre." The area was then under French occupation.

Feb. 1: Poland issued its first Official stamps.

Feb. 20: The plebiscite area of Upper Silesia issued its first stamps.

March 12: The district of Marienwerder issued stamps during a period when the area held a plebiscite to decide if it should remain part of German East Prussia or join Poland. It voted in favor of Germany and German stamps were restored.

March 13: Estonia issued its first air mail stamp. Triangular in shape, it was used for the additional postage required for mail carried by air between Reval (Tallinn) and Helsinki, Finland.

March 15: Pitney-Bowes Postage Meter Co. organized as a result of the merger of Arthur Hill Pitney's American Postage Meter Co. and Walter H. Bowes' Universal Stamping Machine Co.

March 21: North Ingermanland, a tiny area on the Soviet-Finnish border that claimed its independence briefly before being absorbed into the Soviet Union, issued stamps.

April 1: Air mail service was inaugurated in the Belgian Congo when Sabena Airlines began Kinshasa-Gombe service.

April 1: Although stamps of Germany and Bavaria had been issued on Jan. 30 overprinted "SAARE" for use in the Saar, unoverprinted stamps of either area could be used beginning on this date to April 15 (q.v.).

April 4: Spain issued its first air mail stamps. They were regular issues of 1909-10 overprinted "CORREO AEREO."

April 4: The first mail flown in Spain was carried from Barcelona to the Balearic Islands and between Seville and Larache.

April 12: Allenstein (Olsztyn) released its first plebiscite issue.

April 15: Although the Saar had its own stamps from Jan. 30, 1920, unoverprinted German stamps could be used until this date in the former Prussian area of the Saar. In the former Bavarian area, unoverprinted stamps of Bavaria could also be used until this date.

May 7: The first air mail in China was flown between Tientsin and Peking.

May 10: Sweden issued its first coil stamps.

May 18: Czechoslovakia became a member of the Universal Postal Union.

June: Stamps of Greece, overprinted in Greek "Administration of Western Thrace," were placed in use in Western Thrace until the introduction of unoverprinted Greek stamps.

June 20: Bulgaria issued its first semi-postal stamps. The surtax aided ex-prisoners of war of World War I.

July: Former German Samoa was mandated to New Zealand by the League of Nations. Stamps were issued inscribed "Samoa." In 1935, the inscription was changed to "Western Samoa."

July 1: Palestine, which had been under a military administration since being taken from Turkey during World War I, was placed under civilian rule.

July 1: The Belgian Congo issued its first air mail stamps.

July 15: Cilicia, an area of Turkey then occupied by France issued air mail stamps. Some were used on two air mail flights between Adana and Aleppo.

Aug. 1: Memel, under occupation by the Allied powers following World War I, issued stamps.

Aug. 18: Latvia issued its first semi-postal stamps. These stamps were printed on the backs of unfinished bank notes that had been prepared by the Workers' and Soldiers' Council at Riga. The surtax went to the Red Cross.

Aug. 23: Stamps inscribed "RAROTONGA" were issued for use in the Cook Islands. Stamps of New Zealand overprinted "RAROTONGA" had been in use since April 1919. Stamps inscribed "COOK ISLANDS" were restored in 1932.

September: The Far Eastern Republic in Siberia issued stamps.

Sept. 1: Palestine's civilian administration released its first stamps.

Sept. 1: The US Post Office Department ap-

proved use of the Pitney-Bowes postage meter. The Universal Postal Union gave international approval effective on Jan. 1, 1922.

Sept. 8: Transcontinental air mail service began between New York and San Francisco. The westbound mail left Mineola, N.Y., at 6:14 a.m. and arrived in San Francisco late in the afternoon of the next day, according to the *American Air Mail Catalogue* (see Sept. 10, 1920).

Sept. 10: The United States inaugurated its eastbound transcontinental air mail service. It had been intended to begin the flight of Sept. 8, but weather conditions made it impossible. The mail arrived in New York on Sept. 12.

Sept. 15: The first air mail was flown in Peru.

Sept. 17: Sweden issued its first air mail stamps on this date. They consisted of Official stamps of 1911-19 overprinted "LUFT-POST" and surcharged.

Sept. 29: The Free City of Danzig, established following World War I, issued its first air mail stamps. As with the city's regular issues, they were overprints on stamps of Germany. Their first use is reported by Billig as being on Oct. 1 on a Berlin-Koenigsberg-Danzig air mail service.

Oct. 1: The seventh congress of the Universal Postal Union convened in Madrid, Spain. It included the surviving belligerent states and its work was largely that of repairing the damage to the international mail system by World War I. It adopted the gold franc as the standard unit of currency. At this congress, the matter of air mail was first considered and provision was made for air mail service. Spain issued a set of 13 stamps to mark the congress.

Oct. 5: Air mail service began between Prague, Czechoslovakia, and Paris.

Oct. 7: On this date, Lt. Col. R. Leckie left Halifax, Nova Scotia, on the first flight to span Canada. The flight reached Vancouver, British Columbia, on Oct. 17. Several different aircraft and pilots flew stages of the flight. The 3,340-mile flight was made in a little over 49 hours flying time. It carried a small amount of mail.

Oct. 15: Foreign Air Mail Route Number Two (FAM-2) was established on this date between Seattle, Wash., and Victoria, British Columbia. It was intended to speed mail to ships by catching them at Victoria after they had sailed from Seattle. Mail was also picked up from incoming ships. Despite its FAM-2 designation, it is the earliest of the FAM routes. The service was discontinued June 30, 1937.

Oct. 20: Central Lithuania issued stamps while under Polish occupation.

Oct. 29: Free franking for US armed forces overseas ended.

November: Stamps were first issued by rebels in Turkey during the uprising against the sultan by Mustafa Kemal Pasha. As the rebel republican movement spread across Turkey, these issues eventually became the forerunners of the modern issues of the Turkish Republic.

November: Jordan issued its first stamps under a League of Nations mandate to Great Britain. Jordan, then known as Transjordan, had been liberated from Turkish rule in world War I.

Nov. 1: Foreign Air Mail Route Number One (FAM-1) was established. This was the second FAM route authorized (FAM-2 from Seattle to Victoria was begun Oct. 15, 1920). Florida West Indies Airways flew the route between Key West, Fla., and Havana, Cuba, until June 1921, when it was suspended. During January 1923, Aeromarine operated it. The route then

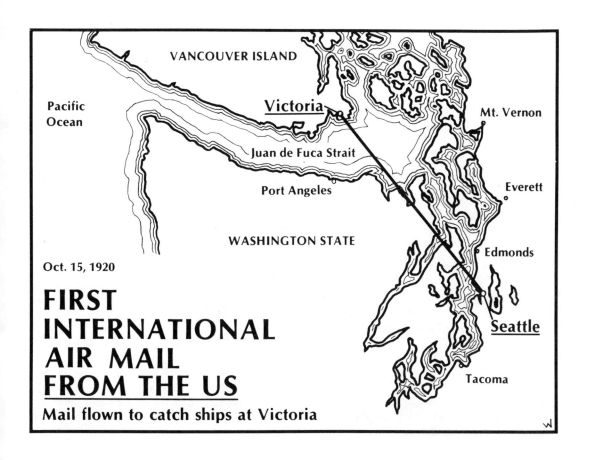

Oct. 15, 1920

FIRST INTERNATIONAL AIR MAIL FROM THE US
Mail flown to catch ships at Victoria

lapsed until Oct. 19, 1927 (q.v.), when Pan American Airways received the contract and the route was re-assigned as FAM-4 because FAM-1 had been re-assigned to the Montreal, Quebec service. It is now merged with FAM-5.

Nov. 11: The first Swiss air mail stamp was issued to frank mail carried on the Basel-Frankfurt air service. A second stamp with a similar overprint was issued April 30, 1919 for mail carried on a Zurich-Berne-Lausanne service. The stamps were withdrawn on March 1, 1923, according to Musson.

Nov. 16: The first setting of a postage meter took place in the office of the Stamford, Conn., postmaster.

Nov. 18: The island of Arbe issued stamps. They were issues of Fiume oveprinted "ARBE."

Nov. 18: The island of Veglia, using issues of Fiume overprinted "VEGLIA," placed its first stamps on sale.

Nov. 27: The Russian post office in Shanghai closed. All other Russian post offices in China closed about the same time.

Dec. 1: The Portuguese African colony of Mozambique released semi-postal stamps. The stamps were used on this date in place of regular stamps. The proceeds were devoted to war relief.

Dec. 1: The Republic of China issued its first semi-postal stamps to help victims of the 1919 Yellow River flood.

Dec. 10: The first metered mailing took place from Pitney-Bowes headquarters in Stamford, Conn.

Dec. 14: Syria issued its first air mail stamps. They consisted of a boxed overprint reading POSTE/ PAR/ AVION."

1921

From this year until May 12, 1926, the New Zealand and British governments agreed as

"an act of grace" to receive and deliver unfranked letters from Pitcairn Island with the recipient paying the normal postage, waiving the usual "double postage due" on international mail.

The Indian feudatory state of Barwani issued stamps.

Stamps of Dahomey were overprinted "TOGO" when the French received a League of Nations mandate over the ex-German colony of Togo.

The French colony of Niger issued its first stamps. They were stamps of Upper Senegal and Niger overprinted "TERRITOIRE/ DU NIGER."

A "floating safe stamp."

The Netherlands issued a set of Marine Insurance stamps. They were the so-called "floating safe stamps." The stamps franked mail carried in a special safe on the decks of ships, so that in the event of the ship sinking, the safe would float free and the mail could be saved. The safe was equipped with light and sound signalling devices. In the following year, a similar set was issued for the Netherlands Indies.

Jan. 2: The first flight of a daily air mail service between Camp Borden, Ontario, and Toronto, Ontario, took place. The daily flights, which lasted until April, 1921, were an attempt by the Royal Canadian Air Force to persuade the Canadian Post Office to begin air mail service.

Jan. 16: A general stamp issue was released for use throughout Yugoslavia. They picture King Alexander and were intaglio printed by the American Bank Note Co. Since Yugoslavia had been formed at the end of World War I, stamps had been issued by the various areas of the country including Bosnia and Herzegovina, Croatia, and Slovenia.

Jan. 30: Yugoslavia issued its first semi-postal stamps. They were sold at double face value to aid disabled soldiers.

Feb. 1: The New Zealand Post Office opened a postal agency on Washington Island. It operated until March 30, 1934. From the amount of stamps sent to the island one can guage the mail volume. Initially, £20 face value was sent. Four years later, it was only necessary to send stamps with a total face value of £1! Although New Zealand operated the postal facilities, the island was part of the British Gilbert and Ellice group.

Feb. 18: The Saar issued definitive stamps inscribed "SAARGEBIET." Since Jan. 30, 1920, stamps of Germany and Bavaria had been overprinted for use in the territory of the Saar.

Feb 22: James H. "Jack" Knight, an air mail pilot, made history when he flew the first night mail a distance of 680 miles from North Platte, Neb. to Chicago, arriving at 8:40 a.m. on Feb. 23. This flight took place during an experiment designed to keep the mail moving on the transcontinental route by day and night. Thanks to Knight, the experiment was deemed a success and Congress provided the funds to continue air mail service.

March 5: President Warren G. Harding appointed Will H. Hays US postmaster general. He succeeded Albert S. Burleson.

March 6: The first regular air mail service in South America began between Tulcan, Ecuador, and Pasto, Colombia.

March 28: The first in a series of trial flights was made to study the idea of internal air mail service during winter in Newfoundland. The flight was from Botwood to Fogo, and return.

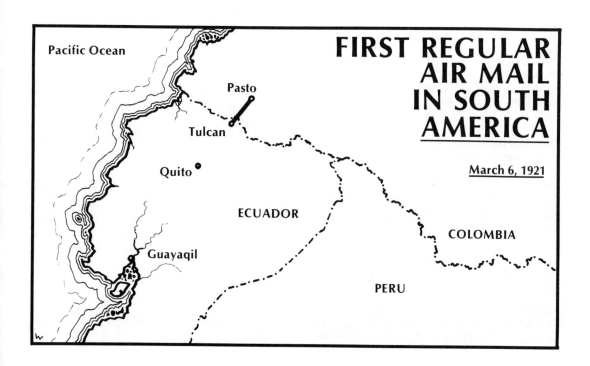

Pacific Ocean

Pasto

Tulcan

Quito

ECUADOR

Guayaqil

PERU

COLOMBIA

FIRST REGULAR AIR MAIL IN SOUTH AMERICA

March 6, 1921

April 1: The first air mail was flown from Memel, in what is now Lithuania. It inaugurated a service between Memel, Konigsberg, and Danzig. Special air mail stamps were not introduced until July 6, 1921.

April 15: The first air mail flight in Costa Rica left San Jose for Managua, Nicaragua, but the aircraft did not complete its flight.

April 27: A small amount of mail was flown on the first air mail flight in French Indo-China. A Breguet aircraft piloted by Lt. Payeroux flew from Vientiane, arriving at an airfield near Saigon on May 2. Only two covers are known to have survived, according to Jean Gravelat.

May 1: The Netherlands issued its first air mail stamps.

June: La Aguera, a Spanish possession on the west coast of Africa, issued its first stamps.

June 25: Lithuania issued its first air mail stamp. It was a one-auksinas denomination of the first issue and was imperforate. The rest of the issue followed in July and October. Those stamps were perforated.

July: Nicaragua issued its first postal tax stamps.

July 1: The Republic of China issued its first air mail stamps. The design pictures an aircraft flying over the Great Wall of China. It has been reported to depict a Curtiss Jenny.

July 6: The first air mail stamps were issued for the port of Memel, later included within the territory of Lithuania and renamed Klaipeda. The Allies administered the port after World War I. They used stamps of France overprinted "FLUGPOST," for use on a Memel-Koenigsberg-Danzig service.

July 8: Crude air mail stamps, locally printed, were issued for use on air mail flights between Saint Laurent and Cayenne, French Guiana. Although the stamps are not listed in some general catalogs, Sanabria included them and an article in the October 1965 *Aero Philatelist*

Annals gives information on them. The stamps had to be used in addition to the regular postage stamps of French Guiana as they paid only the air mail fee. Gibbons notes that they were only used until October 1921.

July 30: Latvia issued its first air mail stamps. They are triangular in shape with the point down and depict what appears to be a Bleriot aircraft.

August: British post offices in Turkey surcharged stamps of Great Britain in Turkish currency for use during the post-World War I occupation of Turkey.

August: Uruguay issued its first special delivery stamp.

Nov. 7: The 35c stamp in Newfoundland's 1897 issue was overprinted "AIR MAIL/ to Halifax, N.S./ 1921" to frank mail on an unsuccessful flight from Newfoundland to Halifax, Nova Scotia.

Dec. 9: The Philatelic Agency of the US Post Office Department was established in Washington, D.C. It is now known as the Philatelic Sales Division. In its first year, sales amounted to $21,900. During Fiscal 1984, sales at the Philatelic Sales Division amounted to $26.5 million.

Dec. 21: The Kingdom of the Hejaz, later part of the Kingdom of Saudi Arabia, issued stamps.

Dec. 24: Yugoslavia became a member of the Universal Postal Union.

1922

The French colony of Chad issued stamps, which were stamps of the Middle Congo overprinted "TCHAD."

Stamps picturing the head of a giraffe were issued for the former German East Africa, which had been mandated to Great Britain as Tanganyika.

The League of Nations headquarters in Geneva, Switzerland, issued stamps.

Jan. 1: The Universal Postal Union's approval for the international use of the Pitney-Bowes postage meter took effect.

Jan. 1: The Philippines became a member of the Universal Postal Union.

Jan. 1: The first air stamps of French Morocco were issued. They depict an aircraft over Casablanca.

Jan. 15: Uruguay issued its first parcel post stamps.

Jan. 31: A shortlived independent administration in Karelia issued a series of 15 stamps. The stamps were valid until Feb. 16, 1922. This was an area in the northwestern part of Russia near Finland. It is now part of the Soviet Union.

Feb 17: The Provisional Government of Ireland issued stamps prior to the Dec. 6, 1922 formation of the Irish Free State. They were overprints on the stamps of Great Britain.

March 1: Albania became a member of the Universal Postal Union.

March 4: Hubert Work was appointed US postmaster general by President Warren G. Harding succeeding Will H. Hays.

April 1: Control of the Post Office in the newly formed Irish Free State was handed over to Irish authorities. Overprinted British stamps had been issued on Feb. 17.

April 2: Mexico issued its first air mail stamp.

April 5: An agent acting on behalf of Arthur Hind bought the British Guiana 1c magenta of 1856 for about $32,500 at the Ferrary sale in Paris. The underbidder was Maurice Burrus.

April 22: The first air mail flight in Algeria took place.

May 15: Finland issued its first semi-postal stamps.

May 25: British stamps bearing this date and the name "Gough Island" are reported by Robson Lowe. They resulted from an expedition to the island, located about 280 miles southeast of Tristan da Cunha. The island was formally annexed by Great Britain on March 29, 1938.

The first air mail stamp of French Morocco (Jan. 1, 1922) and a British stamp overprinted for use by the provisional government of Ireland (Feb. 17, 1922).

June 1: Uruguay issued its first newspaper stamps.

July 7: Estonia joined the Universal Postal Union.

July 13: The Caribbean island of Barbuda, a dependency of Antigua, placed stamps on sale. Following this issue, it released no more stamps until Nov. 19, 1968.

Sept. 5: The first postage meter went into use in Great Britain at the offices of the Prudential Assurance Company. It was made by Pitney-Bowes.

Oct. 2: The US Post Office Department re-established about 22 miles of pneumatic tube mail lines in New York, following the 1918 closure of all pneumatic tube service in US cities.

Nov. 1: Stamps inscribed "Kenya and Uganda" went on sale.

Nov. 2: The South Atlantic island of Ascension released stamps.

Nov. 7: The first air mail stamp was issued by what soon became the Soviet Union. It marked the fifth anniversary of the Russian revolution and was used for a flight between Moscow and Konigsberg (Kaliningrad). Musson reports that it was on sale only at the Moscow Post Office.

Nov. 30: The American Bank Note Company of Canada became the Canadian Bank Note Company.

Dec. 6: When the Irish Free State was formed, it repainted all the country's mailboxes bright Irish green!

Dec. 6: The Irish Free State issued its first stamps.

Dec. 31: The US Postal Agency at Shanghai was closed, according to Konwiser.

1923

Italy issued stamps for Saseno, an island off the Albanian coast that it occupied. Following World War II, the island was restored to Albania.

The Swiss-based International Labour Office issued its first stamps.

The Aero Philatelic Society of America was formed. In October 1926, it became the American Air Mail Society.

Jan. 2: Stamps of South Africa were issued overprinted for use in South West Africa.

March 4: President Warren G. Harding appointed Harry S. New US postmaster general. He succeeded Hubert Work.

April: The Transcaucasian Federation, which comprised Armenia, Azerbaijan, and Georgia, placed stamps in use.

April 1: The 10c basic US registration fee for a $50 indemnity remained in effect, but a 20c fee for up to $100 indemnity was introduced. This applied to first-class mail. Second class could now be registered, but without indemnity.

April 1: Kuwait issued its first stamps, which consisted of the word "KUWAIT" overprinted on stamps of India.

May: Canada issued stamps perforated "O.H.M.S." for use by the Receiver General's office on Ottawa and at offices of his assistants in various Canadian cities. According to Wrigley, the perforating, which had been done

A selection of Bureau precancels.

by the Receiver General's office, was taken over by the Canadian Post Office on March 11, 1935.

May 3: The US Post Office Department introduced Bureau precancels. This is the name given to the precancelation device that the Bureau of Engraving and Printing prints on the stamp at the time it is created. The process involves adding a printing unit to the press and thus the precancelation becomes a step in the stamp's production. The device took the form of a city and state designation between two horizontal lines. Some ₜexperimental Bureau

precancels had been created in 1916 (q.v.), although some sources give the year as 1917. The city and state designation has been omitted since Sept. 21, 1978 (q.v.).

May 11: A French aircraft carried the first air mail in Senegal on a flight from Dakar to Casablanca.

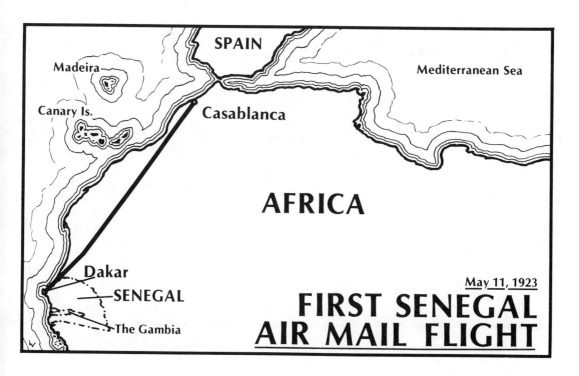

May 11, 1923
FIRST SENEGAL AIR MAIL FLIGHT

July: The Canadian Post Office authorized the use of postage meters (see Aug. 7, 1923 and Sept. 29, 1923).

July 6: The Union of Soviet Socialist Republics, commonly called the Soviet Union or the USSR, was formed.

July 6: The USSR absorbed the Transcaucasian Federation and replaced the federation's stamps with Soviet issues.

July 16: Italian Somaliland issued its first special delivery stamp.

Aug. 7: The first dispatch of mail franked by a postage meter in Canada was made by the Pitney Bowes representative in Toronto, Ontario.

Sept. 1: What is generally accepted to be the first commercially produced cacheted first-day cover was made by George Linn for the US Harding Memorial issue. The cachet consists of a five-line inscription on a black-bordered envelope.

Sept. 6: Ireland became a member of the Universal Postal Union.

Sept. 20: San Marino issued a semi-postal special delivery stamp.

Sept. 23: The League of Nations placed Palestine under British mandate.

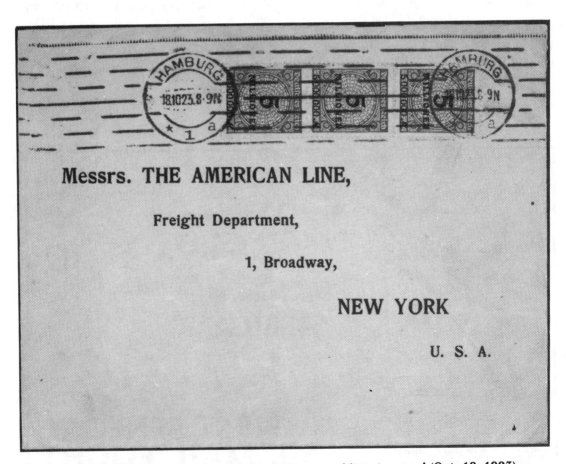

It cost 15,000,000 marks to mail this letter — and it got worse! (Oct. 18, 1923).

Sept. 29: The T. Eaton Co. in Toronto installed the first commercial postage meter in Canada.

Sept. 30: Corfu, under Italian occupation issued stamps.

Oct. 18: It cost 15 million marks to mail a letter from Germany to New York on this date during the inflation period.

Oct. 24: Stamps were first issued for the Italian North African colony of Tripolitania. The colony continued to issue stamps until the mid-1930s, when it merged with Italian Libya.

Nov. 1: Jamaica issued its first semi-postal stamps. The surtax was to benefit the Child Saving League of Jamaica.

Nov. 20: On this date, the German mark stood at 4,200,000,000,000 to one US dollar.

Dec. 18: Great Britian, France and Spain established the International Zone of Tangier around the city on the Moroccan Atlantic coast. The three countries issued stamps for use at their post offices there at various times during the zone's 1923-1956 existence. A British post office had operated in the city as early as 1857. Its mail was taken to Gibraltar for postmarking with its "A-26" canceler. From 1886 to 1907, stamps of Gibraltar were sold at Tangier.

1924

The first stamps were issued for Spanish Sahara.

Algeria issued its first stamps. They were stamps of France overprinted "ALGERIE."

January: The first air mail stamps of Lebanon were issued. They were overprints on regular stamps.

January: The Bureau of Engraving and Printing in the United States issued its precanceled coil stamps, according to correspondence from James Kingman.

Jan. 1: The first stamps were issued for Lebanon under French mandate.

February: Lithuania issued its first semi-postal stamps.

Feb. 2: Carl Ben Eielson was granted the first contract from the US Post Office Department to carry mail by air in Alaska. The contracted route was between Fairbanks and McGrath, a distance of about 300 miles. The department shipped him a DH-4 aircraft and paid him $2 a mile for hauling the mail. On his first flight on Feb. 2, he carried 500 pounds of mail from Fairbanks. After a few months, and several crashes, the Post Office canceled the contract and requested its airplane back.

The first stamp of Algeria is shown at the left (1924) and the righthand stamp was issued by Monaco in 1964 to mark the US Army's round-the-world flight (March 17, 1924).

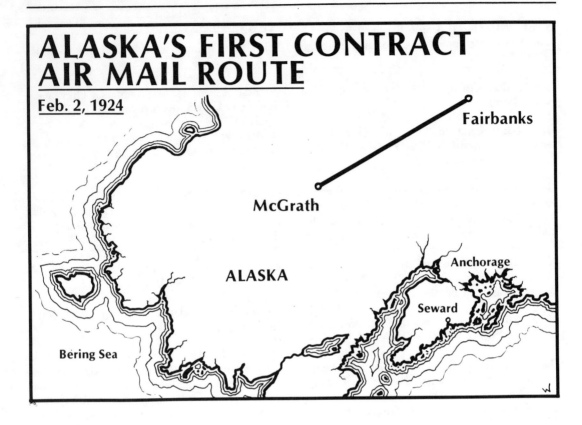

ALASKA'S FIRST CONTRACT AIR MAIL ROUTE

Feb. 2, 1924

Fairbanks

McGrath

Anchorage

ALASKA

Seward

Bering Sea

Feb. 16: Air mail was carried for the first time in Guatemala when US Army aircraft on a visit to the country carried 28 letters on a flight to Balboa, Canal Zone, according to the *American Air Mail Catalogue.*

March 13: The Mexican state of Yucatan placed its first stamps in use.

March 17: The US Army four-plane round-the-world flight began at San Diego, Calif. Covers were carried on the first leg to Seattle, where they were backstamped March 20. The globe-circling flight made its official start on April 6 in Seattle, returning to the city on Sept. 28. The only mail carried on the Seattle-to-Seattle flight comprised three letters carried from England on the return flight to Seattle.

April 1: Southern Rhodesia was created from that part of Rhodesia south of the Zambezi River. Southern Rhodesia, now called Zimbabwe, released its first stamps on this date.

April 16: The new Republic of Greece, marking the centenary of the death of Lord Byron, issued its first stamps.

July 1: Day and night flying on a regular schedule over the US transcontinental air mail route started in a test of the lighted airway system between Cleveland, Ohio, and Rock Springs, Wyo. The tests proved successful. In conjunction with this service, three new air mail stamps were issued in denominations of 8c, 16c, and 24c to cover the three eight cents-per-ounce zones of the route. The zones were New York to Chicago, Chicago to Cheyenne, and Cheyenne to San Francisco. Aircraft left each end of the route simultaneously, making stops at 13 intermediate cities.

July 4: The Eighth Congress of the Universal Postal Union convened in Stockholm, Sweden. It reduced maximum and minimum international rates. Sweden issued a set of stamps to

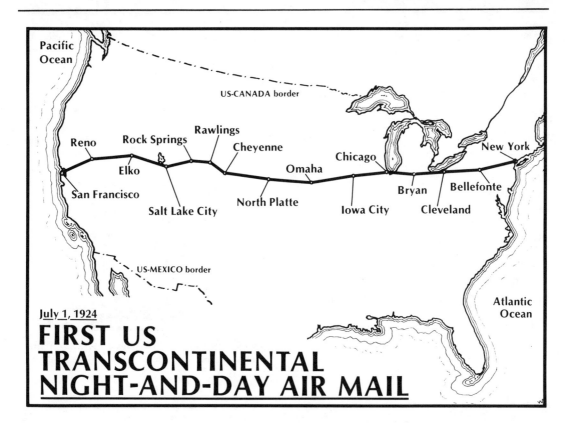

Pacific
Ocean

US-CANADA border

Rawlings

Reno   Rock Springs   Cheyenne   Chicago   New York

Elko   Omaha

San Francisco   Bryan   Bellefonte

Salt Lake City   North Platte   Iowa City   Cleveland

US-MEXICO border

Atlantic
Ocean

July 1, 1924

FIRST US TRANSCONTINENTAL NIGHT-AND-DAY AIR MAIL

mark the congress. The signing date of Oct. 9, 1874 was recognized as the anniversary date of the UPU, rather than the effective date of July 1, 1875 used formerly.

August: Mongolia issued its first stamps.

Sept. 21: The first Canadian company to operate an air service using a semi-official air mail stamp authorized by Canadian postal authorities was Laurentide Air Services Ltd., which inaugurated service between Haileybury, Ontario, and Rouyn, Quebec, on this date.

Oct. 8: The US dirigible USS *Shenandoah* made a transcontinental flight from Lakehurst, N.J., to Seattle, Wash. Some mail was carried, which received a special marking.

Oct. 12: Zeppelin LZ-126 left on its delivery flight to the United States where it was handed over as war reparations and renamed USS *Los*

Angeles. It was the first transatlantic flight by a Zeppelin dirigible and concluded at Lakehurst, N.J. on Oct. 15. It carried considerable mail on the flight, including some that was dropped over the Azores.

Oct. 12: The dirigible USS *Shenandoah* began its return trip to Lakehurst, N.J., from the West Coast. It carried mail and arrived at Lakehurst on Oct. 28.

Nov. 14: The first air mail in Burma was flown from Calcutta, India, to Akyab. It comprised 25 letters.

Dec. 14: A plane flying between Tehran and Enzeli carried the first air mail in Persia (Iran).

1925

Alaouites, an area of Syria under French mandate following World War I, placed its first stamps on sale.

Stamps were issued inscribed for the Territory of New Guinea. Administered by Australia, this territory was the area of the former German New Guinea, which had been taken by Australian forces at the beginning of World War I.

Jan. 1: The first air mail stamps were issued for use in Alaouites on a route between Latakia, Homs, and Damascus, thence on to Marseilles, France.

Jan. 5: Poland issued its first stamps overprinted "PORT/ GDANSK" for use at a Polish post office in the free city of Danzig.

Jan. 14: A survey air mail flight was made from Rio de Janeiro, Brazil, to Montevideo, Uruguay. It carried Brazil's first air mail.

Feb. 2: Legislation introduced by US Congressman Clyde M. Kelly to authorize the postmaster general to contract for air mail service was approved by Congress. The Kelly Act led to the formation of a network of air routes flown by private airlines that carried US mail on regular schedules (see Feb. 15, 1926).

Feb. 21: The Zeppelin USS *Los Angeles* made a flight to Bermuda. Bad weather prevented the dirigible from landing and, although mail was dropped, none was picked up.

Feb. 26: South Africa issued its first air mail stamps for use on a service inaugurated March

This cover was carried by Zeppelin LZ-126 on the first transatlantic flight by a Zeppelin dirigible (Oct. 12, 1924).

2, 1925 (q.v.). They picture the type of aircraft used and are in denominations of 1d, 3d, 6d, and 9d.

March: The Sultanate of the Nejd, later the Kingdom of Saudi Arabia, issued its first stamps.

March 2: South Africa inaugurated regular air mail service on an experimental basis between Cape Town and Durban, with stops at Oudtshoorn, Port Elizabeth, East London, and Mossel Bay. It abandoned the service in June, 1925. Four air mail stamps were issued for this service, which was operated by the South African Air Force.

March 19: The first US postage stamp in a denomination including a fraction of a cent went on sale. It is a 1½c stamp featuring the profile of President Harding and is part of the 1922-25 definitive series.

Bermuda marked the flight of USS *Los Angeles* with these stamps (April 21, 1925).

This cover was carried on the second flight to Bermuda of USS *Los Angeles* (April 21, 1925).

April 1: Northern Rhodesia issued its first stamps.

April 1: The US issued a 25c Special Handling stamp, the use of which ensured that fourth class mail would be handled as first class. On June 25, 1928, 10c, 15c, and 20c denominations were added.

April 8: The first air mail flight in Curacao, Netherlands Antilles, took place when mail was flown from Willemstadt to La Guaira, Venezuela.

April 15: The basic US registration fee went to 15c for $50 indemnity for first-class mail. There was no indemnity for second class and up to $25 for third class. A 3c charge was introduced for a return receipt previously furnished at no charge. The 20c fee for $100 indemnity remained in effect.

April 21: The USS *Los Angeles* made a second flight from Lakehurst, N.J., to Bermuda and moored at the mast of the ship USS *Patoka*. It flew mail to Bermuda and also picked up mail for the return flight.

April 23: The USS *Los Angeles* made the return flight from Bermuda to Lakehurst, N.J.

May 1: A post office opened on the English Channel island of Herm. The large household staff maintained by Lord Perry during the period that he leased the island made the postal facility necessary. It was a sub-post office of the

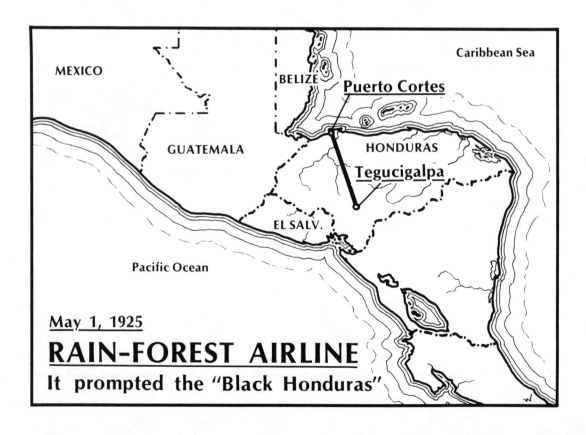

May 1, 1925

RAIN-FOREST AIRLINE
It prompted the "Black Honduras"

Bailiwick of Guernsey, of which the island was part. The office, located in the Mermaid Tavern, closed Nov. 30, 1938.

May 1: The first air mail flight of a new service between the Honduran capital city of Tegucigalpa and Puerto Cortes, on the Caribbean coast took place. The service was not successful and ended after a final forced landing on Dec. 21, 1925. The brief service is notable in that among the stamps overprinted and surcharged to frank mail carried was the famous *Black Honduras*, only one example of which is known. It is overprinted and surcharged "AERO. CORREO. 25" on the 10c dark blue denomination of the 1915-16 definitive series. The Honduran government had given Dr. T.C. Pound, an American resident who held the air mail contract, permission to make his own overprints on stamp it supplied, since it could not produce them in time. The work was done in the Tegucigalpa home basement of job printer Karl Snow.

May 3: The dirigible USS *Los Angeles* flew from Lakehurst, N.J. to Mayaguez, Puerto Rico, mooring to the ship USS *Patoka*.

May 8: The dirigible USS *Los Angeles* made the return flight from Mayaguez, Puerto Rico, to Lakehurst, N.J., arriving on May 10.

May 30: Albania issued its first air mail stamps.

June 6: The dirigible USS *Los Angeles* made a flight from Lakehurst to Minneapolis, Minn. Some mail was carried.

July 1: The US Post Office Department established overnight air mail service between New York and Chicago. It set a rate of 10c per ounce. Daytime service between these cities as a zone in the transcontinental air mail service continued at the zone rate of 8c per ounce.

July 3: The US dirigible USS *Shenandoah* made a so-called "Governors' Conference Flight" from Lakehurst, N.J., to Bar Harbor,

Maine. It carried mail on this flight and on its return flight the following day.

July 29: Stamps were issued for Jubaland (Oltre Giuba). The Italian colony is now part of the Somali Democratic Republic.

Aug. 19: The Italian pilot Marquese Francisco de Pinedo arrived on the Philippine island of Mindanao during a round-the-world flight. He carried mail on several flights within the Philippines.

Aug. 31: Two US Navy flying boats making a flight from San Francisco to Hawaii carried mail. Both aircraft were forced down at sea, one being towed to Kauai after being missing for nine days.

Sept. 10: Poland issued its first air mail stamps.

Sept. 16: The Italian pilot Francisco de Pinedo left Manila for Tokyo on his round-the-world flight. He carried mail to Aparri.

Oct. 5: The principality of Liechtenstein issued its first semi-postal stamps.

Oct. 25: The Netherlands introduced coil stamps with perforations in groups separated by a "bridges" where a perforating pin had been removed. These are called syncopated, or interrupted perforations and represented a successful attempt to prevent premature separa-

tion. Variations of the groupings were tried until 1934, when the idea seems to have been abandoned, according to Cabeen.

Nov. 3: Postal tax stamps were issued for the Portuguese colony of Macao.

Nov. 4: The Tokelau Islands were transferred from the Gilbert and Ellice group to New Zealand administration. Until May 6, 1946, they were known as the Union Islands. The islands did not issue stamps until June 22, 1948 (q.v.).

1926

The Kingdom of Yemen, now the Yemen Arab Republic, issued its first stamps.

Turkey began the use of air mail postal tax stamps.

Jan. 1: Norway issued its first official stamps.

Jan. 19: A US Post Office Department order of this date established air mail rates on contract air mail routes at 10c per ounce for up to 1,000 miles, 15c for up to 1,500 miles, and 20c for over 1,500 miles. The rates applied to mail carried on each CAM route. It cost 5c additional per ounce for carriage on a connecting route over each zone or part zone. Air mail stamps were issued for these rates: 10c (Feb. 13, 1926), 15c (Sept. 18, 1926), and 20c (Jan. 25, 1927).

February: The first stamps were issued for the Kingdom of Hejaz-Nejd, now the Kingdom of Saudi Arabia.

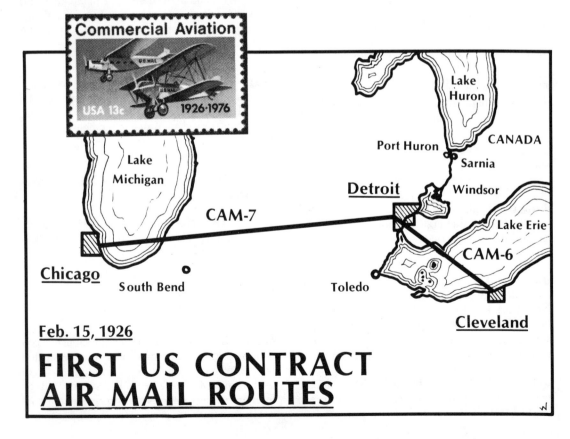

Feb. 15, 1926

FIRST US CONTRACT AIR MAIL ROUTES

Feb. 15: The first air mail routes flown in the United States under private contract started when Contract Air Mail Routes Six and Seven were first flown by the Ford Motor Company between Detroit and Cleveland (CAM-6) and Detroit and Chicago (CAM-7).

March 10: Egypt issued its first air mail stamp. It, and a subsequent stamp, depict what appears to be a De Havilland DH-54 aircraft, but no reference to the type operating in the Middle East can be found.

March 27: The first official government air mail flight in Canada was made from Toronto, Ontario, to Red Lake during the delivery flight of a Curtiss Lark aircraft to Patricia Airways.

Mail was picked up enroute at Sudbury, Pogomasing, and Sioux Lookout. Arrival date was April 12.

April: Syria issued its first semi-postal stamps. The surtax went to the relief of refugees of the Djebel Druze War.

April 1: Syria issued its first semi-postal air mail stamps.

April 5: Civilian air mail service began between Egypt and Baghdad, Iraq.

April 6: Contract Air Mail (CAM) Route #5 began operating between Elko, Nev., and Pasco, Wash.

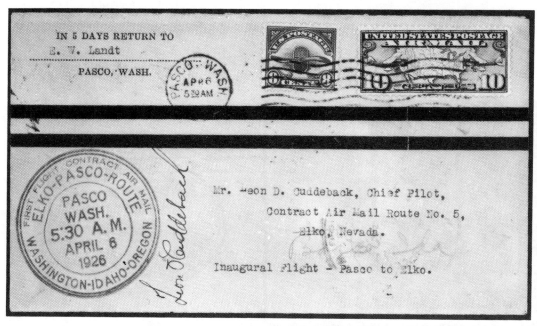

A cover carried on the first flight of CAM 5. The "Commercial Aviation" stamp shows a monoplane that flew CAM 6 and 7, while the biplane was used on CAM 5 (Feb. 15 and April 6, 1926).

April 10: Charles A. Lindbergh and Philip R. Love made test flights in De Havilland DH-4 aircraft over Contract Air Mail Route Two (CAM-2) between St. Louis, Mo., and Chicago. Some covers were flown and signed by Lindbergh.

April 10: The Italian dirigible *Norge* left Rome on a transpolar flight. To be used by the Amundsen-Ellsworth-Nobile polar expedition, it made several European stops on its flight to King's Bay, Spitsbergen. From there it flew to Teller, Alaska. The dirigible carried mail and a semi-official stamp was applied in addition to regular postage.

April 15: Charles A. Lindbergh flew the inaugural flight of Contract Air Mail Route Two (CAM-2) between Chicago and St. Louis, Mo.

May 1: Lebanon issued its first semi-postal stamps. The surtax went to refugee relief.

May 13: The first air mail stamps of the Philippines were issued in honor of the Madrid-to-Manila flight of Gallarza and Loriga. It was a 15-stamp set of overprints on regular stamps.

June 1: Jubaland placed its first semi-postal stamps on sale.

June 4: Costa Rica released its first air mail stamp.

June 18: The Federation Internationale de Philatelie (FIP) or International Philatelic Federation, was founded in Paris. Its present headquarters is in Geneva, Switzerland. Only the chief national philatelic organization in a country may become a member. The American Philatelic Society represents the United States.

July 2: The first international rocket flight carrying covers took place when Robert H. Goddard launched a rocket from McAllen, Texas, that landed at Reynosa, Mexico. It carried 1,072 covers that bear Mexican postage stamps and are postmarked at Reynosa.

July 18: A flight from Sibu to Kuching carried the first air mail in Sarawak.

Aug. 1: Pneumatic tube mail service was reestablished in Boston following the 1918 closure of all pneumatic tube service in US cities.

Aug. 23: The first air mail of the Straits Settlements was flown between Singapore, Kuala Lumpur, and Port Swetenham.

This is the semi-official stamp used on mail carried by *Norge*. The handstamp marking on the back of the item is seen at the right (April 10, 1926).

Sept. 15: A US air mail rate of 15c per ounce for distances of 1,000-1,500 miles went into effect.

Sept. 15: Spain placed in use its first semi-postal stamps and first air mail semi-postal stamps.

Sept. 16: Charles A. Lindbergh bailed out of his aircraft after becoming lost in fog and running out of fuel while flying CAM-2 from St. Louis, Mo., to Chicago (see Nov. 3, 1926).

Sept. 18: The first air mail in Portugal was flown on a flight from Alverca to Tangier, Morocco.

October: The American Air Mail Society was formed from the Aero Philatelic Society of America.

October: Tuva, sometimes called Tannu Tuva or Tuva Autonomous Region, and now known as Tuva Autonomous Soviet Socialist Republic, issued its first stamps.

A stamp of Tuva (October 1926).

Oct. 16: An international philatelic exhibition began in New York City and continued to Oct. 23. In conjunction with this show, the United States issued its first souvenir sheet.

Oct. 18: The US Post Office Department issued the White Plains souvenir sheet in conjunction with an international philatelic exhibition held Oct. 16-23, 1926 in New York City. It comprised 25 of the Battle of White Plains commemorative stamps and the selvedge bears a commemorative inscription referring to the exhibition. It is the first souvenir sheet issued by the United States.

The White Plains souvenir sheet; the first souvenir sheet issued by the United States (Oct. 18, 1926).

Oct. 20: The first Greek air mail stamps, comprising a set of four stamps, were issued. They were used on a service between Brindisi, Athens, Constantinople, and Rhodes.

Oct. 25: The Saar issued its first semi-postal stamps.

Nov. 3: Charles A. Lindbergh bailed out of his aircraft near Covell, Ill., after running out of fuel during bad weather, while flying CAM-2 between St. Louis and Chicago. This is the second time he had abandoned his plane on this route (see Sept. 16, 1926).

Nov. 25: Ship-to-shore mail was flown off SS *Homeric* by Sir Alan Cobham flying a De Havilland Moth seaplane. He landed at Battery Point in New York City. Covers bear a British stamp canceled "HOMERIC" and also bear US postage.

Nov. 28: Egypt issued its first special delivery stamp.

December: Official stamps were issued for South West Africa.

Dec. 20: The Philippine Islands issued its first Official stamps. They are the Legislative Palace issue of 1926 overprinted "OFFICIAL." Subsequent Officials featured the overprint "O.B."

1927

Stamps of Great Britain were overprinted "TANGIER" for use at the British post office in the International Zone of Tangier.

Jan. 1: Saudi Arabia joined the Universal Postal Union.

The first Greek air mail stamps were issued to frank mail on an air mail service between Italy, Greece, and Turkey (Oct. 20, 1926).

Jan. 25: A US air-mail rate of 20c per ounce for the maximum distance over contract air mail routes went into effect and a 20c air mail stamp was issued.

Feb. 1: A US air mail rate of 10c per half-ounce or fraction for mail carried on government or contract air mail routes went into effect.

Feb. 8: Iran issued its first air mail stamps. They consisted of overprints on stamps of 1909.

Feb. 15: The Italian colony of Libya placed semi-postal special delivery stamps in use.

May 21: The 60c stamp in Newfoundland's 1897 series was overprinted "Air Mail/ DE PINEDO/ 1927" to frank mail carried by Francesco De Pinedo on his transatlantic flight (see May 23, 1927).

May 23: Commander Francesco de Pinedo, an Italian, left Newfoundland for Rome in his seaplane *Santa Maria II.* He made a forced landing at sea near the Azores, but was found and towed to land. He resumed the flight and arrived June 16 at Rome. Newfoundland postal authorities issued a stamp to frank mail carried on the flight. It was an overprint on the 60c value of the 1897 Cabot issue.

June 1: While under British mandate from the League of Nations, Palestine issued stamps showing various scenes of the Holy Land.

June 7: The New Zealand Post Office established a postal agency on Pitcairn Island with R.E. Christian as postmaster. Stamps of New Zealand were used, according to Simpson.

June 13: Norway issued its first air mail stamp. It depicts an aircraft flying over Akershus Castle.

June 25: France issued air mail stamps comprising two stamps in the Merson design of 1900-06 issue overprinted with a Bleriot type aircraft and "Poste Aerienne." The stamps commemorated the First International Aeronautical Exhibition at Marseilles and franked air mail carried between Marseilles and Algiers, and Marseilles and Paris.

July 1: The Republic of Lebanon issued its first stamps while under League of Nations Mandate to France.

July 14: Beginning on this date, West Indian Aerial Express made an experimental mail flight between Barahona, Dominican Republic, Port-au-Prince, Haiti and Santo Domingo, Domincan Republic.

From left to right are the 20c US air mail stamp of Jan. 25, 1927, one of Palestine's June 1, 1927 series showing scenes of the country, Norway's first air mail stamp of June 13, 1927, and one of the first French air mail stamps issued June 25, 1927.

July 31: Clarence D. Chamberlin flew mail from the USS *Leviathan* off Fire Island, N.Y. to shore. Covers flown bear a special commemorative cachet.

Sept. 1: The American Railway Express Co. made the first air express flight in the United States from New York to Chicago.

Sept. 1: The Hague Air Mail Conference convened in the Dutch capital city. Thirty-eight postal administrations plus 14 air transport companies and other interested organizations attended. The conference set rates and devised a simple system of international accounting. The systems took effect Jan. 1, 1928 so that one year of experience could be gained before the next Universal Postal Union conference.

Oct. 3: Floating Safe stamps (q.v.) had been prepared for Curacao in a similar design to that used by the Netherlands and the Netherlands East Indies, but they were never issued. On this date, they were released overprinted "FRANKEERZEGEL" and surcharged in

denominations suitable for regular postal use. They were demonitized Jan. 23, 1930.

Oct. 4: The first Canadian Air Stage Service was flown when Western Canada Airways carried mail between the towns of Lac du Bonnet and Wadhope. Air Stage Service provided that all letter mail and parcel mail would be carried by air at regular surface rates on a space-available basis. This service was extended to numerous other routes. In many cases a special cachet was applied to mail carried on the first flights.

Oct. 10: French postage dues were overprinted for use in Martinique.

Oct. 19: Pan American Airways inaugurated its foreign air mail service when flights began

Pan American Airways

First overseas air mail route

Oct. 19, 1927

Gulf of Mexico

Miami

BAHAMAS

Key West

Havana

CUBA

Caribbean Sea

INAUGURACION CORREO AEREO OCT. 28 - 1927 KEY WEST - HABANA CUBA 12¢ AEREO

between Key West, Fla., and Havana, Cuba. The service had been operated briefly in 1920 by Florida West Indies Airways and by Aeromarine Airways for three weeks in 1923. The first Pan American flight was something less than auspicious, since by Oct. 19 the airline's Fokker trimotor aircraft had not been delivered. The first mail was actually carried to Havana by Cy Caldwell, who had stopped at Key West to refuel his Fairchild seaplane and was prevailed upon to drop the mail off at Havana! The story is told by Henry Ladd Smith in his book *Airways Abroad.* On Sept. 15, 1928, the US terminus was changed from Key West to Miami.

Nov. 1: Cuba issued its first air mail stamp.

Dec. 1: The US Post Office Department began to supply stamps in coils of 3,000 with the gummed side out, for use in machines which required either private coils or rewound Post Office coils. At this time the supply of imperforate stamps ceased.

Dec. 3: West Indian Aerial Express made its first regular air mail flight between the Dominican Republic and Puerto Rico. It began service to Haiti on Dec. 6 and to Cuba on Feb. 21, 1928.

Dec. 6: West Indian Aerial Express included Port-au-Prince, Haiti, in its air mail service between the Dominican Republic and Puerto Rico.

Dec. 10: Peru issued its first air mail stamp.

Dec. 28: Brazil placed its first air mail stamps on sale. They were overprints and surcharges on the country's 1913 Official stamps.

1928

During 1928, the US Post Office Department gave approval for the use of advertising slogans in conjunction with postage meters. These were called "postmark ads" by the meter manufacturers.

The first topical collection was exhibited, according to Hornung. A collector named Bernard Fetter of Luxembourg showed a topically arranged collection at a European exhibition that caused much head-scratching among the judges. It is not recorded whether it received an award.

Turkey began to use postal tax stamps.

Jan. 1: Lundy, an island in the Bristol Channel off the north coast of Devon, ceased to be served by the British Post Office following a dispute with the island's owner, Martin Coles Harmon. Harmon had bought the island for £16,000 in 1925. On Nov. 1, 1929, he began the release of local stamps inscribed for the island, which franked mail carried to the nearest British post office on the mainland.

Jan. 1: The Spanish Postal Administration opened a post office in Andorra at Andorra la Vieja, and set up postal agencies in a number of other communities. Stamps for Andorra were not immediately available and stamps then current in Spain were sold. The Spanish postal authorities and later, the French, agreed that both countries would recognize the freedom from postal charges of regular correspondence within the country. Thus, Andorra is the only country to enjoy free domestic mail service.

Feb. 6: Charles A. Lindbergh carried mail on a goodwill flight in the *Spirit of St. Louis* between the Dominican Republic, Haiti, and Cuba.

Feb. 20: On this date and the following day, Charles A. Lindbergh flew his old CAM-2 route from St. Louis to Chicago and return. So much souvenir mail was sent on the flights that several aircraft were required, but it is reported that Lindbergh flew each aircraft for a portion of the route. He made stops at Peoria, Ill., and Springfield, Ill.

This cover was on a flight over CAM-2 route from St. Louis to Chicago, when Charles A. Lindbergh made a special flight over the route he once flew as an air mail pilot (Feb. 20, 1928).

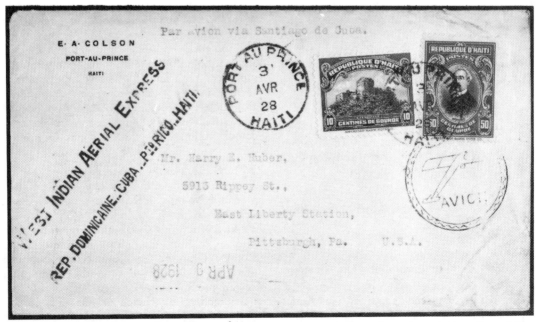

A cover carried by West Indian Aerial Express on its Cuba-Haiti-Dominican Republic-Puerto Rico route (Feb. 21, 1928).

Feb. 21: West Indian Aerial Express included Santiago-de-Cuba, Cuba, in its Haiti-Dominican Republic-Puerto Rico air mail service.

Feb. 25: Lt. James Doolittle made one of several survey flights in South America to demonstrate the possibilities of air mail service. This one carried mail from Lima, Peru, to La Paz, Bolivia. Subsequent flights were from La Paz to Santigo, Chile (March 22-24); Santiago to Buenos Aires, Argentina (May 8); plus Buenos Aires to Asuncion, Paraguay, and Asuncion to Rio de Janeiro, Brazil, on unrecorded dates.

March 1: Argentina issued its first air mail stamps, a 19-value set depicting various symbols of flight.

March 28: The Spanish post office in Andorra placed the first Andorran stamps on sale. They were Spanish stamps overprinted "CORREOS ANDORRA" in two lines. Denominations of 2c, 10c, 15c, 20c, 30c, 40c, and 1p are overprinted in red, and the remainder in black.

April 1: Afghanistan joined the Universal Postal Union.

April 1: Malta's first air mail stamp was issued on this date. The stamp franked mail sent by sea to Egypt for onward transmission by air.

May 21: The Canal Zone Postal Service issued its first air mail stamped envelope. It comprised a 2c stamped envelope of the 1924 series overprinted with red and blue horizontal bars.

May 31: Iceland issued its first air mail stamp.

May 31: The Dominican Republic released its first air mail stamp.

June 25: Special Handling stamps were issued in 10c, 15c, and 20c denominations by the US Post Office Department. Their use on fourth-class mail secured first-class handling. A 25c stamp had been released April 1, 1925 (q.v.).

July 1: The United States set registration fees in a range of from 15c (indemnity not more than $50) to $1 (indemnity not more than $1,000). Fees and indemnities were the same for first, second, and third classes. There was a 3c charge for a return receipt.

July 25: The United States issued the 5c Beacon air mail stamp to pay the 5c rate effective Aug. 1, 1928.

July 26: The first semi-postal air mail stamps were issued for French Morocco.

Aug. 1: An air-mail rate of 5c per ounce went into effect in the United States. The 5c Beacon air mail stamp had been released on July 25, 1928 to pay this rate.

Aug. 7: The US Post Office Department ordered the first precanceled stamped envelopes from contractors, according to James Kingman (personal correspondence).

Aug. 13: The first catapult mail flight was flown to New York from the French passenger liner *Ile de France* , designed to get the mail to the ship's destination or other point earlier than if it arrived on the ship. Only four such flights were made from the French vessel.

Aug. 28: Ecuador issued its first air mail stamps.

Sept. 1: Romania placed its first air mail stamps on sale. They depict a French-built Bleriot Spad 33 aircraft used on an early air route across Europe from Paris to Constantinople.

Sept. 18, 1928 - Sept. 24, 1928

The first air mail stamps of Romania (Sept. 1, 1928) and the Saar (Sept. 19, 1928).

Sept. 18: The German dirigible LZ-127 *Graf Zeppelin* made its first test flight. Some souvenir mail was carried.

Sept. 19: The Saar issued its first air mail stamps. They were used for service between Saarbrucken and Paris, and Saarbrucken and Frankfurt.

Sept. 20: The Netherlands Indies issued its first air mail stamps.

Sept. 20: The LZ-127 *Graf Zeppelin* made a flight over southwest Germany. A special "on board" handstamp was used for the first time on the dirigible.

Sept. 20: The first mail was flown from the Saar.

Sept. 21: Canadian postal authorities issued the first official Canadian air mail stamp.

Sept. 24: During Civic Week in Liverpool, England, F.J. Bailey flew an experimental air mail between that city and Belfast, Northern Ireland. The aircraft was a Short Calcutta flying boat. Flights continued until Sept. 29.

A cover carried on the LZ-127 *Graf Zeppelin* on its Oct. 29-Nov. 1, 1928 flight from Lakehurst to Friedrichshafen, Germany. This was the dirigible's first west-to-east transatlantic flight.

Oct. 11: The German dirigible LZ-127 *Graf Zeppelin* set out on its first transatlantic flight, arriving at Lakehurst, N.J. on Oct. 15. It dropped mail over Constance, Rheinfelden, Basel, the Azores, and Bermuda. The mail dropped at Bermuda fell into the sea.

Oct. 29: The LZ-127 *Graf Zeppelin* left Lakehurst, N.J., on the return from its first North American flight, arriving at Friedrichshafen, Germany, on Nov. 1.

Nov. 9: A flight of Royal Air Force seaplanes carried mail when they arrived in Manila on a good-will flight. Mail was also carried by these aircraft when they left for Hong Kong, Bangkok, and Singapore on Nov. 16.

Nov. 22: San Marino issued its first parcel post stamp. It is in the same format as those of Italy.

1929

In this year, the US Post Office Department recognized ordinary (non-permit) metered mail when regulations ceased to require a minimum number of identical pieces per mailing.

Pitney-Bowes introduced its first multi-denominational postage meter and used meter tape for the first time.

Jan. 1: Paraguay issued its first air mail stamps.

Jan. 2: The first air mail was flown from Paraguay to Buenos Aires, Argentina.

Jan. 6: Canada's famous stamp depicting the schooner *Bluenose* was issued on this date.

Some sources note the date as Jan. 8, but Jan. 6 is cited by Scott, Gibbons, and Robson Lowe.

Jan. 12: The US Post Office Department issued its first air mail stamped envelope. It has an indicium featuring a contemporary high-wing monoplane similar in arrangement to Lindbergh's *Spirit of St. Louis.*

Feb. 4: Charles A. Lindbergh flew the inaugural flight of air mail route FAM-5 from Miami to Cristobal, Canal Zone, and return. He arrived back in Miami on Feb. 13.

Feb. 8: Panama placed its first air mail stamps on sale.

March 6: Walter F. Brown became US postmaster general, succeeding Harry S. New.

March 9: Charles A. Lindbergh flew the inaugural air mail route FAM-8 from Mexico City to Brownsville, Texas, and back to Mexico City.

March 25: Belgium released its first special delivery stamps.

March 25: The so-called Orient Flight of the LZ-127 *Graf Zeppelin* began. The airship dropped mail over Palestine and returned to Friedrichshafen, Germany on March 28.

April 1: The United States issued the first air mail stamp for the Panama Canal Zone. It was an overprint on a regular stamp of the Canal Zone.

April 15: The earliest known use of some values of the US Kansas and Nebraska overprints bear this date. Their official issue date of May 1, 1929 is the date on which the two

Long considered one of the world's great stamps, Canada's *Bluenose* stamp continues to delight lovers of ships and ships on stamps. It has rendered immortal the beautiful vessel that ended its days on a Caribbean reef.

stamp issues were placed on sale at the Philatelic Agency in Washington, D.C.

April 22: The Universal Postal Union admitted Iraq to membership.

April 23: The LZ-127 *Graf Zeppelin* left on a Mediterranean flight. It dropped mail at Seville, Tangiers, and San Remo. The airship returned to Friedrichshafen, Germany, on April 25.

May 1: The United States placed Kansas and Nebraska overprints on sale at the Philatelic Agency in Washington, D.C. The stamps had

been distributed to post offices in the two states beginning April 13 and the earliest known use is April 15. The stamps were issued as an ex-

A postcard dropped from the *Graf Zeppelin* over Seville, Spain, during its Mediterranean flight (April 23, 1929).

periment to combat post office robberies by making it impossible to sell stolen stamps outside the state in which they are stolen. The experiment was deemed a failure and the "control" overprints were discontinued. The stamps involved were the 1c, 1½c, 2c, 3c, 4c, 5c, 6c, 7c, 8c, 9c, and 10c values in the current definitive series. The overprints read "Kans." and "Nebr."

May 10: The Ninth Congress of the Universal Postal Union convened in London, England. It adopted the air mail regulations established by the Air Mail Conference in 1927 at the Hague. A "small package" mail class was initiated.

May 10: Great Britain issued a set of four stamps to mark the Ninth Congress of the Universal Postal Union. This set included the magnificent £1 that is considered a modern classic. However, then and even now, surprise is expressed that Britain should have issued such a high-denomination commemorative stamp. Considering that its very conservative postal administration issued no other commemorative stamps between the 1924-25 British Empire Exhibition issue an the 1935 Silver Jubilee set, it seems even more remarkable.

May 11: Authorized delivery stamps were issued for the Italian colony of Libya.

May 15: Nicaragua issued its first air mail stamps.

May 20: Australia released its first air mail stamp, a 3d value depicting a De Havilland DH-66 three-engined aircraft of the type used on the Adelaide-Perth air mail and passenger service for which the stamp was issued. The aircraft is seen flying over a typical Australian landscape. The service was inaugurated on June 2, according to the *American Air Mail Catalog.* (Rosenblum gives the date as July 2).

May 20: Guatemala placed its first air mail stamps on sale. They were overprints on regular stamps of 1924 and 1926 surcharged in new denominations. The stamps' release coincided with the inaugural Pan American Airways flight to Mexico from Guatemala.

June 1: The Vatican City became a member of the Universal Postal Union.

June 5: Honduras released its first air mail semi-postal stamps.

June 12: The first successful mail delivery and pick-up from an ocean liner was made from the liner *Leviathan,* using the Adams air mail pick-up device.

July 6: The release of the first air mail stamps by Curacao (Netherlands Antilles) coincided with the inauguration of air mail service by Pan American Airways between the United States and the Panama Canal Zone via Curacao. The stamps were overprints and surcharges on regular issues.

July 19: An air mail flight from Vila in the New Hebrides to the French cruiser *Tourville* was made by an aircraft from the cruiser. The ship took the mail to near Noumea, New Caledonia, where it was flown ashore for onward transmission. Some sources note July 16 as the flight's date.

July 20: An aircraft that was catapulted from the French Cruiser *Tourville,* carried mail to Noumea, New Caledonia. The mail consisted of 10 letters.

July 22: The first catapult mail flight was launched from the German liner *Bremen,* a few days out of New York westbound. The mail was flown to the US East Coast and arrived many hours before the ship. This service was operated on a regular basis, except during the winter months, until the mid-1930s. *Bremen's* sister ship *Europa* was also fitted with a catapult (Sept. 15, 1930). In a further attempt to speed transatlantic mail service, mail was flown to the ship after it had left on westbound voyages.

August: Nicaragua issued its first air mail Official stamps.

Aug. 1: The Vatican issued its first stamps. Stamps in a design depicting the crossed keys emblem of the Vatican were in denominations of 5c to 75c, while 80c to 10 lira stamps featured a portrait of Pope Pius XI. The first design was printed by the intaglio process and the second was photogravure printed.

Aug. 1: The dirigible LZ-127 *Graf Zeppelin* left its base at Friedrichshafen for North America. The flight had begun on May 16, but engine trouble developed over France and the dirigible returned to its base for repairs.

Aug. 8: The dirigible *Graf Zeppelin* left

Lakehurst, N.J. on its return flight to Friedrichshafen. North American collectors regard this as the first leg of its globe-circling flight, but European collectors consider the flight began from Friedrichshafen on Aug. 15.

Aug. 15: The dirigible LZ-127 *Graf Zeppelin* left Friedrichshafen eastbound for Tokyo, Japan. It dropped mail at various points along the route.

Aug. 16: South Africa issued its first stamps printed by the government printer in Pretoria. The two stamps were also the country's second air mail issue.

Aug. 17: Ethiopia issued its first air mail stamps.

A cover catapulted from the liner *Bremen* on the first flight from the ship (July 22, 1929).

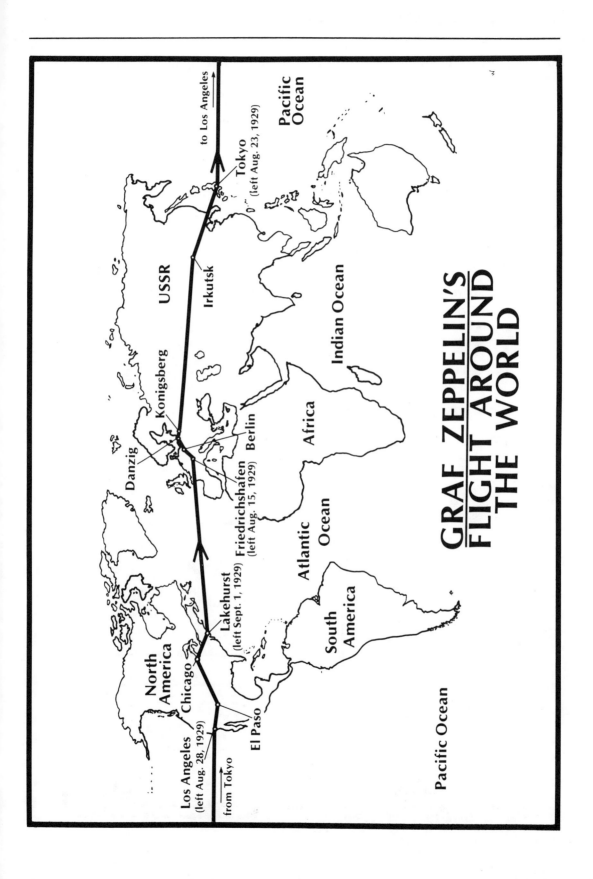

GRAF ZEPPELIN'S FLIGHT AROUND THE WORLD

to Los Angeles

Tokyo (left Aug. 23, 1929)

Pacific Ocean

USSR

Irkutsk

Konigsberg

Danzig

Berlin

Friedrichshafen (left Aug. 15, 1929)

Indian Ocean

Africa

Atlantic Ocean

South America

Lakehurst (left Sept. 1, 1929)

North America

Chicago

Los Angeles (left Aug. 28, 1929)

El Paso

from Tokyo

Pacific Ocean

Aug. 17, 1929 - Nov. 1, 1929

Aug. 17: Imperial Airways flew the first mail from Kuching, Sarawak, to London, via Karachi, in what is now Pakistan.

Aug. 23: The LZ-127 *Graf Zeppelin* left Tokyo on its round-the-world flight. It made the first nonstop crossing of the Pacific Ocean to Los Angeles, Calif.

Aug. 28: The LZ-127 *Graf Zeppelin* left Los Angeles for Lakehurst, N.J. overflying El Paso, Texas and Chicago and arriving at Lakehurst the following day. Collectors in the United States regard this as the completion of the round-the-world flight.

Aug. 29: South Africa's second and final air mail stamp issue comprised a pair of stamps issued Aug. 16, 1929 for a second regular air mail service between Cape Town and Durban on this date. They consist of two stamps in denominations of 4d and 1/- and had to be used in addition to the regular postage.

Sept. 1: The LZ-127 *Graf Zeppelin* left Lakehurst, N.J., for Friedrichshafen, arriving Sept. 4. German collectors regard this arrival as completion of the round-the-world flight.

Sept. 5: The first air mail was flown in Ethiopia nearly three weeks after the country issued air mail stamps.

Sept. 20: Charles A. Lindbergh flew the extension of air mail route FAM-6 from San Juan, Puerto Rico, to Paramaribo, Suriname. Lindbergh flew one of two Sikorsky S-38 aircraft, accompanied by Mrs. Lindbergh. The Lindberghs left FAM-6 on the return trip at Port of Spain, Trinidad. Southbound, stops had been made at St. Thomas, St. Kitts, St. Johns, Castries, Port of Spain, and Georgetown.

Oct. 14: A flight from France to Madagascar and Reunion carried mail both on the outward flight and the return flight to Paris. Outbound mail was backstamped Oct. 27 at Madagascar and on the return trip on Nov. 20 at Paris.

Oct. 22: India issued its first air mail stamps.

Nov. 1: Martin Coles Harmon, the owner of Lundy, an island off the North Devon coast of England, issued the island's first private local

These stamps from St. Lucia, Nevis, and Trinidad and Tobago mark the 50th anniversary of Lindbergh's flight extending FAM-6 from Puerto Rico to Suriname. The Trinidad and Tobago stamp shows the Lindberghs at Port of Spain, the islands' capital (Sept. 20, 1929).

stamps. The British post office on the island had been closed following a dispute with Harmon.

The stamps, denominated in "puffins" (one puffin was equal to one pre-decimal penny) became popular with both tourists visiting the island and collectors of local stamps.

Nov. 9: The last of the street car postal services, that in Baltimore, Md., ended on this date.

Nov. 25: The first set of specially printed stamps for the Spanish Post Office in Andorra went on sale. They depict various views of the country.

Nov. 28: Richard E. Byrd and two companions flew over the South Pole from a base on the Ross ice shelf in their aircraft *Floyd Bennett*. About 50 souvenir covers were carried on the flight.

Dec. 11: New Zealand issued its first semi-postal stamps. Since then, it has issued annual semi-postal stamps, the surtax of which has been devoted to providing health care and for the welfare of the country's children.

Dec. 28: El Salvador released its first air mail stamps.

1930

Jan. 1: The Kingdom of Yemen became a member of the Universal Postal Union. The country is now the Yemen Arab Republic.

Feb. 19: The New York, Rio, and Buenos Aires Airline (NYRBA) inaugurated through air mail service from Santiago, Chile, to Miami, Fla., via Buenos Aires, Rio de Janeiro, Pernambuco, Para, Georgetown, Port of Spain, and various stops in the Caribbean area. The failure of NYRBA to receive a contract to carry mail from the United States was its death blow. In August 1930, the airline was absorbed by Pan American Airways, which had already been granted the US mail contract.

March 15: One of the better-known stamps of France is the semi-postal issue depicting a smiling angel from Reims cathedral and known as *The Smile of Reims*, issued on this date.

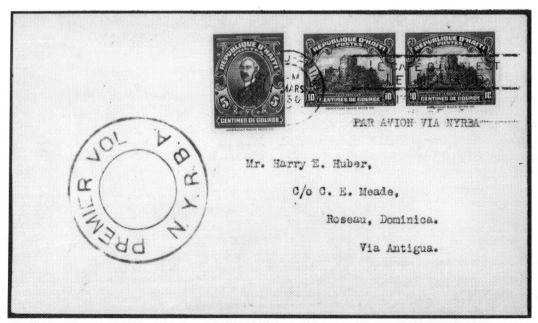

This cover was carried by the New York, Rio, and Buenos Aires Airline (NYBRA) on its service through the Caribbean (Feb. 19, 1930).

The Smile of Reims.

March 21: The first regular air mail flight from Brazil to Germany by German aircraft took place. The covers were canceled in Rio de Janeiro on March 21.

April 1: Jordan issued its first semi-postal stamps. They were overprints on definitive stamps and the surtax was used to combat a plague of locusts.

April 5: Venezuela released its first air mail stamps.

April 8: The Guam Guard Mail was inaugurated and operated "within the territorial limits of the Naval Government of Guam," according to an announcement on April 1, 1930 by the Governor and Naval Commander of the island, Commander Willis W. Bradley, Jr. A US naval officer was in charge of the postal service. Its first route was between Agana and Agat, including the towns of Asan, Piti, and Sumay. The first stamps were issues of the Philippines overprinted "GUAM/ GUARD/ MAIL."

April 19: The United States issued a three-stamp set of air mail stamps featuring the *Graf Zeppelin*. They were released for use on a North American flight by the dirigible. The stamps bear denominations of 65c, $1.30, and $2.60.

April 30: Belgium issued its first air mail stamps. They show an aircraft flying over various Belgian cities. The stamp designer must have utilized a photograph of a Fokker F.VIIa-3m aircraft without realizing the significance of its markings, since it bears the Italian registration I-BDEC!

May 12: French pilot Jean Mermoz flew from Paris to Rio de Janeiro to make the first French commercial flight across the South Atlantic Ocean. Covers were carried from France, Morocco, and Senegal.

May 18: The LZ-127 *Graf Zeppelin* left its base at Friedrichshafen, Germany, for Seville, Spain, on a flight to South America, north to the United States, and then east to Germany. The dirigible returned to Friedrichshafen on June 6.

May 19: The LZ-127 *Graf Zeppelin* left Seville, Spain, for Pernambuco, Brazil.

May 24: The LZ-127 *Graf Zeppelin* flew from Pernambuco, Brazil, to Rio de Janeiro.

The trio of US air mail stamps issued to frank mail on a North American flight by the *Graf Zeppelin* (April 19, 1930).

May 26: Latvia issued its first air mail semipostal stamps. It used the surtax to build a memorial to J. Rainis (Jan Plieksans 1865-1920), a writer and politician.

May 26: The LZ-127 *Graf Zeppelin* left Rio de Janeiro for Pernambuco, Brazil.

May 28: The LZ-127 *Graf Zeppelin* left Pernambuco, Brazil for Lakehurst, N.J. after picking up mail sent to Pernambuco from Argentina, Bolivia, Paraguay, and Uruguay.

May 29: Postmaster General Walter F. Brown authorized the use of Mailers Postmark Permit postmarks. At first authorized only to cancel postal stationery items, the regulations were changed on Sept. 21, 1978 to allow permit postmark holders to cancel definitive stamps. The cancelation of all US postage stamps has been permitted since July 30, 1979.

June 2: The LZ-127 *Graf Zeppelin* left Lakehurst, N.J. for Friedrichshafen via Seville, Spain. It arrived at Friedrichshafen on June 6.

June 28: Norway issued its first semi-postal stamps. They depict the North Cape and the surtax went to the Tourist Association.

June 29: The Central American country of Guatemala issued an aerogramme, then called an air letter sheet, in conjunction with a domestic air mail service. It had no franking value, according to Jennings, and is what is known as a formula item, to which postage stamps must be affixed.

The specially designed stamp for the Guam Guard Mail (July 1930).

July: Two specially designed stamps were issued for the Guam Guard Mail. Known as the second issue, they bear denominations of 1c and 2c. The design reproduced the seal of Guam, which features a beach scene and palm tree. On Aug. 10, 1930, the service reverted to the use of overprinted Philippine stamps, until it was discontinued on April 8, 1931.

July 9: The LZ-127 *Graf Zeppelin* made a flight north over Svalbard (Spitsbergen) where it dropped mail. It returned to Friedrichshafen on July 11.

July 16: Germany inaugurated a connecting air mail service to fly mail to the German liner *Europa* at sea or in an English Channel port, thus cutting westbound transatlantic time for mail.

July 22: Paraguay issued its first semi-postal stamps. The surtax went to the Red Cross.

July 26: Italy issued the first air mail stamps for its North African colony of Tripolitania. They consisted of the overprint "TRIPOLITANIA" on Italian air mail stamps of 1930.

July 29: The British dirigible R-100 left its base in England on a flight to Canada. It arrived at Montreal, PQ on Aug. 1.

Aug. 12: The Principality of Liechtenstein issued its first air mail stamps.

Aug. 13: The British dirigible R-100 began its return flight from Montreal, PQ, to England. No mail was officially carried, but a few letters are known to have been taken by crew members. Canadian postal authorities applied a special marking to mail posted at the airport at St. Hubert, PQ, during the dirigible's visit, but this was not flown.

Aug. 31: The first air mail was flown from Liechtenstein.

Sept. 9: The LZ-127 *Graf Zeppelin* began a flight to Moscow, returning to its base at Friedrichshafen on Sept. 11. The Soviet Union issued two stamps to mark the flight.

Sept. 15: The first catapult mail flight was made from the German liner *Europa* on a westbound voyage to New York. The flights, which cut hours from mail transit time, continued during the summer until 1935. Such flights had been inaugurated by *Bremen* on July 22, 1929.

Sept. 24: Finland issued its first air mail stamp. It consists of a regular postage stamp overprinted "ZEPPELIN/ 1930" and was issued to frank mail carried by the *Graf Zep-*

pelin on a flight from Finland to Germany on this date. The stamp was valid only for this flight.

Sept. 25: The 36c stamp in Newfoundland's 1919 issue was overprinted 'Trans-Atlantic/ AIR MAIL/ By B.M./ "Columbia"/ September/ 1930/ Fifty Cents,' to frank mail carried on the transatlantic flight by Boyd and Conner. See Oct. 9, 1930.

Oct. 9: The aircraft *Columbia* was flown by Capt. J. Errol Boyd and Lieut. Harry P. Conner from Newfoundland to England. The plane was forced to land on a beach in the Scilly Isles off Land's End, but completed the flight to

A cover flown from the German liner *Europa* during the period it was launching an aircraft to speed the mail ashore. The aircraft landed this cover at Southampton, England from an eastbound voyage.

Croydon. Newfoundland issued a special stamp on Sept. 25, 1930 to frank mail carried.

Nov. 5: The 12-engine flying boat Dornier DO-X left Altenrhein on Lake Constance in Germany to begin a flight that would take it to South America, the United States and back to Germany via Newfoundland. Considerable mail was carried beginning at Lisbon, Portugal.

Nov. 13: Uruguay issued its first semi-postal stamps, with the surtax going to a fund for the aged.

Nov. 15: This was the final closing date for mail to be received at Friedrichshafen, Germany, to be carried on the transatlantic flight of the flying boat Dornier DO-X. The mail was delivered to the aircraft while it was at Lisbon, no mail having been carried on the flight to that point, according to Hoffman.

December: The Dominican Republic issued its first postal tax stamps.

Dec. 3: The Dominican Republic issued its first Official air mail stamps and air mail postal tax stamps.

Dec. 17: A flight of 14 Italian Air Force aircraft under the command of Italo Balbo flew from Italy to Brazil, arriving at Rio de Janeiro on Jan. 22, 1931. A quantity of special mail was carried and Italy issued a stamp commemorating the flight.

1931

Jan. 2: Newfoundland issued a $1 air mail stamp depicting the routes of various historic transatlantic flights to and from the island.

Jan. 24: The Curtiss-Wright Flying Service of Glendale, Calif. flew mail to the SS *City of Los Angeles*. The ship had sailed from San Pedro, Calif. the previous day, bound for Honolulu. The mail was postmarked at Honolulu on Jan. 30.

Jan. 31: The flying boat Dornier DO-X left Lisbon and took 7½ hours to fly to the Canary Islands. It had been delayed at Lisbon when fire damaged the aircraft.

Feb. 2: The first rocket mail in Austria was flown when Friedrich Schmiedl launched a rocket containing 102 covers from the summit of Schoeckel Mountain to Radegund, located in the valley below.

Feb. 15: Sudan issued its first air mail stamps. They consisted of Camel Postman stamps overprinted "AIR MAIL."

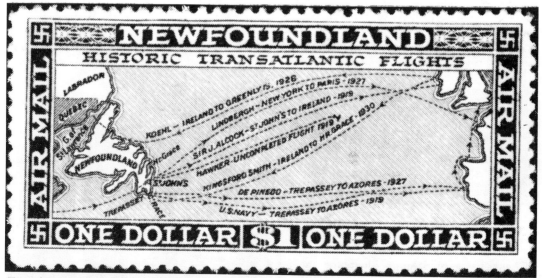

This $1 air mail stamp issued by Newfoundland traces the routes of various early transatlantic flights (Jan. 2, 1931).

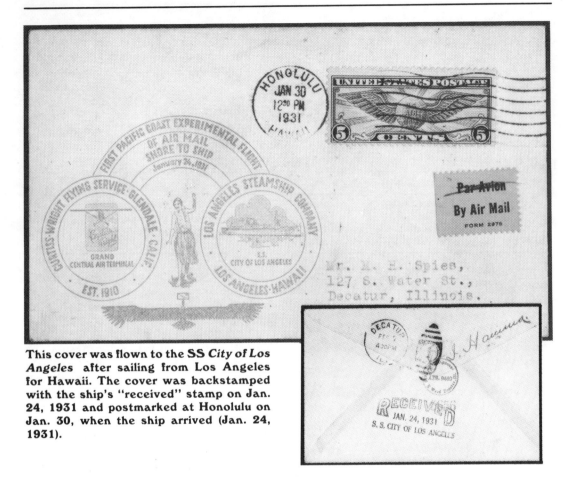

This cover was flown to the SS *City of Los Angeles* after sailing from Los Angeles for Hawaii. The cover was backstamped with the ship's "received" stamp on Jan. 24, 1931 and postmarked at Honolulu on Jan. 30, when the ship arrived (Jan. 24, 1931).

March: An authorized delivery stamp was issued for the Italian colony of Tripolitania.

March 5: The first specially designed stamps for use in South West Africa (Namibia) were issued. Since 1923 the territory mandated to South Africa following World War I had used South African stamps overprinted with "South West Africa" and "Zuid-West Afrika" in bilingual se-tenant pairs or with "S.W.A."

These pairs of stamps illustrate the two forms of overprint plus the stamps inscribed for South West Africa (March 5, 1931).

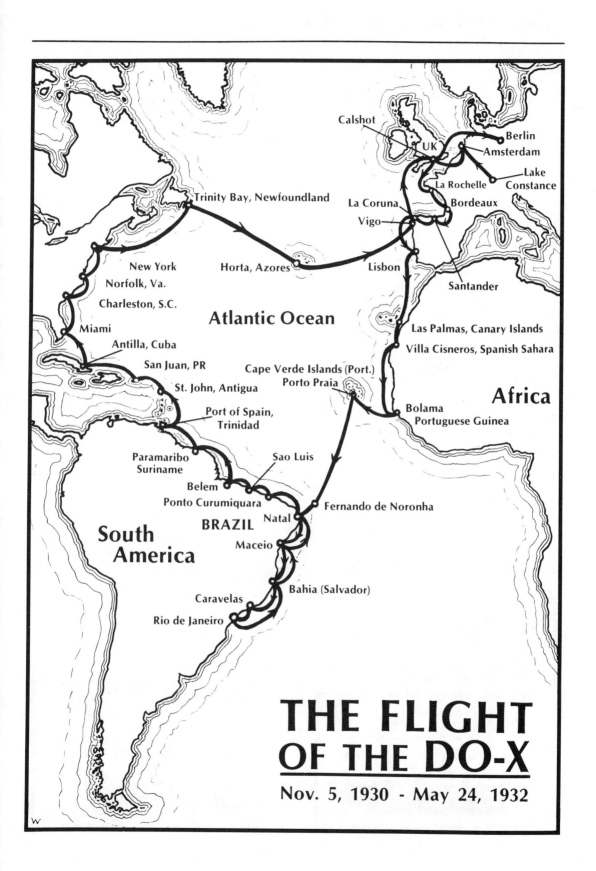

Calshot
Berlin
UK
Amsterdam
La Rochelle
Lake Constance
Trinity Bay, Newfoundland
La Coruna
Bordeaux
Vigo

New York
Horta, Azores
Lisbon
Norfolk, Va.
Charleston, S.C.
Santander

Atlantic Ocean

Miami
Las Palmas, Canary Islands
Antilla, Cuba
Villa Cisneros, Spanish Sahara
San Juan, PR
Cape Verde Islands (Port.)
St. John, Antigua
Porto Praia
Africa
Port of Spain,
Trinidad
Bolama
Portuguese Guinea

Paramaribo
Sao Luis
Suriname
Belem
Ponto Curumiquara
Fernando de Noronha
Natal
South
BRAZIL
America
Maceio

Caravelas
Bahia (Salvador)
Rio de Janeiro

THE FLIGHT
OF THE DO-X
Nov. 5, 1930 - May 24, 1932

March 18: US registration fees remained as of July 1, 1928 (q.v.) and the fee for a return receipt showing to whom and when delivery was made, remained at 3c. However, a return receipt showing also the address where delivery was made became available for a 23c fee. A return receipt could also be requested after mailing for a 5c fee.

April 1: The Indian feudatory state of Morvi issued stamps.

April 4: Imperial Airways of Great Britain began a test flight to Australia. The aircarft crashed at Kupang, Malaya, and Kingsford Smith flew in *Southern Cross* to pick up the mail, which he took to Darwin, Australia. There it was taken over by Queensland and Northern Territory Air Service for delivery to destination cities.

April 6: The first air mail from Brunei was flown to Singapore.

April 8: A notice in the *Guam Recorder* of April announced the end of the Guam Guard Mail. It noted that remaining stamped paper

was to be taken by the Naval Government of Guam and sold with the proceeds to be applied to the public benefit.

April 9: The LZ-127 *Graf Zeppelin* began a flight to Egypt and Palestine. It returned to Friedrichshafen on April 13.

April 14: Britain's Imperial Airways began passenger and mail service from London to Australia. It carried cacheted covers on the Rangoon-Darwin leg. It also carried mail that originated at Singapore.

April 15: The first rocket flight carrying a number of imprinted postcards took place in Germany near Osnabruck. The rocket rose to about 5,000 feet and landed near the launch site.

April 23: The first official air mail flight from Australia to London began. The flight originated at Melbourne and carried some mail from New Zealand.

May 1: The flying boat Dornier DO-X flew to Villa Cisneros in Rio de Oro, on the African

Stamps of many countries have honored that lumbering giant of the sky, the Dornier DO-X (May 1, 1931).

This cover was carried on the first Pacific ship-to-shore flight (June 12, 1931).

coast. It had been delayed in the Canary Islands while repairs were carried out to damage sustained during a Feb. 3 takeoff attempt.

May 3: The Dornier DO-X left Villa Cisneros and flew to Bolama in Portuguese Guinea.

May 16: A naval aircraft flew from USS *Chicago* at sea near Samoa and carried about 150 covers to Pago Pago in American Samoa.

May 30: The flying boat Dornier DO-X flew to the Cape Verde Islands from Portuguese Guinea.

May 31: Australia issued Official stamps, which comprised the definitive issue of 1931 overprinted "OS."

June 4: The Dornier DO-X left the Cape Verde Islands and flew across the Atlantic to Fernando de Noronha, Brazil, where it arrived the next day.

June 5: The Dornier DO-X flew from Fernando de Noronha to Natal on the Brazilian mainland.

June 11: San Marino issued its first air mail stamps. The stamps franked mail carried by air from an Italian airfield.

June 12: The first Pacific Ocean ship-to-shore flight took place when the Goodyear Blimp *Volunteer* met the SS *City of Los Angeles* 50 miles off San Pedro, Calif. Mail was transferred to the blimp, which carried it to the roof of the San Pedro Post Office.

June 16: The new French post office in Andorra issued a set of 36 stamps. Except for three stamps, they were normal French stamps overprinted "ANDORRE." The remaining three were specially printed French stamps similarly overprinted.

June 18: The flying boat Dornier DO-X flew from Natal, Brazil, to Maceio and Bahia (Salvador), also in Brazil.

June 18: The first air mail flight was made from Malta. Its destination was Tripoli, Libya.

June 19: The Dornier DO-X flew from Salvador, Brazil, to Caravelas and San Pedro de Aldea.

June 20: The Dornier DO-X arrived in Rio de Janeiro.

June 24: India issued its first air mail postal card. The indicium reproduced the design of the 1929 Indian air mail stamp and had a denomination of 4 annas.

July: The French mandated territory of Latakia, formerly Alaouites, issued its first stamps.

July 1: The first stamps were issued for Gibraltar showing a view of the famous "Rock." Up to then, all stamps had featured profiles of the reigning monarch.

July 13: British flyer Francis C. Chichester carried mail to Manila when he arrived during his flight from Australia to Japan. See Aug. 3, 1931.

July 24: The LZ-127 *Graf Zeppelin* began a polar flight, which included a transfer of mail with the Soviet icebreaker *Malyguin*. Both Germany and the Soviet Union issued special stamps marking the flight. The dirigible returned to Friedrichshafen on July 31.

July 28: A globe-circling flight by Hugh Herndon and Clyde Pangborn began from Floyd Bennett Field, N.Y. Their return across the Pacific Ocean to Wenatchee, Wash., occurred on Oct. 2 (q.v.).

Aug. 2: Luxembourg issued its first semi-postal stamps. The surtax went to a fund to erect a monument for the soldiers of Luxembourg killed by the Germans during World War I.

Aug. 3: British flyer Francis C. Chichester left Manila for Japan, carrying mail from Australia and the Philippines. The flight ended at Katsura, when he crashed, the aircraft being destroyed. Only part of the mail was recovered.

Aug. 5: The flying boat Dornier DO-X left Rio de Janeiro and flew north to Caravelas and Bahia (Salvador), Brazil.

Aug. 6: The Dornier DO-X flew to Natal, Brazil, from Bahia (Salvador).

Aug. 7: Dornier DO-X flew from Natal, Brazil, to Ponto Curumiquara and Sao Luis, both also in Brazil.

Aug. 8: The Dornier DO-X flew from Sao Luis to Belem (Para), Brazil.

Aug. 18: The Dornier DO-X arrived at Paramaribo, Suriname, from Belem (Para) in northern Brazil after being delayed by an engine failure.

Aug. 19: The Dornier DO-X arrived at Port of Spain, Trinidad.

Aug. 20: The Dornier DO-X flew from Port of Spain, Trinidad, to St. John's, Antigua and San Juan, Puerto Rico.

Aug. 21: The Dornier DO-X flew from San Juan, Puerto Rico, to Antilla, Cuba.

Aug. 22: The Dornier DO-X flew from Antilla, Cuba, to Miami, Fla.

Aug. 25: The Dornier DO-X flew to Charleston, S.C., from Miami.

Aug. 26: The Dornier DO-X flew from Charleston, S.C., to Norfolk, Va.

Aug. 27: The Dornier DO-X arrived at New York on its flight from Norfolk, Va.

Aug. 29: The LZ-127 *Graf Zeppelin* left on the first of three flights to South America during 1931. Brazil issued two stamps marking the flight.

Sept. 18: Between this date and Sept. 28, LZ-127 *Graf Zeppelin* made its second 1931 flight to South America.

Oct. 1: The Vatican issued its first parcel post stamps. They were regular stamps overprinted "PER PACCHI". Postage due labels were also issued on this date.

Oct. 2: Herndon and Pangborn flew nonstop from Japan to Wenatchee, Wash. On Jan. 2, 1981, the United States issued a postal card commemorating the 50th anniversary of the flight. Despite its inscription "FIRST TRANSPACIFIC FLIGHT," the Pacific had been flown twice previously; by Kingsford Smith in 1928 and by the dirigible *Graf Zeppelin* in 1929. It was, however, the first nonstop flight across the Pacific by a heavier-than-air craft.

Oct. 17: LZ-127 *Graf Zeppelin* began its third 1931 flight to South America. It returned to base at Friedrichshafen on Oct. 28.

Nov. 11: New Zealand issued its first air mail stamps.

Nov. 12: The first official air mail flight made from New Zealand to Sydney, Australia, connected with an Australia-to-London air mail flight carrying Christmas mail.

Nov. 20: The first air mail from Gibraltar was

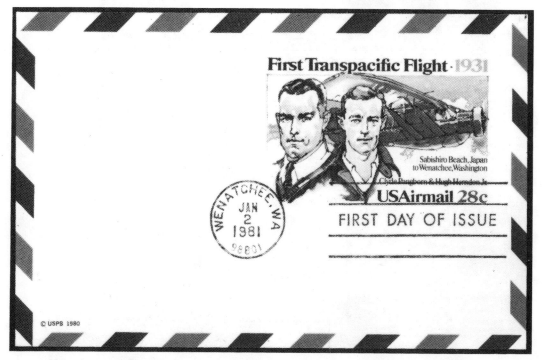

Herndon and Pangborn are remembered, but inaccurately! (Oct. 2, 1931).

Dec. 1, 1931 - Jan. 1, 1932

flown to Tangier by a Saro Windhover amphibian aircraft belonging to M. H. Bland & Co. The firm opened regular service between Gibraltar and Tangier, on the African side of the strait. The aircraft was later sold and is also pictured on a 1985 stamp of Alderney, one of the English Channel islands.

Dec. 1: A Christmas air mail flight left Sydney, Australia, for London on this date. The intention was to deliver the mail in London and pick up mail and return with it to Australia in time for Christmas. The aircraft had mechanical problems at Alor Star, Malaya, and in order to try to meet the schedule, Kingsford Smith picked up the mail and flew it to London, arriving on Dec. 16. He arrived back in Sydney on Jan. 21, 1932.

1932

Jan. 1: The United States issued a set of 12 stamps marking the 200th anniversary of George Washington's birth.

Twelve stamps marked Washington's 200th birthday.

Feb. 18: The Japanese established a puppet government over Manchoukou. The regime was recognized only by Japan's allies, Germany and Italy, plus the Central American country of El Salvador!

March 14: Australia issued what has become a modern classic stamp, the 5/- value marking the opening of the Sydney Harbor Bridge. The set comprises 2d, 3d, 5/- denominations, all in the same design. A quantity of 72,800 of the 5/- stamp is reported by Rosenblum.

March 16: Stamps were released inscribed for the Cook Islands. Since April 1919 the island-group's stamps had been inscribed "Rarotonga", the chief island. Robson Lowe gives the issue date as March 15.

March 19: The LZ-127 *Graf Zeppelin* began the first of nine roundtrip flights to South America during 1932. It returned to Friedrichshafen from the first flight on March 29. Dates of the other South American flights are April 4-13, April 18-27, May 2-10, Aug. 29-Sept. 7, Sept. 12-21, Sept. 26-Oct. 4, Oct. 9-19, and Oct. 24-Nov. 3.

March 20: The Department of Communications of the Japanese government in Manchoukuo (comprising Manchuria and the Chinese province of Jehol) announced that it would take over the postal administration from China on April 1, 1932. Chinese officials were to operate the postal system until Aug. 1, but unrest caused the complete takeover on July 26. This became the issue date of stamps for Manchoukuo.

April 1: Iraq issued its first stamps as an independent kingdom. The British had given up the League of Nations mandate over the area in 1932.

April 7: Inini, comprising the greater part of inland French Guiana, received its own stamps. They were overprints on stamps of French Guiana. It was merged with French Guiana again in 1946, when the entire area became an overseas department of France. The area now uses French stamps.

April 18: The Caribbean island of Montserrat issued a set of stamps marking the 200th anniversary of the island's colonization. It was also the first issue to depict the island as seen from a ship off the main town of Plymouth.

May 8: The dirigible USS *Akron* began a transcontinental flight from Lakehurst, N.J., to Moffat Field, Calif., arriving on May 11. Mail was carried by special arrangement with the US Post Office Department.

May 17: A rather belated Act of the US Congress made legal the reversion of the spelling "Puerto Rico." The spelling had been anglicized to "Porto Rico" upon the expulsion of

Spain from the island by US forces during the Spanish-American War of 1898. However, the spelling was offensive to the inhabitants and the United States postal officials reverted to the original spelling in late 1899.

May 19: The flying boat Dornier DO-X left New York after an overhaul and extended visit since Aug. 27, 1931. She flew to Newfoundland.

This is the rare inverted overprint.

May 20: A $1 air mail stamp in Newfoundland's 1931 series was overprinted "TRANS-ATLANTIC/ WEST TO EAST/ Per Dornier DO-X,/May, 1932/ One Dollar and Fifty Cents," to frank mail carried by the giant flying boat on its homeward flight.

May 20: The Dornier DO-X left Newfoundland for Horta in the Azores, arriving on the following day.

May 22: The Dornier DO-X flew from Horta, Azores to Vigo, Spain.

May 23: The Dornier DO-X took off from Vigo, Spain, for Calshot, England.

May 24: The Dornier DO-X flew from Calshot, England to Berlin, thus completing a journey that had begun on Nov. 5, 1930 from the waters of Lake Constance. It carried a large amount of mail on the flight. Newfoundland and Suriname issued special stamps to mark its visit and to frank mail carried during the various stages of the flight.

June 2: Italy issued air mail special delivery stamps.

June 16: The first specially designed stamps for Andorra were issued by the French post office in that country. There were 22 denominations in five different designs featuring scenes of Andorra.

June 28: The LZ-127 *Graf Zeppelin* visited Switzerland and Liechtenstein on its 250th flight. Mail was carried.

July 1: The basic US registration fee of 15c remained in effect, but some adjustments were made in the graduated scale. All were upward except for the not-more-than $900 indemnity fee, which went from $1 to 95c. From this date, the actual value of an item had to be declared and if it was in excess of the indemnity value, had to be paid for. This was done as a surcharge based on the amount of the excess and distance carried.

July 6: The US air mail letter rate became 8c per ounce plus 13c per ounce for each additional ounce or fraction.

July 11: Italy issued stamps for general use in its colonies. They were stamps of Italy overprinted "COLONIE ITALIANE," in both regular and air mail denominations.

July 21: Captain Wolfgang von Gronau left the island of Sylt, Germany, on a round-the-world flight. He carried mail and the Philippines issued overprinted commemorative stamps to mark his visit to that country. Von Gronau completed the flight on Nov. 10, 1932.

July 26: The Japanese puppet government of Manchoukou issued its first stamps.

July 30: The LZ-127 *Graf Zeppelin* began a flight to Danzig in conjunction with LUPOSTA, an international stamp exhibition in that city. The airship made the return flight to Friedrichshafen on Aug. 1.

August: Aerial Transport Company, operating in Thailand, created a lightweight air letter sheet called an "Air O Gram." It was a formula item, in that adhesive postage stamps had to be affixed. An employee of the company, R.B. Jackson, is credited with the design.

Aug. 1: The dirigible USS *Akron* made a training flight from Lakehurst, N.J., returning the next day. Mail was carried.

Aug. 31: This was the departure date planned for a passenger and mail flight from Wayzata, Minn., to London, England, via Toronto, Montreal, St. Pierre and Miquelon, Newfoundland, Greenland, Iceland, Norway, Sweden, Finland, Leningrad, Latvia, Germany, and Denmark. A stamp was issued to help finance the ambitious scheme and the Newfoundland government agreed to sell the stamps, but backed out on Sept. 13, 1932, after strong opposition had developed.

Newfoundland stated the reason for its withdrawal was that the flight had not begun on the scheduled date. The flight plans were eventually canceled and some of the stamps were placed on the philatelic market, while the Newfoundland Post Office destroyed those it held.

Sept. 22: German flyer Wolfgang von Gronau left Shanghai, China, for Manila, Philippines. He carried mail and arrived there Sept. 24. The Philippines issued special stamps marking the globe-circling flight. They consist of overprints showing his Dornier Wal aircraft.

Sept. 29: After 5 days in the Philippines, German flyer Wolfgang von Gronau left to continue his round-the-world flight. He carried some mail to Surabaya, Java and a reported 471 pieces of mail to Friedrichshafen, Germany. Most of the latter "went missing" and the American Air Mail Catalog notes that only 27 covers were delivered.

Sept. 30: The first contract air mail flights in the Territory of Papua were made by Guinea Airways Ltd. from Port Moresby to Salamaua, the nearest landing ground to the Papuan goldfields. Individual flights had been made previously, the first on March 16, 1928.

A cover carried on Britain's Great Western Railway air service (April 12, 1933).

Oct. 6: Italy issued air mail special delivery stamps for general use in the Italian colonies.

Oct. 27: The dirigible USS *Macon* made a mail-carrying flight from Moffat Field, Calif. to San Francisco, Los Angeles, and San Diego.

Nov. 1: Letter seals were issued for use by British forces stationed in Egypt. Commonly called NAAFI seals because they were obtained from Navy, Army, and Air Force Institutes (NAAFI) canteens (the British version of the American PX), letters bearing these seals on the back were transmitted at a reduced rate.

1933

Jan. 2: Swaziland issued its first stamps as a British protectorate.

March 4: President Franklin D. Roosevelt, appointed James A. Farley as US postmaster general. He succeeded Walter F. Brown.

April 12: Britain's Great Western Railway inaugurated an air service carrying mail and passengers between Cardiff and Plymouth, with a stop at Haldon Aerodrome to serve Torquay and Teignmouth. A special stamp was issued by the railway company on May 15, 1933. The service was not a success and ended on Sept. 9, 1933.

April 28: Iceland placed its first semi-postal stamps on sale. The surtax funded Icelandic charitable organizations.

May 1: Tibet issued a new series of stamps in five denominations. Because Tibet did not belong to the Universal Postal Union, letters to other countries had to bear stamps of another country, usually India.

May 6: The LZ-127 *Graf Zeppelin* left on the first of nine flights to South America during 1933. It returned on May 17. Dates of the other flights are June 3-13, July 1-12, Aug. 5-15, Aug. 19-29, Sept. 2-12, Sept. 16-26, Sept. 30-Oct. 10, and Oct. 14-Dec. 2. The final flight returned via the Century of Progress Exposition in Chicago.

The Austrian WIPA souvenir sheet (June 23, 1933).

May 29: The LZ-127 *Graf Zeppelin* flew to Italy, returning to Friedrichshafen the next day. Commemorative stamps were issued to mark the flight by Italy, San Marino, Greece, Aegean Islands, Cyrenaica, and Tripolitania.

June 23: Austria issued a souvenir sheet to mark the international philatelic exhibition held in Vienna. It contains four 50g stamps reproducing a mailcoach from a painting by Moritz von Schwind. This sheet is now a major rarity. It is known as the WIPA Sheet from the acronym of the exhibition.

July 1: A mass flight of 24 Italian flying boats commanded by Italo Balbo, left Italy for the Chicago Century of Progress Exposition. Italy and its colonies issued a number of special stamps marking the flight. The return flight began July 23.

July 15: Iraq issued the first aerogramme that included an indicium in the form of a 15-fil imprinted stamp featuring King Faisal. Previously, Guatemala had issued an air letter sheet in 1930, one had been issued in Thailand in 1932, and as long ago as 1870-71 France had issued an air letter sheet for use on its balloon air mail service from Paris during the seige. All three items had required the use of adhesive postage stamps and thus are correctly known as formula items. Major D.W. Gumbley is credited with the development of the Iraq aerogramme when he set up an air mail service from that country to Great Britain that operated at the regular letter rate of 15 fils.

July 23: The mass flight of Italian flying boats began its return flight to Italy after visiting the Century of Progress Exposition in Chicago.

July 24: The 75c stamp in Newfoundland's

1933 air mail series was overprinted "1933/GEN. BALBO/ FLIGHT./ $4.50" with the original denomination blocked out. They were used to frank mail on the mass flight of flying boats under Italo Balbo's command returning to Italy from a visit to the Chicago Century of Progress Exposition (see Aug. 8).

Aug. 8: The flight of flying boats commanded by Balbo left Newfoundland for Rome via the Azores. They carried mail franked by a special stamp issued by Newfoundland (see July 24) and most covers are postmarked at St. John's on July 26 and with Aug. 12-15 arrival markings.

Aug. 10: Bahrain issued its first stamps. They were stamps of India overprinted "BAHRAIN."

Aug. 22: Monaco's first air mail stamp consisted of an overprint of a Bleriot aircraft and the surcharge "1F50" on a definitive stamp of 1925.

One of the triptychs issued by Italy to mark the flight of aircraft to the Chicago Century of Progress Exposition (July 1, 1933).

Sept. 17: Postal tax stamps were issued by Yugoslavia. The surtax went to the Red Cross.

Oct. 1: Brazil issued its first postal tax stamp. Its use was compulsory on mail to the Americas and Spain, and optional to other countries. The money raised went to fund airport construction in Brazil.

Oct. 2: A single 50c US air mail stamp picturing the *Graf Zeppelin* was issued to mark the dirigible's visit to the Chicago Exposition. It is sometimes referred to as the "Baby Zep" to distinguish it from its three more expensive cousins.

Oct. 14: The LZ-127 *Graf Zeppelin* left on its ninth South American flight of 1933. The return flight to Germany included a visit to the Chicago Century of Progress Exposition. This flight represented *Graf Zeppelin's* fifth visit to the United States and its 50th transatlantic crossing. The dirigible flew via Recife, Rio de Janeiro, Recife, Miami, Chicago, and Seville, returning to Friedrichshafen on Dec. 2.

Oct. 23: Italy issued its first air mail semipostal stamps.

Nov. 20: French Guiana released its first air mail stamps.

Dec. 1: The British Protectorate of Basutoland placed its first stamps on sale.

1934

The British Post Office experimented with an optical scanner in an attempt to automate the segregation and facing of mail. The device proved unsuccessful.

Jan. 1: The Kingdom of Saudi Arabia, formerly the Kingdom of Hejaz-Nejd, issued its first stamps on this date.

Jan. 27: Stamps were issued for use on mail originating from the headquarters of the permanent Court of International Justice at The Hague in the Netherlands.

Feb. 1: The 10th Congress of the Universal Postal Union and the first to be held in Africa, convened in Cairo, Egypt. It discussed standardizing sizes of mail items and reduced transit charges. The Congress made its decisions effective Jan. 1, 1935. Egypt issued a set of commemorative stamps marking the event.

Feb. 2: Air mail service began between Germany and South America via The Gambia and a supply ship stationed in the middle of the South Atlantic crossing.

Feb. 17: Pilot C. T. P. Ulm flew the aircraft VH-UXX *Faith in Australia* across the Tasman Sea from New Zealand to Australia. New Zealand issued a commemorative overprint to mark the flight.

Feb. 19: The US Army began to fly the mail following President Franklin D. Roosevelt's cancelation of air mail contracts. Its unsuitable equipment and lack of experience caused numerous accidents. The experiment was quickly terminated and new civilian mail-carrying contracts negotiated.

Feb. 20: The United States introduced revenue stamps indicating payment of a tax on profits realized from the sale of silver. They were used until June 4, 1963.

Feb. 28: The British naval vessel HMS *Milford* with Admiral Evans aboard, returned to Cape Town from a visit to Bouvet Island, a

A cover carried by the aircraft *Faith in Australia* from New Zealand to Australia (Feb. 17, 1934).

Norwegian possession in the South Atlantic, about 1,350 miles southwest of Cape Town. A small supply of Norwegian stamps had been obtained from the Norwegian consul there and were overprinted "BOUVET/ OYA" with the consul's approval. Mail was franked with the stamps and accepted by the Cape Town Post Office on the ship's return on this date. However, the Norwegian government repudiated the action and requested that the stamps not be regarded as official. About 1,200 stamps of various denominations were postally used, according to Pirie.

March 16: The creation of US Federal Migratory Waterfowl Hunting stamps was authorized by Congress on this date. The first Duck stamp was issued on Aug. 14, 1934.

March 30: The New Zealand postal agency on Washington Island closed.

April 12: C. T. P. Ulm flew the aircraft VH-UXX *Faith in Australia* from Australia to New Zealand on an official air mail flight.

May: Mail was flown by an autogiro for the first time. The flight was from Hanworth, London to Windsor, Berks., England. The autogiro was the ancestor of the helicopter, although its large rotor was unpowered and produced lift from its free-wheeling rotation.

May 1: The Italian colony of Tripolitania issued air mail special delivery stamps.

May 26: The LZ-127 *Graf Zeppelin* began the first of 12 flights to South America during 1934. The dirigible returned to Friedrichshafen on June 5. The dates of the other 1934 South American Flights are June 9-19, June 23-July 6, July 21-31, Aug. 4-14, Aug. 18-28, Sept. 1-11, Sept. 15-25, Sept. 29-Oct. 9, Oct. 13-23, Oct. 27-Nov. 6, and Dec. 8-19. It made a number of flights in Europe between the dates of the South American flights.

May 28: Air France inaugurated air mail service between France and South America. Jean Mermoz left Toulouse, France, on this date for Natal, Brazil via Senegal, Africa. Monthly flights in both directions followed.

May 31: The United States, which had used

June 6, 1934 - Aug. 14, 1934

military aircraft to carry mail since Feb. 19, restored the job to civilian airlines operating under new contracts. There had been many accidents and public outcry forced the government to revert to use of the commercial airline system.

June 6: The first rocket mail flight in England took place at Rottingdean, near Brighton, when Gerhard Zucker launched a rocket which covered a distance of about 900 yards. Two flights were made carrying a total of 2,864 souvenir covers.

June 15: Yugoslavia issued its first air mail stamps.

July 1: A US domestic air-mail rate of 6c per ounce went into effect. This represented a reduction of 2c from the previous rate.

July 9: Although the scale of US registration fees was not changed, a 10c charge for delivery restricted to addressee only was inaugurated. This service had previously been provided without charge.

July 15: Turkey issued its first air mail stamps. They were overprints and surcharges on definitive stamps of the period.

July 19: The dirigible USS *Macon* flew mail and state papers to the USS *Houston* which was some 1,200 miles off the Pacific coast with President Franklin Roosevelt on board. Apart from the official mail, 16 covers are known, according to *The American Air Mail Catalogue*. The President autographed these covers.

Aug. 2: The autonomous Republic of Syria issued stamps.

Aug. 14: The first in the series of US Migratory Bird Hunting stamps, commonly known as Duck stamps, was issued. It had a denomination of $1 and had to be affixed to a hunting license and signed by the holder of the

This cover marks the introduction of the 6c US domestic air mail rate (July 1, 1934).

license. Revenue from the sale of Duck stamps is used in conservation of wetlands, to purchase refuge areas, to enforce the Migratory Bird Hunting Stamp Act, and other conservation-related purposes. Over the years, the cost of stamps has increased and in 1979-80 went to $7.50. The stamps are issued every July 1 and become void on June 30 of the following year, hence they are usually identified as the 1934-35 stamp, etc. All stamps feature different species of waterfowl and are popular for their fine engraving and attractive colors.

Aug. 20: Great Britain issued its first photogravure-printed stamp. It is a 1½d stamp in the 1934-36 definitive series.

Aug. 30: The United States issued its first air mail special delivery stamp. It is a 16c stamp depicting the Great Seal of the United States and was printed in dark blue. It was intended to pay both the air mail charge and special delivery fee.

Sept. 16: Brazil issued its first semi-postal stamps. The surtax went to support a national philatelic exhibition.

Sept. 29: Switzerland issued the NABA souvenir sheet, commemorating the Swiss National Philatelic Exhibition at Zurich.

Sept. 30: A rocket flight carrying mail was attempted from a ship off the Indian coast. The missile exploded in flight, but most of the mail was recovered from the sea and delivered to the keeper of the Saugor Island lighthouse. This and later more successful rocket experiments were made by Stephen H. Smith.

October: Air mail stamps were first issued for Italian Somaliland.

Oct. 8: Inter-Island Airways flew the first air mail between the four major islands of Hawaii. These are Kauai, Oahu, Maui, and Hawaii. The airline used two Sikorsky S-38 amphibians. The US Post Office Department applied official cachets to mail.

Oct. 11: Covers were postmarked in London on this date and carried by Col. Roscoe Turner and Clyde Pangborn, the third-place finishers in the MacRobertson Air Race from Mildenhall, England, to Melbourne, Australia. They bear a rubber-stamp cachet and are backstamped Melbourne, Oct. 23.

Illustrated here are Britain's first photogravure-printed stamp (Aug. 20, 1934), the first air mail special delivery stamp issued by the US (Aug. 30, 1934), and the Swiss NABA souvenir sheet (Sept. 29, 1934).

Oct. 19: Covers postmarked in the Netherlands, were carried by second-place finishers K. D. Parmentier and J. J. Moll in the MacRobertson Air Race from Mildenhall, England to Melbourne, Australia. This Dutch entry was a standard Douglas DC-2 of KLM named *Uiver*, carrying mail and three passengers.

Oct. 20: Covers postmarked on this date at Mildenhall, England were carried in the MacRobertson Air Race to Australia by the winners, C. W. A. Scott and Campbell Black in their De Havilland Comet aircraft named *Grosvenor House.*

Oct. 30: The first Italian rocket flight carrying mail was made at Trieste by Gerhard Zucker. About 1,600 covers were flown.

Nov. 5: Italian Tripolitania commemorated the 65th birthday of Italian King Victor Emmanuel III on its first air mail semi-postal stamps. The stamps also marked a nonstop flight from Rome to Mogadiscio, Italian Somaliland.

Nov. 5: The French Oceanic Settlements, now French Polynesia (q.v.), placed its first air mail stamps on sale.

Nov. 5: Italian Somaliland issued its first semi-postal air mail stamps.

Nov. 11: Italian Somaliland released its first air mail Official stamp.

Dec. 4: The first rocket mail was flown in Australia from a ship to the shore at Brisbane, Queensland. The container carrying 897 letters fell into the Brisbane River, but was recovered.

Parmentier and Moll carried this cover in their KLM DC-2 aircraft that came in second in the MacRobertson Air Race from England to Australia (Oct. 19, 1934).

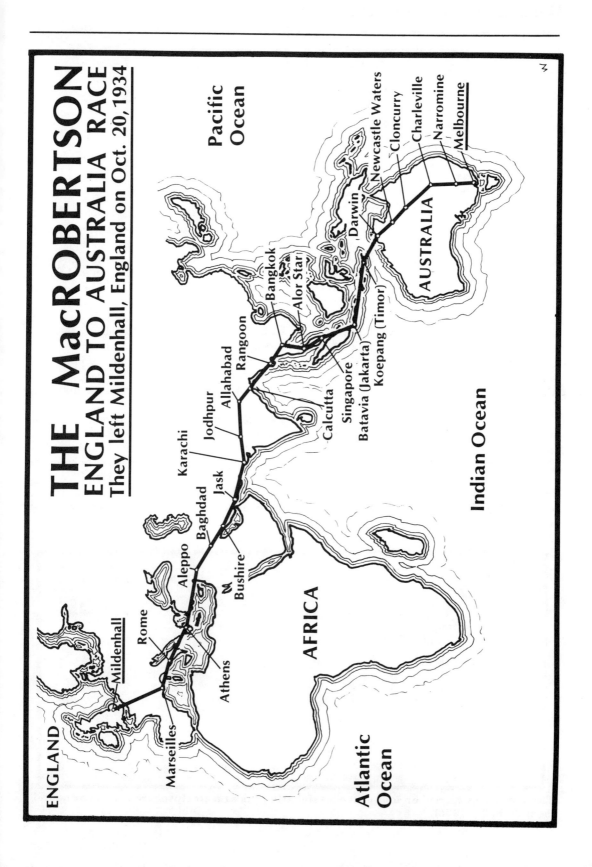

THE MacROBERTSON
ENGLAND TO AUSTRALIA RACE
They left Mildenhall, England on Oct. 20, 1934

Dec. 10, 1934 - Feb. 22, 1935

The aircraft *Snip* and a map of its route from the Netherlands to Curacao is shown on these two stamps from the Netherlands Antilles (Dec. 17, 1934).

Dec. 10: Britain's Imperial Airways inaugurated regular air mail service between Britain and Australia via Greece and India.

Dec. 17: The Dutch airline KLM inaugurated air mail service between the Netherlands and the Netherlands Antilles. The KLM Fokker aircraft *Snip* flew from Amsterdam on this date to the island of Curacao via the Cape Verde Islands and Dutch Guiana (Suriname).

1935

Jan. 1: Until this date, China refused to recognize the Japanese puppet administration in Manchoukuo and did not accept its stamps as valid. It charged postage due on mail coming into China from Manchoukuo.

Jan. 2 A man named Perron experimented with a mail-carrying rocket near Paris, France, according to Smith.

Jan. 19: KLM used the Fokker tri-motor aircraft *Snip* for the first regular air mail flight between Curacao and Aruba. During 1935, KLM carried 675 pounds of mail on 471 flights between the two islands. The 75-mile flight took less than one hour.

Feb. 1: The Dominican Republic issued insured letter stamps. They comprised the Merino issue of 1933, with an overprint converting them to their new role. During 1935, Mexico also issued insured letter stamps.

Feb. 22: Wiley Post made the first of four attempts to make a nonstop stratosphere coast-to-coast flight. He was forced to land only 57½ miles from takeoff at Los Angeles. Subsequent flights landed at Cleveland, Ohio; Lafayette, Ind.; and Wichita, Kansas. Souvenir covers were carried on the attempts and later received an Aug. 20, 1935 cancel at Los Angeles.

This cover was carried on four unsuccessful attempts at a stratosphere transcontinental flight (Feb. 22, 1935).

March 1: The Saar became a province of the German Third Reich and ceased issuing stamps. The Saar had begun issuing stamps in 1920 while under League of Nations administration.

March 15: In an attempt to quiet the philatelic uproar over the presentation by Postmaster General Farley to a favored few of imperforate sheets of US stamps, the US Post Office Department placed on sale at the Philatelic Sales Agency, a number of stamps imperf and without gum. These "special printings" remained available to the public only until June 15, 1935. The stamps included the Peace of 1783 issue, the Byrd Antarctic stamp, the Mothers of America stamp, the Wisconsin Tercentenary stamp, the National Parks series, the 16c air mail special delivery stamp, and the souvenir sheets of the Century of Progress, Byrd, and National Parks stamps.

April 1: Local stamps were first used to frank mail carried by Atlantic Coast Air Services between the island of Lundy and an aerodrome near Barnstaple, Devon, in England. The air mail local stamps paid only the air mail fee and letters from Lundy were also franked by Lundy local stamps and regular British postage stamps. A later stamp depicts a map and air route.

April 6: The LZ-127 *Graf Zeppelin* began the first of 16 flights to South America made during 1935. It returned to Friedrichshafen on April 16. The dates of the other South American flights are April 20-May 1, May 4-14, May 19-28, June 1-11, June 15-25, June 29-July 9, July 14-25, July 29-Aug. 7, Aug. 13-22, Aug. 27-Sept. 5, Sept. 9-18 (the return leg of this flight was LZ-127's 100th Atlantic crossing), Sept. 23-Oct. 2, Oct. 7-16, Oct. 23-Nov. 4, and Nov. 7-Dec. 10. While in South America on the last flight, LZ-127 made three shuttle flights between Pernambuco, Brazil and Bathurst, The Gambia.

April 8: An attempt was made to carry mail by rocket from Belgium across the English Channel to England. Two rockets were launched, each carrying about 200 letters. Both came down in the sea and were recovered. It is not known what the British authorities thought

about this and it was perhaps fortunate that the missiles did not arrive at a destination already occupied by a local inhabitant! Less than 10 years later rockets were to arrive in England carrying much less welcome payloads.

April 17: Pan American Airways made an air mail and passenger proving flight between San Francisco and Hawaii prior to the establishment of regular service across the Pacific Ocean.

April 23: The French colony of Madagascar issued its first air mail stamps.

May 1: Stamps were issued inscribed for Kenya, Tanganyika, and Uganda.

May 6: Antigua issued its four-stamp segment of the 1935 Silver Jubilee issue celebrating the 25th anniversary of the reign of King George V and Queen Mary of Great Britain. Other British Commonwealth colonies and dominions joined in this first of the modern omnibus issues. The majority of the issues, especially of the crown colonies, used the handsome design depicting Windsor Castle.

May 7: Great Britain marked the 25th anniversary of the reign of King George V and Queen Mary with a set of four stamps. These were the first British commemorative stamps since the May 10, 1929 Universal Postal Union Congress issue.

May 14: A glider train consisting of an airplane towing two gliders flew from Miami, Fla., to Havana, Cuba. Jack O'Meara piloted the plane and E. Paul DuPont served as flight manager. Names of the two glider pilots are not known, although one is believed to have been Elwood Keim. See next entry.

May 19, 1935 - June 29, 1935

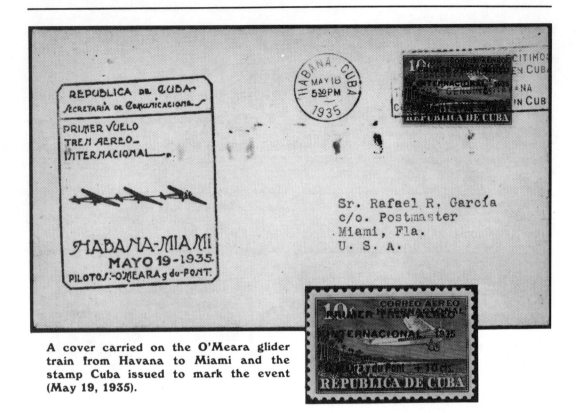

A cover carried on the O'Meara glider train from Havana to Miami and the stamp Cuba issued to mark the event (May 19, 1935).

May 19: The O'Meara glider train made the return flight from Havana, Cuba, to Miami, Fla. Cuba issued a commemorative overprint to mark the flight and mail also bears a commemorative cachet. The stamp was issued both perforated and imperf. See previous entry.

May 27: The Republic of Colombia issued its first postal tax stamp.

June 1: With the release of a new definitive series, Canada introduced the practice of incorporating a tiny year date somewhere within the stamp design.

June 7: The first mail-carrying rocket flight in Switzerland was made by Gerhard Zucker. The rocket carried about 450 items from a ship on Lake Constance to Rheineck.

June 13: A Pan American Airways Clipper under the command of Capt. Edward Musick made a proving flight from Honolulu to Midway Island as part of the preparations for the in-

auguration of a regular mail and passenger service between San Francisco and Manila, Philippines. Only a few covers were carried on this flight.

June 23: The so-called OSTROPA souvenir sheet was issued by Germany to mark an international stamp exhibition held in Konigsberg, East Prussia, then part of the Third Reich. The expensive item has gained notoriety because the sulphuric acid content of the gum has destroyed many of them and will without doubt cause the early destruction of any that still exist bearing gum. Many collectors have already removed the gum and thus saved the sheets. The Scott catalog notes that its mint price for the sheet is in unused condition with the gum removed.

June 29: The first rocket flight carrying living creatures as well as mail was made across the River Damoodar in India. The flight was successful, both mail and a cock and hen arriving unharmed.

July 1: The Indian feudatory state of Bijawar issued stamps.

July 17: The first mail-carrying rocket flight in Luxembourg took place when 300 covers were flown.

Aug. 7: Stamps inscribed "Western Samoa" went on sale in the former German Samoa, which had been mandated to New Zealand following World War I.

Aug. 17: A Pan American Airways proving flight was completed between San Francisco and Wake Island, stopping at Honolulu and Midway Island in each direction. The flight, which carried some mail, had left San Francisco on Aug. 9.

Aug. 19: A mail-carrying rocket launched at Maribor, Yugoslavia made the first such flight in that country. It carried 187 covers.

Aug. 20: Cacheted covers that had been carried by Wiley Post on four unsuccessful attempts to make a coast-to-coast stratosphere flight were canceled at Los Angeles (see Feb. 22, 1935).

Sept. 22: Two mail-carrying rockets launched at Astoria, on Long Island in New York, carried several hundred covers. Both rockets exploded in the air and much of the mail was destroyed. These were the first such flights in the United States.

Oct. 2: The last catapult mail flight was made from the German liner *Europa* to Southampton, England. This was the final flight of the season and the flights were not resumed in the spring of 1936 because the Zeppelin *Hindenburg* had inaugurated an air mail service to North America on May 6, 1936. *Hindenburg* made 10 flights to North America during 1936.

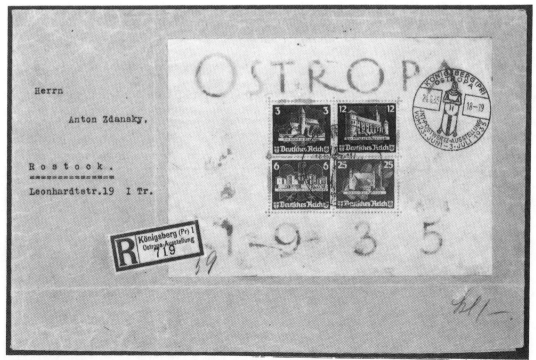

An **OSTROPA** souvenir sheet on cover. This example has had its gum removed and is reaffixed to the cover. Had this not been done, the item would have eventually been destroyed.

A Mexican insured letter stamp.

The Mozambique Company's first air mail issue.

Oct. 2: Mexico issued its first insured letter stamp.

Oct. 5: A Pan American Airways Clipper began a proving flight between San Francisco and Guam, arriving at Guam on Oct. 13. It returned to San Francisco on Oct. 24. Mail was carried.

Oct. 9: The final catapult mail flight was made from the German liner *Bremen* to Southampton, England. This was the last flight of the season and flights were not resumed the following spring, because the Zeppelin *Hindenburg* had inaugurated an air mail service to North America on May 6, 1936.

Nov. 1: The Mozambique Company issued its first air mail stamps. They depict a British Armstrong Whitworth "Atalanta" aircraft of Imperial Airways over the town of Beira.

Nov. 9: A regular air mail service started between France and Madagascar. The service flew by way of Algiers and the Congo. The return flight began Nov. 21.

Nov. 15: Belgian Sabena Airlines inaugurated the first direct flight from Brussels to Elizabethville, Belgian Congo, and Madagascar.

Nov. 15: The Philippines became a commonwealth of the United States.

Nov. 22: The Martin M-130 *China Clipper* flying boat left San Francisco Bay, off Alameda to inaugurate air mail service to the Philippines. It flew via Honolulu, Midway, Wake, Guam, and Manila, where it arrived Nov. 28. A total of 110,866 pieces of mail are reported to have been carried. The United States issued a 25c air mail stamp for the service and the Philippines overprinted two stamps to mark the flight. The return flight began on Dec. 2, 1935 (q.v.).

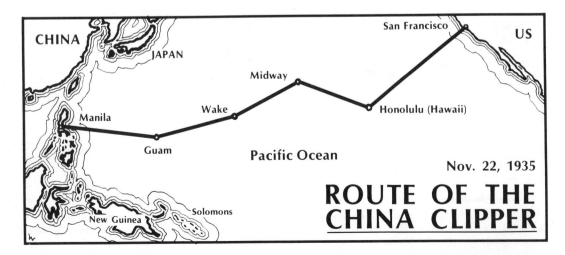

Nov. 22, 1935

ROUTE OF THE CHINA CLIPPER

Above is a cover carried on the first leg of the Nov. 22 flight to the Philippines from California. To the left is an air mail stamp showing the clipper being loaded and below is a postal card picturing the aircraft. Both latter items were issued Feb. 15, 1985 (Nov. 22, 1935).

© USPS 1985

Nov. 24: The newly restored monarchy in Greece issued stamps.

Dec. 2: The Martin M-130 aircraft *China Clipper* left Manila for San Francisco carrying mail for Guam, Honolulu, and North America. The flying boat was commanded by Captain Edwin Musick.

1936

During this year, Spanish revolutionary forces issued stamps at Cadiz, Malaga, Orense, San Sebastian, Santa Cruz de Tenerife, and Seville.

Italian East Africa was formed, but did not issue its first stamps until Feb. 7, 1938.

Coin-operated postage meter devices were tested in the United States. These tests led to the introduction of Mailomats on May 17, 1939 (q.v.).

Jan. 20: King George V of Great Britain died. He was succeeded by the Prince of Wales who became King Edward VIII.

Feb. 16: Visiting Royal Air Force flying boats carried mail from the Philippines to Hong, Kong, Amoy, Shanghai, and Tokyo.

Feb. 25: Ethiopia issued its first semi-postal stamps. The surtax went to the Red Cross.

Feb. 28: The first air mail flight in Liberia took place when the Firestone Tire and Rubber Company sponsored a 322-mile flight from Monrovia to Harper via Cape Palmas. The Liberian Post Office stated that the flight carried 4,000 letters.

March 1: Egypt issued Military stamps to frank a concession rate for British forces stationed in Egypt. This provided a lower rate on mail from servicemen. See NAAFI seals.

March 16: French Equatorial Africa issued stamps that were overprints on stamps of Gabon.

March 23: The Zeppelin LZ-129 *Hindenburg* carried its first mail on a trial flight.

Special stamps had been issued March 16 for use on mail carried by *Hindenburg* and they were first used on this flight.

March 26: Between this date and March 29, the German dirigibles LZ-127 *Graf Zeppelin* and LZ-129 *Hindenburg* took part in a propaganda flight over Germany during which leaflets were dropped urging Germans to "vote" for Hitler during a so-called "election" in that country.

March 27: An Imperial Airways first flight from Hong Kong carried mail to connect with the Sydney-London service at Penang, Malaya.

March 31: The Zeppelin LZ-129 *Hindenburg* left Friedrichshafen on the first of seven 1936 roundtrips to South America. It returned to base on April 10. Dates of the other six flights are May 25-June 3, July 20-July 29, Aug. 27-Sept. 8, Oct. 21-Nov. 2, Nov. 5-Nov. 16, and Nov. 25-Dec. 7.

April 13: The LZ-127 *Graf Zeppelin* began the first of 13 flights to South America during 1936. It returned to Friedrichshafen on April 24. Dates of the other 12 flights are April 27-May 8, May 11-21, June 8-18, June 24-July 6, July 9-20, July 30-Aug. 20, Aug. 13-24, Sept. 9-21, Sept. 23-Oct. 5, Oct. 8-19, Oct. 29-Nov. 9, and Nov. 11-Dec. 1. A shuttle flight to Bathurst, The Gambia, was made during the last trip.

May 6: The Zeppelin LZ-129 *Hindenburg* left Friedrichshafen on the first of ten 1936 roundtrips to the United States. It returned to its base on May 14. Dates of the other nine flights are May 17-May 23, June 19-June 26, June 30-July 6, July 10-July 17, Aug. 5-Aug. 11, Aug. 14-Aug. 22, Sept. 17-Sept. 24, Sept. 26-Oct. 3, and Oct. 5-Oct. 12.

May 9: TIPEX, the Third International Philatelic Exhibition, began in New York City and continued until May 17. The United States released a souvenir sheet consisting of four contemporary commemorative stamps in conjunction with the show.

A cover carried on the LZ-129 *Hindenburg*'s first flight to North America.

May 11: The city of Frankfurt became a base for the German dirigible LZ-127 *Graf Zeppelin*. The airship made shuttle flights between Frankfurt and Friedrichshafen between this date and Sept. 9.

May 18: Uruguay issued a set of late fee stamps. Such stamps are used to frank letters accepted after the normal closing of a mail.

May 29: Philippine pilots Antonio Arnaiz and Juan Calvo carried mail on a good-will flight from Manila, Philippines to Madrid, Spain. They arrived on July 11.

July 25: Austria issued a stamp honoring Engelbert Dollfuss who tried to maintain his country's independence in the face of an aggressive Germany. He had been murdered by Austrian Nazi rebels on July 25, 1934. The

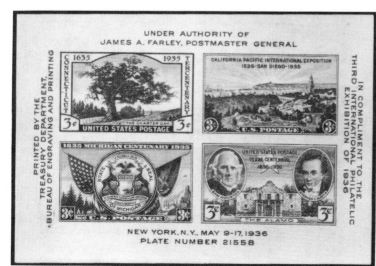

The US Post Office Department issued this souvenir sheet in conjunction with TIPEX, the third US international stamp exhibition held in New York City May 9-17. The sheet was not perforated.

Aug. 1, 1936 - Oct. 26, 1936

Dollfuss issue has become a modern Austrian classic stamp.

Aug. 1: The Zeppelin LZ-129 *Hindenburg* made a flight over Berlin during the Olympic Games being held there.

Sept. 1: Great Britain issued ½d, 1½d, and 2½d stamps depicting King Edward VIII. A 1d denomination was released Sept. 14. The stamps attracted much attention because of their attractive and uncluttered design; a very great departure from the traditional designs used up to that time.

Sept. 14: The 1d denomination in Great Britain's King Edward VIII definitive series was issued.

Sept. 14: The Zeppelin LZ-129 *Hindenburg* made a flight over Nuremberg during a Nazi rally there.

Sept. 30: At a ceremony at London's General Post Office, the British postmaster general inaugurated the first British mobile post office. The vehicle made its first public appearance at the Marden Fruit Show in Kent on Oct. 6-8. The post office on wheels provided postal, telegraph, and telephone services. A second one came into service on April 16, 1938 and both served until the outbreak of World War II on Sept. 3, 1939. The second post office did, however, attend a race meet in northern England during November 1939. The mobile post offices used special postmarks.

Oct. 14: The first Pitney-Bowes "Mailomat" was placed in experimental use at the Stamford, Conn., Post Office. It remained in use there until Oct. 11, 1937. The machine printed a meter stamp different from that of the first regular machine which went into regular use at New York on May 17, 1939 (q.v.).

Oct. 15: KNILM (Royal Netherlands Indies Airways) made its first flight from Manila, Philippines, to Batavia, Netherlands Indies.

Oct. 26: The British King Edward VIII stamps overprinted and surcharged for the Morocco Agencies went on sale at British post offices at Tangier and the French and Spanish zones of Morocco.

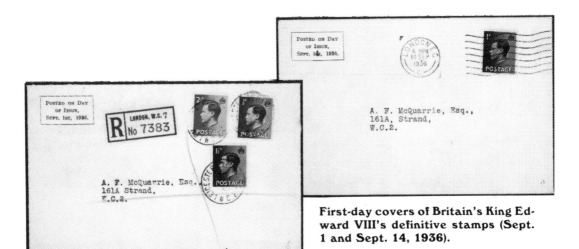

First-day covers of Britain's King Edward VIII's definitive stamps (Sept. 1 and Sept. 14, 1936).

Oct. 27: During the Spanish Civil War, revolutionary forces issued stamps for the Canary Islands.

Dec. 1: Revolutionary forces issued stamps at Burgos during the Spanish Civil War.

Dec. 10: King Edward VIII of Great Britain abdicated. He was succeeded by his brother, the Duke of York, who became King George VI.

1937

Post offices of the Aden Colony Postal Department were opened in the Qu'aiti State of Shihr and Mukalla and the Kathiri State of Seiyun.

Jan. 23: The French island of Reunion's first air mail stamp was an overprint on a regular issue to mark the flight of the aircraft *Roland Garros* from the island to France by Laurent, Lenier, and Touge.

Feb. 28: Stamps of Latakia were withdrawn and the area began to use the stamps of Syria, of which Latakia is now a part.

March 1: Czechoslovakia issued its first personal delivery stamp. The triangular adhesive was affixed to mail by the sender to indicate that personal delivery to the addressee was desired.

The Post Office applied a second type of stamp when a mail recipient requested personal delivery. In that case, the fee was collected on delivery. Similar stamps were issued later by the Germans during their World War II occupation of Czechoslovakia.

March 15: Guatemala issued its first semi-postal and air mail semi-postal stamps. They commemorated the first philatelic exhibition held in that country.

March 16: The Zeppelin LZ-129 *Hindenburg* began its first South American flight of 1937, returning to Germany on March 27.

April 1: Burma issued its first postage stamps. They were stamps of India overprinted "BURMA."

April 1: The Crown Colony of Aden issued its first stamps. They depict an Arab dhow. Stamps of India had been used at Aden since the mid-1800s.

April 13: The LZ-127 *Graf Zeppelin* began the first of its two flights to South America during 1937. It returned to Friedrichshafen on April 25.

April 15: French Equatorial Africa placed its first specially designed stamps on sale.

April 27: The LZ-127 *Graf Zeppelin* began its second and final flight to South America. It returned to Germany on May 8.

April 28: Pan American Airways carried mail on its first regular flight from Manila to Macao and Hong Kong, using the flying boat *Hong Kong Clipper.*

Both Aden's and Burma's first stamps were issued April 1, 1937.

April 29: The *Hong Kong Clipper* made the first air mail flight from Hong Kong to Manila (see April 28, 1937).

May 3: The Zeppelin LZ-129 *Hindenburg* began its final tragic flight to North America. It had been intended that a flight within Germany would be made on May 1 and mail had been accepted. However, bad weather had forced cancelation of the flight and the mail was dropped over Cologne as the dirigible flew over on its way to Lakehurst, N.J. The dropped mail received an explanatory marking.

May 6: The Zeppelin *Hindenburg* caught fire and was destroyed while landing at Lakehurst, N.J. Only 357 pieces of mail were salvaged and forwarded to addressees. It received special handling and is now among the most highly prized of all crash mail.

May 8: Dick Merrill and Jack Lambie made a goodwill coronation flight from New York to London for the coronation of King George VI, returning to New York on May 14. Although it carried mail, the flight's main purpose was to expedite the delivery of British coronation stamps to the US market.

May 8: On the return from its second 1937 flight to South America, the German dirigible LZ-127 *Graf Zeppelin* was retired from commercial service.

May 10: Great Britain issued the first denominations in the King George VI definitive series. They were the ½d, 1d, and 2½d stamps.

Hong Kong Clipper carried this cover on its first flight from Hong Kong to the Philippines. The Hong Kong stamp was issued in 1984 and shows the Clipper at Hong Kong (April 29, 1937).

May 12: British Guiana issued a set of three stamps to mark the coronation of King George VI and Queen Elizabeth. It was part of an omnibus issue in which many other British areas joined. With a few exceptions, all were in the common design shown.

June 1: Japan issued its first semi-postal stamps, using the surtax for the Patriotic Aviation Fund to build civil airports.

June 1: Regular air mail service between Southampton, England, and the English Channel island of Jersey was inaugurated by Jersey Airways. The first flight to the island carried 229 pounds of mail and took about one hour.

June 16: Imperial Airways started regular air mail service between Bermuda and New York using the Short Empire Class flying boat *Cavalier.*

July 5: The Imperial Airways flying boat *Caledonia* made a survey flight from Foynes, Ireland, to Botwood, Newfoundland, carrying souvenir mail. Between July 5 and Sept. 28, *Caledonia* and *Cambria* made 10 Atlantic crossings in the course of the survey for a later regular service. The Pan-American Airways' *Clipper III* also made survey flights on this route during the same period.

July 12: The first stamp of the British Commonwealth King George VI era was issued when Grenada released a ¼d stamp featuring the new king's portrait.

July 13: The United States used the words "First Day of Issue" for the first time on a first-day cancelation for the 3c Ordinance of 1787 commemorative stamp. The ordinance provided for the organization of the Northwest Territory. The stamp was issued at New York City; Marietta, Ohio; and Washington, D.C.

July 30: Great Britain issued 1½d and 2½d denominations in the King George VI definitive series. The series replaced stamps bearing the profile of King Edward VIII issued the previous year.

Dec. 29: Ireland declared itself a sovereign democratic state.

1938

Jan. 8: Great Britain relinquished extraterritorial rights in French Morocco and withdrew British stamps surcharged in French currency.

Feb. 7: Italian East Africa issued its first stamps. A grouping of Italian colonies in East Africa, plus the independent country of Ethiopia that had recently been invaded and subjected by Italy, the area included Eritrea, Italian Somaliland, and Ethiopia. The British Protectorate of Somaliland was incorporated during a brief occupation.

March 6: Pan American Airways began contract air mail service between Baltimore and Bermuda.

Shown are British Guiana's coronation stamp design (May 12, 1937), the first King George VI British Commonwealth stamp (July 12, 1937), the British King George VI definitive design (July 30, 1937), and the flying boat *Cavalier* at Bermuda (June 16, 1937).

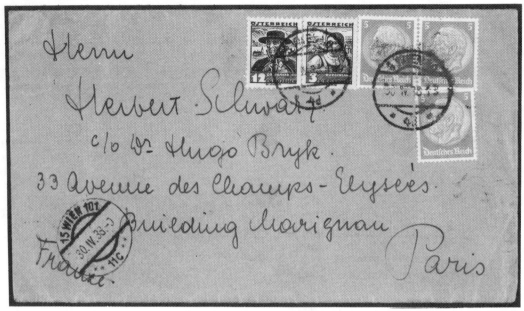

A mixed franking cover from Austria following the German takeover (March 13, 1938).

March 13: Austria became part of Germany as a result of the German invasion and takeover. German stamps were introduced April 4. Tranmer notes that stamps of the Hindenburg series in denominations of 5pf, 6pf, 8pf, 12pf, 15pf, and 25pf were used. All current German stamps were placed in use on June 23. Austrian stamps remained valid until Oct.31, thus permitting mixed franking from April 4 to Oct. 31, 1938.

April 4: German stamps were placed on sale in Austria following the German occupation of that country.

April 16: Italy issued special delivery stamps for Italian East Africa.

The first Presidential (April 25, 1938).

April 16: Stamps were issued for the Turkish area of Hatay during the period of French occupation.

April 25: The United States released the 1c denomination in the Presidential series. It was the first in this definitive issue.

June: The US Post Office Department began to use postage meters in post offices according to Roscoe.

June 1: The Spanish colony of Cape Juby issued its first air mail stamps. They were stamps of Spanish Morocco overprinted "CABO JUBY."

June 11: Germany issued an air letter sheet on the occasion of Philatelist's Day in Bremen. It was imprinted with a 10pf air mail and 3pf Hindenburg indicia.

June 17: The Netherlands Antilles authorized use of postage meters.

June 22: The Vatican issued its first air mail stamps.

July 1: The US Post Office Department required that all matter bearing precanceled stamps where the postage was 6c or more include the user's initials and the month and year on the stamp. This was the beginning of what came to be called "dateds" by precancel collectors.

July 20: The British seaplane *Mercury* made its first commercial flight from Great Britain to the United States. The four-engined aircraft loaded with mail had been carried aloft on the back of the flying boat *Mayo*, before separating to make the transatlantic crossing.

This extended the range of the heavily loaded aircraft, since vital fuel did not have to be used to gain altitude. It also made possible the flight of an aircraft that was too heavy to have taken off under its own power.

July 26: The former Portuguese colony of Cape Verde issued its first air mail stamps.

July 26: Angola placed its first air mail stamps on sale.

July 27: An Imperial Airways flying boat left Southampton to start the so-called "all-up" air mail service between Great Britain and Australia.

By September 1938 five mails a week were

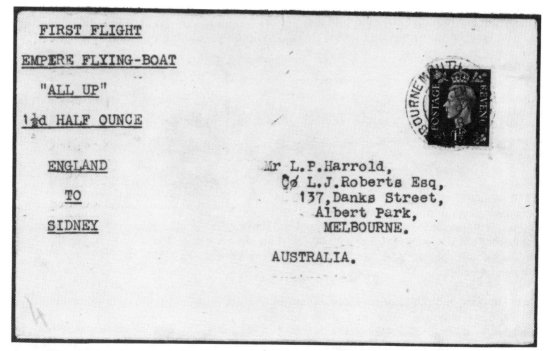

A cover carried on the first "all-up" air mail service between Britain and Australia (July 27, 1938).

operating to India and three to Australia, with a branch service to Hong Kong. The service was extended to New Zealand in 1940.

The rate was 1½d per half ounce. This amazingly low rate was an innovation as remarkable as the introduction of the Penny Post by Rowland Hill in 1840.

Aug. 10: A Lufthansa Focke-Wulf Condor fitted with extra fuel tanks left Berlin for New York. The flight took almost 25 hours. The return flight was made on Aug. 14. The plane carried mail in both directions.

Aug. 12: A submarine carried mail from the Spanish port of Barcelona to the Balearic island of Menorca during the Spanish Civil War. The island was the only one left in Republican hands and it is doubtful that a surface vessel could have made the voyage, since the rebels were blockading the island.

The idea for the mail run seems to have been to justify the release of special submarine mail stamps to raise foreign currency. Of the six stamps and souvenir sheet, only the low values were placed on sale at the post office and they sold out within a few days, according to S. Nathan of Barcelona (*Stamp Collector,* Oct. 7, 1978).

The submarine *C4* carried more than 300 registered covers and 100 covers bearing full sets, plus 100 maximum cards and 200 Agencia Filatelica Oficial covers, some of which were franked with the souvenir sheet and some only with the 1p stamp.

Aug. 14: The Spanish submarine *C4* began the return trip from Menorca to Barcelona, docking there on Aug. 18. Although the motive for the trip was almost certainly philatelic, the submarine carried ordinary mail. See Aug. 12, 1938.

Sept. 1: Portuguese India issued its only set of air mail stamps.

Sept. 14: The Zeppelin LZ-130, named the *Graf Zeppelin II,* made its first test flight. No mail was carried.

Sept. 19: Portuguese Guinea issued its only set of air mail stamps.

Oct. 1: Portuguese Timor released its first air mail stamps.

Oct 15: The Netherlands Indies placed its first semi-postal air mail stamps on sale. The surtax went to the Air Service Fund. The stamps also marked the 10th anniversary of Dutch East Indies Royal Airlines (KNILM) and depict a Douglas DC-2 aircraft operated by the airline.

Oct. 24: Semi-postal stamps were first issued by Niger.

Oct. 24: French Equatorial Africa issued its first semi-postal stamp.

Oct. 31: Austrian stamps ceased to be valid in that country, having been replaced by stamps of Germany following the March 1938 invasion and occupation.

Nov. 15: Burma released its first specially designed stamps. Previously, stamps of India overprinted "BURMA" had been used.

Nov. 23: Cuba issued its first semi-postal stamps.

Nov. 30: The post office was closed on the English Channel island of Herm. It had been opened May 1, 1925, during the period when Lord Perry leased the island and maintained a large staff. The office was located in the Mermaid Tavern and was a sub-post office of Guernsey.

Dec. 1: Greenland produced its first stamps. Until this date, domestic mail and that from Greenland to Denmark was transmitted free. Parcel post had to be paid and stamps had been used for this purpose since 1905.

Dec. 22: Afghanistan issued its first postal tax stamps. They were compulsory on all mail from Dec. 22-28 and the funds were used for hospital facilities.

1939

Hatay was transferred from French to Turkish administration and stamps were issued by the Turks. The area now uses stamps of Turkey. It had previously been called Alexandretta.

Jan. 18: Slovakia's first stamp was an overprint and surcharge on a stamp of Czechoslovakia. It commemorated the opening of the Slovakian parliament.

Feb. 2: The Bureau of the Chief Inspector of the US Post Office Department was established with three divisions of investigation — mail, financial, and administrative. The department had previously been assigned to one of the assistant postmasters general or the postmaster general himself.

Feb. 13: Although the Gilbert and Ellice Islands had administered Fanning Island since Jan. 27, 1916, the New Zealand Post Office operated a postal agency using New Zealand stamps until this date, when Gilbert and Ellice Island stamps went into use.

Feb. 14: The Gilbert and Ellice Post Office opened a post office on Christmas Island (Pacific Ocean). At that time, planners thought that the island would become an important link in traspacific air services and a refueling jetty and weather station were established.

Feb. 21: The Indian feudatory state of Idar issued stamps.

Feb. 22: A flying boat of Pan American Airways inaugurated a New York-Manila, Philippines, service.

March 15: The Carpatho-Ukraine placed on sale the only stamp it issued. It was used following separation from Czechoslovakia and prior to Hungarian takeover.

March 26: Pan American Airlines' *Yankee Clipper* began a proving flight from Baltimore to the Azores, Lisbon, Biscarosse, and Marseilles. From there it flew to Southampton, Foynes, and back to Southampton. The return flight was from Southampton via Lisbon, Azores, and Bermuda, to Baltimore. Regular service to Marseilles began on May 20. Mail was carried on the various legs of the flight.

April 1: The 11th and last congress of the Universal Postal Union before World War II, convened in Buenos Aires, Argentina. A 20 percent basic rate reduction was agreed upon. The effective date would have been July 1, 1940, had not the war intervened.

April 1: The Argentine Post Office demonstrated its Fonopost service at the Universal Postal Union Congress in Buenos Aires. This was a service that permitted a "mailer" to make a recorded message on a small phonograph record 20 cm in diameter, which was then mailed in a special envelope.

April 12: The National Assembly of Albania surrendered the country to Italian invasion forces and the first stamps issued under Italian occupation note that event.

April 29: Guatemala issued its first air mail Official stamps.

May 8: Air mail service between England and the English Channel island of Guernsey was inaugurated when a Guernsey Airways aircraft left Southampton, England. The flight took 59 minutes.

May 12: The first service using the Adams air mail pick-up system began at a number of small communities in the Eastern United States that lacked airport facilities. The system permitted pick-up and dropping of mail from an aircraft in

An Adams pick-up air mail cover (May 12, 1939).

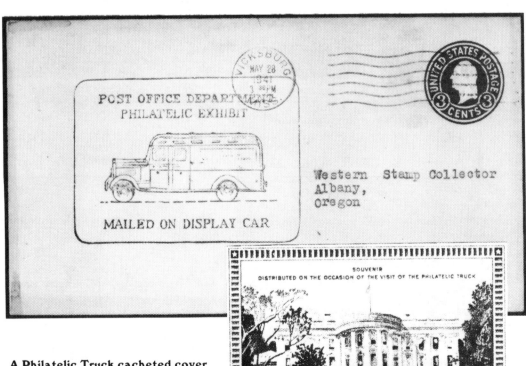

A Philatelic Truck cacheted cover
and the souvenir sheet vignette
(May 15, 1939).

flight. Experimental routes #1001 and #1002, later combined as Route #49, served communities in Pennsylvania, West Virginia, and Delaware. All American Aviation, Inc., operated the routes using Stinson Reliant aircraft.

May 15: The US Philatelic Truck began a tour of the United States that ended soon after the country entered World War II on Dec. 7, 1941. Fitted with exhibits, the truck offered visitors a free souvenir in the form of a non-postal souvenir sheet. The sheet was printed in blue and depicts a view of the White House. The item came both with and without gum, the latter being the most common, and is considered to be a forerunner to the current series of souvenir cards begun in 1954.

May 17: The first Mailomat was placed in regular use in New York. Pitney-Bowes made the combination franking and mailing machine and claimed that it was an unattended miniature post office. A number of these facilities were installed at various locations. They proved uneconomic and World War II halted further development. See Oct. 14, 1936.

June 27: Pan-American Airways inaugurated regular transatlantic service via Newfoundland to Southampton, England.

July: The Canadian Post Office introduced a perforating machine to perforate stamps "O.H.M.S." for official use. The new equipment created the "H" and "M" four holes high. They had previously been five holes high (see May 1923).

July 5: The French Oceanic Settlements issued a semi-postal air mail stamp.

July 5: The French colony of Wallis and Futuna Islands released its first semi-postal stamps.

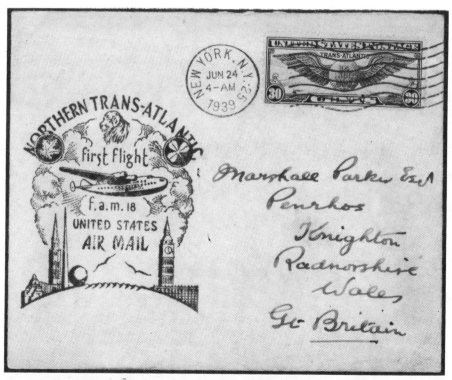

A cover carried on Pan-American Airways first regular transatlantic service via Newfoundland to Southampton, England (June 27, 1939).

July 5: French Guiana placed a single semi-postal air mail stamp on sale.

July 5: The French colony of Madagascar issued a single semi-postal air mail stamp.

July 6: Mail service by autogiro between the Philadelphia Post Office roof and Camden Airport began. The carrier was Eastern Air Lines.

July 9: The Zeppelin LZ-130 *Graf Zeppelin II* carried its first mail during a flight from Friedrichshafen to the German city of Leipzig. Three other flights carrying mostly souvenir mail within Germany were made during July.

July 15: The Czech provinces of Bohemia and Moravia issued stamps following the German invasion and occupation.

Aug. 5: Britain's Imperial Airways inaugurated regular transatlantic service between Southampton, England and New York via Foynes, Ireland; Botwood, Newfoundland; and Montreal, Quebec.

Aug. 6: The Zeppelin LZ-130 *Graf Zeppelin II* made a mail-carrying flight to Wurzburg, Germany. Two other domestic flights carrying souvenir mail were made during August.

Aug. 16: What is claimed to be the world's only undersea post office was opened in the Bahamas. During its period of operation, a special postmark was used.

A cover carried on Imperial Airways' first flight in its transatlantic service (Aug. 5, 1939).

Oct. 1: Afghanistan issued its first air mail stamps. In three denominations, the stamps depict an aircraft over Kabul.

Oct. 3 Haiti issued its first semi-postal stamps, both regular and air mail.

Oct. 15: Cuba issued what is claimed to be the first, and possibly only, government-issued postage stamp intended to frank rocket mail. It was a 1931 air mail stamp overprinted "Experimento del Cohete Postal Ano de 1939." Dr. Arthur Delaney reports that 200,000 were produced.

It had been intended that the stamp should be used during experimental rocket flights to get mail to remote villages. However, Delaney notes that the idea was not pursued and the stamps never used for their intended purpose.

Nov. 6: Slovakia, while under German protection, issued its first semi-postal stamp.

Nov. 20: Slovakia issued its first air mail stamps.

Dec. 1: The first German occupation stamps were issued in Poland.

EXPERIMENTO DEL
COHETE
Postal
AÑO DE 1939

Cuba applied this overprint to convert the stamp to one for rocket mail, but it never got off the ground (Oct. 15, 1939).

1940-1949
War and aftermath

1940

Jan. 12: A cacheted cover was introduced for sale from the US Philatelic Truck during its nationwide tour prior to US entry into World War II. The first covers were sold from the truck at Raleigh, N.C.

Jan. 12: Frederick John Melville died at the age of 57. He was the best-known British philatelic journalist of his day. Author of many books about various aspects of our hobby, his final work was not published until after his death.

Feb. 1: The Canadian Post Office issued free labels that would frank a parcel weighing up to 25 pounds from anywhere in Canada to Axis prisoners of war being held in Canada. There are two designs, one inscribed "Canada, Internment Operations, Postage, Free" and the other is inscribed "Canada, Prisoner of War Mail." Both are about 2½x1½ inches in size, printed in black on red paper, and are rouletted except for the first two printings of the "Internment Operations" design, which are imperforate. There were six printings of both types, according to Holmes. They ceased to be valid Jan. 31, 1947.

Feb. 8: Ivory Coast issued its first air mail stamps.

Feb. 8: The French colony of Mauritania released its first air mail stamps.

Feb. 8: The French colony of Niger placed its first stamps on sale.

Feb. 12: The first direct flight from the Cayman Islands in the West Indies, to the United States carried mail. The flight originated at Grand Cayman and ended at Miami, Fla.

March: The LZ-127 *Graf Zeppelin*, famous in philately for its mail-carrying flights to so many countries, was broken up at Frankfurt, Germany.

March: The LZ-130 *Graf Zeppelin II*, the last of the great German dirigibles, was broken up at Frankfurt. It had never made any international flights, but had carried a considerable amount of souvenir mail on flights within Germany during July and August 1939.

March 1: Chile issued its first semi-postal stamps. They mark the 50th anniversary of Chile's ownership of Easter Island.

April 9: On this day and April 10, the Germans used rockets to distribute propaganda leaflets over Copenhagen and other Danish towns, announcing their occupation of the country.

April 27: Trans-Tasman service between Auckland, New Zealand, and Sydney, Australia, was inaugurated. This represented the final link in the New Zealand-England service.

April 30: The *Government Gazette* at Suva, Fiji, published King's Regulation #4 of 1940 for the "establishment and regulation for a Post Office in Pitcairn Island." A proclamation later set the establishment date as Oct. 15, 1940.

May 6: The 100th birthday of the world's first adhesive postage stamp, the *Penny Black*, was marked by a six-stamp set from Great Britain. The stamps feature profiles of Queen Victoria and King George VI.

May 17: Egypt issued its first semi-postal stamp. It features a portrait of the baby Princess Ferial.

Egypt's first semi-postal stamp (May 17, 1940).

June: Guatemala released its first special delivery stamp.

July 1: The German commander of the Dunkirk (Dunkerque) area in northern France opened a provisional civilian postal service following the withdrawal of the British Expeditionary Force and the surrender of French and Belgian forces. He ordered an overprint be applied to French stamps. It took the form of a three-line boxed inscription reading "Besetztes/ Gebiet/ Nordfrankreich." This was overprinted over two stamps, it being too large for one. It is reported to have been applied to the stamps already affixed to letters. The postal service lasted until Aug. 9, 1940. Scott mentions the items without giving them a listing.

July 12: Pan American Airways inaugurated Foreign Air Mail Route 19 between San Francisco and Auckland, New Zealand, using the new Boeing B-314 flying boat *American Clipper*. The route was via Los Angeles; Honolulu; Canton Island; and Noumea, New Caledonia. At that time the Los Angeles-Honolulu segment was the world's longest over-water route flown by commercial aircraft.

July 14: The United States established a post office on Canton Island. It closed April 23, 1965 and reopened in 1971 as a branch of Honolulu, according to Murphy. It is now part of the country of Kiribati (formerly the Gilbert Islands).

Aug. 15: German occupiers issued stamps for Alsace, France.

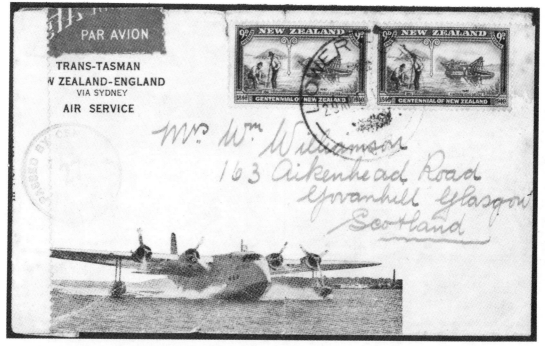

A cover carried on the New Zealand-England air mail service (April 27, 1940).

Aug. 15: The last stamp to be issued by independent Estonia was released.

Aug. 17: German occupiers issued semipostal stamps in Poland.

Sept. 11: President Franklin D. Roosevelt appointed Frank C. Walker to be US postmaster general, succeeding James A. Farley.

Sept. 30: The last government-owned flag canceling machine was retired from use at the Valley Falls, R.I., Post Office. See May 24, 1941.

Oct. 15: The Pitcairn Post Office opened and issued its first stamps on this date.

Nov. 2: The Faroe Islands were cut off from Denmark during the German occupation on this date and made a large number of provisional surcharges to maintain stamp supplies during shortages. The islands were under British protection during this period.

Dec. 1: Romania issued its first semi-postal air mail stamps.

Dec. 1: The Germans occupying Poland issued rural delivery stamps.

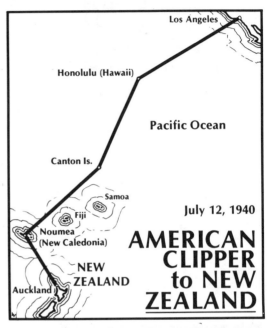

July 12, 1940

AMERICAN CLIPPER to NEW ZEALAND

This cover flew on the Boeing B-314 American Clipper over what was then the world's longest commercial over-water route — the Los Angeles-Honolulu segment of the San Francisco-Auckland, New Zealand service of Pan American Airways (July 12, 1940).

Dec. 10: Stamps were issued by Greece for its occupation of Albanian territory, following the ill-fated Italian attack from bases in Albania.

Dec. 23: Spain released its first air mail postal tax stamp.

Dec. 24: From this date until Feb. 22, 1941, postal authorities on the island of Guernsey permitted the use of bisected 2d stamps as 1d denominations to pay the domestic rate. The German occupation of the island had caused a stamp shortage. The English Channel islands were the only portion of the United Kingdom to be invaded by the Germans during World War II. Robson Lowe gives the date of authorization for the bisect as Dec. 27.

1941

Stamps were issued for the Spanish colony of Ifni. They are Spanish stamps overprinted "Territorio de Ifni."

Slovenia, under Italian occupation, issued stamps.

The German occupiers of Serbia placed stamps on sale.

Stamps of Greece and Italy were overprinted and used by the Italian occupiers of the Ionian Islands during World War II.

Montenegro, under Italian occupation, issued stamps.

Jan. 31: Estonian stamps were withdrawn and demonitized following the Soviet Union's takeover of the country.

Feb. 4: North Borneo issued a pair of war tax stamps.

Feb. 10: The first US Highway Post Office (HPO) began operating on a route between Washington, D.C. and Harrisonburg, Va. The next routes were between South Bend and Indianapolis, Ind. (May 3, 1941) and San Francisco and Pacific Grove, Calif. (Aug. 4, 1941). The HPO system was a shortlived service that covered the period between the decline of railroad service and the general carriage of mail by air. In many cases, the HPO vehicles replaced a similar rail route, but there was considerable improvement in mail service where communities with no rail service gained an

A Highway Post Office first-trip cover (Feb. 10, 1941).

HPO route. The greatest HPO expansion came in the late 1940s and early 1950s. HPO serviced terminated in 1972.

March 14: A US post office opened at the US military base in Bermuda, which had been leased for 99 years from the British government as part of the deal that provided Britain with 50 old US destroyers. The post office was located on Tucker's Island. A US Army Post Office also opened on April 18, 1941. It was numbered 802, later changed to 856.

April 1: The English Channel island of Jersey issued stamps while under German occupation.

April 3: The first aerogrammes for use by British forces were issued. They were designated Army Form W 3077.

April 12: The Croatian state, a puppet state set up when the Germans overran Yugoslavia, of which Croatia had been a part, issued stamps. Following liberation, it again became a state within that country.

April 21: The British introduced an Airgraph service from Cairo to London in an attempt to handle the large volume of mail from troops while using the least amount of aircraft space. This was similar to the V-Mail service introduced by the United States in June 1942. The service involved the photographic reduction of letters and the shipping of the film. On arrival, the film was enlarged and printed before being delivered to the addresses. This enabled many thousands of letters to be flown in the restricted aircraft space available.

May 10: Croatia issued its first semi-postal stamp.

May 20: The British Post Office announced the introduction of a special marking to be applied to mail delayed by enemy action (the bombing of British communities by the Germans). The marking took the form of a bomb in a circle formed by the inscription "DELAYED BY ENEMY ACTION." A variety of other markings with similar inscriptions in a box were also used at various times.

May 24: The last US flag canceling machine was withdrawn from service. The postmaster at Sidney Center, N.Y., owned the machine. Langford reports philatelic specimens dated as late as Dec. 1, 1941.

June: The first stamps were issued for Guernsey under German occupation.

June 1: Mexico issued its first parcel post stamps.

June 5: Corfu, under Italian occupation, placed its first stamps on sale.

July 1: Bulgaria released its first parcel post stamps.

July 1: Stamps of Aden were placed on sale at Berbera, British Somaliland, following its liberation from a brief Italian occupation. They were used until April 27, 1942, when a new King George VI definitive series was released.

July 10: Air mail stamps were first issued for Serbia during the German occupation in World War II. They are overprints on stamps of Yugoslavia.

July 18: The charter of the Mozambique Company expired and the area reverted to Portuguese colonial government.

July 21: Great Britain issued an aerogramme with an imprinted 2½d indicium. It was specifically intended for use in writing to British prisoners of war in Germany and Italy.

July 28: South Africa issued its first aerogramme for use to or from military personnel. Not until 1944 did South Africa issue an aerogramme for general use.

August: Airgraph service was introduced

from London to Cairo after the Egyptian city had been supplied with the necessary equipment for enlarging and printing the messages (see April 21, 1941). More than eight million airgraphs were transported by the end of 1941.

Aug. 2: The British Post Office announced the trial use of a mobile post office. It was set up in east-central London.

The facility took the form of a tent, which could be operational within 20 minutes in an area where the regular post office had been put out of action by German bombing.

These post office "kits" were sent to cities around the country and a number were used at various times. The one available at Tunbridge Wells, Kent, the writer's home at that time, was used on July 28, 1944, when an unexploded flying bomb (V-1) fell near the High Brooms Post Office.

The emergency post offices used a circular date stamp reading "MOBILE POST OFFICE", together with a number and the date.

Oct. 1: Stamps were issued for Eastern Karelia by Finnish forces during their World War II occupation of the Soviet territory west of Lake Onega.

Nov. 1: Finland issued its first military stamps.

Nov. 17: New Zealand's first aerogramme was issued for use in writing to prisoners of war.

Nov. 17: Southern Rhodesia made available aerogrammes for correspondence with men on active service.

Dec. 1: Stamps of Germany overprinted "Ostland" were placed on sale in Estonia following the German invasion and occupation.

Subsequent to the German defeat, the Soviet Union again took over Estonia and its stamps continue to be used.

Dec. 10: The Japanese captured Guam. Until Allied liberation in 1944, the Japanese operated the island's postal services.

Dec. 11: Curacao issued its first air mail semipostal stamps. They included the inscription "The Netherlands Shall Rise Again," referring to the mother country, then under German occupation.

Dec. 13: The nationwide tour of the US Post Office Department's Philatelic Truck came to an end in San Diego, Calif., halted by the wartime need to conserve rubber and fuel. The truck was stored and later dismantled.

Dec. 15: The Polish government-in-exile in Britain issued stamps for use from Polish ships and, on certain days, from Polish military camps in Great Britain.

1942

The Japanese occupiers of Sarawak introduced stamps.

The Indian feudatory state of Jasdan placed stamps on sale.

Jan. 2: Suriname issued its first air mail semipostal stamp. The surtax went to the Red Cross.

February: Motor Vehicle Use revenue stamps were introduced in the United States. They were gummed on the face so they could be applied to a vehicle's windshield as evidence that the tax had been paid on that vehicle up to the expiration date indicated. They were discontinued in 1946.

March 2: British military forces issued British stamps overprinted "M.E.F." in ex-Italian territory they occupied. This included Eritrea, Italian Somaliland, Cyrenaica, Tripolitania, and some of the Dodecanese Islands.

March 4: Japanese occupation authorities reopened postal service in the Philippines. Limited postal service with rigid censorship lasted until Japanese forces were expelled and the islands liberated. The Japanese abandoned the Manila Post Office on Feb. 3, 1945.

March 16: The Japanese invaded and occupied the Straits Settlements and issued occupation stamps overprinted on Straits Settlements stamps.

March 16: The Japanese occupation forces in Malaya issued stamps.

March 23: The Andaman Islands in the Bay of Bengal were taken by the Japanese and occupation stamps issued. The stamps comprised stamps of India surcharged. The Japanese also occupied the adjacent Nicobar Islands during 1942.

May: The Burma Independence Army under Japanese authority issued stamps in Burma.

May 1: Trans-Canada Airlines inaugurated regular service between Moncton, New Brunswick and St. John's, Newfoundland, via Sydney, Nova Scotia and Gander, Newfoundland.

May 18: The Japanese occupying the Philippines issued a stamp commemorating their victories on Bataan and the island of Corregidor. It was an overprint on the 4c denomination of the Philippines' 1935 issue.

June: North Borneo, under Japanese occupation, issued stamps.

June 1: Bulgaria issued its first Official stamps.

June 15: The US Post Office Department introduced V-Mail, which was similar to the British Airgraph service (q.v.). By the photographic reduction of letters, the vast amount of mail could be more easily transported and did not take up so much precious aircraft space. Scheele notes that 2,575 pounds of mail could be reduced to 45 pounds, using one mailbag instead of 37. The postal rate was the same as for domestic letters.

June 15: An aerogramme service was established between Canada and Great Britain.

July: The Kathiri State of Seiyun, now part of the People's Democratic Republic of Yemen, placed stamps on sale.

A Philippine occupation stamp celebrating a US defeat (May 18, 1942) and stamps of the Kathiri State of Seiyun and the Qu'aiti State of Shihr and Mukalla (July 1942).

July: Stamps were issued inscribed for the Qu'aiti State of Shihr and Mukalla, now part of the People's Democratic Republic of Yemen.

Aug. 17: St. Pierre and Miquelon issued its first air mail stamps.

Sept. 18: Lebanon issued its first stamps as an independent nation.

October: Germany conducted a so-called "European Postal Conference" in Vienna, Austria. The conference established a European Postal and Telecommunications Union in the countries occupied by Germany. This union had no affiliation with the Universal Postal Union and ceased to exist after the liberation of Europe and defeat of Germany. The countries that accepted the German invitation to the conference were Albania, Bulgaria, Croatia, Denmark, Finland, Hungary, Italy, the Netherlands, Norway, Romania, Slovakia, and San Marino. Spain, Turkey, Vatican City, and Switzerland sent observers. Portugal and Sweden declined to attend.

Oct. 4: Croatia issued its first postal tax stamps.

Dec. 7: The British Post Office sold aerogrammes similar to the April 3, 1941 issue with a 6d stamp affixed for use in sending Christmas greetings to troops overseas.

Dec. 17: Venezuela issued its first semi-postal stamp and its first air mail semi-postal stamp. The surtax was used for a monument to Simon Bolivar.

1943

The first stamps were issued for French West Africa, according to Scott. They were surcharged stamps of Senegal. Gibbons notes December 1944 as the issue date.

The German occupiers of the Ionian island of Zante issued overprinted Italian occupation stamps.

The first stamps for Fezzan, in the interior of what is now Libya, were Italian stamps overprinted for the French occupation. General Leclerc's Free French forces liberated the area beginning in 1943.

Jan. 15: Britain overprinted stamps "E.A.F." (East African Forces) for use in British Somaliland and the former Italian Somaliland.

February: A US Armed Forces Post Office was opened on Fanning Island, part of the Gilbert and Ellice British colonial group. It closed in July 1945, according to Kyle.

February: Kouang-Tcheou (Kwangchow) reverted to China. France had leased it in April 1898.

March 9: Japanese occupiers of the island of Java in the Netherlands Indies issued stamps.

Germany issued this set of stamps to mark the European Postal Conference of the countries it then occupied (October 1942).

April 1: Provisional stamped envelopes were issued by Japanese occupation authorities in the Philippines. They consisted of prewar envelopes obliterated and revalued.

April 20: The so-called "Afrika Korps" postal label was placed in use. It filled a need for use on feldpost parcels from the large number of German troops in Tunisia. The number of troops had increased because of the British pursuit of Rommel's army west along the African coast and the need for forces to oppose the Allied landings in North Africa. The labels were produced locally under primitive conditions. The design features a palm tree and swastika.

May 19: To ease stamp shortages when the Faroe Islands were cut off from the normal supply of Danish stamps by the German occupation of Denmark, Britain supplied a Neopost postage meter. Apparently, it did not work well and was only used to frank tax bills in June 1943 and June 1944.

June 18: Great Britain introduced aerogrammes for general use, although one had been issued in 1941 for mail sent to prisoners of war, according to Mackay. The denomination of the 1943 aerogramme was 6d.

June 22: The first in a series of US stamps picturing the flags of enemy-occupied countries of World War II was issued on this date. The stamps are the first US issues produced in a combination of intaglio (frame) and lithography (vignette). They are also the first US postage stamps printed by a private printer (the American Bank Note Company) since the Bureau of Engraving and Printing began printing US stamps in 1894.

July 10: The Germans began to require a label inscribed "THERESIENSTADT" on parcels addressed to victims in the German concentration camp there. The sender had to make application to the Gestapo for a permit to send a package and present the permit in order to purchase a label. The cost was equivalent to about $20. Upon the package's arrival, guards removed the wrapping and label and examined the contents. There was, of course, no guarantee that the victim would ever receive the contents. This procedure accounts for the scarcity of the labels in used condition, according to Van Handel.

Aug. 1: Stamps were issued for Sumatra in the Netherlands Indies by its Japanese occupiers.

Sept. 15: The Italian Socialist Republic was proclaimed with Mussolini as head of a German-controlled puppet government. It comprised an area of northern Italy.

Oct. 18: The Malayan states of Kedah, Kelantan, Perlis, and Trengganu were handed over to Thailand after being invaded and occupied by its ally, Japan.

Stamps were issued during the Thai occupation for use in Kelantan (five stamps on Nov. 15, 1943), Trengganu (28 stamps beginning Oct. 1, 1944), and a set of six released in December 1943, which were apparently valid in all four occupied states. The states were liberated in 1945.

Nov. 22: German forces occupying the Montenegren area of Yugoslavia issued occupation stamps.

December: Thailand issued stamps for use in occupied Malaya.

Dec. 20: Italian stamps overprinted "GNR" were issued for use in the shortlived Italian Socialist Republic, a puppet state under Ger-

The United States issued this set of stamps to honor the countries then under Axis occupation (June 22, 1943).

man control. "GNR" stands for Guardia Nazional Repubblicana (Republican National Guard), an organization loyal to the government's leader, Mussolini.

1944

The Swiss-based International Bureau of Education released its first stamps.

Jan. 5: Argentina issued its first semi-postal stamps with the surtax going to the Postal Employees Benefit Association. Subjects of the stamps include Samuel F. B. Morse, Alexander Graham Bell, and Sir Rowland Hill. One denomination shows the globe and the top value depicts the landing of Columbus in the Americas.

February: The South Shetland Islands issued stamps.

Feb. 12: Graham Land in the Falkland Islands Dependencies released its first stamps.

Feb. 21: The South Orkneys placed its first stamps on sale.

March 7: Great Britain issued an air mail

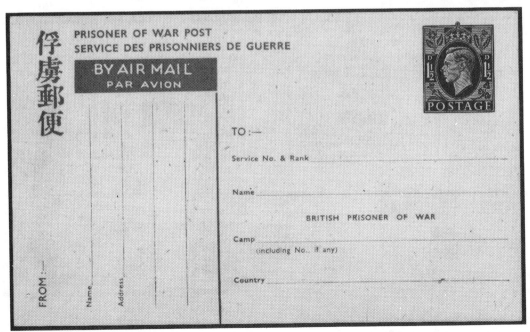

This postal card was issued by Great Britain for use in corresponding with prisoners of war being held by the Japanese (March 7, 1944).

postal card intended for correspondence to British prisoners of war in Japan.

March 26: US registration fees were raised from 20c (indemnity not more than $5) to $1.35 (for indemnity not over $1,000). A basic return receipt went to 4c from 3c and the return receipt showing the address at which delivery was made, was raised from 23c to 31c. The restricted delivery fee doubled to 20c.

March 26: The US domestic air mail rate of 8c per ounce became effective.

April 3: South Georgia issued stamps.

April 25: San Marino issued its first semi-postal air mail stamp. The surtax went to a workers' housing fund.

May 9: Ecuador released its first semi-postal stamps and air mail semi-postal stamps.

May 20: Campione d'Italia, an Italian enclave within Swiss territory, issued a set of five stamps as a gesture of support for the Italian government under King Victor Emmanuel.

It was opposed to the German-dominated puppet state of the Italian Socialist Republic, which cut it off from the former's territory. Because of speculative buying between the issue date and May 23, when the stamps became valid for use, a second issue was released on June 23.

June: Greece placed its first semi-postal air mail stamps on sale.

June 23: A second stamp issue was released by the Italian enclave of Campione d'Italia,

located in Switzerland on Lake Lugano. Speculators had bought out the initial May 20 issue (q.v.) and the new stamps were required for postal use.

A third issue followed on Sept. 7, 1944 (q.v.). The stamps were treated as valid to destinations within Switzerland. Mail destined for addresses outside Switzerland had to be franked with Swiss stamps to the correct rate.

June 27: A set of stamps was issued by the Polish government-in-exile in Great Britain to commemorate the capture of Monte Cassino, Italy, by Polish forces taking part in the campaign.

Aug. 16: Haiti issued its first postal tax stamps.

Aug. 18: From this date, the Falkland Islands accepted mail for onward air mail transmission from Montevideo, Uruguay, to any destination to which air mail service was available.

Sept. 7: A set of seven stamps issued by the Italian enclave of Campione d'Italia, located on Lake Lugano in Switzerland, depict local scenes and artworks. They remained in use until June 1952, when Swiss stamps went into use. The stamps of Italy resumed in 1957 and remain in use.

Sept. 18: Bermuda introduced aerogrammes. As in a number of other British areas, aerogrammes bearing an indicium were not immediately available and blank forms (formula aerogrammes) were initially used, to which adhesive stamps were added.

Sept. 18: Aerogrammes were first used in British Guiana (Guyana). The residents used locally printed formula aerogrammes until the first aerogrammes bearing a 12c indicium arrived from the Crown Agents.

Oct. 11: The Tuva Autonomous Region was annexed to the Soviet Union.

Oct. 25: Southern Rhodesia issued its first aerogramme for general use. Aerogrammes for use to or from military personnel on active service had been used since Nov. 17, 1941.

Oct. 28: The first aerogramme for civilian use was issued in Palestine.

Nov. 1: Ceylon (Sri Lanka) released its first specially printed aerogramme. It had four impressions of a 10c indicium to make up the 40c rate.

Nov. 8: Postal services were resumed by the Allied forces as they liberated areas of the Philippine Islands. All available stamps and postal stationery were overprinted "VICTORY." See Feb. 3, 1945.

Nov. 20: Stamps of India were overprinted for use in Muscat.

Dec. 20: Egypt issued its first aerogramme for general use. Formula aerogrammes had been available for armed forces use since 1941.

1945

The Japanese occupiers of Formosa (Taiwan) issued stamps when the Allies disrupted Japanese communications with the island and a shortage of Japanese stamps developed. The three-stamp set features a large figure of denomination and the chrysanthemum symbol of Japan.

Stamps of the Straits Settlements were issued overprinted "BMA/ MALAYA" for use in the Malay Peninsula, including Singapore, following liberation from Japanese occupation.

Yugoslavia issued stamps inscribed "ISTRIA" for its occupation of the Istrian and Slovene Coast areas of Zone B, former Italian territory south of Trieste. Yugoslavia occupied the areas at the end of World War II.

Feb. 1: The United States issued postal note stamps. Intended to be used on money orders to make up odd amounts, they were discontinued on March 31, 1951.

Feb. 3: The Japanese-controlled Philippine postal service ended as all the islands were liberated.

Feb. 3: The Polish government-in-exile in Great Britain issued a stamp to honor the Poles who died during the Aug. 1 to Oct. 3, 1944 Warsaw Uprising.

March 2: The New Zealand Post Office opened a post office at Raoul Island in the Kermadec island group located about 600 miles from Auckland.

March 10: Aerogrammes were introduced in the Falkland Islands. They were of the "formula" type and adhesive postage stamps had to be affixed.

March 19: Military Government stamps, prepared ahead of time, were placed in use at Aachen and later in the British and American occupation zones of Germany.

March 27: Monaco used the surtax from its first air mail semi-postal stamp released on this date to aid prisoners of war.

April 25: All stamps of the Repubblica Sociale Italiana (Italian Socialist Republic), puppet government under German control in northern Italy, became invalid.

May: The Iranian province of Azerbaijan, while under Soviet control, issued stamps from this month until December 1946. This Iranian province should not be confused with the area known as Azerbaijan in the Soviet Union, which was briefly independent following the World War I Russian Revolution.

May 9: The German Third Reich surrender; ending World War II in Europe.

June 5: A pair of stamps in 5pf and 8pf denominations depicting the Berlin Bear was issued by the Soviet administration in Germany. These were the first new stamps issued in conquered Germany at the end of World War II, according to Wolfe, although the British and Americans had placed on sale the Military Government stamp issue on sale March 19 and there were a number of local uses of obliterated Hitler heads. The Soviet occupation zone of Berlin is now part of East Germany.

Two stamps issued by the Soviet occupiers in what is now East Germany (June 5, 1945).

June 23: Soviet occupation authorities approved the release of a 12pf stamp inscribed with the German and Russian-language words for "post" ("POST/ NOYTA") in the Dresden Postal District (OPD Dresden). The stamp was withdrawn after only eight hours on sale.

The reasons for the withdrawal is not known, although German complaints about the Russian-language inscription have been cited. However, such Soviet sensitivity seems rather out of character.

The same design without the Russian inscription was issued beginning on June 30. Other issues followed until February 1946, when a general issue was released. Dresden is now part of East Germany.

June 27: The first Swedish transatlantic flight was made from Stockholm to New York, via Iceland and Goose Bay, Labrador.

July: The US Armed Forces Post Office on Fanning Island was closed.

July 1: President Harry Truman appointed his first postmaster general. He was Robert E. Hannegan, who succeeded Frank C. Walker.

July 31: The British airgraph service ended. More than 350 million airgraphs had been transmitted since the service opened April 21, 1941.

Aug. 28: Soviet occupation authorities issued stamps in the Mecklenburg-Vorpommern Postal District (OPD Schwerin). The issues continued until replaced in February 1946 by a general issue. The area is now part of East Germany.

Sept. 2: The Democratic Republic of Vietnam was proclaimed by Viet Minh nationalists on Sept. 2, 1945 and stamps issued. They took the form of overprints on stamps of French Indo-China. France recognized the regime on March 6, 1946. According to Scott, the stamps had no international validity. it lists the first stamps valid for international use as being issued in 1951.

Sept. 7: A civilian mail service for intra-island mail was established on Okinawa, in the Ryukyu Islands, following its occupation by US forces.

Sept. 28: Western Saxony in the Soviet occupied Leipzig Postal District (OPD Leipzig) issued stamps. They were used until replaced in February 1946 by a general Soviet-occupied area issue. The Western Saxony stamps were invalidated on Oct. 31, 1946, according to Wolfe. The area is now part of East Germany.

Oct. 1: A provisional stamp was issued on Kume Island in the Ryukyu Islands. Inscribed "KUME/ SHIMA," it had a 7 sen denomination. The stamp was produced by the postmaster with the help of the US Navy. The postmaster placed his seal in the center of the stamp.

Oct. 1: Italy began the release of its first post-World War II set of air mail stamps. Five of the nine stamps used a design showing the Caproni-Campini CC-2 jet aircraft. This aircraft began flying in 1940 and earned a place in aviation history by becoming the first jet aircraft to make a cross-country flight, when it flew from Milan to Rome on Nov. 30, 1941. There are reports that it carried a bag of mail on that flight, but none is known to have survived. The aircraft eventually proved unsuccessful and was not developed further.

Oct. 1: Stamps were first issued for Thuringa in the Erfurt Postal District (OPD Erfurt) of the Soviet occupation zone. They were replaced by a general issue in February 1946 and invalidated Oct. 31, 1946, according to Wolfe. The area is now part of East Germany.

Oct. 10: Stamps were first issued in the Province of Saxony (Halle Postal District). Six denominations were released in a common design featuring the coat of arms of Saxony. Other issues followed, being replaced in February 1946 by a general issue for Soviet-occupied Germany, the area that later became the German Democratic Republic (East Germany).

Oct. 24: The allied occupying powers gave permission to the Berlin Postal Administration to begin mail service to and from the rest of occupied Germany.

November: Java issued stamps prior to the formation of the United States of Indonesia on Jan. 17, 1950.

Nov. 4: The Chinese government of Formosa (Taiwan) issued stamps following its liberation from Japanese control at the end of World War II.

Nov. 6: During the liberation of Sarawak from Japanese occupation in World War II, Australian troops arrived in that country, which was in the Australian zone of liberated territory. During a shortage of stamps, Australian stamps were used from this date to Dec. 16, 1945 at the capital city of Kuching and at two other post offices, according to Rosenblum. Thus, Australian stamps bearing Sarawak cancels dated during this period are of considerable interest.

Nov. 24: Austria released its first general issue of stamps following the country's liberation from German occupation.

Dec. 1: Nicolas Sanabria died. A well-known dealer, air mail authority, and publisher of the *Sanabria World Air Mail Catalogue*, Sanabria had come to the United States following a period as a political prisoner in Venezuela.

1946

Hungary experienced a period of unbelievable inflation and issued a stamp bearing the highest face value ever. The stamp had a denomination of 500 million million pengos!

Feb. 1: South Korea, under US military administration, issued stamps.

Feb. 1: The first stamps inscribed "Falkland Islands Dependencies" were issued on this date. They feature a map of the British-controlled area of the south polar region.

Feb. 19: The Dutch airline, KLM, made a mail-carrying proving flight from Suriname to the Netherlands.

March 12: The first stamps were issued for North Korea under Soviet occupation.

April 30: A letter postmarked on this date in Looe, Cornwall, England, shows evidence of having once had a stamp affixed, but which is no longer present. It is endorsed "Stamp found/ eaten off by Snails." According to Hopkins, it is common in country districts of Cornwall for snails to hibernate in wall-mounted letter boxes. In the spring they awaken hungry and are attracted to the gum of postage stamps on letters that may be in the box!

May: Manchoukuo restored to China. The area had been occupied by the USSR following the defeat of Japan. With the restoration of Chinese authority its stamps were placed in use.

May 6: The Union Islands were renamed the Tokelau Islands. They were then under the administration of Samoa, but are now administered by New Zealand.

May 8: The French colony of Wallis and Futuna Islands issued its first air mail stamp. It commemorated World War II victory in Europe.

May 15: Syria became a member of the Universal Postal Union. It had been a member beginning in 1931 while under French administration and, jointly with Lebanon from 1936.

May 15: Independent Lebanon joined the Universal Postal Union. It had been a member since 1931 as a French colony and jointly with Syria from 1936.

May 25: The independent Kingdom of Jordan issued its first stamps.

June 15: Belgium issued its first air mail semipostal stamps.

June 20: Algeria placed its first air mail stamps on sale. The six stamps show an airplane over Algiers harbor. There are two types of the 20-franc denomination.

June 22: The first mail was carried in the United States by a jet aircraft on flights from Schenectady, N.Y., to Washington, D.C., and Chicago.

June 22: Air France made the first flight of a regular service between Paris and Santiago, Chile. Mail was carried.

July 4: The newly independent Philippine Republic released its first stamps.

July 5: The first commercial delivery of mail by helicopter was from the Bridgeport, Conn., Post Office to a nearby airport. The aircraft used was a Sikorsky S-51.

Aug. 6: The Dutch airline KLM, made a mail-carrying survey flight from Amsterdam to Buenos Aires, Argentina.

Sept. 17: The first flight by Scandinavian Airlines from Stockholm, Sweden to New York was made on this date. The return flight from New York began on Sept. 26. Mail was carried.

Oct. 1: A US domestic air mail rate of 5c per ounce was introduced. It had previously been 8c per ounce.

Oct. 1: American Airlines made a demonstration flight from Los Angeles to Boston of its Flying Post Office. Mail was worked enroute and nine stops were made between the two cities.

Oct. 1: Trinidad and Tobago issued a pair of stamps to mark victory and the end of World War II. Known as the Peace Issue, most other British areas joined in this omnibus series. The common design shown was shared by the crown colonies.

Oct. 6: The Dutch airline, KLM, made a survey flight from Amsterdam to Johannesburg, South Africa. Mail was carried.

Oct. 7: Cyprus introduced its first aerogramme. From 1941 to this date, a Middle East Forces (MEF) form and the "Empire" formula form had been used.

Oct. 11: Australian stamps in denominations of ½d, 1d, and 3d were overprinted "B.C.O.F./ Japan/ 1946" and issued to Australian occupation forces in Japan. The BCOF stood for "British Commonwealth Occupation Force." However, the stamps were withdrawn after two days and re-issued on May 8, 1947 (q.v.) together with additional denominations.

Nov. 1: Yugoslavia issued its first Official

stamps. They depict the coat of arms of the Federated People's Republic of Yugoslavia.

Nov. 30: Scandinavian Airlines made its first flight from Stockholm, Sweden to Montevideo, Uruguay. Mail was carried.

1947

The American Revenue Association was formed.

The Saar came under French administration and its second stamp-issuing period began. This period lasted until the Saar's reunion with Germany on Jan. 1, 1957.

March 1: The Allied Control Council finally abolished the state of Prussia.

April 16: Sarawak became a crown colony.

April 24: Ethiopia issued its first special delivery stamps. The two stamps picture a motorcycle messenger and a view of the Addis Ababa Post Office.

April 24: British Commonwealth Pacific Air Service made its first flight from Auckland, New Zealand, to Vancouver, B.C. The return flight began on May 3, according to the *American Air Mail Catalog*. Mail was carried.

April 29: The United States issued its first aerogramme. It bore a 10c indicium.

April 30: Norway issued its first aerogramme.

May 2: The Swiss airline, SWISSAIR, made an inaugural flight from Geneva to New York. A 2.50fr Swiss stamp was issued to mark the event and was valid to frank mail only on this one flight.

May 7: Originally scheduled for Paris in 1944, the start of the 12th Congress of the

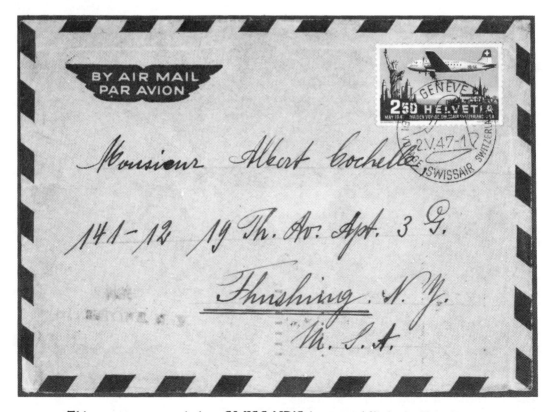

This cover was carried on SWISSAIR'S inaugural flight to New York.

Universal Postal Union was delayed until this date by World War II. It was the largest to date, with 272 delegates attending. Allied commissions represented the powers defeated in WWII and Spain and Spanish Morocco were excluded because of pro-German attitudes during the war. The Congress considered completion of items from the 1939 Congress and the vast expansion of air mail made possible by wartime technological developments being applied to civilian purposes. The UPU was also made an agency of the United Nations effective November 1947. The Congress made its decisions effective on July 1, 1948. France and Lebanon issued commemorative stamps for the Congress.

May 8: Australian stamps overprinted "B.C.O.F." were placed in use for Australian troops occupying Japan at the end of World War II. The Australian stamps were overprinted to prevent them from being used to transfer black market profits back to Australia, where the stamps could have been sold back to the Post Office. The overprint stands for "British Commonwealth Occupation Forces." They were withdrawn from use on Feb. 12, 1949. See also Oct. 11, 1946.

May 13: The Byelorussian Soviet Socialist Republic and the Ukrainian SSR became members of the Universal Postal Union, despite both being states within the Soviet Union.

May 16: The Universal Postal Union added Jordan to its membership.

May 17: An international philatelic exhibition was held in New York City from this date to May 25 to mark the centennial of the first US stamp issue. A souvenir sheet reproducing the two 1847 stamps in colors differing from the originals was issued in conjunction with the exhibition.

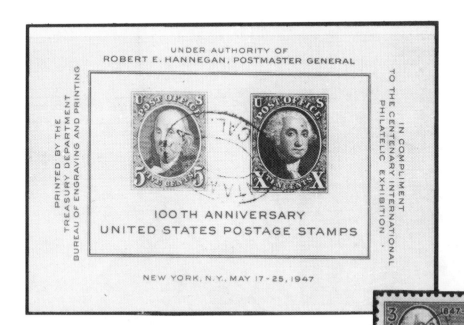

The souvenir sheet and stamp issued to mark the international stamp exhibition held in New York May 17-25.

May 17, 1947 - Nov. 15, 1947

May 17: The United States issued a 3c stamp to commemorate the 100th anniversary of the first US postage stamps, the 5c and 10c stamps of July 1, 1847.

June 10: Norfolk Island issued its first stamps.

June 11: Hungary placed its first air mail semi-postal stamps on sale.

June 24: Newfoundland issued its final stamp prior to becoming the 10th Canadian province on April 1, 1949. The stamp marked the 450th anniversary of John Cabot's discovery of the island.

July 1: Turkey issued its first Official stamps, according to Gibbons. Scott notes only the year "1948" as the issue date.

July 16: Regular air mail service to and from the New Hebrides was inaugurated when a Catalina flying boat of TRAPAS (Transports Aeriens Pacifique, Sud) flew to Vila from Noumea, New Caledonia.

July 21: Jamaica issued its first aerogramme.

Aug. 15: The state of Bahawalpur, located between the then-Dominions of India and Pakistan, placed its first stamps on sale. It is now part of Pakistan.

Sept. 1: Spain's first aerogramme, consisting of a privately printed formula aerogramme bearing a postage meter impression, was issued.

Sept. 1: North Borneo issued its first stamps as a crown colony.

Sept. 18: The first aerogramme of the Philippines was issued.

Oct. 1: Helicopter air mail service began between Los Angeles International Airport and the downtown, San Fernando, San Bernardino, and Newport Beach post offices. This was the first regularly scheduled helicopter air mail service. Experimental services had operated briefly in Chicago and New York.

Oct. 1: South Korea issued its first air mail stamp.

Oct. 1: Stamps were first issued for the Dominion of Pakistan.

Oct. 10: Stamps issued for use in the British and US Occupation Zone A of former Italian territory including Trieste and the Istrian peninsula.

Nov. 10: Pakistan became a member of the Universal Postal Union.

Nov. 15: Brazil issued a triangular semi-postal postal tax stamp to mark Aviation Week, Nov. 15-22, and it made it compulsory on all mail during that week.

From the left are the first Norfolk Island stamp (June 10, 1947), Newfoundland's last stamp (June 24, 1947), and a semi-postal postal tax stamp from Brazil (Nov. 15, 1947).

Nov. 21: The Dominion of India issued its first stamps.

Dec. 16: Jesse M. Donaldson succeeded Robert E. Hannegan as US postmaster general.

Dec. 25: The Australian post office on Heard Island, located in the southern Indian Ocean about 300 miles southeast of the Kerguelen Archipelago, opened on this day and canceled mail.

1948

The Ryukyu Islands, which had been taken from Japan by US forces late in World War II, issued stamps. These stamp issues continued until the island group was returned to Japan on May 15, 1972.

Jan. 3: The Saar achieved a semi-independent status following a period of French control from the end of World War II.

Jan. 6: Burma issued its first stamps as an independent state.

Jan. 19: France placed its first air mail semi-postal stamps on sale.

France's first air mail semi-postal stamps (Jan. 19, 1947).

Jan. 20: Stamps of South Africa went on sale at Marion Island, a small island about 1,400 miles south of Cape Town. Only three first-day covers are known, according to Robson Lowe. A weather station was established on the island.

Jan. 30: Iran issued its first semi-postal stamps. The surtax went to the reconstruction of the tomb of Avicenna at Hamadan.

February: Definitive aerogrammes were issued by Hong Kong, which has used military and formula aerogrammes since its liberation from Japanese occupation at the end of World War II.

April: Fiji issued its first aerogramme.

April 1: Stamps of Great Britain were surcharged for use at British postal agencies in Eastern Arabia. These stamps were used at Muscat (April 1, 1948-April 29, 1966); Dubai (April 1, 1948-Jan. 6, 1961); Doa, Qatar (from August 1950); Umm Said, Qatar (February 1956-March 31, 1957); Abu Dhabi (March 30, 1963-March 29, 1964); and Das Island, Abu Dhabi (December 1960-March 29, 1964). The stamps were also used at Kuwait and Bahrain.

April 1: The first specially printed stamps were issued by Bahawalpur. They had been preceded by Indian stamps overprinted. The stamps were only valid within the state, which is now part of Pakistan.

May 1: Stamps were issued for Zone B, former Italian territory occupied by Yugoslavia following World War II.

May 1: Trans-Canada Airways (now Air Canada) began service between Bermuda and Toronto, via New York. Mail received a commemorative cachet, according to Robson Lowe.

May 1: The Soviet Union established a puppet regime in the northern portion of the Korean Peninsula that it had occupied at the end of World War II.

May 6: The first automatic stamp-vending machine went into service at the General Post

May 10, 1948 - May 16, 1948

Office in New York City, according to Konwiser.

May 10: The Republic of South Korea was formed.

May 14: The British terminated their mandate over Palestine and British administration ceased.

May 14: The state of Israel was formed. It comprised about 75 percent of what had been the British mandated territory of Palestine, liberated by Britain from the Turks during World War I.

Israel's first stamp design (May 16, 1948).

May 15: Egypt issued stamps overprinted for use in occupied areas of Palestine.

May 16: Israel issued its first stamps.

A cover carried on an Air France flight from Geneva, Switzerland to Martinique, in the West Indies. The stamp of Martinique depicts the giant, six-engine flying boat used. The aircraft disappeared on the return flight (June 14, 1948).

May 27: Stamps of Great Britain overprinted "B.M.A./ SOMALIA" were issued by the British administration of the former Italian Somaliland.

May 28: Israel released its first postage due labels.

June: British stamps overprinted "B.M.A./ ERITREA" went into use in the former Italian colony of Eritrea.

June 1: Egypt issued stamps overprinted for use in the occupied Gaza Strip.

June 14: A special flight of an Air France Latecoere 631 six-engined flying boat was made from Geneva, Switzerland, to Fort de France, Martinique in the West Indies. It carried mail and a special cancel was applied. The aircraft disappeared on its return flight.

June 22: The first stamps were issued for the Tokelau Islands. Until May 6, 1946 they were known as the Union Islands. With an area of about four square miles, the islands are located about 300 miles north of Samoa and are now administered from New Zealand. Western Samoa administered them when they issued their first stamps (see Jan. 1, 1949).

June 24: The Swiss-based World Health Organization issued stamps.

July 1: Gold Coast (Ghana) issued its first aerogramme. Since 1941, it had used military formula aerogrammes.

July 1: Postal cards were issued for use in the Ryukyu Islands by the four individual gunto (district) governments established by the United States at the end of World War II. The cards had a 10 sen indicia featuring the stylized deigo blossom design. Although the 10 sen denomination did not meet any local rate, the cards served as the basis for provisional surcharges.

July 1: Great Britain overprinted its stamps "B.M.A./ TRIPOLITANIA" for use in the occupied ex-Italian colony.

July 3: Stamps were issued for use throughout the Soviet occupation zone of Germany. On Oct. 9, 1949, the zone became the German Democratic Republic (q.v.)

July 26: Liberian International Airways inaugurated air mail service from Monrovia, Liberia, to Dakar, Senegal.

July 29: Great Britain issued its first commemorative aerogramme. It commemorated the Olympic Games, held in Britian in 1948.

Aug. 1: The first stamps of the Republic of South Korea were issued.

Aug. 17: The first aerogramme released for use from West Berlin went on sale.

Sept. 1: Stamps were issued for use in the British, French, and US occupation zones of Berlin (West Berlin).

Sept. 1: The Crown Colony of Singapore issued its first inscribed stamps.

Sept. 9: The communist state of North Korea was established. It had been occupied by the USSR at the end of World War II.

Oct. 1: Yugoslavia issued its first aerogramme.

Oct. 12: The Saar designated the surtax for flood relief when it issued a semi-postal air mail stamp.

Oct. 17: Zone B, the former Italian territory occupied by Yugoslavia following World War II, issued air mail stamps.

Nov. 14: The first Qantas flight from Australia to South Africa began on this date. The return flight arrived at Sydney on Dec. 1. Mail was carried.

Dec. 1: A small, blue label went into use in the US and British occupation zones of Germany.

It had to be affixed to all mail within the two zones, and later, in the French zone. It cost 2pf (about ½c) and was instituted to help defray the high cost of the airlift into Berlin during the 1948-49 blockade, when the Soviet Union attempted to force its ex-allies out of their occupation zones in Berlin.

Mail to Berlin and foreign countries was exempt from the tax, which was initially intended to be in effect until February 1949. The Western Allies did not end the tax until March 31, 1956, according to Herman Halle. The label exists in a number of varieties as well as perforated, imperf, and rouletted.

Dec. 1: The Malay state of Penang issued stamps. Previously, it used stamps of the Straits Settlements. The state is now part of Malaysia.

Dec. 1: The first stamps were issued bearing the name of the Malay state of Perlis. Previously, the area had used stamps of Kedah, except for the Japanese occupation period during World War II.

Dec. 1: The Malay state of Malacca released stamps. Previously part of the Straits Settlements, Malacca is now a state of Malaysia.

Dec. 20: British Guiana (now Guyana) released its contribution to the omnibus series marking the silver wedding anniversary of King George VI and Queen Elizabeth. Most British

areas took part and the crown colonies shared the two illustrated designs. The high values aroused great resentment among collectors and subsequent omnibus issues in the British Commonwealth have been in more modest denominations.

Dec. 21: Ireland declared itself a republic and withdrew from the British Commonwealth.

1949

South Korea rejoined the Universal Postal Union as the Republic of Korea. It had previously been a member under the name of Chosan, while occupied by Japan.

During this year, The French island of Reunion began to release stamps overprinted "C.F.A." and surcharged. "C.F.A." stands for "Colonies Francaises d'Afrique" and indicates that the denomination was expressed in French African fancs, which had a different value than the French franc.

The American Topical Association was formed.

Rajasthan, formed from a number of Indian states including the stamp-issuing feudatory states of Bundi, Jaipur, and Kishangarh issued stamps.

The United States of Saurashtra, which included the former stamp-issuing Indian states of Jasdan, Morvi, Nawanager, and Wadhwan, placed its own stamps on sale.

Jan. 1: A US registration fee scale was set at from 25c (indemnity not more than $5) to $1.50 (indemnity not more than $1,000). The basic return receipt charge went to 5c.

Jan. 1: A US domestic air mail rate of 6c per ounce went into effect.

Jan. 1: On this date, the US Post Office Department introduced a 4c air mail rate for postal cards/ postcards. The rate previously had been the same as for one-ounce air mail letters.

Jan. 1: Spanish Morocco issued its first aerogrammes.

Jan. 1: The Tokelau Islands, formerly the Union Islands, became a dependency of New Zealand. They had previously been administered by Western Samoa.

Jan. 10: The United States placed its first air mail postal card on sale.

Jan. 14: Grenada's first aerogramme was released.

Feb. 1: Iraq issued its first air mail stamps.

March 1: Japan placed on sale its first aerogramme for general use.

March 9: Venezuela issued its first express stamp.

April 1: Newfoundland became the 10th province of Canada. For years plagued by financial troubles, after World War II the people of the island faced the choices of renewed dominion status, a continuation of government by commission, or union with Canada as a province. They opted for the latter.

April 1: The Philippines issued its first semipostal stamps and used the surtax to restore war-damaged public libraries.

May 23: The Federal Republic of Germany was formed.

May 26: A pigeon mail service operated from the English Channel island of Herm to Guernsey. Messages were written on a special form and franked with a 1/- Pigeon Service stamp. The service was discontinued upon the completion of a radio-telephone link, according to Newport.

May 26: Private local stamps were issued on the English Channel island of Herm to frank mail carried to Guernsey by a boat belonging to the tenant of the island. The stamps were used for nine years, according to Newport.

June 14: The former French territories of Annam, Tonkin, and Cochin China joined to form the independent state of Vietnam within the French Union.

July 1: The United States of Travancore-Cochin issued stamps.

July 13: Ceylon (now Sri Lanka) became a member of the Universal Postal Union.

July 13: Canadian Pacific Airlines inaugurated air mail and passenger service between Vancouver, B.C.; Honolulu; Fiji; and Sydney, Australia. An official cachet was applied to the mail.

July 19: Laos became an independent country. It had previously been part of French Indo-China.

July 26: Stamps were first issued inscribed "NEDERLANDSE ANTILLEN" (Netherlands Antilles). The area's stamps had previously been inscribed "CURACAO."

September: The Canadian Post Office began to overprint "O.H.M.S." on stamps used by government departments. Canadian Official stamps had previously been perforated with the initials.

Sept. 1: The denomination of US Federal Migratory Waterfowl Hunting stamps (Duck stamps) was increased to $2 from the original $1.

Sept. 7: The Federal Republic of Germany issued its first stamps.

Oct. 4: Burma joined the Universal Postal Union.

Oct. 8: The first general issue of stamps for the People's Republic of China was released on this date.

Oct. 9: Iceland issued its first aerogramme.

Oct. 9: The first Danish aerogramme went on sale.

Oct. 9: Spanish West Africa issued stamps for the first time.

Oct. 9: The Universal Postal Union celebrated its 75th anniversary and countries around the world issued stamps marking the event.

Oct. 9: The German Democratic Republic (GDR or DDR) released its first stamps.

Oct. 10: The British Crown Colony of Trinidad and Tobago issued a set of four stamps to mark the 75th anniversary of the Universal Postal Union. This was an omnibus design shared by other British crown colonies. Gibbons notes Oct. 10 as the issue date, while Scott gives it as Oct. 9. The illustrated first-day cover supports the Oct. 10 date.

Nov. 1: The Postal Transportation Service started operating in the United States. The letters "PTS" replaced "RMS" (Railway Mail Service) and "HPO" (Highway Post Office) in the killer portions of the postmarks used. The PTS included railroad, railroad terminal, highway, and air-mail field post offices.

Nov. 19: Argentina issued the first stamp to be printed on a Giori press. Designed by

Gualtiero Giori, the press was capable of printing up to five colors in one pass and was similar to the three-color press used by the Bureau of Engraving and Printing to produce the first Giori press-printed US stamp issued on July 4, 1957 (q.v.).

Nov. 23: Spanish West Africa issued its first air mail stamps.

Dec. 1: The Netherlands issued its first aerogramme for general use. Aerogrammes for use to military personnel had been available since April 14, 1947.

Dec. 15: Nigeria's first aerogramme for general use was issued on this date.

Dec. 24: The Universal Postal Union accepted Israel as a member.

Dec. 27: The United States of Indonesia was formed, but did not issue its first stamps until Jan. 17, 1950.

The British crown colonies issued this four-stamp set to mark the 75th anniversary of the Universal Postal Union (Oct. 10, 1949).

1950 - 1979
The age of independence

1950

Netherlands New Guinea placed its first stamps on sale.

Jan. 1: The first stamps were issued by the Republic of China (Taiwan), the government of which had been driven from the mainland by Chinese communist forces.

Jan. 10: The Vatican's first aerogramme went on sale.

Jan. 16: The autonomous state of Cyrenaica, which in 1951 was incorporated in the newly formed state of Libya, issued its first stamps.

Jan. 17: The United States of Indonesia, which had been formed in late 1949, released its first stamp.

Jan. 20: West Berlin's stamps became valid for use in the Federal Republic of Germany.

Jan. 26: The Republic of India issued its first stamps.

Feb. 1: Swiss stamps were overprinted for use from the European office of the United Nations.

Feb. 1: The Swiss-based International Refugee Organization issued stamps.

Feb. 1: Trinidad and Tobago issued its first

aerogramme with a 12c indicium. It had previously used a formula aerogramme, to which adhesive stamps had to be affixed.

Feb. 15: The Ryukyu Islands released air mail stamps and a special delivery stamp.

Feb. 20: The French postal administration of Andorra issued a 100 franc air mail stamp.

March 10: The first Austrian aerogramme was specially prepared for release on this date in conjunction with the opening of the Austrian Centenary Stamp Exhibition held in Philadelphia.

March 24: The United Nations placed Somalia (the former Italian Somaliland) under Italian administration during a period in which it prepared for independence. Stamps were issued inscribed "SOMALIA."

April: A post office opened at Alert, on the north coast of Ellesmere Island, in Canada's North West Territories. Only 450 miles from the North Pole, it is claimed to be the world's most northerly post office.

April 18: The first official air mail carried by a commercial jet aircraft and the first international mail carried by a jet aircraft was flown from Toronto to New York during a demonstration flight of North America's first commercial jet aircraft, the Canadian Avro C-102 *Jetliner*. The flight took one hour. No mail was carried on the return flight.

April 24: Somalia, under Italian administration, issued its first special delivery stamp.

April 28: Pneumatic tube service across the Brooklyn Bridge between post offices in New York and Brooklyn was discontinued.

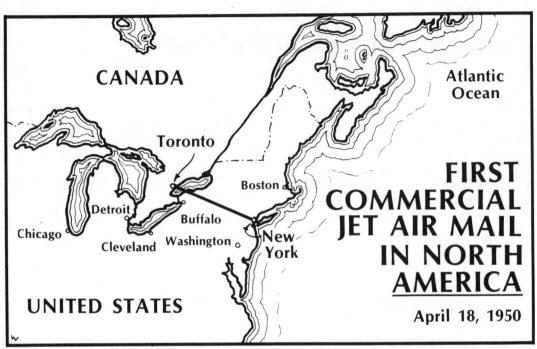

CANADA

Atlantic Ocean

Toronto

Boston

Detroit

Buffalo

Chicago

Cleveland Washington New York

UNITED STATES

FIRST COMMERCIAL JET AIR MAIL IN NORTH AMERICA

April 18, 1950

FIRST OFFICIAL AIRMAIL
• • •
JETLINER
TORONTO
TO
NEW YORK

VIA AIR MAIL

William V. Egbert
P. O. Box 261
New Baltimore, Michigan
U.S.A.

A cover carried on the first commercial jet air mail flight in North America and a Canadian stamp picturing the Avro C-102 *Jetliner* that made the flight (April 18, 1950).

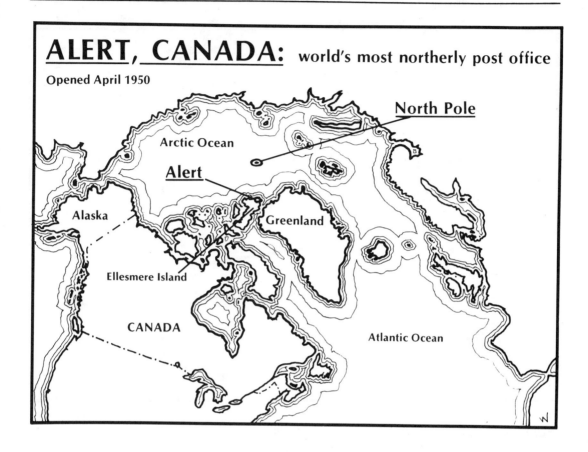

ALERT, CANADA: world's most northerly post office

Opened April 1950

North Pole

Arctic Ocean

Alert

Alaska

Greenland

Ellesmere Island

CANADA

Atlantic Ocean

May 15: The Comoro Islands issued its first stamps.

June 25: Israel placed its first air mail stamps on sale.

July 2: The first aerogramme issued by Israel went into use.

July 3: Sierra Leone released its first aerogramme.

July 12: Colombia overprinted its air mail stamps with a letter "A" beginning on this date for use on mail flown by Avianca, a Colombian airline.

July 18: Colombian air mail stamps were overprinted with a letter "L" beginning on this date for use on mail flown by Lineas Aereas Nacionales Sociedad Anonima, a Colombian airline.

Aug. 17: The Republic of Indonesia issued its first stamps. The country had been formed on Aug. 15 from the United States of Indonesia.

Sept. 4: San Marino issued its first aerogrammes in denominations of 20 lira for use to Italy and 55 lira to other countries.

Sept. 6: Canadian stamps overprinted "G" replaced those/ overprinted "O.H.M.S." on this date, according to Wrigley.

Sept. 16: Jordan issued its first air mail stamps.

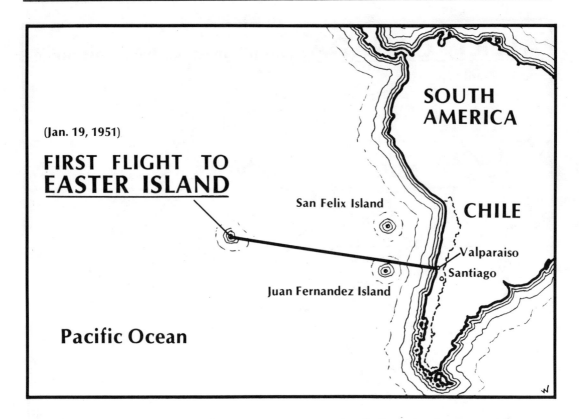

(Jan. 19, 1951)

FIRST FLIGHT TO EASTER ISLAND

SOUTH AMERICA

San Felix Island

CHILE

Valparaiso

Santiago

Juan Fernandez Island

Pacific Ocean

Sept. 26: The Republic of China released its first air mail stamps following its move to Taiwan.

Oct. 17: Aerogrammes were first issued for Portuguese Guinea.

Oct. 21: Portuguese India issued its first aerogrammes.

Nov. 11; The Portuguese colony of St. Thomas and Prince issued its first aerogramme.

Dec. 15: The first Albanian stamps issued under the name of the People's Republic of Albania were released.

Dec. 17: The US Treasury Department began its prohibition of the purchase of North Korean stamps and their importation into the United States. The ban was still in effect at the time of this book's publication.

Dec. 31: The pneumatic tube system for mov-

ing mail in Boston was discontinued.

1951

Beginning this year, most stamps of Afghanistan printed locally were sold in imperforate condition at double face value.

Indonesia became a member of the Universal Postal Union. It had joined in 1877 while known as the Dutch East Indies.

Jan. 2: The Republic of Indonesia issued its first semi-postal stamps.

Jan. 19: About 100 covers were carried on the first flight from Chile to Easter Island.

Feb. 1: Portuguese Timor issued its first aerogramme.

Feb. 1: Israel released its first Official stamps.

Feb. 16: British Guiana (now Guyana) placed on sale a pair of stamps marking the inauguration of the University College of the West In-

University College of the West Indies issue (Feb. 16, 1951).

dies. This was an omnibus issue in which Antigua, Barbados, British Honduras Dominica, Grenada, Jamaica, the Leeward Islands, Montserrat, St. Kitts-Nevis, St. Lucia, St. Vincent, Trinidad and Tobago, and the Virgin Islands also participated. A common design was used showing the arms of the college and the regent, Princess Alice of Athlone.

March 1: Spanish West Africa issued a special delivery stamp.

March 31: The United States discontinued use of postal note stamps. They had been introduced Feb. 1, 1945.

April 2: The Virgin Islands issued a set of stamps inscribed ''BRITISH VIRGIN ISLANDS.'' Up to then its stamps had been inscribed ''VIRGIN ISLANDS.'' It resumed the latter inscription following this issue and used it until 1968, when the ''BRITISH'' was restored. The ''BRITISH'' has been continued with only a few exceptions, when the abbreviation ''BR.'' has been used.

April 14: Finland released its first aerogramme.

May 1: The United States established a post office on Wake Island, which it had annexed in 1898. The post office has ZIP Code 96798.

May 1: The People's Republic of China issued its first air mail stamps.

May 3: Although it is generally true that Great Britain's name does not appear on its stamps, there has been at least one exception. On this date it issued a pair of stamps to mark the Festival of Britain and this appeared as an inscription on both stamps.

June 27: A single 1p air mail stamp was issued by the Spanish postal administration of Andorra.

July 1: US post offices were established in various groups of the US Trust Territories in the Pacific Ocean when civil governments took over administration from the military. The post offices were at Majuro (Marshall Islands), Ponape and Truk (Eastern Caroline Islands), Koror and Yap (Western Caroline Islands), and Saipan (Mariana Islands). All except Yap, which remained a fourth-class office, were raised to third class status on Oct. 1, 1951, according to Murphy. Additional offices were subsequently opened.

Aug. 16: The independent state of Vietnam, later divided into North and South Vietnam, issued its first stamps.

Sept. 17: Fiji placed its first semi-postal stamps on sale.

Great Britain's name appears on this Festival of Britain set (May 3, 1951).

Canada marked the centenary of its first stamp with this set of four (Sept. 24, 1952).

Sept. 24: Canada issued a set of four stamps marking the centenary of that country's first stamps. They were issued in conjunction with the first Canadian international stamp exhibition held in Toronto.

Oct. 1: Singapore's first aerogramme went on sale.

Oct. 21: What was then called South Vietnam became a member of the Universal Postal Union.

Oct. 24: The United Nations headquarters at New York issued its first postage stamps.

November: The Kingdom of Cambodia placed its first stamps on sale.

Nov. 13: The first stamps were issued for the Kingdom of Laos.

Nov. 17: Ethiopia released its first aerogramme.

Dec. 1: Somalia's first aerogramme was issued.

Dec. 21: Kampuchea (Cambodia) joined the Universal Postal Union.

Dec. 24: The independent Kingdom of Libya, which included Cyrenaica, Fezzan, and Tripolitania, issued its first stamps. They comprised stamps of Cyrenaica overprinted and surcharged.

1952 ————————————————
Jan. 1: A US registry fee of 30c, which pro-

These two stamps marked the first direct flight to the Falklands from the UK (April 28, 1952).

vided for no indemnity, was introduced. The scale of charges for indemnity ranged from 40c (indemnity not more than $5) to $1.75 (indemnity not more than $1,000). The basic return receipt fee went to 7c.

Jan. 1: The first stamps issued for Tristan da Cunha took the form of the overprint "TRISTAN. DA CUNHA" on stamps of St. Helena.

Feb. 6: King George VI of Great Britain died. He was succeeded by his eldest daughter, who became Queen Elizabeth II.

April 12: Laos issued its first air mail stamps.

April 28: The first direct air mail flight arrived at the Falkland Islands. It was a survey flight by Aquila Airways, using a Short Sunderland flying boat.

It left on its return flight on May 2. A special cancel was used on mail carried on the flight back to England.

May 5: The French protectorate of Tunisia released its first air mail semi-postal stamps.

May 14: The 13th Congress of the Universal Postal Union convened in Brussels, Belgium. It agreed to abolish the international requirement that stamps be blue for letters, red for postcards, and green for printed matter. The UPU adjusted air mail rates and set a minimum size of 4x2.75 inches for letters. The effective date of the Congress's decisions was July 1, 1953.

May 15: Thailand issued its first modern-style aerogramme.

May 20: Laos joined the Universal Postal Union.

May 30: Italy's first aerogramme was for use only within Europe and bore a 60-lira indicium.

May 30: The first aerogramme for general use was issued for Trieste, Zone A, by Allied occupation authorities. It was an overprinted aerogramme of Italy.

June 4: The Universal Postal Union accepted Libya as a member.

June 14: Stamps inscribed for St. Christopher (St. Kitts), Nevis, and Anguilla went on sale.

June 16: South Vietnam issued its first postage due labels.

July 12: Afghanistan placed its first semi-postal stamps on sale.

July 25: A helicopter carried ship-to-shore mail from the USS *Midway* to the Royal Canadian Air Force Station at Dartmouth, Nova Scotia.

Aug. 12: The first aerogramme was issued by Kuwait.

Aug. 12: A British aerogramme was overprinted for use at Muscat, Dubai, and Oman.

Aug. 29: The United Nations issued its first aerogramme. The release coincided with the annual convention of the American Air Mail Society in New York.

Oct. 30: Papua and New Guinea (now Papua New Guinea) issued its first stamps as an Australian Trust Territory.

Nov. 1: The Ryukyu Islands released its first aerogramme.

Nov. 10: South Vietnam issued its first semi-postal stamp. The surtax went to the Red Cross.

Nov. 11: St. Lucia placed its first aerogramme on sale.

Nov. 17: The first aerogrammes were issued for St. Christopher, Nevis, and Anguilla.

Nov. 19: Scandinavian Airlines made an experimental polar flight from Los Angeles to Copenhagen, Denmark, via Canada and Thule, Greenland. Mail was carried.

Nov. 21: On this date, the United States

Dec. 5, 1952 - Dec. 17, 1953

The first US stamp printed in a combination of intaglio and letterpress (Nov. 21, 1952), Britain's Wilding photograph design (Dec. 5, 1952), and the Queen Elizabeth II coronation omnibus design (June 2, 1953).

issued the first postage stamp printed in a combination of intaglio and letterpress. The commemorative stamp honored the International Red Cross. The red cross in the stamp design was printed in letterpress.

Dec. 5: Great Britain began the release of definitive stamps featuring a portrait of Queen Elizabeth II. The portrait is from a photograph by Dorothy Wilding.

1953

Jan. 21: Arthur E. Summerfield was appointed US postmaster general by President Dwight Eisenhower. He succeeded Jesse M. Donaldson.

Feb. 9: Netherlands New Guinea issued its first semi-postal stamps. The surtax went to the relief of flood victims in the Netherlands.

May 4: Haiti released its first special delivery stamps.

June 2: British Guiana (now Guyana) issued a single 4c stamp to mark the coronation of Queen Elizabeth II. This was an omnibus issue in which the British crown colonies shared a common design. Other members of the British Commonwealth also issued stamps marking the event.

June 18: Following a revolution in Egypt and the ouster of King Farouk, Egyptian stamps bearing his portrait were overprinted with three black bars to obliterate his features. This was done until new stamps could be prepared and released.

July: The US Post Office Department ended a series of tests of postage meters for postage due use. Shortly thereafter, it installed 50 meters in post offices around the country, according to Roscoe.

July 14: Laos issued its first semi-postal stamps, which had a surtax that went to the Red Cross.

Aug. 1: The People's Republic of China released military stamps.

Aug. 1: South Korea gave the surtax from its first semi-postal stamps issued on this date to the Red Cross.

Oct. 6: Four airlines carried regular first-class mail between New York, Chicago, and Washington on an experimental basis. The objective was to speed mail services.

Oct. 17: Indian stamps were overprinted for use by Indian Custodial Forces in Korea as part of a United Nations miliary operation.

Dec. 8: Honduras placed its first air mail special delivery stamps on sale.

Dec. 17: A Royal Air Force Canberra jet transport flew from Northern Ireland to Kitty Hawk, N.C. After overflying Kitty Hawk, the aircraft landed at Elizabeth City, N.C., from where a US Coast Guard helicopter flew pilots and mail to Kill Devil Hills, N.C. The event celebrated the 50th anniversary of the Wright brothers' first successful powered flight.

A cover bearing Egyptian stamps overprinted to obliterate the features of deposed King Farouk (June 18, 1953).

Dec. 31: The New York pneumatic tube service, the last in the United States, was discontinued on this date and the mail moved by truck.

1954

Jan. 1: Stamps were issued for Riouw Archipelago (Riau-Lingga Archipelago), islands belonging to Indonesia off the southern tip of the Malay Peninsula. They consisted of stamps of Indonesia overprinted "RIAU" in vertical or horizontal format.

Jan. 2: Tristan da Cunha released its first stamps showing scenes of the islands and their flora and fauna. Denominations range from ½d to 10/-

Jan. 9: The famous Camel Postman design of the Sudan made its most recent appearance on a stamp on this date. The issue marked the granting of self-government. The design had been introduced March 1, 1898.

March 3: Al Van Dahl, founder and publisher of *Western Stamp Collector* (now *Stamp Collector* newspaper) died at the age of 70 following a heart attack. Together with his wife Arlene, he had founded the periodical in 1931, first as a supplement to *The Mill City Logue*, then as a separate publication. His wife continued to publish it until its sale in 1976.

Born in the Netherlands, Van Dahl grew up in Sweden, attending Uppsala and Heidelberg universities. Moving to North America, he spent some time in Canada before coming to the United States in 1911.

March 13: The Bureau of Engraving and Printing issued its first souvenir card at the

Postage Stamp Design Exhibition at the National Philatelic Museum in Philadelphia. The 1938 Philatelic Truck souvenir sheet is considered a forerunner to the souvenir card series (see May 15, 1939).

April 27: An exhibition of the forgeries of Jean de Sperati took place in London beginning on this date until May 5, 1954. The British Philatelic Association, which had bought Sperati out for between $14,000 and $40,000, staged the show. The BPA also published a two-volume account of Sperati's work.

June 24: The Liberty definitive series was inaugurated by the United States with the release of a 3c stamp depicting the Statue of Liberty.

July 1: Stamps inscribed "Rhodesia and Nyasaland" for use in a federation of Northern Rhodesia, Southern Rhodesia, and Nyasaland Protectorate were introduced.

July 21: French forces withdrew from the northern part of Vietnam and Ho-Chi-Minh created North Vietnam north of the 17th parallel.

Oct. 25: Stamp issues for occupation Zone B ceased as the area was incorporated into Yugoslavia.

Nov. 15: The use of Allied Military Government (AMG-FTT) stamps in Trieste Zone A came to an end as the territory was restored to Italy.

Nov. 30: Savings stamps redeemable for United States savings bonds were issued by the Post Office Department. The stamps were discontinued on June 30, 1970.

Dec. 1: Indian stamps were overprinted for use by Indian members of the International Commission in Indochina.

1955

The American First Day Cover Society was formed.

Jan. 31: Not until this date did the United States Post Office discontinue the last horse-drawn postal vehicle. It had been used in Philadelphia, according to Scheele.

June 6: The United States inaugurated Certified Mail service. A 15c stamp picturing a mailman was issued for this service. The registration rate of 30c, which had provided for no indemnity was eliminated with the introduction of the Certified Mail service. Beginning on this date the 40c registration fee covered zero through $5 indemnity.

June 8: Canadian Pacific Airlines made the first regular flight from Sydney, Australia, to Amsterdam via the north polar route. Mail was carried.

July 20: The independent country of South Vietnam placed its first stamps on sale.

July 26: The first US mail was flown on a regularly scheduled service by turbo-prop aircraft when British Vickers Viscount aircraft began service for Capital Airlines between Norfolk, Va.; Washington, D.C.; Pittsburgh, Pa.; and Chicago.

Sept. 1: Stamps inscribed for the Qu'aiti State in Hadhramaut were issued.

Sept. 25: Cambodia left the French Union and became an independent kingdom.

Oct. 12: Monaco joined the Universal Postal Union.

Oct. 28: The French Southern and Antarctic Territories issued its first stamps.

1956

Stamps were first issued for the Swiss-based World Meteorological Organization.

March 1: The independent Kingdom of Tunisia placed its first stamps on sale.

April 7: The protectorate of Spanish Morocco ceased issuing stamps as the area became part of the new Kingdom of Morocco.

April 25: The first air mail stamps for French Southern and Antarctic Territories were placed in use.

A cover flown on the first scheduled US airline service of the British Vickers Viscount turbo-prop passenger aircraft (July 26, 1955).

April 28: FIPEX, the Fifth International Philatelic Exhibition in the United States, opened in New York City. It ran until May 6. A souvenir sheet reproducing two US stamps depicting the Statue of Liberty in denominations of 3c and 8c and a commemorative postal card were issued.

April 28: Louise Boyd Dale became the first woman member of an international stamp exhibition jury at FIPEX.

April 30: The United States issued a 3c commemorative stamp marking FIPEX, the Fifth International Philatelic Exhibition, held at the New York Coliseum from April 28-May 6. The stamp depicts the show site and the Columbus Monument.

May 4: The first United States multicolored single postal card went on sale. This was also the first US postal card produced in multicolor offset and the first US commemorative postal card. The card commemorated FIPEX, the international stamp exhibition in New York City.

May 10: Ceylon, now Sri Lanka, issued its first semi-postal stamps.

July 1: General stamp issues for the Leeward Islands became invalid on this date. Since their introduction in 1890, the stamps had used the same key type design depicting the reigning monarch. The only variety in design had been provided by the various British Commonwealth omnibus issues beginning with the 1935 Silver Jubilee issue.

The Leeward's sole commemorative issue other than the omnibus participations was the 1897 set marking the diamond jubilee of Queen

The FIPEX souvenir sheet issued by the US on April 28, 1956 and the 3c commemorative stamp issued on April 30.

Victoria — and even that was an overprint on the key type stamps!

July 27: Sudan joined the Universal Postal Union.

Aug. 17: The first stamps issued for the Kingdom of Morocco were intended for use in its Southern Zone (formerly French Morocco) and were denominated in French currency.

Aug. 23: Stamps were issued for use in the Northern Zone of the Kingdom of Morocco. The zone was formerly the protectorate of Spanish Morocco and the stamps were denominated in Spanish currency.

Sept. 15: A stamp issue marked independence for the Sudan on Jan. 1, 1956.

Sept. 15: Six European countries issued the first in what has become an annual stamp issue commemorating the *Conference Europeenne des Administrations des Postes et des Telecommunications* (CEPT). The stamps have come to be known as Europa stamps and the first countries were Belgium, France, West Germany, Italy, Luxembourg, and the Netherlands.

Now, virtually all European countries are members and issue annual Europa stamps. At first, participating countries used a common design, but this was changed in 1974 to a common theme, with each country using an individual design based on that theme. An exception was 1984, when Europa stamps featured a common stylized bridge design to mark the 25th anniversary of CEPT.

Oct. 11: Nepal joined the Universal Postal Union.

Oct. 15: Morocco became a member of the Universal Postal Union. From Oct. 1, 1920 the area had been a member as French and Spanish Morocco.

Nov. 1: Tunisia became a member of the Universal Postal Union as an independent nation. It had become a member under French control on July 1, 1888.

Nov. 16: The United States issued its first multicolored international single and reply postal card. It bears a 4c Statue of Liberty indicium.

Dec. 7: The kingdom of Laos left the French Community.

Dec. 14: Laos issued its first stamps as an independent country. They comprised a set of four regular and two air mail stamps marking the first anniversary of the country's admission to the United Nations.

Dec. 17: The area of Northern Morocco released its first air mail stamps.

Dec. 29: Italy marked the first anniversary of its membership in the United Nations with a

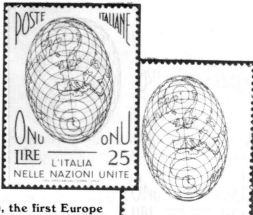

The Leeward key type design (July 1, 1956), the first Europe omnibus design (Sept. 15, 1956), and Italy's steroscopic stamps (Dec. 29, 1956).

pair of stereoscopic stamps, which, when viewed with special glasses take on a three-dimensional effect. The glasses were supplied with an Italian ministerial bulletin that described the printing process.

1957

The Swiss-based International Bureau of the Universal Postal Union issued its first stamps.

Jan. 1: The Saar united with the Federal Republic of Germany. However, stamp issues continued until 1959.

Jan. 11: The New Zealand-administered Antarctic territory of Ross Dependency issued stamps.

Feb. 8: The Dominican Republic placed its first semi-postal and air mail semi-postal stamps on sale.

March 6: Ghana, which had been the British colony of the Gold Coast, issued its first stamps.

March 27: The Australian Antarctic Territory released its first stamps.

March 28: Poland commemorated a philatelic exhibition with its first air mail semi-postal stamp.

April 1: The British postal administration operating for the skeikdom of Qatar released its first stamps.

April 28: The world's most famous stamp forger, Jean de Sperati, died. Although he had promised not to create any more forgeries when he sold his stock, dies, etc. to the British

Philatelic Association, he was working on more forgeries at the time of his death, according to Tyler.

April 30: British stamps overprinted "TANGIER" were withdrawn from use in the International Zone of Tangiers.

May 4: Morocco issued its first air mail stamps as an independent nation.

May 5: The Malayan Federation issued its first stamps.

June 8: The first stamps were issued for the Republic of Togo.

July 1: US registration fees ranged from 50c (indemnity not more than $10) to $2 (indemnity not more than $1,000). A basic return receipt cost 10c and an address return receipt (see March 18, 1931) fee was 35c. The restricted delivery fee was 50c.

Since this date, the registration fee has been determined by the declared value, and full value must be declared. Previously, the fee was determined by the indemnity the mailer chose to pay for, except that from July 1, 1932 (q.v.), the actual value had to be declared and if in excess of indemnity value, paid for as a surcharge based on amount and distance to be carried.

July 4: The United States depicted its flag on the first stamp produced by the Bureau of Engraving and Printing on its new Koebau-Giori press. This press enabled stamps to be intaglio printed in up to three colors in one pass. The various colors were applied to the printing plate by inking rollers cut away so as to apply ink to a specific area of the design. In the case of this stamp, red and blue inks were applied to the plate.

July 15: Stamps were issued inscribed for the Galapagos Islands, a province of Ecuador. The stamps were also valid for use in the rest of the country.

July 25: The Kingdom of Tunisia became a republic.

Aug. 8: The Republic of Tunisia issued its first stamps two weeks after being established.

Aug. 14: The 14th Congress of the Universal Postal Union convened at Ottawa, Canada. Although air transport charges were reduced, some mail rates were increased. The effective date of the UPU's actions was April 9, 1959.

Oct. 10: Ghana joined the Universal Postal Union.

Nov. 19: Stamps bearing graphite lines on their backs were introduced by Great Britain as part of an automatic mail sorting experiment. They were used briefly at Southampton.

Nov. 30: Somalia, under Italian administration, issued its first semi-postal air mail stamps.

Dec. 13: The German Democratic Republic released its first air mail stamps.

1958

Jan. 14: The first Council of Europe stamp to frank mail from the organization's office at Strasbourg, France, went into use. It was a French stamp overprinted "CONSEIL/ DE L'EUROPE."

Jan. 17: The Universal Postal Union admitted Malaysia to membership.

Feb. 12: Following the Feb. 1 union of Syria and Egypt, the resulting United Arab Republic issued its first stamps.

April 3: The United Arab Republic issued its first air mail stamps for use in the Syrian portion of the country formed by the merger of Egypt and Syria.

April 22: Trinidad and Tobago issued a set of three common-design stamps commemorating

The Council of Europe's first stamp (Jan. 14, 1958) and a stamp marking the shortlived Federation of the West Indies (April 22, 1958).

the formation of the West Indies Federation. This was part of an omnibus issue in which the other federation members participated. They were Antigua, Barbados, Dominica, Grenada, Jamaica, Montserrat, St. Kitts-Nevis, St. Lucia, and St. Vincent. The federation dissolved on May 31, 1962.

May 10: Air mail service was introduced from the South Atlantic island of Ascension to Great Britain. Mail first went to Piarco Airport, Trinidad, for onward transmission. Later, mail was routed via Antigua and also via Miami, Florida.

May 19: Colombia issued its first air mail special delivery stamp.

June: The US Post Office Department introduced the first vinyl precancel devices. These now comprise the majority of all devices in use, according to correspondence from James Kingman.

Aug. 1: The US first-class domestic letter rate went to 4c per ounce on this date. Domestic air mail rates were revised to 7c per ounce for letters and 5c for postal cards/ postcards.

Aug. 18: Regional stamps were issued for the Baliwick of Guernsey. They feature the Wilding portrait of Queen Elizabeth II and the emblem of the baliwick.

Aug. 18: The Isle of Man released regional stamps. They feature the Wilding portrait of Queen Elizabeth II and the three-legged emblem of the island.

Aug. 18: Jersey featured the Wilding portrait of Queen Elizabeth II and the arms of Jersey on its first regional stamps.

Aug. 18: Regional stamps, which feature the Wilding portrait of Queen Elizabeth II and the Red Hand emblem of Ulster, were issued for Northern Ireland.

Aug. 18: Regional stamps were issued for use in Scotland. They feature the Wilding portrait of Queen Elizabeth II and the thistle emblem of Scotland.

Aug. 18: The Principality of Wales released Regional stamps. They feature the Wilding portrait of Queen Elizabeth II and the dragon emblem.

Sept. 22: The Swiss-based International Telecommunications Union issued stamps.

Oct. 4: The first transatlantic air mail was carried by a jet aircraft in regular service, when two British De Havilland Comet 4 aircraft inaugurated service between London and New York.

British Regional stamps for (from the top left) Guernsey, Isle of Man, Jersey, Northern Ireland, Scotland, and Wales (Aug. 18, 1958).

The Comet, first transatlantic jet (Oct. 4, 1958).

Oct. 15: The first stamps were issued for Christmas Island in the Indian Ocean.

Oct. 16: Nepal released its first air mail stamp, which was used for mail flown on a domestic service.

Oct. 26: The first transatlantic air mail flown by a US jet aircraft was carried between New York and Paris when Pan American Airways inaugurated its Boeing 707 service (see Oct. 4, 1958).

Nov. 1: The first air mail postal card issued by the Canal Zone Postal Service went on sale.

Nov. 3: French Polynesia first issued stamps inscribed with its new name. The area had previously been known as French Oceania.

Dec. 4: The first globe-circling flight by a De Havilland Comet jet aircraft began on this date. The Royal Air Force aircraft left the United Kingdom and circled the earth in 72 hours flying time. It carried souvenir covers.

Dec. 10: The Malagasy Republic, formerly the French colony of Madagascar, released its first stamps.

Dec. 19: The Republic of Niger was proclaimed. Its first stamps were issued during 1959.

1959

The Philatelic Society of Canada was given permission to use the prefix "Royal."

Jan. 1: New Caledonia issued its first Official stamps.

Jan. 2: The United Arab Republic issued its first semi-postal stamp for use in the Syrian portion of the country. The surtax went to a social fund for postal employees.

Jan. 3: Alaska became the 49th state of the United States.

Jan. 5: The Republic of Guinea placed its first stamps on sale.

Jan. 17: The Mali Federation was formed from the former French colonies of French Sudan and Senegal. The first stamps were not issued until Nov. 7, 1959 and the federation broke up in June 1960. The above dates are noted in the Scott catalog, but the *Encyclopedia Britannica* gives the federation's effective date as April 4, 1959, with complete independence coming on June 20, 1960 and dissolution occurring on Aug. 20, 1960.

Jan. 25: The first regular transcontinental air mail was flown by a jet aircraft when American

The first Christmas Island stamp (Oct. 15, 1958) and the first US transatlantic jet mail (Oct. 26, 1958).

Airlines inaugurated Boeing 707 service between Los Angeles and New York.

Feb. 1: The Government of Kuwait assumed responsibility for its postal service. It had been run on behalf of Kuwait by the British.

April 15: Nepal issued its first aerogramme.

May 6: The People's Republic of Guinea joined the Universal Postal Union.

June 8: Regulus I training guided missile was launched from the US submarine *Barbero* in the Caribbean. It carried 3,000 letters and made a controlled landing at the Naval Air Station at Mayport, Fla., according to US Postmaster General Arthur Summerfield. Jane's *All the World's Aircraft, 1960-1961* says the flight covered a distance of 110 miles. The controller would either have been at the landing site or in an aircraft accompanying the Regulus. In appearance, the Regulus was similar to the World War II German flying bomb. It was fitted with a retractable undercarriage and braking parachute to render recovery possible when used for training purposes.

July 1: The first US Federal Migratory Waterfowl Hunting stamp (Duck stamp) produced in multicolor on the Giori press was issued. This added the beauty of color to the outstanding quality of the engraving and was a combination that made the stamps even more popular among collectors. The Duck stamps are frequently cited as an example of the design and production quality desirable for US postage stamps. With this stamp, the denomination was raised to $3 from $2.

July 13: The Republic of Guinea placed its first air mail stamps on sale.

July 17: The Philippines helped finance a Scout jamboree with its first semi-postal air mail stamps issued on this date.

Aug. 21: Hawaii became the 50th state of the United States.

Sept. 9: One of Canada's most exciting philatelic stories began to unfold with the discovery in Winnipeg, Manitoba, of 30 copies

of the Canadian Seaway commemorative stamp issued June 26, 1959, with the center inverted. The stamps had been bought by an office worker at the post office in Eatons department store. Three of the stamps had been used on mail before the error was spotted. A check with the post office revealed that the remaining 20 from the 50-stamp pane had already been sold. Canada Post officials made a search of post office stocks and discovered six more panes. They estimated that three full sheets of 200 stamps, each containing four panes of 50, had received an inverted blue impression. With the Winnipeg pane, this left five more panes unaccounted for. The quantity known to be in philatelic hands is usually stated to be "less than 100." Winnipeg stamp dealer Kasimir Bileski is reported to have accounted for 92 copies. Of the six panes discovered in CP stock, one half pane of 25 was stolen from a CP exhibit in Montreal in 1980.

Oct. 1: The Republic of the Ivory Coast issued its first stamps.

Nov. 1: Nepal released its first Official stamps.

Nov. 7: The Mali Federation issued its first stamps. The federation had been formed by the merger of the French West African colonies of French Sudan and Senegal. It broke up on

Aug. 20, 1960, according to the *Encyclopedia Britannica*.

Nov. 17: Stamps were first issued for use throughout the Kingdom of Morocco. Previously, stamps in Spanish currency had been used in the northern area and in French currency in the southern area of the country.

Nov. 18: Britain issued stamps bearing phosphor bands as part of an automatic sorting procedure.

Nov. 28: The Congo Republic, formerly the French colony of Middle Congo, issued its first stamps.

Nov. 28: The Republic of Chad released a pair of stamps marking the first anniversary of independence.

Dec. 1: The newly independent Central African Republic placed its first stamps on sale.

Dec. 10: The Republic of Upper Volta's first stamps commemorated the new republic's first birthday.

Dec. 11: The Mali Federation issued its first air mail stamp.

Dec. 18: The Republic of Niger released its first stamp.

Dec. 29: Uruguay issued its first semi-postal air mail stamps. The surtax was intended to aid the national treasury.

1960

Stamps were issued for the Spanish colony of Rio Muni, located on the southwestern coast of Africa. Together with Fernando Po, Rio Muni had formed Spanish Guinea and up to this date had used Spanish Guinea stamps. The colony is now part of the Republic of Equatorial Guinea.

Jan. 1: The independent Republic of Cameroon issued its first stamps.

Jan. 20: The Islamic Republic of Mauritania placed its first stamps on sale.

Feb. 16: Kuwait became a member of the Universal Postal Union.

March: Morocco issued its first semi-postal stamps and used the surtax to aid victims of adulterated cooking oil.

March 1: The Republic of Dahomey, now the People's Republic of Benin, issued its first stamps.

April 1: The United States issued Federal Boating stamps in denominations of $1 and $3. The $1 stamp paid a charge to cover replacement of a certificate while the $3 stamp represented the initial cost of a certificate.

April 11: The Republic of Niger placed its first air mail stamps on sale.

June 6: The Congo Democratic Republic (formerly the Belgian Congo) released its first stamps. They are overprints on Belgian Congo stamps.

June 26: The independent Republic of Somalia was formed from Somalia, which had been under Italian administration since 1950.

July 1: The Congo Democratic Republic joined the Universal Postal Union under its new name. It had been a member as the Congo Free State and the Belgian Congo.

July 1: Sheik Sulman bin Hamed al-Khalifa is seen on the first stamps designed for the Sheikdom of Bahrain.

July 1: Somalia became a member of the Universal Postal Union as an independent republic. It had been a member since April 1, 1959 while under Italian administration.

July 1: Ghana became a republic on this date. It had formerly been a dominion of the British Commonwealth.

July 11: Katanga, a rebel province of the Congo Democratic Republic (Zaire), issued stamps. The republic reunited in 1963. The Scott catalog does not list these stamps, since they were not issued by a recognized government. However, Gibbons and Minkus provide listings.

July 23: Gabon issued its first air mail stamp. It honors Dr. Albert Schweitzer.

July 26: Cameroon became a member of the Universal Postal Union.

Aug. 20: The Mali Federation ended and split into the republics of Senegal and Mali.

Sept. 3: The Central African Republic released its first air mail stamps.

Oct. 1: Stamps were issued for use in Southern Cameroons prior to it becoming part of the Republic of Cameroon on Sept. 30, 1961. The area had been part of the ex-German Kamerun and was mandated to Great Britain following World War I. The population had been given the option of joining Nigeria or the newly independent Republic of Cameroon.

The northern portion voted in favor of becoming Nigerian and the southern part opted for union with the republic. The stamps were used following the vote and before union. The stamps were also used in the northern area, according to Gibbons.

Nov. 21: Haiti released parcel post stamps, both regular and air mail.

Nov. 28: Although the Islamic Republic of Mauritania issued its first stamps on Jan. 20, 1960, full independence did not come until Nov. 28, 1960. In October 1961, Mauritania became a member of the United Nations.

December: The British established a postal service for Das Island in the Persian Gulf. The organization used the stamps of the British postal agencies of Eastern Arabia and operated until March 29, 1964. The island is now part of Abu Dhabi, one of the United Arab Emirates.

Dec. 15: The Republic of Chad commemorated the 1960 Olympic Games on its first air mail stamps.

Dec. 18: The Republic of Mali released its first air mail stamps.

1961

Jan. 7: The only stamp issue for the Trucial States was released on this date. It comprises 11 denominations. A single aerogramme was also issued. The Trucial States comprised the seven sheikdoms of Abu Dhabi, Ajman, Dubai, Fujeira, Sharjah, Ras al Khaima, and Umm al Qiwain. The only post office was in Dubai and the stamps and aerogramme were in use until Sept. 30, 1963. See under individual sheikdoms, also United Arab Emirates.

Jan. 9: The British printing firm of De La Rue & Co. took over the security printing operations of Waterlow & Sons Ltd.

Jan. 11: The Republic of Chad issued a set of three stamps marking its admission to the United Nations.

Jan. 15: The Republic of Mali's first stamps

comprised three stamps of the Federation of Mali overprinted "REPUBLIQUE DU MALI."

Jan. 21: President John Kennedy appointed J. Edward Day US postmaster general, succeeding Arthur E. Summerfield.

Jan. 23: The first stamps were issued by the United Nations Educational, Scientific, and Cultural Organization (UNESCO). They were intended for use on mail from the organization's Paris headquarters. The design features the figures of Buddha and Hermes.

March: Haiti released its first air mail Official stamps.

March 4: The Republic of Upper Volta placed its first air mail stamps on sale.

March 18: The Republic of Mali issued its first specially designed stamps, Official stamps and postage due labels.

March 23: Ivory Coast became a member of the Universal Postal Union.

April 21: Mali joined the Universal Postal Union.

April 27: Then known as the Republic of Dahomey, the Republic of Benin became a member of the Universal Postal Union.

April 27: Sierra Leone marked its independence on its first stamps.

April 29: The first Chilean air mail semipostal stamps were printed by Spain and were a gift to Chile. The surtax aided earthquake victims and increased the pay of teachers.

April 29: The United Arab Republic (Syria) released a semi-postal air mail stamp. The UAR also included Egypt.

May 31: The Union of South Africa became the Republic of South Africa and, because of general condemnation of its racist policies by other British Commonwealth countries, ceased to be a member of the Commonwealth.

June: South Vietnam issued its first military stamp.

June 5: Mongolia featured mail handling on its first air mail stamps. The set marked the 40th anniversary of independence.

June 12: Niger became a member of the Universal Postal Union.

June 14: Senegal joined the Universal Postal Union.

June 23: The Universal Postal Union admitted Chad as a member.

June 28: The Central African Republic became a member of the Universal Postal Union.

July 1: The Islamic Republic of Mauritania issued its first Official stamps.

July 5: The People's Republic of the Congo joined the Universal Postal Union.

July 10: The Universal Postal Union added Nigeria to its membership.

July 17: Gabon became a member of the Universal Postal Union.

July 29: The French colony of Wallis and Futuna Islands became a French Overseas Territory.

Aug. 15: The US registration fee for indemnity of not more than $10 went to 60c from 50c. The rest of the scale of fees was unchanged. Beginning on this date, only first-class matter, including that sent by air mail, could be registered.

Sept. 18: Senegal placed its first Official stamps into use.

Oct. 10: Tristan da Cunha was evacuated because of volcanic eruptions. The islanders returned in 1963.

Oct. 12: The South Atlantic island of St. Helena issued a set of semi-postal stamps for the aid of inhabitants of Tristan da Cunha, driven from their island home by volcanic eruptions. The set was withdrawn after only eight days and is consequently a major rarity. Gibbons notes that only 434 sets were sold.

Nov. 2: Madagascar (Malagasy) became a member of the Universal Postal Union.

Nov. 2: The first stamps of the Syrian Arab Republic were issued following breakup of United Arab Republic, during which it had been united with Egypt.

Nov. 3: The Federal Republic of Germany (West Germany) became the first country to introduce a post code to enable mail sorting to be done using automated equipment.

Nov. 23: The Universal Postal Union added the Republic of Cyprus as a member.

Dec. 9: The independent country of Tanganyika issued its first stamps. It formerly had been called German East Africa and then the British Protectorate of Tanganyika. Tanganyika later merged with Zanzibar and is now Tanzania.

Dec. 18: Portuguese India was annexed by India.

Dec. 20: Panama issued a set of three semi-postal air mail stamps to aid the World Health Organization's anti-malaria program. During 1961-1962, many of the world's postal administrations issued stamps with this theme.

1962

Jan. 1: The Central African Republic released a Military stamp.

Jan. 1: Western Samoa became independent and inscriptions on its stamps were changed to "Samoa i sisifo." The first such stamps, which were released to mark the country's new status, were issued on July 2, 1962.

Jan. 13: Canada issued "tagged" stamps at Winnipeg, Manitoba, for use with experimental sorting equipment that went into use there on March 13, 1962.

Jan. 15: Indian stamps were issued overprinted "U.N. FORCE (INDIA) CONGO." They were for use by members of the United Nations peace-keeping force stationed in the Congo.

Jan. 26: Sierra Leone became a member of the Universal Postal Union.

Feb. 7: Tonga began using air mail Official stamps. The stamps also commemorate the centenary of emancipation.

Feb. 10: Ghana placed its first air mail stamps on sale.

Feb. 20: The United States issued a "surprise" commemorative stamp to mark the first orbital space flight by John Glenn. The 4c

This US stamp was issued nationwide, without advance notice, to mark the first US orbital space flight by John Glenn (Feb. 20, 1962).

stamp had been prepared and distributed to all US post offices in great secrecy and was placed on sale nationwide the moment the space flight ended. It depicts the Project Mercury capsule in orbit.

March 21: Togo joined the Universal Postal Union.

April 7: The Republic of Mali released its first semi-postal stamps. The country used surtax funds for an anti-malaria project. Similar issues were produced by a number of countries.

April 7: The Republic of Upper Volta released its first semi-postal stamps. The surtax went to the World Health Organization's anti-malaria campaign.

April 7: The Central African Republic placed its first semi-postal stamps on sale. The surtax was used to fight malaria.

April 7: The Republic of Chad used the surtax from first semi-postal stamps towards fighting malaria. It released the stamps on this date.

April 7: The Republic of Niger placed its first semi-postal stamps on sale. The surtax went to the World Health Organization's anti-malaria program.

April 13: Liechtenstein became a member of the Universal Postal Union.

May 16: The first stamps of Bhutan were issued. According to Scott, the stamps became valid for international use on Oct. 10, 1962.

July 1: The newly independent Republic of Rwanda issued its first stamps.

July 1: The first stamps were released by the newly independent Kingdom of Burundi.

July 2: The former Western Samoa, now Samoa, introduced its first stamps as an independent state.

July 2: The United States issued a commemorative Documentary revenue stamp marking the centenary of the Internal Revenue Service. The stamp depicts the IRS building in Washington, D.C.

July 2: Algeria's first stamps as an independent country went into use.

July 20: A hovercraft carried its first mail from Rhyl in North Wales, to Wallasey, England.

Aug. 29: Jamaica joined the Universal Postal Union.

Aug. 31: Stamps marking the independence of Trinidad and Tobago were issued. The 5c denomination purports to depict an underwater scene at Buccoo Reef off the island of Tobago. However, collectors discovered after the stamp was issued that the design had been taken from a mural behind the bar of the Hotel Normandie in Port of Spain! None of the fish depicted are found in the waters of the reef. The mural artist was Carlisle Chang, who is said to have received his inspiration from the *National Geographic Magazine*.

At the left is the only US commemorative documentary revenue stamp, issued to mark the centenary of the Internal Revenue Service. On the right is the regular version of the same stamp, issued in 1963. It was the last one, since documentary revenue stamps were not required after Dec. 31, 1967 (July 2, 1962).

Trinidad and Tobago's independence stamps (Aug. 31, 1962).

The stamp from the barroom wall!
This stamp was supposed to picture an underwater scene from Tobago's Bucco Reef. However, it was discovered that the stamp designer had utilized a mural from the bar of a Port of Spain hotel, which in turn was derived from the *National Geographic Magazine!*

Sept. 15: A US post office was established on Christmas Island in the Pacific, as a branch of the Honolulu Post Office. The Christmas Island office closed Sept. 21, 1963. The island is part of Kiribati.

Oct. 1: The United Nations began administration of the former Netherlands New Guinea, before the area joined Indonesia as West Irian on May 1, 1963. The UN administration used stamps of Netherlands New Guinea overprinted "UNTEA" (United Nations Temporary Executive Authority).

Oct. 9: Stamps marking the independence of Uganda were issued.

Nov. 1: The US Post Office Department issued the country's first Christmas stamp. It is a 4c stamp depicting a Christmas wreath and candles.

Nov. 16: The US Post Office Department committed one of its most unpopular philatelic acts when it deliberately reprinted and placed on sale the Dag Hammarskjold commemorative stamp with the yellow background color inverted. The original stamp had been issued on Oct. 23, 1962 and some genuine errors were discovered with the yellow lithographed background inverted. The US postmaster general, J. Edward Day, decided that all collectors should be able to have a copy and reprinted a large quantity. The outrage at this strange act was such that when a similar reprinting was contemplated with a Canal Zone stamp, legal action was instituted and a court ruling prevented its reprinting. But for the unfortunate discoverers of the Hammarskjold "invert" it came too late and the "error" is priced at little more than the normal stamp.

Nov. 19: The United States' first precanceled postal card bears a 3c Statue of Liberty indicium and is precanceled with three horizontal lines, the top two of which are broken. A paid reply card was also issued on this date with a 4c Lincoln indicium and similar precancelation.

The "missing bridge" error was not reprinted.

The reprinted "error" of the Dag Hammarskjold commemorative. This plate block clearly shows the inverted background.

1963

Most of the inhabitants of Tristan da Cunha returned following the end of volcanic activity. The population had been evacuated to the United Kingdom on Oct. 10, 1961.

Jan. 7: The US domestic first-class letter rate went to 5c per ounce. The domestic air mail rate was set at 8c per ounce and the air mail rate for postal cards and postcards rose to 6c.

Jan. 15: Katanga rejoined the Congo Democratic Republic.

Feb. 1: The British Antarctic Territory issued its first stamps. Various antarctic scenes and forms of transportation are depicted.

Feb. 15: Burundi issued its first semi-postal stamps. The surtax was to be used for a stadium and monument to Prince Louis Rwagasore.

March 21: The Congo Democratic Republic issued its first semi-postal stamps. The surtax was for the Freedom from Hunger campaign.

March 29: The Universal Postal Union admitted Tanzania as a member.

March 29: Upper Volta (now Bourkina Fasso) became a member of the Universal Postal Union.

April 1: Great Britain introduced its first local publicity slogan machine cancel on this date. Used at the Sussex town of Hastings, it included a figure referred to as "Happy Harold" and the invitation "We're ready for your invasion at Hastings," the reference being, of course, to

King Harold and the Norman invasion of 1066 that took place nearby. During the early 1930s, when the writer lived there, the summers saw a constant series of invasions by vacationing Londoners and it continues as a popular seaside resort.

April 6: Rwanda joined the Universal Postal Union.

April 27: Sierra Leone placed its first air mail stamps on sale.

May 1: West Irian, formerly the Netherlands New Guinea, became part of Indonesia.

May 23: The postal administration of Qatar was taken over by the Qatar Post Department. Qatar's postal administration had been operated by Great Britain.

May 24: Algeria placed its first semi-postal stamp as an independent state on sale and designated the surtax for the National Solidarity Fund.

June 11: The Cocos (Keeling) Islands released its first stamps.

June 15: The Sheikdom of Dubai, now one of the United Arab Emirates, began issuing stamps.

June 16: Trinidad and Tobago became a member of the Universal Postal Union.

June 17: Tonga issued its first free-form, self-adhesive postage stamps. They are circular and reproduce gold coins. The stamps began a long run of self-stick stamps in all manner of shapes and sizes. The country also released the stamps in air mail denominations, which constitute the country's first air mail stamps.

July 1: The Federal Republic of Cameroon issued a single Military stamp.

July 1: The US Post Office Department introduced its post code. It is called ZIP code, where "ZIP" stands for Zoning Improvement Plan. While there had previously been zone numbers used in major cities, this system is a five-digit (currently being expanded to nine) national coding system identifying each postal delivery area. The figure of Mr. ZIP was created to publicize the system.

July 8: On this date, the United States Treasury Department banned the purchase abroad and importation into the United States of Cuban stamps. The director of the Office of Foreign Assets Control, confirmed this date although it differs from the Feb. 7, 1962 date widely published. The ban is still in effect. The major US stamp catalogs do not list Cuban stamps after the Feb. 7, 1962 date.

July 10: The postal administration of Sharjah and Dependencies, now part of the United Arab Emirates, issued its first stamps.

July 17: From this date until May 4, 1980, stamps were issued for South Georgia. Stamps had previously been overprinted for South Georgia on April 3, 1944 (q.v.).

Aug. 24: The Universal Postal Union added Mongolia as a member.

Sept. 16: Malaysia placed its first stamps on sale.

Sept. 18: Saba, an island in the Netherlands Antilles, received air mail service beginning on this date.

Sept. 30: John A. Gronouski succeeded J. Edward Day as US postmaster general.

Oct. 1: Thailand issued its first Official stamps.

Nov. 25: The South Arabian Federation began to issue stamps.

Dec. 1: Northern Rhodesia, now Zambia, reassumed responsibility for its own postal service following the 10-year period when it was part of the Federation of Rhodesia and Nyasaland. The other federation partners were Nyasaland (now Malawi) and Southern Rhodesia (now Zimbabwe).

Dec. 10: Newly independent Zanzibar issued its first stamps.

Dec. 10: The first stamp issue of Northern Rhodesia was released, following the dissolution of the Federation of Rhodesia and Nyasaland, according to Drysdall. Some catalogs note the issue date as Dec. 1.

Dec. 12: Recently independent Kenya placed its first stamps on sale.

1964

Jan. 3: On this date, the Canadian government discontinued the use of stamps overprinted "G" for official use. Government departments adopted a policy of prepaying postage in bulk based on mail volume, according to Hansen. Wrigley gives the final date of use as Dec. 31, 1963.

Jan. 10: The United States issued its first stamps bearing the figure of Mr. ZIP in the selvedge. This is the 5c commemorative marking the death centenary of Sam Houston.

Jan. 14: Post offices in Zanzibar reopened following the revolution that made the country a republic.

Feb. 13: Uganda joined the Universal Postal Union.

At the upper left is the first appearance of the "Mr. ZIP" figure. The other stamps depict the variations that have been used on the selvedge of US stamps since then (Jan. 10, 1964).

Feb. 19: Stamps inscribed "Rhodesia and Nyasaland" were withdrawn when the constituent territories of Northern and Southern Rhodesia and Nyasaland resumed separate stamp issues.

March 9: Gabon used the surtax from its first air mail semi-postal stamps for a campaign to save the Nubian monuments along the River Nile. The stamps went on sale on this date. A number of countries issued stamps for this project.

March 9: The Republic of Chad issued its first semi-postal air mail stamps. The surtax went to an international campaign to save the Nubian monuments.

March 30: The Sheikdom of Abu Dhabi released its first stamps. It is now one of the United Arab Emirates.

April 23: The 400th anniversary of the birth of William Shakespeare prompted a set of commemorative stamps from Great Britain. This set is noteworthy for being the first British stamps to depict an identifiable portrait of an individual other than a monarch.

April 23: The 400th anniversary of the birth of William Shakespeare was marked by an omnibus issue from 12 British crown colonies. The stamps depicts Shakespeare and the Memorial Theater at Stratford-on-Avon. The

participating colonies were Antigua, Bahamas, Bechuanaland Protectorate, Cayman Islands, Dominica, Falkland Islands, the Gambia, Gibraltar, Montserrat, St. Lucia, Turks and Caicos Islands, and the Virgin Islands. Other countries, including Great Britain, also issued stamps marking the anniversary.

May 5: The United States Treasury Department banned the purchase abroad and importation into the United States of stamps of North Vietnam. The ban, which now includes all of Vietnam, was still in effect at the time of publication.

May 29: The 15th Congress of the Universal Postal Union convened in Vienna, Austria. It had been originally scheduled for Rio de Janeiro, Brazil in 1962, but political unrest caused it to be rescheduled to New Delhi, India. However, India was having problems with the People's Republic of China and the UPU decided to move the meeting to Vienna. The con-

Great Britain honored Shakespeare's 400th birthday with this set; the first to depict an identifiable person other than a British monarch (April 23, 1964).

Austria issued this magnificently engraved set of eight stamps to mark the 15th Congress of the Universal Postal Union held in Vienna in May 1964 (May 29, 1964).

gress increased mail transit charges and some postal rates, but air mail rates remained unchanged. The effective date for the UPU's actions was Jan. 1, 1966. Numerous countries issued stamps marking the Congress.

June 20: Stamps inscribed for the Sheikdom of Ajman, now one of the United Arab Emirates, went on sale.

June 29: Umm al Qiwain issued its first stamps. The sheikdom is now one of United Arab Emirates.

July 1: Sabah issued its first stamps. Formerly known as North Borneo, Sabah is now part of Malaysia.

July 2: Burundi released its first air mail stamps.

July 6: Malawi, formerly the British Protectorate of Nyasaland, began to issue stamps.

July 7: Stamps were issued inscribed "Tanzania" marking the union of Tanganyika and Zanzibar.

July 25: The French postal administration of Andorra issued a single 25c+10c semi-postal stamp with the surtax benefitting the Red Cross.

Sept. 21: Malta received independence. It had been granted self-government in 1961, a status that had been delayed by World War II. In 1974, the Mediterranean island country became a republic.

Sept. 22: The first stamps issued by the Sheikdom of Fujeira went on sale. The sheikdom was one of the Trucial states and is now a member of the United Arab Emirates.

Oct. 1: Kenya issued its first Official stamps.

Oct. 14: Canada released its first Christmas stamps. The 1898 Map stamp is often cited as the first Canadian Christmas stamp, but despite its "Xmas 1898" inscription it was not issued to commemorate Christmas.

Oct. 21: The East African Postal Administration placed stamps on sale for use in Uganda, Kenya, and Tanganyika (later Tanzania), but excluding Zanzibar.

Oct. 24: The first stamps were issued for the African nation of Zambia, formerly Northern Rhodesia.

Oct. 25: The independent postal administration of Qatar released its first stamps.

Oct. 27: The Universal Postal Union admitted Kenya as a member.

Oct. 29: The United Republic of Tanganyika and Zanzibar was renamed the United Republic of Tanzania.

Dec. 12: The Republic of Kenya released its first stamps.

Dec. 21: Ras al Khaima, now one of the United Arab Emirates, placed its first stamps on sale.

The first Canadian Christmas stamps were issued Oct. 14, 1964. Despite its inscription, the 1898 Map stamp was not intended to celebrate Christmas.

1965

Jan. 13: The Sheikdom of Sharjah began to issue Official stamps. They are definitive stamps overprinted "ON STATE SERVICE" in English and Arabic.

Jan. 15: Indian stamps were overprinted "UNEF"for use by Indian members of the United Nations force in Gaza.

Feb. 18: The Gambia released its first stamps following independence.

March 20: Stamps were issued inscribed for Khor Fakkan, a dependency of Sharjah and now included in the United Arab Emirates.

March 31: Stamps of Aden were withdrawn and replaced by those of the South Arabian Federation.

April 15: The East African Common Services Organization issued stamps inscribed for use in Kenya, Uganda, and Tanzania.

May 21: Malta joined the Universal Postal Union.

Aug. 16: Fujeira placed its first air mail stamps on sale.

Aug. 19: The United States introduced postal insurance labels. The first was placed on sale from a vending machine at the Canogo Park, Calif. automated post office, which opened on this date. The label, contained in a booklet, is placed on a package and pays insurance. The booklet also contains a receipt form for use when making a claim.

Sept. 1: The independent sultanate of the Maldive Islands issued it first stamps.

Sept. 16: The Cook Islands issued stamps following granting of self-government.

Oct. 14: Fujeira released its first Official stamps.

Nov. 3: Lawrence F. O'Brien was appointed US postmaster general. He succeeded John A. Gronouski.

Nov. 10: Fujeira introduced air mail Official stamps.

Nov. 11: The British colony of Southern Rhodesia declared itself to be independent, an action not recognized by Great Britain. This act resulted in an economic boycott, including postage stamps, of the colony by Great Britain and the United States. (See July 29, 1968).

Nov. 15: As a state of Malaysia, Malacca participated in several omnibus issues beginning on this date. The stamps for Malacca were inscribed "Melaka."

Nov. 15: Burundi placed its first air mail semipostal stamps on sale.

Nov. 19: The Prominent Americans definitive series was launched by the United States when it released a 4c stamp in black depicting a profile of Abraham Lincoln.

Dec. 9: Stamps were issued inscribed for the United Republic of Tanzania.

Dec. 29: Western Samoa's first air mail stamps were issued.

1966

Jan. 1: Austria introduced a system of postal zone numbers and on Jan. 14 issued a stamp featuring a map of Austria showing the various zones.

Jan. 8: Singapore became a member of the Universal Postal Union.

Jan. 14: Austria issued a stamp depicting a map of the country indicating the various postal zones in a system introduced Jan. 1 (q.v.).

Austria's postal zones (Jan. 14, 1966).

Jan. 21: The independent postal administration of Bahrain issued its first stamps.

Jan. 24: The death of Sir Winston Churchill in 1965 prompted nations around the world to issue stamps in his honor. Included was an omnibus issue from a number of British colonies. They are Antigua, Ascension, Bahamas, Barbados, Basutoland, Bechuanaland Protectorate, Bermuda, British Antarctic Territory, British Honduras, Brunei, Cayman Islands, Dominica, Falkland Islands, Fiji, Gibraltar, Gilbert and Ellice Islands, Grenada, Hong Kong, Mauritius, Montserrat, New Hebrides, Pitcairn, St. Helena, St. Kitts-Nevis, St. Lucia, St. Vincent, Seychelles, Solomon Islands, South Arabia, Swaziland, Tristan da Cunha, Turks and Caicos Islands, and Virgin Islands.

Feb. 14: Australia changed its currency from pounds, shillings, and pence to decimal cents and dollars.

March 1: Singapore issued stamps commemorating its new status as an independent republic.

March 26: The basic US registration fee, hereafter providing for indemnity of not more than $100, became 75c. Fees for indemnity up to $1,000 remained unchanged, but the maximum indemnity was increased to $10,000, with fees increasing by 25c for each additional $1,000 of value to a maximum fee of $4.25.

March 27: George Linn died. He was a philatelic publisher, editor, and founder of the United States weekly philatelic newspaper that bears his name.

April 22: The Cook Islands issued its first air mail stamps.

April 26: Colombia released its only semipostal stamp to date. It is a single 5c + 5c stamp with the surtax going to the Red Cross.

April 29: The first stamps were issued for Muscat and Oman.

May 21: SIPEX, the Sixth International

The souvenir sheet and stamp issued to commemorate SIPEX, the international stamp exhibition held in Washington, D.C. (May 21, 1966).

Philatelic Exhibition opened in Washington, D.C. on this date. It ran until May 30. A 5c commemorative stamp in regular sheet and souvenir sheet format was issued by the USPOD.

May 26: Guyana, formerly British Guiana, issued its first stamps. The country's full name is now the Cooperative Republic of Guyana.

May 27: The United States featured four views on its first pictorial postal card. It is an 11c air mail card with an indicium featuring the US flag, map, and globe and is inscribed "Visit the USA." It is also the first international air mail postal card issued by the United States. The views are of Mt. Rainier, New York, an Indian, and Miami Beach.

July 5: Stamps issued inscribed Manama, a dependency of Ajman and now included in the United Arab Emirates.

Aug. 16: Peru used the surtax from its first semi-postal stamps issued on this date for tourist publicity.

Sept. 1: Western Samoa released its first semi-postal stamp. It raised funds for the replanting of plantations destroyed in the hurricane of Jan. 29, 1966.

Sept. 30: Botswana, the country that had been known as British Bechuanaland, issued stamps inscribed with its new name.

Oct. 4: Lesotho, formerly known as Basutoland, issued its first stamps.

Oct. 25: The Universal Postal Union admitted Malawi as a member.

December: Philatelic forger Raoul ch. de Thuin's implements and cliches, plus most of his stock, were bought by the American Philatelic Society for an undisclosed sum. De Thuin was a longtime forger and faker of postal material.

Dec. 1: Nigeria issued its first semi-postal stamps and dedicated the surtax to the Nigerian Red Cross.

1967

Jan. 1: Ivory Coast issued a Military stamp that bears a coat of arms and has no denomination.

Jan. 1: In the United States, mandatory presorting by ZIP code of second and third-class bulk mail became effective.

March 1: St. Lucia achieved associated state status and issued stamps March 7 to commemorate the event, including the island's first air mail stamp.

March 12: Stamps were issued by the Mahra Sultanate of Qishn and Socotra.

March 22: Guyana became a member of the Universal Postal Union.

March 22: Mauritania became a member of the Universal Postal Union.

March 22: Zambia became a member of the Universal Postal Union.

May 25: The Bahamas adopted decimal currency.

May 30: The Caribbean island of Anguilla proclaimed its independence from the island of St. Kitts, which had been responsible for its administration. Anguilla issued stamps on Sept. 4, 1967.

June 5: Great Britain introduced the so-called Machin Head definitive design. It is widely considered one of the most handsome definitive designs of all time, especially the intaglio-printed high values.

July 1: Italy placed on sale a set of four stamps in a common design to publicize the new Italian

This magnificent head of Queen Elizabeth II provided the inspiration for Great Britain's Machin series of definitive stamps. Introduced on June 5, 1967, it gets its name from Arnold Machin, whose plaster cast of the Queen is seen at the upper left. Initially, the March 5, 1969 four high values of 2/6, 5/-, 10/-, and £1 were intaglio printed by Bradbury, Wilkinson & Company, using the superb engraving featured here.

postal code. The design features a letter with an arrow pointing to the postal code.

July 27: The US Post Office Department eased restrictions to make it possible for collectors to purchase precanceled stamps from post offices. Previously, only permit holders could do so.

Aug. 15: The Maldive Islands joined the Universal Postal Union.

Aug 21: The French territory of Afars and Issas issued stamps. It had formerly been the French Somali Coast and on June 27, 1977 became the independent Republic of Djibouti.

Sept. 4: Anguilla released its first stamps following its break with the administration of St. Christopher, Nevis, and Anguilla on May 30, 1967.

Sept. 6: The Universal Postal Union admitted Lesotho as a member.

Sept. 18: Rwanda issued its first air mail stamps.

Sept. 29: The so-called "Space Twin" stamps were issued by the United States. The two 5c stamps mark US achievements in space and take the form of a horizontal se-tenant pair showing an astronaut during a walk in space.

Nov. 2: The United States released its first photogravure-printed stamp. It reproduces the

painting *The Biglin Brothers Racing* by Thomas Eakins. Printed by Photogravure and Color Co. of Moonachie, N.J., it is not a successful example of the printer's craft.

Nov. 2: The first mail carried by hovercraft in the Falkland Islands was taken from Stanley to Green Patch. The craft later made a circuit of the islands, covering a distance of 600 miles.

Nov. 11: Barbados became a member of the Universal Postal Union.

Dec. 22: Mongolia issued its first semi-postal stamps.

Dec. 31: The United States ceased to use adhesive documentary revenue stamps. They had been introduced in 1862.

1968

Jan. 1: Stamps of Zanzibar were withdrawn and replaced by stamps inscribed for Tanzania.

Jan. 7: The US first-class domestic letter rate went to 6c per ounce. The domestic air mail

Called the "Space Twins," these two se-tenant 5c US stamps were issued to commemorate US achievements in space (Sept. 29, 1967).

rate became 10c per ounce, and air mail postal cards and postcards rose to 8c.

Jan. 12: The Universal Postal Union accepted Botswana as a member.

Jan. 17: The British Indian Ocean Territory's first stamps were released.

Jan. 31: Nauru issued stamps overprinted "REPUBLIC/ OF/ NAURU" to mark its independence on this date.

Feb. 5: Biafra, a rebel area of Nigeria, began to issue stamps.

Feb. 12: The Cook Islands issued its first semi-postal stamps and applied the surtax to a hurricane relief fund.

March 12: Stamps marking the independence of Mauritius were issued on this date.

March 30: The US stamp commemorating the Hemisphere 1968 Exposition in San Antonio, Texas, was the first to incorporate the inscription "Mail Early in the Day" as a selvedge marking.

April 1: The first stamps were issued by the People's Republic of Southern Yemen, now the People's Democratic Republic of Yemen. They are overprints on stamps of the South Arabian Federation, formerly Aden and the various sheikdoms of southern Arabia.

April 26: President Lyndon Johnson ap-

pointed W. Marvin Watson as US postmaster general. He succeeded Lawrence F. O'Brien.

June 28: The People's Democratic Republic of Yemen became a member of the Universal Postal Union.

July 1: Japan introduced its postal code.

July 29: The United States Treasury Department banned the purchase abroad and importation into the United States of Rhodesian stamps. The department lifted the ban on Dec. 16, 1979.

Sept. 6: Swaziland marked its independence by issuing stamps.

Oct. 12: The Republic of Equatorial Guinea, formerly the Spanish Overseas Provinces of Rio Muni and Fernando Po, issued stamps.

Oct. 14: Ireland began the release of a definitive series known as the Gerl series for its designer, Heinrich Gerl. It replaced a series that had been in use, in the case of the low values, for 45 years. Like the contemporaneous British Machin series, the Gerl series has made the switch from sterling to decimal currency and has given birth to numerous variations.

Nov. 19: Barbuda, an island dependency of Antigua, resumed issuing stamps after a single issue on July 13, 1922.

Dec. 3: The Netherlands Antilles issued its first air mail stamps. Previous air mail issues had been inscribed "Curacao."

1969

Jan. 22: Winton M. Blount was appointed US postmaster general by President Richard Nixon. He succeeded W. Marvin Watson.

Jan. 31: Qatar joined the Universal Postal Union.

March 5: Great Britain completed the initial range of Machin definitives, with the release of the intaglio-printed high values of 2/6, 5/-, 10/-, and £1. See June 5, 1967.

March 7: Bhutan became a member of the Universal Postal Union.

March 19: The first US postal card bearing an isolated tagged rectangle to the left of the indicium was issued.

April 17: Nauru became a member of the Universal Postal Union..

May 9: The Universal Postal Union admitted Burundi as a member.

June 30: Spain returned the colony of Ifni to Morocco.

July 1: Japan issued a pair of stamps commemorating the first anniversary of the country's postal code. The stamps depict the postal code symbol, similar to the Mr. ZIP figure used in the United States to publicize the ZIP code.

July 14: The scale of fees for US registered mail was set at from 80c (indemnity not more than $100) to $4.45 (indemnity not more than $10,000). The cost of a basic return receipt went to 15c.

July 20: During the Apollo 11 flight that made the first landing on the moon, astronaut Neil Armstrong canceled a cover on the moon with a canceler reading "Moon Landing, U.S.A."

Aug. 29: Mauritius joined the Universal Postal Union.

Sept. 9: The US Post Office Department issued a 10c air mail stamp commemorating the first landing by man on the moon. The stamp shows an astronaut, presumably Neil A. Armstrong, stepping onto the moon's surface. The Bureau of Engraving and Printing used a die that had been taken to the moon on the Apollo 11 flight to make plates for printing the stamp.

Oct. 1: The 16th Congress of the Universal Postal Union convened in Tokyo, Japan. South Africa was not permitted to attend the meetings because of its internal racial policies and several smaller countries introduced a resolution to have the United States expelled from both the Congress and the UPU! Meanwhile, in postal business, the Congress simplified the tariff structure of letter post by reducing the number of letter-mail classifications to letters, postcards, small packets, printed matter, and literature for the blind. The UPU granted compensation for situations where areas received more mail than

Shown here are Japan's two stamps marking the first anniversary of its post code introduction (July 1, 1969), a stamp from The Gambia showing the cover canceled on the moon (July 20, 1969), and the US stamp commemorating the Apollo 11 moon landing (Sept. 9, 1969).

was originated. Previously, it had been assumed that mail received would generate an equal amount of mail dispatched and thus revenue would be balanced.

Oct. 1: The newly independent postal administration of the British Channel island of Jersey issued its first stamps.

Oct. 1: The Baliwick of Guernsey in the British Channel Islands became a regular stamp-issuing entity when its new postal administration released stamps.

Oct. 4: The United Nations issued stamps for use from its Geneva, Switzerland, office.

Oct. 27: St. Vincent released stamps marking the achievement of Associated State status.

Nov. 3: The US Christmas stamp for this year was issued precanceled with the names of four cities in addition to the normal unprecanceled version. Part of an experiment to reduce mail handling during the Christmas mail rush, the stamp was precanceled for Atlanta, Ga.; Baltimore, Md.; Memphis, Tenn.; and New Haven, Conn. The precanceled stamps were on general sale and could be used at any US post office, for any class of mail.

Nov. 7: Swaziland joined the Universal Postal Union.

Nov. 8: Malta released its first semi-postal stamps.

1970

Jan. 15: Rebel forces in Biafra surrendered, bringing an end to the area as a stamp-issuing entity. The area again became part of the Federal Republic of Nigeria.

Feb. 2: Trinidad and Tobago issued the first postage stamps produced by the British security printing firm, The House of Questa. The stamps are the Carnival issue.

April 22: The first stamps of the Somali Democratic Republic were issued. The government of the country, previously known as the Republic of Somalia, had been taken over by leftists in a coup on Oct. 21, 1969.

May 1: Laos issued a set of air mail semipostal stamps to aid victims of war in Indo-China.

May 20: A new headquarters building for the

The US Post Office Department experimented with Christmas stamps precanceled for four US cities (Nov. 3, 1969).

Universal Postal Union was dedicated. It is located in the Muri, a suburb of Berne, Switzerland. Construction had started in early 1968. A total of 66 stamp-issuing entities issued stamps marking the dedication.

May 20: Costa Rica placed in use its first air mail special delivery stamp.

June 17: Although Great Britain did not convert to decimal currency until Feb. 15, 1971, it issued a 10 pence, 20p, 50p, and a new £1 stamp in the decimal Machin series ahead of time to accustom the public to the change.

July 24: Equatorial Guinea became a member of the Universal Postal Union.

Aug. 12: President Richard Nixon signed HR 17070, the Postal Reorganization Act of 1970, which created the US Postal Service from the old US Post Office Department. The new organization became effective on July 1, 1971.

Oct. 10: The newly independent Dominion of Fiji issued a set of four stamps marking its independence.

Nov. 5: The US Christmas stamps were issued precanceled with lines as well as unprecanceled. The precanceled versions were supplied to 68 cities as an experiment in reducing mail handling during the Christmas mail rush.

1971

Jan. 16: The Sultanate of Oman placed its first stamps on sale. They were overprints on the June 27, 1970 issue of Muscat and Oman.

Feb. 1: The first stamps were issued by the People's Democratic Republic of Yemen' formerly the People's Republic of Southern Yemen.

Feb. 15: Great Britain converted to decimal currency in which 100 new pence are equal to £1. Previously, 12 pence equalled one shilling, 20 of which made up £1.

March: The US Post Office Department released a stamp booklet containing stamps gummed with a resin-dextrin dry gum that had a dull surface, making it almost invisible, but which rendered the use of interleaving between the panes unnecessary. The experimental booklet contained four panes of eight 6c Eisenhower definitives and one pane of eight of the 1c Jefferson definitive of the Prominent Americans Series. This was the first time the dull gum had been used and a note on the inside of the cover invited the comments of users. This dull gum has since become widely used on US stamps.

This experimental US Christmas precancel was supplied to 68 cities in an attempt to speed the Holiday Season mail flow (Nov. 5, 1970).

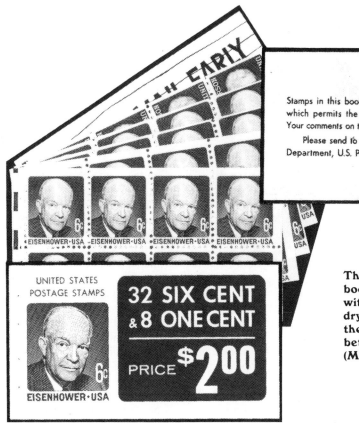

Stamps in this book have been gummed with an adhesive which permits the elimination of the separator tissues. Your comments on this type of gumming will be appreciated.

Please send to Accountable Paper Branch, Facilities Department, U.S. Postal Service, Washington, D.C. 20260.

The US experimental booklet featuring stamps with a new resin-dextrin dry gum that eliminated the need for interleaving between the panes (March 1971).

April 1: Canada introduced its post code system. It comprises two groups of three letters and numerals where the first group is always letter-numeral-letter and the second is always numeral-letter-numeral. The first group designates a large postal area and the second group can pinpoint the address down to a specific home or place of business.

April 30: The United States repealed its narcotic tax and ceased using Narcotic Tax revenue stamps. They had been introduced on Feb. 25, 1919.

May 8: The first US photogravure-printed stamp produced by the Bureau of Engraving and Printing went on sale. It is an 8c commemorative marking the sesquicentennial of Missouri statehood and reproduces a detail from the mural *Independence and the Opening of the West* by Thomas Hart Benton. The painting is located in the Harry S. Truman Library, Independence, Mo.

The Canadian post code stamps (April 1, 1971) and a typical US Narcotic Tax revenue stamp (April 30, 1971).

May 16, 1971 - Dec. 25, 1971

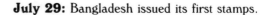

The first BEP-printed US photogravure printed stamp (May 8, 1971).

May 16: US registration fees ranged from 95c (indemnity not more than $100) to $5.15 (indemnity not more than $10,000).

May 16: The US domestic first-class letter rate went to 8c per ounce. Domestic air mail rates were raised to 11c per ounce for letters and 9c for postal cards/ postcards.

June 18: Fiji joined the Universal Postal Union as the independent Dominion of Fiji.

July 1: The United States Postal Service came into existence. It was formed from the old US Post Office Department, in an attempt to place mail operations on a more modern and efficient basis. An 8c stamp featuring the new Postal Service logo was issued.

July 29: Bangladesh issued its first stamps.

Aug. 17: The Sultanate of Oman became a member of the Universal Postal Union.

Sept. 1: The Persian Gulf country of Qatar became independent following a 103-year period during which Great Britain had protected the country and looked after its defense and foreign affairs.

Oct. 8: The Congo Democratic Republic became the Republic of Zaire.

Dec. 2: On this date, the sheikdoms of Abu Dhabi, Ajman, Dubai, Fujeira, Sharjah, and Umm al-Qiwain joined to form the United Arab Emirates. Ras al Khaima joined Feb. 10, 1972.

Dec. 7: The board of governors of the new US Postal Service appointed Elmer T. Klassen as first postmaster general of the new Postal Service. He succeeded Winton M. Blount, who had been appointed by President Richard Nixon prior to the establishment of the Postal Service.

Dec. 18: The Republic of Zaire issued its first stamps bearing its new name. It had previously been the Congo Democratic Republic.

Dec. 25: The Sultanate of Oman placed its

The 8c US stamp was issued to mark the inauguration of the United States Postal Service (July 1, 1971) and the Swiss stamp is that country's first semi-postal air mail stamp (Feb. 17, 1971).

first semi-postal stamp on sale and used the surtax for the United Nations' International Childrens' Fund.

1972

Jan. 26: Tonga joined the Universal Postal Union.

Feb. 3: Grenada issued its first air mail stamps.

Feb. 10: On this date, Ras al Khaima joined the United Arab Emirates.

Feb. 17: Switzerland marked the 50th anniversary of the first Swiss international flight from Zurich to Nuremberg, Germany, and the 25th anniversary of the first Zurich to New York flight with a semi-postal air mail stamp. The surtax went to the training of young airmen and the Swiss Air Rescue Service.

Feb. 22: A French court ruled that the 1968 finder of a river Seine *boule* containing several hundred letters postmarked in January 1871, could keep them, but that he could not dispose of them until 1998 in case any claims were made by descendants of the writers. *Boules* are zinc spheres into which letters were sealed that were addressed to Paris during the siege of 1870-71 by the Prussians. Since the Seine flowed through the encircled city it seemed logical to use it to "float" mail in. Unfortunately, what was logical to the French, was also logical to the Prussians and they placed nets across the river. None of the containers are known to have reached the addressees. The containers were placed in the river at Moulins and are thus known as *Boules de Moulins*. To

fool the enemy, letters intended for this service were inscribed "Par Moulins." Several of these containers have been found along the river in recent years. A French stamp shows letters in a boule and features a map of the route they were supposed to take.

March 20: Costa Rica's first special delivery stamp was issued.

May 15: This is the earliest known use date of the new US Postal Service Officially Sealed label bearing the USPS logo instead of the familiar Head of Liberty.

May 15: The United States returned the Ryukyu Islands to Japan and the islands ceased issuing stamps.

May 22: The Republic of Sri Lanka, formerly the Dominion of Ceylon, issued its first stamps.

July 1: The denomination of the US Federal Migratory Waterfowl Hunting stamps (Duck stamps) was increased to $5 from $3.

August: The newly formed United Arab Emirates issued its first stamps. They are overprints on stamps of Abu Dhabi and comprise the letters "UAE" and an Arabic inscription.

This stamp shows one of the *Boules de Moulins* used by the French in attempts to float mail down the Seine and into besieged Paris during the Franco-Prussian War of 1870-71.

Aug. 9, 1972 - Sept. 6, 1974

Aug. 9: Stamp issues for the island of Aitutaki in the Cook Islands were resumed. Previously, stamps of the Cook Islands had been used. The most recent Aitutaki stamps had been in 1924.

1973
Bahrain became a member of the Universal Postal Union.

Jan. 1: Hungary issued a stamp marking the introduction of a postal code. The stamp features a map of the country showing the postal zones and pictures the raven postal code symbol.

Feb. 7: Bangladesh joined the Universal Postal Union.

March 30: The Universal Postal Union admitted the United Arab Emirates as a member.

June 1: The colony of British Honduras changed its name to Belize and issued stamps overprinted with the new name. Independence followed on Sept. 21, 1981.

June 11: Although the Crown Agents in London had released the first stamps for Belize (formerly British Honduras) on June 1, they were released in Belize on this date.

July 5: The independent postal administration of the Isle of Man released its first stamps.

Aug. 23: Rwanda issued its first semi-postal stamp and used the surtax for drought relief.

Sept. 25: Nicaragua released its first semi-postal air mail stamps. The surtax went to a hospital building fund.

Oct. 24: After a lapse of many years, Penrhyn Island in the Cook Islands decided to resume the release of its own stamps.

Oct. 31: Great Britain discontinued its "printed to private order" service, whereby the public could have the official postal indicia imprinted on paper submitted.

Nov. 14: The first stamps inscribed "Grenadines of St. Vincent" went on sale.

Dec. 29: The first stamps were issued for the Grenadines of Grenada.

1974
The Bahamas became a member of the Universal Postal Union.

Guinea-Bissau became a member of the Universal Postal Union.

Jan. 1: Ivory Coast issued a set of Official stamps.

Feb. 7: The Caribbean island of Grenada was granted independence on this date. Stamps then in use were overprinted with "INDEPENDENCE" and the Feb. 7 date.

March 2: A first-class letter rate of 10c per ounce was established for the United States. Domestic air mail went to 13c per ounce and postal cards/ postcards rose to 11c.

May 22: The 17th Congress of the Universal Postal Union convened in Lausanne, Switzerland, to celebrate the centenary of the organization. A total of 141 countries sent representatives. The congress ran until July 4.

July 20: Turkish forces invaded the island of Cyprus and occupied the northern part of the island. Stamps for use in the Turkish-Cypriot communities, which had been issued Oct. 29, 1973, became the first issue of the Turkish-occupied part of the island on July 27, 1974.

Sept. 6: The first Mailgram messages were transmitted on this date. An earth station at Glenwood, N.J., transmitted the messages via the satellite Westar, to a station at Steele

MGMSAT USA
2=121030U249519 09/06/74
ICS MGMNCSA XBBC
JKPJK USPS WU
ZIP 10467

ARMANDO MASSONE
2440=12=M=BOSTON RD
BRONX   NY   10467

YOU HAVE PARTICIPATED IN AN EXCITING FIRST IN AMERICAN HISTORY.
AS A RECIPIENT OF THE FIRST MAILGRAM MESSAGE SENT VIA SATELLITE,
YOU SHARE IN THE OPENING OF A NEW FRONTIER IN COMMUNICATIONS.

YOUR MAILGRAM WAS TRANSMITTED ELECTRONICALLY FROM NEW YORK TO
LOS ANGELES VIA WESTAR I, AMERICA'S FIRST DOMESTIC COMMUNICA-
TIONS SATELLITE. IT TRAVELED 47,000 MILES AT THE SPEED OF LIGHT.

YOUR MAILGRAM SPACE PACKAGE ALSO CONTAINS THE FIRST OFFICIAL
LAUNCH COVER EVER ISSUED BY THE U.S. POSTAL SERVICE.

THIS SPACE PACKAGE MARKS AN IMPORTANT STEP IN ELECTRONIC TRANS-
MISSION OF LETTER MAIL. IT IS THE FIRST OF THE POSTAL PROGRESS
SERIES, COMMEMORATING ADVANCES IN COMMUNICATIONS AND MAIL SERVICE.

E.T. KLASSEN   R.W. MCFALL, CHAIRMAN AND PRESIDENT
POSTMASTER GENERAL   WESTERN UNION CORPORATION
UNITED STATES POSTAL SERVICE

SEPTEMBER 6, 1974

MGMSAT USA

MAILGRAM SERVICE CENTER
MIDDLETOWN, VA. 22645   POSTAGE PAID BY SENDER

western union Mailgram   UNITED STATES POSTAL SERVICE U.S. MAIL

THIS MAILGRAM WAS TRANSMITTED ELECTRONICALLY BY WESTERN UNION SATELLITE

FIRST MAILGRAM TRANSMISSION VIA WESTAR,
FIRST DOMESTIC U.S. COMMUNICATIONS SATELLITE
SEPTEMBER 6, 1974

WESTAR Launched April, 1974
MAILGRAM Transmission via Satellite
Postal Progress Series

This is the contents of the special commemorative Mailgram package that inaugurated Mailgram service on Sept. 6, 1974. Included was a message from Postmaster General E.T. Klassen and R.W. McFall, chairman and president of Western Union and a commemorative cover marking the launch of the satellite Westar, which were enclosed in the cacheted Mailgram envelope.

This pane is unusual in that it has two of everything in the selvedge! (Oct. 10, 1974).

Valley, Calif. A special commemorative package containing the first message was prepared. The project was developed jointly by the US Postal Service and Western Union.

Sept. 10: Guinea-Bissau achieved independence. It had formerly been the colony of Portuguese Guinea.

October: The Gambia joined the Universal Postal Union.

Oct. 10: The US Postal Service, in an experiment designed to help plate block collectors, issued the Legend of Sleepy Hollow commemorative stamp in the American Folklore series with plate numbers in diagonally opposite corners on each pane of 50 stamps, instead of only at the outside corner. The USPS said it wanted to assist collectors of the four position blocks by providing two per pane instead of one. Unfortunately, the plan backfired because the blocks from the four pane corners at the center of the sheet were identifiable and collectors thus faced the task of collecting eight blocks per four-pane sheet, instead of the traditional four. The experiment was not repeated.

Oct. 19: Niue marked the gaining of self-government by issuing stamps. The island had been a dependency of New Zealand and its previous stamps were overprints on New Zealand stamps. Niue maintains an association with New Zealand.

Nov. 15: The US Postal Service released its first self-adhesive stamp. Issued for Christmas mail, it depicts the dove weather vane on George Washington's home at Mount Vernon. Reports from numerous collectors in recent years state that the stamps are deteriorating, seemingly caused by the adhesive as brown blotches appear on the face of the stamps.

1975

Jan. 22: Great Britain issued its first semi-postal stamp. The surtax went to various unspecified charities. Sales were reported to be disappointing and it has released no further semi-postal stamps.

Jan. 30: The Faroe Islands began the release of their own postage stamps. Although a stamp-issuing entity, the Danish Post Office continued to be responsible for the overall operation of the system, according to the Wowern catalog.

Feb. 15: Benjamin Franklin Bailar succeeded Elmer T. Klassen as postmaster general of the US Postal Service.

March 17: The Cook Islands issued its first Official stamps.

April 17: The US Treasury Department prohibited the purchase abroad and importation into the United States of Cambodian stamps. The ban is still in effect.

April 18: US registration fees went to $1.25

At the left is the first US self-adhesive stamp, including a used example that is evidencing brown blotches (Nov. 15, 1974); Britain's first semi-postal stamp (Jan. 22, 1975); and one of the first modern stamps of the Faroe Islands (Jan. 30, 1975).

(indemnity not more than $100) to $6 (indemnity not more than $10,000). A basic return receipt was set at 20c, an address return receipt cost 45c, and there was a 60c charge for restricted delivery.

April 23: Raoul ch. de Thuin, the philatelic forger who had been bought out by the American Philatelic Society, died in Ecuador.

April 30: The US Treasury Department banned the purchase abroad and importation into the United States of South Vietnamese stamps. Although North and South Vietnam have been under one administration since the Communist takeover of South Vietnam, the Treasury Department lists them separately. The ban is still in effect and applies to stamps issued after this date. The ban on North Vietnamese stamps has been in effect since May 5, 1964.

May: The government of Laos fell to the rebel Pathet Lao.

June 23: Japan installed a coin-operated postage label vending machine at the Shibuyai Post Office. This is believed to represent the first use of such a device. A possible forerunner of this type of installation might be the Mailomat, a coin operated postage meter introduced in the United States on May 17, 1939 (q.v.).

June 25: The independent People's Republic of Mozambique released its first stamps.

July 12: The islands of St. Thomas and Prince, formerly a Portuguese colony, became independent as the Democrat Republic of Sao Tome and Principe.

July 15: In a rare instance of cooperation, United States and Soviet Union postal authorities released a "twin stamp" issue to mark the joint Apollo-Soyuz space flight. The two issues each feature two stamps using the same designs and showing the US and Soviet space craft before and during link-up.

Sept. 16: Papua New Guinea gained independence.

Oct. 11: Beginning on this date, US domestic first-class mail received the same level of service previously given to domestic air mail.

Oct. 14: The United States issued its first undenominated stamps in the form of two Christmas stamps. At the time they were printed, the US Postal Service did not know whether a new 13c postal rate would be in effect so it omitted the figure of denomination. The stamps were finally considered to be 10c stamps as the 13c rate did not become effective

Cooperation in a stamp issue reflects US-Soviet cooperation in space (July 15, 1975).

Dec. 2: The Lao People's Democratic Republic was formed.

Dec. 19: The Cape Verde Islands issued its first stamps as an independent republic.

Dec. 28: Although all domestic US first-class mail had been carried routinely by air since Oct. 11, 1975, the Postal Service introduced a domestic air mail rate of 17c for the first ounce and 15c for subsequent ounces.

Dec. 31: The US first-class domestic letter rate went to 13c for the first ounce and 11c for subsequent ounces up to 13 ounces.

1976

Papua New Guinea became a member of the Universal Postal Union.

The Republic of Cape Verde became a member of the Universal Postal Union.

The Comoros became a member of the Universal Postal Union.

Suriname joined the Universal Postal Union.

Jan. 1: The first stamps issued inscribed for Tuvalu, formerly the Ellice Islands of the Gilbert and Ellice Islands colony, went into use.

Jan. 2: The new British crown colony of the Gilbert Islands, which had been separated from

until Dec. 31, 1975. Since then there have been several undenominated issues, including the "A," "B," "C," and "D" stamps. Strictly speaking, these stamps must be classed as local postage stamps, since they are not valid in the international mails, although their use on international mail seems to have been tolerated. A figure of denomination must appear on postage stamps used for international mail.

Oct. 31: The first stamp in the Americana definitive series was a 13c stamp featuring the Liberty Bell. The United States issued it in booklet pane format.

Nov. 11: An independent Angola placed its first stamps on sale.

Nov. 30: The People's Republic of Benin, previously called the People's Republic of Dahomey, was proclaimed.

The first design in the Americana definitive series (Oct. 31, 1975).

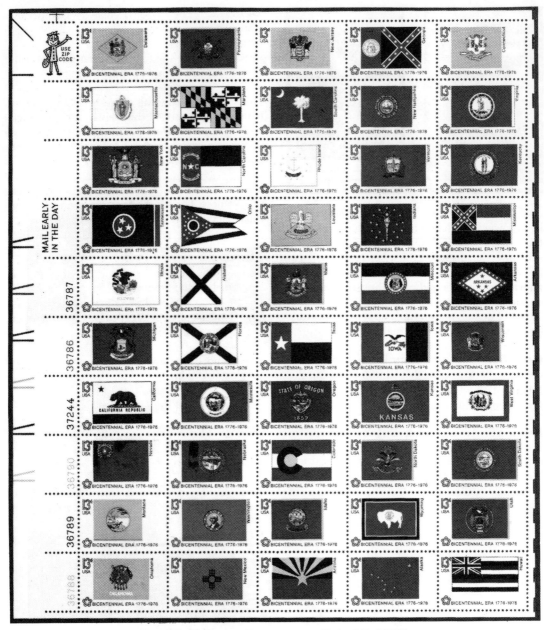

The US 50-stamp flag stamps (Feb. 23, 1976).

the Gilbert and Ellice Islands in Jan. 1, began the release of stamps.

Jan. 17: The US Postal Service issued a 13c stamp to publicize INTERPHIL '76, the international philatelic exhibition held May 29-June 6 in Philadelphia.

Feb. 23: The US Postal Service issued its first pane of 50 stamps, with each stamp bearing a different design. The design took the form of the flags of the 50 states. This was followed in 1982 by a similar issue featuring the 50 state birds and flowers.

April 1: The Faroe Islands assumed responsibility for its postal service. It had previously been administered by Denmark.

April 12: The Caribbean island of Montserrat's first Official stamps consist of definitive stamps overprinted "O.H.M.S."

May 3: The Portuguese colony of Timor was incorporated into Indonesia.

May 29: INTERPHIL '76, an international philatelic exhibition opened in Philadelphia. It ran until June 6. The event celebrated the bicentennial of the United States. The Postal Service marked the exhibition with the Jan. 17 release of a special 13c stamp to publicize the event. During the show, the United States also issued a series of four bicentennial souvenir sheets. They contained either five 13c, five 18c, five 24c, or five 31c stamps. They are noteworthy for the fact that it is virtually impossible to make out the denominations and other inscriptions on the stamps that feature details of the larger overall designs of the sheets. The poor quality of the printing produced many freak items.

June 29: Stamps were issued marking the independence of the Seychelles.

July 18: New US registration fees were set at $2.10 (indemnity not more than $100) and ranged up to $7.40 (indemnity not more than $10,000). The basic return receipt fee went to 25c.

Aug. 8: Coin-operated postage-label-vending

Swiss Frama labels used on cover (Aug. 8, 1976).

The first US stamp booklet to contain stamps printed se-tenant. The cover is also shown (March 11, 1976).

devices manufactured by FRAMA were placed in operation by Swiss postal authorities, which installed the first one at Zurich. Designated as SSVTA (Self-Service Value Ticket Automatons), they represent the first use of the FRAMA device.

Oct. 26: The South African homeland of Transkei issued its first stamps. Since the area is part of the Republic of South Africa, the stamps are not officially recognized as having more than local validity.

1977

Angola joined the Universal Postal Union.

March: From this date until the issue of Nov. 11, 1979, stamps of the Central African Republic were labeled "Central African Empire."

March 11: The first US stamp booklet containing stamps printed se-tenant went on sale. The pane contains seven 13c Flag-over-White House definitives and one 9c Capitol Building stamp in the Americana Series design. The stamps are slightly smaller than their sheet-format counterparts. Most of the panes were perforated 11x10½, but some have been found to be perforated 10. The latter are considerably more scarce and command a much higher price.

June 1: Mongolia issued its first semi-postal air mail stamp.

June 9: The first Official stamps of French Polynesia depict various tropical fruit.

June 27: The Republic of Djibouti was formed on this date. It had previously been the French Territory of Afars and Issas.

June 30: The sole remaining Railway Post Office in the United States ended its 113-year history with a final run on this date. Train #3 made the last southbound run and Train #4 the northbound run on this route between New York and Washington, D.C.

Dec. 6: Stamps were issued for the South African homeland of Bophuthatswana. Since the area is part of the Republic of South Africa, these stamps have not been officially recognized as having more than local validity.

1978

Jan. 16: Harry L. Lindquist, philatelic journalist and publisher, died at the age of 93. He is best remembered as founder of *Stamps Magazine*, first published on Sept. 17, 1932.

He also published a number of classic works on US stamps.

March 1: The US Postal Service Board of Governors appointed William F. Bolger as postmaster general, succeeding Benjamin Franklin Bailar.

March 14: The Netherlands issued two stamps to publicize the country's new postal code.

March 15: Niue issued its first semi-postal stamps and devoted the surtax to the benefit of the island's schoolchildren.

May 22: The US Postal Service issued the "A" stamp. This is the first in a series of "alphabet" stamps bearing no figure of denomination for use during a period of rate uncertainty (see Oct. 14, 1975). It has since been followed by "B," "C," and "D" stamps.

May 29: The US first-class domestic letter rate went to 15c for the first ounce and 13c for subsequent ounces up to 12 ounces.

May 29: US registration fees were set at $3 (indemnity not more than $100) and ranged to $14.50 (indemnity not more than $25,000). A basic return receipt cost 45c and an address return receipt jumped to 55c. The restricted delivery fee was raised to 80c.

June 10: Canada issued its first souvenir sheet. It features 14c, 30c, and $1.25 stamps reproducing early Canadian classic stamps and

The US "A" stamp. It was issued in sheet, booklet pane, and coil formats (May 22, 1978).

was released in conjunction with CIPEX '78, an international stamp show held June 9-18 in Toronto.

July 7: The Solomon Islands issued a set of four stamps marking the island group's independence. It had achieved self-government in 1975 and at that time stamps had been inscribed "Solomon Islands" instead of the previous "British Solomon Islands."

July 24: The Comoro Islands issued stamps overprinted to mark its name change to The Federal Islamic Republic of the Comoros.

Canada's first souvenir sheet (June 10, 1978).

The Commonwealth of
Dominica's first stamp
issue as an
independent nation
(Nov. 3, 1978).

Sept. 13: The US Postal Service announced plans to add four more digits to the existing five-digit ZIP code.

Sept. 21: US Bureau precancel impressions omitted the city and state designation beginning on this date, leaving only two black lines across the stamp.

Nov. 3: The Commonwealth of Dominica released its first stamps as an independent country, according to the Gibbons catalog of the British Commonwealth. Scott gives the date as Nov. 1.

Dec. 2: Norway placed in service its first Frama coin-operated postage label vending machine.

1979

Djibouti became a member of the Universal Postal Union.

Dominica joined the Universal Postal Union.

Mozambique was admitted as a member of the Universal Postal Union.

The US Postal Service introduced "PRESORTED FIRST-CLASS" bureau precancels, the first of several "special service precancels," according to correspondence from James Kingman.

During this year, the Antigua Post Office began to issue stamps inscribed for Redonda, an uninhabited rock in the Caribbean with an area of one square mile. No facilities exist on Redon-

da for the use of these items, but they are understood to be valid in Antigua.

Seychelles became a member of the Universal Postal Union.

The Caribbean island of Grenada joined the Universal Postal Union.

Feb. 22: St. Lucia became independent.

April 30: Stamps for the federal district of Kuala Lumpur, the capital city of Malaysia, went on sale.

May 1: Denmark granted home rule to Greenland. The former Danish colony had become part of the Kingdom of Denmark in 1963.

July 1: The denomination of US Federal Migratory Waterfowl Hunting stamps (Duck stamps) was increased to $7.50 from $5.

July 11: The Gilbert Islands, formerly part of the Gilbert and Ellice group, became independent as the Republic of Kiribati.

July 12: The first stamps issued under the name of Kiribati, formerly Gilbert Islands, were released.

August: The British Indian Ocean Territory withdrew its stamps.

Aug. 24: The United Nations issued the first stamps for use from its Vienna Office.

Sept. 12: The 18th Congress of the Universal Postal Union convened in Rio de Janeiro, Brazil. It included a class of insured letters in the universal postal convention. The Congress ended Oct. 22.

Sept. 13: Since the South African homeland of Venda is part of the Republic of South Africa, its stamps are not officially recognized as having international validity. Its first stamps were issued on this date.

Sept. 15: Brazil placed in service until Sept. 25 a coin-operated postage label vending machine at the Universal Postal Union Conference at Rio de Janeiro. It made its first regular installation on June 10, 1981, but discontinued it on Dec. 20, 1981.

Sept. 15: St. Pierre and Miquelon, located off the south coast of Newfoundland, became a department of France and began to use French stamps.

Sept. 30: The Panama Postal Service took over operation of the US Canal Zone Postal Service.

Oct. 27: St. Vincent issued stamps marking independence.

Nov. 14: An embargo on trade with Iran resulted in the prohibition on the purchase abroad and importation into the United States of Iranian stamps. The US announced on Jan. 19, 1981, that it would lift the embargo beginning on Feb. 24, 1981.

Dec. 16: The US ban on the purchase abroad and importation of Rhodesian stamps was lifted on this date.

1980-1994

The electronic age

1980

St. Lucia became a member of the Universal Postal Union.

Jan. 2: After using Portuguese stamps for many years, Portugal began to issue stamps inscribed for the Azores and Madeira. Both are a part of Portugal.

Jan. 15: The Cook Islands issued its first semi-postal air mail stamps.

April: Zimbabwe, formerly Rhodesia, joined the Universal Postal Union.

April 5: The famous British Guiana 1c magenta of 1856 was sold for $850,000 to an anonymous buyer at a Robert A. Siegel auction. This made it the highest-priced single stamp off cover. It had previously been owned by a group headed by Irwin Weinberg, which had bought it in 1970 for $280,000.

April 18: The first stamps were issued for the independent nation of Zimbabwe, formerly Rhodesia.

May 5: The Falkland Islands Dependencies, which then comprised South Georgia and South Sandwich Islands, released its first stamps.

June 20: The outer islands of the Seychelles placed their first stamps on sale. They were initially inscribed "Zil Eloigne Sesel," then "Zil Elwagne Sesel," later changed to "Zil Elwannyen Sesel."

June 23: The Caribbean island of Nevis released its own stamps. Stamps had been previously issued for Nevis from 1861 to 1890.

June 23: The Caribbean island of St. Kitts issued stamps. Stamps had been previously issued for St. Kitts from 1870 to 1890 under the name of "St. Christopher."

July 30: Vanuatu, formerly the New Hebrides, placed its first stamps in use.

Sept. 10: Luxembourg issued a stamp introducing a postal code to that country. The stamp depicts an envelope bearing the code as part of the address.

At the left is the famous British Guiana 1c magenta of 1856, the most costly single stamp off cover (April 5, 1980) and above is the stamp issued by Luxembourg to mark the introduction of its post code (Sept. 10, 1980).

Oct. 10: The sports set issued on this date by Great Britain represents the first British stamps to be printed by The House of Questa.

Nov. 20: South Korea released its first locally produced intaglio-printed stamps.

Dec. 27: A 19c stamp featuring Sequoyah began the Great Americans series of definitive stamps.

1981

During 1981, stamps were produced inscribed for the Caicos Islands of the Turks and Caicos Islands. The general catalogs do not list these because, as Gibbons notes, "while a separate philatelic bureau was set up, there is no other evidence that a separate political or postal administration exists and stamps of the Turks and Caicos Islands continue to be valid in the Caicos Islands."

The South African homeland of Ciskei issued stamps. Since the area is part of the Republic of South Africa, these stamps are not officially recognized as having more than local validity.

The Universal Postal Union admitted St. Vincent as a member.

Jan. 1: The US Postal Service introduced a new system of identifying printing plates that it had worked out with the Bureau of Engraving and Printing. Instead of the up to six five-digit numbers being printed adjacent to the same number of stamps in the selvedge, each plate for a given stamp would be identified by a single-digit number, all being printed adjacent to only one stamp. This single-digit number (becoming two digits when more than nine plates are used) would be keyed to a five-digit number still used to control printing plates and cylinders. The big advantage to collectors is the fact that the new system reduced the number of stamps that constituted a plate number block. Increasing denominations and proliferating plate numbers as multicolored stamps required more and more plates, and had pretty much brought to an end the collection of plate number blocks. This system brought this branch of philately back into the realm of possibility for the average collector.

Jan. 2: The Federal Republic of Germany (West Germany) placed in service 15 Frama coin-operated postage label vending machines.

Jan. 19: President Carter lifted the embargo on trade with Iran on this date, but it did not

Korea's first locally printed intaglio stamp (Nov. 20, 1980), a US coil pair showing the single-digit plate number below the lefthand stamp (Jan. 1, 1981), a stamp from Ciskei (1981), and the first stamp in the US Great Americans definitive series (Dec. 27, 1980).

become effective until Feb. 24, 1981, after newly inaugurated President Reagan approved the measure. The embargo had applied to the purchase abroad and importation into the United States of Iranian stamps.

Feb. 24: President Reagan approved the Jan. 19 order by President Carter lifting the embargo on trade with Iran, which had included the importation of Iranian postage stamps.

March 15: The United States Postal Service issued the so-called "B" stamps. These were undenominated stamps that had been prepared ahead of time to meet a new rate at shorter notice than would have been required to print new-rate stamps. Upon release they were designated as 18c stamps to meet the first-class letter rate that went into effect on March 22, 1981.

The stamps come in sheet, coil, and booklet formats. The sheet stamps are photogravure printed, while the coil and booklet items were intaglio printed.

Because they bear no figure of denomination, the stamps are only valid within the United States, although they have been accepted internationally.

March 22: The US first-class domestic letter rate went to 18c for the first ounce. Subsequent ounces up to 12 were set at 17c each.

March 22: US registration fees were adjusted. The basic fee went to $3.30 (indemnity not more than $100) with the top charge being reduced to $11.10 (indemnity not more than $25,000). There were other reductions at the high end of the scale, but raises were made at the lower end. Beginning on this date, it was not possible to secure registration without postal insurance at fees ranging from $3.25 for a value of not more than $100, to $9.85 for a value of not more than $25,000. The basic return receipt charge went to 60c, the address return receipt rose to 70c, and the restricted delivery fee was raised to $1.

May 8: The first philatelic item to be sold for $1 million was the cover bearing a copy of the Alexandria, Va., postmaster's provisional. The record price was paid at an auction held by David Feldman Ltd. in Geneva, Switzerland. It had sold for $10,000 at the 1955 Caspery Sale. The cover is known as the *Blue Alexandria,* or *Blue Boy.*

June 10: Brazil placed in service a coin-operated postage label vending machine. Its use was discontinued Dec. 20, 1981.

Sept. 1: Portugal began using its first Frama coin-operated postage label vending machine.

Sept. 21: Belize, formerly the crown colony of British Honduras, became independent.

Philately's first $1 million item, the Alexandria, Va. postmaster's provisional (May 8, 1981).

Oct. 11: The United States Postal Service issued its undenominated "C" stamps. These had been prepared ahead of time to meet a new rate at shorter notice than would have been required to print new-rate stamps. Upon release, the "C" stamps were designated as 20c stamps for the first-class letter rate that went into effect on Nov. 1, 1981.

The stamps came in sheet, coil, and booklet formats. The booklet stamps are in a much smaller size than the sheet and coil versions. Because they bear no figure of denomination, the stamps are officially only valid within the United States, although they have been passed in the international mails.

Nov. 1: The US first-class domestic letter rate went to 20c for the first ounce. Subsequent ounces cost 17c.

Nov. 16: Belgium placed in service Frama coin-operated postage label vending machines at six unspecified locations.

Nov. 30: Grenada issued its first semi-postal stamps.

Dec. 29: Because of uncertainty about a forthcoming postal rate increase, Canada Post issued an undenominated "A" stamp. Instead of a figure of denomination, the stamp bears an "A" and was treated as a 30c stamp. It came in sheet and coil formats.

1982

This was the year of the dog in the Oriental calendar, which runs in a 12-year cycle featuring a different animal after which the year is named. The others are indicated for the next 11 years. See Oriental calendar in index.

Jan. 4: The US Postal Service inaugurated its Electronic Computer-Originated Mail (E-COM) service. It enables mailers to enter the text of a bulk mailing letter into a computer terminal and

An E-COM electronic message envelope (Jan. 4, 1982).

send it by telephone line to one of 25 large post offices throughout the nation. There, postal workers print the letters, place them in special blue and white E-COM envelopes and put them in the mail stream for delivery.

Feb. 15: Western Airlines issued the first stamp in a series designed to frank letters carried between cities for deposit in the mailstream at a destination city for normal delivery. It called its system "Western Airletter" and it was in the nature of a mail forwarding service. The first stamp has a denomination of $1 and depicts a Douglas M-4 mail-carrying aircraft produced in the mid-1920s. Subsequent stamps feature other, more modern aircraft used by Western Airlines. The service sparked similar operations by Burlington Northern, American Express, and PRIDE. Denominations of the stamps varied, depending on the class of service desired. In all cases, the appropriate US postage had to be affixed to the items.

Feb. 26: Stamps of the independent country of Samoa were inscribed "Samoa" beginning with the issue marking the 250th birth anniversary of George Washington.

April 1: Finland placed in service Frama coin-operated postage label vending machines at the

Helsinki railway station, the Helsinki airport, and outside the Turku 10 Post Office.

April 14: Tonga devoted the surtax from its first semi-postal stamp to cyclone relief. The stamp went on sale on this date.

May 20: Tuvalu issued its first semi-postal stamps. The surtax was for Tongan cyclone relief.

July 15: Grenada released its first Official stamps.

Sept. 13: The Falkland Islands used the surtax from its first semi-postal stamps to assist in the rebuilding made necessary by the Argentine invasion of the island group. The stamps went on sale on this date.

1983

This was the year of the pig in the oriental calendar.

Jan. 12: The United States began issuing Official stamps for the first time since previous Officials were declared obsolete July 5, 1884. Department stamps inscribed for use by specific government departments had been introduced July 1, 1873. These new stamps were in-

The first stamp issued by Western Airlines for its Western Airletter service (Feb. 15, 1982).

troduced in an attempt to render a better accounting of government postal costs. They are in denominations of 1c, 4c, 13c, 17c, 20c, $1, and $5, plus a 13c postal card and #10 20c stamped envelopes in both plain and window types. At first called Official Mail stamps, they were subsequently named Penalty Mail stamps (see Feb. 4, Feb. 26, and May 15, 1985).

Feb. 1: Austria placed in service its first Frama coin-operated postage label vending machines.

March 10: The Republic of Palau issued its first stamps.

May 11: The island of Niuafo'ou, better known to philatelists as Tin Can Island, issued its first stamps. Although part of the Tonga group, it lies about 400 miles to the north, roughly in a line between Samoa and Fiji.

June 14: The English Channel island of Alderney, which is part of the Bailiwick of Guernsey, began to issue its own stamps.

June 29: Iceland began using a Frama coin-operated postage label vending machine.

July 18: The US Postal Service introduced its Express Mail "Next Day" two-pound package service. Express mail had been started as a pilot project on a limited basis in June 1970 and a national test with advertising was made beginning in October 1972.

The "Next Day" service brought the release on Aug. 12, 1983, of the $9.35 stamp to frank the special two-pound envelopes developed for the service.

July 18: Luxembourg introduced its first

A cover carried on the eighth space shuttle mission (Aug. 30, 1983).

A USPS "next day" cover using the two-pound pack envelope (July 18, 1983).

Frama coin-operated postage label vending machine.

Aug. 12: The US Postal Service issued a $9.35 stamp to frank its Express Mail "Next Day" service for packages weighing up to two pounds. The stamp was issued in booklet panes comprising three-stamp horizontal strips.

Aug. 30: The United States launched its eighth space shuttle flight, which carried 261,900 covers franked with the $9.35 Express mail stamp. The flight landed on Sept. 5 and after being canceled the covers were placed on sale by the US Postal Service at $15.35 each. Of the 261,900 covers carried, 2,523 were damaged, 1,000 were carried in the crew cabin for USPS use, one bearing a cylinder proof was retained for the Hall of Stamps, a Postal Service museum, and the balance of 258,376 was eventually sold to the public.

Oct. 31: The Society of Philatelic Americans was disbanded. Financial problems were cited as the reason.

Nov. 21: Canada Post placed what it called "Stick 'n Tick" labels on sale at Winnipeg,

Manitoba. It designed these labels to be placed on the face of a greeting card envelope and they combined an indicium at the upper right with a series of post-code boxes at the bottom. The user peeled off the paper backing, applied the label to the envelope and ticked off the appropriate boxes to indicate the post code, writing the rest of the address either above, or to the left if there was room on the envelope. The piece of mail could then have its post code read by an optical scanner, thus speeding the sorting process. To encourage the test use of the labels, they were on sale at $3.49 for a packet of 12 (less than 30c each, 2c under the regular rate) or in packets of 25 at a saving of about 4½c per piece. See Nov. 5, 1984.

1984

The year of the rat in the oriental calendar.

Feb. 22: Australia placed in service Frama coin-operated postage label vending machines at main post offices in the capital cities of the Australian states.

Feb. 22: The island of Bequia in the St. Vincent Grenadines had stamps issued bearing its name, even though it is part of St. Vincent.

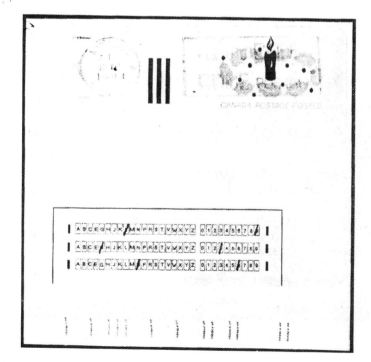

At the left is Canada's first "Stick 'n Tick" label (Nov. 21, 1983) and above is shown Australia's Frama vending machine postage label (Feb. 22, 1984).

March 1: The first stamps were issued by the Aland Islands, a province of Finland.

March 10: Stamps were issued bearing the name of Vaitupu, one of the islands forming the country of Tuvalu.

March 19: Stamps bearing the name of Nui, one of the islands forming the country of Tuvalu, were released.

March 29: Union Island, in the St. Vincent Grenadines, had stamps issued bearing its name, despite the fact that it is part of St. Vincent.

March 30: The pneumatic mail service in Paris closed after operating for 117 years. The system comprised 153 miles of tube connecting the post offices of the city. A letter could be mailed at one post office and delivered across the city by hand from the receiving post office within a few hours. The cost of about $1.80 at the time the service closed, was less than that of a telegram. From four million letters a year as recently as 1960, to 648,000 in its final year, the deteriorating system could no longer compete with telephone and telecopier, and so the postal service that carried the letters of countless lovers, the "romantique pneumatique", came to an end.

April 9: The islands of Funafuti, and Nanumea, which are part of Tuvalu, issued stamps inscribed for them.

April 12: Nukulaelae, one of the islands forming the country of Tuvalu, began the release of stamps.

April 16: Stamps were issued inscribed for the island of Niutao, which is part of Tuvalu.

April 23: Nukufetau, and Nanumaga islands in the Tuvalu group, had stamps issued inscribed for them.

May 1: Great Britain placed in service Frama

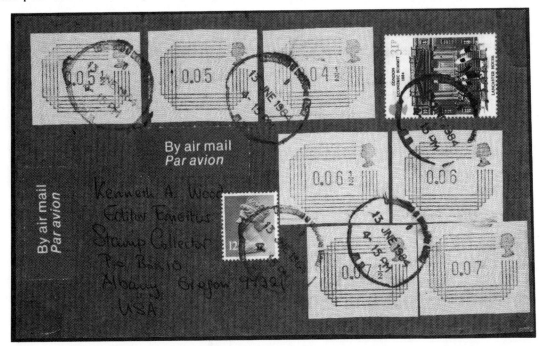

Great Britain's Frama vending machine postage labels (May 1, 1984).

coin-operated postage label vending machines at four locations in England. These locations are the General Post Office in London, and post offices at Windsor, Southampton, and Cambridge. Denominations offered ranged from ½p to 16p.

May 2: The Republic of the Marshall Islands released its first stamps on this date. The island group had been part of the US Pacific Trust Territory since it had been taken from Japan during World War II. The islands had been originally a Spanish colony, then, after the Spanish-American War, the group had been bought by Germany, which lost it to Japan during the First World War. Japan had received a League of Nations mandate over the area after that war.

While the new republic has a British-style

The first integrated intaglio-photogravure US stamp (May 23, 1984).

parliamentary form of government, and has internal independence, the US remains responsible for defense and foreign affairs. As a US possession, the Marshall Islands had used US stamps, but as its own stamps were released, corresponding denominations of US stamps were withdrawn from sale.

May 23: The Douglas Fairbanks, Sr., commemorative stamp issued on this date, was the first US stamp produced using a fully integrated combination of intaglio and photogravure printing. It was printed on the combination A press at the Bureau of Engraving and Printing and represented a final step in achieving a merging of the two printing methods. The BEP applied an intaglio element completely over a photogravure background, instead of producing a stamp with separate areas printed by different methods, as had been done previously. The smaller figure of Fairbanks as D'Artagnan is photogravure with intaglio detail and the larger portrait is completely photogravure.

June 6: The 19th Conference of the Universal Postal Union was held in Hamburg, Federal Republic of Germany, beginning on this date. It ended June 27.

July 12: The Federated States of Micronesia, formerly part of the US Trust Territory of the Pacific, released it first stamps. The entity comprises the four states of Truk, Pohnpei (Ponape), Yap, and Kosrae. The federation capital is on Pohnpei.

Aug. 2: The British Post Office staged a reenactment of the first mailcoach run from Bristol to London, England, using a restored 18th-century mailcoach. During the course of the 17½-hour journey, several records were broken. The record time for changing a team of horses was reduced from 46 seconds, set in 1888, to 41 seconds from wheel stop to wheel start. Another record was set when driver John Parker made the reenactment run singlehanded. Two hundred years ago the trip required two drivers. Twenty-four horses were required to make the 132-mile journey. See Aug. 2, 1784.

Aug. 7: The African country of Upper Volta changed its name to Bourkina Fasso.

The reenactment run of the first British mailcoach leaves Bristol for London on Aug. 2, 1984 (photo courtesy of Bristol United Press and Albert Bath).

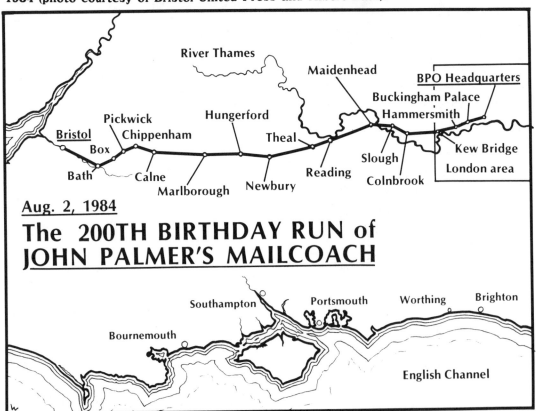

Aug. 2, 1984

The 200TH BIRTHDAY RUN of JOHN PALMER'S MAILCOACH

Cancels commemorating the rebirth of the US mail train (Oct. 30, 1984).

Aug. 13: The US 20c Smokey Bear commemorative stamp issued on this date was the first to be printed on the Bureau of Engraving and Printing's new combination offset/intaglio "D" press.

Oct. 29: The Aland Islands, part of Finland, placed a Frama postage label vending machine in use.

Oct. 30: The US mail train was reborn when a special mail-only train began to run between Boston and Washington, D.C. The northbound train was named *The Fast Mail* and the southbound train, *The Mail Express*. The trains are specifically scheduled to meet US Postal Service requirements and run Tuesdays through Sundays carrying first-class, second-class, and express mail, with principal intermediate stops at New York and Philadelphia. The Monday mail is carried by a regularly scheduled Amtrak train.

Nov. 5: Canada Post placed its Christmas "Stick 'n Tick" labels on sale in Edmonton, Alta; Halifax, N.S.; Hull, Quebec; London, Ont.; Ottawa, Ont.; Quebec City, Quebec; Victoria, B.C.; and Winnipeg, Man. Although similar in purpose and principle to the 1983 labels, the 1984 labels were in two pieces, an indicium for the upper right corner of the envelope and a post code section to be placed at the bottom. They were priced slightly lower than the 1983 labels, at 12 for $3.39 (about 28c each). See Nov. 21, 1983.

1985

The year of the ox in the oriental calendar.

Jan. 1: Great Britain demonetized its ½p coin and the British Philatelic Bureau noted that sets involving an odd ½p in their total face value would be sold for the next higher even penny and a ½p stamp would be included.

Jan. 1: Paul N. Carlin became US postmaster general. He had been appointed by the US Postal Service Board of Governors to succeed William F. Bolger.

Feb. 1: The US Postal Service issued undenominated "D" stamps in its continuing series of "alphabetical" stamps. Like their predecessors, they were issued to ensure an adequate supply of stamps during a rate-change period, when it may not be possible to produce a sufficient stock of new-rate stamps in time. Since the stamps do not conform to Universal Postal Union requirements that stamps used in

Stamp issues from South Korea, the Repubic of China (Taiwan), and Japan marking 1985 as the year of the ox (1985).

the international mails shall bear a figure of denomination, these stamps are valid only within the United States, thus making them local postage stamps. The stamps are in sheet, coil, and booklet format.

Feb. 1: US Postmaster General Paul N. Carlin announced the appointment of William D. Dunlap and Ann DeWitt Harvey to the Citizens' Stamp Advisory Committee.

Dunlap, chief executive officer of a Minneapolis advertising agency was deputy special assistant to the postmaster general for special projects in the last year of the old US Post Office Department, prior to the formation of the US Postal Service in 1971.

Harvey is an artist and graphic design specialist who owns a design firm in Sudbury, Mass. They bring to 18 the total membership of the committee, which reviews suggestions for stamp and postal stationery subjects and recommends subjects and designs to the postmaster general.

The current membership includes: Clinton Andrews of Anchorage, Alaska; Edward A. Beard of Washington, D.C.; Wilbur J. Cohen of Austin, Texas; Belmont Faries of Clifton, Va.; John E. Foxworth, Jr. of West Bloomfield, Mich.; Robert Leuver of Washington, D.C.; C. Douglas Lewis of Washington, D.C.; Edward Mallek of Honolulu, Hawaii; James A. Michener of Austin, Texas; Norma J. Niehoff of New York, N.Y.; Virginia Noelke of San Angelo, Texas; Mary Ann Owens of Brooklyn, N.Y.; Richard "Digger" Phelps of South Bend, Ind.; Jerry Pinkney of Croton-on-Hudson, N.Y.; John Sawyer III of Kingwood, Texas; and John C. Weaver of Rancho Palos Verdes, Calif.

Feb. 4: The US Postal Service issued Penalty (Official) Mail "D" stamps in coil format to frank the 22c first-class letter rate that went into effect on Feb. 17, 1985. Also released was a

The US "D" stamps in sheet, coil, and booklet format and the "D" stamped envelope (Feb. 1, 1985).

Feb. 16, 1985 - Feb. 28, 1985

14c Penalty Mail "D" stamp to cover the 14c postal card effective on the same date. See Jan. 12, 1983.

Jackie Strange.

Feb. 16: Jackie Strange assumed the office of deputy postmaster general. She is the first woman appointed to this level of US Postal Service management.

Feb. 17: The United States increased its postal rates. First-class letters went to 22c per ounce for the first ounce, but the 17c rate for subsequent ounces remained unchanged. Postcards were boosted from 13c to 14c.

International rates were also increased. Aerogrammes went to 36c from 30c. The 40c half ounce air mail rate to Europe, Asia, Africa, and South America except Venezuela and Colombia, went to 44c.

The half ounce air mail rate to Venezuela, Colombia, Central America, the Caribbean islands, Bahamas, Bermuda, and St. Pierre and Miquelon, as well as from American Samoa to Western Samoa, and Guam to the Philippines went to 39c.

International air mail postcards were raised to 33c and an international surface mail postcard increased to 25c, except to Canada and Mexico, for which US domestic rates apply.

Registration fees were raised to $3.60 ($3.55 without postal insurance) for a value not over $100, to $4.25 ($4.15) for a value not over $1,000, and $12.65 ($10.15) for a value not over $25,000.

The basic return receipt cost went to 70c, a return receipt showing address became 90c, and the restricted delivery cost was set at $1.25.

Also raised was the two-pound Express Mail "Next Day" service, which went from $9.35 to $10.75. A new stamp in the latter denomination was issued April 29.

Feb. 17: The US Postal Service abolished the forwarding fee it had charged on second-class mail. Up to this date, magazines and newspapers had been forwarded for 90 days at the second-class transient rate. This rate was only one cent below the first-class rate for each of the first two ounces, increasing to $1.35 for one pound.

Feb. 28: The British Post Office discontinued its redemption of pre-decimal denominated postage stamps. The stamps had been replaced with decimal currency stamps in 1972 and had been demonetized several years ago, according to Edgar Lewy, British philatelic writer.

March 1: Canada Post closed the National Postal Museum in Ottawa, citing the need for expanded office space by members of the Canadian parliament.

April 29: The US Postal Service issued a $10.75 Express Mail stamp to frank the Express Mail "next day" service, which had been increased from $9.35 on Feb. 17, 1985. The design is similar, but varies in detail from the previous stamp.

May 6: The purchase abroad and importation into the United States of postage stamps of Nicaragua was prohibited effective on this date as part of President Reagan's total trade embargo against Nicaragua.

May 15: The US Postal Service issued 14c and 22c Penalty (Official) Mail stamps to frank the new postal rates that went into effect on Feb. 17, 1985 (q.v.). The 14c stamp was released in sheet format and the 22c item was a coil stamp. See Jan. 12, 1983.

June 30: Stamps inscribed for Upper Volta were withdrawn on this date. On Aug. 7, 1984, the country's name was changed to Bourkina Fasso.

1986
The year of the tiger in the oriental calendar.

May 22: AMERIPEX, the international philatelic exhibition, is planned to run from this date to June 1 in Chicago, Ill.

1987
The year of the hare in the oriental calendar.

1988
The year of the dragon in the oriental calendar.

1989
The year of the snake in the oriental calendar.

1990
The year of the horse in the oriental calendar.

1991
The year of the sheep in the oriental calendar.

1992
The year of the monkey in the oriental calendar.

1993
The year of the rooster in the oriental calendar.

1994
The year of the dog in the oriental calendar.

errata

Page heading

1150-June 19, 1464 — Column 2, line 18 "addressee"

1659-June 13, 1668 — "postmarks" in line one of caption should read "postmark"

May 26, 1840-1841 — "honor" in line three of caption should read "humor"

Jan. 1, 1855-July 18, 1855 — Column 1, line 25 "1853" should read "1852"

Oct. 6, 1893-June 30, 1894 — Column 1 illustration shows a 10c surcharge on original undenominated label.

July 22, 1897-April 21, 1898 — Column 1, line 1 "Leeward" should read "Leeward Islands"

May 10, 1929-July 22, 1929 — Column 1, line 25 "an" should read "and"

Sept. 13, 1979-Dec. 16, 1979 — Second Sept. 15 item should read: "St. Pierre and Miquelon became a department of France on July 1, 1976 and used French stamps from April 1, 1978."

Index page 18 — Head should read "Confederation Post Office-Dongan."

Bibliography

Argenti, Nicholas, *The Postage Stamps of New Brunswick and Nova Scotia,* Quarterman edition, Lawrence, Mass. 1976.

Attwood, J.H., *Ascension: The Stamps and Postal History,* Robson Lowe, London, 1981.

Barefoot, John, *GB Revenue Compendium,* J. Barefoot Investments Ltd., York, England, 1981.

Barnes, Robert, *The Postal Service of the Falkland Islands,* Robson Lowe, London, 1972.

Batchelor, L.E. and D.B. Picton-Phillips, *Pre-Victorian Stamps and Franks,* Picton Publishing, Chippenham, England, 1971.

Billig's Philatelic Handbooks, various, Fritz Billig, Jamaica, N.Y. and HJMR & Co., North Miami, Fla.

Billing, R.R., *Mexicana,* October 1984.

Bleeker, Tom R., *Japanese Occupation Issues of the Dutch East Indies (1942-1945),* Philip Cockrill, Newbury, England, 1982.

Boerger, Alfred G., *Handbook on Luminescent Stamps,* Boerger, Ft. Lauderdale, Fla., 1973.

Boggs, Winthrop S., *Ten Decades Ago.,* American Philatelic Society, 1949.

Boggs, Winthrop S., *The Postage Stamps and Postal History of Canada,* Quarterman Publications Inc., Lawrence, Mass., 1974.

Bowker, H.F., "Guam Guard Mail," *The Stamp Specialist, Vol. 1, Part 1,* Lindquist, New York, 1939.

Bowley, R.E., *Sir Sandford Fleming and the Unfolding of Canada (1845-1915): A Philatelic Study,* Peterborough, Ontario, Historical Society, 1983.

Bowyer, Mathew J., *They Carried the Mail,* Luce, New York, 1972.

Brett, George W., *The Giori Press,* Bureau Issues Association, 1961.

Cabeen, Richard McP., *Standard Handbook of Stamp Collecting,* Crowell, New York, 1979.

Castle, Wilfrid T.F., *Cyprus: Postal History and Postage Stamps,* Robson Lowe, London, 1971.

Chaintrier, Louis A., *Balloon Post of the Siege of Paris, 1870-71,* American Air Mail Society, 1976.

Chapman, Kenneth F., *Good Stamp Collecting,* Routledge and Kegan Paul, London, 1959.

Codding, George Arthur Jr., *The Universal Postal Union,* New York University Press, New York, 1964.

Coffey, William A., editor, *Historical Sketches of Watercraft on Stamps,* Ships on Stamps Unit, ATA.

Cohn, Ernst M., *The Flight of the Ville d'Orleans,* Collectors Club of Chicago, 1978.

Cohn, Ernst M., "The French Commissars Airmail of 1793," *The Postal History Journal,* May 1971.

Collins, Peter, *Stamp Collector,* Oct. 31, 1983.

Combs, W.V., *First Federal Issue 1798-1801: U.S. Embossed Revenue Stamped Paper,* APS, 1979.

Confederate Postal History, An Anthology, edited by Francis J. Crown Jr., Quarterman, Lawrence, Mass., 1976.

Crampon, L.J., *Aerophilatelic Flights Hawaii & Central Pacific, 1913-1946,* Hawaiian Philatelic Society, Hawaii, 1980.

Crouch, Col. G.R. and Norman Hill, *British Army Field Post Offices, 1939-1950,* LAVA, New York, 1951.

Davis, Gerald and Denys Martin, *Burma Postal History,* Robson Lowe, London, 1971.

Davis, J.D., *The Falklands War,* published by author, Andover, England, 1983.

Dehn, Roy A., *Italian Stamps,* Heinemann, London, 1973.

Delaney, Dr. Arthur A., *Stamp Collector,* Feb. 18, 1985.

Dickey, Budd W., "The Beginning of Postage Stamp Production by the Bureau of Engraving and Printing," *United States Specialist,* November 1984.

Dougan, Charles W., *The Shanghai Postal System,* American Philatelic Society, 1981.

Drysdall, Alan R., *The Stamps and Postal History of Northern Rhodesia and Zambia, 1963-1965,* Robson Lowe, London, 1976.

Eichenthal, Villem, *Eesti, Specialized Catalogue of Estonia,* Philatelic Specialists Society of Canada, 1962.

Eisendrath, Joseph L., *Crash Covers: An Aerophilatelic Challenge,* American Air Mail Society, 1979.

Federal Republic of Germany, Bernard Davis, National Philatelic Museum, Philadelphia, 1952.

Floyd, F.G., "The Machine Commats of Boston, Mass., 1876-1886," *Billig's Philatelic Handbook, Volume XII,* Fritz Billig, Jamaica, N.Y., 1950.

Foster, Thomas, *The Postal History of Jamaica, 1662-1860,* Robson Lowe, London, 1968.

Funk, Eugene M. and Arthur H. Bond, *Barry Machine Cancels,* U.S. Cancellation Club, Denver, Colo., undated.

Geldhof, A.E., *Stamps of the Orange Free State,* American Philatelic Society, 1938.

Glasgow, Eric, "Postal History in Denmark," *Gibbons Stamp Monthly,* October, 1980.

Gobie, Henry M., *U.S. Parcel Post: A Postal History,* Postal Publications, Miami, Fla., 1979.

Goodkind, Henry M., *The First Air Mail Stamps of the United States,* The Collectors Club, New York, undated.

Gravelat, Jean, *The Aero Philatlic Annals,* July, 1964.

Green, Irving I., *The Black Honduras,* The Collectors Club, New York, 1962.

Greenwood, Richard, Dr. Romano Camara, and Philip Cockrill, *Portuguese Shipping Companies, Paquebot & Ship Cancellations,* Cockrill, England, undated.

Griffenhagen, George B., "The Orangeburg Coil — Revisited," *The United States Specialist,* Bureau Issues Association, January, 1985.

Guide to Precancel Collecting, Gunesch Precancel House Inc., Roselle, Ill., undated.

Hafen, LeRoy R., *The Overland Mail,* Quarterman, Lawrence, Mass., 1976.

Halle, Herman L., *Stamp Collector,* May 6, 1985.

Hallgren, Mauritz, *All About Stamps,* Alfred A. Knopf, New York, 1940.

Hals, Nathan and Phil Collas, *The New Hebrides: Their Postal History and Postage Stamps,* Collectors Club Handbook #20, New York, 1967.

Hamilton, Patrick, *Stamp Collecting,* April 5, 1963.

Hansen, Glenn, *The Guidebook and Catalogue of Canadian Stamps,* first edition, Regency, Winnipeg, Canada, 1970.

Harlow, Alvin F., *Paper Chase,* Henry Holt & Co., New York, 1940.

Harris, L.H., *World's First Air Stamp, Italy 1917,* European Philatelic Library, 1959.

Haverbeck, Harrison D.S., *The Postage Stamps and Postal History of Tibet,* The Collectors Club of New York, 1958.

Haverbeck, Harrison D.S., *The Postage Stamps of Nepal,* Collectors Club, New York, undated.

Heartwell, James C., *Air Stamp Records,* American Air Mail Society, 1942.

Heinmuller, John P.V., *Man's Flight to Fly,* Aero Print Co., New York, 1945.

Hertsch, Max, *Famous Stamps of the World,* Taplinger Publishing, New York, 1968.

Hicks, J. Maurice, "Anthony Trollope: An Unsung Hero of the British Postal Reform," *Congress Book 1977,* American Philatelic Congress.

Historical Sketches of Watercraft on Stamps, William A. Coffey, editor, Ships on Stamps Unit, ATA.

History of the Postal Inspection Service, leaflet, U.S. Government Printing Office, Publication 259, January, 1982.

Hoffmann, George W., "The Dornier DO-X," series, *Airpost Journal,* April 1971 and subsequent issues.

Holmes, Donald B., *Air Mail: An Illustrated History, 1793-1981,* Crown, New York, 1981.

Holmes, L. Seale, *Specialized Philatelic Catalogue of Canada and British North America, Ninth Edition,* Ryerson, Toronto, 1960.

Hopkins, A.E., *A History of Wreck Covers,* Robson Lowe, London, undated.

Hornadge, Bill, *Local Stamps of Australia,* Review Publications, Dubbo, NSW, Australia, 1982.

Hornadge, Bill, *The Pitcairn Islands Stamp Catalogue,* Review Publications, Dubbo, NSW, Australia, 1976.

Hornung, Otto, *Illustrated Encyclopedia of Stamp Collecting,* Hamlyn, London, 1970.

Houseman, Lorna, *The House That Thomas Built,* Chatto & Windus, London, 1968.

Howland, W.G., *Philatelic History of the War Between Peru and Chile, 1879-1884,* American Philatelic Society, 1966.

Hurt, E.F. and Denwood N. Kelly, *The Danube Steam Navigation Company,* American Philatelic Society, 1950.

Ireland, Stamps of, 1980 edition, David MacDonnell and David Feldman, Dublin, Ireland.

Jacques, W.A., *Andorra/Andorre: The Story of its Stamps and Postal History,* Robson Lowe, London, 1974.

Jarrett, Fred, *Stamps of British North America,* first pub. 1929. Reprinted in 1975 by Quarterman Publications Inc., Lawrence, Mass.

Jennings, Peter, *Aerogrammes,* Picton, London, 1973.

Julsen, Frank W. and A.M. Benders, *A Postal History of Curacao,* Van Dieten, The Hague, the Netherlands, 1976.

Kandaouroff, Prince Dimitry, *Collecting Postal History,* Larousse, New York, 1974.

Kehr, Ernest A. and Philip Cockrill, *Egypt: The Posta Europa and 1984 Kehr Catalogue of Interpostals,* Cockrill Series Booklet #33, 1984.

Kehr, Ernest A., "Egypt, The Interpostal Seals," *Billig's Philatelic Handbooks, Volume 21,* Fritz Billig, Jamaica, N.Y., 1954.

Kehr, Ernest A., *The Romance of Stamp Collecting,* Crowell, N.Y., 1947.

Kingman, James, personal correspondence and columns in *Stamp Collector.*

Konwiser, Harry M., *American Philatelic Dictionary and Colonial and Revolutionary Posts,* Minkus, New York, 1947.

Konwiser, Harry M., *The American Stamp Collector's Dictionary,* Minkus, 1949.

Kricheldorf, H., "Germany," *Billig's Philatelic Handbooks, Volume 28,* Fritz Billig, Jamaica, N.Y., 1960.

Krieger, Richard, *The Trans-Mississippi Mails After the Fall of Vicksburg,* Philatelic Foundation, New York, 1984.

Kronstein, Dr. Max, *Pioneer Airpost Flights of the World 1830-1935,* American Air Mail Society, 1978.

Kyle, James, *Gibbons Stamp Monthly,* July, 1975.

Lagerloef, Col. Hans, "Russian Zemstvos," *The Stamp Specialist, Coral Book,* Lindquist, New York, 1945.

Lamb, W. Kaye, *History of the Canadian Pacific Railway,* Macmillan, New York, 1977.

Langford, Frederick, *Flag Cancel Encyclopedia,* published by the author, 1976.

Langford, Frederick, *Standard Encyclopedia of Doremus Machine Cancels,* published by the author, 1968.

Lesgor, Raoul, *France 20th Century Specialized,* Lesgor, Holmes, N.Y., 1955.

Lithuania, Postage Stamps of, Collectors Club, New York, 1978.

Loso, Foster W., *The Stamp Collectors Round Table,* Frederick A. Stokes, N.Y., 1937.

Ludington, M.H. and Geoffrey Osborn, *The Royal Mail Steam Packets to Bermuda and the Bahamas,* Robson Lowe, London, 1971.

Mackay, James A., *Airmails 1870-1970,* Batsford, London, 1971.

Mackay, James A., *The Guinness Book of Stamps, Facts and Feats,* Guiness Superlatives, London, England, 1982.

Mackay, James A., *The Story of Malta and Her Stamps,* Philatelic Publishers, London, 1966.

Markovits, Robert L., *United States: The 10c Registry Stamp of 1911,* Quality Investors Ltd., Middletown, N.Y., 1973.

Marriott, John B., Keeper of the Queen's Collection, "The Royal Philatelic Collection," *Stamp News,* (Australia), September 1984.

Matsumoto, Jun Ichi, *The French Post Office of Yokohama,* Japan Philatelic Publications, Tokyo, 1984.

Mechem, Thomas Owen, *Canadian Philatelic Handbook,* Northwest Stamp Association, Kent, Wash., 1975.

Morgan, Ian C., *The Specialized Catalogue of Canadian Air Mail Stamps,* published in Montreal by the author, 1934.

Morris, Thomas F., "History of the Bureau of Engraving and Printing," *The Stamp Specialist, Gray Book,* Lindquist, New York, 1943.

Mott, Dr. Rodney L., *Postal Stationery,* United Postal Stationery Society, 1968.

Mueller, Edwin, *Handbook of the Pre-Stamp Postmarks of Austria,* Collectors Club, New York, 1960.

Murphy, Robert T., *A Postal History Cancellation Study of the U.S. Pacific Islands (Including the Trust Territories),* Lyndon B. Johnson Space Center Stamp Club, Houston, 1974.

Nathan, M.C. and W.S. Boggs, *The Pony Express,* The Collectors Club, New York, 1962.

Newport, William, *Herm: History and Stamps,* Channel Islands Specialist Society, Sidcup, Kent, England, 1961.

Norris, G.N., "The Phoenix Islands," *Billig's Philatelic Handbooks, Volume 28,* Fritz Billig, Jamaica, N.Y., 1960.

O'Sullivan, Thomas J. and Karl B. Weber, *History of the United States Pioneer and Government-Operated Air Mail Service 1910-1928,* American Air Mail Society, 1973.

Patrick, Douglas and Mary Patrick, *The Musson Stamp Dictionary,* Musson, Toronto, Canada, 1972.

Perkal, Adam and Seymour Kazman, *The Post Office Seals of the United States, Volume One, The Regular Issues,* George Alevizos, Santa Monica, Calif., 1983.

Pernes, Rufino R., *Crown Stamps of the Portuguese Colonies,* J-B Publishing, Crete, Neb., 1976.

Piri, Dr. J.H. Harvey, *Antarctic Posts,* Hayes, West Yorkshire, England, 1982.

Polish Prisoner of War Posts, Polish Philatelic Society of Boston, Mass., 1970.

Poole, Bertram W.H., *The Pioneer Stamps of the British Empire,* D. Van Nostrand, New York, undated.

Postage Stamps of the United States, current edition, US Postal Service.

Postal History of the AEF, 1917-1923, American Philatelic Society, 1980.

Postal Stationery of the United States Possessions and Administrative Areas, United Postal Stationery Society, 1971.

Preston, R.B. and M.H. Sanborn, *The Postal History of Puerto Rico,* American Philatelic Society, 1950.

Prigara, S.V., *The Russian Post in the Empire, Turkey, China, and the Post in the Kingdom of Poland,* translated by David M. Skipton, Rossica Translation #1, 1981.

Private Post, The., Peter S. Thornton, editor, Cinderella Stamp Club, London, 1982.

Reiche, Hans, *A Large Queen's Report,* Canadian Wholesale Supply, Brantford, Ont., 1977.

Reiche, Hans, *The Canadian Lathework Design,* Unitrade Associates, Toronto, undated.

Reynolds, Mairead, *A History of the Irish Post Office,* MacDonnell Whyte, Dublin, 1983.

Bhein, Francis, *The Postal History of the Grand Duchy of Luxembourg,* Chambers, Kalamazoo, Mich., 1941.

Rich, Joseph S. and Stephen G. Rich, *United States Telegraph Issues,* Society of Philatelic Americans, 1947.

Rich, Wesley Everett, *The History of the United States Post Office to the Year 1829,* Harvard University Press, 1924.

Riddell, John D. and Sheila, *U.S.A. Consular Post Offices in Japan,* Robson Lowe, London, undated monograph.

Robertson, Alan W., *Great Britain, Post Roads, Post Towns, and Postal Rates 1635-1839,* published by the author, 1961.

Robinson, Howard, *Carrying British Mails Overseas,* New York University Press, 1964.

Robinson, Howard, *The British Post Office: A History,* Princeton University Press, Princeton, N.J., 1948.

Robson Lowe, *The Encyclopedia of British Empire Postage Stamps, Volumes I-V,* Robson Lowe Ltd., London.

Rock, P.M.C., *Gibbons Stamp Monthly,* June, 1975.

Rodriguez, J.L., *The Story of Gibraltar and Her Stamps,* Philatelic Publishers Ltd., London, 1968.

Rogers, Col. Henry H., *A Century of Liberian Philately,* Bileski, Canada, undated.

Rohrbach, Peter T. and Lowell S. Newman, *American Issue, The U.S. Postage Stamp, 1842-1869,* Smithsonian Institution Press, 1984.

Roscoe, Ernest J., *Stamp Collector,* April 10, 1976.

Roscoe, Ernest J., *Stamp Collector,* Sept. 4, 1976.

Rosenblum, Alec A., *The Stamps of the Commonwealth of Australia,* Acacia Press, Melbourne, 1966.

Rowcroft, William, *Local Post Issues,* published by the author, undated.

Rowe, Kenneth, *The Postal History of the Forwarding Agents,* Hartmann, Louisville, Ky., 1984.

Samuel, R.D., *New Zealand Stamps With Perforated Initials,* Postal History Society of New Zealand, 1968.

Satfield, Garret W., *Canadian Secret Marks Stamps,* published by the author, undated.

Scheele, Carl H., *A Short History of the Mail Service,* Smithsonian University Press, 1970.

Schoen, Robert H and James T. DeVoss, *Counterfeit Kansas-Nebraska Overprints on 1922-34 Issue,* American Philatelic Society, 1973.

Shelley, Ronald G., *The Postal History of the Spanish Civil War 1936-1939,* Shelly, 1967.

Simmons, David J., *Basic Israel Philately,* Society of Israel Philatelists.

Simpson, R.L., *Pitcairn Islands: The Stamps and Postal History,* published by the author, Manly, NSW, Australia, 1972.

Sloat, Ralph L., *Farley's Follies,* Bureau Issues Association, 1979.

Smith, Stephen H., "Rocket Mail Catalogue," *Billig's Philatelic Handbooks, Volume 23,* Fritz Billig, Jamaica, N.Y. 1956.

Staff, Frank, *The Transatlantic Mail,* Harrap, London, 1956.

Stern, Edward, *History of the "Free Franking" of Mail in the United States,* Lindquist, New York, 1936.

Stone, Michael, "Remember the DO-X," *The Airpost Journal,* August, 1971.

Stone, Robert G., *A Key to the Lozenge Obliterators of French Colonies 1860-1892,* The France and Colonies Philatelic Society, New York, 1977.

Stone, Robert G., *French Colonies: The General Issues,* Collectors Club, New York, 1961.

Summerfield, Arthur E., *U.S. Mail: The Story of the United States Postal Service,* Holt, Rinehart, and Winston, New York, 1960.

Taylor, Morris F., *First Mail West,* University of New Mexico Press, Albuquerque, 1971.

ter Braake, Alex L., *Texas: The Drama of Its Postal Past,* American Philatelic Society, 1970.

The Stanley Gibbons Centenary 1856-1956, Stanley Gibbons Ltd., London, 1956.

Thorp, Prescott Holden, *Thorp-Bartels Catalogue of the Stamped Envelopes and Wrappers of the United States,* Prescott Holden Thorpe, Netcong, N.J., 1954.

Traanberg, J.P. and Philip Cockrill, *Netherlands and Colonies: Maritime and Ship Cancelations — 1793-1939,* Cockrill, England.

Tranmer, Keith, *Austrian Post Offices Abroad, Part Eight,* published by author, 1976.

Tranmer, Keith, *The Postal History of Austria, 1938-1946,* published by the author, 1972.

Tyler, Dr. Varro E., *Philatelic Forgers: Their Lives and Works,* Robson Lowe, London, 1976.

Tyrrell, M. William, *The Universal Postal Union: Members and Stamps,* Van Dahl Publications, 1974.

United States Bureau Precancels, Fifth Edition, George Klein, Vincennes, Ind., 1981.

Vallancey, F. Hugh, *British Postmarks,* Vallancey Press, London, 1935.

Van Dam, Theo., *A Postal History of Spain, Collectors Club Handbook #24,* Collectors Club, New York, 1972.

Van Handel, Ray, *Bohemia, Moravia, and Slovakia,* Czechoslovak Philatelic Society, 1958.

Van Vlissingen, Arthur and Morrison Waud, *New York Foreign Mail Cancellations, 1870-76,* Collectors Club of Chicago, 1968.

Velek, John, *First Issue of Czechoslovakia: The Hradcany,* Billig, undated.

Wang, Shih-ying, *Postal Service Today,* Taiwan, May, 1980.

Ward, W., *The Postage Stamps of France, 1840-1925,* Harris Publications, London, 1926.

Warren, Brian and Edward Fitzgerald, *The Gerl Definitives,* Ian Whyte, Dublin, 1978.

Waterfall, Arnold C., *The Postal History of Tibet,* 1981 edition, Robson Lowe, London, 1981.

Watson, James, *Stamps and Aircraft,* Faber and Faber, London, 1961.

Wells Fargo: A Brief History, The History Dept., Wells Fargo Bank, San Francisco, 1976.

Wierenga, Theron, *United States Incoming Steamship Mail, 1847-1875,* published by the author, Muskegon, Mich., 1983.

Williams, L.N. and M., *Fundamentals of Philately,* American Philatelic Society, 1971.

Williams, L.N. and M., *The Postage Stamp: Its History and Recognition,* Pelican Books, London, 1956.

Williams, L.N., *Gibbons Stamp Monthly,* August, 1978.

Williams, L.N., *Scott's Monthly Journal,* January 1981.

Williams, L.N. and M., *Stamps of Fame,* Blandford Press, London, 1949.

Williams, L.N., "The Official Issues of Great Britain," *Stamp Collector,* April 23, 1984.

Wilson, H.S., *T.P.O., A History of the Travelling Post Offices of Great Britain,* Railway Philatelic Group, England, 1971.

Wiltsee, Ernest A., *The Pioneer Miner and The Pack Mule Express,* California Historical Society, 1931, Quarterman Publications, Lawrence, Mass., 1976.

Wolfe, Fred S., *Berlin: Its Fate and Mission,* American Philatelic Society, 1974.

Wolfe, Fred S., *Germany's Post-War Local Post Issues: 1945-48,* APS, 1964.

Wood, Kenneth A., *This is Philately,* Van Dahl Publications, 1982.

Wood, Kenneth A., *Where in the World?* Van Dahl Publications, 1983.

World Air Posts, Francis J. Field, England, 1948.

Wowern, Eric V., *Faroe Islands: Postage Stamps and Postmarks,* GF Frimaerker, Denmark, 1984.

Wrigley, Roy, *The Catalogue and Guidebook of Canadian Official Stamps,* Canadian Wholesale Supply, Paris, Ont., Canada, 1977.

Zinsmeister, Marian Carne, *Liechtenstein Stamps and Their Background, 1912-1973,* Society of Philatelic Americans, 1975.

Zinsmeister, Marian Carne, *Switzerland 1850-1958,* Society of Philatelic Americans, 1959.

Zinsmeister, Marian Carne, *The Stamps of Austria 1850-1957,* Van Dahl Publications Inc., 1958.

Zirkle, Helen K., *The Postage Stamps and Commemorative Cancellations of Manchoukuo,* The Collectors Club, New York, 1964.

Catalogs

American Air Mail Catalogue of Air Letter Sheets, 1953 Edition, American Air Mail Society.

American Air Mail Catalogue, Fifth Edition, The American Air Mail Society, Washington, D.C.

American Stampless Cover Catalog, E.N. Sampson, Van Dahl Publications Inc., 1971.

Australian Commonwealth Specialists Catalog, current edition, Hawthorn Press, Melbourne.

Billig's Specialized Postage Stamp Catalogue of Austria, Billig Stamp Co., New York, 1942.

Catalogue of British Local Stamps, Rosen, B.L.S.C. Publishing Co., London, England, undated.

Channel Islands Stamps and Postal History, Stanley Gibbons Publications Ltd., London, England, 1979.

Dworak Specialized Catalog of U.S. and Canadian Air Mail Covers, 1931, The Gossip Printery, Holton, Kansas.

France Catalogue, Pierre de Brimont, Barclay Press, Montreal, Canada, 1946.

Jhingan, Madhukar, *Post Card Catalogue: India and Indian States, 1879-1979,* We Philatelists, Delhi, India, 1979.

Morgan, Ian C., ***The Specialized Catalogue of Canadian Airmail Stamps, 1934-35,*** The Collector's Magazine, Quebec, Canada.

Mussons Airmail Catalog, 1946, Europe, Musson & Co., London.

Sanabria, ***The World Airmail Catalogue,*** Nicholas Sanabria Co., Ridgefield, Conn., 1966.

Switzerland, Stamp Catalogue of, current edition, The Amateur Collector, London.

United States Postal Card Catalog, 1970, United Postal Stationery Society.

Plus current editions of catalogs published by Gibbons, Michel, Minkus, Scott, Yvert, and Zumstein.

Index

Albania: June 16, 1913; May 1917; March 1, 1922; May 30, 1925; April 12, 1939; Dec. 10, 1940; Dec. 15, 1950.

Album, stamp: 1862.

Alderney: Aug. 23, 1823; Oct. 5, 1919; June 14, 1983.

Alert: April 1950.

Alexandria: 1820; 1830; Jan. 8, 1835; 1842; 1899.

Alexandria Blue Boy: Nov. 25, 1846; May 8, 1981.

Alexandrie: See Alexandria.

Alexandroupolis: See Dedeagh.

Algeria: Oct. 1, 1907; April 22, 1922; 1924; June 20, 1946; July 2, 1962; May 24, 1963.

Allahabad flight: Feb. 18, 1911.

Allan, Ralph: 1720.

Allenstein: April 12, 1920.

Alsace and Lorraine: September 1870; Aug. 15, 1940.

Alwar, Indian Feudatory State of: 1877.

American Air Mail Society: 1923; October 1926.

American Bank Note Company: May 1, 1858; Feb. 4, 1879; July 2, 1894.

American Bank Note Company of Canada: Nov. 30, 1922.

American colonies: 1590; Nov. 5, 1639; 1660; 1661; Jan. 1, 1673; 1683; 1684; Nov. 23, 1685; July 1690; Feb. 17, 1692; April 4, 1692; Nov. 11, 1692; May 1, 1693; June 5, 1693; 1707; 1709; June 1, 1711; 1721; 1730; 1737; 1742; Aug. 10, 1753; May 1, 1755; Nov. 15, 1755; February 1756; Jan. 1, 1757; 1758; 1761; August 1763; Jan. 16, 1764; Dec. 19, 1764; January 1765; Oct. 10, 1765; Nov. 1, 1765; Sept. 7, 1768; November 1772; Jan. 31, 1774; July 2, 1774; March 1775; May 29, 1775; July 26, 1775; Sept. 30, 1775; Nov. 13, 1775; Dec. 25, 1775; Jan. 9, 1776; Aug. 30, 1776; Nov. 7, 1776; Oct. 17, 1777; July 9, 1778; April 16, 1779; Dec. 28, 1779; 1780; May 5, 1780; Dec. 12, 1780; Feb. 24, 1781; Jan. 28, 1782; Oct. 18, 1782; Sept. 3, 1783. See American General Post Office, state headings, and "US" headings.

American Express Airletter Mail Express service: Feb. 15, 1982.

American First Day Cover Society: 1955.

American General Post Office: Oct. 18, 1782; April 5, 1788; July 3, 1788; Aug. 29, 1788; Sept. 22, 1789; Sept. 26, 1789; Feb. 20, 1792; June 1, 1792; May 8, 1794; 1800; January 1803. See American colonies and various listings under US headings.

American Philatelic Association: See American Philatelic Society.

American Philatelic Society: Sept. 13, 1886.

American Philatelist, The: Jan. 10, 1887.

American Postage Meter Co.: Oct. 14, 1902; May 9, 1912; March 15, 1920. See Meter, postage; Pitney, Arthur Hill; and Pitney-Bowes Postage Meter Co.

American Revenue Association: 1947.

American Samoa: See Samoa, American.

American Topical Association: 1949.

Amoy (Treaty Port): Aug. 29, 1842; Feb. 5, 1890; June 8, 1895.

Ancachs: April 1884.

Andaman and Nicobar Islands: March 23, 1942.

Andorra (French): 1877; 1887; June 16, 1931; June 16, 1932; Feb. 20, 1950; July 25, 1964.

Andorra (Spanish): 1837; 1877; Jan. 1, 1928; March 28, 1928; Nov. 25, 1929; June 27, 1951.

Anglo-American Occupation zones of Germany: March 19, 1945.

Angola: Jan. 20, 1798; July 1, 1870; July 26, 1938. See Angola, People's Republic of.

Angola, People's Republic of: Nov. 11, 1975; 1977.

Angora (Ankara): Nov. 1920.

Angra: 1892.

Anguilla: May 30, 1967; Sept. 4, 1967.

Anjouan, French colony of: November 1892.

Annam and Tonkin: Jan. 21, 1888.

Annobon: See Eloby, Annobon, and Corisco.

Antigua: August 1862; May 6, 1935.

Antioquia: 1868.

Arbe: Nov. 18, 1920.

Archer, Henry: Jan. 28, 1854.

Arequipa: January 1881.

Argentina: May 1, 1858; Jan. 11, 1862; April 1, 1878; May 1, 1910; Feb. 25, 1928; March 1, 1928; April 1, 1939; Jan. 5, 1944; Nov. 19, 1949.

Arizona, State of: Feb. 14, 1912.

Arizona, Territory of: Feb. 24, 1863.

Arkansas, State of: June 15, 1836; May 6, 1861; June 22, 1868.

Arkansas, Territory of: March 2, 1819.

Armenia, Republic of: May 28, 1918.

Arwad: See Rouad.

Ascension: 1673; March 3, 1867; Nov. 2, 1922; May 10, 1958.

Assyria: 3000 BC.

Auction, stamp: Dec. 29, 1865; May 28, 1870; March 18, 1872.

Austin, Stephen F.: May 18, 1826.

Australia: Jan. 1, 1901; March 1, 1901; July 1902; Oct. 1, 1907; July 1909; Jan. 13, 1911; May 1, 1911; Jan. 1, 1913; July 16, 1914; Nov. 12, 1919; May 20, 1929; April 23, 1931; May 31, 1931; Dec. 1, 1931; March 14, 1932; Nov. 6, 1945; Oct. 11, 1946; May 8, 1947; Nov. 14, 1948; Feb. 14, 1966; Feb. 22, 1984. See New South Wales; Queensland; South Australia; Tasmania; Victoria; Western Australia; Melbourne.

Australian Antarctic Territory: March 27, 1957.

Australian colonies: Oct. 10, 1843. See also under individual colony names.

Austria: April 1, 1772; Nov. 18, 1817; 1850; June 1, 1850; Jan. 1, 1851; March 1, 1853; June 1, 1867; Oct. 1, 1869; Oct. 4, 1914; Oct. 6, 1914; April 28, 1915; March 6, 1916; March 1, 1917; Nov. 1, 1917; March 20, 1918; March 30, 1918; Feb. 2, 1931; June 23, 1933; July 25, 1936; March 13, 1938; April 4, 1938; Oct. 31, 1938; Nov. 24, 1945; March 10, 1950; Jan. 1, 1966; Jan. 14, 1966; Feb. 1, 1983.

Austrian Italy: See Lombardy-Venetia.

Austrian PO in Crete: March 1903.

Austrian PO in Cyprus: June 1, 1864.

Austrian POs in Turkish Empire: June 1867.

Austro-German Postal Union: 1850; Jan. 1, 1852.

Autogiro mail: May 1934; July 6, 1939.

Automatic mail handling: 1934.

Aviation meets and early mail flights: Feb. 6, 1910; Aug. 6, 1910; Aug. 14, 1910; Sept. 23, 1910; Feb. 18, 1911; Sept. 2, 1911; Sept. 9, 1911; Sept. 26, 1911; Oct. 2, 1911; Oct. 13, 1911; Oct. 17, 1911; Dec. 27, 1911; Feb. 18, 1912; May 25, 1912; June 1912; June 1, 1912; June 2, 1912; July 1912; Aug. 25, 1912; Feb. 11, 1913; March 9, 1913; March 30, 1913; April 13, 1913; May 1913; Jan. 4, 1914; Feb. 17, 1914; Feb. 24, 1914; April 1, 1914; July 16, 1914; Oct. 6, 1914; May 1917; May 22, 1917; June 28, 1917; July 6, 1917; March 20, 1918; May 15, 1918; June 24, 1918; July 9, 1918; Aug. 24, 1918; Aug. 26, 1918; Dec. 13, 1918; Jan. 30, 1919; Feb. 17, 1919; March 1, 1919; March 3, 1919; April 4, 1919; April 12, 1919; May 14, 1919; May 18, 1919; May 18, 1919; June 9, 1919; June 14, 1919; July 2, 1919; July 3, 1919;

July 9, 1919; July 17, 1919; Aug. 7, 1919; Aug. 25, 1919; September 1919; Oct. 5, 1919; Nov. 12, 1919; Dec. 16, 1919. For subsequent air mail events see under country and individual headings. See also US Pioneer flights.

Ayacucho: February 1881.

Azerbaijan: May 27, 1918.

Azerbaijan, Iranian province of: May 1945.

Azores: 1868; Jan. 2, 1980.

Bache, Richard: July 26, 1775; Nov. 7, 1776; Jan. 28, 1782.

Baden: May 1, 1851; Jan. 1, 1872.

Baghdad, British Occupation of: September 1917.

Baghdad-Egypt air mail route inaugurated: April 5, 1926.

Bahamas: June 10, 1859; Jan. 1, 1916; May 18, 1917; Feb. 21, 1918; Jan. 30, 1919; Aug. 16, 1939; May 25, 1967; 1974.

Bahawalpur: Aug. 15, 1947; April 1, 1948.

Bahrain: Aug. 10, 1933; April 1, 1948; July 1, 1960; Jan. 21, 1966; 1973.

Bailar, Benjamin Franklin, US PMG: Feb. 15, 1975.

Balbo, General Italo: Dec. 17, 1930; July 1, 1933; July 23, 1933; July 24, 1933; Aug. 8, 1933.

Balearic Islands: April 4, 1920.

Balloon mail: Jan. 9, 1793; May 1793; June 1793; June 2, 1808; July 2, 1808; Aug. 4, 1808; Aug. 17, 1859; Sept. 5, 1870; Sept. 23, 1870; Nov. 24, 1870; June 18, 1877; Oct. 19, 1897; Aug. 9, 1902; Sept. 20, 1902; Sept. 5, 1903; July 12, 1905; Oct. 14, 1907.

Bamra, Indian Feudatory State of: 1888.

Bangkok: April 27, 1882; July 1, 1885; Feb. 17, 1919.

Bangladesh: July 29, 1971; Feb. 7, 1973.

Baptista, Johann: 1520.

Barbados: April 15, 1852; Jan. 25, 1907; Nov. 11, 1967.

Barbuda: July 13, 1922; Nov. 19, 1968.

Barcelona: 1160; July 20, 1444; April 4, 1920.

Barnard, Joseph: Sept. 21, 1847.

Barr, Desire Albert: December 1842.

Barr, Jean Jacques: December 1842.

Barry, William T., US PMG: April 6, 1829.

Barwani, Indian Feudatory State of: 1921.

Basel: 1845; July 1, 1845.

Basutoland, Protectorate of: Dec. 1, 1933.

Batum: April 4, 1919.

Bavaria: Nov. 1, 1849; June 1, 1905; March 31, 1914.

BCOF Japan: Oct. 11, 1946; May 8, 1947.

Beachey, Lincoln: Oct. 21, 1911.

Beaver: April 23, 1851.

Bechuanaland, Protectorate of: Aug. 7, 1888.

Belgian Congo: Nov. 15, 1908; Jan. 1, 1909; April 1, 1920; July 1, 1920; June 6, 1960.

Belgium: July 1, 1849; Jan. 1, 1871; 1882; June 1, 1893; Dec. 2, 1893; June 1, 1910; 1913; May 1913; March 25, 1929; April 30, 1930; June 15, 1946; Nov. 16, 1981.

Belize: June 1, 1973; June 11, 1973; Sept. 21, 1981. See British Honduras.

Benadir: See Italian Somaliland.

Benin: 1892.

Benin, People's Republic of: Nov. 30, 1975. See Dahomey.

Bequia: Feb. 22, 1984.

Bergedorf: Nov. 1, 1861; Aug. 8, 1867; Jan. 1, 1868.

Berlin: January 1827; November 1865; June 5, 1945; Oct. 24, 1945; Aug. 17, 1948; Sept. 1, 1948; Jan. 20, 1950.

Berlin-New York flight: Aug. 10, 1938.

Bermuda: Jan. 31, 1784; 1848; Sept. 25, 1865; April 1, 1877; Feb. 21, 1925; April 21, 1925; April 23, 1925; June 16, 1937; March 6, 1938; March 14, 1941; Sept. 18, 1944; May 1, 1948.

Berne, Postal Congress of: Sept. 15, 1874.

Bhopal, Indian Feudatory State of: 1876.

Bhor, Indian Feudatory State of: 1879.

Bhutan: May 16, 1962; March 7, 1969.

Biafra: Feb. 5, 1968; Jan. 15, 1970.

Bider, Oscar: March 9, 1913; March 30, 1913.

Bijawar, Indian Feudatory State of: July 1, 1935.

Biscay: July 1, 1873.

Bishop, Col. Henry, named PMG of England: June 1660; Aug. 12, 1661.

Bishop Mark: Aug. 12, 1661; Aug. 13, 1670; 1758.

Bissell, Wilson S., US PMG: March 7, 1893.

Black Honduras: May 1, 1925.

Black Jack: July 1, 1863.

Black Swan: Aug. 1, 1854.

Black Swan invert: Aug. 1, 1854.

Blair, Montgomery W., PMG: May 10, 1813; March 9, 1861; May 28, 1861; July 12, 1861; Aug. 26, 1861; Aug. 4, 1862; May 11, 1863; Oct. 1, 1864; July 23, 1883.

Blanchard, Jean-Pierre: Jan. 9, 1793.

Blizzard mail: See US blizzard mail.

Blount, Winton M., US PMG: Jan. 22, 1969.

Blue Alexandria: Nov. 25, 1846; May 8, 1981.

Blue Boy: Nov. 25, 1846; May 8, 1981.

Bluenose stamp: Jan. 6, 1929.

"B.M.A./ERITREA": June 1948.

"BMA/MALAYA" on Straits Settlements stamps: 1945.

"B.M.A./ SOMALIA": May 27, 1948.

"B.M.A./TRIPOLITANIA": July 1, 1948.

Bohemia and Moravia: July 15, 1939.

boite mobile: See Moveable boxes.

Bolger, William F., US PMG: March 1, 1978.

Bolivar: 1863.

Bolivia: March 18, 1863; 1866; April 1, 1886; April 13, 1913; Feb. 25, 1928.

Booklet, stamp: See Stamp booklet, US stamp booklet.

Booty, Frederick: April 1862.

Bophuthatswana: Dec. 6, 1977.

Bordeaux Issue of France: Nov. 13, 1870.

Bosnia and Herzegovina: July 1, 1879.

Botswana: Sept. 30, 1966; Jan. 12, 1968.

Bottle post office: 1673.

Boules de Moulins: Feb. 22, 1972.

Bourkina Fasso: Aug. 7, 1984; June 30, 1985. See Upper Volta.

Bouvet Island: Feb. 28, 1934.

Bowes, Walter H.: March 15, 1920. See Meter, postage; Pitney-Bowes Postage Meter Co.

Boyaca, Department of Colombia: 1899.

Brazil: Jan. 20, 1798; Nov. 29, 1842; Aug. 1, 1843; July 1, 1877; Feb. 1, 1889; Nov. 15, 1906; Jan. 14, 1925; Dec. 28, 1927; Feb. 25, 1928; March 21, 1930; Oct. 1, 1933; Sept. 16, 1934; Nov. 15, 1947; Sept. 15, 1979; June 10, 1981.

Bremen, catapult mail from: July 22, 1929.

Bremen, Free City of: 1150; 1855; Jan. 1, 1868.

Brewster, William: 1590.

Britannia, British steamship: July 4, 1840.

British and North American Royal Mail Steam Packet Company: See Cunard Line.

British Antarctic Territory: Feb. 1, 1963.

British Bechuanaland: Sept. 30, 1885; December 1885;

Aug. 7, 1888; Sept. 11, 1890; April 1, 1893; April 9, 1900.

British Central Africa: April 1891; July 6, 1907.

British Central African Protectorate: Feb. 22, 1893; July 6, 1907. See Nyasaland Protectorate.

British Columbia: 1847; July 1858; May 4, 1859; July 30, 1860; June 20, 1864; Oct. 26, 1864; Nov. 1, 1865; Nov. 19, 1866; July 1, 1870; July 20, 1871; July 3, 1886.

British Columbia and Vancouver Island: July 1858; July 30, 1860; July 20, 1864; Oct. 26, 1864; Nov. 19, 1866; July 20, 1871.

British Consular Mail: See Madagascar.

British East Africa: May 1890.

British Forces in Egypt, seals of: Nov. 1, 1932.

British Guiana: July 1, 1850; Aug. 5, 1851; 1856; April 5, 1922; May 12, 1937; Sept. 18, 1944; Dec. 20, 1948; Feb. 16, 1951; June 2, 1953; April 5, 1980. See Guyana.

British Guiana 1c Magenta: 1856; April 5, 1922; April 5, 1980.

British Honduras: Oct. 31, 1809; 1858; April 1, 1860; January 1866; April 1, 1879; Jan. 1, 1888; June 1, 1973. See Belize.

British Indian Ocean Territory: Jan 17, 1968; August 1979.

British Levant: Aug. 1, 1885; Aug. 15, 1905; Feb. 28, 1916.

British New Guinea: Sept. 4, 1888; July 2, 1892; July 1, 1901; Nov. 8, 1906. See Papua.

British Postal Agencies, Eastern Arabia: April 1, 1948.

British postal reform royal assent: Aug. 17, 1839.

British Post Office Act legalized penny postal rate in London and established boundaries: June 1, 1711.

British Post Office bought out postal service in American Colonies: 1707.

British Post Office Charter: 1660.

British Post Office parcel service: Aug. 1, 1883.

British post offices in China: Jan. 1, 1917.

British post offices in the Turkish Empire: Aug. 15, 1905; Feb. 28, 1916; August 1921.

British Solomon Islands Protectorate: Feb. 14, 1907; September 1907; October 1911. See Solomon Islands.

British Somaliland: June 1, 1903; July 1, 1941.

British South Africa Company: Jan. 2, 1892.

British stamps first issued perforated: Jan. 28, 1854.

British stamps first issued: Jan. 28, 1854.

British Virgin Islands: 1866; April 2, 1951.

Brown, Aaron V., US PMG: March 7, 1857.

Brown, Walter F., US PMG: March 6, 1929.

Brunei: July 1895; Oct. 11, 1906; Jan. 1, 1916; April 6, 1931.

Brunswick, German State of: 1852; Jan. 1, 1868.

Brunswick Star cancel: September 1857; Feb. 3, 1863.

Bucco Reef: Aug. 31, 1962.

Buenos Aires, city of: Jan. 2, 1929.

Buenos Aires, province of Argentina: April 29, 1858.

Buffalo balloon: June 18, 1877.

BUITEN BEZIT: June 1908.

Bulgaria: June 1, 1879; July 1, 1879; December 1919; June 20, 1920; July 1, 1941; June 1, 1942.

Bundi, Indian Feudatory State of: May 1894.

Bureau of Engraving and Printing: July 11, 1862; Aug. 29, 1862; January 1869; July 1, 1880; July 2, 1894; July 18, 1894.

Burleson, Albert S., US PMG: March 5, 1913.

Burlington Northern Airletter service: Feb. 15, 1982.

Burma: Nov. 14, 1924; April 1, 1937; Nov. 15, 1938; May 1942; Jan. 6, 1948; Oct. 4. 1949.

Burrus, Maurice: April 5, 1922.

Burundi, Kingdom of: July 1, 1962; Feb. 15, 1963; July 2, 1964; Nov. 15, 1965; May 9, 1969.

Bushe, Carle: 1884.

Bushire: Aug. 15, 1915; Oct. 16, 1915.

Bussahir (Bashahr), Indian Feudatory State of: June 20, 1895.

Butchers' Post: See Metzger Post.

Butterfield Overland Mail: 1857; Sept. 16, 1857; Sept. 15, 1858; December 1858; March 2, 1861; July 1, 1861; Sept. 16, 1875.

Byelorussian SSR: May 13, 1947.

By letter: 1720.

By post: 1720.

Byrd, Richard E.: Nov. 28, 1929.

Cabinda: See Portuguese Congo.

Caicos Islands: 1981.

Cairo: 1842.

California: Oct. 1, 1848; Feb. 28, 1849.

California: Nov. 1, 1848; Feb. 28, 1849; Sept. 9, 1850; May 1, 1851; July 30, 1851; July 1858; Oct. 27, 1858.

Cambodia, Kingdom of: Dec. 21, 1951; November 1951; Sept. 25, 1955; April 17, 1975.

"Camel Postman" design of Sudan: March 1, 1898; Jan. 9, 1954.

Cameroon: July 1915; Jan. 1, 1960; July 26, 1960; July 1, 1963.

Cameroons, Southern: Oct. 1, 1960.

Cameroun: See Cameroon.

Campbell, James, US PMG: March 8, 1853.

Campeche, Mexico: 1875.

Campione d'Italia: May 20, 1944; June 23, 1944; Sept. 7, 1944.

Canada: 1705; 1734; April 27, 1754; April 28, 1755; August 1763; 1764; Dec. 15, 1768; November 1772; Jan. 31, 1774; Nov. 13, 1775; Jan. 11, 1784; July 7, 1784; 1787; June 1, 1792; 1801; 1807; Aug. 18, 1833; December 1840; May 1841; Dec. 1, 1843; April 2, 1844; 1847; Nov. 16, 1847; May 14, 1849; May 25, 1849; April 6, 1851; April 7, 1851; April 23, 1851; June 14, 1851; August 1853; Feb. 28, 1855; May 31, 1855; Oct. 1, 1856; July 1858; Jan. 1, 1859; May 4, 1859; July 1, 1859; March 16, 1860; Nov. 19, 1866; July 1, 1867; April 1, 1868; Feb. 1, 1869; Nov. 1, 1870; May 1, 1871; July 20, 1871; July 1, 1873; October 1874; Oct. 15, 1875; Nov. 15, 1875; Oct. 6, 1877; July 1, 1878; July 4, 1886; June 14, 1895; June 19, 1897; June 28, 1898; July 1, 1898; Dec. 7, 1898; Dec. 25, 1898; Dec. 29, 1898; Jan. 5, 1899; November 1912; Jan. 1, 1916; 1917; June 24, 1918; July 9, 1918; Aug. 26, 1918; March 3, 1919; May 18, 1919; Aug. 7, 1919; Aug. 25, 1919; Oct. 7, 1920; Jan. 2, 1921; Nov. 30, 1922; May 1923; July 1923; Aug. 7, 1923; Sept. 29, 1923; Sept. 21, 1924; March 27, 1926; Oct. 4, 1927; Sept. 21, 1928; Jan. 6, 1929; June 1, 1935; July 1939; Feb. 1, 1940; May 1, 1942; June 15, 1942; May 1, 1948; April 1, 1949; July 13, 1949; September 1949; April 1950; April 18, 1950; Sept. 6, 1950; Sept. 24, 1951; July 25, 1952; June 8, 1955; 1959; Sept. 9, 1959; Jan. 13, 1962; Jan. 3, 1964; Oct. 14, 1964; April 1, 1971; June 10, 1978; Dec. 29, 1981; Nov. 21, 1983; Nov. 5, 1984; March 1, 1985. See British Columbia and Vancouver Island; British Columbia; New Brunswick; Newfoundland; Nova Scotia; Prince Edward Island; Stamp, Official; plus other Canadian headings: Fleming, Sir Sandford.

Canadian "A" stamp: Dec. 29, 1981.

Canadian Bank Note Co.: Nov. 30, 1922.

Canadian *Bluenose* stamp: Jan. 6, 1929.

Canadian Pacific Airlines Sydney-Amsterdam Polar flight: June 8, 1955.

Canadian Seaway Invert: Sept. 9, 1959.

Canadian special delivery service: July 1, 1898.

Canadian "Stick'n Tick" labels: Nov. 21, 1983; Nov. 5, 1984.

Canal Zone: See US Canal Zone.

Cancelation, flag: Oct. 31, 1894; Sept. 30, 1940; May 24, 1941.

Cancelation, Maltese Cross: May 6, 1840.

Cancelation squared circle: September 1879.

Canceler, duplex: 1850; June 1853.

Canceling machine: Oct. 12, 1827; September 1857; April 1869; March 6, 1875; Jan. 6, 1876; March 28, 1876; March 1888; Jan. 2, 1894; Oct. 31, 1894; June 30, 1895; July 19, 1899; Dec. 30, 1899; Jan. 24, 1912; Sept. 30, 1940; May 24, 1941.

Canton Island: July 12, 1940; July 14, 1940.

Canton (Treaty Port): Aug. 29, 1842.

Cape Breton Island: 1801.

Cape Juby: 1916; June 1, 1938.

Cape of Good Hope: 1619; Dec. 28, 1791; 1798; June 1803; Sept. 1, 1853; October 1871; April 1, 1893; Aug. 10, 1900; May 31, 1910.

Cape Verde Islands: Jan. 1, 1877; July 26, 1938; Dec. 19, 1975; 1976.

Cappadocia: 3000 BC.

Carlin, Paul N., US PMG: Jan. 1, 1985.

Carlist stamps (Spain): July 1, 1873; April 15, 1874; September 1874.

Caroline Islands: 1899.

Carpatho-Ukraine: March 15, 1939.

Casablanca: May 11, 1923.

Catalog, stamp: Dec. 21, 1861; April 1862; May 1862; November 1865.

Catalonia: April 15, 1874.

Catapult air mail: Aug. 13, 1928; July 20, 1929; July 22, 1929; Sept. 15, 1930; Oct. 2, 1935; Oct. 9, 1935.

Cauca, Colombian Department of: 1879.

Cavalla: 1893; 1913.

Cavallini (Little Horseman): Nov. 17, 1818.

Cayman Islands: April 1889; November 1900; Feb. 12, 1940.

Censorship of AEF mail: July 13, 1917; July 11, 1919.

Central African Republic: Dec. 1, 1959; Sept. 3, 1960; June 28, 1961; Jan. 1, 1962; April 7, 1962; March 1977.

Central Lithuania: Oct. 20, 1920.

Central Overland California and Pike's Peak Express: February 1860; May 11, 1860.

Certified Mail in US: See US Certified Mail inaugurated.

Ceylon: April 1, 1857; 1877; Sept. 9, 1906; Nov. 1, 1944; July 13, 1949; May 10, 1956; May 22, 1972. See Sri Lanka.

Chachapoyas: April 1884.

Chad: 1922; Nov. 28, 1959; Dec. 15, 1960; Jan. 11, 1961; June 23, 1961; April 7, 1962; March 9, 1964.

Chala: April 1884.

Chalmers, James: April 5, 1838.

Chalon portrait: June 14, 1851.

Chamba, Indian Convention State of: 1886.

Chamberlin, Clarence D.: July 31, 1927.

Chandhaburi: Feb. 17, 1919.

Chaplin, William: 1838.

Charkhari, Indian Feudatory State of: 1894.

Charles I of England limits postal service to royal and government business: July 1637.

Chavez, Jorge: Sept. 23, 1910.

Chefoo (Treaty Port): Aug. 29, 1842; Oct. 6, 1893.

Cherifien Administration of Posts: See Morocco, French.

Chiapas, Mexican State of: 1867.

Chichester, Francis C.: July 13, 1931; Aug. 3, 1931.

Chiclayo: April 1884.

Chihuahua, Mexican State of: 1872.

Chile: July 1, 1853; April 1, 1881; Jan. 1, 1919; Feb. 25, 1928; March 1, 1940; Jan. 19, 1951; April 29, 1961.

China: 4000 BC; 1122 BC; 551 BC; 221 BC; 206 BC; 105 BC; AD 220; 1402; 1689.

China, British post offices in: See British Post Offices in China.

China, People's Republic of: Oct. 8, 1949; May 1, 1951; Aug. 1, 1953.

China, Republic of (now Taiwan): 1912; Dec. 14, 1912; March 1, 1914; May 7, 1920; Dec. 1, 1920; July 1, 1921; Jan. 1, 1950; Sept. 26, 1950.

China, Treaty Ports in: Aug. 29, 1842.

Chinese Government Post: Jan. 2, 1897; Feb. 2, 1897. See Shanghai.

Chinese Imperial Maritime Customs Post: 1876; October 1878.

Chinkiang: Aug. 6, 1894.

Chios: May 1913.

Christmas Day delivery: Dec. 17, 1902.

Christmas Island (Indian Ocean): Oct. 15, 1958.

Christmas Island (Pacific Ocean): July 1916; Feb. 14, 1939; Sept. 15, 1962.

Christmas seals: 1904; Dec. 7, 1907.

Chungking: Nov. 1, 1893.

Cilicia: March 4, 1919; July 15, 1920.

Ciskei: 1981.

Citizen's Stamp Advisory Committee: See US Citizen's Stamp Advisory Committee.

City Despatch Post: See US, City Despatch Post.

Clapper Post: April 1, 1772.

Clay tablet letters: 3000 BC.

Coamo, Puerto Rico: Aug. 14, 1898.

Cochin, Indian Feudatory State of: April 1, 1892.

Cocos (Keeling) Islands: June 11, 1963.

Coil stamps: See Stamp, coil.

Colding, Johann Peter: June 2, 1808; July 2, 1808; Aug. 4, 1808.

Colding's Balloon Mail: June 2, 1808; July 2, 1808; Aug. 4, 1808.

Collamer, Jacob, US PMG: March 8, 1849.

Collectors Club (of New York): Oct.5, 1896.

Collection and Distribution Wagon Service: See US Collection and Distribution Wagon Service.

Cologne: March 1, 1919.

Colombia, Republic of: 1886; June 18, 1919; March 6, 1921; May 27, 1935; July 12, 1950; July 18, 1950; May 19, 1958; April 26, 1966.

Colombia, United States of: 1862; July 1, 1881; Aug. 4, 1886.

Colorado, State of: Aug. 1, 1876.

Colorado, Territory of: Feb. 28, 1861.

Columbian issue: Jan. 2, 1893.

Comoro Islands: May 15, 1950; 1976; July 24, 1978. See also Grand Comoro.

Concord coach: 1858.

Confederate States of America: Feb. 9, 1861; Feb. 21, 1861; May 28, 1861; June 1, 1861; July 12, 1861; Aug. 26, 1861; Oct. 16, 1861; Jan. 1, 1862; Oct. 20, 1863; June 1, 1864. See Alabama, Arkansas, Florida, Georgia, Louisiana, Mississippi, North Carolina, South Carolina, Tennessee, Texas, Virginia.

Confederation Post Office: July 9, 1778; 1780.
Confucius: 551 BC.
Congo Democratic Republic: June 6, 1960; July 1, 1960; March 21, 1963. See Zaire, Republic of.
Congo Free State: Jan. 1, 1886; Nov. 15, 1908.
Congo Republic: Nov. 28, 1959; July 5, 1961; Jan. 15, 1962.
Connecticut: May 10, 1694; Jan. 9, 1788.
Connell, Charles: Nov. 1, 1858; May 9, 1860.
Continental Bank Note Company: May 1, 1873; Feb. 4, 1879.
Continental Congress: Aug. 30, 1776; Oct. 17, 1777; April 16, 1779; Dec. 28, 1779; May 5, 1780; Dec. 12, 1780; Feb. 24, 1781; Oct. 18, 1782.
Continental Post Office: July 26, 1775; Sept. 30, 1775; Jan. 9, 1776; Oct. 17, 1777.
Cook Islands: April 19, 1892; April 1919; Aug. 23, 1920; March 16, 1932; Sept. 16, 1965; April 22, 1966; Feb. 12, 1968; March 17, 1975; Jan. 15, 1980. See Aitutaki, Penrhyn.
Corbould, Henry: June 1839.
Cordoba, province of Argentina: Oct. 28, 1858.
Corfu: Sept. 30, 1923; June 5, 1941.
Corisco: See Eloby, Annobon, and Corisco.
Coronation Aerial Post: Sept. 9, 1911; Sept. 26, 1911.
Coronation balloon flight: Aug. 9, 1902.
Coronation flight: May 8, 1937.
Correos: 1263.
Corrientes, province of Argentina: Aug. 21, 1856.
Corrieri Bergamaschie: 1290.
Cortelyou, George B., US PMG: March 7, 1905.
Costa Rica: April 1863; Jan. 1, 1883; April 15, 1921; June 4, 1926; May 20, 1970; March 20, 1972.
Cotton Reels: July 1, 1850.
Council of Europe: Jan. 14, 1958.
Courland: Oct. 10, 1919.
Court of International Justice: Jan. 27, 1934.
Courvoisier SA, Helio: December 1880.
Cracow: March 20, 1918.
Creswell, John A.J., US PMG: March 6, 1869.
Crete: Nov. 25, 1898; May 1899; 1900; March 1, 1900.
Croatia: April 12, 1941; May 10, 1941; Oct. 4, 1942.
Cromwell, Oliver: 1657.
Cross post: 1720.
Cross post letter: 1720.
Cuautla, Mexican State of Morelos: 1867.
Cuba: April 1855; Dec. 19, 1898; Jan. 1, 1899; Sept. 30, 1902; Oct. 4, 1902; Feb. 24, 1914; Nov. 1, 1927; Feb. 6, 1928; Feb. 21, 1928; May 19, 1935; Nov. 23, 1938; Oct. 15, 1939; July 8, 1963.
Cuernavaca, Mexico: 1867.
Cunard Line: May 16, 1840; July 4, 1840.
Cunard, Samuel: May 4, 1839; July 4, 1840.
Cundinamarca, Colombian State of: 1870.
Curacao: April 26, 1827.
Curacao: 1634; Aug. 27, 1807; Aug. 2, 1808; April 26, 1827; November 1863; May 23, 1873; Aug. 23, 1905; April 8, 1925; Oct. 3, 1927; July 6, 1929; Jan. 19, 1935; June 17, 1938; Dec. 11, 1941. See Netherlands Antilles.
cursus publicus: cAD 100; 1160.
Cuzco: February 1881.
Cypher stamp: Jan. 1, 1701.
Cyprus: June 1, 1864; 1868; July 27, 1878; April 1, 1880; July 1, 1881; Oct. 7, 1946; Nov. 23, 1961; July 20, 1974.
Cyprus, Turkish state in: July 20, 1974.
Cyrenaica: Jan. 16, 1950.
Cyrus of Persia: c559 BC.
Czechoslovakia: Dec. 18, 1918; Dec. 12, 1919; May 18, 1920; Oct. 5, 1920; March 1, 1937.

Dahomey: 1899; March 1, 1960; April 27, 1961. See Benin, People's Republic of.
Dakar: May 11, 1923.
Dakota, North: Nov. 2, 1889.
Dakota, South: Nov. 2, 1889.
Dakota, Territory of: March 2, 1861.
Dale, Louise Boyd: April 28, 1956.
Dalmatia: May 1, 1919.
Danish West Indies: Nov. 10, 1855; March 31, 1917.
Danube Steam Navigation Company: Aug. 16, 1846; April 15, 1866; March 24, 1868.
Danzig: 1920; Sept. 29, 1920.
Das Island: April 1, 1948; December 1960.
Day, J. Edward, US PMG: Jan. 21, 1961; Nov. 16, 1962.
DDR (Deutsche Demokratische Republik): See GDR (German Democratic Republic).
Dedeagach: See Dedeagh.
Dedeagatch: See Dedeagh.
Dedeagatz: See Dedeagh.
Dedeagh: 1893; July 18, 1913.
De La Rue & Co.: March 24, 1793; April 1853; Oct. 14, 1854; July 31, 1855; June 27, 1879; Jan. 9, 1961.
De La Rue, Thomas: See De La Rue & Co.
Delaware, State of: Dec. 7, 1787; Aug. 29, 1788; Oct. 1, 1793.
Demonetization: See US stamps, demonetization of.
Denmark: Dec. 24, 1624; July 16, 1653; Dec. 8, 1685; Sept. 25, 1711; June 2, 1808; July 2, 1808; Aug. 4, 1808; April 1, 1851; April 1, 1871; Sept. 2, 1911; March 31, 1912; Oct. 9, 1949.
Dennison, William, US PMG: Oct. 1, 1864.
De Pinedo, Marquese Francisco: Aug. 19, 1925; Sept. 16, 1925; May 21, 1927; May 23, 1927.
Deseret, unofficial state of: March 5, 1849.
De Sperati, Jean: Oct. 14, 1884; April 27, 1954; April 28, 1957.
De Thuin, Raoul Ch.: December 1966; April 23, 1975.
Detroit: 1803.
Detroit River mail service: July 17, 1895.
Deutschland, **German submarine:** June 23, 1916.
De Villayer, Jean-Jacques Renouard: Aug. 8, 1653.
Dhar, Indian Feudatory State of: 1897.
Dickinson, Don M., US PMG: Jan. 17, 1888.
Diego Suarez: 1890.
Dirigible *Norge:* See *Norge.*
Dirigible R-34: July 2, 1919; July 9, 1919.
Dirigible R-100: July 29, 1930; Aug. 13, 1930.
Dirigibles, US: See USS *Akron,* USS *Los Angeles,* USS *Macon,* and USS *Shenandoah.*
Djibouti: 1894.
Djibouti, Republic of: June 27, 1977; 1979.
Doa (Qatar): April 1, 1948.
Dockwra, William: April 1, 1680; Nov. 23, 1682; May 1690.
Dole, Sanford Ballard: July 4, 1894.
Dollfuss Memorial Issue: July 25, 1936.
Dominica: May 4, 1874; Nov. 3, 1978; 1979.
Dominican Republic: Oct. 19, 1865; Oct. 1, 1880; Feb. 25, 1902; July 14, 1927; Dec. 3, 1927; Feb. 6, 1928; May 31, 1928; December 1930; Dec. 3, 1930; Feb. 1, 1935; Feb. 8, 1957.
Dominion of India: See India.
Donaldson, Jesse M., US PMG: Dec. 16, 1947.
Dongan, New York Governor: 1684.

Doolittle, James, South American flights: Feb. 25, 1928.

Dornier DO-X: Nov. 5, 1930; Jan. 31, 1931; May 1, 1931; May 3, 1931; May 30, 1931; June 4, 1931; June 5, 1931; June 18, 1931; June 19, 1931; June 20, 1931; Aug. 5, 1931; Aug. 6, 1931; Aug. 7, 1931; Aug. 8, 1931; Aug. 18, 1931; Aug. 19, 1931; Aug. 20, 1931; Aug. 21, 1931; Aug. 22, 1931; Aug. 25, 1931; Aug. 26, 1931; Aug. 27, 1931; May 19, 1932; May 20, 1932; May 22, 1932; May 23, 1932; May 24, 1932.

Double-stamp markings: June 1853.

Douglas Fairbanks commemorative stamp: See US, Douglas Fairbanks commemorative stamp.

Downey Head: June 22, 1911.

"D" press: Aug. 13, 1984.

Dubai: April 1, 1948; Jan. 7, 1961; June 15, 1963; Dec. 2, 1971.

Dublin, Ireland, Penny Post established: 1765.

Duck stamp: See US Federal Migratory Waterfowl Hunting stamp.

Duke of York (later King George V): 1893.

Dummer, Edward: Oct. 21, 1702; July 1705; July 20, 1711; April 1713.

Dunkirk (Dunkerque) provisional issue: July 1, 1940.

Duplex postal marking: 1850; June 1853; September 1879.

Dutch East Indies: See Netherlands Indies.

Duttia (Datia), Indian Feudatory State of: 1893.

"E.A.F." on British stamps: Jan. 15, 1943.

East Africa and Uganda: 1903.

East African Common Services Organization: April 15, 1965.

East African Postal Administration: Oct. 21, 1964.

Easter Island: Jan. 19, 1951.

Eastern Arabia: April 1, 1948.

Eastern Karelia: See Karelia.

Eastern Pony Express: See Pony Express, Eastern.

Eastern Rumelia: 1880.

East Germany: See German Democratic Republic.

East India Co.: Oct. 14, 1854; Oct. 11, 1855.

E-COM: See US E-COM.

Ecuador: 1865; July 1, 1880; May 4, 1889; March 6, 1921; Aug. 28, 1928; May 9, 1944; July 15, 1957.

Edinburgh, Duke of: May 19, 1890.

Edward IV of England, post system set up by: 1481.

Edward VII of Great Britain: Jan. 22, 1901; Jan. 1, 1902; May 6, 1910.

Edward VIII of Great Britain: Jan. 20, 1936; Sept. 1, 1936; Sept. 14, 1936; Dec. 10, 1936.

Egypt: 3000 BC; 2000 BC; 1550 BC; 1820; 1830; Jan. 8, 1835; 1842; June 1858; March 5, 1862; 1864; 1865; Jan. 1, 1866; Jan. 1, 1893; Feb. 6, 1910; Jan. 4, 1914; Feb. 17, 1914; March 10, 1926; April 5, 1926; Nov. 28, 1926; Nov. 1, 1932; March 1, 1936; May 17, 1940; Dec. 20, 1944; May 15, 1948; June 18, 1953. See NAAFI seals.

Eielson, Carl Ben: Feb. 2, 1924.

Electronic Computer-Originated Mail: See US E-COM.

Elizabeth II of Great Britain: Feb. 6, 1952.

Eloby, Annobon, and Corisco: 1903.

El Salvador: 1867; April 1, 1879; May 4, 1889; Dec. 28, 1929.

Empire "all-up" air mail: July 27, 1938.

Encased postage stamps: Aug. 12, 1862.

England: 1481; 1571; 1573; 1598; 1633; April 1633; July 1637; 1652; 1657; 1659; 1660; June 1660; 1661; Aug. 12, 1661; June 13, 1668; April 1, 1680; Nov. 23, 1682; Oc-

tober 1689; May 1690; 1705; June 1, 1711.

English and Scottish Post Offices united: June 1, 1711.

English Channel islands: Oct. 5, 1919.

Envelope, first mention of: 1675.

Enzeli: Dec. 14, 1924.

Epirus: February 1914.

Equatorial Guinea, Republic of: Oct. 12, 1968; July 24, 1970.

Eritrea: 1892; June 1948. See also B.M.A./ERITREA.

Eslof: June 1, 1912.

Estonia: Nov. 19, 1918; Nov. 22, 1918; March 13, 1920; July 7, 1922; Aug. 15, 1940; Jan. 31, 1941; Dec. 1, 1941.

Ethiopia: 1894; Nov. 1, 1908; Aug. 17, 1929; Sept. 5, 1929; Feb. 25, 1936; April 24, 1947; Nov. 17, 1951.

Etiquette, Air Mail: Aug. 17, 1918.

Eugene Alexander von Taxis: 1676.

***Europa,* flight to:** July 16, 1930; Sept. 15, 1930.

Europa stamps: See Stamps, Europa.

European Postal and Telecommunications Union: October 1942.

European Postal Conference: October 1942.

Exhibitions, stamp: See Stamp exhibitions; US, international philatelic exhibitions.

Fairbanks, Douglas, commemorative stamp: See US, Douglas Fairbanks commemorative stamp.

Fairbanks, Richard: Nov. 5, 1639.

Faith in Australia: Feb. 17, 1934; April 12, 1934.

Falkland Islands: June 19, 1878; Feb. 11, 1880; Nov. 20, 1909; Aug. 18, 1944; March 10, 1945; April 28, 1952; Nov. 2, 1967; Sept. 13, 1982.

Falkland Islands Dependencies: Feb. 1, 1946; May 5, 1980.

Fanning Island: Nov. 29, 1902; Jan. 27, 1916; Feb. 13, 1939; February 1943; July 1945.

Far Eastern Republic: September 1920.

Faridkot, Indian Convention State of: Jan. 1, 1887. See also Faridkot, Indian Feudatory State of.

Faridkot, Indian Feudatory State of: 1879. See also Faridkot, Indian Convention State of.

Farley, James A., US PMG: March 4, 1933.

Farley's Follies: See US Special Printings.

Faroe Islands: 1880; Jan. 3, 1919; Nov. 2, 1940; May 19, 1943; Jan. 30, 1975; April 1, 1976.

Federal Republic of Germany: See Germany, Federal Republic of.

Federated Malay States: July 1, 1896; 1900; July 16, 1900. See Negri Sembilan, Pahang, Perek, and Selangor.

Federation Internationale de Philatelie (FIP): See International Philatelic Federation.

Fernando Po: September 1868; Oct. 12, 1968.

Ferrary Sale: April 5, 1922.

Fezzan: 1943.

Fiji: Nov. 1, 1870; Oct. 11, 1871; Dec. 3, 1871; May 8, 1872; 1891; April 1948; Sept. 17, 1951; Oct. 10, 1970; June 18, 1971.

Finland: March 1, 1856; Oct. 1, 1870; Feb. 12, 1918; May 15, 1922; Sept. 24, 1930; Nov. 1, 1941; April 14, 1951; April 1, 1982. See Aland Islands.

Finlay, Hugh: November 1772; Jan. 31, 1774; July 7, 1784.

FIP: See International Philatelic Federation.

First adhesive newspaper stamp: Jan. 1, 1851.

First adhesive postage stamp: May 6, 1840.

First adhesive postage stamp for British colony:

April 24, 1847.

First adhesive postage stamp outside Great Britain: Feb. 1, 1842.

First adhesive postage stamp use: May 2, 1840.

First aerogramme: 1870; June 29, 1930; August 1932; July 15, 1933.

First African aviation meet cancelation: Feb. 6, 1910.

First air mail carried by civilian jet airliner: April 18, 1950.

First air mail label (etiquette): Aug. 17, 1918.

First air mail stamp: May 16, 1917.

First air mail stamped envelope: 1913.

First airplane mail carried officially: Feb. 18, 1911.

First airplane on stamp: Dec. 16, 1912.

First British aviation meeting cancelation: Aug. 6, 1910.

First British local publicity slogan machine cancel: April 1, 1963.

First British machine slogan cancel: Dec. 10, 1917.

First British mailcoach route: Aug. 2, 1784.

First British photogravure printed stamp: Aug. 20, 1934.

First Canadian air mail: June 24, 1918.

First canceling device: May 6, 1840.

First commemorative adhesive postage stamp: 1888.

First commercially produced cacheted cover: Sept. 1, 1923.

First duplex canceler: 1850.

First Contract Air Mail Route (CAM) inaugurated in US: Feb. 15, 1926.

First cover with an adhesive stamp: May 2, 1840.

First-day cover, first commercial: Sept. 1, 1923.

First England-Australia flight: Nov. 12, 1919.

First flag cancel: Oct. 31, 1894.

First Frama coin-operated postage label vending machine: Aug. 8, 1976.

First franchise stamp: 1869.

First government-issued, adhesive commemorative stamps: 1888.

First government-issued commemorative postal item: 1876.

First helicopter mail: July 5, 1946.

First hovercraft mail: July 20, 1962.

First insured letter stamp: Feb. 1, 1935.

First late-fee stamp: Jan. 1, 1855.

First letter by air in North America: Jan. 9, 1793.

First Letter card: 1882.

First machine canceler: September 1857.

First mailbox: Aug. 8, 1653.

First military stamps: April 21, 1898.

First $1 million item: May 8, 1981.

First modern omnibus issue: May 6, 1935.

First milticolored stamp: July 1, 1845.

First municipal post: AD 1150.

First newspaper stamp: Jan. 1, 1851.

First newspaper wrapper: October 1861.

First numeral obliterators: May 1844.

First Official stamps: July 1, 1854.

First omnibus issue: 1898.

First overprint designating purpose: 1869.

First packet boat service: 1633.

First paper: See Paper, invention of.

First parcel post stamp: July 1, 1884.

First perforated stamps issued in Britain: Jan. 28, 1854.

First philatelic advertisement: March 22, 1851.

First philatelic periodicals: 1862; 1863; May 1, 1863;

Feb. 15, 1864; Jan. 1, 1896.

First photogravure-printed stamps (Bavaria): March 31, 1914.

First pictorial postmark in British Isles: 1750.

First postage due label: January 1859.

First postage meter: Aug. 24, 1900.

First postal card: Oct. 1, 1869.

First postal convention between nations: June 1, 1792.

First postal stationery item: 1608.

First post horn: AD 1100.

First precanceled stamp: Sept. 1, 1847.

First railway mail: Sept. 15, 1830.

First railway post office: Jan. 24, 1838.

First registered envelope: Jan. 1, 1878.

First rocket mail: Feb. 2, 1931.

First roundtrip Atlantic flight: July 2, 1919.

First semi-postal stamps: June 22 and 28, 1897.

First ship-to-shore air mail carried by dirigible: June 12, 1931.

First ship-to-shore mail: Nov. 25, 1926.

First shore-to-ship mail: Aug. 14, 1919.

First slogan postmark: 1661.

First souvenir sheet: Nov. 26, 1906.

First special event cancelation: 1855.

First special event cancelation in Great Britain: May 1862.

First specially designed air mail stamp: May 13, 1918.

First stamp album believed published: 1862.

First stamp booklet: 1895.

First stamp catalog: Dec. 21, 1861.

First stamp-collecting ad: March 22, 1851.

First stamp collector: 1774. See US, first stamp collector.

First stamp dealer: 1852. See US, first stamp dealer.

First stamp exhibitions: 1852; 1870; March 11, 1889.

First stamp printed in multicolor: July 1, 1845.

First stamp printed in two-color intaglio: April 2, 1869.

First stamp showing airplane: Dec. 16, 1912.

First stamp showing a jet aircraft: Oct. 1, 1945.

First stamps of the 19th century: Great Britain (May 6, 1840), Zurich (March 1843), Brazil (Aug. 1, 1843), Geneva (Oct. 1, 1843), Basel (July 1, 1845), United States (July 1, 1847), Mauritius (Sept. 21, 1847), France (Jan. 1, 1849), Belgium (July 1, 1849), Bavaria (Nov. 1, 1849), Spain (Jan. 1, 1850), New South Wales (Jan. 1, 1850), Victoria (Jan. 3, 1850), Switzerland (April 5, 1850), Austria (June 1, 1850), Austrian Italy (June 1, 1850), Saxony (June 29, 1850), British Guiana (July 1, 1850), Prussia (Nov. 15, 1850), Schleswig-Holstein (Nov. 15, 1850), Hanover (Dec. 1, 1850), Sardinia (Jan. 1, 1851), Denmark (April 1, 1851), Tuscany (April 1, 1851), Canada (April 23, 1851), Baden (May 1, 1851), Trinidad (Aug. 14, 1851), Nova Scotia (Sept. 1, 1851), New Brunswick (Sept. 5, 1851), Hawaii (Oct. 1, 1851), Wurttemberg (Oct. 15, 1851), Brunswick (1852), Reunion (1852), Netherlands (Jan. 1, 1852), Roman States (Jan. 1, 1852), Oldenburg (Jan. 5, 1852), Barbados (April 15, 1852), Modena (June 1, 1852), Parma (June 1, 1852), India — Scinde Dawk (July 1, 1852), Luxembourg (Sept. 15, 1852), Portugal (July 1853), Chile (July 1, 1853), Cape of Good Hope (Sept. 1, 1853), Van Dieman's Land — Tasmania (Nov. 1, 1853), Philippines (Feb. 1, 1854), Western Australia (Aug. 1, 1854), British India (Oct. 1, 1854), Bremen (1855), Cuba and Puerto Rico (April 1855), Norway (January 1855), South Australia (Jan. 1, 1855), Sweden (July 1, 1855), New

Zealand (July 18, 1855), Danish West Indies (Nov. 10, 1855), St. Helena (Jan. 1, 1856), Finland (March 1, 1856), Mecklenburg-Schwerin (July 1, 1856), Mexico (Aug. 1, 1856), Corrientes (Aug. 21, 1856), Uruguay (Oct. 1, 1856), Newfoundland (Jan. 1, 1857), Ceylon (April 1, 1857), Natal (May 26, 1857), Peru (Dec. 1, 1857), British Honduras (1858), Russia (Jan. 1, 1858), Tasmania (January 1858), Naples (Jan. 1, 1858), Buenos Aires (April 29, 1858), Argentina (May 1, 1858), Moldavia (July 15, 1858), Cordoba (Oct. 28, 1858), Hamburg (January 1859), Lubeck (Jan. 1, 1859), Sicily (Jan. 1, 1859), Venezuela (Jan. 1, 1859), Ionian Islands (May 15, 1859), Bahamas (June 10, 1859), Granada Confederation (August 1859), Romagna (Sept. 1, 1859), Sierra Leone (Sept. 21, 1859), Liberia (1860), Poland (Jan. 1, 1860), New Caledonia (Jan. 1, 1860), India, Crown Colony of (May 9, 1860), British Columbia and Vancouver Island (July 30, 1860), Queensland (Nov. 1, 1860), Jamaica (Nov. 23, 1860), Malta (Dec. 1, 1860), St. Lucia (Dec. 18, 1860), Nevis (1861), Prince Edward Island (Jan. 1, 1861), Neapolitan Provinces (February 1861), St. Vincent (May 8, 1861), Grenada (June 1, 1861), Greece (Oct. 1, 1861), Confederate States of America (Oct. 16, 1861), Bergedorf (Nov. 1, 1861), United States of Colombia (1862), Italy (March 1862), Antigua (August 1862), Nicaragua (Sept. 2, 1862), Hong Kong (Dec. 8, 1862), Bolivar (1863), Wenden (1863), Turkey (Jan. 1, 1863), Costa Rica (April 1863), Holstein (March 1, 1864), Netherlands Indies (April 1, 1864), Mecklenburg-Strelitz (Oct. 1, 1864), Ecuador (1865), Schleswig (1865), Romania (Jan. 1, 1865), Vancouver Island (Sept. 19, 1865), Bermuda (Sept. 25, 1865), Dominican Republic (Oct. 19, 1865), British Columbua (Nov. 1, 1865), Bolivia (1866), British Virgin Islands (1866), Serbia (1866), British Honduras (January 1866), Egypt (Jan. 1, 1866), Honduras (Jan. 1, 1866), Jammu and Kashmir (March 1866), El Salvador (1867), Turks Islands (April 4, 1867), Heligoland (April 15, 1867), Straits Settlements (Sept. 1, 1867), Antioquia (1868), Azores (1868), North German Confederation (Jan. 1, 1868), Persia (1868), Madeira (Jan. 1, 1868), Orange Free State (Jan. 1, 1868), Fernando Po (September 1868), Gambia (1869), St. Thomas and Prince (1869), Transvaal (1869), Sarawak (March 1, 1869), Cundinamarca (1870), Tolma (1870), St. Christopher (April 1, 1870), Angola (July 1, 1870), Paraguay (Aug. 1, 1870), Alsace and Lorraine (September 1870), Fiji (Nov. 1, 1870), Afghanistan (1871), Guatemala (March 1, 1871), Japan (April 20, 1871), Hungary (May 1871), Portuguese India (Oct. 1, 1871), German Empire (Jan. 1, 1872), Puerto Rico (1873), Suriname (1873), Iceland (January 1873), Curacao (May 23, 1873), Montenegro (May 1874), Dominica (May 4, 1874), Lagos (June 10, 1874), Griqualand West (September 1874), Gold Coast (July 1875), Johor (July 1876), Mozambique (July 1876), Montserrat (September 1876), San Marino (1877), Cape Verde Islands (Jan. 1, 1877), Samoa (Oct. 1, 1877), Sungei Ujong (1878), Panama (1878), Perak (1878), Falkland Islands (June 19, 1878), Labuan (May 1879), Bulgaria (June 1, 1879), Bosnia and Herzegovina (July 1, 1879), Tobago (Aug. 1, 1879), Eastern Rumelia (1880), Cyprus (April 1, 1880), Portuguese Guinea (1881), Selangor (1881), Nepal (May 16, 1881), Haiti (July 1, 1881), Bangkok (April 27, 1882), Tahiti (June 9, 1882), North Borneo (June 1883), Siam — Thailand (Aug. 4, 1883), Santander (1884), Stellaland (Feb. 1, 1884), Guadeloupe (Feb. 23, 1884), Madagascar —

British Consular Mail (March 1884), Macao (March 1, 1884), Korea (November 1884), Guanacaste (1885), Monaco (1885), St. Pierre and Miquelon (January 1885), British Bechuanaland (December 1885), Colombia (1886), Gabon (1886), Tonga (1886), Congo Free State (Jan. 1, 1886), Gibraltar (Jan. 1, 1886), New Republic (Jan. 1, 1886), Portuguese Timor (February 1886), Martinique (July 1886), French Guiana (December 1886), Senegal (1887), Annam and Tonkin (Jan. 21, 1888), Zululand (May 1, 1888), Tunisia (July 1, 1888), Bechuanaland (Aug. 7, 1888), Madagascar (1889), Pahang (January 1889), French Indo-China (January 1889), Nossi Be (May 1889), Swaziland (Oct. 18, 1889), Diego Suarez (1890), Leeward Islands (1890), Seychelles (April 5, 1890), British East Africa (May 1890), French Congo (1891), French Morocco (Jan. 1, 1891), British Central Africa (April 1891), Negri Sembilan (August 1891), Benin (1892), Eritrea (1892), Horta (1892), Mayotte (1892), Mozambique Company (1892), Ponta Delgada (1892), British South Africa Company — Rhodesia (Jan. 2, 1892), Obock (Feb. 1, 1892), Funchal (April 1, 1892), Cook Islands (April 19, 1892), Oil Rivers (July 20, 1892), French Oceanic Settlements (November 1892), Anjouan (November 1892), French Guinea (November 1892), French India (November 1892), Ivory Coast (November 1892), Cavalla (1893), Dedeagh (1893), German East Africa (1893), Vathy (1893), Port Lagos (April 1, 1893), Abyssinia — Ethiopia (1894), Djibouti (1894), Lourenco Marques (1894), St. Marie de Madagascar (April 1894), French Sudan (April 12, 1894), Portuguese Congo (Aug. 5, 1894), Zambezia (November 1894), Majunga (Feb. 28, 1895), Uganda (March 20, 1895), Inhambane (July 1, 1895), Zanzibar (Nov. 10, 1895), German New Guinea (1897), German South West Africa (1897), Grand Comoro (1897), Marshall Islands (1897), Nyassa (1897), Chinese Government Post (Jan. 2, 1897), Sudan (March 1, 1897), German Cameroon (April 1, 1897), Morocco Agencies (1898), Portuguese Africa (April 1898), Thessaly (April 21, 1898), Crete (Nov. 25, 1898), Alexandria (1899), Boyaca (1899), Caroline Islands (1899), Dahomey (1899), Guam (July 7, 1899), Mariana Islands (September 1899). See Indian convention states and Indian feudatory states.

First steam-powered mail road vehicle: 1897.
First stereoscopic stamps: Dec. 29, 1956.
First telegraph stamps: 1851.
First "too-late" stamp: Jan. 1, 1855.
First topical exhibit: 1928.
First transatlantic air mail: June 14, 1919.
First transatlantic air mail by jet aircraft: Oct. 4, 1958.
First transatlantic crossing by a dirigible: July 2, 1919.
First transatlantic steamship mail: April 4, 1838.
First use of the word "philately:" Nov. 3, 1864.
First use of paper: 105 BC.
First US: For first US events, see under various US headings.
First war tax stamps: Jan. 1, 1874.
First wreck cover: June 5, 1817.
Fiume: Dec. 2, 1918.
Flag cancel, first: Oct. 31, 1894.
Fleming, Sir Sandford: Jan. 7, 1827; June 5, 1845; April 23, 1851; July 22, 1915.
Floating safe stamps: 1921; Oct. 3, 1927.
Florida, State of: March 3, 1845; Jan. 10, 1861; June 25, 1868.

Florida, Territory of: March 30, 1822.
Flying post office: Oct. 1, 1946.
Fonopost: April 1, 1939.
Foochow (Treaty Port): Aug. 29, 1842; Jan. 1, 1895; Aug. 1, 1895.
Formosa: See Taiwan.
Forwarding agents: 1673; 1742; Jan. 8, 1835.
Fournier, Francois: April 24, 1846; July 12, 1917.
Foxcroft, John: 1761.
Frama coin-operated postage label vending machines: Aug. 8, 1976; Dec. 2, 1978; Sept. 15, 1979; Jan. 2, 1981; June 10, 1981; Sept. 1, 1981; Nov. 16, 1981; April 1, 1982; Feb. 1, 1983; June 29, 1983; July 18, 1983; Feb. 22, 1984; May 1, 1984; Oct. 29, 1984.
France: June 19, 1464; 1477; 1627; 1633; Aug. 8, 1653; 1801; 1830; 1843; Jan. 1, 1849; 1855; January 1859; 1868; Dec. 19, 1868; 1870; September 1870; Nov. 13, 1870; April 1, 1903; Aug. 14, 1910; Aug. 11, 1914; May 14, 1919; June 25, 1927; March 15, 1930; May 12, 1930; Jan. 19, 1948; June 14, 1948; Jan. 14, 1958; Jan. 23, 1961.
Franking privilege in US abolished: July 1, 1873.
Franklin, Benjamin: 1737; Aug. 10, 1753; 1761; Jan. 16, 1764; Jan. 31, 1774; May 29, 1775; July 26, 1775; Nov. 7, 1776.
Free franked mail: 1715; 1764; Jan. 9, 1776; Oct. 18, 1782; July 1, 1873; Oct. 3, 1917; Oct. 29, 1920.
French Congo: 1891.
French Equatorial Africa: March 16, 1936; April 15, 1937; Oct. 24, 1938.
French Guiana: December 1886; July 8, 1921; Nov. 20, 1933; July 5, 1939.
French Guinea: November 1892.
French India: November 1892.
French Indo-China: January 1889; April 27, 1921.
French Morocco: Aug. 1, 1914; Jan. 1, 1922; July 26, 1928.
French Oceanic Settlements: November 1892; Nov. 5, 1934; July 5, 1939. See Tahiti, French Polynesia.
French Polynesia: Nov. 3, 1958; June 9, 1977. See Tahiti, French Oceanic Settlements.
French post office in Alexandria: 1899. See Alexandria.
French POs in China: 1894.
French POs in Crete: Oct. 3, 1902.
French POs in Egypt: 1899.
French POs in Morocco: Jan. 1, 1891.
French POs in Port Said: 1899.
French POs in Turkish Empire: Aug. 5, 1885.
French POs in Zanzibar: 1894.
French Somali Coast: July 1902. See Obock, French Territory of Afars and Issas, Republic of Djibouti.
French Southern and Antarctic Territories: Oct. 28, 1955; April 25, 1956.
French Sudan: April 12, 1894; Jan. 17, 1959.
French Territory of Afars and Issas: Aug. 21, 1967.
French West Africa: 1943.
Frere, Sir Bartle: July 1, 1852.
Fresno Bicycle Mail: July 6, 1894.
Fujeira: Jan. 7, 1961; Sept. 22, 1964; Aug. 16, 1965; Oct. 14, 1965; Nov. 10, 1965; Dec. 2, 1971. See Trucial States, United Arab Emirates.
Funafuti: April 9, 1984.
Funchal: April 1, 1892.

Gabon: 1886; July 23, 1960; July 17, 1961; March 9, 1964.
Galapagos Islands: July 15, 1957.

Gambia, The: January 1869; Jan. 1, 1879; Feb. 18, 1965; October 1974.
Garbage card: May 27, 1902.
Garcia, Justiniano: March 18, 1863.
Garden City, N.Y. airplane mail: Sept. 23, 1911; Sept. 30, 1911.
Gary, James A., US PMG: March 6, 1897.
Gaza: June 1, 1948; Jan. 15, 1965.
GDR (German Democratic Republic): Oct. 9, 1949.
General Postal Union: Sept. 15, 1874; July 1, 1875; Sept. 15, 1875; Jan. 18, 1876; July 1, 1876; May 2, 1878.
General Post Office, London: June 1, 1711; September 1829; April 6, 1831; Oct. 11, 1841; July 1, 1851; April 1, 1860; May 1, 1860.
Geneva: Oct. 1, 1843.
George V of Great Britain: May 19, 1890; 1893; May 6, 1910; Jan. 20, 1936.
George VI of Great Britain: Dec. 10, 1936; Feb. 6, 1952.
Georgia: Jan. 2, 1788; Jan. 19, 1861; June 25, 1868.
Georgia, National Republic of: May 26, 1918; 1919.
German Cameroon: Feb. 1, 1887; April 1, 1897; July 1915. See Cameroon.
German Democratic Republic: Oct. 9, 1949; Dec. 13, 1957.
German East Africa: 1893; May 29, 1916; 1917.
German Empire: Jan. 1, 1872; Jan. 25, 1884; April 1, 1900.
German Inflation period: Oct. 18, 1923; Nov. 20, 1923.
German Kamerun: See German Cameroon.
German Mariana Islands: See Mariana Islands.
German Marshall Islands: See Marshall Islands.
German New Guinea: 1897; Oct. 17, 1914. See Northwest Pacific Islands and Territory of New Guinea.
German post offices abroad: Jan. 25, 1884; 1897; Dec. 20, 1899.
German Samoa: Dec. 2, 1899; March 1, 1900; Sept. 3, 1914. See Samoa and Western Samoa.
German South Atlantic air mail: Feb. 2, 1934.
German South West Africa: 1897; July 9, 1915.
German surrender in WWII: May 9, 1945.
Germany: 1100; 1615; 1801; January 1827.
Germany, East: See German Democratic Republic.
Germany, Federal Republic of: May 23, 1949; Sept. 7, 1949; Jan. 20, 1950; Nov. 3, 1961; Jan. 2, 1981.
Germany, occupation of: March 19, 1945; June 5, 1945; June 23, 1945; Aug. 28, 1945; Sept. 28, 1945; Oct. 1, 1945; Oct. 10, 1945; July 3, 1948; Dec. 1, 1948.
Germany, Republic of: May 1, 1919; Nov. 10, 1919; Nov. 20, 1923.
Germany, Third Reich: June 23, 1935; June 11, 1938; April 9, 1940; Aug. 15, 1940; May 9, 1945.
Ghana: March 6, 1957; Oct. 10, 1957; July 1, 1960; Feb. 10, 1962. See Gold Coast.
Gibbons, Edward Stanley: 1840; 1856; Feb. 13, 1913.
Gibbons, Stanley: 1856; June 15, 1864; November 1865; July 1890.
Gibraltar: Dec. 2, 1806; January 1876; Jan. 1, 1886; July 1889; Oct. 1, 1898; July 1, 1931; Nov. 20, 1931.
Gilbert and Ellice Islands, British Protectorate of: Jan. 1, 1911; June 1918.
Gilbert Islands: Jan. 2, 1976. See Kiribati.
Giori press: Nov. 19, 1949; July 4, 1957.
Glider mail: May 14, 1935; May 19, 1935.
Goddard, William: July 2, 1774.

Gold Coast: July 1875; Jan. 1, 1879; June 1918; July 1, 1948. See Ghana.
Gombe: April 1, 1920.
Gosforth, England: Feb. 11, 1913.
Gough Island: May 25, 1922.
Graf Zeppelin: See Zeppelin LZ-127 *Graf Zeppelin*.
Graham Land: Feb. 12, 1944.
Granadine Confederation: August 1859.
Grand Comoro: 1897.
Granger, Francis, US PMG: March 8, 1841.
Granger, Gideon, US PMG: Nov. 28, 1801.
Graphite lines, Great Britain: Nov. 19, 1957.
Great Barrier Pigeon Post: May 14, 1897; Nov. 17, 1898; Sept. 5, 1908.

Great Britain: 1481; 1510; 1533; 1571; 1573; 1590; 1598; 1633; April 1633; July 31, 1635; July 1637; 1652; 1657; 1659; 1660; June 1660; 1661; Aug. 12, 1661; June 13, 1668; Aug. 13, 1670; April 1, 1680; Nov. 23, 1682; October 1689; May 1690; Jan. 1, 1701; Oct. 21, 1702; 1705; June 1, 1711; 1712; 1715; 1720; 1742; December 1745; 1750; February 1756; 1764; January 1765; Aug. 2, 1784; March 28, 1785; October 1786; Feb. 28, 1787; Feb. 15, 1794; March 22, 1794; Dec. 3, 1795; Sept. 10, 1799; 1801; 1816; 1819; September 1829; 1830; Sept. 15, 1830; August 1833; 1835; January 1837; June 20, 1837; September 1837; Nov. 23, 1837; 1838; Jan. 24, 1838; April 5, 1838; May 4, 1839; June 1839; July 1839; Aug. 17, 1839; Aug. 23, 1839; Dec. 5, 1839; Jan. 10, 1840; March 26, 1840; April 15, 1840; May 1, 1840; May 2, 1840; May 6, 1840; May 8, 1840; Jan. 6, 1841; Jan. 17, 1841; Feb. 10, 1841; 1843; Oct. 10, 1843; May 1844; Dec. 17, 1845; April 3, 1846; December 1846; May 14, 1849; 1851; June 1853; 1854; Jan. 28, 1854; Oct. 11, 1854; March 1855; July 1, 1855; Oct. 8, 1855; May 1, 1856; September 1857; 1862; April 1862; May 1862; Feb. 3, 1863; 1864; Jan. 1, 1868; April 1869; October 1870; Oct. 1, 1870; March 18, 1872; 1874; Jan. 1, 1878; April 1, 1879; June 27, 1879; Aug. 27, 1879; September 1879; Jan. 1, 1880; Aug. 1, 1883; July 2, 1890; 1893; Dec. 25, 1898; Jan. 22, 1901; Jan. 1, 1902; Aug. 9, 1902; Sept. 20, 1902; Dec. 17, 1902; Sept. 5, 1903; July 12, 1905; Oct. 14, 1907; Oct. 1, 1908; May 6, 1910; Aug. 6, 1910; Aug. 17, 1910; June 22, 1911; Sept. 9, 1911; Sept. 26, 1911; Oct. 13, 1911; Oct. 17, 1911; Jan. 24, 1912; May 25, 1912; June 1912; July 1912; Feb. 11, 1913; June 30, 1913; April 20, 1914; June 30, 1915; Dec. 10, 1917; Dec. 13, 1918; March 1, 1919; May 14, 1919; July 2, 1919; July 9, 1919; September 1919; Oct. 5, 1919; Nov. 12, 1919; April 1, 1922; Sept. 5, 1922; Sept. 24, 1928; May 10, 1929; Aug. 13, 1930; April 4, 1931; April 12, 1933; Aug. 20, 1934; May 7, 1935; Jan. 20, 1936; Sept. 1, 1936; Sept. 14, 1936; Sept. 30, 1936; Dec. 10, 1936; May 10, 1937; July 20, 1938; July 27, 1938; May 6, 1940; Dec. 24, 1940; May 20, 1941; June 1941; July 21, 1941; August 1941; Aug. 2, 1941; Dec. 7, 1942; June 18, 1943; March 7, 1944; April 30, 1946; July 29, 1948; May 3, 1951; Feb. 6, 1952; April 28, 1952; Dec. 5, 1952; Dec. 17, 1953; Nov. 19, 1957; Aug. 18, 1958; Dec. 4, 1958; Nov. 18, 1959; April 1, 1963; June 5, 1967; March 5, 1969; Oct. 1, 1969; June 17, 1970; Feb. 15, 1971; Oct. 31, 1973; Jan. 22, 1975; Oct. 10, 1980; May 1, 1984; Jan. 1, 1985; Feb. 28, 1985.

Great Britain "blitz" mobile POs: Aug. 2, 1941.
Great Britain "blitz" postal markings: May 20, 1941.
Great Britain, local publicity slogan cancel: April 1, 1963.
Great Britain mobile POs: Sept. 30, 1936.

Great Britain, Official stamps: Oct. 1, 1882; July 1, 1883; March 24, 1896; Sept. 1, 1896; Feb. 19, 1902; March 3, 1903; May 1904.
Great Britain Sea Horses: June 30, 1913.
Greece: 1828; Oct. 1, 1861; April 6, 1898; October 1911; Feb. 5, 1917; April 16, 1924; Oct. 20, 1926; Nov. 24, 1935; June 1944.
Greenland: 1905; Dec. 1, 1938; May 1, 1979.
Grenada: June 1, 1861; July 12, 1937; Jan. 14, 1949; Feb. 3, 1972; Feb. 7, 1974; 1979; Nov. 30, 1981; July 15, 1982.
Grenada Grenadines: Dec. 29, 1973.
Grenadines of Grenada: See Grenada Grenadines.
Grenadines of St. Vincent: See St. Vincent Grenadines.
Gresham, Walter Q., US PMG: April 11, 1883.
Grilled stamps: See US grilled stamps.
Griqualand West: October 1871; September 1874; October 1880; May 31, 1910.
Grodno: See Lithuania, South.
Gronouski, John A., US PMG: Sept. 30, 1963.
Guadalajara, Mexico: 1867.
Guadeloupe, French colony of: Feb. 23, 1884; May 1915.
Guam: July 7, 1899; Aug. 15, 1899; March 29, 1901; March 30, 1901; April 8, 1930; April 8, 1931; Dec. 10, 1941.
Guam Guard Mail: April 8, 1930; July 1930; April 8, 1931.
Guanacaste: 1885.
Guatemala: May 31, 1866; March 1, 1871; Aug. 1, 1881; Dec. 18, 1902; May 3, 1919; Feb. 16, 1924; May 20, 1929; June 29, 1930; March 15, 1937; April 29, 1939; June 1940.
Guernsey: Feb. 13, 1794; March 22, 1794; Aug. 23, 1823; Sept. 24, 1856; Oct. 5, 1919; May 8, 1939; Dec. 24, 1940; June 1941; Aug. 18, 1958; Oct. 1, 1969.
Guinea-Bissau: 1974; Sept. 10, 1974.
Guinea, Republic of: Jan. 5, 1959; May 6, 1959; July 13, 1959.
Guipuzcoa: July 1, 1873.
Gumbley, Major D.W.: July 15, 1933.
Guyana: May 26, 1966; March 22, 1967. See also British Guiana.
Gwalior, Indian Convention State of: 1885.

Habersham, Joseph, US PMG: Feb. 25, 1795.
Hadhramaut: Sept. 1, 1955.
Hague Air Mail Conference: Sept. 1, 1927.
Haiti, Republic of: July 1, 1881; July 14, 1927; Dec. 3, 1927; Dec. 6, 1927; Feb. 6, 1928; Oct. 3, 1939; Aug. 16, 1944; May 4, 1953; Nov. 21, 1960; March 1961.
Hakodate or Hakodadi (Japanese Treaty Port): Aug. 29, 1842.
Halifax: April 27, 1754; April 28, 1755; Jan. 11, 1784; 1787; May 4, 1839; April 2, 1844.
Hall, Nathan K., US PMG: July 23, 1850.
Hamburg, Free City of: January 1859; Aug. 8, 1867; Jan. 1, 1868.
Hamilton, Andrew: April 4, 1692; Nov. 11, 1692; May 1, 1693; May 15, 1693; May 10, 1694.
Hamilton Bank Note Co.: May 4, 1889.
Hamilton, John: May 1, 1693; 1707; 1709; 1721.
Hammarskjold Invert: Nov. 16, 1962.
Handstamped Paid markings: Feb. 28, 1787.
Hankow (Treaty Port): Aug. 29, 1842; May 20, 1893.
Hannegan, Robert E., US PMG: July 1, 1945.

Hanover (Hannover): Dec. 1, 1850; Oct. 1, 1866.
Hanseatic League: 1150.
Harnden, William: February 1839; Jan. 14, 1845.
Harrison and Sons (High Wycombe) Ltd.: 1557; 1750; Aug. 20, 1934.
Harrison, Richard: 1557.
Hatay: April 16, 1938; 1939.
Hatton, Frank, US PMG: Oct. 14, 1884.
Hawaii: Oct. 1, 1851; 1882; July 4, 1894; Aug. 12, 1898; June 14, 1900; Jan. 18, 1914; July 3, 1919; Aug. 31, 1925; Jan. 24, 1931; Oct. 8, 1934; Aug. 21, 1959.
Hays, Will H., US PMG: March 5, 1921.
Hazard, Ebenezer, Continental PMG: Jan. 28, 1782; Dec. 31, 1785.
Heard Island: Dec. 25, 1947.
Hejaz: August 1916; Dec. 21, 1921.
Hejaz-Nejd, Kingdom of: February 1926. See Saudi Arabia.
Heligoland: July 1, 1866; April 15, 1867; June 1, 1879; Aug. 10, 1890.
Herm: May 1, 1925; Nov. 30, 1938; May 26, 1949.
Herodotus: c500 BC.
Herrfeldt, J. von: 1841.
Herrmann, Dr. Emanuel: Jan. 26, 1869; Oct. 1, 1869.
Herzegovina: See Bosnia and Herzegovina.
Hidden dates, Canada: June 1, 1935.
Highest face value stamp: 1946.
Highway Post Offices: See US Highway Post Office service.
Hill, John, proposes a Penny Post: 1659.
Hill, Pearson: September 1857.
Hill, Sir Rowland: Dec. 3, 1795; January 1837; Nov. 23, 1837; Jan. 10, 1840; March 26, 1840; December 1846; 1854; Jan. 28, 1854; Oct. 11, 1854; March 1855; 1864; Aug. 27, 1879.
Hind, Arthur: April 5, 1922.
Hindenburg: See Zeppelin, Hindenburg.
Hiogo (Japanese Treaty Port): Aug. 29, 1842.
Hitchcock, Frank H., US PMG: March 6, 1909.
Hohen Blum, Josef von: Feb. 14, 1835.
Holstein, Duchy of: March 1, 1864; Jan. 1, 1868.
Holt, Joseph, US PMG: March 14, 1859.
Homelands of South Africa: See South Africa, homelands of.
Homem, Luis: 1525.
Honduras: Jan. 1, 1866; April 1, 1879; May 4, 1889; May 1, 1925; June 5, 1929; Dec. 8, 1953. See Black Honduras.
Hong Kong: November 1842; May 1, 1860; Dec. 8, 1862; Jan. 1, 1917; March 27, 1936; February 1948.
Horta: 1892.
Hovercraft mail: July 20, 1962.
Howe, Timothy O., US PMG: Jan. 5, 1882.
HPO service: See US Highway Post Office service.
Huacho: April 1884.
Hubbard, Samuel D., US PMG: Sept. 14, 1852.
Hungary: June 1, 1867; May 1871; Nov. 20, 1913; July 4, 1918; June 14, 1919; Nov. 16, 1919; 1946; June 11, 1947; Jan. 1, 1973.
Hunter, William: Aug. 10, 1753; 1761.
Hyderabad, Indian Feudatory State of: Sept. 8, 1869.

Icaria: October 1911.
Iceland: Jan. 1, 1873; Nov. 15, 1919; May 31, 1928; April 28, 1933; Oct. 9, 1949; June 29, 1983.
Ichang: Dec. 1, 1894.
Idaho, State of: July 3, 1890.
Idaho, Territory of: March 3, 1863.
Idar, Indian Feudatory State of: Feb. 21, 1939.

Ifni, Spanish colony of: 1941; June 30, 1969.
Ile de France, catapult mail from: Aug. 13, 1928.
Illinois, State of: Dec. 3, 1818.
Illinois, Territory of: March 1, 1809.
Imperial Airways: April 4, 1931; Dec. 10, 1934; March 27, 1936; June 16, 1937; July 5, 1937; July 20, 1938; July 27, 1938; Aug. 5, 1939.
Imperial Penny Post: Dec. 25, 1898.
Independence, Mo.: July 1, 1850.
India: July 1, 1852; Oct. 1, 1854; Oct. 14, 1854; Oct. 15, 1854; Oct. 11, 1855; Nov. 1, 1858; May 9, 1860; 1861; Aug. 1, 1866; July 1, 1876; July 1, 1879; Feb. 18, 1911; Dec. 13, 1918; Oct. 22, 1929; June 24, 1931; Nov. 21, 1947; Jan. 26, 1950; Oct. 17, 1953; Dec. 1, 1954; Jan. 15, 1962; Jan. 15, 1965.
Indian Convention states first stamps: Patiala 1884; Gwalior, 1885; Jind, 1885; Nabha, May 1885; Chamba 1886; Faridkot, Jan. 1, 1887.
Indian feudatory states, first stamps of: Soruth (November 1864, Jammu and Kashmir (March 1866), Hyderabad (Sept. 8, 1869), Jind (1874), Bhopal (1876), Poonch (1876), Sirmoor (June 1876), Nowanuggur (1877), Alwar (1877), Faridkot (1879), Bhor (1879), Rajpipla (1880), Jhalawar (1887), Bamra (1888), Wadhwan (1888), Travancore (Oct. 16, 1888), Nandgaon (February 1892), Cochin (April 1, 1892), Duttia (Datia) (1893), Charkhari (1894), Bundi (May 1894), Bussahir (Bashahr) (June 20, 1895), Indore (1896), Dhar (1897), Las Bela (1897), Kishangarh (1899), Jaipur (1904), Orchha (1913), Barwani (1921), Morvi (April 1, 1931), Bijawar (July 1, 1935), Idar (Feb. 21, 1939), Jasdan (1942).
India, four-anna inverted head: Oct. 15, 1854.
Indiana, State of: Dec. 11, 1816.
Indiana, Territory of: July 4, 1800.
Indian Territory: June 30, 1834.
India, Official stamps: Aug. 1, 1866.
Indian PO in Zanzibar: 1868.
Indo-China: See French Indo-China.
Indonesia, Republic of: Aug. 17, 1950; 1951; Jan. 2, 1951.
Indonesia, United States of: Dec. 27, 1949; Jan. 17, 1950. See Indonesia, Republic of.
Indore, Indian Feudatory State of: 1896.
Indus valley civilization: 4000 BC.
Inhambane: July 1, 1895.
Inini: April 7, 1932.
Insured letter stamp: Feb. 1, 1935.
Intaglio printing: See Printing, intaglio.
International and Colonial Postage Association: 1851.
International Bureau of Education: 1944.
International Bureau of the Universal Postal Union (UPU): 1957.
International Court of Justice: See Court of International Justice.
International Labour Office: 1923.
International Philatelic Exhibitions, US: See US, International Philatelic Exhibitions.
International Philatelic Federation (FIP): June 18, 1926.
International Refugee Organization: Feb. 1, 1950.
International Reply Coupon: April 7, 1906.
International Telecommunications Union: Sept. 22, 1958.
Interpostal Seals: 1864; 1865.
Ionian Islands: May 15, 1859; May 30, 1864; 1941; 1943.
Iowa, State of: Dec. 28, 1846.
Iowa, Territory of: July 4, 1838.

Iran (Persia): 1868; Sept. 1, 1877; Dec. 14, 1924; Feb. 8, 1927; Jan. 30, 1948; Nov. 14, 1979; Jan. 19, 1981; Feb. 24, 1981.

Iraq: Sept. 1, 1918; April 5, 1926; April 22, 1929; April 1, 1932; July 15, 1933; Feb. 1, 1949. See Baghdad, Mosul.

Ireland: 1562; 1564; 1573; 1598; 1653; Aug. 13, 1670; June 1, 1711; 1765; May 14, 1784; Jan. 6, 1818; April 6, 1831; April 1, 1879; Feb. 17, 1922; April 1, 1922; Dec. 6, 1922; Sept. 6, 1923; Dec. 29, 1937; Dec. 21, 1948; Oct. 14, 1968.

Irish Free State: See Ireland.

Isle of Man: Aug. 18, 1958; July 5, 1973.

Israel: May 14, 1948; May 16, 1948; May 28, 1948; Dec. 24, 1949; June 25, 1950; July 2, 1950; Feb. 1, 1951.

Istria, Slovene Coast: See Zone B.

Italian Austria: Nov. 3, 1918; February 1919.

Italian Colonies: July 11, 1932; Oct. 6, 1932.

Italian East Africa: 1936; Feb. 7, 1938; April 16, 1938.

Italian post office in Crete: 1900.

Italian Socialist Republic: Sept. 15, 1943; Dec. 20, 1943; April 25, 1945.

Italian Somaliland: October 1903; July 16, 1923; October 1934; Nov. 5, 1934; Nov. 11, 1934. See Somalia.

Italy: March 1862; Feb. 11, 1863; Jan. 1, 1868; July 1, 1884; June 1, 1903; September 1908; Sept. 23, 1910; April 1913; Nov. 15, 1915; May 16, 1917; May 22, 1917; June 28, 1917; Nov. 3, 1918; Aug. 19, 1925; April 10, 1926; Dec. 17, 1930; June 2, 1932; July 1, 1933; July 23, 1933; July 24, 1933; Aug. 8, 1933; Oct. 23, 1933; Oct. 1, 1945; May 30, 1952; Dec. 29, 1956; July 1, 1967. See Italian Socialist Republic, plus various Italian states.

Ivory Coast: November 1892; Feb. 8, 1940; Oct. 1, 1959; March 23, 1961; Jan. 1, 1967; Jan. 1, 1974.

Jaipur, Indian Feudatory State of: 1904.

Jamaica: Oct. 31, 1671; July 1705; April 1713; March 20, 1840; Nov. 23, 1860; Nov. 1, 1923; July 21, 1947; Aug. 29, 1962.

James, Thomas L., US PMG: March 8, 1881.

Jammu and Kashmir: March 1866.

Japan: AD 645; 1650; April 20, 1871; April 1, 1873; Dec. 1, 1873; Jan. 5, 1875; April 5, 1876; May 17, 1876; June 1, 1877; March 31, 1880; June 1, 1887; March 9, 1894; Jan. 1, 1899; Dec. 1, 1910; June 2, 1912; July 30, 1912; Oct. 3, 1919; June 1, 1937; March 1, 1949; July 1, 1968; July 1, 1969; Oct. 1, 1969; June 23, 1975. See also Yokohama, Japan.

Japan, Treaty Ports in: Aug. 29, 1842; July 1, 1860.

Jasdan, Indian Feudatory State of: 1942.

Java: June 1908; March 9, 1943; November 1945.

Jefferson Territory: Oct. 24, 1859.

Jersey: Feb. 13, 1794; Feb. 15, 1794; Nov. 23, 1852; Sept. 24, 1856; June 1, 1937; April 1, 1941; Aug. 18, 1958; Oct. 1, 1969.

Jewell, Marshall, US PMG: Sept. 1, 1874.

Jhalawar, Indian Feudatory State of: 1887.

Jind, Indian Convention State of: 1885. See also Jind, Indian Feudatory State of.

Jind, Indian Feudatory State of: 1874. See also Jind, Indian Convention State of.

Johnson, Cave, US PMG: March 7, 1845.

Johore: July 1876; 1916.

Jordan: November 1920; April 1, 1930; May 25, 1946; May 16, 1947; Sept. 16, 1950.

Jubaland (Oltre Giuba): July 29, 1925; June 1, 1926.

Jugoslavia: See Yugoslavia.

Jupiter **balloon:** Aug. 17, 1859.

Kampuchea: See Cambodia.

Kanagawa (Japanese Treaty Port): Aug. 29, 1842.

Kansas and Nebraska overprints: See US Kansas and Nebraska overprints.

Kansas, State of: Jan. 29, 1861.

Kansas, Territory of: May 30, 1854.

Karachi: Dec. 13, 1918.

Karelia: Jan. 31, 1922; Oct. 1, 1941.

Kashmir: See Jammu and Kishmir.

Katanga: July 11, 1960; Jan. 15, 1963.

Kathiri State of Seiyun: 1937; July 1942.

Kedah: 1883; 1909; July 1912; Oct. 18, 1943.

Kelantan: July 1909; January 1911; Oct. 18, 1943.

Kendall, Amos, US PMG: May 1, 1835; Dec. 1, 1835.

Kentucky, State of: June 1, 1792.

Kenya: Dec. 12, 1963; Oct. 1, 1964; Oct. 27, 1964; Dec. 12, 1964; April 15, 1965.

Kenya and Uganda: Nov. 1: 1922.

Kenya, Tanganyika, and Uganda: May 1, 1935.

Kenya, Uganda, and Tanzania: April 15, 1965.

Kerguelen Island: March 28, 1909.

Kermadec Islands: March 2, 1945.

Kewkiang: June 1, 1894.

Key, David McK., US PMG: March 13, 1877.

Khor Fakkan: March 20, 1965.

Kiautschou: May 9, 1900.

King Edward VII Land: Jan. 1, 1908.

King, Horatio, US PMG: Feb. 12, 1861.

King, Samuel Archer: June 18, 1877.

Kingsford Smith: April 4, 1931; Dec. 1, 1931.

Kinshasa: April 1, 1920.

Kionga: May 29, 1916.

Kiribati (formerly Gilbert Islands): July 11, 1979; July 12, 1979. See also Canton Island.

Kishangarh, Indian Feudatory State of: 1899.

Kiungchow (Treaty Port): Aug. 29, 1842.

Klassen, Elmer T., US PMG: Dec. 7, 1971.

KLM (Konninklijke Luchtvaart Maatschappij): Dec. 17, 1934; Jan. 19, 1935; Feb. 19, 1946; Aug. 6, 1946; Oct. 6, 1946. (KLM is the Dutch national airline and is the oldest airline currently in operation).

Knight, James H. "Jack:" Feb. 22, 1921.

Kobe, Japan (Treaty Port): Aug. 29, 1842.

Korea, Kingdom of: November 1884; Jan. 1, 1900; June 1, 1905.

Korea, North: March 12, 1946; May 1, 1948; Sept. 9, 1948; Dec. 17, 1950.

Korea, South: Feb. 1, 1946; Oct. 1, 1947; May 10, 1948; Aug. 1, 1948; 1949; Aug. 1, 1953; Oct. 17, 1953; Nov. 20, 1980.

Koschier, Laurenz: July 29, 1804; Dec. 31, 1835; Aug. 7, 1879.

Kosrae: See Micronesia, Federated States of.

Kouang-Tcheou (Kwangchow): April 1898; February 1943.

Kuala Lumpur: Aug. 23, 1926; April 30, 1979.

Kume Shima: Oct. 1, 1945.

Kuwait: April 1, 1923; April 1, 1948; Aug. 12, 1952; Feb. 1, 1959; Feb. 16, 1960.

La Aguera: June 1921.

Labuan: May 1879; Jan. 1, 1890; Oct. 30, 1906.

Lady McLeod **local stamp of Trinidad:** April 24, 1847.

Lagos, British colony of: Jan. 29, 1852; June 10, 1874; 1879.

La Guaira: November 1863; April 8, 1925.

Lallier, Justin Henri: 1862.
Lamoral von Taxis named hereditary Postmaster General of Germany: 1615.
Lao People's Democratic Republic: Dec. 2, 1975.
Laos: July 19, 1949; Nov. 13, 1951; April 12, 1952; May 20, 1952; July 14, 1953; Dec. 7, 1956; May 1, 1970; May 1975; Dec. 2, 1975.
La Paz: April 13, 1913.
Larache: April 4, 1920.
Las Bela, Indian Feudatory State of: 1897.
La Semeuse: April 1, 1903.
Latakia: July 1931; Feb. 28, 1937.
Lathework: 1917.
Latvia: Dec. 19, 1918; Oct. 10, 1919; Aug. 18, 1920; July 30, 1921; May 26, 1930.
League of Nations: 1922.
Leavenworth and Pike's Peak Express: May 7, 1859; February 1860.
Leavitt, Thomas: Oct. 12, 1827; Jan. 6, 1876; March 28, 1876.
Lebanon: January 1924; Jan. 1, 1924; May 1, 1926; July 1, 1927; Sept. 18, 1942; May 15, 1946.
Leeward Islands: 1890; July 1, 1956. See also Antigua, Dominica, Montserrat, Nevis, St. Christopher, St. Kitts-Nevis, and British Virgin Islands.
Lemberg: March 20, 1918.
Lemnos: 1912.
Lesotho: Oct. 4, 1966; Sept. 6, 1967.
Letter card: 1882.
Letter sheet: Nov. 17, 1818; May 6, 1840; August 1861; Aug. 18, 1886; June 30, 1894.
Levant: See British Levant.
Liberia: Jan. 20, 1850; 1860; April 1, 1879; December 1893; Feb. 28, 1936; July 26, 1948.
Libya: 1912; November 1915; Feb. 15, 1927; May 11, 1929; Dec. 24, 1951; June 4, 1952.
Liechtenstein, Principality of: Jan. 29, 1912; Oct. 5, 1925; Aug. 12, 1930; Aug. 31, 1930; April 13, 1962.
Lincoln, Abraham: May 7, 1833.
Lindburgh, Charles A.: April 10, 1926; April 15, 1926; Sept. 16, 1926; Nov. 3, 1926; Feb. 6, 1928; Feb. 20, 1928; Feb. 4, 1929; March 9, 1929; Sept. 20, 1929.
Lindquist, Harry L.: Jan. 16, 1978.
Lines, payment to: June 1, 1792.
Linn, George: Sept. 1, 1923; March 27, 1966.
Lithuania: Dec. 27, 1918; Jan. 29, 1919; Feb. 17, 1919; June 25, 1921; February 1924.
Lithuania, Central: Oct. 20, 1920.
Lithuania, South: March 4, 1919.
Lombardy-Venetia: June 1, 1850.
London: Dec. 13, 1918; May 14, 1919.
London-Paris air mail service: May 14, 1919.
London Penny Post becomes Twopenny Post: 1801.
Long Island: May 7, 1916; May 26, 1916.
Los Angeles: See USS Los Angeles.
Louisiana, District of: Oct. 1, 1804.
Louisiana, State of: April 30, 1812; Jan. 26, 1861; June 25, 1868.
Louisiana, Territory of: July 4, 1805.
Louis XI of France, courier system: June 19, 1464.
Lourenco Marques: 1894.
Lovelace, New York Governor: Jan. 1, 1673.
Lubeck, Free City of: Jan. 1, 1859; Aug. 8, 1867; Jan. 1, 1868.
Luff, John N.: Nov. 16, 1860.
Lundy: Jan. 1, 1928; Nov. 1, 1929; April 1, 1935.
Luneville, Peace of: 1801.
Lutine, **HMS:** June 5, 1817.

Luxembourg, Grand Duchy of: Jan. 1, 1852; Sept. 15, 1852; Sept. 1, 1870; July 1, 1875; 1895; Nov. 26, 1906; Aug. 2, 1931; Sept. 10, 1980; July 18, 1983.
Lydenburg: September 1900.

Maberly, Col. W.L.: 1854.
MacAdam, John Loudon, English road builder: 1816.
Macao: March 1, 1884; Aug. 11, 1919; Nov. 3, 1925.
Machin definitives of Great Britain: June 5, 1967; March 5, 1969; June 17, 1970.
Machine, canceling: See Canceling machine.
Macon: See USS Macon.
MacRobertson England-Australia air race: Oct. 11, 1934; Oct. 19, 1934; Oct. 20, 1934.
Madagascar: March 1884; 1889; January 1895; February 1915; Oct. 14, 1929; April 23, 1935; July 5, 1939; Dec. 10, 1958; Nov. 2, 1961. See Malagasy.
Madagascar, British Consular Mail: March 1884; January 1895.
Madeira: Jan. 1, 1868; July 1, 1876; Jan. 2, 1980.
Madura: June 1908.
Mafeking: Sept. 11, 1890; Oct. 12, 1899; March 24, 1900; April 9, 1900.
Mafia Island: January 1915; Aug. 6, 1918.
Mahra Sultanate of Qishn and Socotra: March 12, 1967.
Mailbox: Aug. 8, 1653; 1845; Nov. 23, 1852; 1858; Dec. 6, 1922. See pillar box.
Mailcoach: Aug. 2, 1784; March 28, 1785; 1838; Dec. 17, 1845; April 3, 1846; May 10, 1869; 1874; March 31, 1912; Aug. 2, 1984. See US mailcoach.
Mailcoach reenactment: Aug. 2, 1984.
Mail delivery in several US cities begun: July 1, 1851.
Mailers Postmark Permit markings authorized: May 29, 1930.
Mailgram: Sept. 6, 1974.
Mailomat: 1936; Oct. 14, 1936; May 17, 1939.
Maine, State of: March 15, 1820.
Majunga: Feb. 28, 1895.
Malacca (Melaka): Dec. 1, 1948; Nov. 15, 1965.
Malagasy Republic: Dec. 10, 1958.
Malawi: July 6, 1964; Oct. 25, 1966.
Malaya, Japanese occupation of: March 16, 1942; December 1943.
Malayan Federation: May 5, 1957.
Malaysia: Jan. 17, 1958; Sept. 16, 1963.
Malay States, Federated: See Federated Malay States.
Malay, Thai occupation of: December 1943.
Maldive Islands: Sept. 9, 1906; Sept. 1, 1965; Aug. 15, 1967.
Mali, Federation of: Jan. 17, 1959; Nov. 7, 1959; Dec. 11, 1959; Aug. 20, 1960.
Mali, Republic of: Dec. 18, 1960; Jan. 15, 1961; March 18, 1961; April 21, 1961; April 7, 1962.
Malta: Dec. 2, 1806; Dec. 1, 1860; Jan. 1, 1885; April 1, 1928; June 18, 1931; Sept. 21, 1964; May 21, 1965; Nov. 8, 1969.
Maltese Cross cancel: May 6, 1840.
Managua, Nicaragua: April 15, 1921.
Manama: July 5, 1966.
Manchoukuo: Feb. 18, 1932; March 20, 1932; July 26, 1932; Jan. 1, 1935; May 1946.
mansiones: cAD 100.
Mariana Islands: September 1899; May 1900.
Marienwerder, District of: March 12, 1920.
Marine Insurance stamps: See Floating Safe stamps.
Marion Island: Jan. 20, 1948.

Marshall Islands: 1897; May 2, 1984.
Marshall, Jas. W., US PMG: July 7, 1874.
Martin, Glenn L.: Jan. 20, 1912.
Martinique: July 1886; May 15, 1915; Oct. 10, 1927.
Maryland, State of: April 28, 1788; May 1, 1818; May 10, 1845.
Mary Sharpe: Oct. 10, 1843; June 11, 1844.
Mashonaland Mail Service: Sept. 11, 1890.
Massachusetts: 1639; June 9, 1693; Feb. 6, 1788.
Master of the Posts in England: August 1512.
Match and Medicine **stamps:** 1862.
Mauritania: 1906; Feb. 8, 1940; Jan. 20, 1960; Nov. 28, 1960; July 1, 1961; March 22, 1967.
Mauritius: Sept. 21, 1847; 1877; 1903; March 12, 1968; Aug. 29, 1969.
Maxwell, Edward, possibly first US envelope maker: 1835.
Maynard, Horace, US PMG: Aug. 25, 1880.
Mayotte: 1892.
McLean, John, US PMG: July 1, 1823.
Mecca, Sherifate of: August 1916.
Mecklenburg-Schwerin, German State of: July 1, 1856; Jan. 1, 1868.
Mecklenburg-Strelitz, German State of: Oct. 1, 1864; Jan. 1, 1868.
"M.E.F." on British stamps: March 2, 1942.
Meigs, Return J., US PMG: April 11, 1814.
Melbourne: June 10, 1841; Aug. 10, 1841; Aug. 1, 1842.
Melville, Frederick J.: 1883; Jan. 12, 1940.
Memel: Aug. 1, 1920; April 1, 1921; July 6, 1921.
Meratti, Carlo: 1820; 1842.
Mermoz, Jean: May 12, 1930; May 28, 1934.
Merry Widow, **US special delivery stamp:** Dec. 12, 1908.
Mesopotamia: See Baghdad and Mosul.
Metelin (Mytilene): November 1912.
Meter, postage: 1884; Jan. 24, 1899; Aug. 24, 1900; Dec. 9, 1901; Oct. 14, 1902; June 15, 1903; 1904; June 1904; July 11, 1904; Sept. 10, 1904; Feb. 8, 1906; 1910; Oct. 11, 1911; Jan. 24, 1912; May 9, 1912; Jan. 28, 1914; May 18, 1914; March 15, 1920; Sept. 1, 1920; Nov. 16, 1920; Dec. 10, 1920; Jan. 1, 1922; Sept. 5, 1922; July 1923; Aug. 7, 1923; Sept. 29, 1923; 1928; 1929; 1936; Oct. 14, 1936; June 1938; June 17, 1938; May 17, 1939; July 1953.
Meter slogans: 1928.
Metz, French town of: Sept. 5, 1870.
Metzger Post: AD 1100.
Mexico: 1830; Aug. 1, 1856; October 1856; May 12, 1875; April 1, 1879; Sept. 16, 1915; July 6, 1917; Dec. 25, 1918; April 2, 1922; Feb. 1, 1935; Oct. 2, 1935; June 1, 1941.
Meyer, George L. von, US PMG: March 4, 1907.
Michigan, State of: Jan. 26, 1837.
Michigan, Territory of: July 1, 1805.
Micronesia, Federated States of: July 12, 1984.
Middle Congo, French colony of: 1907.
Million dollar item: May 8, 1981.
Mineola, N.Y.: Sept. 23, 1911.
Minnesota, State of: May 11, 1858.
Minnesota, Territory of: March 3, 1849.
Missionaries **of Hawaii:** Oct. 1, 1851.
Mississippi, State of: Dec. 10, 1817; Jan. 9, 1861; Feb. 17, 1870.
Mississippi, Territory of: May 7, 1798.
Missouri, State of: Aug. 10, 1821.
Missouri, Territory of: Dec. 7, 1812.
Miss Rose Cover: Aug. 5, 1851.

Mixed franking, US-Canada: April 23, 1851.
Modena, Italian State of: June 1, 1852; Feb. 1, 1853; Oct. 15, 1859.
Moens, Jean-Baptiste: 1852; 1863.
Moldavia (Romania): July 15, 1858.
Moldavia-Walachia (Romania): June 25, 1862.
Monaco: 1885; October 1914; Aug. 22, 1933; March 27, 1945; Oct. 12, 1955.
Monaco Air Rally, cards for: April 1, 1914.
Mongolia: March 23, 1870; August 1924; June 5, 1961; Aug. 24, 1963; Dec. 22, 1967; June 1, 1977.
Montana, State of: Nov. 8, 1889.
Montana, Territory of: May 26, 1864.
Montenegro: May 1874; October 1895; March 1, 1917; 1941; Nov. 22, 1943.
Montevideo, Uruguay: Jan. 14, 1925.
Montserrat: September 1876; April 12, 1976.
Montreal: 1763; August 1763; 1764; Dec. 15, 1768; Nov. 13, 1775; 1807.
Moquegua: February 1881.
Morocco Agencies: Jan. 1, 1886; 1898; 1907; Oct. 26, 1936; Jan. 8, 1938.
Morocco, French: September 1911; May 1912; Aug. 1, 1914; Jan. 8, 1938.
Morocco, Kingdom of: Aug. 17, 1956; Aug. 23, 1956; Oct. 15, 1956; Dec. 17, 1956; May 4, 1957; Nov. 17, 1959; March 1960.
Morocco, Northern: Aug. 23, 1956; Dec. 17, 1956.
Morocco, Southern: Aug. 17, 1956.
Morocco, Spanish: See Spanish Morocco.
Morvi, Indian Feudatory State of: April 1, 1931.
Moss, Ernest: June 1904.
Most northerly post office: April 1950.
Mosul: February 1919.
Mount Athos: Jan. 25, 1916.
Moveable boxes: 1843; Sept. 24, 1856.
Mozambique: July 1876; Dec. 1, 1920. See Mozambique, People's Republic of.
Mozambique Company: 1892; Nov. 1, 1935; July 18, 1941.
Mozambique, People's Republic of: June 25, 1975; 1979.
Mulready envelope and letter sheet: Aug. 17, 1839; May 6, 1840.
Municipal postal service: 1322.
Muscat: Nov. 20, 1944; April 1, 1948; Aug. 12, 1952.
Muscat and Oman: April 29, 1966.
mutationes: cAD 100.
Mytilene: See Metelin.

NAAFI Seals: Nov. 1, 1932.
Nabha, Indian Convention State of: May 1885.
Nagasaki, Japan (Treaty Port): Aug. 29, 1842.
Nandgaon, Indian Feudatory State of: February 1892.
Nanking: Sept. 20, 1896.
Nanumaga: April 23, 1984.
Nanumea: April 9, 1984.
Naples: June 28, 1917.
Naples, Kingdom of: Jan. 1, 1858.
Natal: 1846; May 26, 1857; 1869; June 30, 1898; May 31, 1910.
National Bank Note Company: April 1870; May 1, 1873.
Nauru: July 14, 1905; Oct. 23, 1916; Jan. 31, 1968; April 17, 1969.
Navarre: July 1, 1873.
Neale, Thomas: Oct. 31, 1671; Feb. 17, 1692; April 4, 1692; Nov. 11, 1692; May 1, 1693; May 15, 1693; June

5, 1693; June 9, 1693; May 10, 1694.
Neapolitan Provinces: February 1861.
Nebraska, State of: March 1, 1867.
Nebraska, Territory of: May 30, 1854.
Negri Sembilan: August 1891; 1899.
Nejd (later Saudi Arabia): March 1925.
Nepal: May 16, 1881; Oct. 11, 1956; Oct. 16, 1958; April 15, 1959; Nov. 1, 1959.
Netherlands: June 13, 1668; March 1815; Jan. 1, 1852; Jan. 1, 1871; Aug. 23, 1905; Dec. 1, 1906; 1921; May 1, 1921; Oct. 25, 1925; Dec. 17, 1934; Aug. 6, 1946; Oct. 6, 1946; Dec. 1, 1949; March 14, 1978.
Netherlands Antilles: Dec. 17, 1934; June 17, 1938; July 26, 1949; Sept. 18, 1963; Dec. 3, 1968. See Curacao.
Netherlands Indies: April 1, 1864; June 1908; June 10, 1915; Sept. 20, 1928; Oct. 15, 1938; March 9, 1943; Aug. 1, 1943.
Netherlands National Post established: March 1815.
Netherlands New Guinea: 1950; Feb. 9, 1953; Oct. 1, 1962; May 1, 1963.

Nevada, State of: Oct. 31, 1864.
Nevada, Territory of: March 2, 1861.
Nevis: May 1, 1860; 1861; June 23, 1980.
New Amsterdam: See New York.
New Britain: See German New Guinea.
New Brunswick: 1783; July 6, 1851; Sept. 5, 1851; Nov. 1, 1858; July 1, 1867. See Connell, Charles.
New Caledonia: Jan. 1, 1860; June 24, 1892; July 20, 1929; Jan. 1, 1959.
New Carlisle, Quebec, Canada, postmaster's provisional envelope: April 7, 1851.
Newfoundland: April 18, 1805; July 14, 1840; April 2, 1844; July 1, 1851; May 30, 1856; Jan. 1, 1857; Nov. 15, 1865; Jan. 1, 1879; April 12, 1919; May 18, 1919; June 9, 1919; June 14, 1919; July 17, 1919; March 28, 1921; Nov. 7, 1921; May 21, 1927; May 23, 1927; Sept. 25, 1930; Oct. 9, 1930; Jan. 2, 1931; May 20, 1932; July 24, 1933; Aug. 8, 1933; July 5, 1937; June 27, 1939; May 1, 1942; June 24, 1947; April 1, 1949.
New France: 1705; 1734.
New Guinea, Territory of: Oct. 17, 1914; 1925. See German New Guinea, Northwest Pacific Islands, Papua and New Guinea.
New Hampshire: June 5, 1693; June 21, 1788.
New, Harry S., US PMG: March 4, 1923.
New Hebrides: March 17, 1897; Oct. 6, 1906; Oct. 29, 1908; Nov. 21, 1908; March 1, 1911; July 19, 1929; July 16, 1947.
New Jersey: 1709; Dec. 18, 1787.
New Mexico, State of: Jan. 6, 1912.
New Mexico, Territory of: Sept. 27, 1850; Dec. 13, 1850.
New Republic: Jan. 1, 1886; May 31, 1910.
New South Wales: July 10, 1803; Nov. 1, 1838; 1840; June 10, 1841; Oct. 10, 1843; June 11, 1844; Jan. 1, 1850; March 3, 1852; Oct. 20, 1853; 1888; Oct. 1, 1891; June 22 and 28, 1897. See Australia.
Newspaper stamp: See Stamp, newspaper.
Newspaper wrappers: Feb. 27, 1861; October 1861; October 1870.
New York: 1660; Jan. 1, 1673; 1684; Nov. 11, 1692; February 1756; Jan. 1, 1757; 1763; Dec. 25, 1775; March 3, 1784; April 25, 1785; July 26, 1788; Feb. 1, 1842; July 15, 1845; Nov. 2, 1845; May 15, 1918.
New York Foreign Mail Cancels: 1870.

New York, Rio, and Buenos Aires Line (NYRBA): Feb. 19, 1930.
New York, State of: April 25, 1785.

New Zealand: January 1840; Oct. 11, 1841; September 1852; July 18, 1855; Dec. 17, 1863; June 15, 1866; Jan. 1, 1873; Jan. 2, 1891; February 1893; May 14, 1897; Nov. 19, 1901; Nov. 29, 1902; 1904; June 1904; July 11, 1904; Sept. 10, 1904; Feb. 8, 1906; Oct. 1, 1907; Nov. 29, 1910; May 18, 1914; Dec. 16, 1919; Nov. 4, 1925; Dec. 11, 1929; Nov. 11, 1931; Nov. 12, 1931; Feb. 17, 1934; April 27, 1940; Nov. 17, 1941; March 2, 1945; April 24, 1947.

Nicaragua: Dec. 2, 1862; May 1, 1882; May 4, 1889; April 15, 1921; July 1921; May 15, 1929; August 1929; Sept. 25, 1973; May 6, 1985.
Nicobar Islands: See Andaman and Nicobar Islands.
Niger: 1921; Oct. 24, 1938; Feb. 8, 1940; Dec. 19, 1958; Dec. 18, 1959; April 11, 1960; June 12, 1961; April 7, 1962.
Niger Coast Protectorate: November 1891; May 12, 1893; Jan. 1, 1900. See Oil Rivers Protectorate.
Nigeria: Jan. 1, 1914; Dec. 15, 1949; July 10, 1961; Dec. 1, 1966.
Niles, John M., US PMG: May 26, 1840.
Ningpo (Treaty Port): Aug. 29, 1842.
Niuafo'ou (Tin Can Island): May 11, 1983.
Niue: Nov. 19, 1901; Jan. 4, 1902; Oct. 19, 1974; March 15, 1978.
Niutao: April 16, 1984.
Norfolk Island: 1840; June 10, 1947.
Norge **(Italian dirigible):** April 10, 1926.
North Borneo: June 1883; February 1891; Feb. 4, 1941; June 1942; Sept. 1, 1947. See Sabah.
North Borneo Company: See North Borneo.
North Carolina, State of: Nov. 21, 1789; May 21, 1861; June 25, 1868.
North Dakota, State of: Nov. 2, 1889.
Northern Ireland: Aug. 18, 1958.
Northern Nigeria: March 1900; Jan. 1, 1914.
Northern Rhodesia: Jan. 2, 1892; April 1, 1925; July 1, 1954; Dec. 1, 1963; Dec. 10, 1963; Feb. 19, 1964; Oct. 24, 1964. See Rhodesia and Nyasaland, Zambia.
North German Confederation: Jan. 1, 1868; April 1871.
North Ingermanland: March 21, 1920.
North Korea: See Korea, North.
Northwest Pacific Islands: March 15, 1915. See German New Guinea; New Guinea, Territory of; and Papua and New Guinea.
Norway: January 1855; Dec. 25, 1871; Jan. 1, 1872; July 1, 1889; Oct. 26, 1905; Oct. 2, 1911; Jan. 1, 1926; June 13, 1927; June 28, 1930; April 30, 1947; Dec. 2, 1978.
Nossi Be, French colony of: May 1889.
Nova Scotia: April 27, 1754; April 28, 1755; 1801; July 4, 1840; Sept. 1, 1851; Oct. 19, 1854; Jan. 1, 1860; July 1, 1867; April 1, 1868.
Nowanuggur (Nawanagar), Indian Feudatory State of: 1877.
Nui: March 19, 1984.
Nukufetau: April 23, 1984.
Nukulaelae: April 12, 1984.
Nyasaland Protectorate: July 6, 1907; July 22, 1908. See Rhodesia and Nyasaland, Malawi.
Nyassa: 1897.
NYRBA: See New York, Rio, and Buenos Aires Line.

Obock: Feb. 1, 1892. See also French Somali Coast, French Territory of Afars and Issas, and Djibouti, Republic of.

O'Brien, Lawrence F., US PMG: Nov. 3, 1965.

Official stamp: See Stamp, Official.

Ohio, State of: March 1, 1803.

Oil Rivers Protectorate: November 1891; July 20, 1892; May 12, 1893; Jan. 1, 1900. See Niger Coast Protectorate.

Oklahoma, State of: Nov. 16, 1907.

Oklahoma, Territory of: May 2, 1890.

Oldenburg: Jan. 5, 1852; Jan. 1, 1868.

Oldest postal service: 4,000 BC.

Oldest stamp design still in use: Dec. 25, 1871.

Oldest State Postal Service: June 19, 1464.

Olsztyn: See Allenstein.

Oltre Giuba: See Jubaland.

Oman, Sultanate of: Jan. 16, 1971; Aug. 17, 1971; Dec. 25, 1971.

Orangeburg coil: Jan. 24, 1911.

Orange Free State: Jan. 1, 1868; March 19, 1900.

Orange River Colony: March 19, 1900; Aug. 10, 1900; March 1903; May 31, 1910.

Orchha, Indian Feudatory State of: 1913.

Oregon, State of: Feb. 14, 1859.

Oregon, Territory of: Aug. 14, 1848.

Oriental calendar: Dog, 1982; Pig, 1983; Rat, 1984; Ox, 1985; Tiger, 1986; Hare, 1987; Dragon, 1988; Snake, 1989; Horse, 1990; Sheep, 1991; Monkey, 1992; Rooster, 1993; Dog, 1994.

Orleans, Territory of: Oct. 1, 1804.

Osgood, Samuel: Sept. 26, 1789; Jan. 22, 1790.

Ostland: See Estonia.

OSTROPIA souvenir sheet: June 23, 1935.

Overland Mail: See Butterfield Overland Mail.

Ovington, Earle L.: Sept. 23, 1911.

Packet boat service: 1633; June 13, 1668; October 1689; Oct. 21, 1702; June 1, 1711; July 20, 1711; April 1713; December 1745; Nov. 15, 1755; February 1756; January 1765; Sept. 7, 1768; Feb. 13, 1794; Dec. 2, 1806; April 26, 1827; Aug. 18, 1833; September 1837; April 4, 1838; May 4, 1839; March 20, 1840; May 16, 1840; Jan. 1, 1842; Oct. 10, 1843; April 2, 1844; June 11, 1844; June 1, 1847; July 1852; May 30, 1856; June 1858; November 1863; Dec. 17, 1863; June 15, 1866.

Pahang: January 1889.

Paita: April 1884.

Pakistan: Oct. 1, 1947; Nov. 10, 1947.

Palau, Republic of: March 10, 1983.

Palermo: June 28, 1917.

Palestine: Feb. 10, 1918; July 1, 1920; Sept. 1, 1920; Sept. 23, 1923; June 1, 1927; Oct. 28, 1944; May 14, 1948.

Palmer, John: 1742; Aug. 2, 1784; March 28, 1785; October 1786.

Panama: June 8, 1872; 1878; Nov. 10, 1903; June 11, 1904; Feb. 8, 1929; Dec. 20, 1961; Sept. 30, 1979.

Panama Canal Zone: See US Canal Zone.

Pan American Airways: Oct. 19, 1927; Feb. 19, 1930; April 17, 1935; June 13, 1935; Aug. 17, 1935; Oct. 5, 1935; Nov. 22, 1935; Dec. 2, 1935; April 28, 1937; April 29, 1937; March 6, 1938; Feb. 22, 1939; March 26, 1939; June 27, 1939; July 12, 1940; Oct. 26, 1958.

Pan-American Postal Union: Feb. 2, 1911.

Paper, invention of: 105 BC.

Papua: Nov. 8, 1906; Sept. 30, 1932. See British New Guinea.

Papua and New Guinea (now Papua New Guinea): Oct. 30, 1952; Sept. 16, 1975; 1976. See British New Guinea; German New Guinea; Papua; New Guinea, Territory of; and Northwest Pacific Islands.

Paraguay: Aug. 1, 1870; July 1, 1881; Aug. 20, 1886; Feb. 25, 1928; Jan. 1, 1929; Jan. 2, 1929; July 22, 1930.

Parcel post stamp: See Stamp, parcel post.

Parcel service, British: Aug. 1, 1883.

Paris: Aug. 8, 1653; May 14, 1919; Oct. 5, 1920.

Paris, balloon mail flights from: Sept. 23, 1870; Nov. 24, 1870.

Pairs Postal Conference: Aug. 4, 1862; May 11, 1863.

Parma, Italian State of: June 1, 1852; August 1859; February 1860.

Pasco: April 1884.

Pasto, Colombia: March 6, 1921.

Patiala, Indian Convention State of: 1884.

Payne, Henry C., US PMG: Jan. 15, 1902.

Peking: May 7, 1920.

Penang: Dec. 1, 1948.

Peninsula and Oriental Steam Navigation Company: September 1837; June 1858.

Pennsylvania: May 1, 1693; May 15, 1693; Dec. 12, 1787.

Penn, William: 1683.

Penny Black: June 1839; April 15, 1840; May 1, 1840; May 2, 1840; May 6, 1840; Feb. 10, 1841.

Penny Black becomes *Penny Red:* Feb. 10, 1841.

Penny Black **VR:** March 26, 1840.

Penny Postage anniversary envelope: July 2, 1890.

Penny Post, Great Britain-US: Oct. 1, 1908.

Penny Post, Ireland: 1765.

Penny Post, London: April 1, 1680; Nov. 23, 1682; 1801.

Penny Red: Jan. 17, 1841; Feb. 10, 1841.

Penrhyn: June 11, 1901; May 5, 1902; Oct. 24, 1973.

Perak: 1878.

Perfins: September 1858; March 13, 1868; March 1, 1869; May 8, 1908.

Perforated stamps: Jan. 28, 1854; July 1, 1855; Feb. 6, 1857; Oct. 25, 1925.

Perkins, Bacon, and Petch: June 1839; April 15, 1840; Aug. 14, 1851. See Perkins, Jacob.

Perkins, Jacob: July 9, 1776; 1819; July 13, 1849.

Perlis: 1909; 1912; Oct. 18, 1943; Dec. 1, 1948.

Permit mail: See US permit mail.

Perot, W.B.: 1848.

Persia: See Iran.

Persian Empire: c559 BC; c500 BC.

Perth Lamb: 1750.

Peru: Dec. 1, 1857; March 1, 1858; April 1, 1879; February 1881; April 1884; Feb. 2, 1890; Sept. 15, 1920; Dec. 10, 1927; Feb. 25, 1928; Aug. 16, 1966.

Philadelphia: 1683; 1737; July 3, 1788; Jan. 9, 1793; May 15, 1918.

Philatelic exhibitions: See Stamp exhibitions; US, international exhibitions.

Philatelic periodicals: 1862; 1863; May 1, 1863; Feb. 15, 1864; Jan. 1, 1896.

Philatelic Society, London: April 10, 1869; 1906. See Royal Philatelic Society, London.

Philatelic Truck: See US Philatelic Truck.

Philately, first use of name: Nov. 3, 1864.

Philippine Islands: Feb. 1, 1854; May 24, 1898; July 30, 1898; May 1, 1899; June 30, 1899; Aug. 16, 1899; Aug. 18, 1899; February 1900; Sept. 28, 1901; Oct. 15, 1901; April 4, 1919; Nov. 25, 1919; Jan. 1, 1922; Aug. 19, 1925; Sept. 16, 1925; May 13, 1926; Dec. 20, 1926; Nov.

9, 1928; July 13, 1931; Aug. 3, 1931; Sept. 22, 1932; Sept. 29, 1932; Nov. 15, 1935; Dec. 2, 1935; Feb. 16, 1936; May 29, 1936; Oct. 15, 1936; April 28, 1937; Feb. 22, 1939; March 4, 1942; May 18, 1942; April 1, 1943; Nov. 8, 1944; Feb. 3, 1945; July 4, 1946; Sept. 18, 1947; April 1, 1949; July 17, 1959.

Phillips, Charles J.: July 1890.

Phosphor bands on British stamps: Nov. 18, 1959.

Photogravure printing: See Printing photogravure.

Pickering, Timothy, US PMG: Aug. 12, 1791.

Picture postcards: April 7, 1906.

Piedmont, in Duchy of Savoy: Jan. 10, 1561.

Pietersburg, Stamps for: March 20, 1901; April 9, 1901.

Pigeon mail, Herm: May 26, 1949.

Pigeon mail, Great Barrier Island: May 14, 1897; Nov. 17, 1898; Sept. 5, 1908.

Pillar box: November 1851; Nov. 23, 1852; Oct. 11, 1854; March 1855.

Pioneer flights in the US: See US Pioneer flights.

Pisco: April 1884.

Pitcairn Islands: March 17, 1830; September 1844; Oct. 6, 1873; 1921; June 7, 1927; April 30, 1940; Oct. 15, 1940.

Pitney, Arthur Hill: Dec. 9, 1901; Oct. 14, 1902. See Meter, Postage.

Pitney-Bowes Postage Meter Co.: March 15, 1920; Sept. 1, 1920. See Meter, postage; American Postage Meter Co.; Pitney, Arthur Hill.

Pittsburgh: July 3, 1788.

Piura: April 1884.

Pneumatic mail service: Feb. 14, 1835; November 1865; 1867; April 1913; March 30, 1984. See US pneumatic mail lines.

Pohnpei (Ponape): See Micronesia, Federated States of.

Poland: Dec. 14, 1850; Jan. 1, 1851; Jan. 1, 1858; Jan. 1, 1860; April 1, 1865; Nov. 17, 1918; Dec. 5, 1918; Jan. 10, 1919; Jan. 27, 1919; May 1919; May 1, 1919; May 3, 1919; Aug. 5, 1919; Feb. 1, 1920; Sept. 10, 1925; Dec. 1, 1939; March 28, 1957.

Poland, General Gouvernement: Dec. 1, 1939; Aug. 17, 1940; Dec. 1, 1940.

Poland, Government-in-exile: Dec. 15, 1941; June 27, 1944; Feb. 3, 1945.

Polish post offices abroad: May 1919; Jan. 5, 1925.

Ponce provisional, Puerto Rico: 1898.

Ponta Delgada: 1892.

Pony Express: 1860; April 3, 1860; April 21, 1860; November 1860; April 1, 1861; May 1, 1861; July 1, 1861; Oct. 24, 1861; Aug. 11, 1862. See Pony Express, Eastern and Pony Express (Virginia City).

Pony Express, Eastern: 1836; July 1839.

Pony Express (Virginia City): Aug. 11, 1862; March 17, 1865.

Poonch, Indian Feudatory State of: 1876.

Porte de Mar: May 12, 1875.

Port Hood provisional: Dec. 29, 1898; Jan. 5, 1899.

Port Lagos: April 1, 1893.

Porto Rico: See Puerto Rico.

Port Said: 1899.

Port Swetenham: Aug. 23, 1926.

Portugal: 1525; 1705; Jan. 20, 1798; July 1853; 1898; Oct. 4, 1911; Sept. 18, 1926; Sept. 1, 1981. See Azores, Madeira.

Portuguese Africa: April 1, 1898.

Portuguese Congo: Aug. 5, 1894.

Portuguese Guinea: 1881; May 20, 1919; Sept. 19, 1938; Oct. 17, 1950; Sept. 10, 1974. See Guinea-Bissau.

Portuguese India: Oct. 1, 1871; April 15, 1919; Sept. 1, 1938; Oct. 21, 1950; Dec. 18, 1961.

Portuguese Timor: February 1886; Oct. 1, 1938; Feb. 1, 1951; May 3, 1976.

Posta Europa: 1864; 1865.

Postage label vending machine: June 23, 1975. See also Frama coin-operated postage label vending machine.

Postage meter: See Meter, postage.

Postal card: Jan. 26, 1869; Oct. 1, 1869; Sept. 1, 1870; Oct. 1, 1870; Nov. 15, 1870; Jan. 1, 1871; April 1, 1871; May 1, 1871; Jan. 1, 1872; May 12, 1873; May 13, 1873; Dec. 1, 1879; March 1, 1893; Feb. 9, 1907; July 1913; April 24, 1916; March 7, 1944; Jan. 10, 1949; May 4, 1956; Nov. 16, 1956; Nov. 1, 1958; Nov. 19, 1962; May 27, 1966; March 19, 1969.

Postal card, reply paid: February 1872. See US, first postal card, reply paid.

Postal Congress of Berne: Sept. 15, 1874.

Postal rates in American colonies: August 1763; Oct. 10, 1765; July 2, 1774; July 26, 1775; Sept. 30, 1775; Oct. 17, 1777; April 16, 1779; Dec. 28, 1779; May 5, 1780; Dec. 12, 1780; Feb. 24, 1781; Oct. 18, 1782; April 5, 1788; Sept. 22, 1789. See US postal rates, US air mail rates, and US registration fees.

Postal stationery: Feb. 1, 1608; Aug. 8, 1653; Nov. 17, 1818; Nov. 1, 1838; Aug. 17, 1839; May 6, 1840; May 9, 1847; Dec. 1, 1848; Dec. 14, 1850; July 1, 1853; March 16, 1860; August 1861; October 1861; Oct. 1, 1869; 1870; Sept. 1, 1870; Oct. 1, 1870; Jan. 1, 1871; April 1, 1871; Jan. 1, 1872; February 1872; May 13, 1873; Dec. 1, 1873; 1876; Oct. 6, 1877; Jan. 1, 1878; April 1, 1879; Dec. 1, 1879; 1882; Aug. 18, 1886; July 2, 1890; Oct. 25, 1892; March 1, 1893; Dec. 13, 1898; Aug. 18, 1899; February 1900; Sept. 28, 1901; May 27, 1902; Feb. 9, 1907; 1913; July 1913; April 24, 1916; May 21, 1928; Jan. 12, 1929; June 24, 1931; June 11, 1938; April 1, 1943; June 18, 1943; March 7, 1944; July 1, 1948; Nov. 1, 1958. See Aerogramme, plus other postal stationery headings.

Postal Union of the Americas and Spain: Feb. 2, 1911.

Postal Union £1: May 10, 1929.

Postbus: June 1, 1905.

Post code: Nov. 3, 1961; Jan. 1, 1966; July 1, 1967; July 1, 1968; July 1, 1969; April 1, 1971; Jan. 1, 1973; March 14, 1978; Sept. 10, 1980. See US ZIP Code.

Post horn: AD 1100.

Post horn design of Norway: Dec. 25, 1871.

Postmasters' Provisional, first known use of: July 15, 1845.

Postmaster's Provisional stamps: 1845; July 1, 1845; July 15, 1845; November 1845; 1846; Aug. 24, 1846; Nov. 25, 1846; 1858; May 8, 1981.

***Post Office Mauritius* stamps:** Sept. 21, 1847.

Post office, most northerly: April 1950.

Post set up by Edward IV of England: 1481.

Post, Wiley: Feb. 22, 1935; Aug. 20, 1935.

Pourpe, Marc: Jan. 4, 1914; Feb. 17, 1914.

Precanceled stamp: See Stamp, precanceled.

PRIDE Airletter service: Feb. 15, 1982.

Prince Edward Island: April 1, 1855; Jan. 1, 1861; Jan. 4, 1872; July 1, 1873.

Printed to private order: Oct. 8, 1855; Oct. 31, 1973.

Printing, intaglio: May 6, 1840; May 23, 1984.
Printing, photogravure: March 31, 1914; Aug. 20, 1934; Nov. 2, 1967; May 8, 1971; May 23, 1984.
Prohibited stamps: Dec. 17, 1950; July 8, 1963; May 5, 1964; July 29, 1968; April 17, 1975; April 30, 1975; Nov. 14, 1979; Dec. 16, 1979; Jan. 19, 1981; Feb. 24, 1981; May 6, 1985.
Prussia: Nov. 15, 1850; 1864; Oct. 1, 1866; June 30, 1867; Jan. 1, 1868; March 1, 1947.
Przemysl, air mail from: Oct. 6, 1914.
Publication, philatelic: 1862.
PUC £1: See Postal Union £1.
Puerto Principe: Dec. 19, 1898.
Puerto Rico: July 25, 1856; 1873; 1898; August 1898; Aug. 3, 1898; Aug. 14, 1898; Dec. 13, 1898; March 15, 1899; 1900; Dec. 3, 1927; May 17, 1932.
Puno: February 1881.

Qatar: April 1, 1957; May 23, 1963; Oct. 25, 1964; Jan. 31, 1969; Sept. 1, 1971.
Qu'aiti State in Hadhramaut: Sept. 1, 1955.
Qu'aiti State of Shihr and Mukalla: 1937; July 1942.
Quebec: August 1763; 1764; Dec. 15, 1768; 1787.
Queensland: December 1859; Nov. 1, 1860; Sept. 27, 1861; Oct. 1, 1891. See Australia.
Quelimane: 1913.
Questa, The House of: Feb. 2, 1970; Oct. 10, 1980.

R-100: See dirigible R-100.
Railway Air Mail: April 12, 1933.
Railway mail: Sept. 15, 1830; Jan. 15, 1831; Jan. 4, 1838; Jan. 24, 1838; July 7, 1838; Sept. 20, 1838; Oct. 27, 1838; Aug. 1, 1848; April 16, 1851; Jan. 4, 1852; August 1853; July 28, 1862; Aug. 28, 1864; Sept. 16, 1875; July 4, 1886; June 5, 1889; Nov. 1, 1949. See US route agents, US railroads.
Rajasthan: 1949.
Rajpipla, Indian Feudatory State of: 1880.
Randall, Alexander W., US PMG: July 25, 1866.
Raoul Island: March 2, 1945.
Rarotonga: See Cook Islands.
Ras al Khaima: Jan. 7, 1961; Dec. 21, 1964; Feb. 10, 1972. See Trucial States, United Arab Emirates.
Rawdon, Wright, Hatch & Edson: March 1, 1832; Feb. 1, 1842; March 20, 1847; June 26, 1847; May 1, 1858.
Redonda: 1979.
Regional stamps of Great Britain: Aug. 18, 1958.
Registered envelopes, special: Jan. 1, 1878.
Registration service: Jan. 6, 1841; July 1, 1855. See US registration service.
Registration stamp: Dec. 1, 1854; Nov. 15, 1875; Dec. 1, 1911.
Regulus I: June 8, 1959.
Renouard de Villayer, Jean-Jacques: Aug. 8, 1653.
Rethymo: Name given to the area of Crete under Russian administration. See Crete.
Reunion: 1852; Oct. 14, 1929; Jan. 23, 1937; 1949.
RFD: See US Rural Free Delivery.
Rhode Island, State of: May 29, 1790.
Rhodesia: See Zimbabwe and Zambia.
Rhodesia and Nyasaland: July 1, 1954; Feb. 19, 1964.
Rhodesia, Northern: See Zambia.
Rhodesia, Southern: See Zimbabwe.
Riau-Lingga Archipelago: See Riouw Archipelago.
Rio de Janeiro: Jan. 14, 1925.
Rio de Oro: 1905.
Rio Muni: 1960; Oct. 12, 1968.

Riouw Archipelago: Jan. 1, 1954.
RMS: See US Railroads.
Rocket mail: July 2, 1926; Feb. 2, 1931; April 15, 1931; June 6, 1934; Sept. 30, 1934; Oct. 30, 1934; Dec. 4, 1934; Jan. 2, 1935; April 8, 1935; June 7, 1935; June 29, 1935; July 17, 1935; Aug. 19, 1935; Sept. 22, 1935; April 9, 1940.
Rodgers, Calbraith Perry: Sept. 17, 1911.
Roger, Count of della Torre and Tassis and Valassina: 1450.
Rohrpost: See Pneumatic mail service.
Romagna: Sept. 1, 1859; February 1860.
Roman Empire: cAD 100. See *cursus publicus*.
Romania: Jan. 1, 1865; Jan. 14, 1906; Nov. 1, 1917; Sept. 1, 1928; Dec. 1, 1940.
Roman roads: cAD 100.
Roman States: Jan. 1, 1852.
Rome: May 22, 1917.
Ross Dependency: Jan. 11, 1957.
Rouad: Jan. 12, 1916.
Royal Mail Steam Packet Co.: March 20, 1840; Jan. 1, 1842.
Royal Netherlands Indies Airways (KNILM): Oct. 15, 1936.
Royal Philatelic Society, London: April 10, 1869; May 19, 1890; 1893; 1906.
Royal Philatelic Society of Canada: 1959.
Royal William: Aug. 18, 1833.
RPO: See US railroads.
Rural Free Delivery system: See US Rural Free Delivery.
Russia: 1666; 1689; 1716; June 10, 1783; Nov. 14, 1783; Feb. 4, 1788; Oct. 27, 1830; Jan. 17, 1833; April 4, 1838; Feb. 23, 1843; Jan. 1, 1845; Dec. 1, 1845; Dec. 1, 1848; Dec. 14, 1850; Jan. 1, 1851; April 16, 1851; March 1, 1856; Jan. 1, 1858; May 31, 1858; Jan. 1, 1860; January 1863; Jan. 1, 1863; Sept. 3, 1863; 1864; April 1, 1865; April 9, 1867; March 23, 1870; Jan. 1, 1872; 1897; Nov. 7, 1917; Aug. 24, 1918; Nov. 27, 1920. See USSR, Zemstvo.
Russian civil war: 1919; Aug. 1, 1919; September 1919; Oct. 10, 1919.
Russian POs in China: Nov. 27, 1920.
Russian PO in Crete: May 1899.
Russian POs in Turkish Empire: January 1863.
Russian Socialist Federal Soviet Republic: Nov. 7, 1917.
Rustenburg: June 23, 1900.
Rwanda, Republic of: July 1, 1962; April 6, 1963; Sept. 18, 1967; Aug. 23, 1973.
Ryukyu Islands: Sept. 7, 1945; Oct. 1, 1945; 1948; July 1, 1948; Feb. 15, 1950; Nov. 1, 1952; May 15, 1972.

Saar: Feb. 8, 1742; Jan. 30, 1920; April 1, 1920; April 15, 1920; Feb. 18, 1921; Oct. 25, 1926; Sept. 19, 1928; Sept. 20, 1928; March 1, 1935; 1947; Jan. 3, 1948; Oct. 12, 1948; Jan. 1, 1957.
Saba: Sept. 18, 1963.
Sabah (formerly North Borneo): July 1, 1964.
St. Christopher (St. Kitts): April 1, 1870.
St. Christopher, Nevis, and Anguilla: June 14, 1952; Nov. 17, 1952.
St. Helena: Jan. 1, 1856; October 1896; Oct. 12, 1961.
St. Kitts: June 23, 1980.
St. Louis Bears: November 1845.
St. Lucia: Dec. 18, 1860; Nov. 11, 1952; March 1, 1967; Feb. 22, 1979; 1980.

St. Marie de Madagascar: April 1894.
St. Nazaire: Aug. 17, 1918.
St. Pierre and Miquelon: January 1885; Aug. 17, 1942; Sept. 15, 1979.
St. Thomas and Prince Islands: 1869; Nov. 11, 1950; July 12, 1975.
St. Vincent: May 8, 1861; Oct. 27, 1969; Oct. 27, 1979; 1981; Feb. 22, 1984; March 29, 1984.
St. Vincent Grenadines: Nov. 14, 1973; Feb. 22, 1984; March 29, 1984.
Salonica: Feb. 28, 1916.
Salt Lake City: July 1, 1850; May 1, 1851; July 1858; May 11, 1860.
Salvador: See El Salvador.
Samoa: Oct. 1, 1877; Dec. 2, 1899; Sept. 3, 1914; Sept. 29, 1914; July 1920. See German Samoa, Western Samoa.
Samoa, American: July 20, 1900; May 16, 1931.
Samos: November 1912.
Sanabria, Nicolas: Dec. 1, 1945.
Sanitary Fair stamps: See US Sanitary Fair stamps.
San Marino: Aug. 1, 1877; April 25, 1907; July 1, 1915; Dec. 15, 1917; Sept. 20, 1923; Nov. 22, 1928; June 11, 1931; April 25, 1944; Sept. 4, 1950.
Santa Fe: Oct. 1, 1849.
Santa Fe Trail: March 3, 1847; Oct. 1, 1849; July 1, 1850; July 1, 1854; July 1, 1858; Aug. 22, 1859; Dec. 23, 1860; June 4, 1863; June 15, 1863; Jan. 21, 1865; April 13, 1866; Sept. 1, 1876; Jan. 24, 1880.
Santander, Colombian Department of: 1884.
Santiago: Jan. 1, 1919.
Sarawak: March 1, 1869; June 26, 1897; July 18, 1926; Aug. 17, 1929; 1942; Nov. 6, 1945; April 16, 1947.
Sardinia, Kingdom of: Nov. 17, 1818; Jan. 1, 1851.
Sark: 1857.
Saseno: 1923.
Saudi Arabia: August 1916; Dec. 21, 1921; Jan. 1, 1927; Jan. 1, 1934.
Saurashtra, United States of: 1949.
Savoy, Duchy of: Jan. 10, 1561.
Saxony: June 29, 1850; Jan. 1, 1868.
Scandinavian Airlines: Sept. 17, 1946; Nov. 30, 1946; Nov. 19, 1952.
Schleswig, Duchy of: 1865; Jan. 1, 1868.
Schleswig-Holstein: Nov. 15, 1850.
Schleswig, Plebiscite area of: Jan. 25, 1920.
Schweizer Renecke: August 1900.
Scinde Dawk: July 1, 1852.
Scotland: June 1, 1711; 1750; Aug. 18, 1958.
Scott, Captain Robert Falcon: Nov. 29, 1910.
Scottish Post Office united with English Post Office under British Post Office Act: 1711.
Scott, John Walter: Nov. 2, 1845; July 27, 1863; July 1867; July 1868; May 28, 1870; March 18, 1872; 1916.
Sea Horses: See Great Britain Sea Horses.
Seaway Invert: See Canadian Seaway Invert.
Seebeck, Nicholas F.: May 4, 1889.
Selangor: 1881.
Senegal: 1887; May 11, 1923; Jan. 17, 1959; June 14, 1961; Sept. 18, 1961.
Senegambia and Niger: July 1903.
Serbia: 1866; March 6, 1916; 1941; July 10, 1941.
Seville: April 4, 1920.
Seychelles: Dec. 11, 1861; 1877; April 5, 1890; June 29, 1976; 1979.
Shackleton, Ernest Henry: Jan. 1, 1908; Nov. 29, 1910.
Shanghai (Treaty Port): Aug. 29, 1842; July 1863; 1865; July 27, 1868; April 5, 1876; May 24, 1919; Nov. 27,

1920; Dec. 31, 1922. See Amoy, Chefoo, Chinkiang, Chungking, Foochow, Hankow, Ichang, Kewkiang, Nanking, Wuhu, Chinese Government Post.
Sharjah: Jan. 7, 1961; July 10, 1963; Jan. 13, 1965; Dec. 2, 1971. See Trucial States, United Arab Emirates.
Shenandoah: See USS *Shenandoah.*
Shibaura: June 2, 1912.
Ship Letter Office: Sept. 10, 1799.
Ship-to-shore mail: Nov. 25, 1926; July 31, 1927; July 20, 1929; May 16, 1931; June 12, 1931; July 25, 1952. See Catapult mail, US ship-to-shore mail.
Shore-to-ship mail: Aug. 14, 1919; July 19, 1929; July 16, 1930. See Catapult mail; US shore-to-ship mail.
Siam: See Thailand.
Sicily: Jan. 1, 1859.
Sierra Leone: Sept. 21, 1859; July 3, 1950; April 27, 1961; Jan. 26, 1962; April 27, 1963.
Singapore: Aug. 23, 1926; Sept. 1, 1948; Oct. 1, 1951; Jan. 8, 1966; March 1, 1966.
Sirius, **British steamship:** April 4, 1838.
Sirmoor, Indian Feudatory State of: June 1876.
Slogan cancel: 1661; December 10, 1917.
Sloper, Joseph: September 1858; March 13, 1868.
Slovakia: Jan. 18, 1939; Nov. 6, 1939; Nov. 20, 1939.
Slovenia: 1941.
Smile of Reims: March 15, 1930.
Smith, Charles Emory, US PMG: April 22, 1898.
Snail-damaged mail: April 30, 1946.
Society of Philatelic Americans: Oct. 31, 1983.
Solomon Islands: July 7, 1978.
Solomon Islands, British Protectorate of: See British Solomon Islands Protectorate.
Somalia: March 24, 1950; April 24, 1950; Dec. 1, 1951; Nov. 30, 1957; June 26, 1960. See Somali Democratic Republic.
Somali Coast: See French Somali Coast.
Somali Democratic Republic: June 26, 1960; July 1, 1960; April 22, 1970.
Sonora: May 25, 1913.
Soruth, Indian Feudatory State of: November 1864.
South Africa: May 31, 1910; June 1, 1910; Nov. 4, 1910; Sept. 1, 1911; Dec. 27, 1911; Feb. 26, 1925; March 2, 1925; Aug. 16, 1929; Aug. 29, 1929; July 28, 1941; May 31, 1961.
South Africa, homelands of: Bophuthatswana (Dec. 6, 1977), Ciskei (1981), Transkei (Oct. 26, 1976), Venda (Sept. 13, 1979).
South African Republic: See Transvaal.
South American Postal Union: Feb. 2, 1911.
South Arabian Federation: Nov. 25, 1963; March 31, 1965.
South Australia: 1836; Jan. 1, 1855; April 1, 1868; Oct. 1, 1891. See Australia.
South Bulgaria: Sept. 22, 1885. See also Eastern Rumelia.
South Carolina, State of: May 23, 1788; Dec. 20, 1860; June 25, 1868.
South Dakota, State of: Nov. 2, 1889.
Southern Cameroon: See Cameroon, Southern.
Southern Cross: April 4, 1931.
Southern Nigeria: Jan. 1, 1900; March 1901; Jan. 1, 1914.
Southern Rhodesia: See Zimbabwe.
Southern Yemen, People's Republic of: April 1, 1968. See Yemen, People's Democratic Republic of.
South Georgia: Nov. 20, 1909; Dec. 3, 1909; April 3, 1944; July 17, 1963; May 5, 1980.
South Korea: See Korea, South.

South Lithuania: See Lithuania, South.
South Orkneys: Feb. 21, 1944.
South Sandwich Islands: May 5, 1980.
South Shetlands: February 1944.
South West Africa: July 9, 1915; Jan. 2, 1923; December 1926; March 5, 1931.
Souvenir card, first US: March 13, 1954.
Souvenir sheet: Nov. 26, 1906; Oct. 18, 1926.
Soviet Union: Nov. 7, 1922; July 6, 1923. See Russian Empire.
Sower, The: April 1, 1903.
Space Shuttle cover: Aug. 30, 1983.
Spain: 1160, 1263; July 20, 1444; Jan. 18, 1505; October 1689; 1706; Dec. 7, 1716; Jan. 1, 1850; Jan. 23, 1850; June 20, 1852; July 1, 1854; 1869; Jan. 1, 1874; April 4, 1920; Sept. 15, 1926; Aug. 12, 1938; Aug. 14, 1938; Dec. 23, 1940; Sept. 1, 1947. See Carlist stamps, Spanish Civil War.
Spanish Civil War issues: 1936; Oct. 27, 1936; Dec. 1, 1936.
Spanish Guinea: 1902.
Spanish Morocco: July 22, 1914; Jan. 1, 1949; April 7, 1956.
Spanish post office in Morocco (Tetuan): 1908.
Spanish Sahara: 1924.
Spanish West Africa: Oct. 9, 1949; Nov. 23, 1949; March 1, 1951.
Special delivery service: See US Special Delivery Service.
Spotswood, Alexander: 1730; 1737.
Spring-Rice, Thomas: July 1839.
Squared circle cancel: September 1879.
Sri Lanka (formerly Ceylon): May 22, 1972.
Stamp auction: See Auction, stamp.
Stamp booklet: April 17, 1884; 1895; April 16, 1900; March 11, 1977.
Stamp, coil: Feb. 18, 1908; November 1912; May 10, 1920; Oct. 25, 1925.
Stamp dealer: Nov. 2, 1845; 1852; 1856; 1860; June 15, 1864; July 1867; May 28, 1870; March 18, 1872; Feb. 13, 1913.
Stamp dealing illegal: June 20, 1852.
Stamped envelope: Aug. 17, 1839; May 6, 1840; May 9, 1847; July 1, 1853.
Stamp, Europa: Sept. 15, 1956.
Stamp exhibitions: 1852; 1870; March 11, 1889. See US international philatelic exhibition.
Stamp, first: See First stamps.
Stamp, franchise: 1869.
Stamp, insured letter: Feb. 1, 1935.
Stamp, late fee: Jan. 1, 1855.
Stamp, marine insurance: See floating safe stamp.
Stamp, military: April 21, 1898.
Stamp, newspaper: 1712; Nov. 1, 1765; Jan. 1, 1851; Jan. 1, 1873.
Stamp, Official: March 26, 1840; July 1, 1854; July 1, 1873; May 1, 1879; Jan. 2, 1891; May 1923; July 1939; September 1949; Sept. 6, 1950; Jan. 3, 1964; Jan. 12, 1983.
Stamp, parcel post: July 1, 1884; Jan. 1, 1913; July 1, 1913.
Stamp, personal delivery: March 1, 1937.
Stamp, pneumatic mail: April 1913.
Stamp, postmaster's provisionals: July 1, 1845; 1846; Aug. 24, 1846; 1858.
Stamp, precanceled: 1868; Dec. 2, 1893. See US stamp, precanceled.

Stamp, registration: Dec. 1, 1854; Nov. 15, 1875; Dec. 1, 1911.
Stamp, semi-postal: June 22 and 28, 1897.
Stamp, special delivery: Oct. 1, 1885; July 1, 1898; Dec. 12, 1908.
Stamp, telegraph: 1851; 1855; 1861.
Stamp, too late: Jan. 1, 1855.
Stanley Gibbons: See Gibbons, Edward Stanley.
Stanley Gibbons Ltd.: See Gibbons, Stanley.
Steamboat mail: See US steamboat mail.
Stellaland: Feb. 1, 1884; April 4, 1884; Dec. 2, 1885.
Stephen, Heinrich von: Jan. 7, 1831; April 1871; April 8, 1897.
Stinson, Katherine: Sept. 23, 1913.
Stockdale, J.: Jan. 31, 1784.
Straits Settlements: Sept. 1, 1867; April 1, 1877; July 16, 1900; Aug. 23, 1926; March 16, 1942; 1945.
Strasbourg postal service: 1322.
Street car post office cars: See US street car mail services.
Submarine mail: June 23, 1916; May 7, 1919; Aug. 12, 1938; Aug. 14, 1938.
Sudan: March 1, 1897; March 1, 1898; January 1905; Jan. 4, 1914; Feb. 15, 1931; Jan. 9, 1954; July 27, 1956; Sept. 15, 1956.
Suez Canal: July 8, 1868; November 1869; Feb. 17, 1914.
Sumatra: Japanese occupation stamps, Aug. 1, 1943.
Summerfield, Arthur E., US PMG: Jan. 21, 1953.
Sungei Ujong: 1878.
Suriname: 1873; Jan. 2, 1942; Feb. 19, 1946; 1976.
Swatow (Treaty Port): Aug. 29, 1842.
Swaziland: Oct. 18, 1889; Jan. 2, 1933; Sept. 6, 1968; Nov. 7, 1969.
Sweden: 1620; 1636; July 1, 1855; Jan. 1, 1872; Oct. 26, 1905; June 1, 1912; Dec. 21, 1919; May 10, 1920; Sept. 17, 1920; June 27, 1945; Sept. 17, 1946; Nov. 30, 1946.
Swiss-based international organizations: See under individual names.
Swiss Republic: Sept. 3, 1798.
Switzerland: 1845; April 5, 1850; Oct. 1, 1870; Sept. 23, 1910; Dec. 1, 1913; Nov. 11, 1920; Sept. 29, 1934; May 2, 1947; Feb. 17, 1972; Aug. 8, 1976. See Swiss Republic, Basel, Geneva, Zurich.
Sydney Harbor Bridge stamp: March 14, 1932.
Sydney Views: Jan. 1, 1850.
Syria: Nov. 19, 1919; Dec. 14, 1920; April 1926; April 1, 1926; Aug. 2, 1934; May 15, 1946; Feb. 12, 1958; Nov. 2, 1961.

Tagged stamps, Canada: Jan. 13, 1962.
Tahiti: June 9, 1882. See French Oceanic Settlements, French Polynesia.
Taiwan: 1945; Nov. 4, 1945; Jan. 1, 1950.
Tanganyika: Aug. 6, 1918; June 28 1919; 1922; Dec. 9, 1961.
Tanganyika and Zanzibar, Republic of: July 7, 1964. See Tanzania.
Tangier, Morocco: Dec. 18, 1923; Sept. 18, 1926; 1927; April 30, 1957.
Tannu Tuva: See Tuva.
Tanzania, United Republic of: March 29, 1963; Oct. 29, 1964; April 15, 1965; Dec. 9, 1965; Jan. 1, 1968.
Tasmania: January 1858; Oct. 1, 1891. See Van Diemen's Land.
Tasso, Amadeo: 1290.
Taxis, Prince Maximilian Karl von: 1827.

Taylor, S. Allan: Feb. 22, 1838; Feb. 15, 1864.
Tchad: See Chad.
Tehran: Dec. 14, 1924.
Tehuantepec Route: Oct. 27, 1858.
Tennessee, State of: June 1, 1796; May 7, 1861; 1866.
Tete: 1913.
Tetuan: 1908.
Texas: Feb. 15, 1779; May 18, 1826; Feb. 7, 1829; 1830; Oct. 30, 1835; Dec. 7, 1835; Dec. 29, 1845; May 29, 1846; Feb. 1, 1861; May 31, 1861; March 3, 1870.
Thailand (Siam): Aug. 4, 1883; July 1, 1885; January 1918; Feb. 17, 1919; August 1932; Oct. 18, 1943; December 1943; May 15, 1952; Oct. 1, 1963. See Bangkok.
Thames: Jan. 1, 1842.
Theresienstadt concentration camp label: July 10, 1943.
The Sower: April 1, 1903.
Thessaly: April 21, 1898.
"They are stayed by neither snow nor...": c500 BC.
Thies, James H.: 1848.
Thrace: 1913; August 1913; December 1919; June 1920.
Thurn and Taxis: 1290; 1450; 1459; 1489; Jan. 18, 1505; 1512; 1516; 1520; 1548; 1615; April 1633; 1676; 1678; 1700; 1706; Feb. 18, 1742; 1801; March 1815; 1827; May 9, 1847; 1850; March 22, 1851; Jan. 1, 1852; June 30, 1867.
Tibet: April 26, 1903; Dec. 12, 1903; February 1910; December 1912; May 1, 1933.
Tientsin: Aug. 29, 1842; May 7, 1920.
Tierra del Fuego: January 1891.
Tin Can Island: May 11, 1983.
Titanic **disaster:** April 14, 1912.
Tlacotalpan, village in Mexico, issued stamp: October 1856.
Tobago: Aug. 1, 1879.
Togo: Sept. 28, 1914; May 1915; 1921; June 8, 1957; March 21, 1962.
Tokelau Islands: Nov. 4, 1925; May 6, 1946; June 22, 1948; Jan. 1, 1949.
Tolima, Colombian State of: 1870.
Tonga: 1886; Feb. 13, 1893; Feb. 7, 1962; June 17, 1963; Jan. 26, 1972; April 14, 1982. See Niuafo'ou (Tin Can Island).
Topical collecting: June 1, 1863; 1928.
Toppan, Carpenter & Co.: May 1, 1858.
Transcaucasian Federation: April 1923; July 6, 1923.
Transjordan: See Jordan.
Transkei: Oct. 26, 1976.
Transvaal: December 1859; 1866; May 1, 1870; April 1877; Aug. 26, 1878; 1881; 1882; June 18, 1900; May 31, 1910.
Travancore-Cochin: July 1, 1949.
Travancore, Indian Feudatory State of: Oct. 16, 1888.
Treasury Competition: Aug. 23, 1839.
Treaty of Paris: Sept. 3, 1783.
Treaty ports in China and Japan: Aug. 29, 1842; July 1, 1860; 1897; Jan. 1, 1917.
Trengganu: 1910; Oct. 18, 1943.
Trentino: Nov. 3, 1918.
Trieste: Nov. 3, 1918.
Trieste, Zone A: Oct. 10, 1947; May 30, 1952; Nov. 15, 1954.
Trinidad: April 24, 1847; Aug. 14, 1851.
Trinidad and Tobago: 1913; Sept. 18, 1914; Oct. 1, 1946; Oct. 10, 1949; Feb. 1, 1950; April 22, 1958; Aug. 31, 1962; June 16, 1963.
Tripolitania: Oct. 24, 1923, July 26, 1930; March 1931;

May 1, 1934; Nov. 5, 1934.
Tristan da Cunha: Jan. 1, 1952; Jan. 2, 1954; Oct. 10, 1961; 1963.
Trollope, Anthony: April 24, 1815; November 1851; Nov. 23, 1852; March 1855; June 1858; March 1868.
Trondheim, mail dropped at: Oct. 2, 1911.
Trucial States: Jan. 7, 1961.
Truk: See Micronesia, Federated States of.
Tuke, Sir Brian: 1510; 1533.
Tulcan, Ecuador: March 6, 1921.
Tunisia: March 1, 1956; Nov. 1, 1956; July 25, 1957; Aug. 8, 1957.
Tunisia, French Protectorate of: July 1, 1888; February 1915; April 1919; May 5, 1952. See Tunisia.
Turin: May 22, 1917.
Turkey: Jan. 1, 1863; April 9, 1867; November 1920; 1926; 1928; July 15, 1934; July 1, 1947.
Turkey in Asia: November 1920.
Turks and Caicos Islands: 1900; 1916. See Caicos Islands, Turks Islands.
Turks Islands: April 4, 1867.
Tuscany, Italian State of: April 1, 1851; Oct. 1, 1854; Jan. 1, 1860.
Tuscumbia: 1858.
Tuva (now Tuva Autonomous Soviet Socialist Republic): October 1926; Oct. 11, 1944.
Tuvalu (formerly Ellice Islands): Jan. 1, 1976; May 20, 1982. See Funafuti, Nanumaga, Nanumea, Niutao, Nui, Nukefetau, Nukulaelae, and Vaitupu.
Twelvepenny Black: June 14, 1851.
Twopenny Blue: May 8, 1840.
Tyner, James N., US PMG: July 13, 1876.

Ubangi-Shari-Chad: 1915.
Uchermann, Karl: June 15, 1903.
Uganda: March 20, 1895; 1903; Oct. 9, 1962; Feb. 13, 1964; April 15, 1965.
Ukraine: July 1918; May 13, 1947.
Umm al Qiwain: Jan. 7, 1961; June 29, 1964; Dec. 2, 1971. See Trucial States, United Arab Emirates.
Umm Said (Qatar): April 1, 1948.
Undersea post office: Aug. 16, 1939.
UNESCO: Jan. 23, 1961.
Unicorn, **British steamship:** May 16, 1840.
Union Island: March 29, 1984.
Union Islands: See Tokelau Islands.
United Arab Emirates: Dec. 2, 1971; Feb. 10, 1972; August 1972; March 30, 1973.
United Arab Republic: Feb. 12, 1958; April 3, 1958; Jan. 2, 1959; April 29, 1961.
United Nations: Feb. 1, 1950; Oct. 24, 1951; Aug. 29, 1952. See also UN, Geneva: Oct. 4, 1969; UN, Vienna: Aug. 24, 1979.
United Nations, Geneva: See United Nations.
United Nations, Vienna: See United Nations.
United States: See under various "US" headings.
United States City Despatch Post: See US, City Despatch Post.
United States of New Granada: 1861. See Colombia, Republic of; United States of New Granada; Granadine Confederation.
Universal Postal Union: 1841; Aug. 4, 1862; Sept. 15, 1875; May 2, 1878; Oct. 9, 1880; Feb. 4, 1885; May 20, 1891; May 5, 1897; July 2, 1900; April 7, 1906; Oct. 4, 1909; Sept. 1, 1920; Oct. 1, 1920; Jan. 1, 1922; July 4, 1924; Sept. 1, 1927; May 10, 1929; Feb. 1, 1934; April 1, 1939; May 7, 1947; Oct. 9, 1949; May 14, 1952; Aug. 14,

1957; May 29, 1964; Oct. 1, 1969; May 20, 1970; May 22, 1974; Sept. 12, 1979; Sept. 15, 1979; June 6, 1984.

University messengers: c1200.

Upper Senegal and Niger: 1906.

Upper Silesia: Feb. 20, 1920.

Upper Volta: 1920; Dec. 10, 1959; March 4, 1961; April 7, 1962; March 29, 1963; June 30, 1985. See Bourkina Fasso.

Uruguay: Oct. 1, 1856; June 26, 1859; July 1, 1880; Aug. 25, 1912; August 1921; Jan. 15, 1922; June 1, 1922; Jan. 14, 1925; Nov. 13, 1930; May 18, 1936; Dec. 29, 1959.

US, Adams mail pick-up: June 12, 1929; May 12, 1939.

US airlines carry regular mail: Oct. 6, 1953.

US air mail: Jan. 9, 1793; Aug. 17, 1859; June 18, 1877; Jan. 18, 1914; May 13, 1918; May 15, 1918; July 15, 1918; Aug. 12, 1918; Jan. 30, 1919; March 3, 1919; July 3, 1919; Aug. 14, 1919; Sept. 8, 1920; Sept. 10, 1920; Oct. 15, 1920; Nov. 1, 1920; Feb. 22, 1921; Feb. 2, 1924; March 17, 1924; July 1, 1924; Oct. 8, 1924; Feb. 2, 1925; Feb. 21, 1925; June 6, 1925; July 1, 1925; July 3, 1925; Aug. 31, 1925; Jan. 19, 1926; Feb. 15, 1926; April 6, 1926; April 10, 1926; April 15, 1926; Sept. 16, 1926; Nov. 3, 1926; Nov. 25, 1926; July 31, 1927; Sept. 1, 1927; Feb. 6, 1928; Feb. 20, 1928; Feb. 4, 1929; March 9, 1929; June 12, 1929; Sept. 20, 1929; Nov. 28, 1929; Jan. 24, 1931; May 16, 1931; June 12, 1931; Feb. 19, 1934; May 31, 1934; Oct. 8, 1934; Feb. 22, 1935; April 17, 1935; May 14, 1935; May 19, 1935; June 13, 1935; Aug. 17, 1935; Aug. 20, 1935; Oct. 5, 1935; Nov. 22, 1935; Dec. 2, 1935; April 28, 1937; April 29, 1937; May 8, 1937; March 6, 1938; Feb. 22, 1939; March 26, 1939; May 12, 1939; June 27, 1939; July 6, 1939; July 12, 1940; June 15, 1942; June 22, 1946; July 5, 1946; Oct. 1, 1946; Oct. 1, 1947; Oct. 6, 1953; July 26, 1955; Oct. 26, 1958; Jan. 25, 1959. See Air mail; US air mail rates; US dirigibles *Akron, Los Angeles,* and *Macon;* US pioneer flights; individual airlines; and various Zeppelin headings.

US air mail contract, first: Feb. 2, 1924.

US air mail invert: May 14, 1918.

US air mail postal card: Jan. 10, 1949.

US air mail rates: May 15, 1918; July 15, 1918; Dec. 15, 1918; July 18, 1919; July 1, 1924; July 1, 1925; Jan. 19, 1926; Sept. 15, 1926; Jan. 25, 1927; Feb. 1, 1927; July 25, 1928; Aug. 1, 1928; July 6, 1932; July 1, 1934; March 26, 1944; Oct. 1, 1946; Jan. 1, 1949; Aug. 1, 1958; Jan. 7, 1963; Jan. 7, 1968; May 16, 1971; March 2, 1974; Oct. 11, 1975; Dec. 28, 1975.

US air mail route, first: May 15, 1918.

US Alaska-Yukon-Pacific Exposition issue: June 1, 1909.

US Army began to fly mail: Feb. 19, 1934; ceased May 3, 1934.

US "A" stamp: May 22, 1978.

US "Baby Zep" 50c air mail stamp: Oct. 2, 1933.

US "Beacon" air mail stamp: July 25, 1928.

US begins use of Parcel Post stamps: Jan. 1, 1913.

US blizzard mail: March 12, 1888.

US "B" stamp: March 15, 1981.

US Canal Zone: June 24, 1904; Feb. 9, 1907; April 24, 1916; May 7, 1919; May 21, 1928; Feb. 4, 1929; April 1, 1929; Nov. 1, 1958; Sept. 30, 1979.

US Carriers' stamps: July 1, 1851.

US Certified Mail inaugurated: June 6, 1955.

US Citizens' Stamp Advisory Committee: Feb. 1, 1985.

US, City Despatch Post: Feb. 1, 1842; Aug. 16, 1842; Nov. 28, 1846.

US COD service: July 1913.

US Collection and Distribution Wagon Service: Oct. 1, 1896; April 3, 1899; Dec. 20, 1899.

US commemorative revenue stamp: July 2, 1962.

US Congress abolishes franking privilege: Jan. 31, 1873.

US Congress passes Postal Act: Sept. 22, 1789.

US consular service fee stamps: See US stamp, consular service fee.

US "C" stamp: Oct. 11, 1981.

US Dead Letter Office: 1825; March 16, 1877.

US modern definitive series': Presidential, April 25, 1938; Liberty, June 24, 1954; Prominent Americans, Nov. 19, 1965; Americana, Oct. 31, 1975; Great Americans, Dec. 27, 1980.

US Departmental stamps: See US Official stamps.

US, Douglas Fairbanks commemorative stamp: May 23, 1984.

US "D" stamp: Feb. 1, 1985.

US E-COM: Jan. 4, 1982.

US Express Mail "Next Day" Service: July 18, 1983; Aug. 12, 1983; Feb. 17, 1985; April 29, 1985.

US Federal Boating stamps: April 1, 1960.

US Federal Migratory Waterfowl Hunting stamp (Duck stamp): March 16, 1934; Aug. 14, 1934; Sept. 1, 1949; July 1, 1959; July 1, 1972; July 1, 1979.

US, first adhesive commemorative stamps: Jan. 2, 1893.

US, first adhesive postage stamp: Feb. 1, 1842.

US, first aerial mail delivery and pick-up from ship: June 12, 1929.

US, first aerogramme: April 29, 1947.

US, first air express: Sept. 1, 1927.

US, first air mail by jet aircraft: June 22, 1946.

US, first air mail on regularly scheduled turbo-prop aircraft: July 26, 1955.

US, first air mail postal card: Jan. 10, 1949.

US, first air mail route: May 15, 1918.

US, first air mail special delivery stamp: Aug. 30, 1934.

US, first air mail stamp: May 13, 1918.

US, first air mail stamped envelope: Jan. 12, 1929.

US, first all-different pane of 50 stamps: Feb. 23, 1976.

US, first automatic stamp-vending machine: May 6, 1948.

US, first Christmas stamp: Nov. 1, 1962.

US, first coil stamps: Feb. 18, 1908.

US, first commemorative postal stationery: 1876.

US, first commemorative (Smokey Bear) printed on combination "D" press: Aug. 13, 1984.

US, first commemorative produced in combination of intaglio and letterpress: Nov. 21, 1952.

US, first Contract Air Mail Route (CAM): Feb. 15, 1926.

US, first-day cancel: July 13, 1937.

US, first envelope maker: 1835.

US, first Federal Migratory Waterfowl Hunting Stamp (Duck stamp): Aug. 14, 1934 (see US Federal Migratory Waterfowl Hunting stamp).

US, first 50 all-different stamps issued in one pane: Feb. 23, 1976.

US, first Foreign Air Mail route (FAM-2) established: Oct. 15, 1920.

US, first fractional denomination stamp: March 19, 1925.

US, first Giori-printed postage stamp: July 4, 1957.

US, first helicopter mail: July 5, 1946.
US, first intaglio and letterpress stamp: Nov. 21, 1952.
US, first intaglio and offset lithographed stamp: June 22, 1943.
US, first integrated intaglio-photogravure stamp: May 23, 1984.
US, first lettersheet: August 1861.
US, first machine slogan cancel: July 19, 1899.
US, first mailbox: 1858.
US, first multicolor international single and reply postal card: Nov. 16, 1956.
US, first multicolored postal card: May 4, 1956.
US, first nationally valid adhesive postage stamps: March 3, 1847; July 1, 1847.
US, first newspaper wrapper: October 1861.
US, first New York-Paris scheduled air mail: Oct. 26, 1958.
US, first official missile mail: June 8, 1959.
US, first Pacific Coast shore-to-ship mail: Jan. 24, 1931.
US, first perfins authorized: May 8, 1908.
US, first perforated stamps: Feb. 6, 1857.
US, first philatelic auction: May 28, 1870.
US, first photogravure printed stamp: Nov. 2, 1967.
US, first photogravure printed stamp by the Bureau of Engraving and Printing: May 8, 1971.
US, first pictorial postal card: May 27, 1966.
US, first postage due labels: July 1, 1879.
US, first postal card: Nov. 15, 1870; May 12, 1873; May 13, 1873.
US, first postal card, reply paid: Oct. 25, 1892.
US, first postal card with tagged area: March 19, 1969.
US, first post office in Alaska: July 23, 1867.
US, first precancel: Sept. 1, 1847.
US, first precanceled postal card: Nov. 19, 1962.
US, first railway post office: July 28, 1862.
US, first reply paid postal card, international: March 1, 1893.
US, first rotary-press printed stamp: June 30, 1914.
US, first self-adhesive stamp: Nov. 15, 1974.
US, first se-tenant booklet pane: March 11, 1977.
US, first ship-to-shore mail: Nov. 25, 1926.
US, first shore-to-ship mail: Aug. 14, 1919.
US, first souvenir card: March 13, 1954.
US, first souvenir sheet: Oct. 18, 1926.
US, first special delivery stamp: Oct. 1, 1885.
US, first stamp booklet: April 16, 1900.
US, first stamp booklet with dull gum: March 1971.
US, first stamp booklet with se-tenant stamps: March 11, 1977.
US, first stamp collector: 1855.
US, first stamp dealer: 1860.
US, first stamped envelope: July 1, 1853.
US, first stamp exhibition: March 11, 1889.
US, first stamp showing airplane: Dec. 16, 1912.
US, first stamp with Mr. ZIP figure in selvedge: Jan. 10, 1964.
US, first stamp with two plate number positions per pane: Oct. 10, 1974.
US, first transatlantic air mail by US jet aircraft: Oct. 26, 1958.
US, first transatlantic steamship of US registry: June 1, 1847.
US, first transcontinental air mail service by jet aircraft: Jan. 25, 1959.

US, first trancontinental air mail route inaugurated: July 1, 1924.
US, first undenominated postage stamps: Oct. 14, 1975.
US, first use of resin-dextrin dry gum: March 1971.
US, first USPOD motor vehicle test: Dec. 20, 1899.
US, first woman deputy PMG: Feb. 16, 1985.
US flag cancels: Oct. 31, 1894; Sept. 30, 1940; May 24, 1941.
US flying post office: Oct. 1, 1946.
US franking privilege abolished: July 1, 1873.
US grilled stamps: Oct. 22, 1867.
US guided missile mail: June 8, 1959.
US "gummed side out" coils available: Dec. 1, 1927.
US Hammarskjold "invert:" Nov. 16, 1962.
US, helicopter mail: July 5, 1946; Oct. 1, 1947.
US Highway Post Office service: Feb.10, 1941.
US, International Philatelic Exhibitions: Oct. 27, 1913; Oct. 16, 1926; May 9, 1936; May 17, 1947; April 28, 1956; May 21, 1966; May 29, 1976; May 22, 1986.
US Jamestown Exposition issue: April 26, 1907.
US joins UPU: July 1, 1875.
US, Kansas and Nebraska overprints: April 15, 1929; May 1, 1929.
US Kelly Act: Feb. 2, 1925.
US, last horse-drawn postal service: Jan. 31, 1955.
US, Legend of Sleepy Hollow commem.: Oct. 10, 1974.
US letter sheet: August 1861; Aug. 18, 1886; June 30, 1894.
US Louisiana Purchase Exposition issue: April 30, 1904.
US mailcoach: April 25, 1785; Dec. 31, 1785; 1858; May 10, 1869. See Mailcoach, US mail in the West.
US mail delivery: July 1, 1851.
US "Mail Early..." marginal inscription: March 30, 1968.
US Mailgram: Sept. 6, 1974.
US mail in the West: March 3, 1847; Oct. 1, 1848; Feb. 28, 1849; Oct. 1, 1849; July 1, 1850; May 1, 1851; April 22, 1854; July 1, 1854; 1857; July 1, 1857; Sept. 16, 1857; 1858; July 1858; July 1, 1858; Sept. 15, 1858; Oct. 27, 1858; Nov. 23, 1858; December 1858; May 7, 1859; Aug. 22, 1859; 1860; February 1860; April 3, 1860; April 21, 1860; May 11, 1860; Sept. 15, 1860; Dec. 23, 1860; March 2, 1861; July 1, 1861; June 4, 1863; June 15, 1863; Jan. 21, 1865; April 13, 1866; May 10, 1869; Sept. 1, 1876; Jan. 24, 1880. See Butterfield Overland Mail, Pony Express, Wells, Fargo & Co.
US mail prepayment by stamps or postal stationery compulsory: Jan. 1, 1856.
US mail prepayment compulsory: April 1, 1855.
US mail via Panama: March 3, 1847; Oct. 1, 1848; Dec. 1, 1848; Jan. 17, 1849; Feb. 28, 1849.
US money order service: Nov. 1, 1864.
US moon landing cover: July 20, 1969.
US moon landing stamp: Sept. 9, 1969.
US motor vehicles used by Post Office: Dec. 20, 1899; Oct. 1, 1906; Aug. 7, 1912; July 1, 1918.
US motor vehicle use revenue stamps: February 1942.
US national postage stamps: March 3, 1847; July 1, 1847.
US newspaper stamps: September 1865.
US newspaper wrappers: Feb. 27, 1861; October 1861.
US, New York-Paris air mail service using jet aircraft: Oct. 26, 1958.
US, official airplane mail: Sept. 23, 1911.

US, Official postal card: July 1913.
US Officially Sealed labels: March 16, 1877; May 15, 1972.
US, Official stamped envelopes authorized: July 1, 1873.
US, Official stamps for postal savings correspondence: Dec. 22, 1910.
US Official stamps: July 1, 1873; May 1, 1879; July 5, 1884; Jan. 12, 1983; Feb. 4, 1985; May 15, 1985.
US Overrun Countries issue: June 22, 1943.
US Panama-Pacific Exposition issue: Jan. 1, 1913.
US Pan-American Exposition issue: May 1, 1901.
US parcel post: July 22, 1887; Oct. 1, 1899; Dec. 16, 1912; Jan. 1, 1913; July 1, 1913.
US Parcel Post postage due labels: Nov. 27, 1912.
US penalty envelopes: March 3, 1877; May 1, 1879.
US permit mail: April 28, 1904; Oct. 1, 1904.
US Philatelic Agency: See US Philatelic Sales Division.
US Philatelic Sales Division: Dec. 9, 1921.
US Philatelic Truck: May 15, 1939; Jan. 12, 1940; Dec. 13, 1941.
US Pictorial issue of 1869: March 27, 1869; April 2, 1869.
US Pioneer flights: Nov. 3, 1910; Sept. 17, 1911; Sept. 23, 1911; Oct. 4, 1911; Oct. 8, 1911; Oct. 17, 1911; Oct. 21, 1911; Nov. 3, 1911; Nov. 6, 1911; Nov. 16, 1911; Nov. 25, 1911; Dec. 12, 1911; Dec. 28, 1911; Jan. 2, 1912; Jan. 20, 1912; Feb. 17, 1912; March 2, 1912; March 12, 1912; March 24, 1912; April 6, 1912; April 10, 1912; April 21, 1912; May 15, 1912; May 18, 1912; May 30, 1912; June 3, 1912; June 6, 1912; June 7, 1912; June 27, 1912; June 30, 1912; July 4, 1912; July 12, 1912; July 17, 1912; July 19, 1912; July 20, 1912; July 21, 1912; July 22, 1912; Aug. 3, 1912; Aug. 6, 1912; Aug. 10, 1912; Aug. 20, 1912; Aug. 23, 1912; Aug. 28, 1912; Sept. 6, 1912; Sept. 9, 1912; Sept. 10, 1912; Sept. 16, 1912; Sept. 21, 1912; Sept. 26, 1912; Sept. 28, 1912; Oct. 4, 1912; Oct. 12, 1912; Oct. 31, 1912; Nov. 24, 1912; Jan. 13, 1913; March 29, 1913; April 19, 1913; May 17, 1913; Sept. 2, 1913; Sept. 4, 1913; Sept. 9, 1913; Sept. 15, 1913; Sept. 23, 1913; Oct. 4, 1913; Oct. 17, 1913; Jan. 18, 1914; May 30, 1914; June 28, 1914; Sept. 17, 1914; Oct. 17, 1914; Nov. 3, 1914; Feb. 20, 1915; May 20, 1915; Aug. 7, 1915; Aug. 14, 1915; Sept. 6, 1915; Sept. 13, 1915; Sept. 21, 1915; Nov. 4, 1915; July 3, 1916; July 18, 1916; Oct. 5, 1916; Oct. 13, 1916; Nov. 2, 1916.
US pneumatic tube mail lines: March 1, 1893; October 1897; December 1897; 1915; June 30, 1918; Oct. 2, 1922; Aug. 1, 1926; April 28, 1950; Dec. 31, 1950; Dec. 31, 1953.
US POD's Aerial Mail Service: July 15, 1918; Aug. 12, 1918.
US Possessions join UPU: Oct. 1, 1907.
US postage currency: Aug. 21, 1862; May 27, 1863.
US Postage due labels: July 1, 1879.
US postal card: Nov. 15, 1870; May 12, 1873; May 13, 1873; Dec. 1, 1879; March 1, 1893; July 1913; Jan. 10, 1949; May 4, 1956; Nov. 16, 1956; Nov. 19, 1962; May 27, 1966; March 19, 1969.
US postal convention with Germany: Oct. 1, 1899.
US Postal Inspection Service: November 1772; March 6, 1801; June 11, 1880; Feb. 2, 1939.
US Postal Insurance labels: Aug. 19,1965.
US postal note stamps: Feb. 1, 1945; March 31, 1951.
US postal rates: April 5, 1788; Sept. 22, 1789; Feb. 20, 1792; June 1, 1792; June 1, 1794; March 2, 1799; Dec. 23, 1814; Feb. 1, 1815; Feb. 1, 1816; March 31, 1816;

May 1, 1816; May 1, 1825; July 2, 1836; March 3, 1845; July 1, 1845; March 3, 1847; Aug. 14, 1848; March 3, 1849; Sept. 27, 1850; July 1, 1851; Oct. 1, 1852; April 1, 1855; April 3, 1860; June 30, 1863; July 1, 1863; June 30, 1864; Jan. 1, 1868; Jan. 1, 1869; Jan. 1, 1874; July 1, 1875; Oct. 1, 1883; July 1, 1885; Jan. 1, 1893; Oct. 1, 1908; July 16, 1917; Nov. 2, 1917; April 3, 1918; July 1, 1919; July 18, 1919; July 6, 1932; May 14, 1952; Aug. 1, 1958; Jan. 7, 1963; Jan. 7, 1968; May 16, 1971; March 2, 1974; Oct. 11, 1975; Dec. 31, 1975; May 29, 1978; March 22, 1981; Nov. 1, 1981; Feb. 17, 1985. See Postal rates in American colonies, US air mail rates, US registration fees, US ship letter rates, US steamship rates and routes.
US Postal Savings stamps: Jan. 3, 1911.
US Postal Service: Aug. 12, 1970; July 1, 1971.
US, Postal Transportation Service: Nov. 1, 1949.

US postmasters general and appointment dates: Samuel Osgood (Sept. 26, 1789), Timothy Pickering (Aug. 12, 1791), Joseph Habersham (Feb. 25, 1795), Gideon Granger (Nov. 28, 1801), Return J. Meigs Jr. (April 11, 1814), John McLean (July 1, 1823), William T. Barry (April 6, 1829), Amos Kendall (May 1, 1835), John M. Niles (May 26, 1840), Francis Granger (March 8, 1841), Charles A. Wickliffe (Oct. 13, 1841), Cave Johnson (March 7, 1845), Jacob Collamer (March 8, 1849), Nathan K. Hall (July 23, 1850), Samuel D. Hubbard (Sept. 14, 1852), James Campbell (March 8, 1853), Aaron V. Brown (March 7, 1857), Joseph Holt (March 14, 1859), Horatio King (Feb. 12, 1861), Montgomery Blair (March 9, 1861), William Dennison (Oct. 1, 1864), Alexander W. Randall (July 25, 1866), John A.J. Creswell (March 6, 1869), Jas. W. Marshall (July 7, 1874), Marshall Jewell (Sept. 1, 1874), James N. Tyner (July 13, 1876), David McK. Key (March 13, 1877), Horace Maynard (Aug. 25, 1880), Thomas L. James (March 8, 1881), Timothy O. Howe (Jan. 5, 1882), Walter Q. Gresham (April 11, 1883), Frank Hatton (Oct. 14, 1884), Wm. F. Vilas (March 7, 1885), Don. M. Dickinson (Jan. 17, 1888), John Wanamaker (March 6, 1889), Wilson S. Bissell (March 7, 1893), William L. Wilson (April 4, 1895), James A. Gary (March 6, 1897), Charles Emory Smith (April 22, 1898), Henry C. Payne (Jan. 15, 1902), Robert J. Wynne (Oct. 10, 1904), Geo. B. Cortelyou (March 7, 1905), Geo. von L. Meyer (March 4, 1907), Frank H. Hitchcock (March 6, 1909), Albert S. Burleson (March 5, 1913), Will H. Hays (March 5, 1921), Hubert Work (March 4, 1922), Harry S. New (March 4, 1923), Walter F. Brown (March 6, 1929), James A. Farley (March 4, 1933), Frank C. Walker (Sept. 11, 1940), Robert E. Hannegan (July 1, 1945), Jesse M. Donaldson (Dec. 16, 1947), Arthur E. Summerfield (Jan. 21, 1953), J. Edward Day (Jan. 21, 1961), John A. Gronouski (Sept. 30, 1963), Lawrence F. O'Brien (Nov. 3, 1965), W. Marvin Watson (April 26, 1968), Winton M. Blount (Jan. 22, 1969), Elmer T. Klassen (Dec. 7, 1971), Benjamin Franklin Bailar (Feb. 15, 1975), William F. Bolger (March 1, 1978), Paul N. Carlin (Jan. 1, 1985). See also pre-US postmasters general Benjamin Franklin (July 26, 1775), Richard Bache (Nov. 7, 1776), and Ebenezer Hazard (Jan. 28, 1782).

US postmasters' provisionals: See Postmaster's Provisional stamps.
US Post Office Department from 1825 to June 30, 1971: See under individual US headings. See also American General Post Office, US Postal Service.

US post office seals: 1872; March 16, 1877.
US post offices in California: Nov. 1, 1848; November 1849; July 30, 1851.
US post offices in Panama: June 8, 1872.
US post offices on naval ships: July 1, 1908.
US prestamped wrappers: Feb. 27, 1861; October 1861.
US Project Mercury stamp: Feb. 20, 1962.
US, PTS: See Postal Transportation Service.
US railroads: Jan. 15, 1831; Nov. 30, 1832; Jan. 1, 1836; July 7, 1838; Sept. 20, 1838; July 28, 1862; Aug. 28, 1864; Sept. 16, 1875; Nov. 1, 1949; June 30, 1977; Oct. 30, 1984.
US Railway Mail Service: See US Railroads.
US Railway Post Office: See US Railroads.
US registration fees: July 1, 1855; July 1, 1863; Jan. 1, 1869; Jan. 1, 1874; July 1, 1875; Oct. 1, 1878; May 1, 1879; Jan. 1, 1893; July 1, 1898; July 1, 1902; Nov. 1, 1909; July 1, 1911; Dec. 31, 1912; April 1, 1923; April 15, 1925; July 1, 1928; March 18, 1931; July 1, 1932; July 9, 1934; March 26, 1944; Jan. 1, 1949; Jan. 1, 1952; July 1, 1957; Aug. 15, 1961; March 26, 1966; July 14, 1969; May 16, 1971; April 18, 1975; July 18, 1976; May 29, 1978; March 22, 1981; Feb. 17, 1985.
US registration seal: Feb. 14, 1872.
US registration service: July 1, 1855; May 1, 1856; Oct. 1, 1856; Feb. 14, 1872; Jan. 1, 1874; July 1, 1875.
US registration stamp: Dec. 1, 1911; May 29, 1913.
US, reply paid postal card: Oct. 25, 1892.
US revenue act: 1862.
US revenue stamped paper: May 1, 1755; Jan. 1, 1757; Nov. 1, 1765; Oct. 1, 1793; July 6, 1797; July 1, 1798; March 1, 1801; May 1, 1813; Jan. 1, 1814; May 1, 1818; May 10, 1845; Oct. 1, 1862.
US revenue stamps: 1862; Oct. 1, 1862; Feb. 20, 1934; March 16, 1934; February 1942; April 1, 1960; July 2, 1962; Dec. 31, 1967; April 30, 1971.
US round-the-world flight: March 17, 1924.
US Route Agents: May 18, 1838.
US Rural Free Delivery: Oct. 1, 1896; June 30, 1897; Aug. 1, 1900; Aug. 7, 1912.
USS *Akron*: May 8, 1932; Aug. 1, 1932.
US Sanitary Fair stamps: June 18, 1861; Feb. 22, 1864.
US Savings stamps: Nov. 30, 1954.
US, Second-class forwarding fee abolished: Feb. 17, 1985.
US Shanghai Postal Agency: July 27, 1868; May 24, 1919; Dec. 31, 1922.
US ship letter rates: March 2, 1799; Dec. 23, 1814; April 1, 1855; Feb. 27, 1861; June 30, 1863.
US ship-to-shore mail: July 31, 1927; June 12, 1929; June 12, 1931.
US shore-to-ship mail: June 12, 1929; Jan. 24, 1931.
US silver tax stamps: Feb. 20, 1934.
US, single-digit plate numbering system: Jan. 1, 1981.
USS *Los Angeles* (ZR 3, formerly Zeppelin LZ-126): Oct. 12, 1924; Feb. 21, 1925; April 21, 1925; April 23, 1925; May 3, 1925; May 8, 1925; June 6, 1925.
USS *Macon*: Oct. 27, 1932; July 19, 1934.
US-Soviet joint Apollo-Soyuz space flight "twin" stamps: July 15, 1975.
USS *Shenandoah*: Oct. 8, 1924; Oct. 12, 1924; July 3, 1925.
US Space Shuttle *Challenger* flight covers: Aug. 30, 1983.
US "Space Twins" issue: Sept. 29, 1967.
US Special Delivery Service: Oct. 1, 1885; Oct. 1,

1886; Dec. 12, 1908.
US Special Handling stamps: April 1, 1925; June 25, 1928.
US Special Printings: March 15, 1935.
USSR: See Soviet Union.
US stamp agent: May 18, 1855; Feb. 1, 1869.
US stamp booklet: April 17, 1884; April 16, 1900.
US stamp, consular service fee: April 5, 1906; June 1, 1906.
US stamped envelopes: July 1, 1853.
US stamp, precanceled: Aug. 14, 1844; Sept. 1, 1847; Aug. 1, 1879; 1894; May 26, 1903; January 1904; July 1, 1913; 1916; May 3, 1923; Aug. 7, 1928; July 1, 1938; June 1958; July 27, 1967; Nov. 3, 1969; Nov. 5, 1970; Sept. 21, 1978; 1979.
US stamp, precanceled, Christmas: Nov. 3, 1969; Nov. 5, 1970; Nov. 15, 1974.
US stamps, demonetization of: Jan. 1, 1862.
US stamp, self-adhesive: Nov. 15, 1974.
US stamp vending machine: May 6, 1948.
US steamboat mail: Jan. 23, 1812; Feb. 27, 1813; Dec. 1, 1835.
US steamship rates and routes: March 3, 1845; March 3, 1847; July 1, 1851; April 14, 1853; December 1856; June 30, 1864; Oct. 30, 1865; July 1, 1875.
US street car mail service: Dec. 5, 1892; Feb. 3, 1893; Nov. 9, 1929.
US street car RPO cancel: Feb. 3, 1893.
US Trans-Mississippi issue: June 17, 1898. See *Western Cattle in Storm* $1 stamp.
US Trust Territories of the Pacific: July 1, 1951.
US War Savings stamps: Dec. 1, 1917.
US Washington bicentennial issue: Jan. 1, 1932.
US waterways and canals declared post roads: 1823.
US, world's first specially designed air mail stamp: May 13, 1918.
US "Zeppelin" air mail stamps: April 19, 1930.
US ZIP code: July 1, 1963; Jan. 10, 1964; Jan. 1, 1967; Sept. 13, 1978.
Utah, State of: Jan. 4, 1896.
Utah, Territory of: Sept. 9, 1850; Sept. 27, 1850.

Vaitupu: March 10, 1984.
Valencia: September 1874.
Valparaiso: Jan. 1, 1919.
Vancouver Island: 1847; July 1858; May 4, 1859; July 30, 1860; June 20, 1864; Oct. 26, 1864; Sept. 19, 1865; Nov. 19, 1866.
Van Dahl, Al: March 3, 1954.
Van Diemen's Land (Tasmania): Oct. 4, 1828; 1835; Nov. 1, 1853. See Tasmania.
Vanuatu: July 30, 1980.
Vathi: See Vathy.
Vathy: 1893.
Vatican: June 1, 1929; Aug. 1, 1929; Oct. 1, 1931; June 22, 1938; Jan. 10, 1950.
Veglia: Nov. 18, 1920.
Venda: Sept. 13, 1979.
Venezia Giulia: Nov. 3, 1918.
Venezuela: Jan. 1, 1859; November 1863; Jan. 1, 1880; April 8, 1925; April 5, 1930; Dec. 17, 1942; March 9, 1949.
Venice: 1290; Feb. 1, 1608.
Vera Cruz, Mexico, US post office in: May 3, 1914.
Vermont, State of: March 4, 1791.
Victoria: April 13, 1837; June 10, 1841; Aug. 10, 1841; Aug. 1, 1842; Jan. 3, 1850; Dec. 1, 1854; Jan. 1, 1855; Jan. 1, 1884; Oct. 1, 1891. See Australia.

Victoria, Alexandria, Queen of the United Kingdom of Great Britain and Ireland: May 24, 1819; June 20, 1837; 1877; Jan. 22, 1901.
Victoria Land: Nov. 29, 1910.
Vienna: March 30, 1918.
Vietnam, Democratic Republic of: 1945; Sept. 2, 1945; June 14, 1949; Aug. 16, 1951; Oct. 21, 1951; July 21, 1954; April 30, 1975.
Vietnam, North: July 21, 1954; May 5, 1964.
Vietnam, South: Oct. 21, 1951; June 16, 1952; Nov. 10, 1952; July 20, 1955; June 1961; April 30, 1975.
Vilas, Wm. F., US PMG: March 7, 1885.
Ville d'Orleans: Nov. 24, 1870.
Vin Fiz label: Sept. 17, 1911.
Virginia, colony of: 1661.
Virginia, State of: June 26, 1788; May 1, 1813; April 17, 1861; 1870.
Virgin Islands: See British Virgin Islands.
V-Mail: June 15, 1942. See Airgraph service.
Volksrust: March 1902.
Von Gronau, Captain Wolfgang: July 21, 1932; Sept. 22, 1932; Sept. 29, 1932.
VR *Penny Black* **and** *Twopenny Blue* **authorized:** March 26, 1840.
Vryburg: November 1899.

Wadhwan, Indian Feudatory State of: 1888.
Waghorn, Thomas: Jan. 8, 1835.
Wake Island: May 1, 1951.
Waldy, Henry: 1683.
Wales: Regionals, Aug. 18, 1958.
Walker, Frank C., US PMG: Sept. 11, 1940.
Wallace, Robert: August 1833; 1835; January 1837.
Wallis and Futuna Islands: 1920; July 5, 1939; May 8, 1946; July 29, 1961.
Wanamaker, John, US PMG: March 6, 1889.
Washington: June 1, 1847.
Washington, D.C.: May 15, 1918.
Washington Island: Feb. 1, 1921; March 30, 1934.
Washington, State of: Nov. 11, 1889.
Washington, Territory of: March 2, 1853.
Waterlow & Sons Ltd.: Jan. 9, 1961.
Watson, W. Marvin, US PMG: April 26, 1968.
Wayzata flight: Aug. 31, 1932.
Webster, Daniel: June 1840.
Wei-Hai-Wei: Sept. 1, 1899.
Wells, Fargo & Co.: March 18, 1852; May 20, 1852; July 2, 1852; July 1858; April 3, 1860; April 1, 1861; May 1, 1861; Aug. 11, 1862; November 1866.

Wenden: 1863.
West Berlin: See Berlin.
Western Airletter service: Feb. 15, 1982.
Western Australia: Dec. 4, 1829; July 1852; Aug. 1, 1854; June 5, 1889; Oct. 1, 1891; August 1900. See Australia.
Western Cattle in Storm **$1 Trans-Mississippi stamp:** June 17, 1898.
Western Samoa: July 1920; Aug. 7, 1935; Jan. 1, 1962; Dec. 29, 1965; Sept. 1, 1966; Feb. 26, 1982. See Samoa, German Samoa.
Western Thrace: 1913; June 1920.
Western Ukraine: 1918.
West Germany: See Germany, Federal Republic of.
West Indian Aerial Express: July 14, 1927; Dec. 3, 1927; Dec. 6, 1927; Feb. 21, 1928.
West Irian: See Netherlands New Guinea.
West Virginia, State of: June 20, 1863.

White Plains souvenir sheet: See US, first Souvenir sheet.
Wickliffe, Charles A., US PMG: Oct. 13, 1841.
Wilkinson, F.: Jan. 24, 1912.
Willemstadt: April 8, 1925.
Wilson, William S., US PMG: April 4, 1895.
WIPA souvenir sheet: June 23, 1933.
Wisconsin, State of: May 29, 1848.
Wisconsin, Territory of: July 4, 1836.
Wise, John: Aug. 17, 1859.
Witherings, Thomas: April 1633; July 31, 1635.
Wolf, Elmer E.: Jan. 24, 1899.
Wolmaransstad: June 1900.
Woodson, Col. Samuel: July 1, 1850.
Work, Hubert, US PMG: March 4, 1922.
World Health Organization: June 24, 1948.
World Meteorological Organization: 1956.
Worsdell, Nathaniel: Jan. 4, 1838; Jan. 4, 1852.
Wreck covers: June 5, 1817; Feb. 13, 1830.
Wuhu: Aug. 1, 1894.
Wurttemberg, Kingdom of: March 22, 1851; Oct. 15, 1851; February 1872; 1902.
Wynne, Robert J., US PMG: Oct. 10, 1904.
Wyoming, State of: July 10, 1890.
Wyoming, Territory of: July 29, 1868.
Wyon, William: June 1839.

Xerxes: c500 BC.

Yap: See Micronesia, Federated States of.
Yca: April 1884.
Yemen Arab Republic: 1926; Jan. 1, 1930.
Yemen, Kingdom of: See Yemen Arab Republic.
Yemen, People's Democratic Republic of: June 28, 1968; Feb. 1, 1971.
Yemen, People's Republic of Southern: April 1, 1968. See Yemen, People's Democratic Republic of and South Arabian Federation.
Yokohama: Aug. 29, 1842; July 1, 1860; Sept. 7, 1865; July 27, 1867; Jan. 5, 1875; March 31, 1880; June 2, 1912.
Yucatan: March 13, 1924.
Yugoslavia: Jan. 16, 1921; Jan. 30, 1921; Dec. 24, 1921; Sept. 17, 1933; June 15, 1934; Nov. 1, 1946; Oct. 1, 1948.

Zaire, Republic of: Oct. 8, 1971; Dec. 18, 1971.
Zambezia: November 1894.
Zambia: Oct. 24, 1964; March 22, 1967. See Northern Rhodesia, Rhodesia and Nyasaland.
Zante: 1943.
Zanzibar: 1868; Oct. 1, 1875; 1894; Nov. 10, 1895; Dec. 10, 1963; Jan. 14, 1964; Jan. 1, 1968.
Zemstvo postal services: 1864; September 1865; 1874.
Zeppelin LZ-1: July 2, 1900.
Zeppelin LZ-126: See USS *Los Angeles* (ZR3).
Zeppelin LZ-127, *Graf Zeppelin:* Sept. 18, 1928; Sept. 20, 1928; Oct. 11, 1928; Oct. 29, 1928; March 25, 1929; April 23, 1929; Aug. 1, 1929; Aug. 8, 1929; Aug. 15, 1929; Aug. 23, 1929; Aug. 28, 1929; Sept. 1, 1929; May 18, 1930; May 19, 1930; May 24, 1930; May 26, 1930; May 28, 1930; June 2, 1930; July 9, 1930; Sept. 9, 1930; April 9, 1931; July 24, 1931; Aug. 29, 1931; Sept. 18, 1931; Oct. 17, 1931; March 19, 1932; June 28, 1932; July 30, 1932; May 6, 1933; May 29, 1933; Oct. 14, 1933; May 26, 1934; April 6, 1935; March 26, 1936; April 13, 1936; May 11, 1936; April 13, 1937; April 27, 1937; May 8, 1937; March 1940. The nine roundtrip flights by Graf

Zeppelin in 1932 are grouped under March 19, 1932, the nine 1933 South American flights are listed under May 6, 1933, the twelve 1934 South American flights are under May 26, 1934, the sixteen 1935 South American flights are under April 6, 1935, and the thirteen 1936 South American flights are under April 13, 1936.

Zeppelin LZ-129, *Hindenburg:* March 23, 1936; March 26, 1936; March 31, 1936; May 6, 1936; Aug. 1, 1936; Sept. 14, 1936; March 16, 1937; May 3, 1937; May 6, 1937. The 1936 flights of *Hindenburg* to North and South America are grouped under the date of the first departure in each case.

Zeppelin LZ-130, *Graf Zeppelin II:* Sept. 14, 1938; July 9, 1939; Aug. 6, 1939; March 1940.

Zeppelin mail: July 1, 1908; June 19, 1910; May 7, 1911; July 16, 1911; July 19, 1911; March 4, 1912; June 10, 1912; June 28, 1912; Aug. 3, 1912; Oct. 12, 1912; May 4, 1913; Aug. 24, 1919; Oct. 8, 1919; May 8, 1932; Aug. 1, 1932; Oct. 27, 1932; July 19, 1934. For *Graf Zeppelin* flights, see Zeppelin, *Hindenburg.* For *Graf Zeppelin II* flights, see Zeppelin II, Graf. For Zeppelin LZ-126 (ZR3) flights, see USS *Los Angeles.*

Zil Eloigne Sesel: See Zil Elwagne Sesel.

Zil Elwagne Sesel: June 20, 1980.

Zimbabwe: Aug. 7, 1888; Sept. 11, 1890; Jan. 2, 1892; April 1, 1924; Nov. 17, 1941; Oct. 25, 1944; Nov. 11, 1965; July 29, 1968; Dec. 16, 1979; April 1980; April 18, 1980.

ZIP code: See US ZIP code.

Zone A occupation territory: See Trieste.

Zone B: 1945; May 1, 1948; Oct. 17, 1948; Oct. 25, 1954.

Zululand: May 1, 1888; Dec. 31, 1897; June 30, 1898.

Zurich, Canton of: March 1843.